Due

# POLITICS  FROM  INSIDE

*Also by Sir Austen Chamberlain*
DOWN THE YEARS

PUBLISHED ON THE FOUNDATION ESTABLISHED
IN MEMORY OF
WILLIAM McKEAN BROWN

Speaight. 157. New Bond Street. W.

*Mary E. Chamberlain 1909*

# POLITICS FROM INSIDE

An Epistolary Chronicle
1906–1914

BY

## SIR AUSTEN CHAMBERLAIN
K.G., P.C., M.P.

WITH FRONTISPIECE IN PHOTOGRAVURE

NEW HAVEN
YALE UNIVERSITY PRESS
1937

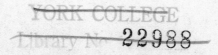

# POLITICS FROM INSIDE

## An Epistolary Chronicle
## 1906-1914

BY

### SIR AUSTEN CHAMBERLAIN

PRINTED IN GREAT BRITAIN

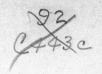

TO

M. E. C.

TO WHOM THESE LETTERS WERE WRITTEN

I DEDICATE THIS BOOK

IN

LOVE AND GRATITUDE

FOR ALL SHE HAS BEEN TO ME AND MINE

# ACKNOWLEDGMENT

I DESIRE to express my thanks to those whose letters are printed here or to their literary executors for the permission to include them.

I must also express my great indebtedness to the *Annual Register*, which I have found invaluable in compiling the introductory notes prefixed to the letters of each year and from which I have been permitted to quote.

A. C.

July, 1936.

6

# CONTENTS

|                                                      | PAGE |
|------------------------------------------------------|------|
| FOREWORD                                             | 9    |
| THE FAMILY CIRCLE                                    | 13   |
| PRELUDE: AN EXCHANGE OF LETTERS, 1904                | 22   |
| LETTERS OF 1906                                      | 35   |
| LETTERS OF 1907                                      | 45   |
| LETTERS OF 1908                                      | 91   |
| LETTERS OF 1909                                      | 133  |
| LETTERS OF 1910                                      | 187  |
| LETTERS OF 1911                                      | 313  |
| LETTERS OF 1912                                      | 401  |
| LETTERS OF 1913                                      | 499  |
| LETTERS OF 1914                                      | 597  |
| INDEX                                                | 649  |

# FOREWORD

I HAVE grave doubts whether this book ought to be published. It consists in the main of letters written to Mrs. Chamberlain for the family circle, and above all for my father at a time when his active life was ended but when his interest in all that concerned public affairs was still as keen as ever and such political ambitions as he may once have entertained for himself were concentrated on his sons, and particularly on his eldest son, whom he had early introduced into politics and for whom he was far more ambitious than he had ever been for himself. The letters, therefore, are full of my doings and sayings, of the part which I took in this or that controversy or event, of the speeches which I made and of the measure of success which they achieved. I am not sure that they will bear the scrutiny of less loving and more critical readers. I am haunted by the fear that they will appear boastful and egotistical, that I shall incur the reproach of having far too good a conceit of myself and that the constant repetition of the first person singular will be not merely wearisome but repellent.

Why, then, it may well be asked, do I make a book of them? I might plead in reply the generous reception of an earlier effort and the kind encouragement of friends who said they found that volume pleasant and interesting reading and added the hope that I should write more of the people among whom I had moved and the scenes in which I had borne a part. Or I might reply more cogently in the words of Dr. Johnson: "Sir, no man ever wrote except for money." I hope that one of these excuses may find acceptance, or that in combination they will at least temper the wind to the lamb who thus rashly shears away the protection which a decent reticence would have afforded him.

But though all these motives have influenced me—not least that which carries the weight of Dr. Johnson's authority—I admit that I cherish the hope that these thumb-nail sketches of the politics of a time so little separated from us in years and yet so far removed in all else may not only be read with interest by the dwindling band of those who can still recall them but may possess some value for

9

the student of Edwardian and early Georgian politics, may help him to recover the atmosphere of those times and to enter into their spirit—that they may, indeed, be accepted, as I claimed for my earlier sketches in *Down the Years*, as sidelights on history.

Such sidelights have their uses for the historian. Lord Morley, who had been in turn historian, critic, biographer, journalist and statesman holding high office and taking a large part in great movements of which we have not yet seen the end, never tired of warning his fellow-historians that there was less of deep-laid plot and counter-plot and more of improvisation in the actions of rulers and Cabinets than the historian was apt to admit. Thus, for example, he writes in *Politics and History* [1] of Taine's account of Napoleon :

> " But then alas ! such unity is for art and not for history. . . . This is not the way in which things really happen. For that it is no wonder that the critic takes down a volume of Cardinal de Retz with the stir and spirit of affairs in full circulation, and the actors as Retz says, ' hot and smoking with violence and faction.' "

" Smoking with violence and faction ! " These letters will not, I hope, incur that condemnation, but they were written amidst the passions which the politics of that time blew into a hot flame to which we have no parallel in a House of Commons more like, as a Member recently said, to " a Mothers' Meeting " than to the fiercely contested arena from which these letters were written.

These were the days when the Unionist Party which had governed the country for ten years returned from the General Election a bare 150 strong, over whose prejudices and convictions the triumphant majority of British Radicals and Irish Nationalists were prepared to ride roughshod, sweeping their leaders before them ; when Lloyd George's Budget appeared a portent of oppressive taxation and social revolution and its rejection by the House of Lords an unavoidable hazard ; the days of King Edward VII's death and King George's accession in the midst of the constitutional crisis which followed and of what was known as the Constitutional Conference—a meeting of four of the leaders on either side, of whom I was one, in an attempt to reach a compromise—and its failure ; of two General Elections in a single year and of the Parliament Act. They were years of slow and often disheartening preparation for the reform of the tariff which has since become

---

[1] *Notes on Politics and History*, quoted by courtesy of Messrs. Macmillan Ltd.

the accepted policy of a National Government. And through them all ran the red strand of the growing tension with Germany and the ever-increasing bitterness of the long struggle over Home Rule, as it neared its end, of the determination of Ulster to fight rather than submit to a Dublin Parliament, of " the mutiny " at the Curragh, and of wars and rumours of war ending in the great crash of August, 1914.

It all seems very distant now. We are living in a different world where all is changed in us and around us; a generation has grown up to whom even the Great War is not a personal memory but only a " tale that is told." It remains to be seen whether the struggles of those days have interest for them, but I believe that the story of these events has still a lesson for us today, if we will seek to disinter it from the dust which has settled upon it.

And so I present these letters as " Sidelights on History "—not history itself nor even, certainly not always, as my own considered opinion of the men and events to which they relate. Where the letters are quoted, I have let them stand as they were written from day to day, in the heat of conflict and amid the passions of the hour, with no thought of their ever being seen by anyone outside the circle to which they were addressed. If they have any value, it is in this freedom and spontaneity that it consists, but that very fact demands additional indulgence from those to whose attention they may now come.

July, 1936.

# THE FAMILY CIRCLE

THE FAMILY CIRCLE

## THE FAMILY CIRCLE

AMONG the many kind things said of my earlier volume, none pleased me more than the comment of a lady who had known my father well. She wrote: "I do so delight in the way your father seems present in every line of the book—his beautiful inspiration," and the proper introduction to these letters would be some account of my early life, of the influences by which I was surrounded from childhood upwards, and above all of the family circle which gathered about my father. Yes, that should be the first chapter, but can I write it?

I was reading a little time ago an account of his early years by an author of individuality and distinction. His childhood seemed to have been unhappy, and he loathed his schools, both private and public. It was a dreary tale, not untinged with bitterness in the telling, which left a bitter taste in the mouth of one reader, but at least it served to deepen my sense of the debt I owe to those who throughout my life have surrounded and shielded me with their untiring love.

And yet it might have been so different. A mere recital of the vicissitudes of my earlier years would seem to preclude such happiness and make impossible the fullness of family life and love. My mother died when I was born, after three short years of perfect happiness, but not without having planted in my father's breast that love of flowers which meant so much to him throughout his life. "You must not laugh at Joe's gardening," she wrote to my grandmother Chamberlain. "I am going to make him a real gardener," and long years afterwards, as I accompanied him on one of his Sunday morning reviews of his orchids, he said to me: "I don't know after all that any flowers ever gave me more pleasure than the first sixpennyworth of red daisies that I bought in the Market Hall and carried home to plant with your mother in our little garden in the Harborne Road."

In accordance with my mother's wish my elder sister and I were placed in charge of her unmarried sister under my grandfather

15

Kenrick's roof, and my father came to live with him at Berrow Court. My grandfather had terrified his own children—when she was over eighty his eldest daughter still shuddered at the recollection of how he used to shout at them—but to us he was always kind and forbearing. My aunt—Auntie she always was to us—was love itself. No mother could have been more devoted, and she made our mother real to us first by stories of her childhood suited to our age and comprehension, and later by making us understand what she had been to her brothers and sisters and to friends, how they had all turned to her in their troubles, how sweet and unselfish she had been, so that for a time all happiness seemed to have flown their lives with her.

In this aunt's charge we stayed until, four years later, my father married again. His bride was my mother's first cousin, Florence Kenrick, and "Cousin Florrie" became henceforth "Mama" to us. I still see her as, on our arrival with my father at his new home, she came running from the rockery where she was planting the ferns they had gathered on their honeymoon in the Lakes, pulling off her gauntlet gloves, with the trowel still in her hand and a loving welcome for her new children which never failed in her short life. She bore my father four children. Between them and us she made no distinction, and amidst all the cares of this growing family and of my father's public life—for he soon became Mayor of Birmingham—she always found time to play with us, to read to us and to watch over us with all a mother's love.

Once again my father enjoyed the perfect companionship of a happy marriage, but again desolation swept down upon his home. Mama died in 1875, leaving him with a family of six young children —the eldest not yet fifteen and the youngest not yet two years old.

For a time friends feared for his reason under this second staggering blow. He saved himself by hard work, but for years it left him desolate to fight a lonely battle with fate and the world, but to us children he was always the same. Only long afterwards did I begin to perceive what these years had been to him and how desperately his sorrows had clung to him throughout them. It was one day in my 'teens that I spoke critically to him of a friend of his, left early a widower with an only child. "He doesn't seem to care much for the boy," I said, "or to see much of him," and my father, quick as always in a friend's defence, blurted out before he saw the implication of what he was saying, "You must remember that his mother died when the boy was born," and in a flash I saw for the first time what he had so carefully concealed from me, that in my earliest years I had been to him the living embodiment of the first tragedy of his life.

So again later, after he became engaged to Miss Endicott, I was sitting talking with him after dinner and he spoke of my mother. As the conversation drew to its close, I said to him, "Do you know, Sir, that this is the first time that you have ever spoken to me about my mother?"

"Yes," he said, "I know. Until happiness came again into my life, I did not dare to—and even now I can't do it without the tears coming into my eyes." And so it was. Men who knew him little or saw him only in the midst of the fierce battles of his public career, thought him made of steel; it was but the armour he wore to protect the secrets of his heart. "We never knew your father," an Irish Member once said to me in the heat of the fight over Mr. Gladstone's Second Home Rule Bill, "until we saw him with you. I can only say I wish that my son's relations with me were like yours with your father."

We next passed to the charge of my father's second sister, who came to live with him, and, on her marriage a little later, to that of his youngest sister. Again we were surrounded with the most loving care, and so the years passed until she too married and my eldest sister took her place as the lady of the house and watched over us all, a brilliant woman, the most like in intellect to himself of all my father's children, "with the mind," as a friend wrote to The Times after her death in 1918, "of a great man and the heart of a great woman." But through all these changes the spirit of the home never changed and the ties of love held us ever more united.

Then, in 1888, my father married Miss Endicott. She was younger than my eldest sister and myself and she came from a different world, but she stepped so naturally into ours that soon she became the centre of our family life almost as much as my father himself. I like to recall that when my father on his first return from his American mission told me of his engagement my first words were: "This is the best news, Sir, that you could have brought us," and that when, eighteeen years later, I returned from Algiers where I had met and become engaged to my wife, he reminded me of these words and added: "and I now repeat them to you."

My sister said of her, "She brought his children closer to him," [1] and the best tribute I can pay to these two remarkable women is that my sister's affection for her was such that she continued to live under my father's roof in Birmingham or London until his death. In after years I once said to my sister : "I never understood why you did not marry X——. He was such a good fellow." "I should have done so," she answered, "if I had been one whit less happy at home." There can be few cases where a daughter, after being for four years mistress of her father's house, can have yielded her place so willingly and with such perfect results to a step-mother younger than herself. It would be impossible to exaggerate the debt we all owe to her or the love that she inspired.

I have just found among the letters which my father had preserved one which I wrote to him for the anniversary of his wedding day, eleven years later :

MY DEAR FATHER,                                        14th November 1899.

Though I cannot be with you tomorrow night, I shall be thinking of you and shall drink your health and Mary's at my lonely dinner.

You reminded me not so long ago that when you told me of your engagement I said that was the best news you could have brought us home from America. I could not know then how true a prophet I was ; but I like to think that that was how the news first appeared to me, and that in the years that have since passed there has been nothing for any of us to change or regret. And now I have only to thank you for the present you brought to us and to wish you and Mary many many happy returns of your wedding day. I don't think there was ever a happier or a more united family and to you and Mary we owe it all.

Ever your affectionate son,

AUSTEN CHAMBERLAIN.

My father was a good talker—one of the best of his day—and a good listener. We learned much from his conversation, for he talked freely to us of all that he was doing, and he encouraged us to talk as freely of all that interested us. Even in our childhood the

---

[1] J. L. Garvin's *Life of Joseph Chamberlain*, ii. p. 373.

actual precepts he enjoined upon us were few. I remember only three :

"Always tell the truth ; everything can be forgiven if you tell the truth." "If a thing is worth doing at all, it is worth doing well." And finally the duty of obedience. "When you are told to do something by Mama, do it at once. When you have done it you may ask why."

I hear his voice now, kindly but firm, as he released me from the corner of the room where I had been stood for dis-obedience. For the rest we learned our lessons from his example and from the atmosphere of the home. He taught us by example, not by precept.

When I was in the Sixth Form at Rugby, my House Master, Henry Lee-Warner, with whom I had formed a friendship that ended only with his death, once told me that when my father entered me for the School he spoke a good deal of my health, but said nothing about my religious instruction. Knowing that my father was a Unitarian (and a Militant Nonconformist in those days) he asked him whether he had any special instructions to give on that subject. My father had replied in the negative, saying that he was quite content that I should attend the Chapel Services and the ordinary Bible teaching and had added : "If his family have not put their ideas into him yet (I was then thirteen) it is time that someone else tried."

"I have often been surprised since to find how little your father ever seems to have said to you on the subject."

"But you don't observe that he has failed to put his ideas into me ?"

"No, indeed !" laughed Lee-Warner, "but how was it done ?"

As the years passed my relations with my father became ever more intimate. I acted as a sort of A.D.C. to him in the General Election of 1886, which the split in the Liberal Party, caused by Mr. Gladstone's acceptance of Home Rule, made peculiarly bitter, as he was separated from and denounced by so many of his old friends. In time I became his colleague in the House of Commons and later in the Cabinet. When he left Balfour's Cabinet in 1903 to act as the pioneer of Tariff Reform, he insisted that I should remain, and I became the main link between him and Arthur Balfour—a link that was sometimes strained almost to breaking point—and I drafted the "Valentine Letter" which made their continued co-operation possible after the disastrous election of 1906.

I did not marry till I was forty-two, and up to that time my home, whether in Birmingham or in London, was his house, except for the two years when first I was Chancellor of the Exchequer in 1904-5, when I occupied 11 Downing Street. From there, on my first night, I wrote to him :

11.1.4.

11 DOWNING STREET,
MY DEAR FATHER,                              WHITEHALL, S.W.

I cannot close my first evening away from your roof in a house for the time at least my own, without writing a line to you. It is so great a change in my life and all about me is so strange that as yet I hardly realise it. But what I do realise is how much I owe to you and how very dear to me is the close friendship which you have encouraged between us. I do not think there are many fathers who have been and are to their sons all that you have been to me ; and my prayer tonight is that the perfect confidence which I have enjoyed for so long may continue unimpaired by our separation, and that I may do something to help you in the great work which you have undertaken. It is at once a great encouragement and a great responsibility to be heir to so fine a tradition of private honour and public duty and I will do my best to be not unworthy of the name.

Ever your affectionate son,

AUSTEN CHAMBERLAIN.

With my father's illness in the summer of 1906 and his retirement from active work, I was necessarily forced more into the position of a protagonist in the Tariff Reform struggle and in the Liberal Unionist wing of the Party. Thus my activities increased as my father's ceased, and he followed my fortunes and those of the political fight with unwearying interest. The one thing that I could do for him when he was abroad or out of London was to send him news of what was happening, and it became my habit to keep a letter always on my table, adding a few words at night or morning after or before my day's work. They thus form a more detailed account of my doings than I have for any other period of my life, but there are gaps in the correspondence, occasionally filled from other sources, whenever we were both in London, or my wife and I went to stay with him at Birmingham.

His passionate interest in the causes for which he fought continued till his last hours.  I saw him on the morning of the day on which he died.  He questioned me about some debate a day or two before.  I spoke of a speech of Asquith's, and he asked what I had replied.  "Quite right," he said, when I told him, and added as I left his room : "Somebody has got to give way, but I don't see why it should be always us."

These words, so characteristic of his dauntless spirit, were the last he spoke to me.

# PRELUDE

## An Exchange of Letters, 1904

*A. C. to A. J. Balfour.*
*Confidential.*

HIGHBURY, BIRMINGHAM,

MY DEAR BALFOUR,                              *24th August* 1904.

. . . Everything therefore tends to confirm me in the opinion which I expressed to you at our last meeting—that it is time that we had a change of Government. I do not think that we have credit or parliamentary strength sufficient to overcome so many difficulties. I do not think that we can in any case last long enough to reach better times, and I do not believe that we shall gain strength or live down unpopularity (earned or undeserved) by attempting to carry on administration through another session.

But, if this is a correct view of the position—and it is at any rate the view taken by so shrewd an observer as Douglas[1]—it is more than ever important that we should use what little time we have left to bring the Party together, to unite it on a common policy which will be our platform for the future, to awaken its enthusiasm and to prepare it and the electors for the fight in which we shall shortly be engaged.

At the present time the Party viewed as a whole is timid, undecided, vacillating. It has no constructive policy. It does not know what is to be its future. It is exposed to a most active and dangerous attack and it stands timidly on the defensive. Now, no party can win on these lines, and, as things stand now, we are already disastrously beaten and every month's delay will only make our case worse. But there is no reason why we should thus sit still and let the tide of disaster swamp us. We cannot win now but we can lay the foundations of future victory, and even now we may profoundly modify the results of the next elections.

What is needed to work this revolution in our fate is only

[1] Right Hon. A. Akers-Douglas, then Home Secretary and for many years Chief Whip of the Conservative Party, afterwards 1st Lord Chilston.

22

that our leaders should be united, and united in support of a positive future policy. You know what I think that policy should be. It need not be my father's. I am convinced that you and he could carry in a shorter period than most people suppose the whole of the Glasgow programme; but I can quite believe that though in general sympathy with his objects, you are not prepared to adopt all his methods, and I do not propose for your adoption anything to which I anticipate that in principle you can have any objection. Let it be your own policy announced by you at Southampton, distinct from his wherever you think a difference necessary, but let it be one on which he and his friends can unite with you. I undertake that you will not find him unreasonable. You would not expect him to pretend—and it is not desirable that he should pretend—that you had given him all he asked or all he wanted. He may still think his own line the best, but I am certain that for the sake of unity, and, above all, for the sake of keeping in close touch with you, he will accept less and loyally work for it.

But, if we are to do any good we must get together quickly. We must plant our batteries at once and open fire on a concerted plan this autumn. I do not think that you have any conception of the results which would be achieved by such combined action even now, though you must see the disastrous effects which will follow from our silence or our half-hearted and discordant utterances during the next few months. The danger is in a nutshell: if we don't now get together, we shall inevitably and fatally drift farther and farther apart. It is a prospect which fills me with consternation on every ground—political and personal. And please allow me to say without offence that you have some personal responsibility in the matter. You encouraged my father to go out as a "pioneer"; you gave your blessing to his efforts for closer union with the Colonies; you assured us who remained that we too thus served the interests of Imperial Union and we were thus induced to leave him for the time almost single-handed at his Herculean task. He undertook this work believing in your sympathy, believing that, when he had proved that the obstacles were not insuperable, you and your Government would be prepared to make some advance; and had he not been led to believe this, I think his course would have been different, and with however profound a regret at seeing

23

so great an opportunity lost, I believe he would never have set out on a course which in such a case could only result in bringing him in conflict with old friends and particularly with yourself.

Are we now to tell him that we can do no more? That because some forty Free Fooders still hesitate, we are unable to move? You know that I cannot take that line, and, believe me, there are many of your colleagues and more of your followers who are in almost as great a difficulty as I am.

Cannot you make a bridge for us all and yet do nothing and say nothing which is not in accordance with your most profound convictions? I think that you might; and it is in the hope that you will, that I give both you and myself the trouble involved in writing and reading this long letter.

I tried to suggest the other day what such a policy might be. The main feature of it would be to announce that, if again returned to power, you would summon a conference of Colonial and Indian representatives to consider the question of Imperial trade and that, if you were satisfied by the result that other portions of the Empire would do their share, you would then propose to Parliament such measures as are necessary to fulfil our part of the common policy.

In this way and in this way only can your doubts as to the attitude of the Colonies be resolved; and please remember that all the members of the late Cabinet, except those who have since resigned, agreed to consult the Colonies and that we were only prevented from doing so by Ritchie and Co.

If the result is not satisfactory, you will not proceed further. If our doubters like Lytton and Maxwell[1] think it unsatisfactory, they will be free to act as they please. If the Colonies are unreasonable, I and others who think with me will have to recognise facts. We must surrender our hopes and we, at any rate, shall give you no further trouble.

I put this point first because it is the concession which I ask of you—a concession not of principle, but of policy only.

On the other hand, you might fix the limit of the duty on *wheat*. You might reduce it to 1s. if you think 2s. too high. You might reject the idea of a "scientific tariff" if that frightens people, and you might substitute for it a fixed 10 per cent. or $7\frac{1}{2}$ per cent.

[1] Sir John Stirling Maxwell, Bart.

to provide the necessary revenue; you might have a fixed addition of 5 or 10 per cent. for retaliatory purposes where needed, or you might deal with each such case separately; and you might graft on any such plan whatever proposals for dealing with dumping seem best to you. In short, in all these matters I think I may safely say that we should all desire to fall into line with you and to meet your wishes in every way.

This is not the Glasgow policy—still less is it the Glasgow policy in its later developments; but if you would put forward some such policy as this, closely in harmony as I believe with all you have ever said or thought, you would rally all our scattered forces, and we should go to the country united and zealous instead of divided and half-hearted.

But I beg you not to proceed with the suggestion you made to me in Downing Street. It will not do to propose a second referendum after the Conference. The more I think of this suggestion, the less I like it; but one practical objection is I think sufficient to cause you to reject it on further consideration. You cannot ask your followers to work hard and long if the only result of success is to be that the fruits of victory are at once to be put to the hazard of a fresh election. No party can be kept together by a policy which promises at best but a succession of dissolutions, and candidates will not be forthcoming if the only result of their election is to be, that, within a year or so, they are to be involved in all the chances and expense of a fresh election.

But such a policy as I have tried to sketch, if put forward by you, would give us all the opportunity we want. It would change the issue. It would be your policy, not my father's. It would make the way easy for all those who wish to rejoin the ranks, and it would be received with enthusiasm by all those who have never wavered in their allegiance to you. And if we are once united I do not think you would have occasion to complain of lack of enthusiasm or of any difficulty in getting unpaid workers. We can get them here [1] though you know how peculiarly the Education Act has hit Unionists and especially Liberal Unionists in these parts. And we should get them elsewhere if we had a definite constructive policy to inspire zeal and evoke effort.

[1] *i.e.* in Birmingham.

25

We doubtless may lose a man or two here and there, and the Party agents may always dwell on the danger of such losses. But in such matters they are the worst advisers. They think only of the few whom they know and forget the many whom they don't know. They never consider the enormous accession of power that comes to any party which can raise a great ideal and touch the spirit of the nation. They overlook the importance of acting on the offensive and substituting an active policy of the future for a mere passive defence of the past. In short, they think only of possible losses and not also of the certain gains.

Mind, I do not say that even on these lines we shall not lose seats. We must lose them after nearly twenty years of almost continuous success; but please observe that we have had no worse defeats since May of last year [1] than we had at Woolwich and Rye before that date; that we have fared no better where our candidate has been a "half-hogger" than where he has been a "whole-hogger"; and that both Bridgeman at Oswestry and Touche at Lanark think they would have done worse with the more restricted policy, and the former (while blaming most of all the lack of organisation) says that he attributes his defeat mainly to education and cannot after careful enquiry find out that the labourers were influenced by dear food, though at first he was inclined to suppose that they were.

Do, I beg you, give your most favourable consideration to these suggestions before the Southampton meeting. If you cannot see your way to a policy which will unite the Party, then we are not only beaten at the next election—we are ruined. Beaten we shall be in any case; but surely what we have to do is to prepare the way for future success. And, if you will raise the standard at Southampton, we can all close up during the autumn, and instead of our present confusion and lethargy, you will inspire us with new life and courage.

It is you and you alone who can work this change and now is the time to do it.

I cannot tell you how deeply I feel all this. It is my only excuse for writing, and if you knew how I hate writing, you would

[1] When my father first raised the question in his speech in Birmingham Town Hall.

be able to measure the reality of my concern by the length of my letter.

I think we are on the brink of disaster. I know that you can save us, and I cannot rest content without at least trying to convey to you some part of my conviction and of the reasons which inspire it.

My present plan is to go abroad immediately after George Duckworth's wedding on 10th September, but I suppose we shall probably have to meet in London before that to consider the very unsatisfactory turn that the naval war is taking in so far as our shipping is concerned. In any case I shall stay—or return—if I am wanted. Meanwhile I shall remain here at Highbury.

Yours very truly,

AUSTEN CHAMBERLAIN.

*Balfour to A. C.*
*Dictated.*

NORTH BERWICK,

MY DEAR AUSTEN, *1st September* 1904.

I cannot put off longer acknowledging the receipt of your letter of 24th August and apologising for not having answered it before. This note is *not* an answer to it; I am writing one which will, I hope, reach you long before you go abroad.

As things are at present, it does not seem likely that we need have a Cabinet before that date; but I want, before it arrives, to get at least one stage further in the discussion which we began just before we separated for the holidays. Both your conversation and your letter have been much in my thoughts.

Yours ever,

ARTHUR JAMES BALFOUR.

*Balfour to A. C.*
*Private.*

WHITTINGEHAME,

MY DEAR AUSTEN, *10th September* 1904.

The agreement between your views and mine on the present political situation is so nearly complete, that the one difference

27

which *seems* to divide us obtains perhaps an undue prominence. I hold as strongly as you do that—apart from old age—our weakness in the country is due chiefly to our divisions on the fiscal question. If it were not for the fact that the elections seem to have gone as much against us before, as after, these divisions made themselves felt, I should indeed have regarded them as the chief cause of our weakness. But, whether they stand first or second in order of importance, their importance is at all events certain.

Now for your remedy. You think, and I agree, that there is nothing very inspiring in the "Sheffield" programme. "Liberty of negotiation" with foreign countries would, I am convinced, be a great gain. But it does not lend itself easily to popular treatment, and such merits as it might otherwise possess from a merely electioneering point of view have been largely discounted by the fact that both "protectionists" and "Free Fooders" have conspired to represent it as a "compromise" or as "a half-way house" on the road to something else. This is not an accurate way of putting the case, since the Sheffield programme is logical and self-contained. But even if it *were* accurate, it is not obvious why it should be damaging. There are many occasions on which a compromise is exactly what the public wants. The present occasion, however, is probably not one of them : if only because it requires considerable skill to "take the offensive" from a position of compromise, and this skill the majority of the Party do not possess. Indeed, they find it hard even to "take the offensive" quite apart from the fiscal question ; and so it must always be when one Party has done much, and the other nothing, for nine years. The latter find themselves naturally in the position of assailants, the former are apt to lapse into a position of mere defence—always a dissipating one except for the best trained troops.

How, then, is this state of things to be remedied ? Remedied completely it cannot be till we have been some time in opposition. But what partial cure can be found for it ? You say, in effect, that what we want is a policy on which, with all due reservations, the Party can agree ; and a policy which, when agreed to, will tap deeper springs of enthusiasm than can ever be reached by the Sheffield programme taken *simpliciter*. Holding the views which you and I share with respect to our Colonial Empire, there can be no doubt that it is in *that* direction we must search for what we want—even if we fail to find it.

There are other reasons lying altogether outside party politics which tend in the same direction. It seems quite impracticable to leave the Colonial question exactly where it is. The possibility of new commercial relations between Canada and the U.S.A.; the awakening of Australia to her increased need for the protection of a powerful, and therefore Imperial, fleet in the face of a victorious Japan; our ignorance as to how far the Colonies are ready to make genuine gaps in their protective wall of tariffs for our benefit—an ignorance which paralyses effort on this side of the water in favour of closer fiscal union, and tends to make Imperialists rely unduly on protectionist support;—all these considerations point to the extreme desirability of having a full and free discussion with our Colonies on the present position and future organisation of the Empire.

Such a discussion may of course be abortive; but, unless it is "full and free," it is, I think, sure to prove abortive. No relevant subject should be excluded from debate; no preliminary fetters must be imposed either on the Colonial or the British representatives. The Colonists must not come here precluded from discussing Imperial free trade in any of its various degrees; the British must not lay down as a condition precedent to discussion that this or that article of consumption must in no case be taxed. Liberty of suggestion, and (I should be inclined to add) privacy of discussion, without which liberty of suggestion is almost certain to be a mere sham, are essential to any fruitful result.

But if I have carried you with me so far, you will see why I do not think it possible to say, as you would wish me to say, that we must go to the country pledged, if we are returned to power, not merely to summon a Conference but also to carry at once into effect any conclusions at which it may arrive, provided they are, in our opinion, reasonable. I do not for a moment believe that the Colonies would enter into a Conference if *they* were required to give any such pledge. Their Ministers would say, and with much reason, that they could not ask their respective electorates to give them a majority which might be used to carry out some new, and, at present, wholly unthought of, plan; that if the Conference and the various Governments concerned were to settle the matter without any further reference to the electors, then each Government must lay down beforehand the general limits beyond which it would not go, and the delegates both of Great Britain and of each Colony must be tightly bound by their instructions to refuse even to discuss any scheme by which those limits would be transgressed. Once anything like this occurs, there is an end of "full and free" discussion; and an end also of all the benefits which such a discussion will, I believe, confer on the cause of Imperial Unity.

And is there reason to think that any greater acceleration of Colonial Union would be obtained by your plan than by mine? I doubt it. I think yours would frighten the Colonies; and it would certainly frighten an important section of opinion in this country;—a reflection which brings us back to the strictly domestic aspect of the problem we have to solve. Would, then, such a scheme as I have thus sketched not do more to unite the Party in respect of fiscal and Colonial policy than any possible alternative? The true protectionists would not much like it; but then I am afraid that, so far as I am concerned, I can propose nothing they *would* much like; and, in any case, they would probably prefer it to mere Cobdenism. The bigoted Free Fooders would regard even the permission to discuss food taxation as trafficking with the "accursed thing." The pedantic Free Traders would regard the removal of even the greatest obstacles to freer trade as too dearly purchased if it involved the imposition of a single customs duty unbalanced by an equivalent excise. But surely the great mass of the Party who belong to none of these sections would not only approve the motives of the policy, but would think it well worth fighting for—the reasonable "whole-hogger" and the reasonable advocate of "Sheffield-but-no-further," while not abandoning their views would be glad to have the whole subject examined in a broader spirit, and with an increase of knowledge which is imposs- ible so long as the Colonies are no parties to our discussions, and so long as those discussions rise but rarely above the level of mere platform recriminations.

My idea, therefore, would be to take the very earliest opportunity

I can find of (1) reaffirming the Sheffield programme, both on its positive and negative side, *i.e.* saying that, if returned to power, we will at once endeavour to make this change in our fiscal policy, but will in the next Parliament make no other; at least, none involving bread taxation; (2) saying that, in our opinion, the Colonial question cannot be left where it is; that we will summon a free and full conference, with power to consider *any* proposals which it may think likely to conduce to closer union, fiscal or other, between different parts of the Empire; (3) it would go without saying that if satisfactory proposals could be devised, we would do our best to induce the country to accept them, and the Party to embody them in its programme; (4) the Imperial and Colonial question thus dealt with to be explicitly dissociated from protection (true protection), with which, indeed, it has no connection, logical or sentimental; protection to remain what it has long been, a doctrine largely held in the Party, but with no place in its official creed.

It seems to me that this scheme is in substantial harmony with your father's views. It differs, perhaps, from some suggestions which he has thrown out from time to time in the course of his Imperial propaganda. But, unless I am much mistaken, these suggestions are not of the essence of his policy, but are in the nature of (as the schoolmen would have said) more or less "separable accidents." What he has fought for, what he has done more than any man to promote, is *Union*—fiscal union, military union, naval union, Union, in short, of every kind which is compatible with the self-government of our free Colonies. I believe that my plan for attaining this great object is the best which can at present be devised, both considered in itself and considered in relation to the future of the only party in the State which is capable of taking a lead in what I hope will one day be a National policy. At present we can hardly hope to carry both parties with us; but at least a great end will have been gained if one of them could be induced to accept it with zeal and without producing serious schism in its ranks.

Yours ever,

Arthur James Balfour.

*Private.*                                              TREASURY CHAMBERS,
                                                        WHITEHALL,
MY DEAR BALFOUR,                          *12th September* 1904.

I cannot help regretting that the very important reply which
you have sent to my letter of 24th August only reached me today
on the very eve of my departure. I had hoped from what you said
that I should have heard from you in plenty of time to allow
both for careful consideration of all you might say and for further
communication with you if necessary. As it is I must content
myself with giving you briefly my first impressions on reading and
re-reading your letter.

They are not cheerful. I am afraid that the difference in our
points of view is greater than I had thought or than you suppose.

I believe in the policy of Colonial Preference. I believe it to
be the greatest object to which we in our time can devote ourselves
not only for itself but for all to which it may lead and which we
cannot realise without it. I believe it to be worth great immediate
sacrifices, if such were called for, both from the Party and the
nation, for the sake of the future advantages it promises. But I do
not believe that in reality such sacrifices are necessary from the
Party, for I think that the mass of the Party and of the nation have
a true and sure instinct in this case as in so many others, and that
such doubt and hesitation as prevails is due not to the question
itself but to the divided counsels of its leaders and the hesitation
of its parliamentary chiefs.

Believing this, you must forgive me for saying that I think
your policy wrong alike from the national and the purely party
point of view; and though it pains me deeply to have to say so,
if this is your last word, I do not see how I can possibly come into
line with you at the next election.

Looked at from the standpoint of party, I fear that the policy
you sketch means further disunion, a prolongation of the present
uncertainty, a controversy over and therefore a hardening of our
views, wherever we disagree among ourselves. The struggle in
the Party will continue, and each section will try, and will be bound
to try, to make itself as strong as possible, by enforcing pledges
and capturing associations and seats. As to the ultimate result of

such a struggle, I have no doubt. But meanwhile it involves the Party in serious divisions, in perpetual controversy and parliamentary impotence.

For the nation it means, I fear, that this great question is put before them not as a noble cause worthy of all that is best in us, calling for great efforts and justifying every sacrifice; but timidly, hesitatingly, amid circumstances of doubt and indecision which obscure the greatness of the issue, which take off the edge of effort, and kill enthusiasm.

Lastly the Conference itself, so summoned, will in my opinion meet, if it meet at all, in circumstances the least favourable to a successful issue of its deliberations. Whether the Colonies would accept an invitation couched in such terms, is, I think, doubtful; but that such a Conference could be successful, is, I fear, more than we have any right to hope. I grant you that Colonial statesmen are timid, but what then? We must have courage for ourselves and for them too. We must know what we want and how we mean to secure it; and, whilst willing and active to meet their difficulties in every way possible to us, we must go into Council with clear and decided views both of the end and the means, and we must feed them with our strength and our enthusiasm. If *we* show doubt and hesitation we are lost, and with us goes the last chance of the permanent union of that Greater Britain of which we are still the centre and the heart.

It is because the policy you sketch appears to me, and will I fear appear to others, timid and uncertain, that I think it will be fatal to us and our cause. I cannot bring myself thus to postpone the great issue. I do not think it wise and I do not think it right. I cannot sit still while colleagues in the Cabinet—Londonderry or another—put such glosses on your utterances as he did in his speech in the north a fortnight ago. I have done my best, believe me I have done my best and under very difficult circumstances, to keep the Party together and to give you all the loyal support which my position under you makes it a pleasure to me to render. What the future has in store, it is now too soon to say. My position in regard to autumn speeches must in any case have been difficult. It will be doubly so now. I will continue to do what I can for you, if you wish it, while this parliament lasts; but its days are numbered

C

and your letter deprives me of the hope that when the election comes I can issue an address indistinguishable in point of policy from your own.

Yours very truly,

AUSTEN CHAMBERLAIN.

*P.S.*—It is hardly necessary for me to add that I write without consultation with anyone as I wrote before. Before leaving B'ham, on my last evening at home, I told my father what I had already written to you without his knowledge. I found as I had expected that he would have acquiesced in such a compromise as I suggested, but you cannot expect him to view more favourably than I do the proposals you intend to make.

*Balfour to A. C.*  BARDBURY PRIVATE HOTEL,
NORTH BERWICK,
MY DEAR AUSTEN,  *22nd September* 1904.

I will not be so unkind as to mar your trip abroad by a fiscal discussion! But I am obstinate in believing that our differences (if differences they are to be called) are neither as great nor as irreconcilable as you suppose. Time will show it. I speak in a few days at a dinner in Edinburgh—and in the sense I told you. But I do not believe that either your father or you will take exception—or at least not serious exception—to anything I have to say.

I hope you will enjoy your holiday—you have most certainly deserved one.

Yours ever,

ARTHUR JAMES BALFOUR.

I go to Balmoral Monday.

34

1906

1906

## INTRODUCTORY TO 1906 LETTERS

THE meeting of the new Parliament of 1906 was preceded by a meeting of the Unionist Party at Lansdowne House. As we had succeeded in winning only 150 seats, it was decided, on my father's urgent insistence, that the defeated candidates should be invited with the successful ones so as to make the gathering more representative. Up to the eve of this meeting, however, the growing gap between my father and Arthur Balfour was unbridged. On his return to London from Scotland, Balfour had dined with my father, but after a prolonged discussion lasting till midnight they parted without reaching any agreement. The next morning they and a few of the leaders met at Balfour's house in Carlton House Gardens, but again the discussion dragged on without bringing them any nearer to one another. They drew exactly opposite inferences from the result of the election. Balfour saw in it a reason for extreme caution ; my father drew from it a very different inference—that a more pronounced Tariff Reform policy would have had greater success and prevented the defeat which was in any case inevitable from becoming a rout. At the last moment I drafted a letter which was approved by Akers-Douglas, formerly Lord Salisbury's trusty Whip and latterly Home Secretary in Balfour's Government, and by Alec Hood, our Chief Whip. Jack Sandars, Balfour's secretary, made some additions to it, and it was accepted by Balfour and my father and published in the papers on the morning of 14th February, from which date it became known as the Valentine letter. It was heralded with relief by everyone except the extreme Free Fooders, and enabled my father to continue his co-operation with Balfour. I attended the early weeks of the new session, but was then ordered abroad by my doctor in consequence of a prolonged attack of sciatica, the result of the strain which I had gone through in the last two or three years.

I chose Algiers for my holiday, and here I met Miss Ivy Dundas and in ten days became engaged to her, thus finding the help and support to which I have owed everything in subsequent years.

We were married at St. Margaret's, Westminster, on 21st July, but my father had been struck down by illness a few days before and was unable to be present. Thereafter, although he encouraged and helped his friends and supporters by his messages and counsel, he could take no further active part in public affairs. His interest in them, however, remained unaffected, and the only return that I could make for all the love he had showered upon me was to supply him with a commentary on public affairs more personal than he would find in the papers and giving him an account of what went on in our party councils behind the scenes.

On returning to town for the autumn session we took a house in Egerton Place, and, whilst that was being prepared for us, stopped at the Hans Crescent Hotel.

The letters which follow were written to Mrs. Joseph Chamberlain whenever we were separated. She and my father spent the early months of the year on the Riviera. They would return for Whitsuntide, which we generally spent with them at Highbury, and we in our turn usually spent our Autumn holiday on the Continent. When we were all together in London or Birmingham the letters ceased and there is a gap in the story.

We have had a dull week in the House, but Plural Voting and Workmen's Compensation have kept us pretty busy. The Government and the Labour Members agreed upon a "compromise" on the number of days which are not to count, viz., seven days, but to count back to the first day if the incapacity lasts fourteen days. This "compromise" is said by the Birmingham Mutual to be the worst thing of all for them, but I am bound to say some of the other Companies do not agree with them and produce very different figures. I opposed the compromise and said I would prefer the Grand Committee's three days with no counting back; but there was some division of opinion among our men, and of course we could do nothing against the combination of the Government and Labour.

One or two of the Government's supporters are restless, but the Bill is rightly being treated as non-contentious.

· · · · · ·

I find both Long and Carson "support me" at Dublin, so though I am to be the "Speaker of the Evening" I can be comparatively brief. But just now, for an Englishman at any rate, a speech on Home Rule is like flogging a dead horse. My last three speeches came very easily, as ease goes in such matters, but this time I feel fairly stuck.

This afternoon we agreed to finish the third Reading of the Irish Town Tenants' Bill on condition that the Government took only two other little departmental bills—one of which I was pressing for in the interest of my constituency. For the purpose of shortening debate it was arranged that we should not provoke the Irish, on condition that the Government was very mild and did nothing to provoke us. In spite of this Cherry, the Irish Attorney-General, made an ill-tempered speech, which caused Balcarres to tell Whiteley that it justified us in throwing up the agreement. To which Whiteley replied, "So it does, but I hope you won't. You fellows play the game, but ours are such d——d fools that they can't play it even when it is explained to them!"

Our house goes on apace. . . . As soon as we can get maid-servants in we shall begin to put in furniture and carpets; so I think we may safely say we shall be in before Christmas.

HOUSE OF COMMONS,
*3rd December* 1906.

The rejection of the Plural Voting Bill is now being moved by Sir H. Kimber in a thin and dull House, where Long and I alone adorn our Bench. I do not like to leave; I find that there will not be occasion for me to speak as both Long and Balfour propose to do so. I am, therefore, not obliged to listen with more than one ear, and I take the opportunity to send you a few lines.

Hewins was a little perturbed by Fielding's Budget Statement. I gathered that the preferential column of F.'s new tariff was pretty much, though not entirely, what he had expected, though there were notable exceptions, *e.g.* tin-plates where the Americans are rapidly capturing the Western-Canadian market and H. had hoped that British tin-plates would be put on the free list. But his real concern was that instead of the minimum duty for foreigners being kept $33\frac{1}{3}$ per cent. above the British Preference rates, he gathers that this difference will form the basis for negotiation with foreigners and will be whittled down and perhaps altogether destroyed in coming negotiations with Germany and the U.S.A. He, of course, asked for the impossible—viz., some action at the Conference next April. I tried to put into his head some idea of what was and what was not possible, and into the hearts of all the others a little more confidence and courage. But the fact is, they lack neither; but they do like at times to lean on someone else's shoulder and transfer their small cares and worries to someone else's keeping. However, they are all keen and all at work; so one cannot be angry with them. Money is coming in pretty well for the dinner. Parker Smith has done well in Glasgow.

No, I cannot write an intelligent or intelligible letter with speeches going on around me, so I will finish with the latest House of Commons story I have heard.

Overheard in the dining-room:

*1st Waiter to second do.*—Ain't you wanted at the Government table?

*2nd Waiter.*—No. There's only two of 'em there.

*1st Waiter.*—Which two?

*2nd Waiter.*—Only old Hugly and the Hemperor!

The listening M.P. looked into the Government dining-room and discovered Cherry, the Irish Attorney-General, and John Burns dining alone!

SHELBOURNE HOTEL, DUBLIN,
*8th December* 1906.

I do not know whether Hilda will have given you any account of our last night's meeting.[1] My own judgment on it would be that, as a Unionist demonstration, it was a great success. The Rotunda was crowded. So was the overflow, and many were turned away unable to get admission to either. It has given the Unionists here the tonic they needed and I hear they are all very happy and pleased. As to my speech, I think the delivery was good and its reception was all I could desire, but its matter was stale. There were no new arguments and no fresh treatment of old ones, and so, though it served the purpose of the moment, it is not an effort of which I feel proud!

As I had to speak at the overflow also (no decent report of this available) I was obliged to be comparatively brief, but the speech lasted fifty minutes as it was and was wholly occupied with Home Rule. I kept the Tariff question and its place in Unionist policy for this morning, when I received a Liberal-Unionist deputation and gave them half an hour on the subject. This will, I hope, be well reported in Monday's *Irish Times* and, if so, you shall have a copy. My argument was that the democracy want two things; imperialism and social reform. We were successful just so long as we combined the two ideals. We lost when we failed to satisfy their aspirations on the second. We can only win by combining them again. Our policy on social

[1] At the Rotunda in Dublin.

reform should not be limited to one question, but the first and greatest branch of it is Tariff Reform. Whatever may at one time have been the case with England, our present fiscal system never suited Ireland. Ireland has a special interest in changing it, but the work of education in Ireland must be done by Irishmen. And with that I commended their efforts and gave them my blessing.

We lunched yesterday with the Provost of Trinity. Ivy dined here with Mr. Power and a party of ladies, and I dined at the Kildare Street Club. After the meetings we had supper with the Campbells and then went very tired to bed at one o'clock.

We have just lunched and are going out driving, but it is wet and stormy with only brief gleams of sunshine.

We dine tonight at the St. George's Yacht Club at Kingstown with Judge Ross, formerly M.P., and then go back to London by the night mail.

I have a very busy week before me. Ivy will lunch with you at the Berkeley at one o'clock on Friday. I will come if I can, but doubt if I shall be able to manage it.

Warm messages to Father pour in from all sides.

HANS CRESCENT HOTEL,
*10th December* 1906.

It was a real joy to me to get your letter this morning with your and Father's commendations. It is true that I have now the something that was lacking in my life—the something that in its way is everything, though it seems ungrateful to all of you at home who have done so much for me to say so. But you and Father know the world of difference there is between my present political missions, with Ivy to help and sympathise and encourage, and my old solitary excursions, with nothing but my own fancies to brood on. The miracle of her love grows deeper, and the miracle of my own! I had so reluctantly, yet so utterly, abandoned the hope of ever finding in my life what I, who had seen my father's happiness and known his sorrows, felt was all life, or at least all that makes life and its battles really worthy of the best a man can give—what indeed alone makes it possible for him to give his best at all times and in all moods.

42

But I did not mean to write you a love-letter! I was going to say that I was glad Hilda was at Dublin, because I have often thought that my family never saw me at my best in point of form and delivery. I often think that the meetings—comparatively small and with, very probably, a little noisy knot difficult to interest or control—which they have visited with me in my own constituency are the most difficult I ever have to deal with, and that in that sense the prophet rightly has more honour outside his own country than within it.

Caillard's suggestion is foolish. He is one of those who does not know what is possible, fixes his heart on the impossible and then gives way to melancholy when he finds he cannot realise it. But he is a good fellow. His heart is in the right place, and we must be patient with him.

I gather they had an excellent meeting and certainly good speeches at the Tariff Reform League on Friday. Well, this week I must dine and dine and be a villain! I ought to be in the House all the time for the Education Bill, but I cannot cut the Duke's dinner or the Cordwainers' salver—I mean banquet!

I am off to do some shopping now. The house may be ready by today week. What a pity you cannot stop to see it on Friday.

Ivy's cook is much excited and perturbed. Her sister has told her that I am "such a big man." She fears her culinary skill may be unequal to pleasing such grandeur!

1907

1907

## INTRODUCTORY TO 1907 LETTERS

THE letters of 1907 are mainly occupied with the struggle to keep Tariff Reform in the forefront of the Unionist programme and with the events of the Colonial Conference, as it was then called, of that year. They ceased with my father's return from the Riviera to England and were not resumed in the autumn, as we spent these months at Highbury, where our eldest son was born.

*Tariff Reform—Preparation for Colonial Conference*

9 EGERTON PLACE, S.W.,
*11th February* 1907.

Balfour's letter is very unsatisfactory. Long opposes a fiscal amendment from the Front Bench. Balfour thinks my proposal won't do for the reason already given by him to Hewins and now elaborated in three pages. The letter concludes:

> "I am much more hopeful of an amendment on lines suggested by Hewins. . . . The essence of the plan is . . . to concentrate attention upon the critical position which this country stands in towards the Colonies, and especially Canada, in view of the Tariff changes which Canada is proposing in her fiscal relations with Germany, with the U.S.A. and with the mother country. To make the British public understand the fiscal perils which are ahead is certainly much more our duty while we are in opposition than to make ourselves responsible for any special scheme for meeting them when they arise. Let us force those who are conducting affairs to say how they mean to deal with the problems which will certainly come up in an acute form at the approaching Conference."

6.15 p.m. I discussed this suggestion with Bonar Law, Gilbert Parker, Ridley and Goulding. We agreed that I must ask A. J. B. to give us the terms of his proposed amendment, but that if it only asked the Government what they would do without indicating what we would do, it was impossible to accept it. We must then have an amendment of our own, and Bonar Law proposed and we agreed that we must call a meeting of all T.R. members and organise at once.

I then saw Robbins[1] and told him to mention no names but that the line for him to take was that he found among Tariff

---

[1] Sir Alfred Robbins, London Correspondent of the *Birmingham Post*.

Reformers a very strong feeling that action must be taken in the House at once, that it was hoped it would be taken by the Front Bench, that indeed it was the necessary corollary of the Hull speech, but that it was certain, in any case, that Tariff Reformers would take the opinion of the House if the Front Bench did not move.

He asked me about the *Morning Post* paragraph in reference to my intentions. I had not seen it. It appears that they said (1) that I wanted an amendment and (2) might move it myself and (3) would in any case support it. I said it was unauthorised. I did not wish any statement made about my intentions; but between ourselves (1) and (3) were true, though (2) was not.

Then I had half an hour for lunch at Brooks and then went to the Goschen service. I walked back to the L.U. offices and talked with Pease and Boraston, telling them the whole story. Pease will go with us, but pressed very hard for unity if possible. I said he could not feel more strongly on the subject than I did.

At 4 went to the Constitutional Club and met the Executive of the T.R. League and about 20 M.P.s.

Ridley explained the desire of the Executive to see Bonar Law and me to urge on us necessity for action.

I agreed it was necessary to take action now. So-called compromise, viz., that in view of other urgent perils Free Fooders and T.R.s should alike be silent on fiscal question, was no compromise. A movement which did not move was dead. Silence would kill T.R. as easily as opposition. The compromise gave everything to the Free Fooders and nothing to us. Besides, the Colonial question at least was urgent.

I had, therefore, discussed the question with a few friends. They agreed with me that we must have a fiscal amendment on the Address; that it was most desirable it should be official; that we might take a less good or less complete amendment if it were official than we should move if left to ourselves, but we must have a definite fiscal issue.

It has occurred to us that something like the enclosed [1] would

[1] *Enclosure.* "And to assure His Majesty of the earnest desire of this House that advantage may be taken of the coming Colonial Conference to secure closer commercial relations with the Colonies upon a preferential basis."

do and I had proposed this to Balfour, and I told them the substance of what I had written to B.

I had hoped to be able to give them his reply. Owing to difficulty of communicating freely in my absence from town I was not able to do so. I asked for their views—especially if anyone dissented, let him speak at once. If there was not a Front Bench amendment I was prepared to speak and vote for any Back Bench one. But this would do no good unless T.R.s acted together and those present would at once set to work to get our friends into the lobby with us.

Dixon Hartland warmly approved—was ready to move himself if no one else did.

*(In first reading, read
words in brackets and
omit words underlined.)*

                                                    12th February 1907.

All morning I fought [1] with beasts, *very* nice beasts, I confess—not a soul with me except, I think, Linlithgow, if I did not mistake his "becks and nods and wreathed smiles."

They at last got to this beautiful composition:

"and express regret that (while domestic reform is apparently to be postponed to threatened constitutional changes) no mention is made in Your Majesty's Gracious Speech of the approaching Colonial Conference (bearing as it does so closely on the hopes the country entertains of more intimate) and the opportunity offered thereby of securing freer trade within the Empire and closer commercial relations with the colonies" on a preferential basis.

I have no time for details of the discussion. Long was actively against my amendment; so was Douglas. I told them there would be an amendment anyway, or at least I would do my best to secure one, etc., etc., etc. I argued up and down. At last they produced the above. I said it would not do and we adjourned till tomorrow at 6.30.

I lunched here and then went to the Tariff Reform League and telephoned to Ridley, Law, Goulding, Lee, Parker, Hills and

---

[1] At our "Shadow Cabinet."

Remnant to join me (Willoughby is not in town). They agreed this would not do. We summoned all T.R.s to meet at 4 o'clock tomorrow at the H. of C. by telegram, instead of Thursday. Alas! Cochrane, Bridgeman and Foster are abroad—and others, I fear, out of reach.

Then we drafted (at least I did and they approved) amendments omitting words in brackets and adding words underlined.

I took this to Balfour as a concession at 8 o'clock. He was not unfriendly. Alec Hood had meanwhile been telling T.R.s that there would be a Front Bench fiscal amendment.

I had an interesting talk with A. J. B., which gives me some hope—no time to detail it. I told him that if we were to have a Front Bench amendment on the Lords (as might seem necessary after C.B.'s speech) I did not at all insist on this being moved from our Bench. What I wanted was that it should be official. He might *give* it to the Back Bencher to move, but *we must have* official tellers.

Meanwhile, I had set Remnant, Parker and Hills to work, telling them that all depended on whether they could get our men to stand firm against Whips' pressure. We have a lot of rotters— as always.

*13th February* 1907.

Well, well, all's well so far, my dear Mary; but it has been hard work.

A. J. B. missed his appointment with me today at 2.45, so I went to our meeting without having seen him again. 43 Members attended—41 stayed to vote—the 2 who left early agreed with the majority.

I told them frankly my opinion and the opinion of the ex-cabinet, where I was alone in my view of the urgency of the question. Bonar Law spoke strongly for action. So did Middle-more, Lockwood, Evelyn Cecil and Captain Craig.

Banbury was for "a clear and distinct amendment" but would give way if Balfour said he did not want it.

Mason thought any fiscal amendment inopportune. Hardy, I think, concurred, though he was not very clear, and in any case only favoured it if official.

51

I said "official" included two things—(1) an amendment moved from the Front Bench and (2) an amendment moved by a Back Bench man at Balfour's request, for which B. would speak and *name opposition tellers.* I had already told B. that I would be content with (2) if we could only have one Front Bench amendment and he desired (as he did) after C.B.'s speech to challenge him at once on the Lords.

We voted and we separated, pledged to secrecy.

At 6.30 the ex-Cabinet met. I was asked to repeat all that had happened and did so. All thought action inopportune and regretted the decision of "my friends." A long and wearisome discussion followed. At last A. J. B. asked Long his opinion. It was that it was a great pity to have any amendment, but he understood that one would now be moved; if it was moved in the form I had suggested, B. must speak on it; if he spoke *on* it, he must speak *for* it; if he spoke for it, our Whips must tell for it. Alec Hood said just the same. Douglas said ditto.

Long asked whom I proposed as mover. I suggested Hills and this was at once approved. Balfour saw Hills after dinner, gave him the amendment and asked him to move it.

Government has got into a mess (and an awkward one) over the New Hebrides Labour Ordinance. Their people don't like it, but swallow it. Winston was very poor and lame in his reply.

I got home to dinner at 8.15, back to the House at 9.20 and spoke on Old Age Pensions without premeditation.

And so to bed.

HOUSE OF COMMONS,
*20th February* 1907.

Well, my dear Mary, it is all over and on the whole I am satisfied. It might, it is true, have been better, but it *was* good.

The arrangements for the debate were thrown out by Winston. I had arranged with Hood that Alfred should speak early on the first day and Bonar Law in the evening; then that I should get the adjournment and A. J. B. wind up. But A. J. B. announced on Tuesday that he would take first place after Winston, who was to reply to the mover. But Winston's speech as prepared was not suitable, so he hung back. A. J. B. hung back also and wouldn't let his colleagues go on, and so all was rather flat, though not bad, till Bonar Law spoke.

Today A. J. B. spoke with great earnestness and very finely. As you will see, he said three things:

1. Use the duties you now have for what they are worth. That is all we ask of *this* Government.

2. We shall have to impose new duties.

3. When they are imposed I will use them for all they are worth in this cause.

There was on the one hand no qualification and no reserve. There was on the other hand no definite statement as to what new duties we should find necessary.

Winston was violent and poor. He gave no answer to B. Law. A. J. B.'s speech was fine and on a very high level of thought and expression. Lloyd George gave no more an answer to A. J. B. than Winston to Bonar Law; he was reckless in statements of fact and showed great ignorance.

I think I got well home, but I was thrust too much into the dinner hour and was hurried. I am *never* happy, however, in the House. But our people were pleased. "We are," as Alfred said to me, "a Colonial Preference Party" and instead of going back (as we should have done had we kept silence) *we have gone forward*.

I have had no time to write to you earlier, though I know how much you will have desired news from the Front.

Yes, I am well pleased with the whole debate, not satisfied with my own performance, but satisfied that I did good and, above all, pleased that we have had a fiscal amendment, a fiscal discussion, and a fiscal division.

9 EGERTON PLACE, S.W.,
*3rd March* 1907.

I shall never get a letter written to you unless I keep one always on the stocks. Or, to put it differently, I must open a sort of Savings Bank Account for you and pay in little by little as opportunity allows. There will henceforth be neither head nor tail to these notes, but you shall be credited day by day as nearly as I can with anything I have to offer in the way of news or comment, and from time to time the balance standing to your credit shall be sent to you.

It was delightful to have you and Father here even for so short a time and to show you *Our House.* I feel more at home in it since Father has been here, and it was splendid to see how easily he got about and how much he noticed. Ivy says that, sitting where he did, *she* can't see the wrinkles in the Wimperis! I think Father's sight is like some deaf people's hearing—surprising you when you least want to be seen or heard.

A big dinner at the Palace. Strathcona spoke of his yacht and would like to hear from you. If you require it, it will take a fortnight to put it in order. He asked me to enquire of you about it.

The King and Prince both asked after Father very kindly.

I found Eldon Gorst and Francis Hopwood talking of Jamaica, so I enquired whether it was usual for the Sec. of State for War to communicate his thanks direct to a Foreign War Minister for aid rendered in a British Colony. Gorst observed: "I read it with great surprise in the papers"; and Hopwood: "Well, it is explained that it was intended as a personal message not for publication. The beauty of it is that it comes to this: that the S. of S. was thanking Mr. Root for protecting his soldiers, but he had taken all his soldiers away beforehand! so there were none to protect."

I think there must have been a little friction over that matter.

The County Council elections are a surprise for everyone. The best opinion on both sides was that the Progressives would have a majority of ten or twelve. The question now is have we the men required to take the Chairmanships of the big Committees— it seems doubtful. Yet those who fought the battle want the spoils and, it is said, will not give them up to anyone whom they might get as Alderman by co-option.

I have been reading Haldane's great Army speech. It seems to me a bad exposition of his intentions, very difficult to follow. If I understand it, I dislike many features of it. It seems to me that he will never get his new voluntary force and, meanwhile, he begins by destroying what exists, instead of by building up the new. And even if he gets this new "Territorial Army," he relies for a successful campaign on its volunteering for service abroad by battalions and even brigades. That seems to me a risky speculation.

NOTE.—I never understood till the Great War came what a magnificent achievement Haldane's army reorganisation was. Confession of my error is the only amends I can offer to his memory.

*5th March* 1907.

Today we have spent on the Navy Estimates. Only interesting for an acceptance wrung from C.B. of the Two Power Standard as we have always understood it, *i.e.* a margin of security over any *two* other Powers at any time. We have without doubt a very good margin just now, because other Powers stopped their building programme to see what the *Dreadnought* was going to be and have not yet decided how to meet it, *i.e.* with what type of ship. Robertson[1] gave on the whole a satisfactory account of the new Home Fleet, of the numbers, of the nucleus crews, etc. We cannot make a strong attack here at present, but I distrust C.B., and his party are ready to give away anything when the pinch comes. C.B. got very angry and restive under Lee's and Balfour's criticisms of his letter to the *Nation*, *i.e.* the *Speaker* redivivus.

*6th March* 1907.

Now that I have got a larger sheet, you will naturally be prepared for its containing less news. That is how these things usually work out—just as when I was a boy and had 6d. I spent the whole of it in buying a purse and an account book and then had nothing to put in the one and a very little to put in the other.

I had my first ride today. Chancellor was in excellent form. I invited Scott[2] to take the opportunity of inspecting our house now it is finished. On my return he said: "You've got a very nice house, sir. I think the dining-room is very nice—and the

[1] Financial Secretary to the Admiralty.
[2] My father's London coachman from 1880 till his death.

drawing-room, too." And then, with much feeling and the friendly smile you know, he added: "I think you ought to be *very* happy, sir!"

Did I tell you that Ivy has joined, by request, the Ladies' Committee of the 1900 Club Albert Hall Banquet to the Colonial Premiers? The other members are Miss Balfour, Lady Lansdowne, Lady Londonderry, Miss Brook Hunt and, on my suggestion to Boyd Carpenter, the Secretary, Mrs. Alfred Lyttelton, whom they had all of them forgotten!

Ivy went to a Colonial tea-party at Mrs. Alfred's today and appears to have been the centre of attraction.

Collings introduced his Land Bill today under the ten minutes' rule, speaking easily and very earnestly, but going on to weak ground on which he is ill-informed, as I think, about war risks and insurance of our food supply. Ramsay MacDonald threatened opposition from the Labour Party at a later stage—quite consistent from their point of view, but very useful from ours.

*7th March* 1907.

This morning Liberal-Unionist Committee at noon. Telephoned for to meet Chaplin and Bonar Law at the Tariff Reform League and went there at 1.15. Settled to have an Albert Hall demonstration in April and agreed to be one of the speakers. At the House all afternoon on the Navy Estimates and said a few words. Brought Collings home to dinner, where I found Col. Dundas, whom we have kept for the night. Collings is in excellent spirits. Got him to talk of old days, Devonshire village life, Brother Tom, his Father, Mother, his sailor brother and their shipwreck off the Dutch coast. Collings has just gone at 11.30 and the Colonel is fascinated. It was indeed most interesting and delightful to see and hear Mr. Collings.

We are commanded to dinner at Marlborough House on the 15th, and Ivy says her whole time is occupied in explaining that we cannot keep engagements because of "commands."

Alfred Lyttelton said today that it was very good of her to come to Mrs. A.'s Colonial tea. She had delighted the Colonials and been the *clou* of the party.

*11th March* 1907.

This morning I received your letter of the 8th. It was delightful to have more news of you and you know I always like to hear from any of you. But remember that you have gone away for a holiday and don't let me become an addition to the already heavy burden of your daily correspondence. I was greatly flattered by the encomiums passed on my chatter. The fact is that the only way to write good letters is to keep the pot always on the fire and throw in any dainty scraps as fast as you meet with them. If you wait till you have got enough, you wait long and then the dish loses its savour. So my writing is to be a hot-pot, or hotch-pot—I fancy the two words are the same in origin, but B. is not here to turn up the dictionary.

11.30 p.m. Well, we have had a very pretty day at the House. From 4 o'clock to 11 one speaker after another has rubbed the noses of the Government in their New Hebrides dirt. Alfred was good, Bonar Law was better, F. E. Smith did well and Arthur surpassed himself. I don't know how it will all read, but I haven't heard our boys cheer so for a long time. And the other side! Dumb dogs, beaten curs, and they knew it! All their men are sick, and the most sick of all are the Government. John Burns told one of our men that at a meeting of his the other night one of his supporters came up to him and said, "We put you in to turn the Chinamen out and now what's this you've done in the New Hebrides?"

A good many people will say the same before they have done with their precious convention. Winston was flippant and thin; Grey was grave, but very weak; and C.B. was pitiable. . . .

*12th March* 1907.

A delightful day—fresh air and bright sun. Had a meeting of my Committee at 10.30 and then walked home through the Parks. Last evening's entertainment bears the morning's reflection. Still very pleased with yesterday's debate.

A dull afternoon at the House and a meeting of the Tariff Reform Executive, at which we did some business and Sam Storey was, as usual, rather cantankerous.

I hear that Freddy Guest, being asked at one of his meetings: "Were not you and all your family Unionists till a short time ago?" replied: "Oh, yes, that is so; but when Mother changed, *we all* changed!" So like the old story, "When father says turn, we all turn together!"

Dined at the Brodricks. St. John in his new capacity as an Alderman of the London County Council entertained Councillors Lord Alec Thynne and Lygon. Both pleasant young fellows.

C.B. today approached Balfour with a proposition to have an informal conversation under the presidency of the Speaker to consider the possibility of appointing a "Committee on the Business of the House," *i.e.* as I understand, Father's proposal for an adaptation of the American Committee on Rules. C.B. proposed to bring with him Ellis, and "I suppose Fowler must come, as he takes an interest in it, though he is rather stupid, and then I had better get someone more nimble-witted, say Asquith."

Balfour accepted, asked me to join him and expressed his doubt whether there was anyone else on our Bench who could help him! I suggested Stuart-Wortley, as the "opposite number" of Ellis, and Walter Long. We are to meet the week after next, I think, or the end of next week. I suggested to Balfour that our representatives must meet and talk the matter over first to prevent our pulling different ways.

11.45 p.m. Ivy and her Father and Mother have been to see *Raffles* and are full of praises of Gerald du Maurier's acting. I dined with the United Club and opened a discussion on Colonial Preference. Maxse and others had particularly begged me to take on the job for fear lest, if I refused, the task would be allotted to someone who would not be "thorough." So I *was* "thorough." Our friends seemed well pleased and the discussion was all one way. I took occasion to tell them that they need not be afraid of the corn tax; but that even if they were, that would not save them. They were all tarred with the food-tax brush and could not escape it. So that they had better face it boldly.

Hewins tells me he thinks it very doubtful whether Laurier will come to the Conference. He is face to face with grave financial scandals, cannot leave Canada if Parliament is still sitting, and

Borden refuses to facilitate the conclusion of business and the closing of the session. Hewins says Fielding will not come in any case, as Elgin has refused to assent to the Canadian proposition that all Ministers who come should be members of the Conference, though with only one vote for each Colony. Surely Elgin ought to have welcomed this? I cannot yet make up my mind whether I wish Laurier to come under the circumstances or not. I think *not*.

*15th March* 1907.

Dined at Marlborough House. Ivy, taken in by the Master of Elibank, whom she found pleasant, had Herbert Gladstone, whom she found dull, on the other side. I sat between Tweedmouth and Sir A. Bigge, with Morley on the other side of the latter. I talked Admiralty affairs with T. He has evidently had some difficulty with the Cabinet about Rosyth and other matters, but thinks the Cabinet will now be all right.

Morley was interesting about India; impressed by the vastness of its problems; not at all inclined to let natives enter the high places of the service—in particular not disposed to admit them to his Council or to Minto's. Said there was a dangerous spirit represented by the National Congress, but Congress was split, as all Progressive parties are; should he attempt, by doing something, to strengthen the hands of the moderate party, or should he do nothing and so throw everything into the hands of the extremists, who would end "by getting knocked on the head with rifles and guns"? It was the old problem, the problem of Ireland again. I said older than that—as old as the French Revolution and older. The extremists always won in the long run. By granting something, you might strengthen the moderates for a year or a few years, but you gave new weapons to the extremists and the struggle began again. He assented, but took up the reference to the French Revolution, observed there was much to be said for the Girondins, though he himself would have been a Jacobin.

Then he asked my view as to a native member of his Council— a representative, as Bigge called it, of Indian opinion. I said I was dead against it; first, because *a* native was no more a representative of India than the Archbishop of Canterbury was of the

59

Baptists or the Unitarians; second, because our whole position in India rested on the admission that we were different from and in a different position from the natives. We could not admit equality. White men could not and ought not to submit to coloured rule, etc., etc. Bigge took the other side, especially in regard to the Army. Morley said he pretty much agreed with my conclusions, though not with all my reasons. He knew *he would not* submit to be governed by a man of colour. Then he spoke of a Leeds Labour M.P., who had asked him when he was going to begin to govern India according to Indian ideas. "Indian ideas! What are they? Caste (not exactly the Labour ideal!), purdah, suttee, child marriages, female infanticide—those are Indian ideas. Govern India according to Indian ideas—what nonsense!"

He thought the Amir's visit a mistake. He was a barbarian. He understood nothing. He learned Bridge and he quarrelled when he played it. But he could no more understand what he saw than he (Morley) could understand some vast and complicated machine. "The new G.C.B." had blown twenty men from the guns since he got back home for giving him bad advice on big things, or trifles, such as whether the officer in attendance on him should sit by his side or opposite him in his carriage. And worse: he has become a Freemason, and the Mullahs are preaching against him, and the Mullahs are the real power. And meanwhile his brother, Nasrullah, who was opposed to the visit but was brought by him, sits sinister and watchful. He and the Mullahs are the danger.

The Aga Khan has been suggesting to the Prince a royal viceroy *en permanence*, with a Prime Minister to do the work of the present viceroy. The idea brings smiles to Bigge and I suppose to the Prince—not so to Morley!

*18th March* 1907.

Rode at 10 o'clock. Very few people were out. Met Leroy Lewis and discussed Army reforms with him. I owe to him a characteristic story of Arnold-Forster as War Minister. He telegraphed for Grenfell to come over from Ireland to advise "on a most important and urgent matter." G. came—reluctantly. On getting to the War Office he was received by A.-F., who said: "I am most grateful to you for coming. The point on which I wished to consult you is most urgent. It is so and so."

"Well," said G. slowly, "my view on that is——"

"One moment, General," interrupted A.-F., and for five-and-forty minutes by the clock he poured out his own views, after which G. returned to Ireland, without having found an opportunity of expressing *his*!

I raised the question of our action on the Passive Resisters' Bill. I want the House of Lords to pass it—it will make some Nonconformists, all the Romans and many Churchmen very sick and will, I believe, start passive resistance on the part of the two last-named, for it forces Romans and Churchmen to pay three times over; first, for their buildings; second, for rates; and third, for their own special teaching. This is grossly unfair, for at least if they are to pay 2 and 3 they ought not to pay 1. But I think the time has come to let a Bill pass which puts our people on their mettle and does not satisfy the extreme Noncons. It will make our men and the Romans fight harder, will remove the grievance of some of the moderate Noncons. and drive a little wedge a little way into their " bloc." My colleagues, I think, agreed—Lansdowne heartily.

I was also anxious that nothing should be done to weaken the position of the Lords in regard to last year's Bill, so well put this session by Balfour—that as amended by them it would still have removed the crucial grievance of the Noncons., including the call on them to pay rates towards Church or Roman teaching. Agreed also, I think.

Long told a story. Tullibardine asked Sinclair to stay with him. Sinclair was very full of his Scottish Land Bill, so T., on one of their walks, called up an old tenant and said: "Come and listen to Mr. Sinclair's account of the Bill the Government are going to bring in."

The tenant came and listened and said nothing while Sinclair poured forth the story of his wonderful measure and expatiated on its merits. Still the tenant was silent and T. began to grow anxious lest, called to curse, he should stay to bless. But at last to Sinclair's repeated question: "Won't that be a grand thing for you and your children?" he replied, "Eh, mon, it's too silly to pass!"

*20th March* 1907.

Rode at 10.

Business at the House—C.B.'s new standing orders. I had been asked to be ready to take part in the discussion and had "wombled" the question a little, but this morning found a note from Hood saying the Chief wished me to follow C.B. So, after dictating letters to Mr. Wilson, I hastily made a few notes and this afternoon delivered myself of an hour's oration of a temperate non-party but unyielding kind. Ellis subsequently quoted a passage from a speech of Father's against me. I had forgotten it; and if it correctly represents his views (apart from its context) I do not, I fear, agree with it under present circumstances. But present circumstances are very different from those of any preceding time and I daresay Father himself would qualify the view quoted by Ellis. The quotation referred to the extension of Grand Committees. My line was that the time at our disposal was sufficient but ill-distributed, and the true remedy was a time-limit fixed by a non-party Committee on Business, as first propounded and often urged by Father.

I am told that C.B. hoped to get his first Standing Order today. He got nothing! The Second Reading Discussion will last at least half Monday, and then there are all the amendments.

*21st March* 1907.

Went to the House at 12 noon for the conference with C.B. on Procedure. The policeman at the Ladies' Gallery entrance, which I always use, said, "They're still at it this morning, sir," and as I had seen a little crowd outside Palace Yard I supposed he referred to the Suffragettes, who were very disorderly last night. So I said, "Drat the women! I wish the Magistrate would give the leaders a good heavy sentence," and passed on. Arrived at C.B.'s room his messenger told me that the conference was put off "on account of these frequent interruptions." Odd, I thought, but I supposed C.B. was receiving deputations from

62

the demonstrators or conferring with the police, so I put on my hat again and came away.

Lunched at home with Col. and Mrs. Dundas. At three went to the House again to ask some questions and then for the first time learned that the House was still sitting on Wednesday's business—there having been a fine row over a breach of faith. Wasn't I a goose?

The sitting finished at 5.30. This beats Father's record on the Army Bill at the time of the flogging discussions. He only kept the question going till 6 a.m. Our boys had maintained the discussion till nearly 6 p.m. There is to be a Saturday sitting to do Thursday's work; but as the Irish have first place with a resolution on primary education in Ireland, the Government and the Irish can "get the Speaker out of the Chair" without our assistance.

*23rd March* 1907.

To the House at 12 to enter a protest against the Government conduct of business, but first had a ride in the Park.

Returned to lunch, where we had Mlle de Nys (very pleasant), Hilda Mary,[1] looking *very* well, and Miss Allison, whom I liked.

Then to the House again and voted against the Metric System (compulsory) Bill. Then to a Tariff Reform Committee. They have disposed of 5000 places for the Albert Hall demonstration already.

Dined with the Loulou Harcourts. Sat between Lady Desborough, pleasant as always, and Mrs. Cavendish Bentinck. On the other side of Lady D. (whom I should have taken in if she had arrived before we sat down) was Birrell, pleasant and amusing. Our conversation led us to the subject of unappreciated jokes and B. cited an example. In speaking last autumn of the arduous duties cast on the Board of Education by the Lords' amendments to the Education Bill he had said no one could be found to undertake them—Not even my noble predecessor would accept such a task, though no impediment has been sufficient to restrain his family from serving the State.—I cannot recall the words, but I remember the incident and the gibe was obvious—the suggestion

[1] My niece.

that they were always office-seekers. Londonderry sought him out and warmly thanked him for his complimentary reference!

Lady D. contributed the following reminiscence. In days gone by, in a pause of the conversation at a dinner at Lady Pembroke's, Lady Brownlow was heard to ask Birrell: "And do *you* think that our Souls should dwell in the Ideal or in the Real?" To which Birrell: "Br-r-r-r!"

Birrell said he remembered the question! "Now how would you have answered it?" he asked Lady D. "Oh, I should have floundered," she replied. "No, I am sure you would have answered charmingly," said he. "But not so epigrammatically!" I ventured.

Many thanks for your letter and Father's message. We shall have time to consider his advice. In any case, we shall fight the Bill on those lines in our House, though of course we cannot reject it there.

1907 : April, May

*Colonial Preference—The Colonial Conference—The Budget*

9 Egerton Place, S.W.,
*9th April* 1907.

We are all pleased with the Colonial resolutions for the Conference. The London Chamber of Commerce on a poll has decided by about two to one in favour of Tariff Reform and Preference.

*10th April* 1907.

The weather here is as vile as exiles on the sunny Riviera could wish!

Lunch time past and gone.

Now it has rained as well as fogged! Well, I shall not go to the House till dinner-time. The Army Debate is proceeding and I shall not be wanted, but I am engaged to dine with Buxton to meet Dr. Jameson. I shall try to nobble him for our little dinner on the 20th.

Now I am going to work on Income Tax reform and taxation of land values. "Isn't that a pretty dish to set before the king?"

*10th April* 1907.

Buxton's dinner last night included Dr. Jameson, Tweedmouth, Dixon Poynder, A. E. Mason and myself, sitting in order named. The talk was rambling but pleasant—House of Commons stories; Winston's indiscretions, of which, said Dr. J., more will be heard at the Conference; South African affairs; characters of Rhodes, Hofmeyer, Malan (the coming Boer leader) and Smuts, the real director of Boer policy in the Transvaal; House of Commons procedure, and Father's suggestion for a Committee on Business, which, Buxton told me, the Cabinet had favoured "but we understood you would not have it"—on what authority I knew not and could not discover. Then in a pause in the conversation, Buxton injudiciously asked the Doctor: "Are you doing anything

E                                        65

to develop the Cape wine trade?" and you can imagine the answer he got. "Yes, all we can, but we want a little help from you," and so on. A good deal of good-natured chaff followed, in the course of which I said: "No, Doctor, don't trust to the late Government. As Buxton says, they were no good. And don't trust to Buxton, who is a hide-bound Cobdenite, or to Tweedmouth, who is absorbed by Admiralty work. But go to the President of the Board of Trade.[1] He is a really open-minded Minister." And in the midst of the laughter with which this sally was greeted I heard Buxton murmur under his breath: "Yes, none of us know what Lloyd George is up to!"

*12th April* 1907.

Well, I had an active day yesterday. Worked here all morning. Duckworth to lunch. Told me again that the Treasury are rather disappointed with Asquith. "If a subject is forced upon him, he gets up the papers like a brief, but he never thinks of anything till it is forced on him." G. H. D. has no hint of what the Budget is likely to be.

Then to the House and took an active part in discussion on new Standing Order, speaking several times. My line always was: "reform is urgent, but you make changes in the wrong places. You should restrict Report, not Committee. Besides, your exception of money bills is pedantic and you are not logical. You should abolish the preliminary resolutions on all money bills. I make my protest. You won't listen, but I console myself with the thought that I will make you stew in your own juice before long. Ha, Ha! A time will come (and a Budget) when your precedent, properly and logically extended, will be most useful— to me!"

I was engaged to dine at the Constitutional Club to honour Bonar Law. Gave up the dinner to hold the fort in the House during the dinner hour. Spoke at 6 o'clock, 7 o'clock, 8.15 and 9. Then hurried to the Club, where the King's health had just been drunk. Called for soup and cold meat. Listened to an admirable speech from B. Law—*all* you would wish it to be, clear, forcible, strong and corn-taxy! Spoke myself, paid him a very warm but

[1] Mr. Lloyd George.

well-deserved tribute and pointed out that some people had political courage, some could be inspired with it and some must be taught that it was less dangerous to fight than to run away.

Back to the House at 11 in time to hear C.B. announce closure of the Procedure Rules for Monday. Spoke again. Home and to bed, satisfied with my day's work, of which, however, you will find no adequate account in any paper!

*15th April* 1907.

A busy day at the House over C.B.'s guillotine motion, but I got off for an hour and dined at home.

Alfred Lyttelton said to me today: "I think we are doing very well with Preference." I find that opinion generally held and I share it. Public interest is keen and the Premiers have kept the subject well to the front. You will have noted Deakin's speech at the Australian dinner.

Haldane, talking to A. J. B. about the time to be allotted to the Army Bill, says the Budget will occupy much time, which means, I suppose, that it will be a big Budget; but I cannot guess *what* it will be. Asquith was not at work at it at Easter. He played two or three rounds of golf a day and bridge at night.

*16th April* 1907.

A cold raw morning. To my Committee [1] at 10.30, where we had a very good witness, but Lord! as Mr. Pepys says, to see how these people do contradict one another. Walked home with Duckworth. Ivy, meanwhile, had been at her Ladies' Committee for the 1900 Club Banquet to the Premiers.

Busy all the afternoon at the House, where I dined and was kept till midnight. I think the Licensing Bill is abandoned and that Asquith is to placate the temperance people with high licensing duties.

On my return home I found B.'s letter, for which many thanks. She is quite right about the stir the Conference is making. There

---

[1] The Government had asked me to take the Chairmanship of a Committee on Marine Insurance in time of war. We reported against a Government scheme, but I told the Prime Minister when the subject was raised again some years later that owing to changed circumstances our conclusions no longer held good.

is, I think, more real interest in it—more expectation of results—than ever before. We Tariff Reformers are keeping our end well up. The Premiers are having Tariff Reform resolutions rained upon them and I have great hopes that they will see and understand the growth and strength of the movement. So far prospects are very encouraging.

*17th April* 1907.

Botha continues to make good speeches, but there is rather too much gush over him for my taste.

11 p.m. John Morley and Anson, who dined quietly with us, have just left. Their talk was very pleasant and interesting, but I never can Boswellise a conversation. We began with House of Commons recollections. Speaking of Davey's [1] speeches, Morley said, "They were like a magnum of soda-water gone flat." Gladstone had once said to him: "Parnell is an admirable speaker; he always says exactly what he wants to say." We recalled many parliamentary incidents, such as parliamentarians love to talk of.

Morley told us that Bryce's ambition was to go to India. He shed tears when he was sent to Ireland. "He didn't want to go, as who would?" Anson told us Birrell's parting words at the Education Office. "Well," said Morant to him, "I think you leave everything in order for your successor." "Yes," said Birrell, "I read a suicide case in this morning's paper. 'The deceased man's affairs were all in perfect order, and no reason can be assigned for his rash act.'"

M. said at the India Office he thought they would rank Kimberley first and George Hamilton second among their chiefs in recent times.

Then we talked of Kitchener. Why had I cheered M.'s statement that K.'s term in India had been extended two years? Because I thought there was a great work of reorganisation urgently needed and K. was the man to do it. Nothing had shocked me more than what I had learnt at the Defence Committee of the unpreparedness and inefficiency of the Army in India. I understood that now that he was no longer fighting Curzon, he was doing very

---

[1] Afterwards Lord Davey.

well. Morley replied doubtfully, "Ye—es, certainly. Yes, officially I think he is doing very good work. And then as there is undoubtedly some unrest now in India—much exaggerated, but still there is some—and as it is desirable to reassure the whites and give somewhat *à penser* to the natives, it is well to have a great figurehead like K. But he was deeply disappointed. He wanted to succeed Cromer, but it was thought he was not diplomatic enough for the foreigners, though he would doubtless impose on the Khedive, who is now the enemy. I need not say," Morley added, "that they did not want him at home."

I criticised Haldane's Army speech as ill-arranged and repeating itself. The whole story could have been better told in two-thirds the time. Morley: "Yes, I remember Bryce once saying to me as we left a Cabinet, 'Don't you find Haldane very hard to follow?' And I confessed I did. 'I'll tell you why it is. His speeches have no paragraphs. There are full stops here and there, faintly marked, but no paragraphs.'"

Morley on the India Office [1] again: "A day or two ago I had Richmond Ritchie with me—the ablest man in the office. (This surprised me. He is a good Civil Servant, but I thought Godley [2] far abler.) The Indian Government wanted a punitive expedition against the Zakka Khels; my Council wanted it. I said no. Then I said to R.: 'Now that has taken us a quarter of an hour, but *that* I call hard work. I'm tired. Do you remember Bowen's definition of hard work—answering yes or no on imperfect information?'"

Morley to Ivy: "Well, politics are very fascinating, but what is the most interesting career? Literature—real literature—a Shakespeare or a Tennyson, if you will—is higher. To be a great artist—a musician, now that attracts me; he suffices to himself."

Anson: "It depends on whether you seek permanent or immediate recognition. The politician, the actor, the orator, who is an actor, get the latter."

Morley: "Well, I think I would sooner 'sit down amid loud cheers' than stop an expedition against the Zakka Khels in my Cabinet!"

[1] See Morley in *Down the Years*.
[2] Afterwards Lord Kilbracken.

69

And I to protest that speeches were a burden, but that there was no pleasure in the world like sitting in some big office of administration, or in Cabinet, and feeling you were helping to mould and direct the policy of your country and make her history.

Was not Morley's utterance a characteristic flashlight on his weakness?

Somehow we touched on the House of Lords. "It is easier," said I, "to strengthen it than to reform it." "Yes," said Morley. "You remember that in the '92 Government Rosebery made a strong speech about it and then a Cabinet Committee was appointed to consider what was to be done. After some weeks, as nothing more was heard of it, Harcourt and I, who were always very good-humoured (another flashlight! I liked this touch), enquired what had become of it, and it then appeared that the Committee had held several meetings, but they were still wrangling as to whether the object was to be to strengthen or to weaken it. For my part, I am dead against a Senate—a house of retired Colonial Governors and worn-out Civil Servants and aged states-men in retreat. I had sooner—and many of our Party would say the same—have the Carlton than the Athenæum to rule over us."

Morley would have liked to be at the Guildhall to see "Botha shaking Roberts's two hands—a wonderful sight." I said, "less wonderful, I think, and far easier than the reconciliation or friend-ship of opposing politicians." Morley demurred. "Surely," I rejoined, "it is far easier to conceive of Lee and Grant meeting as friends after the Civil War than of Jeff Davis and Lincoln doing the same." "Yet," said Anson, "there is a great deal of friendship among opponents in the House." "There is a good deal of *fausse bonhomie!*" retorted Morley.

After all, I think I may sign,

BOSWELL, Jr.

*19th April* 1907.

"Well, what do you think of it all?" For myself, alas, I have no time to *think*, but I note some impressions.

The Budget is a good one and Asquith is preparing a very strong position for next year. I reckon he will have at his disposal, when he makes his next financial statement, roughly :

1,500,000 allotted to Sinking Fund for this year only,
  600,000 of arrears of Income Tax,
  600,000 of Income Tax additional from his new proposals,
  700,000 additional Death Duties,
1,000,000 normal growth of Revenue.

4,400,000
2,000,000 additional taxation on Licences,
  600,000 from Motor Cars.

7,000,000 Total *plus* whatever he can save on the Army and Navy
         Estimates.

Meanwhile he has produced a "sound" Budget and one which, subject to examination in details, is not inequitable. His differentiation of the Income Tax is illogical in execution and involves many administrative difficulties, but it will be popular. His increase in the Death Duties on fortunes over £150,000 is also popular and, I think, right, except in the case of landed estates, where the capital value is out of all proportion to the free income.

On the whole it is a Budget of promise rather than performance, but I think he will be able to fulfil the promise, though not to reduce taxation as well. He will start Old Age Pensions on a pretty handsome scale, but he cannot also greatly reduce food duties, even if he can reduce them at all.

It is not an easy Budget to fight, and the prospects are more favourable to him than I like.

I left the House of Commons about 9 o'clock and got to the Albert Hall in time for the speeches. It was a splendid spectacle and Father's letter was received with great enthusiasm. Ivy sat between Moor[1] and Brodeur,[2] with Smartt[3] just beyond, and found them very pleasant. Ward,[4] Borden,[5] Moor and Botha

---

[1] Prime Minister of Natal.
[2] A Canadian Minister.
[3] One of the South African Ministers.
[4] Prime Minister of New Zealand.
[5] Afterwards Prime Minister of Canada.

(the only Colonials with whom I got a chance of speaking) sent the kindest messages to Father.

Balfour's speech was—well, it was Balfour's speech; but it had no lesson, no inspiration, no effect. Laurier was inaudible a few yards away; but Moor said, "the best he has made yet—the most outspoken." "I have been trying," Laurier said, "since I arrived here to find out what most interests the people of this country in connection with this Conference and it seems to me it is the question of trade Preference." Every favourable allusion to Preference was loudly cheered.

Deakin [1] is wonderfully fluent, but he gives me the idea of a man who means business, who is determined that business shall result, and whose very rhetoric *is* business, because of the faith that inspires it and the force that directs it. He, if any man, will fill Seddon's place. He will compel thought and action, and Jameson, Ward and Moor will respond to every sign and word from him. Laurier will be—is being—pushed and pulled along by them.

Botha made another unexceptionable speech. If he means what he says, it is perfect; and it is really difficult to believe that it is all the *fausse bonhomie* of which Morley spoke in another connection.

As husbands and wives escorted each other up the Hall and I was late, Ivy had to "process" the length of the Hall alone and "I got a cheer all to myself," she says.

This morning I attended a Liberal-Unionist Council Meeting. All goes well there. Then Lilian lunched with us, very busy and active as usual.

Then I go to a Tariff Reform Committee and tonight dine with the Pilgrims to meet the Colonials again. They asked me to speak, but I declined. The Duke of Devonshire speaks. In any case, I have two speeches next week and "that is enough."

*20th April* 1907.

I was very sorry to have to trouble Father for another message, but the feeling of our Committee was *very* strong. "Could you not write one yourself?" they asked, and I replied, "No doubt I *could*; but what would my Father say when he saw it in the papers?" I think the draft I sent has the "Chamberlain touch,"

[1] Prime Minister of Australia.

I thought as I sat in the Albert Hall the other night, what an awful place to speak in! But I also thought what a glorious opportunity Balfour missed. It was cruel to see it so hopelessly lost, and that is, I think, the feeling of all our people. We must see if we can do better.

Last night I went to the Pilgrims. Grey made a fine speech and Deacon made a remarkable one. Watch him. He is the biggest figure in this Conference. I was placed between Shaw (Lord Advocate) and Jack Pease, with Caillard, Spender, of the *Westminster*, and Lord Kinnaird at the same table. Brodeur, who was to have been there, did not turn up. Shaw got very gloomy over Deakin's rather bellicose utterances. "Cheer up, Tommy," said Pease, "war is not yet declared!" "I'm afraid there are no Quakers in the South Seas," retorted Shaw.

Kinnaird is High Commissioner of the Scottish Church, and when he went to open the General Assembly it was the Lord Advocate's duty to attend in his wig and gown. "My known views on disestablishment," said Shaw, "caused my friends to feel some surprise at seeing me in the procession, and as my carriage passed the Guards' band, they struck up ''E dunno where 'e are!'"

I interchanged civilities with Spender [1] and expressed the hope that he would continue to co-operate with me in keeping the food question to the front.

I slipped out after Ward's speech, but even so did not get home till 11.30.

This afternoon I rode down to Richmond with Leo. . . .

Deakin sends warm greetings. I am trying to get him and Mrs. D. to lunch or dine with us.

I must go and dress for our dinner.

*20th April* 1907.

I continue the chronicles of Egerton Place. Our party was Julia Lady Tweeddale and Evans Gordon, the Duckworths, the George Murrays, the Blumenthals, Mrs. Gervase Beckett (he fell off, being obliged to go down to his constituency) and Evelyn

[1] Mr. J. A. Spender, then editor of the *Westminster Gazette*, by far the ablest exponent of Liberal policy in the Press of that time.

Dundas, who stays the night with us. All very pleasant and very talkative, and I think they enjoyed themselves.

I gathered from Murray that he thought Asquith had got a pretty difficult job before him in his attempt to differentiate the Income Tax and that A. himself did not yet know the answer to my questions about pensions, life charges, etc. I have a few more ready for Monday and mean to make some further observations. It is a case for sap and mine before developing an attack in force on the Second Reading with alternatives. . . .

*21st April* 1907.

Dined alone at home and enjoyed our quiet evening. But we were disturbed by strange noises in the kitchen. I rang for Allinson[1] and enquired: "Have you got a puppy downstairs?"

"No, sir."

"Well, what is it then? There's too much noise, anyway."

"It's my son, sir!"

The infant, aged three, was very merry and making the strangest noises. So I sent him a banana and that quieted him, and I hope mollified Allinson's natural disgust at my unpardonable mistake.

*22nd April* 1907.

I got a ride at ten o'clock and have been busy at the Budget ever since. Now I am off to the House. We "bus" to Hyde Park Corner and then Ivy will walk across the Parks with me and cab it home. I propose to make a few more observations on the Income Tax resolution.

How I should like to have half an hour's talk with Father about the précis of the Conference's proceedings published today. I think that what they have done is all to the good, but I wish Deakin had had his way and got its own Secretariat for the Conference. It is curious to see how this question, and the question of the Prime Minister of Great Britain presiding, have come to the front the moment Father's commanding personality is no longer there to make everyone feel that the Colonial Secretary is the biggest President the Conference could have. As long as Father was C.S.

[1] My butler.

no one thought of these matters; and having in mind Father's tenure of office I was at first prejudiced against the change. But apart from his personality, I think the change is right.

11.30 p.m. Well, I delivered myself of an hour's further criticism of Asquith to my own satisfaction and then we dined at Stafford House, a non-party dinner to the Premiers. I sat next Ward, who regretted they had not done more but was pleased with what they had done. They had found Laurier very difficult and it had needed much pressure in private conversations to carry him as far as they had done. Ward hoped they would do something as to defence and talked in the right spirit about Preference. He was sure it would come, hoped they would arrange a $33\frac{1}{3}$ per cent. Preference among all Colonies while over here and believed they would so help the question along, even in this country. Anyway they would put forward their views and they were not discouraged by our election, which was no affair of theirs.

London is laughing over a story of Lady Derby at the Prince's dinner to the Premiers.

"Who," she asked of Sir Wilfred Laurier, "who is the pleasant-looking gentleman next Lady Laurier who is enjoying his dinner so much?"

"That," replied Sir Wilfred, "is *your* Prime Minister!"

I spoke to both the Lauriers tonight. They send their greetings.

I hear the Liberals did not at all like Deakin's speech at the Pilgrims. "One didn't know what was coming next," they say. I fancy they are nearly as much afraid of him as they used to be of Seddon.

*27th April* 1907.

Our object last night was to lead Deakin on, on Preference. Jameson says he is rather shy on that subject when it comes to discussing details, as he is a little afraid of his position at home. On other subjects he has been bold and pressing, especially urging publication of full reports daily and the establishment of a Secretariat of the Conference under the Prime Minister of this country, but paid for by all the Colonies. He demanded to see the gentleman who deals with Australian affairs. "Where is he? I want to see his cage."

75

"His cage? What cage?" asked Elgin.

"The cage in which he is kept. He must be kept in a cage or he couldn't know so little of anything that happens outside."

We baited the Preference hook for him by telling him that Ramsay MacDonald had come back from Australia saying that though D. talked Preference, that was only a political move and Australia would give nothing.

D. retorted scornfully that they were cursed with that kind of traveller in Australia—"the man with eyes bandaged, ears stuffed and only his tongue loose—who knows more about us when he arrives than when he leaves, because he sees only what he wishes to see and hears only what he has come to learn."

The Conference is going to take up Preference on Tuesday. Jameson and Deakin mean to press the Government for a Preference on existing duties.

Laurier has, of course, been against them all through, and Botha falls naturally into line behind Laurier.

People are gushing a great deal too much over Botha, but his speeches, I must confess, are all they should be. Duckworth was told by Bernard Holland that when some Army proposals were under discussion Botha said: "I think we ought to do so and so, because after all what we all want is not only to defend the Empire *but to extend it.*"

Smartt said to me: "There'll be no more fighting in South Africa. They have no idea of that; and it's not necessary. They will make it Dutch without that." I asked what he thought of Smuts's Education speech. "Smuts has a private quarrel with the Predikants," he said, "but he knows they are his best political organisers."

*28th April* 1907.

The Scottish Land Bill is on today, but the division will not be taken till tomorrow, so I stay at home to work. It is a very bad Bill, introducing and making compulsory the worst features of the Irish system. Scottish farmers are actually asking their landlords to raise their rents so as to put them outside its scope! Here for instance is a case. A tenant of Cawdor's, paying £37, 10s. per annum, asks to be raised to £50. "I know you will never ask for the money and it will get me out of the Act. I don't want to be forced into the Court." I hear the same story of the Dukes of Argyll's and Richmond's estates.

I told Mr. Wilson to send you a copy of the Albert Hall programme.

I spoke of the size and the distance of the audience. Said Neville in his pretty way: "It didn't surprise me that you should look so small. What did surprise me was that such a little man could make so much noise!"[1]

*1st May* 1907.

I dined at home quietly with Ivy, and then came downstairs to a pile of uninteresting letters, but also to one which gives me *great* pleasure—I mean of course Father's, with a note added from Ida. You know that there is nothing I value so much as praise from Father. It is a great encouragement to me in the midst of my difficulties and the suspicions with which I am surrounded.

I think we may be confident that Deakin, Ward, Jameson and Moor will *not* give away the Preference case. I pressed C.B. today about full reports, and he practically pledged himself to giving them after the Conference. They are terrified of Deakin and I hear he scarified them again today at the Victoria League, where I should have been but for the Budget.

A. J. B. speaks at the Albert Hall on Friday next and volunteered to me the statement that he meant to deal with the question of broadening the basis of taxation and with Preference. There is no doubt that the speeches of the Premiers are affecting the minds of some of those who were hanging back. S. H. Butcher and Bob Cecil are cited to me as instances of men who now admit that "we must do something." I don't exaggerate the importance of this, but it is worth something.

This is poor stuff, but I am tired and it is late.

*2nd May* 1907.

The King invites Father to his dinner to the Colonial Premiers on May 8th. I have declined on his behalf formally and written privately to Knollys to make his excuses as well.

[1] There were of course no "loud-speakers" in those days.

It was a great pleasure to read Father's views of the situation and of the different proposals which have been made at the Conference. I will wait and see what Balfour says at the Albert Hall before making up my mind about the Compatriots' dinner to him. He *is* impressed by the Premiers' attitude and speeches and is going strong on broadening the basis of taxation, but I do not myself anticipate that he will materially advance his position.

*Later.* Asquith has this morning "point-blank refused Preference in any shape or form." So says Deakin in a private note to Balfour, and evidently he is not only disappointed at the decision, but offended by the form in which it was conveyed. Asquith seems to have been on this occasion, as so often, quite needlessly brutal. At any rate, that is the impression produced.

Deakin also says in the note that full daily publication was vetoed by Laurier. Elgin did not himself veto it, but was evidently glad to range himself behind Laurier, who was with difficulty persuaded to agree to a daily précis; but the précis on Preference is so ludicrously inadequate that Deakin believes he will be able to get a full and early publication of the discussion. *Tant mieux!*

The Clives' cook at Wormbridge says, "You know, mum, my husband is a dreadful radical, but I'll take care that he votes right next election. I never met such a pleasant young lady as Mrs. Austen Chamberlain!"

*3rd May* 1907.

We dined last night with Lady Selborne—half an hour late, having waited for Mr. Moor of Natal, who didn't turn up. Lady Waldegrave, Lady Howick, Duncan, late Colonial Secretary of the Transvaal, and the Selbornes' second son being the company. Lady S. pressed me hard, by Selborne's desire, to "go gently," to leave time for others who were moving to close up, etc. I get plenty of this advice, but I have my own rôle to play, and though I must not neglect altogether that point of view, someone must make the running and that someone must apparently be your humble servant.

Duncan thinks Botha sincere; he does not think that Smuts will or can rule him, as Smuts has no influence with the people and is disliked as a free-thinker by the Predikants.

11.30. Well, the Moors did go to the Naval Review, but they somehow got here by 8.30 and our party was complete—the others being the Lugards, William and Louise (in a *lovely* pink gown), V. Caillard, the Birchenoughs, the Cochranes and Miss Jones. The Lugards speak gloomily of the Colonial Office and, indeed, I think it is evident that the officials are falling back into their old ways; and the old complaints—removed by Father's administration—are reviving. L. was much struck by Winston's keenness and ability, but tells me that Elgin "could hardly sit in his chair" when Winston spoke, snubbed him and interrupted him. All this on the subject of Nigerian railroads. Girouard, consulted before there was any idea of his going out, backed Lugard's views.

Moor tells me that Asquith had some plain speaking today from Lyne and others. They have yet to vote on Preference, "but everyone who has spoken since Asquith has clearly shown his disappointment," and Lyne challenged Asquith to take a referendum to prove his assertion that the people of this country were against it. I gather that Moor thinks the 1902 resolution will be reaffirmed unanimously and the Australian addition will secure the support of New Zealand, the Cape and Natal, but will have against it Great Britain, Canada, Newfoundland and the Transvaal—in spite of Hofmeyer's speech reported today.

Moor is impressed by the numbers of resolutions he has received and notes the progress of the movement here.

*4th May* 1907.

Moor told Ivy that Smartt and Lyne were both furious with Asquith, and even the summary published this morning shows that they pitched into him severely. He appears to have got his figures all wrong besides. Deakin is also said to have been "furious." I am pleased with Balfour's speech last night. It is a great thing that he should, voluntarily and entirely of his own accord, devote a whole speech to Preference and Fiscal Reform. It will help us along, even though he still leaves his "i's" undotted and his "t's" uncrossed. Lloyd George has still to address the Conference on behalf of the Government and is expected to be much more conciliatory. If their words mean anything, they are going to try a policy of shipping subsidies and so on, but this means money and

where is money to come from? By all means let them try. We
will egg them on if we can.

Today the Deakins lunched with us, the rest of our party being
the Hewinses, the Fabian Wares, Leo Maxse and Hilda. Deakin
is righteously angry and at the same time encouraged; thinks that
on the whole the semi-secrecy enforced has stimulated curiosity
and interest about their proceedings and that Asquith's flat refusal
was better for the cause than any pretended concessions, which
would have enabled the Government to say, "See, we are doing
what is wanted!" and yet not to have done it. He sent the
warmest messages to you and Father, and both he and Mrs. Deakin
spoke of the very nice letter she had received from Mary. He is
a *man* and, as Maxse said, "what luck that Australia should have
thrown up a man just when he was so wanted!" He has a very low
opinion of Elgin, as dull and inferior in every way; says John
Burns was red tape personified; evidently thinks badly of, and
is angry with, Laurier for doing "bonnet" to the Government
and is sure that he is being bought by the promise of some
Canadian subsidy.

Hewins says that every figure Asquith used is wrong. He has
written to the papers to point out the errors, and his letter should
appear on Monday. A. J. B. and Hewins appear to be "as thick
as thick." A. J. B. sent for him yesterday afternoon and went
through his Albert Hall speech with him in advance, "and I stiffened
it up throughout," said Hewins.

Ivy and I have just ordered a motor cab and are going to
leave cards on the Bonar Laws at Wimbledon for the sake of
fresh air.

*5th May* 1907.

Lilian came to me yesterday on her way back from the Osterley
garden party. She and some other Tariff Reformers wanted to
know if we could not organise a mass-meeting in the Albert Hall
to be addressed by Deakin and wanted me to sound Deakin as to
his willingness to undertake it. He was so angry with Asquith,
Elgin and Co., so vexed at the denial of publicity etc., that they
thought he would speak out strongly, and the working men had
had no opportunity of hearing him such as a mass-meeting would

give; and, lastly, the Press would report a mass-meeting more fully than a smaller gathering.

I took the night to think the matter over and then replied that I was rather doubtful whether Deakin ought to be asked to come so far into our Party arena and that in any case I was sure that I, a Front Bench man, was not the person to ask him; it would look too much as if I wanted him to pull the chestnuts out of the fire for me. If, however, he felt inclined to deliver a kind of political testament to us before leaving our shores, it would be useful, and we could surely, through our friends, let the Press know the special importance of the speech he was going to make and get him well reported; that the audience mattered nothing but the report was everything. Could not an Australian or Colonial Banquet be arranged in his honour, which should serve him as a rostrum? If so, Amery or Maxse should sound him as to his willingness. Just as I was writing this, Lilian sent me a letter with the same idea. I hope something may come of it.

Lilian says all the Canadians in London are very angry about Laurier's attitude and she thinks it will do him a good deal of harm in Canada. Deakin told me that L. had only taken a fifth-rate part in the Conference. He was evidently angry and disgusted with him.

*5th May* 1907.

Deakin was much pleased by my recalling Father's description of himself as (in Gambetta's phrase) a *Radical Autoritaire*. He evidently felt that he fell into the same category and he observed that a Radical must be "autoritaire" if his radicalism was to serve any purpose.

*A propos* of I know not what remark, Leo Maxse said, "Yet it is the men who were extremist and intransigent who have made great movements possible." To which I replied, "Yes, but is not this the distinction—the man of thought must be intransigent; the man of action must always compromise?" And I think that is true, and a truth that we all have to recognise. But how about Cavour and Garibaldi? In one sense Garibaldi was the "man of thought," the idealogue—to use today's phrase—and Cavour the "man of action." But it is straining words to call them so. I suppose the proper distinction is between the man who is working for an idea pure and simple and the man who, sharing the idea, cares more for immediate realisation of whatever is presently practicable than for symmetrical perfection or logical consistency.

*A propos* of words and phrases, is there anything which more strikingly brings home the novelty of our Imperial problem than the difficulty of finding words to describe facts? "Colonial" "Imperial"—neither really fits the Conference. How are we to say in one word: "The self-governing Dominions" (this is the Conference phrase) "beyond the seas"? And what one word will express the white nations of the Empire including the United Kingdom? and what other word the "Reichs-lands" as I hope we shall in time come to regard the tropical dependencies?

I had some talk with Deakin as to these latter and the possibilities of making "the Colonies" more really partners in them. He would heartily approve and promote simultaneous examination for the Indian Civil Service in all the "Dominions"—not the allocation of so many places to Australia or Canada, but simultaneous holding of the same exam. in the different countries—as has already been done for some educational exams. But he does not see his way to any joint military occupation, as I had hoped—the idea being that *e.g.* Australia might, in addition to its militia, have two battalions of regulars, one in Australia and one on the Indian frontier. He says their development will be on the lines of a "Citizen Army." He does not see his way to any "regulars" at all, though he is confident they would find plenty of volunteers for war.

*6th May* 1907.

Well, after being jolly "under creditable circumstances" for some time, it is pleasant at last to have something to be jolly about! Of course, we here in London and in Parliament always exaggerate the importance of the event of the moment and we are all elated; but, making all allowance for our hot-house atmosphere and the excitement it produces, we have enough to rejoice over sincerely and profoundly. A. J. B.'s speech is recognised as marking an advance for the Party, and the Hayes-Fisher letter adds point and emphasis to it. Our men are merry. I went to the House at question time. Says Arthur Lee: "I say, the sheep are hurrying into the fold." To him succeeds Evelyn Cecil, already concerned with the problem of the future—these labourers of the eleventh hour, the Londonderrys, Stanleys, etc., must not be restored to office at the expense of the workers—"us workers" I think he said.

Then comes Arthur Stanley: "Eddie told me to take the earliest opportunity of telling you that he had become definitely a Tariff Reformer. I transmit the message without comment. You realise, I suppose, that in a short time you will be denounced as a laggard!"

These *voces populi* will give you some idea of the buzz of excited comment on the events of these days.

Then A. J. B.: "Will you consider whether we should raise the question of Preference on the Second Reading of the Budget, or whether we should ask for a day for a Vote of Censure on the Government?"

I said: "Let us have a Vote of Censure after the papers are presented."

"Would you let the Budget go without an amendment then?"

"No, but I would raise the broadening of the basis on that."

We had some further discussion later in the afternoon, again initiated by him, and then I drafted the following amendment to the Budget, which I think I shall move from the Front Bench. "You are the only man who can do it," says A. J. B., with his usual flattery. "We are entirely in your hands."

Here is the draft:

"That this House declines to proceed with proposals based upon the maintenance of all existing taxes at their present high level for several years, and is of opinion that the financial needs of the country as disclosed in the Budget Statement of the Chancellor of the Exchequer require that the basis of taxation should now be broadened, in order that the anomalies and hardships inseparable from the present high rate of particular taxes may be corrected, the necessary revenue collected with fairness to all classes of the community and our fiscal system adapted to the present conditions of national and imperial trade."

I will see if I can touch up the concluding words. I should like them a little more pointed. But at first sight A. J. B. and

83

Lyttelton approved. We are to have a (shadow) cabinet on this and other matters on Wednesday. The draft was intended to be a broad challenge to our whole fiscal system. It is as such that I claimed—no, I did not claim, but expressed the desire that I, as ex-C. of E., should move it. If I move it (even as it stands) we hoist as a Party the flag of Tariff Reform in answer to Asquith's *non possumus*, and we are again committed all along the line.

Good night. It is late and I have spoken twice—very shortly—since dinner.

*9th May* 1907.

When did I last write to you? On Monday, I think; yes, it was Monday and I was in excellent spirits, and so I am still, seeing no reason to abate any of my satisfaction at the course of recent events.

On Tuesday morning it rained hard and was cold and raw. I went to my Committee, but returned with an attack of lumbago and was forced to put myself to bed after lunch, and there I stayed till lunch-time today. . . .

I have seen no one and heard no news since I last wrote, except that a meeting has been arranged for Deakin at the Baltic, which gives him a good non-party platform. The Chairman happens to be a good Tariff Reformer.

Dr. Walker tells me that Robert Cecil will have to "come on" if he means to keep the Marylebone seat. "I see he must—not only among the doctors but when I went canvassing. They all ask questions about it and press him to go further."

Fred Oliver writes, "You must be chortling." So I am! But I was sorry to see Gilbert Parker's letter. By all means avoid gush over the new converts, but since they are converts it is not our business to point out their inconsistency, or to expose the weakness of their reasoning.

*10th May* 1907.

You will have seen from my letters that we also had had the same idea as Father, namely, that there ought to be a formal Vote of Censure on the Government *à propos* of the Conference. We shall, however, wait for the publication of the full reports, now promised, before giving notice of it. I quite agree that Alfred ought to move it; but precedent and Mr. Speaker will together force us to confine it to one day, and I doubt whether, under the circumstances, I shall speak upon it.

Alec Hood called to see me this morning to learn if I was likely to be in my place on Monday. "Otherwise," said he, "we shall be in some difficulty. Bonar Law would much prefer to speak later in the debate and it's more in his line. Walter is not exactly the man to do it, but he would be furious if I put up George Wyndham in front of him. Arnold-Forster is ill again and I don't know to whom to give the motion if you cannot take it."

So I reassured him, saying I thought he might rely on me with confidence.

We had a pleasant and interesting gossip. I extract the following from his observations:

"The Government are in an awful mess with their business. Whiteley[1] came to him the other day. 'I wish you would help us on a little faster with our business,' said he.

"'Why should I?' asked Alec. 'You never helped us. Are you going to have an autumn session?'

"'No, our men won't stand that.'

"'Are you going to sit through August and September?'

"'No, our men won't do that!'"

Loulou is going to take charge of the English Land Bill. "Is it like the Scottish one?" asked Alec.

"No," said Loulou, "as an English landlord I think that's a d——d bad Bill and I don't like it. The English Bill will include compulsory powers, but it will be very moderate and I can tell you that I don't think you, as a landlord, will object to it."

If it carries out Loulou's promise, Alec proposes to move all its provisions into the Scottish Bill—an awkward move for the Government, as they cannot pretend that the lowland Scottish system differs from the English.

I make no comment on Loulou's political honesty.

[1] Patronage Secretary of the Treasury.

85

When I was last in the House, Fred Lambton said to me in the lobby: "Well, Austen, so you have captured Hayes-Fisher?"

"I was very glad," said I, "to see his letter; but Hayes-Fisher always wanted to work with the Party if he could—which I fear some people (pointedly) do not."

"Oh yes, he was always wobbling. I think Hunt is the only consistent man. He ought to be made leader."

"I hear he gets his whips again," said Morpeth.

"Why, even Freddy gets the Whips," rejoined Arthur Stanley.

"Of course," said I. "How else would he know when to vote against us?"

And with that bitter-sweet observation we broke off to go and vote.

*14th May* 1907.

My speech went all right and is fairly reported this morning. Ivy came down to the House to hear it. The rest of the debate, except McKenna's reply, was rather languid. Nowadays the after-dinner speeches hardly get reported and the House gets consequently very slack when it is known that there will be no division. Balfour speaks today. What will he say? He sent for Hewins again last Thursday, saying, "You know this Government is going out—(he is over-sanguine there)—and I want to know to what I am being committed. What shall I have to do?" To which Hewins replied, in the true Balfourian manner: "That depends on a multitude of circumstances and the conditions of the moment, which cannot be foreseen!" But he went on to tell him that the corn duty was the simplest thing; after that the other agricultural duties; and, lastly, the duties on manufactured goods. He says B. is getting very keen and interested, which I think is true.

Fred Oliver writes: "I guess you feel pretty chirpy? The whole army on the run! Into them, my boy; smite them; make the slow ones quick and the quick ones dead men. Yoicks! How your Father must smile as he reads his newspapers. For myself, I am a devout Scotsman and I thank God accordingly and whistle the Old Hundredth."

*Wednesday night:* I don't know how Balfour's speech will have struck you. As heard, it was earnest, clear and definite, and I was well pleased with it. There was one dangerous passage about restricting the growth of protected interests in the Colonies, but it can't do any harm here and will not, I expect, be reported overseas. For House consumption the speech was excellent. About ten men voted with us who have not hitherto been in our lobby.

The debate prevented me from attending a Tariff Reform Committee.

By the way, Balfour sat next McKenna at a City dinner the other night. Something caused B. to say of Lloyd George that he might some day be Chancellor of the Exchequer. "He would be a very unsound one, then," retorted McKenna. "Of course you disagree with us, but you *can* understand our principles. Lloyd George doesn't understand them and we can't make him!" and he went on to say that some question having arisen in Cabinet about purchasing goods abroad for the Government and it having been explained that the Government on their Free Trade principle were bound to do it when they could thus secure them more cheaply, "Well," said Lloyd George, "I call that a rotten argument!"

Did you read Morley's account of the repressive measures he has sanctioned in India? Deportation and imprisonment without trial, suppression of meetings, police reports, power of district judges or resident magistrates—the whole armoury of Irish coercion! Is it not the irony of fate that it should fall to his lot to do all this? I think he is rather proud of his strength in a rather weak man's way.

Mr. Mackrell (of the Cordwainers') is eighty-three but, except that he is deaf, as alert as ever. He had had bronchitis this winter, his cousin told me, and happening during his illness to break an old tea-cup he had used for many years, made up his mind and told his old servant that it was a sign that he should die and, what is more, fixed February 14-15 as the date of his decease. On the 14th he took solemn leave of all his household, sent instructions to the undertaker to call next morning to measure him for his coffin and asked his cousin to sleep in the house that night. His cousin did so, but on waking found that Mr. Mackrell had called for his coffee and an egg and was "much better." He is now perfectly well and, the fatal day being passed, has no intention of following his tea-cup for many years to come.

HIGHBURY,
*16th May* 1907.

So here we are once more at Highbury and very pleasant it is to be here, though I wish you were all at home to give us welcome. Neville seems as busy as ever and looks well, I think. Morpeth said to me, "Your brother made a ripping speech at the Town Hall. He got a great cheer for his Father at the beginning and a great cheer for himself at the end."

*19th May* 1907.

I am glad that you approved the House of Commons speech. I thought myself that the material was all right, but the manner was halting, partly because I was tired and in some pain, still more because I find the strain of a speech in the House tremendous. I am never at my ease with them as I am with a meeting, never feel that I really *command* their attention. However, perhaps that will come some day. Let us at least hope so. Lord Hardinge was there. He said to Ivy at dinner, "Doesn't your husband stammer more than he used to do?"

"He doesn't stammer," said Ivy indignantly.

"Oh, yes, he does. I think you've made him!"

Ivy is not sure that she likes Lord Hardinge.

*25th May* 1907.

Well, Mary, our *causeries de tous les jours* are coming to an end. What shall I do without them? I suppose I shall have to turn to my work, which they have been for so long a delightful excuse for postponing! Seriously I shall regret them. I have enjoyed talking with you—for that is what these letters have been—talk about anything and everything and nothing, and it has given me deep pleasure to think that in this way I could do something to play my part in the family life and be one of your circle even though far away from it. I daresay we shall find occasion again to talk in the same way from London to Birmingham, but I am half regretful at the thought that there will be a break of even a few days in our almost daily gossips. You have all been very kind in saying that you do look forward to them and that they are part of your pleasures. If it had not been for this, I should have felt too selfish in my happiness, although I know that the last thing you or Father would wish is that I should be less happy on the one hand or that I should abandon any part of my work on the other. Well, this I can say: that Father's supporters held their own while the tide ran against them, and that now that the tide is turning he will come back to find that even in his absence we have made progress, that the ground we hold is more our own and that what remains to be won—and it is much—is more within our reach. Our danger now is not Liberalism, but "Labour" working with and through Liberalism. But if we could hold our own and even gain ground before the Conference, everything is possible to us now after the Conference. And I am confident, in a way I have never been before, that whatever the part which Father may take in the work, *his* name will triumph and his labour will not have been in vain.

NOTE.—This letter marks the return of the family to London and concludes the correspondence of the year. My wife and I spent that summer and autumn at Highbury, where our eldest son was born.

half regretful at the thought that there will be a break of even a few days in our almost daily gossip. You have all been very kind in saying that you do look forward to them and that they are part of your pleasures. If it had not been for this, I should have felt too selfish in my happiness, although I know that the last thing you or Father would wish is that I should be less happy; on the one hand or that I should abandon any part of my work on the other. Well, this I can say: that Father's supporters held their own while the tide ran against them, and that now that the tide is turning he will come back to find that even in his absence we have made progress, that the ground we hold is more our own and that what remains to be won—and it is much—is more within our reach. Our danger now is not Liberalism, but "Labour," working with and through Liberalism. But if we could hold our own and even gain ground before the Conference, everything is possible, to us now after the Conference. And I am confident, in a way I have never been before, that whatever the part which Father may take in the work, his name will triumph and his labour will not have been in vain.

Note.—This letter marks the return of the family to London and concludes the correspondence of the year. My wife and I spent that summer and autumn at Highbury, where our eldest son was born.

1908

1908

INTRODUCTORY TO 1908 LETTERS

THE letters of 1908 open with a brief account of a luncheon at the
Hall of the Cordwainers' Company of which my grandfather's
grandfather had become a freeman nearly 170 years earlier. The
connection has continued unbroken down to the present day, when
it is continued by my eldest son and myself. Five of my forebears
have served the office of Master of the Company.

Next comes an account of a conversation with Cecil Spring-
Rice, afterwards the Rt. Hon. Sir Cecil Spring-Rice, Ambassador
at Washington at the outbreak of the Great War, but at this time
Councillor of the Embassy at Berlin.

The progress of Tariff Reform plays a great part in the correspondence of this year when Asquith became Prime Minister on
Campbell-Bannerman's death and Mr. Lloyd George succeeded him
as Chancellor of the Exchequer with the difficult task of piloting
through the House the Budget which his predecessor had just
introduced.

It records, too, my first impressions of Mr. Mackenzie King,
now Prime Minister of Canada.

93

*Luncheon at Cordwainers' Hall—Spring-Rice on Germany—Tariff Reform—Irish University Bill—Mackenzie King and the Oriental immigration into Canada—Resignation of Campbell-Bannerman.*

9 Egerton Place, S.W.,
*7th January* 1908.

Today we went down to Cordwainers' Hall. Ivy was very much struck by the Furse portrait, which she thought a noble picture of Father. She says it is even more like him now than when she first saw him, as he looked so drawn and tired then. I rejoiced in it again and more than ever. It is certainly by far the finest picture done of him. The Master had out all the Company's silver, beginning with a cup of 1666 and including some very nice pieces. Then we lunched with him, Past Master Canham and Mrs. Canham, Mr. Mackrell and the Clerk and his wife, and had up one of the few bottles still remaining of "Chamberlain's Ink"—the port laid down by my Grandfather in 1837.[1]

The Company's records date back to 1279. I saw the entry of William Chamberlain's admission in 1740.

Spring-Rice *speaking*: *9th January* 1908.

"All independence of thought in Germany is gone. Old Virchow said, 'I am not a Professor. I am a *Beamter* (an official). Even if I think about botany I must think like a *Beamter*.' The

---

[1] *i.e.* '34 vintage. It was a magnificent wine, still full of character. The Master who admitted me to the Company in 1896, when I first tasted it, told us that the tradition was that it had got its nickname from its great "body" and deep colour. The Court sampled it from time to time, but finally deciding that it would never be fit to drink, offered it to their wine merchant. He tasted it, and observing that it was a fine wine, regretted that it would not pay him to offer more than 144s. a dozen for it. At that the Court awoke to its merits. "Oho!" they said, "if it is worth that to you to buy, it is worth our while to keep it." If he had offered a third of the amount, the Master concluded, the Court would have sold the lot.

94

whole machinery of German Government through the schools, the Universities, the public services, everywhere, is being used to breed up the young generation in the same conviction that they must fight England that those of the 'sixties had that they must fight France. Tirpitz is terrified. He knows the Navy is not fit for it. You will see, Tirpitz will have to go. The Emperor restrains it. He is our one friend—well friend, no; but he does not want to declare war. He knows he would go down to history with a black mark, and any man hesitates to send thousands and hundreds of thousands of men to their grave by a word or a stroke of the pen. But Bülow is our bitterest enemy. He connives at and encourages the whole anti-English movement. The pressure comes from below. The whole Harden case was an effort to intimidate the Emperor. They were furious with him for not having declared war at the time of the Algeciras Conference. They thought he listened too much to a cosmopolitan clique, the Eulenburgs, etc.

"At one time they used to say and even believe that England would begin a war of defence as soon as she saw the German navy growing strong, but now this is too thin. No one believes it. They know they will have to declare war, but they cannot do this till they have created their navy and educated a generation to regard the war as inevitable. Then their plan will be to have some small quarrel going, suddenly to send an ultimatum, to sow the sea off our coasts with mines dangerous for twenty-four hours (compare their proceedings at the Hague Conference) dropped from merchant vessels previously sent out for the purpose, leaving a strip known only to themselves for the route of their invasion. London will be starved, for its food comes by sea. The essential thing is to lull the British people into false security meanwhile and to prevent her training her citizens for home defence."

*8th February* 1908.

Tell Father I was very pleased with the T.R. Conference and Dinner. The speeches were good and the feeling was excellent. I was quite pleased with my own performances, though this morning's was practically impromptu and the evening's was prepared with my eyes closed, as you found me! But the whole thing went with a swing and every sentence was echoed with cheers. I see the "Sea-green incorruptible" [1] ignores my challenge, but it will no doubt stick a knife in me later. But I owed it one and am glad to have paid my debts!

*Sunday:* Those observations about the meetings and my speeches in particular look very egotistical and boastful, but if I may not say what I think to you, to whom can I say it? and you know that at least I am not always equally self-satisfied, so you will pardon a little jubilation.

Signor Tosti is here. I heard him observing to a group of ugly and admiring females: "*On ne trouvera pas un hôtel plus confortable en Angleterre. Ça m'est sympathique. D'abord la musique est bien. On joue de petites choses agréables, pas trop fort,*" etc. etc.

They were playing his music last night!

*28th February* 1908.

Hewins lunched with us in order to talk over the "Bread" motion with me. I hope to do something with my material tomorrow. He told me of an episode in the House in the Home Rule days as described to him by an old Radical Member, his friend. Gladstone spoke for three-quarters of an hour. He was magnificent in denunciation, most moving in pathos, sweetly persuasive, bitterly humorous—all in turn—carrying the House along with him and concluding amid a storm of excited and enthusiastic cheers. "And then Chamberlain, who had been sitting perfectly impassive, rose to his feet and I must confess that in five minutes there was not a shred of Gladstone's argument left!"

In his later years Gladstone discoursed at the Oxford Union on "Recent discoveries in relation to Homer." "I believe," said Hewins, "that there was not a sentence in his address which was not open to a charge of inaccuracy; but he concluded with a wonderful panegyric on Oxford. 'Well, what do you think of Gladstone?' I asked my old Head, the Master of Pembroke, a violent Tory. 'He almost persuaded me to the use of tears!' was his reply."

[1] My nickname for the *Westminster Gazette*.

"Balfour," said Hewins, "does not like the charge of being obscure. He asked me the other day what I thought of his speeches. I said they were the most lucid utterances I had read on the fiscal question."

"Flatterer!" I interjected.

"Well, I know what causes the obscurity and where the uncertainty comes in. I meant that he was perfectly clear to *me*. He would like to put duties on manufactured goods but fears it is impracticable, and he would like to put a duty on corn but fears the people won't stand it!"

"And so," said I, "he chooses Retaliation, into which morass we have all followed him, so that we might not be thought jealous of or indifferent to his little bantling—the least practicable thing of all."

Hewins sighed and shook his head slightly, saying, "Yes, that's quite impracticable."

And so good night!

*2nd March* 1908.

11.30 p.m. A. J. B. was really admirable.[1] He disclosed the profound difference in the Government ranks. He probed the wound and turned his knife round and round. I have known him to be more "finished" but never happier. And with it all he combined sound good sense on the great issues.

*12th March* 1908.

I told you that yesterday I attended the monthly Executive Committee meeting of the Tariff Reform League. Father will be interested to see the enclosed extracts from the reports laid before them. Royds said the masses in Liverpool were moving decidedly, but they still had great difficulties with merchants and other leading men. Yorkshire, too, is moving since the S. Leeds election. On the motion of Bonar Law it was unanimously decided, in view of the probability of an early by-election in Winston Churchill's constituency through his promotion to the Cabinet, that unless Joynson-Hicks, the accepted Conservative candidate, would un-

[1] In debate on the Navy Estimates.

reservedly accept Balfour's Birmingham programme, we would run a Tariff Reform candidate.

Norwood also is stirring itself up against Bowles. Notts. has got satisfactory assurances out of Lord H. Bentinck.

*13th March* 1908.

We had a pleasant row in the House today between the Labour Party and Burns ("very stiff and proud" and shouting "very loud") over an Unemployment Bill, the principal clause of which embodied the right to work, *i.e.* to have work at standard wages found for any man who registered himself as unemployed. Of course, we supported the Government, but it was a pretty sight for us onlookers. Henderson, sessional chairman of the Labour Party, wound up with a clever and damaging little speech against the Government, and many of their people were uncomfortable, hating the Bill and yet awfully afraid of voting against it.

*14th March* 1908.

I am on the rota at the Bank this week, so it being a bright though cold morning Ivy drove down with me to Cannon Street in a motor cab, and then we had a happy idea and went on to the Tower, which she had never seen and which I last saw when Shaw Lefevre gave a party there in the early 'eighties. There is some splendid gold plate of Charles II's time. The sun was shining brightly and it was pretty on the terrace by the river in front of Traitor's Gate. One no longer sees the dungeons without a special order, but there was a pretty little collection of instruments of torture: thumb-screws, the "scavenger's daughter," the rack, etc.; and there is some fine armour but nothing to match the Wallace or Madrid collections.

*14th March* 1908.

Did I tell you Dilke's story of Bismarck and the London cab-man? You must imagine B. speaking slowly but *very* good English. It relates to his first visit to England. "I took," he said, "a cab to drive a very short distance, but the man saw I was 'green' and he drove me a long way round. At the end I offered him a shilling, for I knew the distance, and he swore at me. I was

98

very angry, but I took out all the silver I had in my pocket and I held it out to him and said: 'If you won't take what I offer you, take what is right for yourself'; and, as I thought, he did not dare to take more than one shilling, but," concluded Bismarck with great satisfaction, "he said, 'what I say is, damn all Frenchmen!'"

*17th March* 1908.

Horace Plunkett dined with us. He talked of his experiences of petticoat government in Wyoming years ago. He said he had been most anxious to find out whether the women exercised an independent judgment, or voted with their husbands, and had sent the enquiry to everyone he could think of. Generally they replied that the women followed their mankind; but one correspondent answered as follows: "Most always with their husbands, except when they are short and red-haired, when they are apt to be independent!"

*26th March* 1908.

Good old Peckham![1] What a smash! I saw Boraston today and he said, "Well, you can make some guess at your own figure, but what you can't calculate is the figure of your opponent. It is evident that *their* men won't vote for the Government just now." The Miners' Eight Hours Bill undoubtedly helped us, especially with the gasworkers, of whom there may be a thousand or more.

So the Duke[2] is gone! I was not surprised, and yet at the moment it was unexpected. Well! he had a fine sense of public duty and worthily continued the traditions of a great family. I think Victor will be as public-spirited, though he is not likely perhaps to play so great a part. Kerry will be Victor's successor in the House of Commons, which is all as it should be.

There is a bad bulletin about C.B. today. He is weaker and the end seems to be expected. I got your note at Barnstaple

[1] The seat which had been lost by 2339 votes in 1906 was won back by a majority of 2494 at a by-election.
[2] The 8th Duke of Devonshire; succeeded by his nephew, who was M.P. for West Derbyshire.

this morning and would have called today on my return to town, but I had no cards.

I will write more fully of our excursion tomorrow. But I am very tired tonight. We had a capital meeting.

*27th March* 1908.

Well, it was a very tired individual who sent off a few hurried lines to you last night, and I am still a little headachy this morning, but nothing worth mentioning. I have cleared my table of letters—or nearly so—having dictated to Mr. Wilson for an hour and a half, and now I will occupy the time till Aunt Lina comes to lunch in talking to you.

I must go back to Tuesday when we left London. In the morning I had the final meeting of my Committee, got my report signed by the whole of the members except Sir G. Clarke, now in Bombay, and subject to a single reservation by Otley that if everything changes the subject might some day be reconsidered. I was pleased with the unanimity, which at one time seemed impossible, and we parted with mutual compliments and congratulations.

Then having half an hour to spare and it being a lovely sunny spring morning, I walked round St. James's Park with Duckworth, spying out the first signs of almond blossom and enjoying the crocuses, which looked lovely in the sun. And then I joined Ivy at Waterloo and off we went to Barnstaple. But alas! as the journey proceeded, the glory of the day departed and by the time we got as far as Salisbury it was raining hard.

We got to Barnstaple at 6.30 and were met by a large and enthusiastic crowd, and driven off to our host's, Sir Bourchier Wrey, ex-Commander in the Navy, who has now grown a moustache, hates the mention of the Navy and chiefly prides himself on being a Lt.-Colonel of Yeomanry. He retired on succeeding to the estate about seven years ago and married some four years later.

There was a pleasant house party and next morning broke fine and sunny. Ivy walked about the grounds and defended me from reporters, whilst I finished my notes. A biggish party came to lunch and then, whilst the other men attended the afternoon conference, Lady Clinton, Ivy and I were motored over to Ilfracombe and back—a lovely drive.

The evening meeting was a great success—5000 people in a long, low, narrow market hall. They said they had not had such a gathering there since the Duke of Devonshire's visit fourteen years ago. It was a difficult place to speak in and I rather tired my throat, which very seldom happens with me, but Ivy said it was not noticeable in my voice. The speech pleased them all, I think, and they were a capital audience. The Devon L.U. agent came up to me afterwards and said, "Your speech will help us to regain our Nonconformists," and immediately afterwards Sir William Acland came up "as a Churchman" to thank me for what I had said on education. So I hope I have done some good.

We returned yesterday, leaving such a lovely morning behind us that it seemed sinful to go back to town. The country was looking its best and the banks and hedgerows were gay with primroses; but after Salisbury it turned wet and London was wrapped in orange-coloured fog.

*31st March* 1908.

We had a very interesting day in the House yesterday, and some good speaking. Redmond's speech was of course exactly what such speeches from him always are, but the speech of the day was Percy's. It was beautifully delivered in a good voice, and besides substance and argument contained much pleasant humour. Birrell was, as always, fluent, discursive, childishly irresponsible. It was, as Balfour said, a new volume of *Obiter Dicta*—indeed I suggested this observation to him—but it had very little real reference to the debate, and it concluded most lamely with an appeal to the Irish party to say what *their* proposals were and what *they* would accept. Read Percy's speech in full, the last paragraph of Birrell's and as much of Balfour's as you like—he was good, at times very good, but not at his best. The Irishmen were very much dissatisfied with Birrell, who sat down amid gloomy silence—not a cheer from any quarter of the House. Asquith did little to retrieve the situation, and Healy was put up on behalf of the reunited Irish party to express its disappointment.

He was evidently uncomfortable, did not feel sure of his party and not certain that he would not be disavowed. Indeed, the party cheered him but little, and Redmond sat behind him in gloomy silence. Douglas told me afterwards: "I hear Redmond is mad with Tim Healy for over-riding the horse." It is expected that there will be a new split among the Nationalists before long and we may console ourselves with the thought that Tim is far more amusing and more interesting as a free-lance!

Ian Hamilton was just back from a flying visit to Berlin and Petersburg. He saw both Witte and Kuropatkine. He thought the latter very industrious, intelligent and scrupulous, but with the "mind of a copying clerk"—incapable of action or thought on a big scale.

Witte told him that he saw Kuropatkine on the eve of the latter's departure for the Far East. K. explained his plan—to concentrate, for a year if need be, at Harbin, to leave Port Arthur to its fate, and not to move forward till he was ready to overwhelm the Japs.

Ah! a curious footnote to the Home Rule debate. You will see that the Government said they could not have accepted Redmond's motion without the addition proposed by Simon of words expressly reserving the supremacy of the Imperial Parliament. Simon's amendment was exactly the one which St. Aldwyn wanted the Opposition to move! He suggested it to me and to Balfour, and we both told him that of course Redmond would accept it and make fools of us all if we moved any such thing. St. A. was not convinced; but, of course, R. did accept in advance Simon's words, no doubt as the result of communications with the Government. It is curious how short-sighted a shrewd man like St. A. can sometimes be.

*1st April* 1908.

You will have seen by the papers that Birrell's Irish University Bill met with general acceptance and much praise. In fact, if anything is to be done in regard to Irish University Education, this is, I think, the best measure that could be devised. Belfast has at last got touched with the desire to have a University of their own. That made them more reasonable. On the other side, the Roman Catholic Hierarchy is also less *intransigeant*. They are at length content to have a University which everyone knows will be Roman Catholic in spirit and atmosphere, without insisting that it shall be placarded all over with portraits of the Pope and memorials to the infallibility of Rome. There will be no tests for teachers or taught, but everyone knows that both will belong entirely or almost entirely to the Roman Church. I meant to vote against the Bill, but shall not do so now that I have seen it. Indeed, there would have been no division yesterday but for two or three Orangemen who forced it against the wish of other Ulstermen. These latter would have been well content to let it go unchallenged, but, on a vote being forced, felt obliged to go into the lobby against it.

*5th April* 1908.

King [1] is a very intelligent and interesting man—Deputy Minister (*i.e.* Permanent Under-Secretary) of Labour in Canada, now over here to discuss with the Home Government the whole question of Oriental immigration into the Pacific slope of Canada. I gather that he has come to an arrangement with Grey, Morley and Elgin which is satisfactory to him; but as far as I could make out, it did not proceed on any general principle, or at least, if there was a principle it was simply that the Canadians would not be swamped and undersold by cheap Oriental labour; but the solution of the problem is, as far as I can gather, different in each case, and different methods are adopted for checking the inflow of Chinese, Japanese and Indians respectively.

Incidentally, it was evident that he had a bad opinion of the Japs. I had written "low," and this is true as far as honesty and truthfulness of either individual or government is concerned; but it was clear, and he did not attempt to conceal it, that he rated highly their power of organisation, etc., and rather feared it.

After the Vancouver riots he was sent by Laurier to hold an enquiry. One of his principal witnesses was the Japanese ex-Consul, now director of a trading or emigration company. He

[1] The Rt. Hon. W. L. Mackenzie King, present Prime Minister of Canada.

caught this gentleman lying and perjuring himself and proved it by papers he seized in his office. The Jap acknowledged it: "I lied to you; you found me out; but if you had not found me out all these gentlemen (with a wave of his hand to his assembled compatriots) would have told you the same story, for they had read my evidence in our Japanese papers published in Vancouver."

Subsequently King had to tell the whole story in his report to his Government. He sent a copy of the report to his Jap friend, saying: "You will see what I have said on pages — and —. I'm sorry to be disagreeable, but I had to tell the whole story."

The Jap replied: "Let us light the lamp of friendship and feed it with the oil of sincerity. Do not let any little personal difference cause a flicker in the flame!"

King spoke with evident feeling of a speech of Father's in which he referred to the Canadian rebellion of '37 and expressed sympathy with the rebels. His grandfather on his mother's side was out with the rebels and his grandfather on the father's side with the troops. All his sympathies historically were with the rebels of that time, and Father's reference (I cannot recall it) had touched him deeply. Lord Grey says he will be a force. He is certainly a clever man and, I think, if a force, will be a force on the right side. I am glad to have seen him.

*6th April* 1908.

C.B.'s resignation is announced today. The House has adjourned till the 14th, when the new Ministers' writs will be moved and a further adjournment made over Easter.

## 1908 : MAY

### Tariff Reform

9 EGERTON PLACE, S.W.,
*5th May* 1908.

There seems a real chance of Winston being beaten at Dundee,[1] but not by our man, though Baxter is proving an excellent candidate. Poor Winston! I have seconded him for Grillions, where I dined last night—a small gathering and rather dull, being much interrupted by poor stories from Sanderson when the conversation showed any chance of getting interesting. Only Selby, Grey, Haldane and myself besides Sanderson.

*6th May* 1908.

I am a false prophet![2]

Alas! I have misled you and misled myself. On getting Vince's telegram yesterday afternoon that our promises were 5645, I estimated our poll at 80 per cent. of that figure, or 4516. I was only ten votes wrong in this, but those ten votes made the difference between victory and defeat. Of course, my real error was in estimating the total poll at 85 per cent. of the electorate or less. I thought this a safe calculation, but it was 87½ per cent. and that made all the difference.

I felt very sick about it, because I expected too much; but it's much more sickening for the Government. The *Daily Mail* describes it as one of the most serious blows that the Government has received since the turn of the tide and it draws from it "the frank confession that Tariff Reform is a growing force." The General Purposes Committee of the T. R. League met this afternoon

---

[1] On standing for re-election, as was then necessary, on becoming President of the Board of Trade.

[2] I had foretold a victory for Mr. Amery in the East Wolverhampton by-election. He was defeated by 8 votes, reducing a hostile majority of 2865 at the General Election to 8 two years later.

105

and passed a resolution drawn up by me which, I hope, treats the situation properly.

I fear it is evident that West Wolverhampton will not take Hewins as its candidate, but Hood asked me yesterday if there was any chance of his caring to stand. "I want him in the House," he said, "not to speak but to coach our boys." I have great hopes of Hood.

Affairs look a little better on the Indian frontier, but they must be giving the Government many anxious moments. I learned from Edward Grey that they do not think that the Amir in any way encourages the raiders, but that his position is too precarious for him to put any effectual stopper on them. Father must be glad to see how well Willcocks is doing. If I remember rightly, the War Office was slow to employ him after Ashanti, and Father pressed his claims and merits.

*9th May* 1908.

What do you think of the Budget? It was a difficult task to follow such a statement without a moment for reflection; but I think what little I said reads pretty well. I have just developed my views a little further for to-morrow's *Observer* to please Garvin, though I hate allowing myself to be interviewed. For the moment the Budget will help them in elections.

I am anxious about the Shropshire seat, and I hear bad accounts of our organisation in Dundee. I expect Winston to win and Baxter to stand third on the poll.

ORWELL PARK,
*16th May* 1908.

We got down here yesterday with just time to dress and dine and then were motored off to Ipswich for our meetings, first some fifteen hundred people in the Town Hall, whom I addressed for forty or fifty minutes on Tariff Reform, and then another fifteen hundred in the Corn Exchange, whom I addressed immediately after on Old Age Pensions, Education and Licensing for fifty minutes, explaining that I had spoken on *our* policy at the other meeting and now wished to speak on the Government's policy. But when I had finished my fifty minutes a voice said, "Tell us *something* about Tariff Reform. We're all full of it"; and the meeting cheered loudly, so I had to give them an extra ten minutes on that! They were good meetings, but the double speech bothered me awfully. It was far worse than the ordinary meeting with an overflow, for both meetings were equally important; and the thought of the second speech bothered me during the delivery of the first, so that I think the second was far the better of the two and the first was not very good. Ivy confesses that I was labouring for the first eight minutes, but says it was all right after that.

Lord and Lady Stradbroke, the Walter Guinnesses, Savile Crossley, Lord and Lady Graham, Captain Peel and Mr. Goldsmith were staying here for the night and the four first are staying over Sunday. This is a big, rather rambling red-brick house, built by the late George Tomlin, overlooking the Orwell, a broad tidal river. There are some splendid ilex on the lawn and in the park and some beautiful old cedars. It has been a warm fine day. We wandered round the gardens and through some of the woods this morning with Pretyman (he is growing bamboos like weeds), and this afternoon we sailed down the river to Shotley Point and Harwich and back in a little yacht belonging to Pretyman. As we landed we saw a couple of sheldrake fly into the cover of a little wood skirting the steep bank of the river and we went off to try and find their nest. This we failed to do, but we came on *orchis maculata* growing beautifully. I never saw bigger spikes or the plants in such profusion.

9 EGERTON PLACE, S.W.,
*18th May* 1908.

Our visit to the Pretymans was very pleasant. I send you the local paper. Please let me have it back as they were sold out and this is my only copy. Sunday was a lovely day. We attended church in the morning in a barn (the church is under repair). It was a lovely summer day with a warm west wind, and gracious! the barn *was* hot. In the afternoon Ivy rested, and the rest of us walked or drove (I walked!) to the Decoy. Of course, at this time of year there were only a few tame "wild duck" and pintail there, but the decoy man and his dog went through all the motions of driving the duck into "the Pipe" and I was very interested to see a real decoy exactly reproducing the features of the one depicted in the *Animated Nature* volumes which delighted Beatrice and me in our childhood. They have taken as many as a thousand wildfowl in one day in a winter's frost in this Decoy—wild duck, widgeon, pintail, etc.

The walk there—only a mile or so—was lovely. The woods were full of bluebells. It was sweltering hot and after tea I sat out in the garden for some time with Ivy. The nightingales were singing, singing everywhere—I have never heard anything like it. At night they were almost too vocal.

The more I saw of the view from the house the more I enjoyed it. The big, almost flat, lawn broken here and there with ilex and cedar; the park beyond, falling away rapidly to the Orwell; the broad estuary of the river; the deer and the pine trees—all reminded me somehow of Turner's pictures of Petworth. In detail it was quite unlike, and yet the spirit and, I think, the colouring of the whole were similar. At any rate, I could not get the comparison out of my mind.

The Guinnesses left before dinner. They were very pleasant. Only the Stradbrokes were left, but the Vicar and his wife dined with us and we found them very attractive. He is Dr. Paget, brother of the Bishop of Oxford and himself Suffragan Bishop of Suffolk (Ipswich). He is extraordinarily like his brother. "My, ain't he ugly!" a woman was heard to exclaim as he arrived at some church for a consecration. He overheard and turning quickly to her, said, "Ah! but you should see my brother!" and passed on.

He was very pleasant and attractive and the Pretymans may well congratulate themselves, as they do, on having him as their Vicar.

In the evening we looked at some of the Pitt treasures. There is a very fine Gainsborough portrait of Pitt (the one exhibited in last winter's Old Masters), a Chatham and Lady Chatham, Pitt's watch, a lock of his hair—fair, but with the powder still clinging to it—and all his correspondence and papers.

Besides this they have found there a number of the *Paston Letters*, separated from the rest of the collection, which I believe is at Windsor. How they came there, no one knows; but in their collection of MSS. are a letter from Warwick the King Maker and a letter from an Eton Boy, dated 1467, asking for a pair of stockings, cost 8d., and recounting a visit to a lady at Windsor, to whom his elder brother had become engaged. "Of her beauty," he says, "I will leave you to judge; but for her hands, I wot me they are somewhat thick!"

*26th May* 1908.

We left Highbury cold and wet yesterday morning. Ivy and I lunched at the Carlton and then we both went down to the House, where I opened the debate on the Budget. Ivy says it was the best speech she has heard me make, which is comforting even if too favourable. Anyway, my colleagues approved and some of the Government also congratulated me, amongst others Lloyd George,[1] who added: "I agreed with a good deal of what you said—with more perhaps than you would think and with more than I can say. I wanted to keep the sugar duty on and use it for pensions!"

I send you a very interesting letter from Joseph Lawrence. I have begged him to write in the same sense to Balfour, who does not yet realise the future which Tariff Reform has in Lancashire. He is afraid that if Education is out of the way, Free Trade will carry Lancashire and says he knows that Spender of the *W. Gazette* (to whose opinion on such matters Asquith attaches importance) has told the Government that if they cannot settle the Education question their chances in Lancashire are hopeless.

Curzon is coming along! He will not, I expect, help us very much, but his speech at the United Empire Club last night definitely places him on the side of the Tariff Reformers and against Cromer and his followers. I am just off to Ridley's to lunch to meet Curzon and discuss India's position.

*27th May* 1908.

Ouf! What a day I have had! Very tired this morning. A late cup of coffee and slice of toast and a hurried survey of the papers in bed. At eleven dictating letters to Wilson. At twelve Committee at Great George Street to meet Sir J. Backhouse and Mr. Matthews and try to settle unfortunate difficulties in the North.

[1] He had just become Chancellor of the Exchequer on Mr. Asquith's accession to the Premiership. The Budget had been framed by Asquith.

This lasted till 1.30 and my chance of lunch vanished. Then to Committee at the Bank; due at 1.45, but the Embankment was blocked half-way down, owing to the President's visit to the Guildhall. Turned back and into Fleet Street, so with difficulty to St. Paul's. Found there an impossible jam of traffic. Got out and ran most of the way up Cannon Street. Arrived late and breathless. Did Committee work. Then an unusually long Board lasting till 3.45. Went straight on to the House and found a discussion started on the financial resolution for the Pensions Bill. Could not leave the Bench for twenty minutes or more. Then got a hasty tea with two boiled eggs. Hurried back to the House and found myself obliged to speak almost before I knew what it was about. Conference with Alec Hood about Marylebone; talk with Bonar Law; meeting with Balfour, Douglas, Long, Hood and Bonar Law about amendment to Second Reading of the Budget. Letter to Ridley about Marylebone. Home at 7.15. Call from Leo Maxse. Dress and go out to dinner at Lady Tryon's. And now it is past midnight and I must go to bed!

*28th May.*

Ivy had her second afternoon At Home last Tuesday and again had fifty visitors. In the evening we dined at Lilian's, who had a reception afterwards for the Women's L.U. delegates. One lady arrived at ten in the morning and was very indignant when her mistake was pointed out to her. "If people mean ten o'clock *at night*, they should put it on their cards," she said and went off in a huff.

*28th May* 1908.

We lunched with Lady Clifford of Chudleigh today and then Ivy went on to the meeting of the Women's Unionist and Tariff Reform League. She says Milner's speech was full of good stuff, but badly delivered, from vast sheaves of notes from which he read largely, losing himself at intervals. The honours of the meeting were divided between Captain Tryon and Lady Edward Spencer Churchill, both of whom, and especially the former, she says were excellent.

I have done a lot of talking in the House these last few days,—

amongst other speeches being one very little reported on Preference for Irish tobacco and home-grown beet sugar, on an amendment moved by an Irishman. I daresay we shall recur to the subject later in the Budget. Lloyd George seemed rather squeezable.

I have not yet found time to tell you of our lunch with Curzon at Ridley's, Hewins and Bonar Law being the only others present. It was very satisfactory. Curzon was very friendly. He began by saying that the attitude of the Indian Government and the meaning of their dispatch had been much misunderstood. They were not in principle hostile to Preference or Retaliation. But their main consideration was the position of India as a debtor country and the vital necessity of maintaining their exports so as to maintain the exchange. They feared three things: the sacrifice of India to Lancashire, as she had been more than once sacrificed before; interference with the Indian revenue from customs, thus upsetting their balance-sheet and destroying the favourable exchange; and retaliation by foreign powers who might attack India to punish England, while England (not herself feeling the strain) might leave India to fight the battle alone and not come to her assistance. Their general conclusion was that India had not much to gain but might have a good deal to lose. They were not hostile as a whole, though Barber, the present Finance Minister, an old-fashioned Cobdenite, probably was; but they were not convinced that the thing was expedient. Even Barber might change if he saw India's interest in a new policy.

We took up his points *seriatim*. India had to gain by Preference on 16 per cent. of her exports—tea, corn, tobacco, being the chief. Curzon rather belittled the value of Preference on tea. "India and Ceylon already had nearly all our trade." True, but Java threatened to become a serious competitor, and in any case India had much to gain from a lowering of the tea duty, which was always followed by an increase of consumption. Corn would become increasingly valuable as irrigation developed. "But," said C., "we are practically at the end of remunerative irrigation and corn is uncertain, because in bad years we need it all ourselves." True again, but then how important to develop the production, to have our markets for your surplus in good years and the increased supply for your own use in bad, etc. etc.

As to Retaliation. Your exports are raw materials. Germany, the U.S.A., etc. cannot penalise your jute and cotton. If they do, they ruin their industries to the gain of Dundee and Lancashire; they divert your raw material to us. You have a different but an equally large market.

"But they might penalise our tea to bring you to reason." Surely not, for they would fear, as you do, that, as that did not touch us directly, we should remain indifferent. If they wanted to hit us they would choose something we should feel at once. If they dared touch raw material, they would tax our coal; but they dare not. We do not fear it for ourselves. You need not fear it for India.

Then about your exchange, your customs duties and Lancashire; "If you ask us," I said, "to say that we will leave on the cotton import duty and take off the excise, I do not deny that there is much to be said for your demand; but I reply that I cannot do it. To propose that in Lancashire would be suicide. We must carry Lancashire to win and we cannot afford to offer that concession, which in fact we should never be given power to make."

"Oh," said Curzon, "but I do not ask that. We don't want it. Barber has always said 'I will not raise the question of Excise Duties, which bring in £250,000, because if I do the Home Government will insist on the abolition of the Customs Duties on cotton, which bring in about one and a quarter millions, and if those go then all the rest of the customs will have to go also, and we lose four millions of revenue.' We do not need to touch excise, but your policy requires you to object to our customs."

"Oh, no, no, no. On the contrary. Leave the customs on British goods where they are, if you please, but raise them on foreign goods. Give us a Preference, a real Preference, but you need not let us in free. Your duties are really very moderate revenue duties. Perhaps you can lower some of them to us if you raise them against the rest of the world; but even this is not absolutely necessary. Preference is the keynote of the situation, and remember that the Preference is for English *and Indian* goods over foreign goods. American and Japanese competition is likely before long to become very serious. Under your present system and ours you cannot protect yourself against it. The Home Government on Free Trade principles would be obliged to forbid it. Grant

Tariff Reform principles and, provided you give us low duties and a good Preference, you may put what duties you like on the foreigner. Your fiscal autonomy is greater, not less, than before. Even if Preference in our market is not in your view very valuable, power to protect your industries against the foreigner may be a great advantage to you."

This was a complete surprise to him, or he chose to treat it as such. It wholly altered the situation. Certainly, on those lines the proposal assumed a very different aspect to that which it had worn when the Indian Government dispatch was penned. "But now, who will say that on behalf of Tariff Reformers?" He would like to examine more closely our case as to the benefits derivable from Preference and as to the remoteness of the danger from Retaliation, and to consult some fresher Indian authorities than himself on the subject, but if this examination proved satisfactory he thought there was little or nothing to divide us, in view of this "new attitude" on our part.

So then I threw my most attractive fly. Hewins should prepare a statement on the lines indicated above for Curzon's consideration. If necessary, we should have a further conference to remove any minor objections C. might feel, but if he were generally satisfied then Bonar Law, I and all of us were ready at any time to make the declaration above set forth. "But that is not the best way to do it. Our speeches may not be reported and, in any case, will not reach India. What I would suggest is that if, after considering the statement that Hewins will send you, you are satisfied that on these general lines the scheme is practicable and desirable, *you* should then take an opportunity of speaking on the whole subject, and that you should lay down these lines as the ones on which any proposals for the co-operation of India must be based; and then Bonar Law and I would take the earliest opportunity of publicly recognising your authority on such a matter and accepting your conditions on behalf of Tariff Reformers."

Well, we talked on a little, Bonar Law emphasised the Tariff Reform view that Free Trade within the Empire was not necessary, perhaps even was not desirable, even if it were possible. Thus, Canada by developing her industries developed her wealth. The more she prospered, the more she bought. It was the surplus

H  113

demand over what she could herself supply which we desired to obtain. So we did not wish to cramp the development of industry either in Canada or in India. The more they developed their industry and their wealth, the more they would buy from elsewhere. Let that elsewhere be the Empire. That is all we ask.

Then we talked of who were to be "the representatives" of India for the purpose of negotiations, and finally, as we were concluding and summing up, Curzon said he thought, if he might say so, that perhaps the suggestion I had made was the most practical or at any rate the best way of proceeding. Of course, what he said would go into the Indian papers and so forth.

*Et voilà!* So now! I think we have fairly hooked that fish. He was very pleasant and cordial throughout.

## 1908: MAY, JUNE, JULY

*The Budget—Old Age Pensions Bill—Germany and the Baghdad Rly.
—Grey's Views—Russian Views on the Anglo-Russian Treaty—
Admiralty Dissensions—Progress of Tariff Reform.*

*Cambridge Political Soc.—The Pepys Club—Walter Harris's Anecdotes
—Delcassé.*

9 EGERTON PLACE, S.W.,
*29th May* 1908.

Well, it's a sad heart that never rejoices! I have made two
more speeches today. The L.U. Club held its annual meeting this
morning and I took the opportunity of warning our people against
falling into the same trap in which the Government is caught by
making promises incapable of fulfilment by any man. I think the
time had come when it was necessary to do this and at least to
clear myself and the leaders of the movement from all responsibility for them. The *Daily Express* and some of our speakers have
been running very wild and will discredit us if not checked. And
after all, it is so unnecessary! Our cause is so good that it does not
need bolstering up by such means. "Cheap food" and "Work
for all" were my text. I might have added "No Income Tax."
We merely discredit the practical reforms we can make by leading
people to expect the impossible.

Beatrice and Mr. Collings lunched with us and B. and we went
afterwards to see Sargent's water-colours. The room was not
large enough for them, being indeed little more than a passage and
crowded, so that it was impossible to see them from the proper
distance. Balfour was just leaving as we entered and commended
the pictures for their "impudence, force and cleverness." I liked
the choice and order of the epithets!

115

CAMBRIDGE,
*31st May* 1908.

I attended the dinner in King's College Hall in honour of Oscar Browning and made them a short speech which satisfied me though I had found it very difficult.

Turning over the old Minute Books of the Political Society last night (I ought to explain that the P.S. was founded by O. B. in 1876, that he has been its Perpetual President, and that it has met weekly in his rooms ever since during the two winter terms), I found that in 1884 "Mr. Austen Chamberlain read a short but practical paper on the Russian Mir in relation to the Irish Land question."

Question propounded:
Would the Irish Land question be solved by a communal system on the lines of the Mir?

| *Noes:* | *Ayes:* |
|---------|---------|
| The President, etc. etc. | The Essayist, etc. etc. |

I appear also at various times and after papers read by others to have declared that a single Chamber system was desirable; that Cobden was "a statesman of a high order" and alas! that it was not desirable that "the United Kingdom should remain the centre of a great Empire."

But even in these salad days I recorded my vote in favour of the proposition that "an Irish Parliament would be a rebel Parliament."

It was curious to see that in 1884 or 1885 the Society unanimously resolved (let me say that I was not present) "that the present constitution of France possesses no element of permanence."

9 EGERTON PLACE, S.W.,
*2nd June* 1908.

I dined at Grillions—a small, dull party. I have had no luck there lately. Last week Sanderson dined *alone*—a thing which has not happened since Mr. Gladstone on a like occasion consumed three bottles of wine unaided.

Bonar Law made a really admirable, closely reasoned and coherent speech today on the Budget [1]—the best thing he has yet done. His speeches are nearly always good, but the argument is usually disjointed. Today it was consecutive and crushing. Winston replied in a very good debating effort—quite the best thing he has done in that line and showing, as Bonar Law observed, the practice he has had at Manchester and Dundee. Indeed it was not difficult to detect the passages which came straight from his election speeches. Balfour made a good and satisfactory declaration and Asquith wound up with the assured approval of his own side but without any real knowledge of the course of the Debate (he had heard only half my speech and none of Bonar Law's) and with no real attempt to meet our arguments. Incidentally, he repeated his taunt that he did not know what Balfour meant to do about corn, but as Bonar Law observed to me, the complaint rang hollow this time and instead of being followed by vociferous applause from his own benches it scarcely elicited a weak "Hear, hear!"

Balfour observed that Lloyd George had no doubt a difficult task with a Budget that was not his own but that he had not done justice to himself in his speeches on it. I could not help whispering to my neighbour, "Well, his position *is* a difficult one. Asquith has begotten the child, and then he has got an affiliation order against Lloyd George, compelling him to maintain it!"

Asquith still talks as if he thought further reductions on the Army and Navy votes possible. I cannot think what he is at. The Defence Committee have been seriously considering our position and have had A. J. B. before them as a witness. B. explained his old views, emphasised the fact that he had never said (as is too often assumed) that an invasion by Germany was impossible, but only that if you had a sufficient and efficient force at home such as to necessitate invasion by a *large* force if the invasion was to have any chance of success, then such an invasion became an impossibility in our *then* condition of naval supremacy, but adding, with reasons, his opinion that the position had gravely changed to our detriment since he spoke and that he viewed with serious

---

[1] On an amendment to the Second Reading of the Finance Bill, calling for a broadening of the basis of taxation.

apprehension the chances of what might happen if we were already engaged elsewhere when the Germans chose to attack.

No questions were asked him and he is told by Esher that Roberts and Fisher, who were both present, highly approved his evidence. But where in all this does Asquith see his chance of avoiding a huge increase? I am loath to believe that he means to content himself with fine words and theatrical attitudes in such vital matters of national security, but both his words and his gestures while B. was speaking today give furiously to think.

*4th June* 1908.

I was detained by a meeting of colleagues to consider what course we should follow on the Second Reading of the Old Age Pensions Bill. We were all agreed that we should not move any amendment at that stage, but that in supporting the Second Reading we would accept this Bill as a temporary bridge to a complete scheme on a contributory basis.

*17th June* 1908.

Arthur Lee took me last night to a dinner of the Pepys Club at Barbers' Hall. The Club was founded in 1903 to commemorate the two hundredth anniversary of Pepys's death and has for its President Mr. Wheatley, the latest editor of the *Diary*, who is now at work tracing the little-known history of Pepys's later days after the close of the *Diary*. There were just fifty of us present which filled the little hall, and we had a most enjoyable evening. Barbers' Hall was built in 1636 by Inigo Jones for the Barber-Surgeons and then consisted of a "Livery Hall" burnt in the Great Fire, a "Theatre" pulled down in 1784 and the "Parlour or Court Room" in which we dined. It is, as I have said, a very small hall lit by a lantern in the ceiling, elaborately decorated with carved and painted garlands looking almost like Dresden China. The oak panelling has alas! been buried in red paint, but on the staircase and in the room above the fine woodwork is still to be seen. It is the only hall in London which still exists as Pepys knew it. On 27th February 1662-3, he records in his *Diary*:

"About 11 o'clock, Commissioner Pett and I walked to

Chyrurgeons' Hall (we being all invited thither and promised to dine there); where we were led into the Theatre; and by and by comes the reader, Dr. Teame, with the Master and Company, in a very handsome manner; and all being settled, he began his lecture . . . which was very fine; and his discourse being ended, we walked into the Hall, and there being great store of company, we had a fine dinner and good learned company, many Doctors of Phisique, and we used with extraordinary great respect. Among other observables we drank the King's health out of a gilt cup given by Henry VIII to this Company, with bells hanging at it, which every man is to ring by shaking after he hath drunk up the whole cup. There is also a very excellent piece of the King, done by Holbein, stands up in the Hall, with the officers of the Company kneeling to him to receive the Charter."

The cup and picture are still there and we too saw them both, though we were not put to the ordeal of emptying the cup to the King's health. The cup, they say, has been pawned, sold and stolen, but has always been recovered. The picture is a vast canvas with some twenty figures in it. The exact share which Holbein took in it is disputed, but it is agreed that it was finished by someone else. On 29th August 1668, Pepys again records:

"To Chyrurgeons' Hall where they are building it new, very fine" (*i.e.* the new hall since pulled down—not the Court Room where we were); "and then to see the theatre which stood all the fire, and, which was our business, their great picture of Holbein's, thinking to have bought it by the help of Mr. Pierce, for a little money. I did think to give £200 for it, it being said to be worth £1000; but it is so spoiled that I have no mind to it, and is not a pleasant, though a good picture."

There were besides in the hall a portrait of Inigo Jones by Vandyck, the fair Stewart (afterwards Duchess of Richmond) of Pepys's *Diary* and the *Grammont Memoirs*—I should think the only fair lady of that Court of whom no evil can be said—and a fine portrait of a Clerk of the Company by Sir Joshua. The Company is very rich too in plate; besides Henry VIII's cup, there is another given by Charles II in 1676 and a large punch-bowl given by Queen Anne. The Company boasts that it is the only one which possesses *three* royal gifts.

All this was described to us and much more besides by a Past Master of the Company, very agreeably and with a pleasant humour. Amongst other things is the record in the Company's register of the coming to life at their hall of a man who had been hanged at Tyburn and whose body they were just going to dissect. He could give no clear account of himself, they said, "but he several times pronounced distinctly the word 'Don't.'" This was in 1668. He was sent back to Newgate, reprieved and transported.

The other speeches were brief, and interspersed with them we had songs, Pepys's own "Beauty Retire" and some others composed by Pelham Humfrey, "lately returned from France, and is an absolute Monsieur, as full of form and confidence and vanity, and disparages everything and everybody's skill but his own. The truth is, everybody says he is very able, but to hear how he laughs at all the King's Musick here, that they cannot keep time nor tune, nor understand anything." So Pepys in his *Diary* on 15th November 1667.

Altogether a very delightful and Pepysian evening, which I thoroughly enjoyed.

*19th June* 1908.

I have been reading *Coke of Norfolk*. Disappointing! But the truth is that I cannot read with patience the biography of a Whig of Fox's school during the American War or the great French struggle. They are too blindly unpatriotic. Incidentally, I have learned the derivation of the "billycock" or "bowler" hat, *i.e.* a form of hat invented by Bowler, a City hatter, and brought into fashion by "Billy" Coke, nephew of Coke of Norfolk. Otherwise the book has not tended to my edification.

*22nd June* 1908.

We did our duty at the Windsor Garden Party without any particular enjoyment of it, though the scene was pretty enough, and then had a pretty motor drive with Arthur Lee over to Camilla where we arrived just in good time to dress for dinner. Besides the Lees and ourselves the only other guest was Leverton's brother, Walter, the Morocco correspondent of *The Times*.

W. H. told one or two amusing tales. The Sultan had promised him a fine horse and saddle, but the horse was never "fat" enough (this is considered a beauty in horses) and the promise remained unfulfilled. One day Harris was dining with Menebbe, the War Minister, who boasted that he held the Sultan in his power. Harris told of the promised horse and how he had never been able to get it. "That's just like the Sultan," said Menebbe, "but I'll make him give it you at once." And there and then he wrote a short letter to the Sultan which he showed to Harris, saying :—"Harris is here enquiring about his horse. You must send it to him at once, or he will make trouble." It was late in the evening; the Sultan was in his harem and they waited an hour or more for the reply. When it came, Menebbe read it, and passing it to Harris, exclaimed, "There ! that's the Sultan all over !" The note said simply, "Give Harris the best horse and saddle in your stable at once."

Next morning Harris called on the Sultan to thank him for his splendid present, and the Sultan gravely replied that he had been specially "fattening" the horse for Harris for months and that the saddle was one which he had had specially made for himself !

On the other occasion, some great Sheikh sent Harris a fine black horse and a black mule. They were brought down to his house by a little black slave boy, and Harris having written a note of thanks gave it to the boy to take back. "But I am part of the present," said he, and since then he has remained in Harris's household. One day, soon after the German Emperor's visit, Harris heard a ring at his bell and saw the French Minister with some of his staff there. His servants had all gone out and there was no one but this small boy to open the door, which he did, clad only in a *very* short cotton shirt.

"Is Mr. Harris at home ?" asked the Minister in French. No answer.

"Don't you speak French ?" asked one of the staff in Arabic. At once the young imp brightened up and replied :

"Oh, no. Since the Emperor's visit, we speak nothing but German !"

Harris speaks highly of the French fighting and of the endurance of the troops from the generals downwards. The Foreign Legion is, he says, largely German—at least 65 per cent. being Germans,

mostly deserters from the German Army. At Casablanca he witnessed a curious scene. A patrol of the Foreign Legion was passing
through the Jews' Quarter where there had been much pillage.
The Jews came out of their houses and cried: "Vive la France!"
The patrol looked up the street and down the street; there was no
officer within sight; and then they turned and thrashed the Jews,
bidding them never utter that cry again!

The British Vice-Consul's house was attacked at Casablanca
and defended as best the inmates could by rifle fire. At last the
French were able to send a reinforcement with a small gun to be
mounted on the roof. "You may put the gun on the roof if you
like," said the Vice-Consul, "but I won't have my polished stairs
scratched. You must lay the drugget first." And in the midst of
fighting, he solemnly insisted, being of the "precise and tidy sort,"
on laying the drugget before going further.

Bravo Pudsey! What a surprise. Pike Pease was very hopeful,
but I simply didn't believe a win to be possible. Alec Hood said
to me today:

"Hughes won that seat. They were going to lose it like South
Leeds. The same man was playing the same game, but I sent
Hughes down and he stopped it"—*i.e.* he stopped the banning of
Tariff Reform.

*23rd June* 1908.

Many thanks to Father for his comments on Metternich's
conversation.[1] I had come to pretty much the same conclusion
myself, with this difference, if difference it be, that I do regard the
state of public opinion in Germany as most dangerous—not as
portending an outbreak at present, for they are not ready for it,
and besides, I believe the Emperor to be pacific—but as tending to
make a conflict some day inevitable. I had some conversation
with Edward Grey on the subject last night. He told me that when
he first came into office, Metternich constantly held similar
language to him, but that for some time past he had ceased to do so.
He had pointed out to M. that as long as the German Press pursued

[1] See *Down the Years*, pp. 48-58.

the line of hostile and menacing criticism which they had adopted
he must not be surprised at the attitude of some English writers.
The whole trouble arose from their insisting on building ships
which were not commerce-protectors and were not suitable for
defensive action in their home waters. Impartial observers—Dutch
naval officers for instance—all inferred that Germany meant to
attack us—not now but about 1915. What other inference was
possible? No neutral thought that we were preparing for aggression. He had sent for M. after the Reval meeting and had told
him that no new alliances were being formed and that the only
subjects of a political nature discussed there were Persian and
Macedonian questions; so M. could not complain that Germany
was again being kept in the dark.

As to the Baghdad Railway he had indicated to Germany the
nature of the terms on which we should be prepared to co-operate.
France was anxious to go in. Russia, however, was very susceptible on the subject, and he would not do anything now to
frighten Russia. He had urged the Russians to say what they
wanted, but so far he could get no answer from them. By inference he had told the Germans that we should not allow the
railway to be completed unless our proposals were accepted; but
of course he had not put it as bluntly as that.

I recalled to his mind how useful and influential in the final
settlement had been his declaration on behalf of Rosebery's Government that a French expedition to the Nile would be "an unfriendly
act" and urged that some public statement now about the Railway and the Persian Gulf might prevent Germany going too far,
or if the worst happened, prepare the mind of our people for the
action they would have to take.

As regards my pet Smyrna-Aidin idea, he said the difficulty
there would be the Sultan, who wanted to keep the European
terminus under his eye. However, it would take some time before the new sections were completed. Meanwhile his policy was
to accumulate as many cards in his own hand as he could. The
question of the renewal of the increased customs duties would be
coming up then, and the Sultan, whose chief interest lay in the
Holy Places, might not be so squeezable after they were passed.
And indeed by that time the Sultan himself might be dead and with

him might go the gang who were now selling the country to the Germans, for that was what it came to.

He did not like the idea of letting the Germans complete the line alone, for he thought there would be great danger in having German influence predominant in that "great Mohammedan wedge between India and Egypt," especially if they began to run branch lines into Persia where they were already beginning to be active, and he dwelt on the way in which the German control would be used to divert trade into German hands. "Where the Germans have the communications, they get the trade and the English are driven out."

Altogether I thought what he said was shrewd and sensible.

Last Sunday we motored over from Camilla to lunch with the Northcliffes at Sutton—a beautiful drive through the most lovely Surrey scenery. Delcassé was there and I found him very pleasant. He asked warmly after Father. He was particularly insistent that we—our Press and speakers—should deal tenderly with the Czar. "He is the best friend you have in Russia," he said, "and he is very sensitive. He reads the English papers and he is very susceptible to their criticisms." He did not think that the Empress had any influence on politics or interested herself in them. We saw him again last night and he is coming to lunch with us today.

Lady Northcliffe's garden was really beautiful. She has now made the whole sloping bank at the end of the plateau on which the house stands into a wild garden, and had besides a very pretty formal rose-garden in addition to the walled gardens. What a magnificent house it is!

*24th June* 1908.

At Lansdowne's dinner Ivy was taken in by Mr. Balfour. He told her he had that afternoon addressed 8000 people of the Pan-Anglican Conference in the Albert Hall on "Religion and Science" and, he added, "I don't believe there was one of them who understood what I meant. I'm not sure that I understood myself." How beautifully characteristic! Delcassé to whom I told the story said it was "true Balfour." "He has a very distinguished mind."

Delcassé was very pleasant and talkative and lavished compliments. He told Beatrice that he had been taking a lesson in French from her, and Ivy that he would be amply satisfied if he could talk English as she speaks French. I wanted to get his opinion of Clemenceau, which I suspected to be unfavourable. I asked him how far Clemenceau still influenced the *Aurore*—how far it represented his feelings. He said:

"I will answer your question by another. How far does Clemenceau influence Clemenceau?"

And he went on to speak of him as guided entirely by the feeling of the moment, very brilliant but with no settled policy and no *suite dans ses idées*.

"He arrived too late," he said, "*il lui manque le long apprentisage de la responsibilité.*"

I was glad to have him here and to be able to show him that small attention and he seemed pleased with it.

*25th June* 1908.

You will have seen that the Government was forced to yield on the question of a sliding scale of income for Old Age Pensions, and again last night on the question of fining old people living together. I am delighted, for these are the two points which I chose for attack as soon as the scheme was promulgated. Incidentally, I may say that I got in a little speech of ten minutes or so on Lloyd George's surrender, on which I have been much congratulated. The report in *The Times* does not do it justice.

*26th June* 1908.

Ivy and I went this morning to Laszlo's Exhibition. I found Lady Frances Balfour there who said, "At last we have a portrait of Arthur!" but I did not quite share her enthusiasm in that case. Still the portrait is good and, like Sargent's, better than anything I had ever seen as a likeness of Balfour, showing his strength of character and not merely his sweetness of disposition. But Laszlo's triumphs are the portraits of Arthur Lee, very stern and grave; of President Roosevelt, giving the impression of immense power and energy with some coarseness but restrained withal; of Mensdorf; and, above all, of Alfred Lyttelton, done absolutely to the life—the most satisfactory *portrait* I have seen of anyone for a long time. I can imagine nothing better.

I have been reading *Coke of Norfolk*—rather poor stuff I think—gushy and too much of it described from or in the style of the *Norfolk Intelligencer*. But fancy! He was born in 1754 and died in 1842 at the age of 88. His son, the present Earl of Leicester,[1] is still living—thus two lives span more than a century and a half, and Father and son together have seen six reigns including the two longest in our history. The present Lord Leicester was born in 1822 (when his father was 68) and his youngest son was born in 1893. If the latter lives to be 60 (very little for so long-lived a family) three generations will have covered two centuries!

HIGHBURY,
*27th June* 1908.

Ivy and I left London at 10 o'clock this morning and stopped at Rugby for the School Speech Day. It was very like old times to see the boys acting and hear their recitations. They have got a very fine Honours List this year which, by the number and diversity of the Honours gained, shows that the School is doing well all round, educationally, and is in a very different condition, as far at least as the teaching is concerned, from what it was in my day. Then we lunched in Old Big School with the Headmaster, and I escaped making a speech by pleading that the senior governor present must propose the Headmaster's health. And after that Ivy and I visited my old house and looked up my study and the dormitories in which I slept, and any other marks of the past we could find.

9 EGERTON PLACE, S.W.,
*30th June* 1908.

Balfour and Douglas both confirm from other sources my story of the row in the Cabinet between Winston and Crewe. B. says he expects that Winston is just playing his father's part again.

Yesterday a question was asked in the House: "Whether the President of the Board of Trade had a room placed at his disposal

[1] The 2nd Earl of Leicester died in 1909.

at the War Office for the purpose of giving him access to departmental papers?" The answer was: "No," but by what mental
quibble it was justified I do not know, for the fact is that Winston
has been sitting daily, or almost daily, at the War Office and that
departmental papers are actually "marked" to him. Balfour says
he has no doubt that Winston has been plunging against the Army
Estimates, that Haldane has declared that any further considerable
reductions are impossible, and that, after Winston had made himself sufficiently objectionable, he has been told to come across to
the War Office and point out how they could be made. B. added:

"I was staying with him in the same house last Sunday. He
did not attempt to conceal that they were in an awful mess about
next year's finance and at their wits' end how to provide for their
expenditure. He said he must leave by an 8 o'clock train on Monday
morning in order to be in time for a Cabinet Committee which
he had to attend 'and where,' he added, 'I intend to make myself
damned disagreeable!'" B. had no doubt the Committee was on
Army Estimates.

It is believed that all the Cabinet, with the possible exception
of Grey, is against Haldane.

The Government had another bad day in the House yesterday.
By basing their scheme on non-contributory lines and at the same
time declaring that the pension is "a right," they have got themselves involved in innumerable absurdities. If we had free debate,
we could worry them almost to death, but the guillotine saves
them and will secure the passage of the Bill in a form which I
believe would be impossible if we had full discussion.

*2nd July* 1908.

I have done three days' hard work at Old Age Pensions, making
a number of short speeches of no particular consequence and one
or two onslaughts on the Government which pleased me as they
were practice in a style I lack and they turned out well. We were
so severely guillotined that much of the Bill went undiscussed, but
the Government were in very considerable argumentative difficulties on several occasions, and we had the satisfaction of at least
seeing the Labour Party chafing under the operation of the closure
for which they had so cheerfully voted. Without any obstructive

debate and with a little ingenuity in arranging our amendments, we got several of our discussions in before them and "rode them off," to use a racing phrase. On Tuesday night we had quite an exciting time one way and another and one of those episodes which, as Ida says, give so much pleasure to the House and no one outside it can understand! I did not get my dinner till 9.45 that night and was back in my place when the row began at 10.15. Alas! when Balfour had to borrow a hat to put a point of order while the division was in progress, it was Sandy Cross's hat that he took. As I told him, it was unlucky, for we are doing our best to oust Cross and now he will be able to say that he is under not merely the same umbrella but the same hat as Balfour!

Did you notice Lloyd George's description of himself? "I have no nest-egg as the Hon. member suggests. Next year I shall have *to rob somebody's hen-roost* and I must consider where I can get most eggs, and where I can get them easiest and where I shall *be least punished.*"

I hear that the Treasury is wincing under this description of himself by a Chancellor of the Exchequer—"the most unfortunate phrase ever used by a Chancellor of the Exchequer and I suppose you won't allow him to forget it." Not likely! The Conservative Office is getting out a picture of Lloyd George in the hen-roost which he finds empty whilst all the hens—capital, labour, investments, wages, etc.—are seen flying away overhead to foreign lands.

*2nd July* 1908.

I asked Sir A. Nicolson whether there was now anything like Cabinet responsibility in Russia, recalling the difficulties of our own Government during the war [1] owing to the fact that *e.g.* the Russian Navy Office habitually acted without consultation with and even in opposition to the Foreign Office in those days. He replied certainly there was. Our treaty was the work of the whole Cabinet and bound them all. It was the first thing of the kind and very important. He could have settled with Isvolski in a few hours, but he and the Emperor wanted to rope in the whole council of ministers, which very nearly upset the whole arrange-

[1] The Russo-Japanese War.

ment. But happily the British Government stood firm and after a continuous sitting of six hours the Russian Cabinet agreed unanimously to the arrangement.

Then I asked, is there anything you can call public opinion in Russia which approves or disapproves the treaty, and again he replied, "Certainly."—The whole Russian Press of all shades of opinion. They were all very much in favour of it and delighted with the King's visit. They disliked Germany and the Germans and wanted to carry the English agreement further; but the Czar said this was a new movement and he wished to go gently. N. thought he was right.

Nicolson has a high opinion of Stolypin and says the Duma is doing very well. The first two were impossible, but the present, which really represents the country gentlemen, is showing moderation, courage and independence.

NUNEHAM,
*6th July* 1908.

Please give my love and best wishes to Father. Every day that passes must give him increasing assurance of the early success of his cause. He "builded better than he knew" in that great campaign of his, and there is increasing evidence that opponents as well as friends know that his policy is going to triumph. He ought never to think of himself as "out of it" so long as his name and his messages are so great a force and so eagerly waited for and so warmly received at all gatherings of our friends. He is playing even now a bigger part in the movement than he knows.

9 EGERTON PLACE, S.W.,
*8th July* 1908.

Father's birthday, and he is much in our thoughts.

London and the House begin to have a winding-up air about them.

"When are you going away?"

"What are you going to do this summer?" and so on—these are the questions with which conversations open. As to news, there is none, and the poor letter-writer is altogether at a loss for material.

I 129

It is true that the scandal of the dissensions in the Navy has burst forth again, stimulated by Arthur Lee's letter in *The Times*; and the friends of Fisher on one side and of Charley Beresford on the other are raging in the columns of all the newspapers. Personally it seems to me that the Admiralty needs a *very* strong First Lord and I doubt it has not got it. I should like to see Lord Charles and Percy Scott both ordered to haul down their flags and Sir John Fisher allowed to retire. I think his usefulness has ceased and that his influence now is mischievous. But nothing can excuse Percy Scott's impudence to Lord Charles, or Lord Charles's insubordination and disloyalty to the Admiralty. The whole quarrel is discreditable to all concerned, and the methods by which it has been carried on on all sides—the Press intrigues and personalities—as well as the quarrel itself are disastrous to the Navy and absolutely contrary to all its traditions since the days of Nelson.

I heard some time ago that Fisher and the Board were seriously considering the issue of an order to Lord Charles to strike his flag; and that Lord C. on his side was equally carefully counting his chances if he should throw up his command and start an open campaign against Fisher. But each side came to the conclusion that the forces were too nicely balanced and that public opinion would incline the scales against the one which appeared the aggressor. So neither side did anything fairly, but both sides continued to intrigue secretly.

Before taking up his command at Plymouth, Fawkes [1] was approached by someone with the question:

"Are you going to be loyal to Fisher?"

His reply was characteristic of the man.

"I'm going to be loyal to the Board of Admiralty. I always have been and I always shall be. But I know nothing of Fisher and don't understand what loyalty to Fisher means."

Would that all others would speak and act the same.

*9th July* 1908.

Asquith gave an excellent answer to questions about the Admirals' quarrels yesterday—that is, it would be excellent if they would act up to it. But Arthur Lee tells me that he only wrote his

---

[1] The late Admiral Sir Wilmott Fawkes.

letter after and because one of the Civil members of the Board told him that they had proposed to deal drastically with those in fault but had been prevented by the Cabinet, who feared the row that would ensue.

We had a meeting of the General Purposes Committee of the T.R. League yesterday. Here are some of the figures laid before us which will, I think, be of interest to Father as showing progress:

*First six months of the year:*

|  | 1906 | 1907 | 1908 |
|---|---|---|---|
| Subscriptions . . . | £2,000 | £6,000 | £8,400 |
| Donations . . . | £3,100 | £2,000 | £2,100 |
| Sale of Monthly Notes . | £55 | £136 | £215 |
| Total Income . . | £6,200 | £8,500 | £12,100 |
| Total Expenditure . . | £7,800 | £5,500 | £8,600 |
| Leaflets issued . . | | 1,000,000 | 3,000,000 |

The last edition of the *Speaker's Handbook* was published in October. 10,000 copies were printed; only 400 remain in hand.

Number of meetings arranged from Victoria Street alone in the past six months was 241—approximate attendance 64,000—average net cost to the League per meeting 10s. 5¼d. Pretty good, is it not?

This includes our Blackpool campaign where, as you know, all working-class Lancashire spends its holidays and where we took a "pitch" on the sands. The agent reports that the experiment was successful beyond all expectations. Thus in one week when the Burnley workmen were there, 291 applications to join a Burnley Branch now about to be formed were received. The Lancashire workman is reported to be "an eager enquirer for information."

*21st July 1908.*

The House has been a little more lively the last two days over the Licensing Bill. I had a fierce brush with Asquith in an angry and excited House on Monday evening. Asquith was rude and

131

offensive in his interruptions of a speech to which he would not reply and to which he did not take the trouble to listen.

I had been dining with the Tariff Reformers and curiously enough the Chairman of the dinner had referred to my first effort in the House—a question to Asquith, then Home Secretary—and I had told the T.R.s how, as I left the House on that occasion after receiving an unsatisfactory answer, the old door-keeper had stopped me and said :

"That won't do, sir. You'll never get on if you submit like that. Mr. Chamberlain wouldn't have put up with it. He'd have gone on worrying him!"

1909

THE year 1909 saw a determined movement to bring the Unionist Party into line on Tariff Reform on the basis of a speech made by Balfour in Birmingham in December 1907, so that a Unionist Government might not again be rendered impotent, if we won a General Election, by internal divisions on this vital article of its programme. A Unionist victory at the polls did not seem so impossible at the time as subsequent events made it appear. The Home Rule majority in 1906 had been swollen to exaggerated proportions by the discontents accumulated by ten years of Unionist Government, by Balfour's Education Act which, whatever its merits, had alienated the great bulk of Nonconformity, and by the split on Tariff Reform. Many Conservatives and Unionists were now returning to their allegiance, by-elections were moving favourably for us, and the Government's supporters in their turn were becoming increasingly restive. In order to obtain the support of the Free Fooders, they had pledged themselves at the General Election not to make Home Rule an issue in this Parliament and their interim policy had satisfied no one and had been repudiated by the Nationalists. The rejection of their Education and Licensing Bills by the House of Lords had stirred no deep feeling, and their prestige was obviously falling. The progress of the Suffragists and their growing hostility to Asquith and his Government added to their troubles.

On top of this came a fierce controversy as to the sufficiency of the Navy in view of the growing fleet of Germany. The demand was crystallised in a jingle coined by George Wyndham which ran through the country:

"We want eight and we won't wait."

Finally, the financial year 1908-9 had ended in a deficit and heavy additional taxation was obviously impending.

It was in these gloomy circumstances that Mr. Lloyd George opened his famous Budget in a speech lasting five hours. Whatever else may be said of it, it must be admitted that its boldness, the new issues which it raised and the passions which it aroused on one side

135

and the other, changed the whole aspect of affairs. It was fought tooth and nail by the Unionist Party at a length commensurate with the time taken by the Chancellor to open it. His Budget statement was made on 2nd April, but the Finance Bill did not receive its Third Reading until 25th November.

"The Bill during its passage through the Commons had expanded from seventy-four clauses to ninety-six and from sixty-two pages to ninety-eight." [1]

It had occupied three days a week during many weeks. The House never rose until after midnight, and not infrequently we returned home when the milkman was going his early rounds. I recall no comparable Parliamentary struggle since the debates on Mr. Gladstone's Home Rule Bill in 1893. The tax on undeveloped minerals had been abandoned and a tax on mining royalties substituted and large changes had been made in the Land Taxes proper. When the Budget eventually became law they had a disastrous effect on the provision of small houses which began the shortage we have only just succeeded in overtaking, and they brought no money to the Exchequer. They were repealed by me when Chancellor of the Exchequer in Mr. Lloyd George's Post-War Coalition Government.

The increase of the Spirit Duties was very unpopular with the Irish, whose opposition, as will be seen, gave the Government a good deal of trouble at subsequent stages, and the increase of the Tobacco Duty was disliked by their Labour supporters.

After this stormy passage through the House of Commons the Bill was at length sent up to the House of Lords only to be refused a Second Reading on 2nd November after three days' debate.

A General Election had now become inevitable. The passions roused by the Budget burned more fiercely than ever, and fresh fuel was added from Radical platforms by violent denunciation of the House of Lords and the demand, first formulated by Rosebery himself, I think, when he was Prime Minister, to "end or mend it," became the most urgent article of the Government's creed. The Constitutional Question had become for the first time a living issue.

I worked harder in the House of Commons this year than ever before or since. Except for ten days or a fortnight when I was laid up with sciatica, I believe I attended and spoke on nearly every day of the Budget discussion. Writing in the following March, I told my father that "from a publication just received I learn that my

[1] *Annual Register* for 1909, p. 237.

speeches filled 526 columns of *Hansard* last session, being exceeded in length only by Balfour with 611 and Lloyd George with 710, whilst only three other men exceeded 300. I trust therefore that you will feel that I fairly discharged my duty to my constituents!"

My wife and I took a short holiday in Holland at Easter, and paid a flying visit, much spoilt by bad weather, to Florence in November.

I fear that my views on Women's Suffrage as expressed at the time will anger some of my readers, but I have let them stand. I am bound to admit that, if the results of its adoption have not realised all its promoters' hopes, neither have they justified my fears.

*Tariff Reform—Fiscal Amendment—Crisis on Naval Estimates—*
*Scottish By-Elections*

HIGHBURY,
*7th February* 1909.

I see that I shall be very busy as soon as I get to town—interviews, committees, Bank, etc. But no more public meetings for a time, thank goodness! Two a week for six weeks, or at least eleven in six weeks, is too much. No, it will be twelve, for they have arranged an "overflow" at Wolverhampton!

*10th February* 1909.

Here are some scraps that may interest you all. I have arranged to see Goulding and Gwynne of the *Standard* (both at their own request) about Bob Cecil as soon as I go to town. I shall tell them what I told Lawrence: "I have nothing to do with Marylebone; but if I were a Marylebone elector I should be ready to make special terms with Cecil in view of his special position; but they would *not* be *his* terms. I would say, 'if you will promise not to oppose a Unionist Government I will not oppose you'; but that is the limit to which I would go. I wouldn't accept Bob's own terms at any price—or advise anyone else to."

Mickey Beach is all right, as I thought.

I had Vince and Jenkins up yesterday. Grogan has made a very good impression in the Potteries and will at any rate give Wedgwood a stiff fight in Newcastle-under-Lyne. I think we have got a man for Lichfield—Dr. Cotes—rather of the Major Darwin type, but "sound on the goose."

I have been busy writing letters all morning and have only time left to scribble this note to you before lunch. Thank goodness my Wolverhampton speech was mostly made yesterday, so my mind is easy.

138

9 EGERTON PLACE, S.W.,
13*th February* 1909.

Wolverhampton was terribly hard work. Alfred Bird called for us in his car at 5.45. I dined at the Club, and Ivy with Mrs. Marston. At 8.15 a meeting in the Agricultural Hall—packed—between two and three thousand. I spoke for 50 minutes and then —hey presto—off to an *overflow* in the Drill Hall, holding twice the number and densely thronged! They had carried away half the barriers in the first mad rush in and were packed like herrings in a barrel.

"What shall I talk about?" I asked.

Shouts of "Tariff Reform" from all parts of the Hall and then a cry: "Tell us how your feyther is!" and loud cheers. So I gave them another half-hour and was *very* tired when I got home again after 11.30, and Ivy says I talked all night in my sleep.

Never mind! it's over now and I am very well and today's post only brought demands for five more speeches. Don't they wish they may get them?

*Sunday*, and a busy day. Goulding came to lunch to report his negotiations with Bob Cecil. They had produced no result. I asked him about the story J. Lawrence told me of the Duke of Sutherland having refused to pay for his Tariff Reform party. Quite untrue as I supposed. It was a misunderstanding arising from another occasion when the Duke had lent Stafford House *as it stood* for a Women's Tariff meeting and the women had under-taken to pay *extra* expenses. It was then that Henderson, being asked to give £50, drew a cheque for the whole £300 required.

Gwynne of the *Standard* came this afternoon—also to talk about Bob Cecil. He thought there was more chance of Bob's being ready to accept a compromise than did Goulding, but had nothing definite to say. I told him that the only compromise possible was that Bob should not be opposed if he undertook not to oppose a Unionist Government and if, apart from the specific terms of his pledge, he meant to be a friend and act as a friend of a Unionist and Tariff Reform Government, and that these terms were for Bob only and not for others. I would do my best to smooth matters on these terms, but I had nothing to do with Marylebone and did not know if my advice would carry any weight. If Bob declined these terms and continued to be an enemy of Tariff Reform, then frankly I would sooner the seat were given to the Radicals or, if that could not be and we could not win, that Bob came in against us as an open foe.

I told G. he might tell Bob all I had said.

*15th February* 1909.

Such a day !

16.2.09. And at that point another man called to see me and then another and then it was time to dress for Balfour's dinner and then there was Lady Londonderry's party and then I was glad enough to get home to bed !

I got your letter yesterday morning and in the course of the afternoon I wired to you that the *Tageblatt* article had aroused no further comment here and that I did not think any further statement necessary. I delayed sending the telegram until I had verified dates, for I confess that I thought the Leicester speech was before the outbreak of the Boer War, and, though as a matter of fact I sent word to the *Mail* Reporter who brought me the *Daily Telegraph* cutting that I had nothing to say, I very nearly decided to issue a contradiction like Father's off my own bat. But I was wrong and Leicester came about a month after the outbreak of war. Of course the *Tageblatt's* account was very inaccurate. I am not certain, but I think it emanates from an old German Foreign Office official who is no friend of Bülow. I think you may safely leave the matter where it stands unless you are forced to take action by further *Tageblatt* "revelations." I have seen no further reference to the matter here since Father's telegram to the *Mail* was published.

You will have seen the King's Speech before this reaches you. After hearing it read last night we had a short preparatory talk about amendments. Balfour said we must have an amendment about Ireland, and Chaplin loudly, and the rest silently, agreed. I said we must have an amendment on Tariff Reform and Unemployment. I agreed that the state of Ireland was a scandal and we ought to discuss it, but unfortunately the country was not interested in it ("All the more reason for having a Front Bench amendment on it," cried Chaplin) and we were not going to win on it. If we won, we would change the condition of Ireland in 48 hours and every constable would be hunting a murderer instead of being hunted by one; but we should win on T.R. It was about T.R. that we had all been talking in the country; it was the only thing the country cared for and therefore we must move about it.

Chaplin rampaged. The country must be made to care about Ireland. T.R. was going so well, it could take care of itself, etc. He had thought of moving a Preference amendment, but Hewins had warned him that the Canadian situation was too delicate, that indiscreet utterances by minor people might do infinite harm there, where, for the moment, they are on the high horse about their treaty-making powers.

Balfour had also thought of this, but desisted for the same reason. He wished to take a fiscal discussion on the new-revenue-necessary line on the Budget. It was the line that brought all wobblers in. Could we take another on the Address?

Arnold-Forster thought this much the best plan.

Harry Chaplin and Arnold-Forster! Thus to be wounded in the house of one's friends!

I pressed my view. If we did not seize on Unemployment at once, the Labour Party would make it their own again. We should be unable to vote on our own issue and should have to follow the Labour Party or abstain as was the case when the Speaker treated the autumn debate on Unemployment as the Labour Members' day, gave their amendment priority and closured the debate at the close of the evening.

Balfour admitted the force of all this (when does he not?) but would the Speaker allow it? would he give us two amendments? We must see. He had no objections if it could be arranged. Of course nothing was settled.

I went on to Londonderry House—many enquiries about you both.

Robbins (of the *Birmingham Post*) tells me the Radicals consider

Central Glasgow as hopelessly lost. Scott Dickson showed Bonar Law a letter from Hood, who apparently had some fear of Scott Dickson wobbling, saying :

"My dear Scott Dickson,

Much as I should like to welcome you back to the House, I had sooner see the seat lost than have a Conservative returned who will not support the whole party programme."

Scottie was furious ! But Bonar Law thought it very good !

Did Goulding tell you that the *Morning Post* article on the Free Fooders was left with Percival Hughes for four days in order that he might "submit it to his superiors" and was then published with his approval?

All negotiations with Bob Cecil are at an end. Gwynne told him of his interview with me and after reflecting on it Bob wrote to say that he could give no pledge to vote or to abstain. I am very sorry on personal grounds, but it is perhaps after all the best thing politically. Gwynne showed me Bob's letter last night, having obtained his permission to do so though it was marked "Confidential."

*16th February* 1909.

Things are looking better ! I find Sandars and Alec Hood anxious to get a T.R. amendment. What is more, Balfour made a very good reference to the subject today in connection with unemployment such as would directly lead up to the kind of amendment I contemplate. I saw him afterwards on another matter and then showed him the amendment which I had drafted.

"Could I have worded it more suitably," I asked, "if I had heard your speech *before* instead of *after* I drafted it?"

He read it and said :

"Of course I agree with every word of it. Indeed the fact is that I knew these fellows would not be satisfied unless I said something about fiscal reform and I was bothered about how to tack it on to the King's Speech. Then I thought of what you said last night and I stole your thunder"—which is a happy fact !

My draft runs:

"But humbly represents to your Majesty that this House views with anxiety the state of trade and employment in this country, the failure of your Majesty's Ministers to recognise the nature and gravity of the situation; and regrets that there is no mention in your Majesty's gracious Speech of any proposals for enlarging the market for British and Irish produce and increasing the demand for labour by a reform of our fiscal system which would promote the growth and stability of our home trade, and would develop our oversea trade through the establishment of a system of mutual preference between the different portions of the Empire."

That will do, won't it?

A. J. B. said he had desired a Preference amendment and Lansdowne had entirely agreed; but Chaplin told him that Hewins was afraid of it for fear of treading on Colonial corns. I was able to tell him that what Hewins feared was that a pure Preference debate would hinge on the Franco-Canadian treaty negotiations, but that he had said last night to me: "If you don't have an amendment on T.R. and unemployment, we are done!"

Curious to see how A. J. B. now hangs on Hewins!

I then said that what I pressed for was that Percy and I should hand in the Irish and Tariff Reform amendments together tomorrow. I did not much care in that case which was moved first. Both would appear on the paper simultaneously, both would stand in Front Bench names, and both would be moved unless the Speaker ruled one out of order or closured debate.

I came home in the train with Sandars, who proposed that I should move first, since if the Speaker closured out the Irish amendment we could force a discussion of Irish grievances by a direct Vote of Censure.

We have a "shadow Cabinet" tomorrow morning to decide our course. I believe they will be substantially of my way of thinking.

My leisure (!) moments yesterday and today were occupied in drafting a reply to Carrington's criticisms (*Times*, 19th February) of my Durham speech. I showed Collings the draft; he is delighted.

143

It will probably go to *The Times* tomorrow; am I wise or foolish to notice them?

Goulding was in high spirits when we called. He who a year ago was all gloom now said we should sweep London.

Talking of Glasgow, which he said we should win, Robbins asked my forecast. I said my information is not complete, but I expect a majority of 50.

"You are rather sanguine."

"Yes, I think so—more sanguine than most. But I believe we are going to win largely in London and recover Lancashire. We shall reverse the position in the Midlands, but I do not at present think we shall gain very much in Scotland. You see I count on success breeding success. Suppose my calculations point to a majority of thirty. Think what losses that means to the Government and what striking successes it means to us in the early days. If then thirty is right on paper, the swing will make it fifty."

He said: "Yes, there was force in that. It was a fair calculation. The Government knew they were losing London and Lancashire; they regarded Central Glasgow as gone, but they believed they would hold nearly all Scotland."

I send you his "London Letter."

*17th February* 1909.

My amendment was accepted by the "shadow Cabinet"—to be moved tomorrow if the Speaker consents. I have just been with Alec Hood to see him and learn "if his intentions are honourable," but he was out.

The pitch is a little queered by a Labour amendment which has got precedence today. If necessary I must move my words from "and regrets" as an addendum to theirs.

*19th February* 1909.

Well, well, well! So here we are again! Our great debate has come and gone and I am well pleased both with its personal and public aspects. But I must go back a little. We held our "shadow

Cabinet" on Wednesday morning. I went prepared for a fight and for another of those long uphill collar strains by which our T.R van has been pulled along. Not a bit of it! A. J. B. opened the proceedings with a friendly statement of the position, but one which left the "van" pretty much where it was before. Chaplin made some observations, slightly sobered by my remarks to him the night before. Wyndham pressed manfully for a T.R. amendment and hey presto! the thing was done! I fancy Londonderry said something, but nobody marked him! I read my amendment (with a Retaliation sentence added), it was accepted *nem. con.* and given first place; and Alec Hood and I proceeded to interview the Speaker and secure his assent. He was out and I had to hurry to my Bank, but Hood saw him later, found him ready to give two days to me as well as two days to Ireland, and clearly and very properly of opinion that my amendment raised an issue quite distinct from Barnes's.

You will have read my speech and I send you some press cuttings. I think I may fairly say that my speech, pieced together between dinner time on Wednesday and lunch on Thursday, was a success. I don't think that the *matter* was any better than some others which have disappointed me and others, but somehow it took on, and even in the accounts of hostile critics who are bound to say, and do say, that I had no case, there is the admission that I "added to my reputation."

You would have enjoyed the momentary triumph I got out of Lloyd George's foolish insistence on my reading the words of Burns's speech (just one of the little dramatic episodes that the House loves, which achieve a success altogether out of proportion to their intrinsic importance) and still more the effect of the couplet thrown at Winston. When I was at Highbury, I wanted (for Wolverhampton) another couplet which I could not remember verbally, so I searched Father's Commonplace Book for it—unsuccessfully. But I came upon these lines of Dryden's and "Chortled in my joy."

"Oh that I had had them at Stechford!" I cried.

"Never mind," said Ivy and Beatrice in a breath, "they are 'handy to have in the house.'"

"Yes," said I, "in *the* House."

As I began :

> "Still violent whatever cause he undertook,"

Winston was leaning forward, smiling amiably. He did not know the couplet !

> "But most against the Party he forsook,"

a roar of cheers from our fellows, and Winston, throwing up his hands, collapsed into his seat and—blushed !

Masterman disappointed his friends. Alfred made a very good but not a really effective speech. Lloyd George, who said he only wanted twenty minutes, clearly had nothing to say.

Bob Cecil played his part with great skill, was excellent in tone and temper and (as Mason remarked to me) conclusively proved the impossibility of the position which he wished to be allowed to occupy.

Today Wyndham spoke very well for fifty minutes and then got out of his depth for ten. Balfour played the game, and Winston, with an enthusiastic backing from his friends, did better than usual.

But the honours remain with us. The House was far more "in hand" than on any fiscal debate in this Parliament ; we had no *contretemps* ; Alfred and Wyndham both declared plainly for taxation of corn, and Balfour, who cheered Wyndham's declaration that you could not have "effective Preference" without taxation of corn and meat, but with whom it is not a point of honour not to *say* that he *will* tax corn, was not even heckled on it.

You will have seen my letter in today's *Times* re Carrington and Small Holdings. I hope I have not slaughtered myself to make a holiday for Collings ! I am comforted by the fact that the *Westminster* makes no comment on it. If they had had an answer ready, they would have jumped on me in their "Notes."

I see *The Times* is not over sanguine about Central Glasgow and Bonar Law tells me that "at any rate Bowles is interesting them." Boraston, a day or two ago, was hopeful about putting up at any rate a good fight in South Edinburgh. But I suppose that with his added prestige Dewar will carry it. Border Burghs are no man's land, but the chances are in favour of the Radicals. Yet I have my hopes.

*20th February* 1909.

I have had a hard week and was very glad to feel my work was done when I got home at half-past five yesterday. Today I had only one political caller at 10.30, then went to the Bank and afterwards joined Ivy at the Leicester Galleries. Here there were two excellent exhibitions of work by William Callow (R.W.S. 1812-1908) and Alfred Parsons. Among Callow's water-colours were pictures as early as 1838 and as late as 1904. They made a very pleasing collection and some were quite attractive. Parsons's exhibition was described as Pastorals. They were mostly very small and all the better, I thought, on that account. We particularly admired half a dozen cloud effects, mainly sunsets, some bright and peaceful, some stormy and foreboding, but all painted with great skill and feeling.

Then we went to a small exhibition of Interiors of Venetian Palaces and Churches by Pierre Bracquemond, at Maclean's, but were very disappointed. His palaces were good and so were some Parisian interiors with bric-à-brac; but his colour scheme for the Venetian Churches was all wrong. St. Mark's looked like a colour-washed barn, the Miracoli marbles like a dully painted wainscoting. This may be "Impressionism" as the catalogue states, but I am sorry for the person whose impressions so entirely miss the characteristic beauty of the buildings.

After lunch we took a walk in the Park and found it a little misty but delightful. In fact we have had a week of dry frosty weather with a good deal of sunshine and not too much wind most days, so that it has really been very good for London at this time of year.

*20th February* 1909.

As far as I can see our division on the fiscal amendment was satisfactory—numbers nothing to boast of, it is true, but as good or better than they usually are; several good men away for sufficient reasons and only Cecil, Bowles, Lambton, Cross and Percy Thornton deliberately staying away. Cross, as you know, already has notice to quit and Thornton is not standing again.

Haddock, who turned out Dick Cavendish, was describing to a select circle his difficulties in the contest.

"I know nothing of politics and I had no one to help me. I had to stand on my own bottom."

"No, no!" said F. E. Smith, "you swam on your own fins, my dear Haddock!"

21st February 1909.

We have just had Monsieur Pernolet, the Duckworths and Beatrice to dinner.

Pernolet was full of interesting talk as always, much about Russia as to which he is at once pessimistic and reassuring, seeing on the one hand no chance of much improvement and on the other no possibility of revolution. He has large industrial interests there, but says there is no development among the people, no natural demand for the products of industry and no progress. The Russian is quick and clever like a child or a negro. The *main-d'œuvre* is very cheap and quick to learn up to a certain point, but it never reaches a high level. It quickly does what is wanted *à peu près* but never does it right. It would be cheaper to pay more and employ good foreign labour if it were possible. All their labour is Russian, but none of their foremen or managers.

"Of course we have to have in our mines a Russian chief engineer *auquel il est expressément défendu de rien faire—mais qui est responsable de tout.*"

They had recently had a very bad explosion in one of their mines—300 lives lost—"and all, as I could see very well, because one of our men—*du reste un garçon très intelligent* (a Frenchman)—*n'avait pas fait son service.*" There was an enquiry of course. "The whole band descended on the spot. There were *trois jours de noces effrénés*"—banquets, lunches, etc. At the end magnificent reports; we were complimented and the Russian staff censured.

"*Ils n'avaient pas vu, ou n'avaient pas voulu voir, ce que je voyais très bien, moi, de Paris.*"

Incidentally, he told us that the Emperor spent his days studying reports—masses of reports in which the truth was buried—painstaking, but quite futile. The Empress had great influence but was silly—"*une bête.*" Her chief adviser and confidant was a butcher from Cannes who had had a local reputation for foretelling whether a child would be a boy or a girl. The Empress had heard of him and summoned him to Petersburg.

"If you turn the key in the lock a certain way, it will be a boy," said he, and it was! He was now the most influential man at the Russian Court. But the trouble had been to find a uniform for him. "*Enfin, il a été nommé 'Vétérinaire de la Cour' et voilà!*"

It is coarse, but I confess I roared at the incongruous title. *Quel pays!*

*22nd February* 1909.

We had a curious debate in the Commons to-day on Ponsonby's amendment for pressing on at once the quarrel with the Lords. The Government forces were obviously ill at ease; Asquith's speech was received in chill silence and Balfour made an admirable debating reply. Incidentally, Goulding produced a good thing. Four years ago Sinclair proposed to reduce Linlithgow's salary on the ground that to have the Secretary for Scotland in the Lords was "an insult to Scotland." Poor Sinclair! that kick upstairs remains a mystery to me. I can understand why Asquith should have wished to fire him out of the Cabinet or out of office, but not why, leaving him in possession of both, he should put him in the Lords. The reason publicly given—that he wanted a competent man to manage Scottish business in the Upper House—is ludicrous to all of us who know Sinclair.

Hewins writes to me today in a postscript to a letter on other matters:

"I understand on high authority (this I heard on Saturday) that there is an absolute deadlock in the Cabinet on Navy Estimates."

I do not know Hewins's authority, but I think he is not far wrong.

*23rd February* 1909.

I am just back from the Levée. Amongst others I saw Cadogan, who will be out at Cannes in a few weeks' time and will call on you. He, Halsbury and many others asked after you and Father.

Then I saw Admiral May, the Second Sea Lord.

*May.* So you are fighting again in the House of Commons.

*A. C.* Yes, and we are not the only people who are fighting!

*May.* N-no. We all have to fight in these days. Well, I hope the Cabinet will soon settle it now.

*A. C.* Well, I don't know what you have asked for, but you will get it if you are firm. Tell Fisher [1] from me that I repeat now what I said to him when we first met fifteen years ago. If the Naval Lords stand firm and are prepared to resign together, they will get their way now as they did then over the Spencer programme.

*May.* Oh! there's no doubt what the Naval Lords will do.

*A. C.* Well, power is in your hands. The Government cannot afford to quarrel with you in their present position. Besides Asquith is on your side.

*May.* Hum! one doesn't know who is on our side in the present state of things!

My conversation recorded above has borne fruit. First a note from Sir John:

"My beloved Austen,
I am sitting tight!
Yours till hell freezes!

J. F."

Next I met him this afternoon in Palace Yard and he renewed his assurances that he was sitting tight, that the Government didn't want to go out, and that therefore he knew he had the whip hand. But he was that moment on his way to the fourth (or fifth) Cabinet on their estimates. The P.M. was behaving "abominably"; he got all the credit for being for a strong Navy, but his action was "abominable." (All this with strong expressions for a desire for secrecy delivered in a loud voice on the island in the middle of Palace Yard!) The much maligned McKenna was the only good

[1] Admiral Sir John Fisher, afterwards Lord Fisher.

man—he and Grey. Grey was a rock. "McK. came in to fire me out. 'I had better be frank, Sir John,' he said, 'we will have three or four new battleships, but no more.' I let him talk and now by Jove! it's 'Fisher, we'll have eight!'"

"Go on and prosper," said I, "but mark my word, financially the greatest difficulty will come next year. You have lived on your fat and postponed action too long. Don't procrastinate any more. The C. of E. will be even less ready to pay your bill next year than he is this year. Get all you want now and suffer no postponement."

And he assures me he will.

### 24th February 1909.

I am still blushing! Harry Chaplin certainly would not recognise my account of his conversation, for he did the mischief without intending it and without knowing that he had done it. However, all's well that ends well! but if there had been anyone who did not wish for a T.R. amendment in our councils, Chaplin would have played straight into their hands. But he is forgiven. It was good of him to write to Father.

Oh! it is 10.30. I must to a Committee (L.U.).

11.00 p.m. I went to my Committee or rather appointment with Savile Crossley and Boraston and did business of the usual kind. Boraston says his reports on election prospects indicate that the Government would have a majority of twenty if they dissolved now, but he thinks these reports too pessimistic. I hear on good authority of a very confidential kind that the Conservative Central Office estimated a majority of twenty *for us* in January. I believe we should do better than either of these estimates. But the pending Scotch by-elections will be significant as indicating whether we have anything to hope from Scotland. I think Bowles is beat, but I don't care to count on either of the other seats.

I stayed at Great George Street till 1.00; then took a hurried lunch at the H. of C. and went to the Bank—no comfort to be found there. Then back to the House, listened to speeches, read magazine articles, voted on the Irish motion and home to dinner at 8.30.

I was sure you would all be pleased with the fiscal debate—quite the best we have had.

There was yet another Cabinet on the Naval Estimates yesterday afternoon, and still no decision reached.

Have you ordered Captain Bagot's *Canning Papers*, reviewed in today's *Times*. If not, I will get them for myself and send them on to you.

*27th February* 1909.

At the Speaker's I heard of Harry Chaplin's prowess. He went to a public dinner, feeling unwell, grew worse, told the Chairman he was so bad he must go home without speaking, was persuaded to stop, ate nothing but a few mouthfuls of soup, drank *a bottle* of champagne but "felt no better—there was no reaction" (Heavens! any other man would have felt decidedly worse), was persuaded to try port, took "four or five glasses," began to feel better and made the speech of his life! Think of it! a bottle of champagne and the best part of a bottle of port on an empty stomach and he didn't go under the table or out of his senses!

Yesterday morning I went to our first Committee on Tariffs—only Hewins, Ridley and myself present. After some discussion about the new French Tariff I dictated at their request a paragraph for Mat to get by heart and deliver to his Manchester audience last night. You will see it in full in today's *Morning Post*, to which and other papers it was sent by Hewins. Our evidence is that the threats of Winston and others to retaliate are producing a very bad effect on public opinion in France and seriously endangering the Entente. Yet our own people here are furious at the threat to their trade involved in the new French proposals, and men like Sir William Holland openly talk of retaliating on French wines and silks. Could anything better illustrate the weakness and the danger of our present system? We have no defence except a direct, provocative attack on French industries—the forging for this purpose only and for use against France alone of a special and arbitrary weapon by special and exceptional legislation wholly alien to our whole accepted system and settled policy. Could anything be worse, more invidious or more clumsy? Even Lord Cromer ought to prefer a "scientific tariff" to this. Of course Winston and the Government will not carry out their threats; but they are obliged to make them, for in no other way can they influence the French Government or pacify angry supporters; and in the meantime they undoubtedly injure our relations with France.

Very serious reports are afloat about the Navy. You will have seen that *The Times* and other papers assert, I fear truly, that the German Government have actually hurried on their new construction in advance of their programme dates as fixed by law, and are bidding high for (if they have not now actually secured) a superiority to us in the latest types of ships about 1911-12. There is more that I do not like to write, but in face of this the *Daily Chronicle* announced on Friday that the Government had settled their programme and composed their differences and that that programme was only four battleships with power to the Government to increase the number later in the year if they thought necessary, "the estimates being presented in an unusual form," and in that case, the extra ships to be paid for by loan.

All this I had confirmed on *very* high, though not naval, authority at the Court last night, except the loan story, which was said to be untrue. The only ray of hope is that I was told that the Naval Lords have not yet agreed. If they do agree, they deserve to be shot, and unless the whole story is false (and its source prevents me from believing that) Asquith deserves to be hung. It is inconceivable how any body of responsible men with the knowledge which the Government have before them can so play with the gravest issue which we have had to face for years. I am not often pessimistic, but I am seriously alarmed now. There is no doubt that Asquith has sold the fort after all his fine words. I expect that his sins as Chancellor are finding him out and that he has no answer to his successor when the latter says, "You have made this naval expenditure *impossible*." I learn on good authority that the repeal of half the sugar duty was decided last year at the last moment, after all the Budget figures were in print, and on the dictation of the Whips, who said, "We are losing seats and votes. Nothing but Old Age

Pensions and repeal of the sugar tax will stem the adverse tide. Do that or we perish ! "

*27th February* 1909.

I think we shall certainly win Central Glasgow. I hear good reports of Hawick, but do not believe we shall win that or either of the other Scottish seats.

*Tariff Reform: its progress during the last few years—Death of Arnold-Forster—Naval Estimates Crisis: New Zealand's offer of a Dreadnought—The Suffragist Movement.*

9 EGERTON PLACE, S.W.,
*8th March* 1909.

I used my presence in the House at question time to ask Asquith a question about a small muddle they have got into with their financial arrangements and had the pleasure of finding out that he thought (in private) that the Chancellor had made a hash of it, and that the Chancellor thought (in private) that the Secretary of the Treasury never ought to have done it, and that that is the way they do their business!

This evening I am going to dine at Grillions and then to the House again.

*10th March* 1909.

Lyttelton tells me that he hears from Selborne that Botha, Smuts and Steyn did very well at the Union Conference and got on well with Jameson. There was no racial fight, but of course each colony struggled its hardest for itself. The men whom B., S. and S. hate are Sauer and Merriman. Hofmeyer's influence has gone. All this was confirmed by Hannon, late of the Cape Agricultural Department (who was sent to me by Jameson), who added that Jameson was the real leader of the Conference and exercised more influence than anyone else.

*11th March* 1909.

Your letter of the 9th. Don't worry about Father's letter to Goulding. I saw how it happened, but it will do very well as it stands "as an extract from a letter received," etc. Goulding wanted me to add a sentence of my own, but *that* I refused to do. No thank you, not if I know it!

I have been at Great George Street this morning to meet a deputation from Edinburgh and discuss Scottish organisation. I hope some good will come of it. They are asking for the appointment of a Chief Agent for Scotland, and, if the West of Scotland agrees, we will make the appointment and then we shall get our finger in the pie, and can I hope teach them something.

Look at the enclosed figures taken from the Executive Committee's report of the Tariff Reform League and dealing with its literature. They are a rather remarkable record I think.

### Literature Dept. Report for December

During December 356,050 leaflets and cartoons were issued as compared with 188,000 in December 1907 and 93,000 in December 1906.

The following is a comparative statement of leaflets, pamphlets and other publications of the League, and stereo-blocks issued during the past three years:

| Leaflets, pamphlets and posters | 1906 | 1907 | 1908 |
|---|---|---|---|
| Leaflets, pamphlets and posters | 1,603,000 | 3,225,000 | 6,034,900 |
| Monthly notes | 60,000 | 62,000 | 120,500 |
| Editor's News Sheets | 17,000 | 17,600 | 23,400 |
| Notes for Speakers | Nil | Nil | 38,500 |
| Stereo-Blocks | — | 3,880 | 7,201 |
| Tariff Reformer's Pocket Book | — | — | 6,500 |

Or again look at these receipts for literature *sold*.

### Jan. and Feb. (2 months only)

| Receipts for literature other than | 1907 | 1908 | 1909 |
|---|---|---|---|
| Monthly Notes | £40 14 0 | £151 16 7 | £478 6 1 |
| For Monthly Notes | £34 13 9 | £52 17 11 | £106 3 5 |

Altogether a very satisfactory growth.

I forgot to say in talking of our Scottish deputation this morning that Cox told us that we had never won S. Edinburgh till after the month of May. In the last election in which a Unionist was successful there were 3000 untraced removals; on this occasion there were less than 300. The May term makes all the difference to us. He would have won last June or next June. This floating residuum is what beats us.

FOLKESTONE,
13*th March* 1909.

Poor Arnold-Forster![1] I feel his death more than I could have believed possible. What a fine character he was! He had defects which all could see, but what indomitable courage he has shown in these last years! What patience in pain and suffering! He was no administrator and had no executive capacity, but what industry, what stores of knowledge and what vast energy! And curiously enough though the "I—I" was so prominent in all his conversation, how little he thought of himself or cared for his own position in comparison with the causes for which he fought! His conversation was egotistical often both in form and matter, but at bottom the man was not, or, to put it otherwise, he was egotistical yet thoroughly unselfish. His great failing was his inability ever to see another man's case or get into another man's mind. He was so full of his own ideas that he scarcely listened to what others had to say or, if he listened, failed to understand it. There was no elasticity about his ideas and his way of putting them; and where he might have had his way in all essentials, he often got nothing or gave up too much because he could not see and adapt himself to the small changes that were necessary to commend those ideas to others.

Balfour made a capital speech to the T.R. League Executive. You will be pleased with it. Note particularly his blame of the Free Fooders for forgetting the whole cause in their hostility to a part. I quite expected him to keep his rebukes for too eager Tariff Reformers or Confederates, and I know a month ago he was thinking of begging us not to go too fast and not to drum anyone out of the party. But I think Salisbury's letter about Abel Smith put the last touch to his irritation with the Cecils, and thank goodness he gave them a wipe.

[1] Right Hon. H. O. Arnold-Forster, Secretary of State for War, 1903-5.

FOLKESTONE,
*13th March* 1909.

I sent off my letter in such a hurry that I had not time to explain why Father's letter was not quoted with verbal accuracy at the T.R. luncheon. Goulding, as you know, copied the passage and sent the copy to Ridley; Ridley sent it to me and I sent it to you. You sent it back to me, and, the thing being settled and the omission of the sentence approved, I filed it away with other papers. But Goulding, it appeared, had relied on Ridley to produce it and had left the original at home, so that when we met at the Club none of us had a copy and we had to put it together from memory! Well, yes. It was rather bad management; but I hope no harm was done. We followed the wording of the original closely and the spirit exactly.

Well, the Government have made a compromise on the Navy question which will satisfy no one, I expect. "*Qui est ce qu'on trompe ici?*" Is it four ships or eight? One thing is clear, I think. They don't mean to pay the bill. D—— them! I feel more strongly about this than about anything they have done—except Birrell's miserable administration of Ireland. They are both so wicked and so unnecessary.

9 EGERTON PLACE, S.W.,
*15th March* 1909.

I dined at Grillions, a small but pleasant party—Asquith and Selby my neighbours; Crewe, Wenlock and Haldane my *vis-à-vis* and Sandown and Birrell to complete our numbers. Somebody mentioned that —— made a record at the Athenæum today, scoring 140 blackballs out of about 180 voting. But this was capped by Crewe telling of a man who at Brooks's got 42 blackballs when only 41 members voted. A waiter subsequently confessed that he had surreptitiously slipped in a blackball lest by any oversight the candidate should get in, "for he was very undesirable, sir."

*16th March* 1909.

What a world it is! I am very busy, yet I accomplish nothing. But it is certain I shall be busier still tomorrow, so I must write a note tonight.

Why shall I be busy tomorrow? Well, because at 11.0 I must attend our Tariff Committee to consider meat duties. Would you tax live meat or dead meat the heaviest? There are seven pages of the summary of evidence, given before the Agricultural Committee of the Tariff Committee, in favour of heavier duties on dead meat and five pages in favour of a higher duty on live meat, with 40 non-summarised witnesses for the former and 70 for the latter. And after carefully reading the whole, I know a good deal more than I did before, but I *don't know* the answer to the original question, which, without any knowledge, I would have answered with a fair degree of confidence. "Where ignorance is bliss" 'tis folly to read the evidence! Well, we shall see!

So at eleven the meat duties. At 1 o'clock, if possible, lunch. At 1.45 Bank Committee; at 2.15 Bank Board. Then House of Commons and, if needed, I will *debate* the Navy Estimates at seven, *i.e.* if Pretyman (who has "got the hump" because Lee is *not* superseded) thinks it *infra dig.* to follow Lee. When I can, I will dine (at the House) and at 8.15 I will be in my place to hear Stanley Baldwin on "The Flight of Capital" and to say a few words, if I can get them in edgewise in a debate which only begins at 8.15 and must end at eleven, and in which a mover and seconder of the motion and a mover and seconder of an amendment must be heard before anyone else can speak. And after that I will go to bed and to sleep as fast as I can get there . . .

I went to the House. It was one of the most deeply interesting and curious scenes I have witnessed for a long time.

McKenna spoke. Then Balfour rose, and at once seized the attention of the House by his evident earnestness and by the gravity of the situation he disclosed. You must read the debate. McKenna was defending himself against the Little Navy men. In a moment the boot was on the other leg. It was no longer a question—Are you doing too much? Everyone was saying—Have you done enough? B. sat down and Asquith rose. The tea hour came and went and not a man stirred. No boisterous cheering; no party recriminations; a deep low murmur of assent from us and some-times from the Liberal benches, to Balfour; cheers greeting "the prave worts" with which Asquith began; silence, or earnest conversations aside, as he proceeded to examine how far his programme fulfilled his promises.

Then he sat down at 6.15. A question from Balfour, a question from me and—no one rose! No one was prepared for the gravity of the issue raised, for the turn the debate had taken—all the more striking because of Balfour's studious avoidance of any party recriminations and narrow restriction of the immediate issue. Someone else put a question. And again silence! Then Lupton rose and the whole of the House trooped into the Lobby to discuss the tremendous issues at stake.

We resume our attack tomorrow. Meanwhile I think the Little Navy men are bowled out. Lobby gossip has it that they don't know what to do. Their amendment will probably not be moved. No one believes in their "too much." We only wish we could believe in the Government's "Enough!"

*18th March* 1909.

Why am I writing now when I said I should have no time? Why, to rest my mind! I am tired. I have to make a speech for Stepney tomorrow evening. I haven't got an idea in my head! I haven't had a moment to think and I don't feel as if I *could* think at this moment! Such a cheerful situation! But the great thing is not to worry and not to get a headache, so let us smoke the evening pipe I have just lit and have a little chat.

If you ask my opinion, the Government are in a very awkward situation about their Navy Estimates. They have produced widespread alarm by their speeches and the whole country is excited and anxious about the situation revealed by Tuesday's debate. The fact is that the Government altogether miscalculated the forces at work. They thought that they had got to justify their estimates against a Radical attack on the size of their programme and they prepared their speeches from this point of view. But they were quite wrong. All they said in their defence against the Little Navy men only served to strengthen the real attack—the charge that they are not doing enough. And today there was obvious on their side very considerable discomfort and uneasiness about their position and in the Prime Minister himself a restlessness and irritation which are perhaps the best possible evidence of his consciousness of the weakness of his case. They can find but little comfort in the Press. But I wish to heaven they would do the right thing even now. But they won't unless the Admirals force them, and the Admirals are a broken reed.

I made my speech as desired by A. J. B.—not very good but not very bad either—good rather than bad, I think.

With Wednesday night's debate I was well satisfied. I did not much like the motion and would not have chosen that subject myself, but we came well out of it and had the honours of the discussion. Stanley Baldwin spoke very well. I think he should develop into a Front Bench man. Mason was thoughtful and knowledgeable, but not effective. I don't quite know why it is, but the same may be said of all his speeches. My own performance, which, owing to the course of the debate and the very short time available to me, was a purely debating one, was satisfactory, and once again I felt how the subject had moved forward in the last twelve months and how profoundly all the situation had changed.

FOLKESTONE,
*21st March* 1909.

. . . Next Mr. Collings. I wrote to you about his accident as soon as I heard of it and I telegraphed (on Wednesday, I think) just when I supposed the news would be reaching you. What has happened to letters and telegrams these last few days one can only guess by our experience at this end. Your telegram of the 17th was only delivered to me yesterday, the 20th. I at once telegraphed again the latest news, but I do not know if you will receive it before you get letters and papers of the same date. The French strikes seem to be spreading rather than contracting. It is like living in days before the penny post or the electric telegraph. One feels terribly cut off from you. The latest bulletin about Collings is that "the processes leading to" mending were going on satis-factorily, but he has had much pain, cannot move an inch, is weary of lying in bed and needs absolute quiet—I expect for the head as much almost as for the body. It is a sad troublesome business; but I gather that the pain is rather a good sign than the reverse as it means that the muscles are pulling the pieces together.

We talk of nothing here but the Navy. I did not go to the House on Friday, but I had a note in the evening from Jack Sandars to say that the "Chief found, when he arrived at the House this afternoon, that there was every prospect of a difficult situation arising on Monday, if he postponed the notice of a Vote of Censure on the Government's naval policy till that day" and he had therefore given his notice at once but wished me to "understand that but for this urgency, he would have acquainted you and his colleagues before Monday when he had intended to give this notice." I have not yet got the key of this enigma. I have no doubt that Balfour has acted wisely, but it is a pity that his hand was forced and that the situation could not have been allowed to develop for another two or three days on entirely non-party lines. I fear that a Vote of Censure will rally to the Government the little band of really dissatisfied Liberals who were preparing to speak out.

I think I wrote to you of my speeches on Wednesday evening and Thursday. I was very tired on Thursday night and on the verge of a headache, could do no work and slept badly. Friday morning slipped away in answering letters first and then in a visit to the Bank, where, as I had so much else to do, I was of course detained an unusually long time. I only got back home at lunch time and retired to my room at 2.30 to think what I would say at Limehouse at 8—with not a note made and not a clear idea in my head. "You will have a meeting of over 4000 people," Leverton had said, "and all East-Enders from the Tower Hamlets. We could have disposed of four or five times the number of tickets. Ordinarily they are not very keen about meetings in the East End, and when one proposes to take a hall like this (the Edinburgh Castle where Father spoke with Pearson in the Chair) they tell you it won't do and that no *ordinary cabinet minister* will fill it, but this time there has been extraordinary interest about it. I have been bombarded with a demand for tickets that I can't supply. They are so keen to hear you."

All very flattering no doubt, but what was I to do with a tired body and a fagged mind, dinner at 6.30, the meeting at 8, not a note prepared and not an idea forthcoming? Well, I thought for an hour, if you can call it thinking, and then I said to myself— We must have something about the Government and something about the Navy, a few words about Asquith's Free Trade speech and a good deal about employment.

And then I went to sleep for two hours! I woke in time for a cup of tea. Then I singled out the notes of an old speech—not for use—but to flourish in my hand at the beginning and so give the meeting the idea that I knew what I was going to say and keep their confidence that it was all right and plain sailing before me.

What the result was you will have seen from the *Morning Post*, which was practically a verbatim report. You will have recognised old ideas and phrases worked up again, but they came out freshly, the audience was a very good one and enthusiastic and (I may say it to you) the delivery was easy and good. We were all very pleased with ourselves and thought we had done a good evening's work. Leverton said, "It was more like your father than like you," so you can imagine that I was gratified.

Altogether a satisfactory week for me, for I made three speeches three days running on different subjects and one may almost say unprepared. My speeches in the House this Session have been easier and I have felt more at home there than ever before in this Parliament.

As we drove to Limehouse, we passed through Queen Victoria Street. "Do you know the name of that church?" asked Leverton. "It used to be 'St. Andrew in the Wardrobe,' but they amalgamated two parishes, and it is now 'St. Andrew in the Wardrobe with St. Anne.'" Rather humorous, but is it quite proper?

Leverton showed me at dinner the first volume of his Grangerised *Fanny Burney*. It is really magnificent, and the insetting of the prints has been beautifully done by Rivière. You know he has been collecting them for years and the whole will make thirty large folio volumes. He has a print of almost every place and every person mentioned. Where no prints of people named in the *Diary* were in existence but portraits were known to be in their descendants' hands, he has asked and obtained permission to have them photographed, so that this copy of his will be quite unique in its completeness. He met with but one refusal and that from Rosebery of all people, who replied rather shortly that he could not allow it and that he had only been able to trace a passing mention of the name which was not of sufficient interest to justify the request. But there Lev. caught him fairly: "Your lordship has probably referred only to the second edition of Fanny Burney's *Diary* and has not noticed the passages in the earlier edition which I have the honour to transcribe: 'They then joined in drawing a most odious character of him (Neil, second Lord Primrose), especially for avarice. After which Mr. Bruce (Abyssinian Bruce) said "and yet this man is my rival" (*i.e.* for the hand of Lady Anne Lindsay). "Really," cried I, "I am sure I wonder that he should venture—I mean on account of his figure!" and again later: "He is the fattest, ugliest and most disagreeable man in London."'"

I think Lev. had the best of that!

9 EGERTON PLACE, S.W.,<br>
22nd March 1909.

It appears that "from information received," as the police say, A. J. B. had reason to think that Asquith intended himself to reopen the debate today and to say that the Government would definitely pledge themselves to begin preparations for the four conditional or "phantom" Dreadnoughts this year; and, founding himself on a not very clearly or happily worded phrase in B.'s speech of Thursday, to claim his support on this basis. Now B.'s intention was to ask not merely that "*may* be laid down" should be changed to "*shall* be laid down" but to "shall be laid down *at the earliest possible moment!*" to which end, indeed, all his argument pointed. But he felt that if A. got in first with his modified proposal (to which, I doubt not, the Sea Lords consider him already pledged) he (*i.e.* Balfour) would appear to be acting with a very bad grace if he did not accept it and if it could be alleged (as A. and the Radicals would allege) that he was raising his terms. So he put his amendment in there and then.

Just afterwards Lyttelton turned up at the House fresh from some matinée to which he had been with Mrs. Asquith and confirmed the information received. "Henry was very worried with all this naval business, but he was going to make a great speech on Monday as soon as the debate was renewed, which would put everything right and be a great triumph for him."

Alfred told me today that "another lady" reported to him that

Mrs. A. was very sick at the turn things had taken and said, "It's either Alfred or Austen who have put him (Arthur) up to this. He would never have thought of it!" As a matter of fact it was Arthur Lee who has been the prime mover all through and supplied Arthur Balfour with his facts and figures. Lee has done very well.

Asquith was very fretful and ill-tempered again today. There were signs of a small Liberal revolt in Ridsdale's speech, and acting with him were Villiers, Beck, Lynch, Rees and one or two others.

Two of our men who were at the Speaker's Levée on Friday told me in almost the same words how Asquith, who was in the Trinity House uniform, came up to each of them separately and said, "Don't you think I should do very well for the Captain of one of the 'Phantom Dreadnoughts'?" They had hinted as politely as they could that a phantom ship was as much as he was to be trusted with!

Neville did well at the Annual Meeting, did he not? What a shame it is that the *Post* will not report him decently!

*24th March* 1909.

Well, it's a mad world, my masters, and strange things happen in it. Yesterday Admiral of the Fleet Sir Gerard Noel came to lunch and talk Navy with me. He was Junior Naval Lord when I first joined the Board—not a very good administrator, but a fine officer and the man who settled the Cretan affair for a time by hanging five Turkish soldiers and deporting the rest. Like so many other officers he profoundly distrusts Fisher and is very hostile to the present Board. In order that he might talk freely and without reserve Mrs. Dundas and Mrs. Rider went out to lunch and left us alone. Noel came early and we were just in the thick of it when who should walk in punctually at 1.30 but Parker Smith? He had written the day before saying he wished to see me and asking if I could give him lunch here or see him at the House at 5. I wired back "Sorry engaged lunch. Come to House of Commons at 5" and then, changing my plans yesterday morning, I wired again, "Please come to Egerton Place instead of House" which he assumed to mean come to lunch whereas I meant come at 5.

Well, in he came. I looked, I fear, surprised; Noel looked vexed and halted short in the middle of a sentence. P. S. said, "I am afraid I am interrupting you" and I sent him up to the drawing-room for ten minutes whilst I explained the situation to Noel and rapidly finished our talk and whilst, as I fondly hoped, Allinson was laying another place and Mrs. B. was cooking another egg. But A. had not caught on, and when we got into the dining-room there were only two places and two eggs! I was mortified!

I did not get much out of Noel and do not suppose that I should have done in any case, for he does not express himself very easily nor, I fear, think very clearly. P. S. hadn't much to say, but we laughed over the misunderstanding and I vowed once again that I would never try to save ha'pence when telegraphing.

I think I know now pretty well what happened about the Naval programme. The Sea Lords asked for six Dreadnoughts to be laid down this year and six more next year. This was refused and they were very near resigning. Then someone hit upon the ingenious idea of four this year and four on April 1st next, material for the latter being collected in advance. The Admirals believe that the second four are definitely promised to them—even saying they have the written promise in their pockets though they of course cannot produce it. Winston, Ll. George and Co., on the other hand, consider there is no such definite promise—only a conditional undertaking. And if they are forced to carry it out, they will of course count these four ships into next year's programme as they are to be wholly financed next year, and will make the two years' programme one of eight or at most ten ships, if they can have their way, instead of the Admiralty twelve.

You see how Fisher and his colleagues have been jockeyed and how this explains his conversation with me in Palace Yard when he exclaimed that McKenna now says: "By Jove, we'll have *eight*." It is the very trap against which I warned him when I told him not to think that the financial situation would be easier next year and urged him to insist on having *this year* whatever he had asked for as being necessary for this year.

McK. has told him—You will get eight ships instead of six. The rest is only a financial arrangement which does not concern

166

us. What does it matter to you and me when or how the Chancellor pays provided he gives us what we ask in ships?

And so Lloyd George's Budget was to be eased, the Little Navy men were to be told it was a programme of only four ships and the Big Navy men were to be assured that it was really eight. And now as a result of all this manœuvring the whole country wants eight and will not be happy with less! Asquith jumps about like a parched pea in a frying-pan and doesn't know which way to face, the Liberal Party is divided and all sections of it dissatisfied and uneasy, and confidence in the Admiralty has received a rude shock. People will watch the Navy estimates narrowly for some time to come.

A sign of the times—Arthur Lee was in a small Berkshire village on Sunday. He asked if people there were at all interested in the discussions and whether they followed them. He was told that the head boys of the village school had gone as a deputation to the schoolmaster two days before to ask him to tell the school about it and exactly how we stand!

And the Colonies! Spirit of Seddon! Bravo New Zealand! How Father must rejoice! And this d——d Government is going to refuse, I bet! I admit that they are in an awkward position for accepting, as the fools have been declaring that they are amply provided; but surely we ought to accept the offer and do more rather than less because it is made to us. I would lay down two extra ships and start a "Dominion Squadron."

But *they* won't. They will tell the Colonies to mind their own coasts! Drat 'em!

I dined with the Arthur Lees last night—a pleasant party and a large company of candidates etc. afterwards. I had to leave early to go on to an evening party at Marlborough House which fell awkwardly as I was specially wanted to parade before the candidates. However, I told Mrs. Lee that I hoped the shortness of my nether-garments would excuse the shortness of my stay and my coronation medal would give *éclat* to her reception!

Alfred, Cawdor and others were there and assured me that I must have made a mistake. They knew of no party at Marlborough House. And I began to think I must have made some silly mistake, and that when I got there, the policeman at the gate would say,

167

"Party, sir. No, sir. Missus's party is next month, sir!" But it was all right. There was a concert and I sat next Mrs. Asquith. She was very fidgety and rather amusing.

"I call this school-room music," she said. "Where did they get these people from? I never heard any of their names before."

A pause and then: "I know! They're from the School of Music." And then confidentially, "I think it so like the Waleses to get their music from the School of Music." And to Derek Keppel, "Where *do* they come from, Derek?" To which he replied, "I don't know, but they are all English. *That's* the point!"

Then to Alfred Rothschild on the other side of me: "Alfred, I think they ought to allow one to smoke on these occasions. Alfred, have you any of your little French bonbons?" and aside to me: "He always carries such delightful little sweetmeats." And Alfred produced a little jewelled gold box and handing it to her quite gravely said, "Soda-mints!" I nearly rolled off my chair.

"I must do something," said Mrs. A., tearing at her programme. "Can you make a dove?" "No," I said, "but I can make a battle-ship, can you?" "I'm going to make a dove," she said. I watched and presently I said, "Why, it's a ship after all. Do make me a Dreadnought." "No, it's a *dove*. There it is for you." "Oh!" I exclaimed, "I asked for a Dreadnought and you have given me a dove!" "Now that's just like your dear Father. Do tell me, how is he? We used to have such delightful chaff."

Supper afterwards and I did not get away till 1 o'clock or go up to bed till 2. I have not been so late since—oh! long years ago before I married.

*24th March* 1909.

So the Government have accepted *not* the offer which New Zealand made but another proposition. N.Z. offers a Dreadnought *at once* for the present emergency, and the Government replies we don't need it now, but in view of future burdens we accept it for later on—not to add strength to the Navy but to relieve our Treasury! Oh, dear! *quelle canaille!*

Do let me know what Father thinks of it all and how he thinks the offer ought to have been treated. I think it ought to have been accepted as an addition to the Government programme, who might well have jumped at this opportunity of getting a changed issue and met the N.Z. offer by making their programme a definite six ships in this year instead of four this year and four (conditionally) on April 1st next.

Alfred "on the whole" was in favour of acceptance. A. J. B. has thought differently. I need not say that he warmly appreciates the spirit shown by the N.Z. offer, but he regards acceptance of it as humiliating for us, as a confession of weakness for which there is no ground and a cowardly shirking of our obligations. "The time will come, no doubt," he argues, "when we cannot alone maintain the whole burden of defence, but it has not come yet. We can still do it; we ought to do it. We conduct the whole foreign relations of the Empire; we make peace or war. As long as this is so, we must pay the piper. We must shoulder the responsibility of naval defence." He would, I gather, have thanked them warmly and declined sympathetically, saying in effect: "It is just like you. It is splendid. If we needed it, we would accept it without hesitation. The time will come when we shall need it and we count on you. But that time has not come yet. This is our obligation. We can meet it, and we should be ashamed to shirk our clear duty and allow you to bear burdens that are rightfully ours as if we were paupers." And he would have us lay down eight Dreadnoughts just as fast as British firms can build them.

He is right about our duty, but I cannot bring myself to think that we should be right to refuse the Colonial offer. Do let me know what Father says.

*26th March* 1909.

Some sunshine but a cold wind blowing bitterly down the streets—so I am told, for I have not put my nose outside, having my Women's Suffrage speech tonight. Lord! how I do dislike the suffragists *en masse*, though there are very charming women among *them*, if not among the screeching sisterhood of suffragettes; and how I hate their whole movement and all it means in politics and social life. The more I think of it, the more my whole soul revolts against it—and I did not need the slight touch of lumbago to which I awoke this morning to stiffen my back against it! However, I think it is passing off—the lumbago, I mean, not the dislike. It has not touched the sciatic nerve so far.

I lunched with Lady Desborough yesterday—a pleasant party; Soveral, Lady Lister Kaye, Lady Ian Hamilton, Lady Cynthia Grahame all asking after you. Ian is taking a holiday in the Balkans and is tremendously impressed by the Bulgarian army. Of course, he is very impressionable, but in this case I believe him to be right. Soveral was very gloomy about peace prospects. How dearly Russia is paying for her Far Eastern adventures and defeats.

Fred Oliver was at the Lees' dinner. I saw him for a moment next day. "I had a very pleasant chat after dinner," he said, "with a nice old gentleman in the corner of the drawing-room and told him all sorts of things he didn't seem to know about the Navy. Later on I discovered that he was Lord Cawdor!" [1]

Just back from the Anti-Suffrage meeting—no trace of lumbago left, whether as the result of aspirin or not I do not know. *Liberavi animum meum*, I hope without offence, but quite clearly. A very good meeting with a sprinkling of noisy suffragettes to emphasise their unfitness for political power. Why do some women suppose that inability to control themselves proves their right and fitness to control others?

FOLKESTONE,
28*th March* 1909.

B. will tell you, I expect, about the Suffrage meeting. Of course they had got too many speakers with the result that no one but Cromer got reported, but the speeches were all pretty good and the speakers walked warily among the pitfalls of a difficult subject.

9 EGERTON PLACE, S.W.,
30*th March* 1909.

That rather egregious person, Cathcart Wason, had prepared an address to Sir J. Ward as follows:
"Members of the House of Commons cordially appreciate magnificent offer of New Zealand Commonwealth."

[1] Cawdor had been First Lord of the Admiralty in Balfour's Government.

and M.P.s of all parties being asked, are naturally signing it, beginning with the Government and Front Opposition Benches. He asked very nicely (I am bound to say) for Father's signature. Will Father authorise me to sign for him? I hope he will. I demurred at first to troubling him as he was abroad and the absence of his signature would be quite understood. But Wason pressed his request and I felt obliged to say I would refer for instructions. Please telegraph "Yes" or "No." I shall understand either word as the answer to this enquiry.

The P.M. and A. J. B. have signed.

*30th March* 1909.

I was delighted to get from your letter Father's views on the Vote of Censure. I told A. J. B., who really was pleased to have this confirmation and approval of his action, for though he has never doubted that it was right, he has, I think, been a good deal troubled with criticism and advice from superior people.

You will see the course of the debate from the papers. Grey's speech has not, I think, reassured anyone. It gave the impression that he did not at all like his task and was speaking against the grain. The signs of Cabinet struggles were evident in it and though it impressed the House, as his speeches always do, it did not reassure them. Asquith only returned to the House ten minutes before he rose, spoke for a short twenty minutes and added nothing to the Government case. Balfour did well and our case stood unshaken at the end of the debate. On any showing and even assuming all their figures and anticipations to be correct, the Government are doing too little. But I think that the feeling in the country is so strong and will be so reinforced by these discussions, that they will have to do more rather than less than they intended.

Ida's letter to B. answered my enquiry about Father's attitude to the New Zealand offer. I enclose a cutting from the *Standard* which will show you Ward's reply. Of course he has very strong Radical sympathies and desires to help the Government all he can. He would certainly have been justified in withdrawing his offer, but on the whole I am glad that he did not. But I fear that our Government have effectually destroyed all chance of further offers from the other Dominions, who will now confine themselves to coast defence.

A. J. B. speaks at a great mass-meeting today at the Agricultural Hall. I suggested to him last night the scheme of a passage in his speech about the New Zealand offer and of a natural transition to Tariff Reform—both of which he said were "good—yes, I like that—that's very good. I shall say that." Will he?

Ivy and I go to Lord St. Oswald's at Nostell on Thursday for my speech at Leeds to the annual meeting of the T.R. League on Friday. We shall return here on Saturday. The *Morning Post* wrote the other day that the Press Association only offered a quarter column report, but that if I were going to make a very important declaration they would send a special reporter. But I was not prepared to say that I *would* make a very important declaration. No, thank you!

Croydon was good, was it not? Acland-Hood was apologetic that it was not better, but my modest demands are satisfied! I have given Boraston standing instructions to wire *all* results to you as soon as known, while you are abroad.

*31st March* 1909.

I am very glad to have Father's views about the New Zealand offer so fully stated. I think A. J. B. dealt with it properly yesterday at the Agricultural Hall. He took pretty much the line I suggested and also used my "transition" to Tariff Reform.

In case you did not notice Lord Farquhar's opening remarks, I attach them. These straws show how the wind is blowing. He has been one of our difficulties in Marylebone.

*1st April* 1909.

What a week Balfour has had. Monday, the Vote of Censure; Tuesday, mass-meeting of 10,000 at the Agricultural Hall; Wednesday, Navy meeting at the Guildhall; and today, Thursday, the India Council's Bill in the H. of C. It makes one ashamed of one's own complaints of hard work. He is in good form and great spirits but very seriously disturbed about the Navy and about German intentions.

We got back from Leeds, or rather from Nostell Priory, about 4.30 yesterday.

The T.R. demonstrations in the West Riding—four mass-meetings and a conference in two days—were a great success and have made some stir up there. I send you the best report of my speech—not a very good one—the report I meant, but it is equally true of the speech. Somehow I was tired and there was no elasticity either in my mind or my voice. Ivy said she noticed it in my voice the moment I began to speak, but that I "warmed up" later on. I got some fun out of a silly poster—"Five questions for Mr. Austen C."—with which the Free Trade Union had placarded Leeds and the meeting was a crowded and good one. The *Morning Post* description hardly does it justice.

You will see from the two Westminster articles that the "Sea-green" is very angry—a good sign. When they are angry, they are uncomfortable!

What a treasure-house Nostell is! Do you remember the magnificent Holbein picture of Sir Thomas More and his family, and the portrait of Rembrandt? And then the Chippendale furniture! How it makes one's mouth water to see it and to read the prices paid to Chippendale for it, for St. Oswald showed me C.'s account—£1500 in all for what would be worth as many thousands now. He appears to have been a regular Selwood to the Winn of the day and such items as the following occur side by side:

| | | | |
|---|---|---|---|
| To a very large writing table for the library in very fine wood, carved, etc. . . . | £73 | 10 | 0 |
| To repairing chair . . . . | 0 | 1 | 6 |
| To taking down your own bed, etc. . . | 1 | 0 | 0 |
| To feather bed for servant, cleaning, etc., and so forth . . . . . . | 0 | 5 | 0 |

Amongst various curiosities collected by the St. O.'s great-grandfather are a lot of relics of Captain Cook. They have no connection with Nostell and he means to give them to a museum.

Miss Winn is very anxious that they should be offered to New Zealand. He hesitates between that and the British Museum.

"They will only be lost there in the vast collection, and New Zealand has done so splendidly," urges Miss Winn.

"Well, will you ask your Father what he thinks ?" they both said, and I promised that I would.

Miss Winn would so much like to see you again, so I encouraged her to call on you in London. She is a very keen politician but *not* a suffragist !

You stayed at Nostell for a Wakefield meeting.

*5th April* 1909.

I am so glad that you all thought as highly of Balfour's speeches on the Navy as I did. They have certainly raised his position in the eyes of the country. I am told by an eye-witness that at the Agricultural Hall he really impressed and captured a London mass-meeting for the first time. I shall convey to him Father's warm appreciation of these speeches for it will give him pleasure. I have also sent a note to Mrs. Arthur Lee to tell her Father's views of Lee's speech. They will both be made happy by them, for there is no one whose praise they would more highly value.

Yes, the action or inaction of the Government is really abominable. They have evidently been thinking only of how to placate their little-Englanders, and apart from the wickedness of this course at such a crisis, it was so silly ! Those little-Englanders don't count at such a moment and the Government have got themselves as well as their country into a great hole. I see that Lucy announced in yesterday's *Observer* that the Government will lay down the four conditional ships this year. I don't suppose that he has any special information, but I think he is right, for I believe that the Government will be forced into action which the Admiralty and Grey evidently think necessary though Winston and Lloyd George may not.

You see I was wise to refuse to make any forecast as to the amount of the deficit and that all the prophets were wrong. The latest rumours that I hear are that the Government have given up the idea of taxing Land Values, having come to the conclusion after prolonged enquiry that they would only get a million to a million and a half out of it and that the game is not worth the candle. It is also believed that they have decided for the same reasons against a graduated income tax and are now contemplating a raid on the Sinking Fund for six or seven millions, twopence on the income tax on all incomes, which would yield some five and a half millions, and two millions or so from licences. This would be very humdrum after their loud professions about the new resources at their disposal and would not make them popular with anyone. But it would be much less pernicious than most of the plans that have been suggested for them. But it is wrong to raise the income tax and lower the Sinking Fund together for that cuts a slice off our war reserve at each end.

Of course you knew that we had no chance of doing anything in Denbighshire. Neither shall we do any good in East Edinburgh which McCrae vacates by accepting office in the Scottish Local Government Board.

By the way, I have good reason for thinking that the Government or at least the Defence Committee are seriously concerned about the amount of systematic German espionage which is going on in this country. I would not give sixpence for the prospects of peace the moment we are not in a position which makes attack on us hopeless. I do not suppose that Germany would declare war then and there, but I do think that her diplomacy would at once become intolerably *exigeante* and we should be thrust into positions of humiliation which might leave *us* no alternative. That after all is the game which Germany has constantly played—with France, with Russia and in minor ways with ourselves. It is cruel to think that with such a foe our Government should take *any* risks and it is wicked to build on "declarations" which do not affect to have any binding force, and, after what we know of Bismarck and German diplomatic methods in his time and since, would be worth nothing as a security even if given in a "binding" form.

I spent a busy day on Sunday tidying up, destroying accumulated papers and studying the Convention of London and the Laws of Maritime Warfare for a possible speech on Wednesday as A. J. B. has asked me to take charge of the discussion to be raised by Leverton on the Holiday Adjournment (see Political Notes in *The Times* of Friday and Saturday).

*The Budget*

9 EGERTON PLACE, S.W.,
*April* 1909.

Here we are at home again. Our good luck continued to the last. We crossed last night over a sea as smooth as one of Holland's own canals and did not know when we left the Scheldt or got into the—what *do* you get into at Harwich? I think it must be the estuary of the Orwell, but I fancy it bears some other name.

Things are much more forward here than in Holland. The primroses in the woods we passed near Harwich this morning were lovely. We longed to get out and pick them.

*27th April* 1909.

What strange doings these are at Constantinople! I did think that that sly old fox, Abdul Hamid, had got the best of it again when the counter-revolution took place; but he is evidently at the mercy of events, and it looks just now as if the prophecy which Percy made to me—that it would all end in a military despotism— might be fulfilled. Did you notice in today's *Times* a telegram from Vienna that the Sultan's fate was not yet settled but that "meanwhile he would pay the Macedonian troops from his own privy purse"! What irony!

*30th April* 1909.

What a Budget it is! All the rumours were wrong and there is the super-tax and the land-values tax and the unearned increment tax, besides countless other changes and increases. We set to work this afternoon to organise some forty or fifty of our M.P.s into four committees to study and deal each with a section of the proposals, and I hope we shall make a good fight all along the line. It is

176

certainly a "great" budget and affords infinite matter for discussion and amendment, if we are allowed time. It will touch up a great number of people and make the Government many enemies, but I should think will be popular with their party gatherings and afford many good texts for their tub-thumpers. But I do not profess to have got its cumulative effect or even its separate provisions clearly in my mind as yet, for it is enormously complicated and was not well explained by Lloyd George. He was fagged before he began. Halfway through he was dead beat and had to ask for a half-hour adjournment. He recovered somewhat after this, but much of the speech was read and badly read. He stumbled over the sentences, rushed past full stops, paused at the commas and altogether gave the impression that at these points he did not himself understand what he was saying. The speech lasted from three to eight including the half-hour interval. The best part of it was the exposition of the large programme with which he began— a regular electoral manifesto, having little or no connection with the Budget.

"Did you notice," said A. J. B., "how I, I, I, recurred in that portion? I can't help thinking that he meant it as a bid for position against Asquith."

Alec Hood told me afterwards that he had been watching the faces of Lloyd George's supporters and colleagues while he spoke. He thought them very unsympathetic and contrasted them, and Asquith's in particular, with the sympathetic and eager faces that surrounded me in my first and most difficult Budget.

You may imagine that I did not envy myself my task of following Lloyd George at 8 o'clock. Of course I only skimmed the surface of his proposals, but even that was difficult enough. However, I was told by the colleagues who were brave enough to stay it out that my speech did very well and Alfred said to me later,

"You know, I suppose, that Arthur was very pleased with it."

I think they were all glad that it was my job and not theirs! [1]

---

[1] At this time it was still the regular custom that immediately after the Chancellor of the Exchequer had finished his statement, the ex-Chancellor should make a speech of substance in which he would give a first sketch of the criticisms of the Opposition. This practice was, I think, first abandoned by Asquith at a later date, with excellent results for all parties.

May 1st and the middle of winter! The newspapers report snow in Yorkshire, snow in B'ham, snow in Gloucestershire and snow I don't know where else. Here in the last two days it has hailed and sleeted and rained. The sun still shines a good deal, but there is no warmth in it and a cold wind blows hard from the north.

I went to the Academy Banquet last night and . . . Schuster came up to me to say that after this Budget he was with me on everything but Tariff Reform; the D. of Somerset shouted his woes into my ear and everyone I saw talked Budget to me. So reposeful! Asquith came up as I was speaking to Ampthill and exchanged friendly greetings. I had had a fierce brush with him on Budget night, but we were very amiable. He said something of the shortness of the speeches. "If you had come up a moment before," I said, "you would have heard me expressing my appreciation of yours."

"You don't often do that, my dear Austen," he replied.

"No," I rejoined, "not in public. I don't think people like the augurs to wink at one another in public!"

I find from Lobby gossip and the Press that Lloyd George's statement is universally considered a failure *as* a statement—tedious, diffuse and confused. "A pitiful exhibition," Burns called it in speaking to Balcarres. "What do you think of it?" asked Douglas of Nicholson, the second clerk at the Table. "Why, I think he reads even worse than Palgrave!" Father will recall Palgrave's reading of documents which had to be "read at the table" and will appreciate the bitterness of the criticism.

The more I look at the Budget itself, the worse I think it—and the more vulnerable. We ought to be able to make them sweat over it, if you will pardon me that very vulgar expression. But, oh, dear! I shall have to sweat too these next few weeks and you must not expect to hear anything of me from Sunday to Sunday.

CHECKENDEN, Nr. READING,
9th *May* 1909.

You will have seen that we have put up a very good fight so far. We have badgered the Chancellor thoroughly at question-time and had far and away the best of the debate. Lloyd George is sharp enough, as we all know, but it really looks as if he were out of his depth this time. I suppose he will get on his feet again as the debate goes on, but his refusal to answer very simple and direct questions and the irrelevance of his arguments in many cases to his proposals makes one feel that at present he does not know what he is doing. "It seems to me," said Leverton Harris to Haldane in the smoking-room on Budget night, "that he read that speech like a man who does not understand what he is reading." "Of course he doesn't," replied Haldane. "Why, we have been trying for weeks to make him understand clause —— of the Bill and he *can't*!"

Balfour opened the debate for us on Monday with a capital speech. He was followed—need I add that he was not answered?—by Buxton. Winston replied to him that evening, but Winston did not know enough to answer him. On Tuesday, Pretyman took up the game and made an admirable speech, full of knowledge, closely reasoned and well expressed. Chaplin began on Wednesday, dull and rather ineffective, for he never really got on to the real points of attack. Asquith's speech was remarkable for a very handsome tribute to Chaplin, paid with something of Chaplin's own old-world stateliness, and then for some excellent chaff on Chaplin's accusation that the C. of E. had stolen his clothes. How this would read, I cannot say; but it was delivered with more lightness than is usual with Asquith and sent us all into roars of laughter at the time. For the rest, his speech was full of big words and well rounded sentences as usual, but he did not touch the case made on our side. I followed him and have got much kudos by my attack. The Government side trooped out *en masse* as I rose, but our men stayed and gave me a good and enthusiastic audience, and compliments were showered on me afterwards, from Balfour's "You did that awfully well, my dear Austen" and then a moment afterwards, "I hope you *know* how well you did it," to Carson's "It is the best speech I have ever heard you make in the 15 years I have been in the House. I am hoarse with cheering," and so on from other good judges. "You hit the nail on the head every time." "You hammered them right on to the end." "It was more like your father than anything you have ever done."

All very pleasing and satisfactory and leaving me with the gratifying consciousness that I had made a good speech this time, though I hope not unduly elated by my success.

On reading this through, I see I have confused the course of the debate. Winston spoke on the first night. The Attorney-General essayed to answer Pretyman and was quite ineffective and Lloyd George himself was no better on the evening of that day. He is ill and overworked and his speech was languid, conciliatory and weak. Undoubtedly we had the best of the fight. Feeling against the Budget is growing in well-informed circles and the populace are angry about the extra halfpenny on their tobacco. I suppose Lloyd George will carry as much of the Budget as he likes (I suspect that some part of it may have been put in to give away) but we shall knock some holes in it, I think, and it will not leave the Government more popular than it found it.

Thursday afternoon was occupied by us in preliminary meetings of the four committees into which we have divided our stalwarts for the Budget fight and I attended them all. Each committee has its draughtsman expert, and I think we have set about our task in a business-like way. We will speak more confidently of results when our work is done—say about the middle of September!

9 EGERTON PLACE, S.W.,
*4th September* 1909.

You will probably have heard from Bessborough that Bob Cecil has accepted the terms approved by him. I understand that this is still very confidential, as nothing is to be said till both sides have consulted their Associations. I confess I am heartily glad. Bob has done so well in the House that it was very disagreeable to fight him outside it and it is a real advantage to present a united front in the country. He may vote against us on Second Reading, but I think it is clear now that he will not give us trouble. Bowles, I understand, gets the same terms though he does not equally deserve them and Abel Smith promises a little better. Fred Lambton we cannot touch. Corbett and Cross will be fought, and that is the whole of the Cave.

This information I had from Alec Hood who also asked,

"Your father is in favour of a fight, is he not? I thought of writing to him and then I thought I should see you and I would not bother him."

"Of course he is," said I, "strongly in favour of a fight and has been so from the beginning."

"Well," said Alec, "I'll tell you what I hear. All our people are spoiling for a fight and will be disappointed if they don't get it. If there is no fight we can't keep them at boiling point. All my reports say that there have been no defections on account of this Budget but that if we allow them time to bring in a *bribing* Budget next year, my agents won't answer for the result."

I hear very confidentially from another source that Rosebery wants to move the rejection of the Budget in the Lords! He has not yet said anything to Lansdowne about it, but it may be difficult for L. to refuse if he does. I am sorry for it. I don't like going tiger-shooting with him.

*Sunday.*

I see that Garvin has got the Rosebery idea in today's *Observer*. My informant was Sandars, and I expect that he got it from Garvin, and Garvin from Rosebery himself. Sandars's own comment was that he wanted the rejection moved by someone who would put Tariff Reform as the alternative clearly in his speech. So do I.

The Government are now persuaded that the Lords will reject the Bill. Hitherto they have not believed it. They have altered their tactics in the House accordingly, and instead of hurrying they are now dawdling. The object is to tide over till January, so as to get an appeal on the new register. They have not had a good time on the Licensing clauses.

HOUSE OF COMMONS,
*20th September* 1909.

Please let Father and Neville see the following:—I did not submit the draft resolution to Balfour but Councillor Brooks sent it to Alec Hood for his approval.

Hood was afraid that the reference to the House of Lords would be interpreted as Balfour signalling to Lansdowne and the Lords, would be bad for Lansdowne and the Lords and perhaps not good for the Party.

Balfour also took this view though he holds that there is "only one policy for us," and thinks that if the Lords did not reject the Bill, he could not continue to lead the Party.

Balfour's idea of his speech is to say nothing directly of the Lords, but to say that those who think we can go on in the old financial ways are in a fool's paradise, there must be a great departure either towards Socialism or to Tariff Reform. This Budget is Socialism, the alternative is Tariff Reform. The people must choose between them. Is this as claimed the poor man's Budget or is Tariff Reform the real poor man's Budget? and so forth—always contrasting the Budget and Tariff Reform.

I felt I could not insist on the resolution as originally drafted in face of Hood and Balfour and the Conservatives on the Joint Committee and accordingly have agreed to one running somewhat as follows:

"This meeting—recognising that the Budget is intended to

postpone indefinitely the policy of Tariff Reform—expresses its determined adherence to that policy as the necessary means for increasing employment at home and strengthening the Empire at large and condemns the Budget as not merely unjust to individuals but injurious to national trade and policy."

Father will, I know, regret the appeal to the House of Lords, but I think we shall get in exchange a good T.R. speech and resolution.

I was afraid that A. J. B. would object to the "Lords" if he heard of it. He is very anxious not to appear to dictate.

9 Egerton Place, S.W.,
*25th September* 1909.

I found all our own people delighted with the meeting, delighted with Father's letter and Balfour's speech. Several of them had sat at the wires in London and heard the speeches "as if they were in the Hall." Is it not wonderful to think of? I did not get to bed till 5.30 yesterday and was at the House again at 12.30 to find to my horror and dismay that there had been a landslide and the tobacco clause was through without a division before anyone knew what Caldwell [1] was doing. So I made a row to save our face and to prevent the Radical Press saying that we only protected Dukes. I must say Lloyd George behaved very well and gave us full satisfaction.

*27th September* 1909.

Did I tell you what Finlay says was Balfour's description of Hicks-Beach at a moment when he was irritated by him—"The manners of a pirate and the courage of a governess"?

"I don't know whether I really said it," observed Balfour, "but I think it is rather good!"

*18th October* 1909.

A. J. B. was not at the House today, so I can't give him your message till tomorrow.

I find our people in good spirits, thinking the tide is setting our way again.

[1] Chairman of Ways and Means.

*22nd October* 1909.

Many thanks for your letter. Balfour told me that he thought Father better than he had yet seen him.

I have had a heavy week but have quite got rid of my lumbago. I think we have employed our time in the House pretty well, keeping the Government on the points which they least like to discuss and thoroughly alarming their agricultural members and some others, with the result that their own men have been speaking against them a great deal.

The week has been full of gossip and doubt as to what course the Government wanted to take and what course we ought to pursue. Should the election be in November or in January?

Gradually our people have come to the conclusion that January is the month for us, partly because the Budget, no longer very hot now, will be quite cold by then; partly because unemployment will have been more felt by then; partly because the new register is said on this particular occasion to be more favourable to us than the old, as we have got on to it large numbers of lodger voters and because the class of voter who usually makes a new register unfavourable to us will on this occasion vote for Tariff Reform and more work; and last but not least because we got pretty clear indications that the Government wanted to have the election in November.

Our fellows are in excellent spirits and those who have been speaking about the country say that there has been a wonderful change and that every day gained is in our favour. The Budget is losing its glamour and Tariff Reform is reconquering its position. George Wyndham for instance writes that we are "as in January, only better." And M.'s lies about Old Age Pensions point the same way. He evidently feels that Land Values alone won't win England!

I hear that Runciman's father, who presided at Lloyd George's Newcastle meeting, was awfully sick at Lloyd George's speech, and it is said to have done harm to the Radical cause up there.

So Jebb and the *Morning Post* are to have their way in Marylebone. I wonder what will come of it. In any case and whatever happens I was very glad to see Father's letter to Freeth.

MOUNT EDGCUMBE,
PLYMOUTH,
*4th December* 1909.

You will no doubt have seen by the papers that we have had a tremendous meeting here last night [1]—eight or nine thousand people—and that all went off splendidly. But you will probably see no report of my observations so I enclose the *Western Morning News*. Both conference and evening meeting were excellent and very large.

Lady Lansdowne said to Ivy, "I am very hopeful now. I was not before. And they did want to hear about Tariff Reform!"

So strange that they should! They quite approved the action of the House of Lords, but were not deeply stirred by it. Rather they took it as a matter of course.

[1] Lord Lansdowne and I were the principal speakers.

1910

1910

*A Year of Crisis*

1910 was one of the stormiest years of my political life. The dissolution necessitated by the rejection of the Budget took place in January and resulted in a gain of one hundred seats to the Unionist Party. In 1906 they numbered only 158 members, including the Speaker. They had won some seats at by-elections, and with the additional hundred gained in January they now numbered 273, only one less than the Liberals who were dependent for a majority on the support of the Labour Party and the Irish Nationalists.

The long-drawn-out struggle over the Budget of 1909 at last came to an end on 8th March, on which day it received the royal assent. Even in the new Parliament its passage was far from smooth. The Irish Nationalists disliked the raising of the Spirit Duties and Labour disliked the addition to indirect taxation. More serious still, the Nationalists, with much Radical support, at first refused to pass the Budget until the proposals of the Government for dealing with the Veto of the House of Lords had been approved, and they sought to exact a promise from the Government that a pledge should be at once obtained from the King that if the House of Lords refused to pass these resolutions or the Bill to be founded on them, sufficient peers should be created to secure a Government majority in the House of Lords. For several weeks the result of this internal struggle was in doubt. Finally agreement was reached between the contending factions and the Finance Bill passed as I have said.

The resolutions on which the Parliament Bill was subsequently founded were then taken into consideration, and the agitation against the House of Lords continued more furiously than ever. It was not a good issue for the Unionist Party, and we sought to press against it a constructive programme of Tariff and Social Reform. This was at first all the easier as we were now a united party, the members of the small Free Food group in the last House having lost their seats at the General Election, so that our Chief

Whip was able to boast that he had 273 members, including the Speaker, and that he could count on 272 of them; but the main subject of public interest continued to be the powers and privileges of the House of Lords.

The struggle was suddenly interrupted by the death of the King. The House had just risen for a short recess, and my wife and I had joined my father at Cannes. We had scarcely arrived when news reached us of the demise of the Crown, and we returned at once to London, but too late for me to be present at the Proclamation Council. Parliament was immediately summoned as required by Statute. The Easter holiday was abandoned and a recess promised for a little later in the year. When this came my wife and I took a motor trip to the Chateaux on the Loire with our friend, Leverton Harris.

There was a general feeling that the new King ought not to be confronted immediately on his accession with a political crisis in which the Crown might have to take a more momentous decision than any recorded since the struggle over the Reform Bill of 1832, and that an effort ought to be made by the political parties to reach agreement on the Constitutional issue. As a result, Asquith proposed to Balfour that four of the leaders of either side should meet in Conference and try to find a settlement. The proposal was accepted, and Asquith named as the Government representatives Lord Crewe, Mr. Lloyd George, the late Augustine Birrell, and himself; Balfour invited Lord Lansdowne, Lord Cawdor and me to join him as representing our party. The Conference met for the first time on 17th June and continued sitting, with some interruption in the Parliamentary recess and with varying fortunes, until 10th November. It held altogether twenty-two meetings, but failed to reach agreement. There were times when we seemed very near agreement on some aspects of the problem, such, for instance, as the treatment of financial measures and general legislation, but the shadow of the Home Rule controversy hung over us all. The Unionists contended that organic measures, that is measures affecting the Crown and the Constitution, must be subject to special safeguards, ensuring that, if the two Houses disagreed, the nation should be consulted before they became irrevocable. As to the Crown and the Constitutional Act which would result from any agreement we might reach, there was I believe no insuperable difference, but Home Rule barred the way. On this point we could obtain no satisfaction and negotiations were finally broken off. We should have liked a full statement made as to the extent of the agreement which had been reached and the grounds on which we ultimately differed, but the Government were averse from any disclosure and, as it had been agreed at the beginning that nothing of our deliberations should be allowed to appear except by common consent, we were obliged to give way. The only announcement made to the public was therefore a brief statement that the Conference had failed to reach agreement.

I may here note an interesting feature of the Conference. At an early stage of our discussions it was agreed that it might be useful to have some evidence as to the State Constitutions of the United States of America, the working of the Nomination System in the Senate of Canada, the American and Dominion methods of dealing with deadlocks between the two Houses and the working of the Referendum.

Dr. Murray Butler, President of Columbia University, and Mr. Fielding of Canada gave evidence on these points. Sir George Reid of Australia was also invited to give evidence but was prevented from doing so.

Before the final decision was taken, the position was reported by Balfour to his principal Unionist colleagues, referred to in the phrase of the day as "the Shadow Cabinet." I find among my papers some notes of this meeting made by Sir Robert Finlay which he communicated to me a week later for my own use and a note of my own which I then added. These are printed on pages 295-297—together with other letters which elucidate the position.

I was not certain at the time, and have never been sure since, whether Asquith really desired a compromise or was only playing for time. Lloyd George certainly desired to reach agreement if possible, and at one time during the Conference made proposals to Balfour for the formation of a National Government, composed of representatives of the two parties. He had found his recent dependence upon the Irish vote irksome and the bargaining with them which it involved humiliating, but much more was he impressed by the growing menace of German rivalry, the number and magnitude of the issues confronting Parliament and the impossibility for either party alone to achieve the best solution of them.

No letters passed between my father and me at this time, for he had returned to London and I was in frequent personal communication with him. Of the discussions in the Conference itself I have notes, the accuracy of which as far as they go was confirmed by Lansdowne, to whom I later submitted them, when he compared them with his own, but of the secret negotiations outside the Conference, which were never even distantly alluded to in the Conference itself, I have no contemporary record. The first approach was made by Mr. Lloyd George to Balfour in terms of such secrecy that Balfour believed it to be known only to Mr. Lloyd George, Mr. Churchill and himself and he did not mention it even to his colleagues in the Conference. The actual memorandum which Lloyd George submitted to him was not shown to any of us at the time, and I only obtained a copy years afterwards from Mr. Lloyd George himself. Outside the Conference, F. E. Smith and Bonar Law were taken into Lloyd George's confidence, and such records as I have are in some correspondence with colleagues, which I have included in this volume.

Mr. Lloyd George has given some account of his proposals in the first volume of his Memoirs,[1] but this account, in a work where the mention of it is merely incidental, is necessarily incomplete, and since the silence which has hitherto shrouded these negotiations has now been broken, I think a fuller disclosure is necessary.

Mr. Lloyd George argued that parties would always disagree on certain vital issues affecting the government of this country, but he contended that at that moment the questions which were of most vital importance to the well-being of the community were all of a character capable of being settled by the action of the two great parties without any sacrifice of principle on the part of either, and he urged with great force and sincerity that the rapid rise of great foreign competitors had put us in a position where no time ought to be lost in repairing the deficiencies of our national system and putting our machinery into better order so as to equip us for a situation with which we had never before been confronted. For the first time in hundreds of years the continent had enjoyed a long period of peace, and foreign nations had used their immunity from internal and external conflicts to develop their industrial and commercial equipment to an extent which menaced our supremacy.

The problems which this new situation raised could not, he held, be dealt with by a single party without its incurring a load of temporary unpopularity within its own ranks which neither side could afford to face if it stood alone, confronted by an opposition resolved to take advantage of every opportunity to oppose and

[1] *War Memoirs,* vol. i. p. 36.

defeat it. He gave as examples of such problems: Housing, the sale of Drink, Insurance, Unemployment, the Poor Law and National Reorganisation, including under this head National Defence, for which he suggested the Swiss militia system as a model, Trade and Tariffs and schemes for uniting the Empire and utilising its resources for Defence as well as for Commerce and Foreign Policy. All of this was very vague and sketchy but much of it was attractive to Unionists. As the conversation developed, however, it appeared that on our side it involved counter-concessions on Home Rule, Education, the Disestablishment of the Welsh Church and other matters, for which the great bulk of our party were wholly unprepared and, so far as Ireland was concerned, would be resented as the betrayal of a cause to which we were committed.

F. E. Smith was strongly in favour of acceptance; Bonar Law was, I think, also favourable, but less vehemently so. Balfour felt it impossible for himself to make the sacrifice demanded. I believe that I was the only Unionist Member of the Conference who would really have wished to pursue the matter further, but in the absence of any other material I cannot speak confidently of my own attitude at the time.

The only members of the late Cabinet outside the Conference whom Balfour consulted on the secret proposal were, I believe, Akers-Douglas and Gerald Balfour. Akers-Douglas, of whom Mr. Lloyd George speaks slightingly, had been Lord Salisbury's Chief Whip and Balfour's Home Secretary. He was a man of shrewd judgment and wide experience. No better opinion as to the attitude of the Party could have been sought.

The idea of Federalism was in the air at the time. F. S. Oliver, the author of the *Life of Alexander Hamilton* and later of *Ordeal by Battle*, my intimate friend since our College days and a publicist of notable originality and distinction, was pressing it in a series of remarkable letters to *The Times* over the signature of "Pacificus," and Mr. Garvin was lending his powerful advocacy to it in the *Observer*. I myself was already turning my thoughts to it and later in 1913-14 I and others tried to revive it, but the passions of both sides were too inflamed, and their opposing standpoints too rigidly defined and fixed, for compromise to be possible to either.

I must add here that I have never regretted my opposition to Gladstonian Home Rule. I did not believe then, nor do I believe

now, that it offered even the slightest chance of affording a permanent solution. It had the fatal defect of creating a Parliament and
a system of government which had no parallel in any part of the
British Empire, and in my considered view, now as then, the Irish
Parliament would for this reason never have rested till it had freed
itself from all the restrictions proposed by Mr. Gladstone and his
successors in the interests of the supremacy of the Parliament of
the United Kingdom.

A Federal system, or system of general devolution of local
affairs to each of the units of the United Kingdom, on the model
of the Canadian Constitution, seemed to me, revolutionary as it
was, less dangerous, just as in later years, when the Dominion system
was fully developed and the position of Ulster safeguarded, I sought
in the Dominion model a cure for the age-long strife between the
two islands.

As I have said, nothing came of these proposals. No agreement
could be reached on them any more than on the problems submitted to the Conference itself. The business of the session was
rapidly concluded and Parliament was dissolved on 28th November.

In the course of the discussions at the Constitutional Conference
the Referendum had been suggested as one alternative method of
settling deadlocks between the two Houses on Bills altering the
Constitution. A section of the Unionist Party was strongly in
favour of the Referendum on its merits. I thought it, on the contrary, injurious to the authority of Parliament, very difficult to work
so as to obtain a judgment on the real issue and capable of great
abuse in times of strong passion and excitement. It was, however,
the only method we could devise for securing an appeal to the
electors which met the condition *sine qua non* of the Liberals that
such deadlocks must be capable of solution within the life-time of a
single Parliament and without recourse to a dissolution. In defer-
ence, therefore, to the wishes of my Unionist colleagues and in the
hope that by the concession agreement might be reached I yielded
my own opinion and consented to accept this device. Had the
Liberals also accepted it, we might have been obliged to extend its
application to a Tariff Reform Budget, at any rate on its first
introduction; but even with this concession, no agreement was
found possible and there was no reason to make further sacrifice.

To my dismay, however, while I was addressing meetings at
Glasgow and Edinburgh, Balfour under great pressure from many
quarters, including some important Tariff Reformers, made a bid

for the Free Trade vote by undertaking, in his opening speech in the campaign at the Albert Hall, that if successful he would submit Tariff Reform to a Referendum.

I was broken-hearted and protested vehemently, but the mischief was done. After the event I examined the effect of this sudden conversion in a memorandum of which I sent copies to Balfour and Lansdowne. It is here published. This surrender disheartened our keenest supporters and failed to conciliate opponents. The result of the elections left the composition of the new House practically unchanged.

The lists were set for the next and bitterest stage of the struggle. The crisis of 1910 was to be followed by the greater crisis of 1911.

## 1910 : JANUARY–MARCH

### *Political Crisis*

I summed up my view of the lesson of the General Election in a letter to Balfour as soon as the results were known :

*Private.*

HIGHBURY,

MY DEAR BALFOUR,                                      *29th January* 1910.

I am very sorry to learn from a letter of Lady Betty's to Beatrice that you are not well. I expect you need a change and rest, but I fear there is little chance of your getting it, for we have stormy times in front of us and shall need your counsel and leadership.

What, I wonder, do you think of it all? Frankly, I am disappointed; but you were less sanguine than I was, so your disappointment should be less. Scotland is very bad; Wales about as good as I hoped, though we have not made the progress in the places in which I expected it; London did not come up to my expectations, nor did Lancashire. The Midlands have done well, though curiously enough we failed to win two of the seats about which, before the contest, we were most sanguine.

The counties generally are very good. In Devonshire we were overwhelmed at the last moment by the weight of oratory on the Government side—three Cabinet Ministers and other lesser lights against whom we could set none but local men. But for this we ought to have won three or four more seats down there. The most curious feature of the whole elections is the singularly complete reversal of by-election results. Seats won at by-elections have always a tendency to swing back, but I have never known them to do so with such unanimity.

I have had a good many letters from candidates both successful and unsuccessful, and from them and from my own experience I draw the following conclusions :

1. Tariff Reform was our trump card. Where we won, we

196

won on and by Tariff Reform. Even where we lost, it was the only subject in our repertoire about which people really cared. In many cases (*e.g.* London) electors said to our canvassers, "Yes, we want Tariff Reform, but we want the Budget (*i.e.* the land taxes) too. We'll have the Budget first, and we'll have Tariff Reform next time."

2. The Food Taxes were, of course, the great difficulty our men met with. On the whole those who faced this difficulty most boldly came off best. But *where the question of food taxation had been shirked or evaded* BEFORE *the contest, it loomed largest* IN *the contest*. It requires time and repetition to beat down the cry of dear food, "black bread and horse-flesh," and to make the people look at the question in the proper light as first and foremost, for working-men, one of employment. But it can be done if once our candidates see that they must do it, if they acquire for themselves and impart to others the necessary information, and deal with this question in frequent speeches, not waiting to be challenged upon it but going to meet their enemy in the gate. The ignorance of their own case shown by many of our candidates was shocking.

3. In London and in Yorkshire (West Riding especially) the Budget was popular and the Lords were not. The electors were interested in Tariff Reform (*e.g.* see Hewins's account of his experience), but they did not vote on it. They voted against the Lords and, above all, against the Landlords.

4. In Scotland the class hatred was very bitter and the animosity against landlords extreme. Nothing else counted very much. Owing to the split in high quarters in Glasgow, such chances as we might have had in that city were ruined. The Free Fooders rallied at the last moment, but they could not undo the mischief they had done.

5. Where a man has become a convinced Tariff Reformer, nothing will shake him. It is a religion and he becomes its ardent missionary. These are our best workers.

All the above is full of hope and encouragement, as far as England is concerned. A little more time, as Hood told me before the election and Balcarres has written to me since, would have made a vast difference in Lancashire. Tariff Reform was making converts daily, but we started it too late in Lancashire owing to the attitude of the leaders in Manchester and there was not time for it to sink in and get sufficient hold of the people. A bolder attitude in the earlier days would have led to much greater success in the elections. The workmen are more advanced than their employers. Scotland presents a more difficult problem, but there also Tariff Reform was held back too long. Our only chance of winning Scotland is to change the issue on which Scotsmen vote. As long as it is the land, the landlords, and the rest of the Radical programme we shall be beaten. We must try to make them think of something else, and that something else can only be Tariff Reform.

But there is one feature of the situation which causes me some anxiety. The combination of the Liberal and Labour Parties is much stronger than the Liberal Party would be if there were no third party in existence. Many men who would in that case have voted with us voted on this occasion as the Labour Party told them, *i.e.* for the Liberals. The Labour Party has "come to stay." It is much stronger than at first appears from the electoral returns, for on this occasion it has chiefly served as a cat's-paw to pull Liberal chestnuts out of the fire. This the Socialists see and are complaining of. It may lead to trouble between the two parties to the coalition in future, but the existence of the third party deprives us of the full benefit of the "swing of the pendulum," introduces a new element into politics and confronts us with a new difficulty. The Irish, of course, everywhere voted against us.

So much for the past, and now as to the future.

I hope you will come up to town in time to allow of careful consideration of our course of action before Parliament meets for business. We ought I think to have more than one "cabinet" to discuss the situation. Meanwhile I give you my own first ideas for what they are worth.

I suppose that if the Budget gets through the House of Commons, it must pass the Lords. I say "if it gets through the Commons," as the Government may come to grief over the whisky tax. Probably, however, they will abandon it to placate the Irish, whose position, if it is insisted upon, will be one of some embarrassment.

To settle the Budget of this year must, I take it, be the first business of the Government though there are some rumours to the contrary. Then comes the question of the powers and constitution of the House of Lords. As to their powers I hope they will stand firm. Nothing can be worse for them or for us than that they should give way and pass a Bill on lines of the Campbell-Bannerman resolution, and one General Election is not sufficient to carry such a grave constitutional revolution. If they must die they had better die fighting. It is not the issue upon which I would choose to take the decision of the country if the choice were ours; but there is nothing to be gained by committing suicide, and to consent to limit their veto to a single session would be suicide pure and simple.

On the other hand, it would be well for them to show their willingness to reform. Could not Lansdowne at once take up the report of Rosebery's Committee? This is one of the questions I should like to discuss with you and him. He might even put forward a proposal for election of a proportion of the House by County Councils.

It is, however, possible that Asquith will at once confront the King with a demand that he shall create, if necessary, sufficient peers to force the Campbell-Bannerman Bill through the House. I do not imagine the King would consent to this without first sending for you and Lansdowne, and I think you ought to advise him to refuse. This would of course mean that you would have to be prepared to take office although in a minority in the House of Commons and to dissolve again the moment you were beaten. In that case, I suggest that you should table one or more Tariff Reform resolutions, take a division on the first and dissolve again at once. It would be a great risk, but I see no other way out, and we ought if need be to risk everything, for if we don't resist we lose everything.

If Asquith does not take this extreme course, which some of his colleagues and many of his followers are sure to press on him, our policy is easier. We must be aggressive all along the line, but above all, like the Anti-Corn Law League in its seventh year, we must transfer the Tariff fight from the country to the House of Commons. As Cobden said, the best platform from which to address the country is the floor of the House of Commons, and we must raise the issue there on every occasion, beginning with an amendment to the Address. This is the only way in which we can educate the people and above all educate our own men. We shall have a united party behind us and we can make a better show both in debate and in the division than we could in the last Parliament. We can riddle Asquith's assertions and we can show up Lloyd George about German conditions both of living and wages. But we must fight out the *whole* question there and be prepared to meet and indeed anticipate every challenge.

I believe the result would be quickly felt in the country. If time is given us we ought also to press our land policy. Your speeches on that subject were a great assistance to our men in country districts and even in many of the towns where the idea of small cultivating ownerships is popular.

There is much more to be said when we meet, but this is enough to show you in what direction my thoughts are tending and more than enough to exhaust your patience.

I am going up to London on Wednesday next when my address will be 9 Egerton Place, S.W.

Yours ever,<br>AUSTEN CHAMBERLAIN.

P.S.—Hood writes to me (27th Jan.):

"My belief is that the decision of the Lords as to payment of members out of Trades Union funds, right though it was, did us infinite harm (in Lancashire and the North). I had a stiff fight, but it will interest you and your father to know that we won purely from the support of the agricultural element, farmers and labourers alike, for Tariff Reform and a strong Navy."

In this district the Lords' decision did not affect us. I don't think we can afford to give away our own men in the Trades Unions.

A. C.

9 EGERTON PLACE, S.W.,<br>20th February 1910.

Balfour was unable to preside at his dinner.[1] He has a cough but it is believed that he will be able to be in the House tomorrow. Heaven send that he may be! It would be disastrous to have him absent.

---

[1] At the opening of the Session.

You will, I suppose, get the King's Speech almost as soon as this letter. It is brief and very much what you will have expected. A reference to foreign affairs and to India, a paragraph on the Prince of Wales's approaching tour in South Africa and on the opening of the Union Parliament. Then the Budget and Supply which must be attended to *at once*—the usual reference to economy but the provision for the Navy is largely increased. Then "*with all convenient speed*" proposals for adjusting the difficulties which long-standing differences between the two Houses have produced. "In the opinion of my advisers" the supremacy of the House of Commons in finance and its predominance in legislation must be secured. There is reference to reform of the House of Lords as well as to restriction of its powers. And so with a very ill-worded paragraph the Speech closes. No other legislation is referred to.

In short, Asquith has his own way. Budget first and Veto after. Asquith has beaten his recalcitrant colleagues and now defies Redmond, Barnes and Co. who, being beaten, will doubtless come to heel.

Robbins tells me he hears from Lloyd George's entourage that Redmond has already been promised that though the Budget must go through without alteration *now*, the whisky tax shall be dropped and the land taxes, as far as they affect Ireland, amended in the new Budget. He thinks that Barnes will get a wigging from the Labour Party tomorrow for speaking in their name without their authority. His manifesto produced a real scare in Liberal circles, but the scare is over. The Labour Party doesn't want another dissolution as yet, but Robbins hears on good authority that the Liberal War Chest is well filled and they are ready. He expects a dissolution in the summer or autumn.

By the way the L.-U. War Chest is also very comfortably lined. Having forgotten on Friday evening to give Father a message from Savile Crossley on the subject, I took on myself to express Father's thanks to Lansdowne last night for his very successful help in raising funds.

I am to move my T.R. amendment on Tuesday if nothing unexpected happens tomorrow. Hood is keen for it and keen to have it at once. "It's like this, Austen," he says, "What I say is, I've got 273 men and I can count on 272 of them, and they just want a fight on it at once." And then we talked of election experience and he summed up his own experience by saying, "We've just got to rub the food duties in—keep on pegging away at them, that's what I say." *Magna est veritas!*

*21st February* 1910.<br>10.30 p.m.

I came home to a rather late dinner and have been hard at work since, but I have just had a telephone message that my amendment cannot be reached till Wednesday, so I have a little breathing time to talk with you. But oh how I wish it were to *talk,* so that I might hear all your views as well as give my own.

Practically, I have heard only Balfour and Asquith. I don't imagine that anything has been said by Redmond or Barnes to change the view I have already formed (which you share) that they and their friends will for one reason or another vote with the Government or at least take care that it is not put in a minority.

If this is so, then here are my first impressions.

This is a very different House from the last—our benches crowded and our men overflowing the gangway. The Labour Party now sit on the Government side and the two front benches below the gangway on our side are occupied by our men and by the Independent Nationalists. But it is a different House in spirit as well as in externals. Our men are keen and full of fight and spirits. The Government side is chastened. There will not be the same brutality as there was in the first session of the last Parliament.

Balfour looked ill but spoke well. I thought his speech very able and quite his own. No one else would have made it in the same way, but it was very effective. Incidentally I think he gave away the O'Brien-Healy game too much and made Redmond's path too easy; but as against the Government position, it was, I thought, very able and original. It was very well heard by the House and very well received by our men.

Asquith also did well. I thought his references to the Crown excellent both in taste and substance. But he was little cheered by his own side. They will follow him because they cannot help it, but Lloyd George is the hero of their fighting forces.

The only surprise of the day was the decision of the Government to proceed by resolution first [1]—very wise but quite unexpected by me, and, I believe, by everyone—at least in the sense explained by Asquith, *i.e.* of resolutions which are to be the real framework of a bill and not mere fulminations against the Lords. Otherwise the situation presents itself much as I expected. I think we have a fair hand, and the chances at the moment are very nearly equal between the Government and ourselves as regards victory at the next election.

*23rd February* 1910.

So I was too hasty in assuming when Redmond rose last night that, as Balfour had put it, he was going to find reasons for voting for the Budget. He is showing more fight than I expected. Will he fight on to the end or is it only bluff when all is said and done? I still suspect the latter and believe that a *modus vivendi* will be discovered by these warring sections of a "triumphant majority"; but it must be admitted that the situation is more critical and more interesting than I had expected. One thing, I think, is clear; that Asquith won't give way in substance and that if Redmond is to be satisfied he will have to be satisfied with a shadow concession—not a reality.

Barnes's speech was very weak and poor from whatever point of view you consider it. Of course he and his friends are going to back the Government whatever the Government do. No one knows even now whether Redmond means business or not. O'Brien took his speech as a surrender today and lashed out fiercely at him, loudly cheered by Healy. They make Redmond's position very uncomfortable but they don't clear up the doubt as to what he will actually do, and negotiations and Cabinets are still proceeding. Balfour tells me that Lloyd George looked very angry yesterday while Redmond was speaking. F. E. Smith made a good speech today—his best for a long time past. His text was— Your quarrel with the Lords culminated in the Budget. You appealed to the people; you are beaten. On its merits the Budget cannot command a majority in the new House. But the Budget

[1] On the relations between the two Houses.

was only the culmination. The quarrel began on Education. Again you are beaten. Not one of your Education Bills commands a majority in this House. The Liberals sat dumb and uncomfortable.

*24th February* 1910.

Father will, I hope, be content with the opening day of the Tariff Reform fight in the new House of Commons. We all feel pretty cheerful about it. We carried the war into the enemy's camp and we showed new power and vigour in our Party. Steel-Maitland and Mackinder both made good speeches and are a real addition to our forces. And there was a general tone of buoyancy and confidence throughout our ranks.

*25th February* 1910.

*Tempora mutantur!*

13*th March* 1906.—The Free Trade resolution was carried in the new House of Commons by 474 to 98.

24*th Feb.* 1910.—The Tariff Reform resolution is beaten in another new House by only 31 votes—285 to 254.

Congratulations to Father!

Balfour made an excellent speech, arguing the corn duty I think for the first time and openly assuming it as the basis of his policy. So we make another great advance and overcome one more difficulty. The rest of his speech on employment was very good and followed with great interest by the House.

Lloyd George replied to me in a clever, unscrupulous and characteristic speech amidst boisterous cheers from his Party and from the Labour men, and Bonar Law wound up the whole debate with an effective and closely reasoned reply, and then came the division—our lobby strangely crowded after the sparse population of last year—and tremendous cheering from our men as the results were announced.

The debate was remarkable for the number and excellence of the maiden speeches—Steel-Maitland, Tryon, Mackinder, Page Croft and George Lloyd,[1] all made their mark. We are enormously strengthened in debating power.

The political situation is very obscure still. The Redmondites are

[1] Now Lord Lloyd of Dolobran.

apparently not prepared to give way and are certainly making it more and more difficult for themselves to do so. Asquith on the other hand is reported to have his back to the wall. He is very sick of the whole business, feels deeply the position in which he is placed and resents his Party's treatment of him. Meanwhile there is, if not a cave, at least great dissatisfaction among the Scottish Radicals and English extremists at the talk of "reforming" the House of Lords, and threats of voting against the Government are widely used. Grey made it a "matter of life and death" that reform of the constitution of the House of Lords should find a place in the King's Speech and would have resigned if it had not done so. This I have as coming to my informant direct from a member of the Cabinet. It is not thought that the Government have even yet settled what their resolutions are to be, and nobody quite sees why they proceed by resolution at all, as time presses and that form of procedure is cumbrous and must involve much waste of time.

Meanwhile Rosebery has given notice of a motion that the Lords shall resolve themselves into a Committee to consider their own reform. Very characteristically he told no one beforehand of his intention, only observing to Lansdowne afterwards, "I didn't tell you because I didn't think you would much like it."

What a delightful man to work with! L. says he knows what R. is at; "The fact is he made a great mess with the Budget speech last year and he is now anxious to wipe out the recollection of that with a great splash on this question."

However L. and Balfour are not sorry to have him move if he adheres to his present plan which is to take the motion for the Committee on the 14th and following days, on which there would be a general discussion, and then in Committee to move first that the possession of an hereditary peerage should not by itself give a right to sit in the Lords. Other resolutions would be tabled later but would not be produced at present. His first motion might therefore come before the Government scheme is introduced and his later resolutions after we know what the Government plans are.

The general feeling in the Lords is in favour of that House taking action early and Rosebery's proposal for a Committee of the whole House will be grateful to them.

I have been discussing plans and possibilities with L. and A. J. B. this afternoon. They are both convinced that considerable change is inevitable. The *Scotsman* has collected replies from all Unionist candidates in Scotland to a series of enquiries about the recent election. They *all* say that the principal cause of our defeat was animosity to the Lords as hereditary legislators, some adding that this feeling was embittered by dislike of them as landlords, and they all say that there is no chance of changing the verdict as long as the issue remains the same.

There was a rumour this afternoon that Asquith surrendered completely to Redmond last night after a prolonged interview, but this we discredit. The rumour went on to say that Asquith would introduce a Veto Bill on Monday, at the same time abandoning all idea of reforming the composition of the House of Lords. But Jack Pease, who is now a Cabinet Minister, like Seely is talking Reform as well as Veto.

On the other hand it is believed that Redmond cannot give way. The feeling against the Budget is steadily rising in Ireland and if it were not for Dillon and Tay Pay he would probably throw the Irish Vote in St. George's in the East against the Government so that Benn would in that case lose his seat. He is battling hard for his life and position with these two colleagues and so far has held his own skilfully. What will come of it all, no one can say. The air is thick with rumours. At present the best opinion is that Asquith will stand firm; that Redmond will not yield; that therefore the Government will be beaten on the Budget; but the Budget will not be reached till after Easter when another Budget is due.

We could not take office at such a time of year in such a financial mess whilst still in a minority. A. J. B. quotes the discredit into which the Tories got after the defeat of Gladstone's Government in 1885 on their Budget when Lord Salisbury took office and his Government were bullied and knocked about before they got to the country whilst the Liberal Party pulled itself together again.

How then is the King's Government to be carried on?

It is thought that the Government would like to be beaten at this moment on some minor issue and then go to the country again on the same issues as before—the Budget and the Veto,

We were in a majority in the House today for a long time during the discussion on hops and it was quite uncertain, even when we divided, who had a majority, so that many of us were kept back in the lobby till it was clear that the Government forces had come up, and only voted when it was clear that we should not put them out.

We might perhaps beat them on Monday by the aid of Irish or Radical malcontents on the question of taking the time of the House; but in spite of your advice that we should get them out at the first moment and on any question, we all feel that this would not do now and that you yourself if here would not advise it at this moment. The situation changes from day to day and from moment to moment. It is extraordinarily difficult and complicated and I quite believe that from your post of observation at Cannes, and with your mind filled with the pictures of things as they were a fortnight or a week ago, you will think us wrong. But all this brings discredit on the Government and discouragement to the Radical Party, and if we do beat them on the Budget that may be the *coup de grâce*. At any rate it would be a tremendous triumph for us and make their attack on the Lords a glaring absurdity. A General Election in June or July would suit us best. August we must strive our hardest to avoid as so many of our supporters are away from home and cannot be brought back.

Don't be surprised if Balfour appears in Cannes before the end of next week. His doctors have been urging him to take a change and rest, and there will apparently be no contentious business in our House before Easter. He is not as well as one would like to see him.

*26th February* 1910.

There is very little more political news. The United Irish League have withdrawn their support from Benn in St. George's in the East. Asquith has seen the King again and there has been another meeting of the Cabinet. So every evening newspaper has its own sensation and purveys its special rumour, but I do not believe that there is as yet any real change in the situation or that there is likely to be one before Easter. Rosebery and A. J. B. are to meet at Belvoir (I think it is) for the week-end, and A. J. B. will see what he can learn of R.'s ideas.

We attended the Court last night. "Well, Winston," said I, "you didn't join in the Tariff Reform Debate."

"No, I should have liked to, but I had my share earlier in the week—and precious hard work it was. There was precious little straw to make bricks with!"

"Yes, and plenty of people to take offence—plenty of people seeking offence indeed."

"Oh, yes," said Winston, "just look at the Irish. You know how ready they are for chaff generally, but you saw how touchy they were on Tuesday. Oh! you won't have to wait long! A few weeks!"

"Oh!" said I. "You'll last longer than that."

"How can we? Why, the Irish send us a fresh ultimatum every day. We're at the fourteenth now! I don't see how we can last beyond April. I thought you might have beaten us on hops today. It would have suited me very well to hop it on hops."

"Yes, I daresay; but it didn't suit us," said I with a laugh.

*27th February* 1910.

From what I have already written, you will know what is my view of the situation at the moment. Briefly, you may summarise it thus: a financial situation of great difficulty and complexity, a parliamentary situation of unstable equilibrium, a Government which might at any moment be upset, an Opposition which is not ready to take office and might be ruined by taking it in such peculiar circumstances, and an electoral situation full of doubt and danger for all parties.

I have not the least doubt that the Government would be glad, mightily glad in fact, to be defeated on a side-issue which left their policy intact—a snap decision, a point of procedure or any-thing of that kind. They would resign at once, shuffle the cards, discard the weak ones and reappear at the elections, united and rehabilitated, with the old issues of down with the Veto of the Lords and down with the landlords and up with the People's Budget. Let the rich pay! The Earth is the Lord's and He has given it to His people. You are His people.

Meanwhile, if we took office, we should have no majority and no one—not even Asquith—could really guarantee to us safe passage of the necessary financial bills. One Budget is nearly twelve months overdue. Another Budget is nearly due and before either can be carried a War Loan Bill, a Treasury Borrowing-powers Bill, Votes A and 1 of the Navy, a vote on account of the Civil Service and of the Army, and a Consolidated Fund Bill must be carried by Easter or the King's Government cannot be carried on. Never have we seen such a financial situation. Never has there been such a congestion of business. There has been nothing comparable to it on previous occasions when both Parties have come to terms to "wind up" necessary business with a view to a dissolution.

What a kettle of fish!

I have ever before me the thought that "he who will not while he may, when he will, he shall have nay." But to defeat the Government on a by-issue and to take office in such a situation would be suicidal. From the moment of the change the fortunes of the Radicals, which are now on the down-grade, would begin to mend, and we should be discredited before we had any real power. It would be April before we could dissolve and late May or June before we could set to work at our offices even if victorious (which under such circumstances I do not think we should be) and a Tariff Reform Budget cannot, in spite of all Hewins may say, be produced at a moment's notice.

It will not do therefore to defeat the Government on a side-issue. We must take the risks of delay—the risk, that is, of their coming together again, finding some *modus vivendi* between the warring sections of the majority and carrying both Budget and Veto Bill through the House of Commons. In that case, the Budget passes, and that question is removed from the electoral campaign. The Veto Bill is rejected by the Lords, but meanwhile they have put forward their own schemes of reform. That question is not removed, but at least the issue is changed and we get a chance in Scotland and the North. The Government retains its majority in the Commons, has no excuse for resignation and no opportunity to drop embarrassing luggage. It is still in office when the new elections come, but discredited by all the hectoring and intrigue of these weeks, by the surrender it will have had to make to secure its majority in the House and by its proved inability to command the various forces which buffet it about and by its general weakness and impotence.

On the whole that seems the best thing that could happen for us.

Well—no; perhaps the best thing is the thing which seems most likely to happen. By our support the Government may carry the absolutely necessary financial and non-controversial measures. This brings us to Easter. Then assume that both Government and Nationalists stand firm. Soon after Easter we defeat the Government with the aid of the Nationalists on the old Budget. Asquith resigns. We have no majority and there is no Budget for 1909-1910 or 1910-1911. What is to happen then?

A. J. B. says he would be *most* reluctant to take office. "What would you do, Austen? How *could* you make a Budget? But if we don't take office what is to happen? I assume that the King will send for me. 'You have defeated my Government,' he will say. 'I think I have some claim to call on you to provide me with another.' Yet I shall be *most* averse to taking office under such circumstances. I remember the lessons of 1885, etc. etc."

So said A. J. B. to L. and me last Friday.

Under the circumstances he saw only two alternatives: "the first you may think so absurd that it is out of the question, viz.: a Government of Permanent Under-Secretaries—which would be on the face of it purely provisional and only for the purpose of 'making' the elections—supported in council and defended in the House by the two Front Benches in combination."

L. and I both shook our heads. "Well then, what other alternative is there but a neutral Government? Rosebery and a Government of affairs to do the necessary business, and then dissolve? I suppose Asquith and I should have to find him colleagues and promise him support."

I said: "I like neither idea. Either Government would get into trouble and we should suffer from their discredit. I don't think the country would stand or understand Government by Under-Secretaries, and as to Rosebery—well, in such a case only one man counts and that man is you; but as far as I am concerned, nothing would induce me to serve under him!"

"Of course not," said A. J. B. "You could not. You and I are too much engaged in the fight, too prominent partisans to take office with him. But one might find others. The difficulty is *Who* ?"

I said again it wasn't possible. Alec Hood and Sandars who had come in nodded approval to me. "There is only one man you could give him," said Hood, "and that's Hugh Cecil!"

"No," I concluded, "I speak off-hand. Circumstances may alter—they change from day to day—and my opinion may change too. But at present I say: Refuse to take office. Tell the King he must send for Asquith again and force him to resume. Asquith knew that it was doubtful whether he had a majority on the Budget. Yet he did not bring the Budget to a vote. Now, in the month of April, not one but two Budgets are due or overdue. No Ministry, fresh to office, without a day for consideration or consultation, can frame a Budget; let alone pass it through a House in which they are in a minority of 120. Asquith got you into this mess. He must pocket his pride and get you out of it. He must drop the obnoxious features of his Budgets, bring in a non-contentious business Budget, pass it with our help and go to the country directly after."

I do not think that the Radical Party could survive such a fiasco and such a humiliation. The "People's Budget" beaten in the People's House, the House of Lords justified, the Government discredited, its Party angry, divided and confused!

"But would Asquith consent to return ?"

"I think he must. You must force him to drink the cup to the dregs. In the circumstances and at that time of year, you are not and cannot be bound to take office. Asquith by his delays and bargainings has made Government impossible except by himself. He must lie on the bed that he has made."

Such was the sense of our conversation.

There is one other alternative—not mentioned by us at this interview—viz.: that Asquith should resign and the King send for Lloyd George! In this case the Government policy would be recast on non-Radical lines, but Grey, Haldane and Crewe at least must go with Asquith, and though the new Government might have a majority in the Commons, such a split would destroy their last chance of a majority in the country.

*28th February* 1910.

What am I to say of the latest political developments? I deliberately sealed my letter this morning before I knew what the day would bring forth so that you might see all my varying moods and share the almost hourly changes of our calculations.

"He who will not when he may, when he will, he shall have nay." So I wrote last night  So Healy said today. I followed Healy; Lloyd George followed me, and hey presto! the trick was done! Lloyd George squared the malcontents and the Government is safe in the House of Commons.

I don't know how to begin the story. On Saturday Balfour got such information from the entourage of the Cabinet that he was awfully afraid that they would resign on the least excuse. "They have now decided that they will all resign together. The danger of partial resignations has passed." So said an intimate lady friend of Ministers, and B. sent a message to Hood that he must not let it be known that we would support Ministers today because if that were known and if it was thought, as a consequence, that the existence of the Ministry was not at stake, Irish, Labour and Radicals would all vote against the Government and they would only be saved by the Opposition. They would say, "We have suffered many humiliations; we might be prepared to endure more. But there is one last humiliation to which we won't sink and that is to be kept in office by our opponents against a majority of our friends!" They would resign. We should be forced to take office to protect the King. We could not dissolve till after Easter and meanwhile we should be at their mercy with an unprecedented financial complication to disentangle and set straight.

Today Asquith made his motion for taking all the time of the House up to Easter. But then he foreshadowed business after Easter. On the 29th, the Government would move its House of Lords Resolutions—short and simple; first, Supremacy of the Commons in finance; second, in effect the C.B. resolution over again; third, but only as a basis for legislation in a subsequent session, reform of the constitution of the House of Lords. These resolutions—and this, said A., is the only change in the Government's programme—will be sent up to the Lords.

And what then? asked Redmond when his turn came. What if the Lords reject them? Will you or won't you then ask for guarantees before you go on with the Bill which is to be founded on them?

On this point Asquith's speech had thrown no new light. The Government had practically abandoned *reform*; Grey had been beaten, given way—accepting the shadow instead of the substance—but neither the Irish nor the Cave were in any way mollified.

Balfour followed Asquith and left things much where they were, which was the proper thing for him to do.

Then came Redmond. "You are living on the support of your enemies."

"I did not say I should support them," exclaimed Balfour. "I only said I didn't see that they could do otherwise than ask for all the time of the House."

"Why do you say that?" I asked. And then followed the explanation of his views with which I began. I said, "I don't believe they mean to resign." "Nor do I now, at least not so much as I did on Saturday. I was speaking under the influence of my feelings of Saturday," replied Balfour. "Well," I said, "they cannot resign unless they are beaten. Or, if they do, you can force them back into office. The only thing that would give them a real excuse for resignation, and leave you no excuse for refusing to take office if they did resign, would be your failure or refusal to support them in those purely business measures which are necessary for *any* Government to carry on the business of the nation. That would be inconsistent with your speech at the Constitutional Club; it would appear factious and unscrupulous and would place them in the right and us in the wrong. My policy would be to let it be known throughout House and lobby that we are going to vote *with* them so as to permit or encourage as many of their own people as possible to vote against them. The very best thing at the moment is for us to be in a position to save them from their own friends. Nothing would be so humiliating to them or so irritating to their party. Let us humiliate them if we can!"

This conversation took place in Balfour's room after Redmond had finished and while Dalziell was speaking. A. J. B. said he entirely agreed if only it did not mean the Government's resignation. Alec Hood said a dissolution *now* would be fatal to us.

"Healy's up!" said someone putting his head through the door. So we went back to hear Healy.

H. was impartially denouncing everyone, but in particular ourselves. "When the Irish vote against the Government the Unionists support them. When the Unionists vote against the Government it is on some question on which they know the Irish will vote with the Government or not vote at all. All is sham and make-believe. If you meant to get the Government out, you would jump at the first chance, no matter what it was."

"This is a splendid opportunity for you. Now is your time to make our position clear," said A. J. B. to me. "You had better follow him."

So I did. I won't recapitulate my speech for it has lost all interest from subsequent events. From the personal point of view it was quite satisfactory.

Lloyd George rose as I sat down. His reply to me was poor and it was not for that he rose. He was put up to pay the price Redmond and the Cave demanded. The Budget would not be touched in the Commons till the Veto resolutions had been passed. These would be at once sent up to the Lords. If they passed them, well and good! If not—well, the Government would not plough the sands. They would not waste time with a bill only to have it rejected. Then would be the time to ask for guarantees and the Government would not hold office without them.

This is my understanding of his speech and so it was understood by Redmond and the Labour people, for when the question was put no one challenged a division. The Government have surrendered. Asquith has eaten his words again. Grey has caved in! Some take a different view of Ll. G.'s speech but that is my reading of it.

*1st March* 1910.

The report of the Debate bears out my impression at the moment. Asquith entirely failed to placate the foes of his own household. His speech left the situation substantially the same though it showed further weakening of the Government, the surrender in substance of Grey and more wobbling by the Prime Minister. But Lloyd George's speech entirely changed the position. He gave the pledge required by the malcontents, and for the present and in the House of Commons the Government is safe. If words mean anything, his words mean that the Budget will not be touched till the Veto resolutions have left our House. This is the first surrender to the Irish and other malcontents. Next, that reform of the Constitution of the House of Lords is not to be concurrent with limitation of the Veto but is to be postponed to the Greek Kalends. Second surrender. Third, that the Resolutions are not only to be sent to the House of Lords but that if they are rejected there, the Government will then ask the King for "guarantees" and will resign if they are not granted. Third and most important surrender, which makes the real change in the situation.

It is too soon as yet to say what is the final result of all these manœuvres. But one thought occurs to one at once. What if the Lords neither accept nor reject the resolutions forthwith? What if they are at that moment engaged in considering their own scheme of reform and defer consideration of the Commons resolutions till they have finished their own proposals? or if they say: "These resolutions are obscure. We do not know what they mean or how you intend to work them. They are very interesting, but we should like to see them in the form of a bill before we express any opinion on them." What then?

This is of course the obvious course for the Lords to take. The Government cannot have overlooked the probability of their so acting, but no provision is made for it or at least none is announced. Would they then go on with the Budget and send it up to the Lords or would they still hold the Budget back? or would they ask "guarantees" without waiting for the decision of the Lords and would they resign if they did not get them?

In the first case, at least, the Budget might be got out of the way and cease to be one of the issues of the election. In any case it would appear that there must be a dissolution in May, June or July in which the House of Lords must be a main issue—perhaps, in spite of all we can do, *the* main issue. Not altogether a comfortable position for us, but as I look back I do not see how we could have bettered it. From later reports I do not think we could have beaten the Government on hops. We certainly could not have beaten them yesterday after Lloyd George's speech. And if we had beaten them, we should have been obliged ourselves as our first act to propose the same resolution and to try to carry the same bills and estimates, and we should have had all our men detained in London while they flooded the constituencies or returned from time to time to put us in a minority or otherwise inflict humiliation on us.

If we could have beaten them, put our own issue at once to the House, got beaten on that and gone at once to the country, I should have been all in favour of doing so. But finance is in such a plight that this was literally impossible. We should have had to struggle on for weeks in the House in a minority. We should never have got a real chance of producing our Budget; we should have had to make shift with some modification of theirs and we should have incurred great humiliation and probably a good deal of enmity without any adequate prospect of ultimate success.

9 EGERTON PLACE, S.W.,
*1st March* 1910.

I am sending you tonight cuttings from the *Westminster Gazette* and the *Birmingham Daily Post* by which you may check my impressions of the debate and the situation. I have written to you in such hot haste and so immediately under the impression of the moment that I scarcely know what I have said; but I felt that the mood, the atmosphere, of the moment was the really interesting thing to you, so I purposely wrote in haste—with the prospect of repenting at leisure.

Now the crisis is over. As a matter of fact I don't think that *we* ever had the power to bring it to an issue. That could only be done by the Government themselves. Saturday's meeting of the Cabinet was the critical point and on Saturday the "moderates" gave way and the situation was saved for the Government. The *B.D.P.* speaks of Redmond's bluff. No doubt both sides were bluffing, but in my opinion it was not Redmond's nerve which gave way under the strain. It is Asquith and Grey who have yielded once more. It is Redmond who triumphs, for the time at least. What will follow and what will be the result of the General Election, which it is now obvious must come in the summer, none of us can say.

The party of Veto first has won. The Government mean to keep finance in confusion and the Budget in suspense, not merely because they would not have a majority for the Budget if it were taken first, but also because they mean to keep the position such that a Government without a majority in the House can neither carry on nor dissolve. It is a very clever but utterly unscrupulous game. Somehow I think that it will not succeed; but, to speak quite frankly, both parties are afraid of an appeal to the country and neither party is reassured by the fears of the other.

At the levée today I saw George Murray.[1]

"I didn't know you were such an autocrat," said I. "To levy taxes without authority for two years is rather a large order."

"Yes," he replied, "I ask everyone what is the use of a Treasury. No one seems to want one now."

"Well, I don't know how long you will go on. One reason why things have gone as smoothly as they have done was because everyone supposed that the collections would be regulated at the first moment."

"Yes, of course," said Murray, "as soon as Parliament met."

"You did very badly with your last issue of Treasury Bills," said I.

"Oh, why do you say that? We placed them at 2½ per cent."

"Yes, but the Bank had to take a lot of them!"

"Who told you that story?" asked Murray.

"Oh! I've been told. Secrets do leak out," said I.

"Well, the Bank sold them the next day. But I was in an awful funk. There were only applications for 3½ millions (I think the figure is right) and no more were coming in and I didn't know what was going to happen. Who told you?"

"Not the Bank and not an official. If you *wish* to know, a newspaper editor told me, but he said he wouldn't publish it for fear of a panic!"

You should have seen Murray's face when he found that I knew, and still more when he found that a newspaper knew!

*2nd March* 1910.

The *Morning Post* is aggravating in its determination to believe the worst of its "leaders." The note which Balfour "tossed across the table, and which is supposed to have acquainted the Prime Minister with the intention of the Opposition to stay their hand," was a line to say that he would rise to order if Asquith travelled beyond the subject-matter of his resolution, not with the object of preventing him from doing so but to secure the Opposition's

[1] The Right Hon. Sir George Murray, G.C.B., then Permanent Secretary of the Treasury.

right to reply! Thus is history written by journalists who won't even take the trouble to ask their friends what they are doing before hanging them.

What would the *Morning Post* have and what does it think we could have done? If we had defeated the Government on Monday and they had resigned, as of course they would have done, what would have been our position? We could not have dissolved. That was the crux of the situation. Putting aside the Budget, there was three weeks' absolutely necessary financial business—necessary that is, not merely to avert confusion but to prevent an act of default and practical bankruptcy, to provide money to pay the Services and to meet the twenty millions of War Loan which are falling due. Dissolution therefore was out of the question and we should have had at once to make the very motion which we had defeated and to sue to Asquith for his support on the very point on which we had refused to support him. How could we have lived or carried through the essential business in such circumstances? We should have been discredited and humiliated and Asquith could have kept us in or put us out as and when he pleased. We should have had all the responsibility and no power. He would have had all the power and no responsibility.

All this assumes that we could have beaten the Government, but as a matter of fact we never had a chance of doing so. Redmond had not the slightest intention of defeating them at any time in that debate. If we had voted against Asquith's motion, he would either have abstained or, after Lloyd George's speech, voted with them. We should have done a rather dirty trick and all for nothing or only to make ourselves look fools.

*3rd March* 1910.

This morning I attended a concourse at Lansdowne House on House of Lords reform—chiefly remarkable for the presence of Rosebery at our councils. There was a good deal of rather discursive conversation and no very definite result. The biggest question raised was whether an elective element should find a place in a reformed House, *i.e.* whether a portion of the House being selected in some manner from the hereditary peers, and a second portion being nominated by the Crown for life or for a term of years, a third portion should be elected by some form of electoral college, probably County Councils singly or grouped where the population was too small for a single county to elect a representative.

Rosebery, George Curzon and I were in favour of this proposal.

"Unless you are prepared for that," said Rosebery, "you might as well give up reform from within. Nothing less will affect public opinion sufficiently to change the situation in Scotland and the North."

With this Curzon and I agreed. Wyndham was, I think, also of this opinion, but he is never very easy to understand. Long agreed and Akers-Douglas, to my surprise, expressed himself strongly in the same sense. Salisbury was entirely hostile to the idea; Midleton was apparently hostile but quite incomprehensible; Lansdowne expressed great reluctance to admit it and a doubt whether he could take any active part in support of it, but spoke before Long, Douglas and, I think, Balfour had given their opinions. Balfour said:

"I agree with what I believe Austen thinks. I dislike the whole thing. I would like to leave things as they are if we could. I don't believe you can make a better House. But that is not the question. The question is: Can you make a Second Chamber strong enough to stand and resist assault? Can you make such changes as will enable our men to fight with success in Yorkshire, Lancashire and Scotland against single-chamber government? I don't think you can in our democratic days unless you admit an elective element, and though at first I thought that the elective and non-elective elements would at once clash and the remaining hereditary element be thrust out I have come to the conclusion on reflection that this danger is not as great as I at first thought and that such a House as we are discussing might stand at any rate for fifty years."

I had previously said, "The question is not whether you can improve the House—I doubt on the whole whether you could get a House of men better qualified for their work—but the question is can you make the House strong enough to do its work successfully?"

"That's exactly it!" said Rosebery. He and George Curzon and I were the active protagonists of an elective element; Salisbury and Midleton the chief opponents.

*5th March* 1910.

Many thanks for your letter of the third received today. I was very glad to get Father's comments, and find myself very much in agreement with them. If we could have turned the Government out on hops (which I do not think that we could) we ought to have done so, and it was a mistake even to hesitate about it, though on that Friday no one would have been more pleased at defeat than the Government itself. It was then more probable than not that there would be either resignation of the whole Government or of a section of it before Monday. It was only on Saturday that the different sections of the Government came to terms and resolved all to hang together.

Except on Friday we never came near to defeating them— never had a chance of it, I mean—and if there was ever a chance on Friday it would only have been by a snap division, *i.e.* by passing round word to our men to stop the debate while the discussion was still in full flow.

And what a mess we should have been in after all! We could not have dissolved; we could not even have adjourned whilst the new ministers were being re-elected, for there is not a day to spare between now and Easter if the necessary financial business is to be done, and we should have had to leave the House sitting in charge of Under-Secretaries.

No, I don't see how it could have been done. There has never been quite such a complicated situation before.

*5th March* 1910.

It is 11.50 and I am only just back from Buckingham Palace— a very good dinner, a quite excellent and very large cigar and pleasant talk.

The King,[1] as always, asked kindly after Father and sent him good wishes. He was very pleased that Father had taken his seat. "Are you going to spoil my holiday with a crisis?" he asked.

[1] H.M. King Edward VII.

"I think not, sir," I replied. "I think Your Majesty is safe till after Easter."

"A General Election in July—July, I think, would be quite early enough," said the King, "but you have a very difficult situation. You must play your cards very carefully."

Loulou [1] and I talked of recent debates. "The trouble with our Lloyd George," said Loulou, "is, as I remarked to my colleague the other day, that he uses figures *exactly as if they were adjectives.*" This in answer to my observation that Lloyd George was so grossly inaccurate even when there was no object in deceiving. "He gives you the first answer that comes into his head and then enquires at the office next day whether by any lucky chance what he said was correct."

I had a good deal of talk with Rosebery. "I hope you were satisfied with my chief's speech in the City last night," I said.

"Yes," he replied. "He was very much against any change at first, but he told me he had been completely converted. I had a long talk with him last Sunday at Belvoir, you know. I am afraid, however, that we shall have great trouble with our host of Thursday" (*i.e.* Lansdowne). "He hates the whole thing. But what I want to know is what was the result of our meeting?" (He left a little early.) I gave him my impressions of it as already written to you. He dwelt on the necessity for radical change. I asked why Scotland was so strong against the Lords. "Because of their opposition to the Reform Bill of '32," he said. "They have never forgiven or forgotten it. But I am certain that as between a Reformed House and Single Chamber Government the people will choose the former and on that issue the Government will be beaten—and they know it. I thought Asquith very dejected on Monday. There had been negotiations with the Irish and he thought he had got them and they sold him."

Something led me to say that my belief was that the Government were all at sixes and sevens on Friday, and then thought resignation as a body or a split in the Cabinet inevitable, and that they only patched up their differences on Saturday.

"What makes you think that?" he asked.

"Well, I hardly know, but putting things together——"

[1] The late Lord Harcourt.

"Oh! I agree with you. I believe that was so, but I wondered how you knew."

"Well, partly from a conversation at the Court on Friday night with Winston—and then ladies will talk!"

"Yes. A lady of high authority said they had decided to announce their resignation on Monday."

Balfour had heard the same—no doubt from the same lady. Who she was, I don't know.

At this point Reid moved up to talk with Rosebery. "Before we are interrupted," said R., "I must tell you. I meant to have called on your Father the other day, but I saw he had left for France. Tell him—it will amuse him—that last year I was driving in the Park in that one-horse carriage I drive and I saw him and Mrs. Chamberlain driving too. He had his arm in a sling and his eyeglass in his eye and a slouch hat on. Oh! thought I, this is my chance to salute him. So I turned round and drove past him and made such a bow that my hat nearly fell into his brougham and then—I saw it wasn't him at all! I don't know what the people thought of me. I could only whip up my horse and run away."

We had altogether a good deal of talk about the House of Lords. I pressed on him not to offer too much at first.

When we left that subject he spoke of Father and asked how he had created and kept such an enormous influence over B'ham. "I could never understand it," he said. "After all he was a very extreme Radical and now——"

I gave reasons. "And you must remember," I added, "that he was always a great imperialist. No doubt you can point to a good deal of surface inconsistency in his speeches, as on Free Trade for instance. But there is a much greater underlying consistency in his career."

"Yes," he said, "that is so. I have always been told that about his early days. I sometimes say that it is not that he is more inconsistent than other people, but his speeches are so epigrammatic that people remember them and that they are worth quoting."

He was going on, but it was at this point (not as I have written above) that he saw we were going to be interrupted and that he turned to the story of his drive in the Park.

Mowatt[1] told stories of Gladstone and others of his chiefs. On one occasion Gladstone had been very much interested in some small bill which got much knocked about and altered in the House. He was sitting in his study eyeing its mutilated form in gloomy despondency when George Russell said to him: "Well, Mr. Gladstone, you must remember that, as the old Greek said, sometimes the half is greater than the whole." Mr. G. sprang to life at the words. "What old Greek said that?" he cried. "*No* old Greek ever said it," he declared with the utmost scorn.

George Russell saw a copy of *Hesiod* on the shelf, got it down and laying it open at the passage before Mr. G. said, "The chance of for once triumphing over you in a point of classical scholarship overcomes my profound respect." Mr. G. eyed the passage fiercely and then snorted out contemptuously, "An evident interpolation!"

Was it not characteristic? Russell afterwards asked Sir A. Godley whether there was any reason to suppose that Hesiod had not written the line. "So little," said Godley, "that I believe it is the only line we have that he ever did write!"

Mowatt thought Gladstone's mind had lost some of its power before his last Government. I said there was no sign of it in the House during those Home Rule debates, but Mowatt stuck to his view. Mr. G. was often to be found in his study in those days looking a weary crushed old man, but he sprang into life and vigour as soon as work was mentioned.

Mowatt once asked Thring (old Thring—not the present one) if he found his work as Parliamentary Draughtsman very hard. "No," said Thring, "I know my trade. You drag the kernel of your bill into the first two or three clauses and then the rest is easy. No, I don't find it difficult—except with Mr. Gladstone; but his mind so envelops you, so closes round yours and presses on you from every side, that I know nothing like it. When I have worked with him for an hour, I am obliged to get up and say, 'Mr. Gladstone, I must stop. I'm tired out!'"

[1] Sir Francis Mowatt, G.C.B., for many years Permanent Secretary to the Treasury.

At lunch on Sunday I found myself between Lord Rothschild and a young lady I did not know. I had only got down there at 12 o'clock.

"I made Mowatt very angry," said Lord R., "by telling him that we were living on the backwash of American prosperity. He didn't like it."

"Of course not," I said, "but it's true. I don't discuss those questions with him."

"Oh, I do. He's very stupid about them, but I like him. He eats a good dinner, drinks his wine and he's very pleasant, tho' he did behave shamefully to Arthur Balfour."

"Yes," I said, "he did behave badly then, but he was always very nice to me and I like him."

"Of course he behaved shamefully," repeated Lord R.

At this point Lady R. who was at another table out of earshot rose, and Vaughan Williams who was on the other side of Lord R. hurried round to tell me that the lady on my left was Miss Mowatt! Wasn't it like Lord R. to discuss her father to her face and mightn't I have put my foot in it under such guidance? My guardian angel must have been specially attentive to me at the moment to bring me so well out of it.

I went to the Lords yesterday to hear Lansdowne and Revelstoke. The Prince of Wales was there and spoke very cordially to me in the waiting-room, undertaking to stop and watch for Lansdowne whilst I went to hunt for him elsewhere!

Have you heard the latest story which is going the rounds? Someone complained that Cabinet discussions leaked out and Winston said:

"Yes, it's a Welsh leak!" Rather good, I think!

*9th March* 1910.

I have dictated a long memorandum of a discussion at dinner at Mat Ridley's last night to Mr. Wilson and told him to send it to you this afternoon. If you get the chance to show it to Balfour I should be very glad. Perhaps if he is not coming to see you, you could send it up to his hotel for him to read and return to you when he has done with it.

*Memo.*

I dined last night at Mat Ridley's with Wyndham, Sam Storey, F. E. Smith, Rupert Gwynne (Mat's brother-in-law, who won Eastbourne for us), Hewins, Goulding and Gwynne of the *Standard*. Bonar Law joined us after dinner. The dinner, I think, was held at Goulding's suggestion in order that we might discuss certain points of party policy and in particular what pronouncement ought to be made by the Unionist leaders on certain prominent questions, in view of another early appeal to the electorate.

We began, however, by discussing the question whether it was to our advantage to turn the Government out if we had an opportunity or whether it would be better to leave them to make the appeal to the country. On this point we were unanimously of opinion that it was of importance to get the Government out if possible on a fair issue, and that if they resigned Balfour ought to take office whatever the situation, propound his own policy either by statement made in the House of Commons or by resolutions, and go to the country on the issue so raised. Bonar Law was alone in at first holding that it would be better for us if the Government remained in office and themselves dissolved, but was converted by our reasons to the other view. The consideration which mainly affected him was one which I put forward, viz.: that our success or failure at the next General Election depended on what the country was thinking about at the moment of the election, and that that would be largely decided by the question of which party was in office at the time, for the Government of the day has the last word in the House of Commons and would really state the issue on which the country had to decide.

This unanimity of opinion, very strongly held by all of us, was the more noteworthy because we were equally agreed that even if it had been possible to beat the Government on hops, or on the motion for the time of the House, it would not have been good policy to do so then. Indeed so strongly had both Storey and F. E. Smith held this view that they had deliberately walked away from the House on Friday when they thought there was a possibility of the Government being beaten, and that without any pressure or suggestion that they should do so from the Whips. It appeared to us that after Easter when the question may again arise we should be in an entirely different position. If the Government can go on without a Budget so could we. The absolutely necessary financial business would have been done and there would be nothing to prevent us from dissolving Parliament as soon as we had stated our policy in the House and challenged a vote of confidence on it. This would of course be refused and would give us the opportunity of appealing to the country.

But before this appeal is made there are some questions which must be settled. I have been pressed on all sides for a clear pronouncement as to our policy in regard to Colonial corn, or rather I should say, Colonial wheat; for I do not think that the same considerations necessarily apply to oats and barley as do to bread stuffs. It is evident that if we had a majority in the present House of Commons we should be obliged to admit Colonial wheat free. So many of our men are pledged to that course that we should not have a majority in our own party for taxing it. These men say that they started on the line indicated by my Father's Glasgow speech—that their arguments have been based on the supposition that Colonial wheat would be admitted free—that they have laid great stress on this feature of the policy, and that it is impossible for them in view of the arguments which they have used in the past now to alter their attitude on this point.

I think this is true, and as far as I can learn it would be a great relief even to those who have hitherto defended a shilling duty on Colonial wheat if they were allowed to promise that it should be admitted free. The editor of *Farm & Home* wrote to both Balfour and myself saying that this suggestion which appeared in the *Standard* was causing great dissatisfaction and alarm in agricultural districts, but I think he is quite mistaken. There may be a few parts of the country where the agriculturists would like Colonial corn taxed, but the representations which have come to me on the subject come largely from country members who find the proposed tax on Colonial wheat unpopular both with labourers and farmers. We grow so little wheat in these days that even the farmer in most parts of the country is to be reckoned a consumer rather than a producer of wheat.

Under all these circumstances I have come to the conclusion—which as Balfour knows is shared by Bonar Law—that we had better make free Colonial wheat definitely a part of our policy. If Balfour agrees I hope that he would be willing to state our policy on this point officially either in a speech or perhaps better still in an interchange of letters which could be easily arranged. So much confusion has arisen from the different language held by different candidates at the last election (a conspicuous illustration of which is the fact that I was saying one thing whilst Father was writing the other) that a pronouncement by our leader is the only way of clearing up doubts, and it is the easier for Balfour to make it because he has never committed himself to either point of view.

At the dinner we were agreed that Tariff Reform must be kept conspicuously in the forefront of our programme. To it would be naturally added the reform of the House of Lords on which those present hoped that our leaders would have given us clear guidance before we again appealed to the electors. Balfour has already spoken of the reform of the Poor Law as being urgent, but he has given no indication of the lines on which he contemplates proceeding. It was felt very desirable that the Party should have some guidance on this point. You will understand that they do not want the details of a Bill, or indeed any details at all, but they do want a lead as to how they are to treat the recommendations of the minority report and what answers they should give to the questions which are showered upon them on the subject. If they do not get this lead soon we shall find our troops committed in detail, and we may easily discover on assuming office that so many pledges have been given by our men that we have not a free hand to do what we think right. I wonder whether Balfour is prepared to formulate the general lines of a policy himself or whether he would get together some of our men with knowledge of the subject under his own guidance to consider and formulate suggestions.

Another question yet remains, to which Goulding, Storey and F. E. Smith attach the very highest importance. They all say that in the English towns we were beaten by the Land Taxes of the Budget. Goulding added that he was convinced that the defeat of the Moderates in the recent London County Council Elections was due to the same cause and that unless we were

prepared to indicate an intention of dealing with this question we
have no chance of winning these towns back. We were all agreed
that we could have nothing to do with the taxing of ground
values or with any general valuation scheme, and that if anything
was to be done by us it must be on the lines of a reform of rating,
not as in the Budget by a new National Tax. Wyndham desired
an Enabling Act permitting Municipalities to rate vacant plots at
their real letting value. This would satisfy the others and they
proposed that we should proceed on the lines of Lord Balfour of
Burleigh's minority report. Bonar Law said that this was so
hedged in with restrictions that he doubted whether it would be
sufficient—certainly there would be very little money in it. On
the whole, however, the others thought that this was an advantage
rather than otherwise. They did not believe there was much
money to be got out of any fair system, but there was a vast
amount of sympathy with the idea which had been attracted to
the Government by the Budget and which we must try to win
back for a saner proposal. Storey and F. E. Smith felt sure that
a proposal on these lines coming from a leader of the Unionist
Party would be very popular with the great Town Councils who
had forced Lloyd George to share his plunder and even now
grudged the Treasury the half which Lloyd George retained. It
is certain that if we do nothing the Radical Party will sooner or
later establish their national taxes, and once established in that
form any Radical in need of money, or any Socialist Chancellor
in pursuit of the policy of nationalisation of the sources of production, will find it an easy task to give a turn to the screw and
raise the levy from year to year. On the other hand, if this source
of revenue, such as it is, is once given to municipalities, the
Treasury will never be able to put its finger in the pie again and
the Chancellor of the Exchequer will have no temptation to
screw up taxes from which he derives no advantage.

It was very strongly pressed upon me before I left that I should
take the earliest opportunity of putting forward reform of Rating
on these lines as the Unionist alternative to the Government Land
Taxes. Those present believed that if it were made clear by
someone speaking with authority that this was the Unionist policy
it would produce an enormous effect on the Boroughs. I believe

that we must do something of the kind, but I scarcely feel sufficiently informed on the subject to deal with it out of hand. I shall, however, make it my business to read again the minority report of the Royal Commission and see how far we can adopt their recommendations. It is evidently a subject of the greatest importance.

Curiously enough since dictating the above I have received a letter from the Rector of Birmingham, Canon Denton Thompson, saying that he has written to Mr. Balfour to suggest that "some definite statement of the inclusion by Unionists of say the proposals made by the Poor Law Commission on which both the majority and the minority agree should be made." He writes as a Unionist and attaches great importance to the suggestion.

A. C.

*Note by A. C.*

I can find no note of Balfour's reply to this if he sent me one. He was then at Cannes and probably did not write. Lansdowne expressed agreement with the proposal that Colonial wheat should be admitted free, and stated that he entirely agreed about the anxiety of keeping Tariff Reform conspicuously in the front of our programme.

He was in favour of a reconstitution of the House, based upon the principle that the possession of a hereditary peerage should not by itself entitle a seat and vote, and that the House must be liberally reinforced from new sources to put an end to the immense disparity of numbers between the two sides, but he feared there would be great difficulties about admitting an elective element.

He did not feel sufficiently informed about the Poor Law to make suggestions for its reform, but favoured an examination by one or two of our own men to form a scheme for consideration, and he suggested the question of Occupying Ownership, upon which Balfour had always laid great stress, as another plank for our platform. As to Land Taxes he wrote:

"I am sure it would be right to do something in regard to Land Taxes. I have always myself, in debate, professed a readiness to deal with cases in which the owner arrested the development of the district and evaded his fair share of taxation by holding up land, and it would certainly be desirable that the product of these taxes should go into the hands of the municipalities instead of the Exchequer. I attach great importance to taking some action which will show the public that the urban landowners are not actuated by purely selfish considerations and are ready to bear their full share of local taxation."

Bonar Law, to whom I also sent a copy of the memorandum, replied that he agreed so fully with it that he would make no written comments. He added that he was returning to London in a few days when he would like to discuss the position with me.

I resume my extracts from my letters to my father.

*11th March* 1910.

Look at the report in today's *Times* of our discussion yesterday on the Vote on Account. The Government have changed their minds again, and that since Wednesday of last week, when they put down the Army Votes. You will see that they are taking a Vote on Account and Navy supply for six weeks only instead of for four or five months. I think the inference is obvious. By about the end of May they expect in some way to have brought matters with the Lords to a crisis upon which they will resign, or to have been beaten in the Commons on their Budget. (The former is the more probable calculation.) In either case they resign. Balfour takes office, forms his Government and in ordinary course would at once dissolve. But though you can carry on Government without a Budget you cannot carry on without supply. The Government plan is therefore to perpetuate financial confusion, to leave the incoming ministers without sufficient supply to tide over a General Election, to force them first to run the gauntlet of by-elections for ministers and then to face a House of Commons in which they are in a minority of 124 whilst they get further Votes on Account and pass another Consolidated Fund Bill before they can carry the appeal to the people.

Very sharp, very unscrupulous and rather clever as you would expect a small attorney to be clever in a small tricky way!

Well, things may yet work out differently from what they expect; but even if they turn out as the Government now plan them, we must take office at all hazards. We may be able to find

231

a way out of the financial dilemma; but if not, we must fight a way through.

I think there is too much "jockeying" about the Government tactics to make them really good policy.

I had a very pleasant dinner at Revelstoke's last night.

*12th March* 1910.

Moberly Bell told a story of a Kentish labourer who was presented to someone as the man who had done most for the Unionist Party in the Division. "Did I canvass 'em? No, not 'xactly. They was a-shouting Down with the Lords—fifteen or twenty of 'em was. What's the use of shouting? I says. 'Taint *no* use. You can't down 'em with shouting, I says. You go and write it on your tickets, I says. Write: Down with the House of Lords there!" And the innocents went off and triumphantly wrote the magic words across their ballot papers and spoiled all their votes!

*14th March* 1910.

Many thanks for two very interesting letters received this morning with an account of Father's comments on what I have written to him. I confess that like him I do not feel the same confidence in the advice I have given about the reform of the House of Lords as I do in my views on other points in the situation. You will notice that today's political notes in *The Times* entirely confirm my views of what the Government are playing for. The moral is obvious: Balfour must be prepared to take office. The financial situation will be more difficult than Garvin perceives, if I may judge by yesterday's *Observer*, for he does not understand the legal difficulty of paying out money without authority, *i.e.* that money can only be issued on a certificate of the Controller and Auditor-General who is not a Treasury official but an independent officer of the House of Commons to whom alone he is responsible. But whatever the difficulties we must be prepared to face them and, as I wrote the other day, to cut our way through them if we cannot escape from them.

Monsieur Pernolet dined with us last night—very pleasant.

We discussed Balfour, whom he contrasted with Father. I quoted Sainte-Beuve on the old Duc de Broglie [1] as very applicable to him.

"It is curious," he said, "that you should quote that, for this morning Cambon said to me: 'Balfour, c'est le duc de Broglie.'"

I could not get to the Lords to hear Rosebery's speech today. "A fine performance" and "too long" were the chief comments I could gather. "Very useful and splendid for us when we go electioneering," Sandars said. Others spoke more doubtfully. Opinion is not yet formed.

*15th March* 1910.

I spent the afternoon at the H. of C. listening to dull Navy debates (a *very* good maiden speech, by the way, from Eyres Monsell,[2] M.P. for the Evesham Division) and attending a very useful and business-like Tariff Reform Committee.

I hear that Newton made a very good speech in the Lords today, but that the House is in a curious and very uncertain mood. It loudly cheers all attacks on the Government and mildly approves reform in general but relapses into stony silence the moment any particular reform is dwelt upon. It doesn't know where it is or what it wants. What will come of it all none can say; I think a great deal depends on Lansdowne. His opinion will carry great weight—all the more perhaps because he is obviously very conservative in this matter and very anxious (and rightly so) to carry the mass of the Lords with him.

*17th March* 1910.

I am ashamed to have no news for you, but I have none and can gather none. The Navy debates in our House are uneventful except for fresh revelations of McKenna's character and temper and for some very good speeches by new members—the best of all being that of young Eyres Monsell who succeeded Col. Long in South Worcestershire. On the whole the Government's naval

[1] See *Down the Years*, p. 214.
[2] Now Lord Monsell.

programme is a good one. They have found out that their Little Navy line did not pay and have altered their policy accordingly. Lambert, the Civil Lord, walked down to the House yesterday with Walter Long and gave him an amusing account of McKenna's conversion, detailing how McKenna at the Treasury had written minutes and memoranda to prove that the Admiralty wasted money and did not require the estimates for which they asked; how he had come to the Admiralty boasting of the reductions he was going to make; how Fisher had played with him and captured him completely, and how under Fisher's guidance and the pressure of public opinion he had completely turned round.

The Lords' debate goes on with some good speeches each day. I was told yesterday that Curzon's was very fine. Algernon West, no friendly critic, said "One of the finest pieces of parliamentary oratory" he had ever heard. It is good, but I confess that after hearing this eulogy, I was rather disappointed when I read it. The debate discloses great difference of opinion and there will certainly be considerable opposition to the introduction of any elective element. Yet I think that on the whole the best men favour it, with the one very big exception of Lansdowne. Even he, I think, is more governed in this matter by anxiety lest he should not carry the great bulk of the House with him than by his own intrinsic dislike of the proposal; but there can be no doubt that he does dislike it.

*19th March* 1910.

I have had it suggested to me that I should give notice of a Vote of Censure on the Government for not collecting Income Tax and for not pressing on the Budget and ask for Tuesday, the 29th, for its discussion, but I have decided against this proposal mainly for two reasons: first, that as we can and shall raise the same question (without dividing) on the Consolidated Fund Bill, Asquith could and probably would refuse. I should then be forced to divide on this Bill on Monday and should get a bad division. Secondly, on the ground that when the majority is notoriously at sixes and sevens, it is bad policy to reunite them in the division lobby unless you are compelled to do so. On any Vote of Censure which we could frame, all the Government's own men, the

Labour Party and the Irish would come together. We had better let them stew as long as possible, though we shall of course be forced to join issue with them very early on the Lords' resolutions. They will probably all be united there in any case, but there is just a chance of some breach somewhere and we had better keep that chance open. I go back for a precedent to '92-'95 when, after full experience of their effect, Father advised dropping Votes of Censure which only recruited the shattered fragments of the majority and trying to beat the Government on some less formal occasion.

*21st March* 1910.

What a tangled situation it is! None of us see our way out of it or know how it will end, and the Government are evidently as uncomfortable as we ourselves are. I hear from Goulding that T. P. O'Connor told him "for his private guidance" that the Irish had now replenished their war chest and would not allow the Budget to pass.

"But you don't think that we shall be such fools," he added, "as to beat the Government on the Budget; we shall beat them on something else."

This bears out my idea that the Government will fall on a time of the House or a guillotine resolution.

*22nd March* 1910.

Bonar Law had got from Lloyd George last night in the smoke-room a statement that a dissolution in May was "inevitable" and the strong impression that the Government would themselves dissolve and not resign. He believes the Irish have been squared.

Alfred Lyttelton said he heard this morning from Bankers in the City that the City had become so jumpy about the Government's financial arrangements that yesterday morning half the applications for the issue of the Exchequer Bonds had been withdrawn and, if the Government had not closed the lists, the remainder would probably have been withdrawn also—an absolutely unprecedented occurrence.

*Secret.*

WHITFIELD,
*24th March* 1910.

I have very good information that Grey had actually resigned last week and that the only question was whether Haldane would resign with him or not. They have patched matters up again and once again there will be no resignations. I believe too that they have squared the Irish, but, as to this, we get the most conflicting evidence. It is, however, evident that the Irish are eager to be squared and will take any excuse which they think sufficient to protect their position in Ireland against O'Brien. Grey has been outmanœuvred altogether, beaten from one position to another and finally, I think, beaten altogether. "Reform," for which he has fought, finds no place in the resolutions and is relegated to the position of a pious opinion only to be named in Asquith's speech. Of course no action will ever be taken on it by that party; but it will enable Grey, and such as wish to, to deny vehemently that they are single-chamber men. I suspect that the old C.B. resolution hung like a millstone round Grey's neck. With his views, he ought never to have assented to that and, having assented to it, he has been in a false position in all these discussions; well, let us hope that he is right and that "death and damnation"[1] will follow on the course they are taking.

WHITFIELD,
*27th March* 1910.

Many thanks for returning Lansdowne's letter and for your interesting account of Father's conversation with A. J. B. I am very glad to have it. You do yourself a great injustice as a correspondent for you gave me all the pith of their talk as the papers would say. I am glad that B. has had a good holiday, for he needed it to refresh his mind as well as to strengthen his body. I am sure that it will make a great difference in his outlook on the political situation and in his willingness to accept responsibility if the moment comes for him to do so; and Father's talks with him will have helped him to prepare and strengthen him for the inevitable. They will dwell in his mind and the seed thus sown will not have fallen on waste places.

[1] Lord Rosebery's words.

236

9 EGERTON PLACE, S.W.,
*30th March* 1910.

. . . We left Whitfield next morning just after nine and got to town just in time for the House of Commons. Asquith was very dull. He read nearly his whole speech from sheaf after sheaf of manuscript produced from a red box. He seemed ill at ease throughout, and though he read well, never seemed to get into his stride or to move with any freedom. His party cheered him as much as they could, but there was no real enthusiasm and an air of unreality and flatness hung around the whole debate.

Balfour's reply was interesting, as he always is, but I thought he seemed tired, though he looked well, and his delivery was more than usually hesitating. Afterwards we retired to his room to consider what amendment should be moved, and decided after a short discussion on the motion which stands in Finlay's name.

Sir Robert Finlay:

Line 1, leave out from "That," to end, and insert "in the opinion of this House a strong and efficient Second Chamber is necessary; (that this House is willing to consider proposals for the reform of the constitution of the existing Second Chamber, but declines to proceed with proposals which would destroy the usefulness of any Second Chamber, however constituted), and would remove the only safeguard against great changes being made by the Government of the day not only without the consent but against the wishes of the majority of the electors."

Balfour tried to draft one, but again he seemed tired and could not produce anything that he liked, so I offered the words within the brackets, to which I added the first sentence because Wyndham was anxious to have it in and the last because, when suggested by Bonar Law, it seemed to me to have merit. Finlay will move it tomorrow. I do not think that I shall take part in the debate till we get to the resolutions in Committee.

Today F. E. Smith opened the ball with a brilliant speech—quite the best thing he has done. Hugh Cecil also spoke with some effective passages but he is not the equal of Bob for debating. . . . Birrell, who followed, entertained Balfour more than he did me, but I suppose may be counted as a success. "I don't suppose,"

237

said Balfour, "that that (his reference to definition of dogmas) [1] interests anyone in the House but me, but it delights me. I think him the most interesting speaker in the House." And again, after some witticism, "The best of the fellow is that all his good things are *blurted* out!"

After his speech and Wyndham's, A. J. B., Long, Lyttelton and myself retired to Balfour's room to consider our attitude to a private member's bill which embodies the policy of the Minority Report of the Poor Law Committee. Balfour, who had not read it or given much consideration to it but who had seen the Webbs, was the most favourably inclined to it. The rest of us, who had gone a little deeper into it, were agreed that it would not do, though I confessed to having been greatly attracted by it before I studied it. I think that our line will be that the first work for Parliament (and quite enough for one Parliament) is to carry out the recommendations on which both the majority and minority are agreed. These alone will work an enormous change and require all the care Parliament can give to them. The popular and *sound* objections to the minority scheme in its entirety are :

1. That it would cost about 50 millions!

2. That it establishes an intolerable bureaucratic tyranny. Five separate inspectors from the Local Authority might descend on any working man's home and carry off himself, his wife or any or all of his children to a municipal institution, feed, clothe or otherwise care for them, utterly ignoring both parental rights and parental responsibility, whilst it would rest with a sixth inspector not appointed by or under the control of the Local Authority to decide without appeal whether any and, if so, what part of the cost of this public assistance should be recovered from the family. And all the inspectors might act without any call for help from the individual, without there being any destitution and without there being anything in the nature of a criminal act or default on the part of the parents.

[1] "Theologians have pointed out again and again in the Councils of the Church that the declaration and definition of a dogma at once increases in a sense the authority of that dogma whilst it may in other directions limit it. It was so said of Papal Infallibility. . . . Here we limit the constitutional and legal powers of the House of Lords in certain directions, but we increase them in certain other directions. . . ."

3. That the whole tendency of the Report is to make the position of the State-aided better than that of the ordinary decent working man taxed to support them.

"The Webbs," said Vivian to Lyttelton, "carry you on logically and imperceptibly from one point to another; but when you look at the whole, it's moonshine!"

Not a bad criticism.

I see that the *B. Post* confirms my impression of Asquith's speech, but praises Balfour's more than I did. Perhaps I was too critical. Ivy's estimate is more like the *B.P.'s* than mine.

*31st March* 1910.

. . . Well, the Government are guillotining their Lords' resolutions pretty sharply. *Tant mieux!* Though they foreshadow a vast constitutional change, they do not in themselves afford a very wide field for discussion; and perhaps the less we discuss them the less we concentrate public attention on them and the better for us. This at least is Bonar Law's view.

The political situation remains fearfully obscure to everyone. No party is really confident; none is really happy, and those who are usually most sanguine can only whistle to keep up their spirits.

Boraston[1] asked my opinion as to the proper policy of the L.-U. office in view of an early election. Some were in favour of "concentration," *i.e.* letting unlikely seats go uncontested. I replied, "Fight every seat!" and he expressed his satisfaction and cordial agreement. . . .

[1] Chief Agent of the Liberal-Unionist Party.

*Reform of House of Lords—The Irish Question—Death of King Edward*

9 EGERTON PLACE, S.W.,
*2nd April* 1910.

I went down to Birmingham yesterday afternoon and addressed my Committee in a short but dull speech which is quite sufficiently reported in *The Times*. Then Chavasse entertained about fifty secretaries and chairmen at the Union Club and we passed a pleasant and useful evening. I made them another speech (without reporters) in a lighter and more personal vein with which they were very pleased. It was intended and had the effect of stimulating the personal feeling between them and me and gave evident satisfaction.

I send you two contradictory cuttings from the *Birmingham Post* of successive days which well illustrate the march and counter-march of rumour. I *think* Redmond will be squared. If not, the Government will fall on the Budget guillotine. No doubt it would be better to beat them on the Budget than on the time of the House, but beat them we must on the first opportunity that offers if one does offer at all. And you need not fear that there is any arrangement, such as the *Post* seems to suggest, for giving them the guillotine without opposition.

*5th April* 1910.

The air is again full of rumours which it is impossible to reconcile one with another and from which it is difficult to disentangle the truth. I believe, however, that the fact of the matter is that there is little if any difference remaining between the Irish and the Government, and that what uncertainty exists is due, as *The Times* lobby correspondent said to me yesterday, rather to the personal equation than to any intrinsic difference of opinion. However, let me begin at the beginning and give you the rumours for what they are worth.

240

In the first place it was announced early last week in the *Freeman* and other Irish papers that Redmond and Dillon would speak at meetings in Ireland last Sunday and would simultaneously make an important announcement, and it is clear from published correspondence that the National League in Dublin specially arranged a meeting for Dillon at short notice. On Friday or Saturday, however, this statement was contradicted, and it was explained that it was all a mistake. The two meetings were held and both Dillon and Redmond spoke, but they made no such pronouncement as had been foreshadowed. Rumour offers as an explanation that they had come to an agreement with Lloyd George in the early part of the week-end, intended to announce it on Sunday, but that when it was submitted to the Cabinet the Cabinet refused its consent.

Second rumour. On Saturday Balfour had "good reason" for thinking that Redmond was squared, or at any rate that the Government believed him to be squared. What the source of his information was I do not know—I should think one of the ladies in the Asquith circle. Redmond's Sunday speech, however, did not bear this out and Balfour reads in it a menace to the Government's existence. On the other hand, Lloyd George last night spoke of the future in a much more confident tone than he or any other minister has done for some time past, and I think it is evident that he believes that the Government have weathered the storm as far as the House of Commons is concerned.

My own inference from all this is that the present difficulty arises from the unwillingness of Redmond to part with the Budget until after the House of Lords has dealt with the Veto resolutions. If the Budget can be kept in the House of Commons until the Veto resolutions were dealt with, one way or another, in the House of Lords, he would apparently be quite content, but it is not easy to see how the Government can arrange their business so as to produce this result. Failing that, Redmond wants a statement from Asquith publicly made in the House of Commons that if the Lords reject the Veto resolutions Asquith will apply to the King to use his prerogative. It seems difficult to believe that Asquith will consent to make any such announcement, though he might be willing to make application to the King. It is thought, however, that a sympathetic person could find and use a form of words that would be sufficient to placate the Irish. But Asquith is not that sympathetic person. Lloyd George would do it, and they would trust him, but Asquith they mistrust and dislike, and it is here that the personal equation of *The Times* correspondent comes in. "They may," he said to me, "be upset by the personal equation; they may be upset by time, but I think that they will come to an arrangement. As to what they will do if the King refuses the guarantees when asked for them," he said, "that is where my head whirls when they try to explain it to me."

I gather from all this that they have not exactly made up their own minds yet what they will do in that most probable eventuality. I think that when they first shortened Supply there can be no doubt that they intended to resign in such an eventuality and that they thought that they could bluff Balfour out of taking office in such a difficult situation. But they are no doubt beginning to realise, as indicated a little time ago in the *Westminster Gazette*, that they might not succeed in bluffing Balfour and that, if he did take office, his position would be enormously strengthened and their own correspondingly weakened. My present view, therefore, is that they will themselves dissolve rather than allow us to come into office and appeal to the country on our own programme.

Balfour called me into consultation about the financial situation with which we should be confronted. He was willing to take office to make the elections, but was not willing to follow what he calls the 1885 precedent and face for months a hostile House of Commons with a Budget and other measures which they might obstruct and manipulate as they pleased. I told him there was no occasion to have a Budget before the election—that all that was required was a new Vote on Account and a Consolidated Fund Bill. I suggested that for this purpose he need not delay long enough even to form his Government if he did not wish to, though I held it to be absolutely necessary that all appointments in the Government should be announced before we went to the electors. After some demur he accepted my reasons on the second point. I observed that if he did not wish to have a series of by-elections, and to delay procedure in the House of Commons until they were finished, he could begin by appointing another Lord of the Treasury besides himself—they two would appoint a Patronage Financial Secretary of the Treasury, who might or might not be the man permanently intended for the office, and the Financial Secretary should at once move in the House of Commons the Vote on Account with money for Old Age Pensions in the forefront of it.

He suggested that if the Radicals wished to make trouble they might obstruct or even refuse this Supply. I said that in that case I believed it would give him the opportunity of playing the part of the younger Pitt with credit to himself and with great effect upon the country, and that if the Radicals refused Supply we should be in a state of revolution. We must be prepared to act in defiance of the law and cut our way through to the electors. How this was to be done I did not know and did not think that anybody could say definitely until we were in a position to go into the offices, see what power we could exert, and what action the Comptroller and Auditor-General—who is the real difficulty—would take. But there must be some way of preventing government being brought to a standstill and we must find that way and take it whatever the risks.

I gave my father's quotation, "*de l'audace, de l'audace, et toujours de l'audace*"—which by the way is from Danton, not Mirabeau. As I say I do not believe that the situation here contemplated will arise; in the first place because I believe the Government will not resign, and in the second place because I believe they would not dare to refuse Supply if they did resign. But if I am proved wrong and the crisis does take this shape I believe that Balfour will be ready to assume all necessary responsibility.

*7th April* 1910.

I have had a very busy week-end and still find myself both pressed for time and oppressed by the thought that I have to speak at Southport on Saturday. Why, why did I undertake that task?

I am rather pleased with my own performances in the House during the last two days. On Tuesday Asquith moved his guillotine motion on the House of Lords Resolutions. He was followed by Balfour, and then the debate got very thin and looked as though it would peter out. However, I arranged a little diversion with George Wyndham, and by the simple expedient of demanding to know from Winston, who was in charge of the Government case, whether they intended to proceed with the discussion of the Bill in our House, succeeded in giving a new turn to the debate and putting vigorous life into a moribund discussion. George Wyndham followed Winston, who was thought by his friends to have been very indiscreet. In my own opinion, however, he gave the only answer that could be given and did as well as it was possible for him to do in the circumstances, but the Government had the appearance of being in a mess. They had to fetch Asquith to explain while we brought in Balfour to follow up Asquith's explanation and dot the i's and cross the t's.

The gist of the whole discussion was—"You, Asquith, say that you have no compunction in limiting the debate on the Resolutions because the Resolutions really commit the House to nothing, and the House will have ample opportunity of discussing the Bill. But, in fact, you do not intend that the House should discuss the Bill at all, and whilst proclaiming in the House that the Resolutions are little more than a formality you intend to use them outside the House as the deliberate and settled expression of the people's will. You cannot have it both ways. You have destroyed the force of your Resolutions, and when you take them to the House of Lords or to the Throne those high authorities are entitled by what you have said to regard them as of no authority."

It was a useful debate from the point of view of future discussions in the House of Lords, though of course points of this kind do not touch the electorate.

Yesterday Haldane moved the first of the Resolutions. I followed him in an impromptu speech in the course of which I succeeded in making Haldane and Asquith very angry and came into sharp conflict with both of them. The fact of the matter is that I feel such a profound contempt for Haldane as a politician that I am unable to speak of him without showing it. He was very ineffective and discursive as usual, and the result was that I was almost equally discursive in my attempt to follow him. I spoke far too long and missed the *beau moment* for sitting down, and felt when I did sit down, that I had not been altogether successful. I was rather pleased, however, when I heard congratulations from unexpected sources. The first was Keir Hardie, who, passing me in the lobby, said he thought it the best thing I had done; and the second came from Bowles, of all people. Bowles said to Bonar Law, "What a good speech Austen made. I had no idea he could speak as well," and Bonar Law in repeating this to me said, "I saw when you sat down that you were not satisfied with yourself, so you may like to hear what Bowles said. It marks the advance you have made in the four years that he was out of Parliament!"

The most amusing feature of the debate was Lloyd George's face whilst Haldane rolled out his interminable washy flood of small talk. Lloyd George, as we caught his eye, clearly expressed his contempt for the performance. He shrugged his shoulders and turned up his eyes as though to say, "What are you to do with a fellow like this—did you ever hear such foolish nonsense?" It was curious too to observe that Haldane had got the whole of his concluding observations typewritten, and read them without shame from the manuscript. This is becoming the common practice of ministers.

In the evening we had a first-rate Tariff Reform debate—only four speeches, for both the mover and seconder of the T.R. motion occupied a long time. The latter was Sam Storey; and the old man really got home this time both on the Liberals and the Labour Party. It was a fine sight to see him with his long beard and venerable aspect thrusting right through the enemy's defences. Radicals and Labour men could not conceal their dismay and irritation. It was a good night's work finely done.

You should read the speech, and if Father feels moved to send a line of congratulation to Storey, old Sam will be gratified.

I think I told you that Balfour consulted me about the financial situation in which we should be placed if we came in. Yesterday I saw Beach at the Bank, and he expressed a very strong opinion that if the Government resigned, "Balfour must take office—no other course was possible for him." This is curious as Beach is not generally in favour of strong action.

While I was talking with Balfour, Lansdowne came in to consider what line he should take on Denbigh's motion in the House of Lords about beet-sugar growing. Balfour is quite prepared to give it protection if good quality sugar beet can be grown in this country, but he has some doubt on this question.

Bonar Law and I, on the other hand, attach great importance to it as one of the most important Tariff Reforms from the agricultural point of view. I think there is no doubt that good beet can be grown here with at least as high a percentage of sugar as they obtain in Germany. I have not had time to read Lansdowne's speech but I hope and believe that it will have been very sympathetic.

In the course of our little discussion I was led to say: "You know I do want to give some protection to British agriculture," on which Balfour interjected, "My dear Austen, you will be obliged to whether you want to or not. The fiscal needs of the Treasury are so great that you cannot avoid it. It is all very lamentable but it cannot be helped"—an observation in which Salisbury, who had joined us, agreed.

We then discussed the Scottish situation in view of a deputation which Balfour was to receive next day, composed of Scottish members and candidates. Incidentally, Lansdowne told a story which amused me, as it would anyone who remembers Charles Parker. We were talking of the kind of candidate that Scottish constituencies like. "Some time ago," said Lansdowne, "a very good Unionist candidate had been beaten in Aberdeenshire, and I was talking with a gillie up there and was asking him the reason for the defeat. 'We did not like the man,' said the gillie. 'Well, what sort of man do you like?' asked Lansdowne. 'Ah!' he said, 'we liked Mr. Parker, there was a sparkle about him!'"

The deputation was interesting and useful. We did no more than listen to their views and ask a few questions, but they were not as downcast as I had been led to believe. Lords and landlords used as practically synonymous terms had been their great difficulty. Reform of the House of Lords and a definite programme of land reform, both in rural and urban districts, were their chief *desiderata*. Tariff Reform, they said, helped and did not hinder them, or as one of them put it, "There are more Tariff Reformers in Scotland than there are Unionists."

The future still remains very obscure, but there is a widespread conviction that the Irish are squared and that no accident will happen to the Government in our House. If this is so, I think we shall get our spring recess after all, though it will come a little later than was expected. I am now very hopeful that at, or before, the end of the month Ivy and I will be able to join you at Cannes. Unless my presence is imperatively required here I shall think myself justified in leaving a few days before the Parliamentary recess, or in other words as soon as possible after the Veto Resolutions are disposed of.

*11th April* 1910.

Nine days since I wrote to you with my own hand! Such a thing has not happened in all our diary correspondence and I feel quite ashamed of myself. And now I have really nothing to talk about. Rumour continues to fill the air; but as rumour has launched every conceivable hypothesis in turn, even she can now provide us with nothing new. No actual bargain has been struck with the Irish, and Irish, Labour members and not a few Radicals still hanker for "Guarantees." If Asquith hasn't got them and won't ask for them now, will he tell the King that the dissolution must be on this point and that if he again has a majority he will *then* ask the King for the guarantees? And will he state in the House, before the Budget leaves it, that this will be his policy? If so, writes "Tay Pay"[1] in *Reynolds'*, all will be well; the King will be kept out of the controversy and the Tories will not be able to pose as the protectors of the Throne—a contingency which he evidently feels would be very dangerous for the Radical Party.

"Tay Pay" also suggests that when the Lords reject the resolutions, Asquith's first step will be to resign, Balfour will probably refuse to form a Government and then Asquith will have this conversation with the King. I wish we could spread that belief that Balfour will "funk." He won't when the time comes; but if the Government believed that he would, it would obviously be to their advantage to show that he could not form a Government and go to the country saying:

"We are the only possible Government. Support to Balfour means a continuation of confusion. We, and we alone, can settle this controversy and give the weary elector rest from elections."

I wish I saw how to tempt them into this trap!

Yes, last Wednesday's speech in the House of Commons *was*

[1] The late T. P. O'Connor.

247

fluffy, but it was real debating, for my only notes were words of Haldane's taken down as he spoke. But it had a greater success than I thought at the time and I have received many congratulations on it. A. J. B. told me next day that several of the Party had spoken to him in its praise and he was himself very cordial about it. The fact is they liked the attack on Haldane. What a fool he was to wriggle so! If only he had sat still and held his tongue, there would have seemed nothing in it—and there wasn't much except for his obvious discomfiture.

Oh! I must be off at once to my Bank and then to lunch with Lansdowne to discuss the House of Lords by his request.

Please tell Father how much I appreciate his praise and encouragement—but he knows it.

*12th April* 1910.

There was an unexpected Cabinet hastily summoned at 12.30 yesterday morning. What it was about I don't know, but Winston and Lloyd George looked very glum when they came into the House, and Crewe and Carrington were met in the Park "looking as if Crewe was breaking to Carrington the news of the death of his nearest relation." Such are the joys of office and the resplendent position of His Majesty's Government! Well, if we ate dirt during our last year, as alas! we did, the Government are having a full meal of it now.

You will have seen in the papers O'Brien's revelations and Lloyd George's anxiously worded rejoinder. We have decided not to touch the matter till O'Brien and Ll. G. have made their statements in the House. One cannot trust either man, but O'Brien's latest declaration seems to confirm the rumour which I reported some days ago that Ll. G. was ready to bargain but that the Cabinet rejected the terms offered. Arthur Balfour still believes that the crash will come next Monday on the guillotine motion on the Budget, but I do not take that view. If there is a breach at all, which I still think unlikely, it will not come till the last moment, say on the Third Reading of the Budget. At least that is my opinion.

We had an interesting gathering at the House of Commons yesterday when the four working men who stood as Unionists at the last Election gave an account of the visit they have since paid to Germany. They were all enormously impressed by the prosperity and well-being of the German workmen. One of them told how he was wearing a "Chamberlain button."

"Is that Chamberlain?" asked one of the German working men whom they met. "Very good man England—no good Germany!"

More of these visits are being arranged.

We went down to Southport on Saturday—a long and tedious journey. I made my notes in the train and you will have seen my speech in *The Times*. Ivy said it was quite satisfactory but I took too long over the first part and had not time enough for Tariff Reform and the cotton trade. I found the meeting a little heavy—partly because I was depressed by a cold and sore throat which I have kept down but not cured with the usual remedies—partly also the fault of the meeting itself. Still it was a very good meeting, but too middle-class.

I lunched with Lansdowne and Lady L. yesterday at his request to discuss the House of Lords position. But he would not say a word while Lady L. was in the room! and we had not much time to ourselves afterwards. He is very averse to any element of election and much troubled by it. I fear that things have gone so far that nothing short of the admission of *some* elected element will do any good, and if the Lords now reject all idea of it, it will be worse than if they had never touched the question of reform at all. Lansdowne desires effective conferences between the two Houses in case of differences, such as were held in the seventeenth century—and in this I agree with him—the Referendum, to which I am rather averse, and a large infusion of men nominated by the Prime Minister for the duration of a Parliament.

I do not see how to work the Referendum so as to decide on the real issues ordinarily in dispute between the two Houses, *i.e.* not for or against a Bill but for or against a whole series of amendments on which the Lords insist and which the Commons refuse to accept. And apart from this objection to it, I fear we should not get people to vote. A Referendum once a year— a kind of General Election without candidates—would disgust all but the most hardened politicians with political contests and weary the whole country, but our part of the country would, I fear, be wearied first. For working a Referendum we have no organisation on our side equal to the Chapel organisation on the other.

I had other objections to urge against allowing the P.M. to nominate any large proportion for a Parliament. This only repeats in the House of Lords exactly the same impulse at exactly the same moment as has formed the House of Commons and is to my mind far less conservative in the broad sense than election say of one-third of the House by County Councils for twelve or fifteen years, one-third retiring every fourth or fifth year. They would reflect the permanent or prolonged movement of public opinion but would not be subject to the same momentary gusts that deflect the House of Commons.

This is badly put and I don't know whether you will be able to discern my meaning, but I must be off to the House.

*12th April* 1910.

11.30 p.m. Just back from the House of Commons where at 10 o'clock I made a short debating speech on an amendment excluding from the Government resolution bills dealing with the composition or functions of the House of Lords. It went off very well and I may score up another success to my credit. Don't think me vain. I write to you as I shouldn't to anyone but the family, and I know that you like to hear all that concerns me. I was much cheered by my own party, felt I had fairly got the attention and interest of other parties and was warmly congratulated by friends afterwards. It all means greater freedom and ease in the House and greater readiness in debate.

Even *The Times* report does not give any idea of the speech. It is too condensed so that part of the argument and all the life have gone out of it.

It was rather amusing that I was chaffing with Ivy and Mrs. Clive at dinner, for which I came home. Mrs. C. had got tickets for the gallery, and Ivy and she had arranged to go down together. I tried to dissuade them. The interest of the debate had passed with the afternoon. Now we were on an amendment, no one would make a speech of interest. They had much better stay quietly at home and discuss children and chiffons, etc. etc. However they insisted on coming and as we drove down I said: "Now I shall have to behave like Flavin." You remember when Flavin was asked one night why he made a speech which both he and others had already made several times, he replied, "Sure, mightn't a man have his girl in the gallery?" And I dare say that my speech lost nothing owing to Ivy's presence in the gallery!

Rumours of the Government coming to smash on Monday are growing in force. A. J. B. said that putting together what Winston said at the close of his speech this afternoon with what he heard from other sources, he thought that they now expected defeat. If so, good-bye to all idea of a holiday! I don't feel certain that they have not got themselves into real difficulty through their negotiations with O'Brien, and I shouldn't wonder if Lloyd George were in trouble with the Cabinet for indiscretions. All their tempers are a little strained.

> HOUSE OF COMMONS,
> *13th April* 1910.

3.30 p.m. For what it is worth!

Croall of the *Scotsman* tells me that Haldane told him yesterday that the Government would be beaten on Monday. The Irish don't care a d—— about the Budget, but they make demands for pledges or guarantees which the Government won't give, said Haldane.

I still disbelieve in the revolt or breach being carried to the length of voting against the Government.

> *Copy of telegram, dated 15th April* 1910.

Government have given way to Irish about guarantees Budget will pass unaltered Hope start for Cannes Thursday 28

> AUSTEN.

> 9 EGERTON PLACE, S.W.,
> *15th April* 1910.

So we shall get a holiday after all! I'm not sure that this is not the thought that was uppermost in my mind yesterday as it became quite evident that the Irish had been squared. The idea of going through another election without any rest or "let up" whatever filled me with horror, and the thought of a holiday consoles me for all disappointments. Indeed I don't think I am disappointed, for, as I believe my letters to you would show, I have long held that the Government would come to terms with the Irish, though I confess that Asquith's surrender was more complete than I expected. Fancy the impudence of trying to make such a statement in the last ten minutes before the guillotine was to fall when not one word of comment would have been allowed to the Opposition! Certainly Balfour's criticism was not a whit too strong. Asquith has lost his last rag of character and stands naked, but I hope not altogether unashamed, at the bidding of his Irish taskmasters. He seemed very nervous; the whole House was excited and electrical and ministers were all fidgety and restless.

*17th April* 1910.

I am glad you thought well of the Southport speech. I was busy all Friday morning—letters, visit to the Bank, etc.—tired all Friday afternoon, and had to dine at Lansdowne's (very pleasant, only I was *very* tired) and attend the Speaker's levée in the evening. So my notes for the speech were only made in the train. We arrived at our host's at six and the meeting was at seven, and we had had a journey of five and a half hours, so it is no wonder that I was not proud of my performance and felt some anxiety when I found that *The Times* had chosen this occasion to give me a verbatim report. Well, I really believe that the more I "let myself go" the better I do; and since I have to speak so much, that is a satisfactory conclusion at which to arrive.

Ida endorsed on her envelope that you had got my telegram. I have been feeling very flat since, for the fight is over for the time. The Government can have what Budget they will, and I imagine from the terms of their guillotine resolution that it is the old one altered only in respect of dates, where necessary. If that is so, the terms of the guillotine make discussion a sham, and the ten days we have still to pass before the holiday will be a weary waste of good time; but I must see it out. But I can think of nothing but the holiday and the pleasure of basking in Cannes sunshine amidst Cannes flowers.

A curious episode: last Friday week Burns rose as soon as Asquith sat down after speaking in the Poor Law discussion. Everyone was surprised at this unusual arrangement of ministerial speeches, especially as Asquith had fairly covered the departmental ground, giving the departmental statistics, etc.

"But no one," said Asquith to Balfour subsequently, "was more amazed than I was. Burns hadn't said a word to me about it!" What a Cabinet!

Balfour's letter on Colonial wheat and on beet-sugar growing is satisfactory, I think. The draft was submitted to Bonar Law and me, and we made one or two verbal alterations. But the substance was right in the original. It was pleasant to see him in his speech to the United Club (or was it the 1900 Club?) dwelling on the necessity for taking the aggressive with Tariff Reform. What an ass Rosebery is! Does he really believe we could win without Tariff Reform? It would be better if he *would* consult someone of common sense before he wrote letters to *The Times* instead of boasting that he had consulted no one. I bet he had had a letter or other urgent plea from Harold Cox, for Cox sent a message to me in exactly the same sense. Lord save us from Superior Persons!

Collings invited the Party to meet him in one of the Committee rooms last Thursday to discuss our Land policy and, as he said, to find out where we stand. I had a brilliant idea and carried Balfour up to the meeting. B. made a useful speech, so did Pretyman, and I also spoke at Collings's request. Altogether it went off very well. I hope Collings was pleased and I think he was, and in any case we did away with all idea of a split, and the Party, which was getting very uncomfortable, is happy again. A good afternoon's work!

*18th April* 1910.

I have of course no more political news to give you. All the Radical papers say "Splendid" to Mr. Asquith's declaration and all our papers cry "Shame." What I wonder do the masses think?

And do they think about it at all? Not much, I expect. I shall have a tedious week of close sitting at the House, I suppose. All the papers seem to expect excitement today, but I expect it will fizzle. O'Brien, if he speaks, is nearly sure to tell his story badly. I see the Government are all swearing assiduously that there has been no bargain. Methinks they do protest too much. After all a nod is as good as a wink in such cases.

I am still astonished at the completeness and abjectness of Asquith's surrender, for I am convinced that Redmond would not have voted against him. He has eaten unnecessary dirt. I suppose the appetite grows!

We were to have dined at the Onslows' tonight. Now Ivy goes alone as I feel I must keep myself free for the H. of C. After working so hard at the Budget last year, I must see the end of the struggle through, but, good Lord! I'm sick of it.

*18th April* 1910.

Things today passed off very much as I expected. O'Brien was prolix, ineffective and unconvincing. I think Lloyd George had the best of it, but he might easily have done much better. Tim Healy made a brilliant speech in his best form. He has done nothing as good for many years. His attack on Redmond was extraordinarily bitter. Asquith was very sensitive and touchy; I should think it is time that he too had a holiday. The House was excitable and apt to be noisy, but when all is said and done there is little wool and much cry.

I dined at Grillions—nothing special to record of the dinner, but Asquith, who was there, said he hoped our holiday would be a full month. In that hope at any rate I cordially concur.

Balfour is convinced that the Government mean, at their own time and at some moment when the Treasury is bare of spending power, to go to the King and demand the creation of Peers on the ground that it is then clear that the Lords will not pass the Veto resolutions. Assuming the King refused, Balfour is confident that they will then demand a dissolution.

"I imagine that the King would refuse if he did the proper constitutional thing (but I don't know whether he will, for I don't know what nerve he has) on the ground that he could not at once dissolve so new a Parliament, and the Government would resign! Then he would, I suppose, send for me, but they count on my being unable to accept because of the financial difficulty and they expect that they could then go back to the King and say, 'You see that we are the only possible Government. Now we must have the guarantees.'"

Balfour proposes to go into the legal position with Finlay [1] and me to see how far we could defy a hostile House of Commons, and what are the legal difficulties and how they could be overcome.

*19th April* 1910.

I do not feel quite certain that I have got Balfour's ideas quite correctly. Our conversation was interrupted. I must renew it at some favourable moment.

*20th April* 1910.

Another good speech from Steel-Maitland yesterday—remarkably good in fact—but a dull day on the whole. I took the opportunity to have a long talk with Balfour in the evening.

He began by saying that Lansdowne wanted another meeting of leaders to consider the further action of the Lords. He had told L. to choose his own Peers and to summon me. Need he summon anyone else from the Commons? Very flattering, but I thought he had better summon the lot! Long never occupied much time and would be furious if he were left out. Akers-Douglas would say nothing unless directly asked his opinion, and then it would be worth having on the electoral aspect of any question. The only person who was apt to take up much time was Wyndham, and I must confess that the trouble with him was that when he had done I never knew what he meant. He agreed: "Our dear George" was apt to monopolise any topic and "monologue" on it. And he was obscure.

"I wonder why. For one thing he talks in metaphors. I believe it's his natural way of talking, but it's a great bore for a person with a non-literary mind like mine. I had him for an hour this

---

[1] Afterwards Lord Chancellor.

afternoon, but by dint of cross-questioning him, I think I got out of him what he did mean. He thinks he has some reason for believing—and I really think he has some—that Asquith now means to have a January election. But I am leading you away from what you wanted to talk about?"

"No," said I, "you are bringing me to it. One of the things I wanted to speak of was our conversation on our way to Grillions. You said something about the King's nerve; you weren't sure whether he had nerve for it."

"Yes, I hear he's ill and very cross."

"Well, did that apply to his possible refusal to create Peers or to give Asquith a dissolution?"

"Oh! to the creation of Peers."

You will see on reference to my letter that I wrote the conversation correctly in the first instance and then altered it into incorrectness. This was because it seemed to me that it was a much stronger thing to refuse Asquith a dissolution than to refuse him the right to nominate 500 Peers. However, Balfour went on:

"My idea is that at some moment when recourse to the H. of Commons for fresh financial powers is urgent A. will go to the King and say, 'It is now evident that the Lords will not pass the Veto resolutions or Bill. Much the best thing is that you should authorise the announcement that you are ready to create whatever number of Peers is required. There would then be no revolution. Everything would be settled quietly. The Throne would not be brought in question. But if you do not wish to do that, then I ask for a dissolution now or in January.'"

If the King refused, Asquith would resign, feeling sure that Balfour *could* not take office in such a financial situation and in a hostile House of Commons. Balfour after a day or two of enquiry etc. would be obliged to return his commission into the King's hands. A. would be sent for again and would be able to dictate terms. "Your Majesty must now see," he would say, "that we are the only possible Government. We now advise and require the creation of Peers."

Such was Balfour's idea of Asquith's present plans. It was, however, complicated by what he had heard from Wyndham of a January dissolution and by his idea that all parties would like to defer another election as long as possible, and the Government and Asquith especially.

"It would give him another six months' office and he likes office."

Asquith might therefore delay the crisis or the dissolution or both.

I pointed out that if Asquith tried to delay the crisis, the Lords could always force it and, if necessary, they must be urged to do so. Further that the delay of the dissolution was an impossible project. The Government would have to announce their intentions as soon as the crisis arose. If they announced in June that they intended to dissolve in January, that would mean a General Election lasting over six months—a preposterous idea. No one would stand it, and the Government Party least of all could afford it. We could make their situation intolerable. They would have to produce another Budget. The Irish whisky grievance would come up again. We could make it so hot in their constituencies that the Government supporters *would* not stay in London, and we could disperse our men over the country with an arrangement to recall them by telegraph at any moment if we needed them. The Government could not live under such conditions.

"Yes," he said, "I think that is so, but you said you thought the Government had intended to resign at one time, but had now decided not to do so. Why?"

"Well," I replied, "they must have contemplated resignation or they would not have formulated the policy of Short Supply. But I think they have given it up, partly because of an allusion in the *Westminster Gazette* some time ago—and the *Westminster Gazette* is generally well-informed—but more, I suppose, because I am so convinced that their resignation and your taking office would be to our advantage and their disadvantage, that I feel that they must be convinced of it too. If only they could be persuaded that you would not take office! Ah! then they might try it."

Balfour then said that of course he would only take office for the purpose of dissolving with as little delay as possible. What financial measures would be necessary? The natural thing would be to tell the King that he could only take office if he had Asquith's

promise to facilitate these, but as it would be A.'s policy to refuse
any assistance, he was not sure that it would be wise to ask for it
and to expose himself to a rebuff. He was quite ready to take office
if he could carry the thing through. But could we? Suppose
we wanted a loan. Natty,[1] who was always sanguine and who
thought our success certain, had told him he could get a loan
from the City easily. But could we? Not if the City saw the
thing as he saw it or conceived of Asquith returning with a majority
and making the kind of speech which he would make if he were
then Prime Minister.

"Here are big financial houses in the City—Tories themselves—
who have aided and abetted a Tory Ministry to defy the House
of Commons and to act in contravention of the will of the House
and the people. They have knowingly and willingly helped a
Ministry, which did not possess the confidence of the House, to
defy that House and to break through all the legal restraints which
Parliament had established to prevent this very thing happening.
They must take the consequences. Their loan to the Government
was in fact a loan to the Tory Party. The public credit was not
and could not be pledged. We refuse to honour Tory bills issued
in despite of the House of Commons and of every parliamentary
safeguard and security."

So Asquith might speak, and if this idea occurred to the City,
they would not give us a loan without parliamentary sanction.

I told him that I did not believe, for reasons which I gave
(though I admitted that I might be wrong), that we should want
a big loan. We might need to borrow a million or two, but
*that* the Bank of England would be bound to give us and Asquith
could not refuse to recognise a loan from this Bank as he might
refuse to recognise borrowings from Rothschilds and other City
Houses. I believed that the only difficulty would be in getting
over the penalties connected with the issue of money and especially
the need for the assent of the Comptroller and Auditor-General.

"Oh, if that's all," said Balfour, "I don't mind that. I don't
regard that as nearly so serious."

"Besides," said I, "I have already got public acknowledgment
from the Government (1) that they have exercised a dispensing

[1] Lord Rothschild.

power in the collection of taxes, and (2) that they have spent money in excess of their parliamentary authority."

"Yes, that is very important."

Finlay is to look into the legal position and ascertain the exact difficulties which have to be overcome.

I again said he must take office if he had the offer, and in fact that is his own view.

"But what then?" he asked. "If we are beaten at the Election, it seems to me that the Constitution is at an end."

"Well," I said, "it doesn't do to look too far ahead when you can't foresee the circumstances. Another election might still be indecisive. Suppose the Government again returned but only by a decreased majority—80, 50, 30 instead of 120. That would not justify a revolution. If I were consulted by the King, which of course I should not be, I should say in such circumstances, 'Your Majesty must still refuse Asquith's demands. Send for Balfour again. He must again take office and, if necessary, make a fresh appeal to the country.' Don't say anything which would suggest that another election, if adverse, puts us out of court and settles the case."

"No, no, of course I won't say anything of the kind."

Then I called his attention to Keir Hardie's speech (*Times* of Monday).

"On Thursday Asquith steps aside and uncovers the Throne. On Saturday Keir Hardie says that if there are any 'obscurantist tendencies on the part either of the House of Lords or the Throne' both will be swept aside. That is the first result of Asquith's betrayal of his trust—of his exposure of the Crown which it was his special duty to guard."

"Oh!" said B. "I think there's a good deal to be said about that and by a curious coincidence I am speaking on Wednesday."

"So it seems to me," I replied, "a great deal to be said both for Biarritz [1] and for the country. It may affect the King's action when the crisis comes if he sees that Asquith is not protecting him. And remember, as Henley said, they will have to fight not only the Tory Party but the most popular man in the Kingdom, namely the King himself."

[1] Where the King was taking a short holiday.

*21st April* 1910.

I saw Tim Healy a couple of days ago in the lobby.

"Your speech," said I, "apart from its matter, gave infinite pleasure to the House. I have never heard you in better form."

"You're very kind," said Healy, and I was passing on when he called, "Mr. Chamberlain, tell me, how is your father?"

I answered and he added, "I've often thought of writing to him, but I feared that from a political opponent it might not be acceptable. But will you tell him that I often think of him, and tell him, Mr. Chamberlain, never unkindly—*never* unkindly."

This was said with obvious sincerity and genuine feeling. What a queer man he is!

How have I spent the day? Well, called (but didn't answer) at 8.30. Coffee and Joe at 9.0. Mr. Wilson at 10.30. Mr. Jenkins at 11.0. Meeting at Lansdowne House 12–1.30. Lunch with Wyndham. Boraston wedding at 2.30 and reception afterwards. Then visit to tailor, and home at 4.0 to see Mr. McVittie of Edinburgh who asked for an interview through Boraston. He came to urge me to put forward my own programme. My practical mind combined with Balfour's philosophical intellect was a most powerful combination but—well you could have too much philosophy and too little practical good sense, and wouldn't I do for the Party what Father used to do? and so on till five.

Five till six Joe and tea. In the House they are discussing "an ass named Anderson" as Healy said the other day, and I haven't been near the place. There is no reason why we should defend Anderson who acted with doubtful propriety in 1896 or 7 and blabs about it now out of mere vanity and folly. He deserves any punishment he gets and it will be a good lesson for the Civil Service. My sympathies are not with him.

Six till seven read. Seven till seven-thirty slept. Eight dined with Ivy quietly—the first time this week. Then walked about the drawing-room admiring all our things—our cabinets, our china, our pictures, our flowers.

Now (11 o'clock), to bed—and nothing to do till Monday!

The Lansdowne House meeting led to a rather rambling discussion on nothing in particular, but it appeared that the House of Lords had better *brusquer le dénouement* rather than delay it.

*22nd April* 1910.

We were to have dined with the Willoughby de Eresbys yesterday but she was ill and the dinner was put off, so we went to the Repertory Theatre to see Irene Vanbrugh in *Trelawny of the Wells*, nothing very special but a pleasant piece of acting in quaint early Victorian costumes—crinolines and chignons. Then on to the Salisburys' evening party, but found it nearly over—the guests who were asked for 10.30 having begun to arrive at 9.40—so pleasant for the hostess! B'ham never treated you as badly as that.

Balfour, who was even later than we were, seized me for a moment to say:

"I must talk to you again. I don't think that you are right about the Government's intentions."

I take this to mean that he thinks he has got confirmation of the rumour that they intend to resign when beaten in the Lords and not to dissolve. But it may mean that they do intend to defer the dissolution till January. I shall hear fully on Monday, I suppose.

I am to see him on Monday morning about the Budget debate that afternoon. He wishes to direct it to the Licensing Clauses.

"Newton and Whitbread are coming to me at 12.50. Can you come too? They tell me it means absolute ruin."

So I expect it does, to the London Breweries at least. I had not meant to speak but this may oblige me to do so, for Pretyman, whom I had told off for the job, would speak on land, but not licences.

A. J. B. has taken to sending me his letters and asking what answer he is to give whenever any question of finance or tariff arises—horse corn, Colonial sugar, beet sugar, wheat and so on— I advise on all.

"It will be your business," he said to me the other day when talking of the financial measures we should have to take.

*24th April* 1910.

I have just been reading Gathorne Hardy's Life by his son— well done almost entirely from the daily diary which G. H. kept all his life. But it would be much more interesting if his idea of what was due to Cabinet secrecy had allowed him to write more freely. There is a curious letter of Lord Salisbury's written to G. H. just *after* the 1900 election.

"I am not sure that the omens are favourable. The phenomenon is without example that a party should twice dissolve, at an interval of five years, and in each case bring back a majority of more than 130. What does it mean? I hope the causes are accidental and temporary. But it may mean that Reform Bills, digging down deeper and deeper into the population, have come upon a layer of pure combativeness. If this is the case I am afraid the country has evil times before it. Of course I recognise the justice of the verdict the country has just given; but that the love of justice should have overborne the great law of the pendulum, I confess, puzzles and bewilders me."

A very curious letter, not very easy to decipher—perhaps only the result of his own growing weariness and detachment.

By the way, this reminds me that as I drove back from Grillions the other night with Balfour and Midleton, B. was talking of Cabinets and Cabinet difficulties.

"You were extraordinarily fortunate, Austen. The Cabinet you sat in was the pleasantest I have ever known. All the others were always quarrelling," he said.

Midleton demurred and as we walked upstairs I heard B. referring to Beach's conduct as justifying what he had said.

"I always regret," I said, "that when Salisbury resigned and you became Prime Minister my father was in London and not in Birmingham. You know he was laid up in bed owing to a cab accident and I carried all the news to him from day to day. Now if only he had been at Birmingham, I should have written to him as I do now, and what a page of history my letters would have made. I shall never forget Beach's strange conduct on the morning of the Party meeting at the F.O.—how five minutes before the meeting he said he would not come and how he stalked in, silent and forbidding, just as we were opening the door of the big room to go into the meeting!"

"He was always like that," said Balfour, "always he would and he wouldn't."

Well, he has always been very pleasant to me—except when he once d——d me violently for bringing in a supplementary estimate which he had ordered!—but he is the one man of whom I have ever heard Balfour say a bitter word. And he certainly behaved extraordinarily meanly on that occasion when he first refused Balfour his help, then said he would give it if Balfour pledged himself in your absence in bed to have nothing to do with your ideas of Colonial Preference and, when this was indignantly refused by Balfour whose sense of loyalty was outraged by the suggestion, finally declined to go on in office or even to attend the Party meeting. It was a fitting climax that as we were going in without him he should stalk in without a word to anyone!

*24th April* 1910.

The meeting at Lansdowne House the other day was not very important. L. opened by enquiring what course it was best for the Lords to take: discuss the resolutions or insist on the Bill? press on or delay? negative the Bill or resolutions or refer them together with the Rosebery resolutions and a proposal for joint sessions or conferences and for the Referendum to a Select Committee of the Lords to consider and report.

A desultory conversation followed and there was some difference of opinion both as to our best course and the Government's intentions. Salisbury wanted us to take up the Referendum. Curzon and Alfred Lyttelton opposed. So did Londonderry and I—my ground (apart from the intrinsic difficulties of working the Referendum in cases of conflict between the two Houses—who should state the case, etc.?) being Londonderry's; that the more frequent appeals to the voter, the worse we shall do. He will get bored and slack and will not come to the poll. We should suffer more from this cause than the other side. Many of our people would get tired sooner. The hardened and keen partisan will nearly always vote, but it is just the moderate man who is most slack. He grumbles, but ordinarily doesn't work, and often doesn't vote. We have no organisation that can compare with the Chapels for the purposes of a Referendum. Further I agreed with Bonar Law that this would not help us electorally in the present contest, and with Curzon that we had better not rush into such changes without careful thought and without knowing exactly what we meant.

L. has leanings to it and Selborne and the Cecils are hot for it.

At intervals I made two observations which were supported particularly by Curzon and which I think carried the day.

1. It must be remembered that, when we talked of delay, it was in the power of the Government always to precipitate the crisis at any moment they chose. We were agreed that August would be a fatal date for us (holiday time for the middle classes). If we delayed till then, would not the Government choose that moment to dissolve or force a dissolution? Answer: Quite possibly.

2. If all these questions were referred to a Select Committee of the Lords, what would come of it? Was there any probability that agreement would result—at any rate satisfactory agreement? Answer: None whatever or very little.

Midleton began to talk about what would happen if we were beaten.

"If we only gained 30 or 40 seats, they would still have a majority of 80, and we should be smashed, etc. etc."

I observed, "I wholly protest against M.'s speculations. In the first place, his arithmetic is wrong; the majority against us would be only 60 or 40, but that's of no consequence. What is of consequence is that we should not admit *anything* as final defeat till *after* we have been finally defeated. If the Government, after losing 100 seats on their first appeal, lose 30 or 40 more on their second, *we have won!* They are defeated and we have won. You can't carry a resolution on such a dwindling support. I don't know what the King *would* do, but I know what he *ought* to do in such circumstances. He ought still to refuse to create Peers, let Asquith resign, and send for Balfour again. And Balfour ought to take office again and dissolve again if necessary. It would be the King and Mr. Pitt against a factious coalition."

The meeting smiled pleasantly and kindly at my boyish enthusiasm and we broke up.

"On the whole," said Balfour, "I gather that the general opinion is in favour of bringing things to a head early after the recess."

What a day! and what shall I do next. Like poor Habakkuk I shall soon be rated as "*capable de tout.*"

Ivy went off at 10.30. I wrote till 12.30 and then went to Balfour's to hear the brewers' case. I arrived five minutes late for the appointment but found Balfour closeted with Lansdowne and the brewers waiting. L. was bowed out and the brewers were bowed in. B. could give them exactly five minutes! Happily their representatives could say what they had to say in that time and B. went off to preside at a lunch to workmen returned from Germany, and I to lunch at the Club with Fred Oliver and Morrison. Lansdowne and I were convoked for 3 o'clock in B.'s room at the House to discuss further the action of the House of Lords. We, or rather L. and I, turned up punctually and began. B. arrived in two minutes—much pleased with the lunch ("I liked the men," he said) and we had an animated discussion till 3.43 when I interrupted him to say:

"Look here! who is going to speak on the Budget and when?"

"Well," said B., "I think one of us two must begin and speak before O'Brien moves his amendment; but we've plenty of time to settle that, haven't we?"

"Just two minutes," said I; "in two minutes one of us must be on his legs."

"Well, you do it!" replied B.

There was no time to argue. I just scurried off. If B. *has* a fault as a H. of C. leader, it is his inability to conceive that everyone's wits are not as nimble as his own!

I was respited for 10 minutes by a division, but seized in the lobby by a provincial brewer who disapproved the policy advocated by the London brewer at one o'clock, disputed the latter's conclusions and had a policy of his own which he wished me to foreshadow though he admitted the trade were not agreed about it— all of which of course made things easier!

And then I was on my legs speaking—without a note and without an idea except such as came to me as I went along. And between ourselves, it was a great success. Words as well as ideas came easily and I was well satisfied when I sat down after 30 or 35 minutes. After all there is nothing like practice. Not in vain did

I make 300 (or was it 400?) speeches last year and in increase of ease and command I have the reward of my labours—in that and in Father's approval and praise, dearest to me of all commendation.

I had many congratulations. I will quote one. As I was leaving the House tonight Bonar Law said to me: "I do not often think when Balfour winds up a debate that anyone else could do better. But between your speech today and his there was no comparison. Yours couldn't have been better and his—in the main—was not effective." Balfour can afford to admit a failure and I am not yet *blasé* about success!

A pleasant dinner at Grillions and a poor speech from Lloyd George completed the day. Now it is bedtime even for a bachelor.

*Tuesday:*

Lansdowne had got the idea that the gathering at L. House wished him to press for the Bill instead of the Resolutions, but on reflection that course did not commend itself to him. I had not so understood our decision, if decision it could be called. Anyway we decided against it now unless circumstances change. A. J. B. said: "Of course the air is full of all manner of rumours, but I think you must take it now that the Government do not mean to follow your course, Austen (*i.e.* to dissolve). They will resign, trusting that they have made it impossible for anyone else to carry on Government."

We discussed possibilities. B. had asked Milner, as an old Treasury man, to look into the matter; but as far as B. could learn, every penny raised must go into the Exchequer and once there could not be got out without a certificate from the Comptroller and Auditor-General and he could not be removed except on address by both Houses.

"Then," said I, "you could only send a corporal and file of soldiers to turn him out and put someone else in possession."

"Yes, I suppose we might do that!" said B.

He was inclined to take office even if we were to be beaten and unable to carry on.

*Death of King Edward VII*

9 EGERTON PLACE, S.W.,
*11th May* 1910.

The House met today, but the Speaker is not yet home, so I was unable to get an answer to Father's question. I must either call upon him after his return or else write to him and in any case I will let you know the result.

I wired to you as soon as Asquith announced his intentions. The House is to adjourn till 8th June. Ivy and I have settled to go motoring in France with Leverton from 22nd May to 11th June or 12th unless anything unexpected happens to alter our plans. We shall probably go to Boulogne, work down to the Loire and return by Brittany and Normandy. At any rate our operations will be within these limits.

The speaking in the House today was good. Asquith, Balfour and Enoch Edwards (Hanley, Labour) were all good. They spoke with evident feeling and sincerity. I thought Balfour's references to the growing importance of the Crown as the link of Empire well and usefully said. He too put the King's real part in Foreign Policy well and impressively. Asquith spoke with much feeling—almost too much; his tears come too easily—and the whole showed the House of Commons at its high level.

The address in reply was ordered to be presented to His Majesty by the M.P.s who are Privy Councillors. None of us could remember that this was formally carried out last time; but after some hesitation we were told that there ought to be five or six Privy Councillors from each side, and four of us who were talking with Balfour at the time accompanied him to Marlborough House. Asquith handed the King the address voted by the House; the King took it and then shook hands with each of us. He said a

267

word on business to Asquith and Harcourt, and as he shook hands with me, asked after Father. To the others he did not speak and left the room again at once.

By the way it would be proper and would be liked if you or Father would write to the Queen Mother. I have enquired and am told that I certainly should do so.

The Government have as yet decided nothing and are all at sixes and sevens. Balfour was given three dates for the resumption of business within the last twelve hours and all on authority from the Government. Winston is for pressing the fight at once. Crewe and others are for delay and perhaps an autumn session. Lloyd George talks as if he were not averse from compromise. For the present there is nothing for us to do but "wait and see."

*12th May* 1910.

I forgot to tell you that I found on my arrival a very nice letter from Mr. Wilson, saying that he had been expecting a telegram to recall him, that he would think it no hardship to interrupt his holiday if I needed help and offering to meet my convenience in every way. I have thanked him but there is no need to call him back, for everything is at a standstill. I had only one letter this morning.

I see no sign in the Liberal Press of the Government desiring or attempting any compromise on the constitutional question. Everything seems to point to a summer session for the necessary business consequent on the demise of the Crown, with a new Budget and Supply, and then an adjournment to the autumn when the Veto resolutions would be taken up again, with a probable election in January.

I send you one of the curious old-fashioned notices sent out to the provincial cities in regard to the proclamation of King George as Sovereign. The old wording is quaint and like so many of these ceremonies carries one's thoughts back into the centuries that are past.

*12th May* 1910.

I have just come back from the Palace. I sent my letter to the Queen Mother by hand this morning and at 5 o'clock received a telephone message that the Queen would receive me at Buckingham Palace between six and seven (of course I had not asked to be received). I accordingly went there at six and after waiting for a quarter of an hour was shown upstairs, conducted by a nurse through a dressing-room or sitting-room to a door beyond, which she opened and motioned me to pass through. The centre of the room was hidden by a screen round which the Queen came, and taking my hand she led me up to the open coffin in which the late King was lying.

"Thank you so much," she said, "for your kind letter. I thought you would like to see him again. He looks so peaceful. Tell your Father. I know he will feel it so much."

I replied suitably, and she said again :

"He is so peaceful. He looks so like himself. He always looked like that when he was sleeping—so like a soldier" (he was in his Field-Marshal's uniform and cloak) "and he died for his country. All this trouble the last year worried him—and perhaps he could have calmed it. Perhaps some word from him would have made them wiser."

Again she said how peaceful he looked and that she had thought I should like to see him.

"Those *were* happy days," she said, alluding to the reference in my letter to the time of our cruise immediately after the Coronation,[1] and with some reference to Ivy she dismissed me.

She was wonderfully restrained and calm herself, and the King's face with its fine features looked, as she said, perfectly peaceful and calm.

You will certainly do well to write to her. It evidently gives some comfort to her to get such letters.

*17th May* 1910.

Today's ceremony was singularly impressive. I went by underground to the House, which assembled at 11.0. At 11.30 the Speaker came in in his State robes—all the members were in morning dress—his usual procession was formed and behind him

---

[1] I had then just entered the Cabinet as Postmaster-General and received the King's Command to accompany him on the *Victoria and Albert* as minister in attendance on His Majesty.

we walked four abreast, Privy Councillors first and the others following, by the Members' Entrance to Westminster Hall.

In the centre of the Hall was the catafalque draped in purple, standing in the centre of a long diamond-shaped dais about six inches high. On either side, 8 or 10 feet from the broadest part of the dais, ran a railing draped also in purple cloth. Behind this we ranged ourselves—the Speaker in the centre, Asquith on his right, Balfour on his left and so on. My place was fourth or fifth on the right just beyond the head of the catafalque. The line of Members stood three or four deep from the steps to nearly the great door.

Then came the Lord Chancellor and the Peers in procession down the steps and took up their position behind the opposite barrier. The choir and a band stood at the highest point of the steps and all the Heralds in their gorgeous mediaeval tabards stood at the great door.

Then followed a long wait. It was ten minutes past twelve before we heard amid the *thick* silence the mournful dirge of the massed bands of the Guards playing the Dead March in *Saul*—all the drums muffled. It was most moving. Through the open doorway I could see the gun-carriage draw up and a state coach soon follow it. Then the procession moved up the Hall—the Heralds, the General Staff, the Board of Admiralty and a long line of officers, filing away on each side of the catafalque and all taking their position on the steps at St. Stephen's end of the Hall.

Then came the bearer party with the coffin and, closely following, the late King's Private Secretaries and Equerries bearing the insignia—crown and orb and sceptre—which they placed upon the coffin. No word of command was spoken, an officer slowly moved his arm and the bearer party moved off. The Royalties were already on and round the low dais. The Queen and the Empress Marie of Russia knelt at a prie-dieu, King George stood beside on the right of Queen Alexandra. Behind them were Queen Mary, her children and the rest.

Then the Archbishop of Canterbury and the Dean of Westminster read a short service with anthem and hymn and all was over. The Queen Mother rose, stepped forward and knelt for a moment beside the coffin. It was singularly touching and moving.

And then they all retired and we filed out again by our side door.

You can imagine how splendid was the scene. The black lines of Members of the two Houses, the deep mourning of the Royal ladies and the brilliant uniforms of the Princes, the fine old hall, the sunshine visible through the great door at one end and the mass of colour on the steps at the other, with Kitchener's great figure standing out conspicuously in the front row and Roberts next him on the one side and Admiral Sir Arthur Wilson on the other.

Ivy went to the Ridleys' house and said the procession was very impressive but most impressive of all was the absence of spoken words of command as the procession approached. The Surrey Regiment and the Argyll and Sutherland Highlanders were on duty there. An officer raised his right arm to the level of his shoulder, slowly moved it round to before his face and dropped his hand on his sword, held on the ground in front of him; then slowly did the same with his left arm, paused and dropped his head on his breast and stood rigid with his eyes on the ground. And as he made each motion, the whole line of soldiers did the same till they all stood with hands on their rifles reversed and with heads bent down. Ivy says it was deeply moving.

There were vast masses of people all along the route, thousands, she says, at that corner by the Duke of York's Steps, who could have seen nothing, but all very orderly, impressed and impressive.

In a way it seems strange, but there can be no doubt that the public feeling is more deeply and more widely stirred this time than even on Queen Victoria's death.

I hear that King George was very dignified though deeply moved at the Proclamation Council, that all the Council proceedings were very badly conducted in great confusion, no arrangements made, summonses not delivered till within an hour of the Council meeting, and Almeric Fitzroy [1] finally reading the wrong proclamation! Today I think everything was just as it should be —a great pageant made noble by a great sorrow.

[1] Clerk of the Council.

271

*Mrs. Chamberlain to A.C.*                              VILLA VICTORIA,
                                                        CANNES,
MY DEAR AUSTEN,                                         15*th May* 1910.

Thank you so much for your letters which are our great stand-by, as ever. Your account of your visit to the Queen Mother touched us very much and I think your Father was *very* glad you had been.

He really is very much moved by it all and is ready to hear all that we can—and to talk of the King and the name he has made during his brief reign with great appreciation and sympathy—while he also is very sympathetic to the new King and looks forward to his developing into a Sovereign who will be a worthy successor to his Father and Grandmother.

We wrote to the Queen yesterday. Your Father dictated the letter to me and insisted on my adding my own signature to his. I hope she will not feel it comes less from him on that account, but I could not persuade him only to speak of me, and have the letter signed with his name alone.

The genuine feeling of the people generally is very striking, and shows how strong was the personality which has called it forth. I cannot but feel that it may tend to alleviate the political situation and at all events make the extremists realise that they cannot involve the Crown in the conflict with impunity.

                                        9 EGERTON PLACE, S.W.,
                                                17*th May* 1910.

My first thought on reading your letter is the great wish that Father should write to King George. If he would put into a letter to him what he has said to you of his sympathy with the King in his great responsibilities and sorrow, and of his assurance that he will be a worthy successor to his Father and his Grandmother, I am sure that King George would be greatly touched and would *value it.* Father could do this and take the opportunity of acknowledging the King's enquiry after him when I went to Marlborough House with the Commons deputation. I urge it very strongly, for I am sure that it would give real pleasure. And Father in writing such a letter would naturally be led to speak of the King and Queen's special knowledge of the Empire and of what that means both to them and to the nation. The King has, I am convinced, a real regard for Father and would value such a letter from him and I think it would help him. Please tell Father that I urge this very strongly. I am sure that a letter from Father would give comfort, pleasure and encouragement.

My second thought is that I have been a very bad correspondent, and the references in your letter and the girls' letters to my own make me blush! Would that I had had more to tell and that I could have told it better. I can describe conversations—more or less—but I have no gift for painting and I cannot make pictures of scenes and pageants.

*18th May* 1910.

I took Aunt Emma and Amy this morning to the Lying-in-State by their special wish. We got there a little before twelve and entered Westminster Hall by the doorway from the passage leading to the Members' entrance. The purple barriers stood as they had stood the day before. The steps at the far end of the Hall were black with people—a cascade always moving and always full. As they reached floor level they divided into two streams, were gradually marshalled into single file and so passed the coffin between the barriers and the catafalque in a quiet, subdued, continuous stream. A few exchanged whispered words, but over all brooded a hushed silence. The whole Hall was carpeted in grey felt and everyone moved noiselessly over it. A ray of sunshine shone through the lantern overhead and fell upon the catafalque. We stood where the Speaker had stood yesterday and watched the stream go by, men, women, children, boy scouts in their uniform —mostly people of the working and lower middle classes, all wearing mourning. So it had been since six in the morning; so it would be till ten at night. So it was yesterday; so it will be tomorrow. Men and women had stood in the queue all night; by 5 a.m. it stretched to St. George's Square; fast as the stream poured past it never lessened in length.

Suddenly just opposite us the policeman stopped the two streams, and as those in front passed on and out of the great North door into Palace Yard we saw the reason. At every half-hour the guard is changed. Men cannot stand the strain longer. Slowly, silently, with measured tread and eyes downcast, an officer and four men of the Corps of Gentlemen-at-Arms issued from the Guard Committee Room in the north-west corner of the Hall, stepped behind the four who stood at the end of the dais facing the great door and took their places whilst these, as slowly and silently, paced away. Then four Yeomen of the Guard with halberds reversed as silently relieved the four motionless figures standing with bowed heads at each corner of the dais. And lastly four officers of the Grenadier Guards took the places of four Life Guardsmen—two on either side of the catafalque—and one Ghoorka officer succeeded another at the foot of the coffin. Not a word had been spoken, not a command given. As the newcomers took their stations, those relieved came, as it were, to life and marched away, and the newcomers with heads bowed, arms reversed and hands on their sword hilts held before them, fell into immobility. It was greatly and grandly impressive.

And then the streams of passing people poured on again. And so it is every half-hour.

I shall take Beatrice and Ivy tomorrow.

18th May 1910.

I told Allinson to send you last Saturday's *Graphic*. I hope you received it for the sake of Luke Fildes's drawing of the late King. It was very true. His death has called forth some fine verses. Those which followed the Poet Laureate's lamentable performance in *The Times* were fine. I suspect they were by Arthur Benson, but I do not know. Rudyard Kipling's poem in today's *Times* is noble. Read also Owen Seaman's Coronation Ode republished in this week's *Punch*—noble and prophetic. It was in some sort a prayer and the prayer has been granted.

The line of people waiting to pass through Westminster Hall stretched out for five miles today—four abreast. Beatrice passed it and says it was profoundly striking.

A detail. Harcourt told me today that the catafalque had been placed just on the spot where the ray of sunshine coming through the lantern of the Hall would fall upon it at 12.30 just as the service was ended. But all yesterday it was overcast and the sun never got through the clouds.

He also told me that he had accompanied the King of Spain to the Hall at 11 o'clock last night after the Hall was closed to the public, and they had witnessed the solemn changing of the guard which I described in my earlier letter—solemn in the midst of the throng of people, almost overpowering in the stillness of the night.

Did you read the article on *The Crowd in Mourning* in this day's *Times*? "They're giving him to us now."

Arthur Balfour told the Geralds that the Queen Mother felt he was being taken from her too soon, that it was very very hard to part with him, but that she must "give him to his people." It was right and she would do it.

So do our Kings and Queens read the hearts of their people and so do their people echo their secret thoughts. It is this communion of thought, this perfect understanding and confidence that their sorrow is the nation's sorrow, which makes our Princes say to the whole nation what other men keep for the closest circle of the family, and it is this which explains, as far as anything can explain, the hold they have on the affections of millions whom they have never seen and who yet know them and love them.

*19th May* 1910.

I took Ivy and Beatrice to Westminster Hall this morning. The same unending streams of people flowed past—all ages, even babies in arms. There were more well-dressed people in the crowd than when I went yesterday and they passed now two abreast— the queue has grown so long that the police are evidently trying to pass them faster. It is a marvellous and touching sight.

All the route of the procession is becoming purple with the hangings on the houses, and wherever there are railings—all around Palace Yard and all along the Piccadilly side of Green Park and at Hyde Park Corner—the railings are hung with thousands of wreaths of laurel, box and yew sent from all over the country. London is congested with people and among all the crowds colour is hardly to be seen.

275

20th May 1910.

The great day is over. As far as I can gather all went well everywhere. The crowds were overwhelming in London but well behaved. The railway to Windsor seemed lined nearly the whole way with people. The scene in St. George's Chapel was as gorgeous and moving as anything could be. The singing of the choir, unaccompanied, was beautiful. We were both in the Choir and by some good chance together, whilst most other husbands and wives were separated. But of all the great pageant four figures stand out before my eyes—King George leading the Queen Mother, followed by the Kaiser leading the Empress Marie of Russia—so dignified, so tender, so solemn. The Queen Mother was marvellous in restraint and dignity and looked *so* young. Madame Kato [1] took her for one of the Princesses and would not believe Ivy when she told her it was the Queen! All the other royal ladies went to the Gallery.

We went down by an 11.10 train, had a buffet lunch afterwards in the Waterloo Chamber, and were back here by 4 o'clock.

The Kaiser was wonderful. He walked up to the Chapel, as he rode through the streets, turning neither to right nor left, his eyes on the coffin, and he stood through the whole service as steady as one of his own Grenadiers till he knelt for the benediction. I never felt so great an admiration for him. His face as he passed was *imposing* and he was conspicuous just because he was so utterly oblivious of all but the King who was gone.

I am glad it is all over. I have felt the strain. London has been *oppressed* in these days, and no one could escape the depression.

20th May 1910.

We went down [2] in the train with the Lansdownes.

"Tell me," he said, "what do you think? I think Rosebery is anxious to do whatever public opinion renders desirable, but his present idea is, not to proceed at once, the moment we come back, with his resolutions, but to take them up very shortly. He regards

---

[1] The Japanese Ambassadress.
[2] To Windsor for the funeral.

them as quite apart from the Veto Resolutions—'as a domestic matter' as he calls it, for the House of Lords. What do you think?"

"I think it most undesirable," I said.

"Oh!" said Lansdowne, "I talked to Arthur and —— (someone else, I forget whom) about it and they saw no objection," and he developed this a little.

"Well," I said, "I answered you at once and without thought 'Most undesirable,' and the more I think of it, the more I hold that view. R. may call it a domestic matter; but for the Government it is not and cannot be such. The country will not so understand it, and it gives the violent men of the Government just the excuse they need for pressing on. They will say: we were willing to wait; you forced the pace and so on. In my opinion it is imperative that R. should now hold his hand till the Government show theirs."

I think this was largely L.'s own instinct though he had been shaken by the opinions expressed by Rosebery, Balfour, etc., for he said,

"That's very important. I shall try to see Balfour and R. to-day after the service and I think I shall quote you."

I said, "Well, it's only my view for what it's worth. But the more I think of it, the more strongly I hold it."

"Oh, it's very important," he said. "I attach great importance to what you say, for after all it's a question of what the effect on public opinion may be."

"Well, you may certainly quote me as holding that view strongly."

Was I not right?

The Speaker will swear in Father any day immediately after Prayers if we give fully a quarter of an hour's notice.

17th June 1910.

You will see in tomorrow's papers that the Conference has met and the only announcement that will be made in regard to its proceedings.

There is no truth in the statement that Balfour and Lansdowne met Loreburn, Asquith and Crewe yesterday. There have been no further *pourparlers* and, as you will see from the notice to be published, we meet to discuss "the constitutional question" and "without conditions or limitations."

## 1910: OCTOBER

### The Constitutional Crisis and Mr. Lloyd George's Overture for a National Government

I fill up the gaps in my correspondence with Mrs. Chamberlain from other sources.

My reply to Mr. Garvin shows my attitude to his appeal for a reconsideration of the Unionist position on the Irish question.

The letter from F. E. Smith on Mr. Lloyd George's proposal, to which mine of 21st October is a reply, is published in the *Life of the Earl of Birkenhead* by the present Earl,[1] vol. i. p. 220.

The other letters explain themselves if read in connection with the introductory remarks prefixed to this year.

*Extract from a letter sent to Balfour by J. L. Garvin, a copy of which was sent by Mr. Garvin to A. C.*

*20th October* 1910.

Now may I attempt to put my case as plainly as I can at the outset without being altogether too long.

There is a new and quieter Ireland. Unionist legislation chiefly carried under your auspices has created it. That legislation is turning a nation of "Have nots" into a nation of "Haves" (putting that antithesis in its crudity only for shortness). Old Age Pensions have strengthened, the coming Invalidity schemes and other now inevitable developments of social policy will further strengthen, the *new and to my mind unbreakable financial links between the two islands.* There is a complete change in the psychology of the Irish question—a great change of material interests—an equal change of view among large sections of Irishmen forming, or ready to form, as I think a majority. Redmond's "Imperial" declarations derive their importance not from the worth of any words of his, but from the facts which have forced them from him. When he has to talk moderation instead of extremism on the other side of the Atlantic where speeches "horribly stuffed" were the only talk to go down,

---

[1] Quoted by kind permission of the publishers, Messrs. Thornton Butterworth and Co.

that is a change indeed. How then can we who have worked the
economic revolution in Ireland say that we will not recognise the
possibility of any Irish administrative change in the direction of
limited self-Government perhaps no more inimical to the parliamentary union of the United Kingdom—perhaps no less advantageous to it—than is the local autonomy of Quebec to the
parliamentary union of Canada.

Other factors still more far-reaching are changed. The Irish-
German alliance in the United States may do something worse than
block absolutely as it does the cause of a permanent Anglo-American
*entente*. If the Japanese alliance should have to lapse owing to the
conditions of feeling in the rest of the English-speaking world,
where should we be? The present state of the Irish question with
its reaction upon the United States is the greatest danger to Canada;
I much fear that in a conflict just on the old lines of 1886 or 1893
—when all the conditions of Ireland itself, in our Imperial policy,
in our Foreign policy, have changed to an extent then inconceivable
—we, the Party of Preference and Imperial Union, shall find ourselves stripped of the sympathy of the Dominions.

These things weigh upon me and have long weighed.

Thinking the present Dublin Castle system now untenable—
some form of devolution inevitable—I cannot think it now impossible to frame a safe constructive compromise between the
Gladstonian Home Rule which has perished—what greater justification of the struggle against it?—and the old Unionist position
which has now lost so much of its old basis. Since then a generation
has passed away; no elector under forty, few under fifty, remember
the conditions and emotions of that fierce decade from 1879 to 1889.
The passions that vitalised the Unionist cause more than arguments,
and carried it to victory, are extinct. The murder of Cavendish and
Burke, the dynamite outrages, the cattle-maiming, the shootings,
the evictions, the holding up of the House of Commons,—it is all
long long past and forever gone, like so many of the once familiar
great figures that battled in the front on both sides. You and
Mr. Chamberlain alone are left. How can we excite such a struggle
as was then waged? Whence is anything like the same motive
power to come? I think we shall fail on that line, and fail because
not only will the strong passions have deserted us, but even reason

will not be to the same extent on our side. Cattle-driving is bad, and should be crushed; it is nevertheless as water unto the wine of wrath that was. I know the follies and fanaticisms of the Sinn Fein and the Gaelic League. They will continue to give trouble. But are they much worse—are they as dangerous to the Empire—as our own anti-naval, anti-militarist and Socialist factions? Would not an Ireland under Federal Home Rule on the Quebec model or so, send a solid *majority* of Conservatives to help defend in the Imperial Parliament nearly all we care for?

I entreat that if the Conference breaks down—and many of us would far rather see it working towards a solution which would do something definite for Imperial Union, even Preference, next year as well as for the Irish pacification—I entreat that if we are to fight another General Election soon we shall fight for a strong Second Chamber as the only bulwark against Socialism and all destruction, but that we shall not close the door to a reconsideration of the Irish question whether we win or nominally lose at the polls.

*A. C. to J. L. Garvin.*

HIGHBURY, BIRMINGHAM,

MY DEAR GARVIN,                                    *21st October* 1910.

I am very glad to have your letter and the explanatory extract from your communication to Balfour. They are much less of a shock to me than I think you anticipate would be the case. There is indeed little with which I disagree in what you have written to him, and that little is rather a question of temperament, proportion, or degree than of principle. I recognise the truth of all you say as to the changed position in Ireland and the circumstances which have brought it about. Indeed, I have in conference with colleagues dwelt upon the very factors of the situation both in Ireland and Great Britain to which you attach so much importance. Nor has the Colonial aspect of the question escaped my notice. I think that Colonial statesmen in their utterances on Irish questions often show ignorance and expect us to do in the United Kingdom what they would be the first to repudiate in United Canada or Australia. But their opinion, whether well or ill-founded, whether honestly formed with such knowledge of the facts as they have or merely the result of Irish pressure in their own electorate, is a factor which

we cannot afford to neglect. I therefore do not at all close my mind
to the suggestion of a great development in Unionist policy towards
Ireland, or rather, as I would prefer to say, a reversion to the line of
policy which my father was laying before the country before
Mr. Gladstone introduced his mischievous and destructive scheme.

But if such an operation is to be successfully carried out, we must
act with careful thought and with moderation both in speech and
writing. I think it unwise to lay stress on the American side of the
case. We never have done any good, and we never shall do any good,
by touting for American sympathy or kowtowing to American
opinion, and if our domestic policy appears to be directed by a
desire to secure an American *entente* or alliance, it will only earn the
amused contempt of the American people. Let us do the right thing,
but let us do it in the right way. Let us do it because it is the right
thing and not to please foreign, even American opinion. And let
us remember that the more moderately we state our case—the less
there is about it of hyperbole and superlatives—the greater will
be the impression made upon the British electorate and the more
likely they are to understand and to appreciate the greater consistency which underlies our apparent change of attitude.

You must remember too—and this is important—that much
depends upon the attitude of the Liberal Party. I attach very little
importance to the utterances of Redmond, which by the way,
he has already repudiated. That, however, would not affect me
at all if the two great Parties were united in opinion as to the extent
to which they would go in conceding Devolution within the United
Kingdom. Much which would be safe, and indeed the highest
wisdom and prudence under such circumstances, would be unsafe
if the Liberal Party treated it merely as a minimum from which
under Irish pressure they would advance to further concessions. It
was this reflection which caused my father to abandon his own
suggested reforms when Parnell put the Irish vote up to auction
and Mr. Gladstone agreed to pay a fancy price for it.

If we were in office we might perhaps, with the experience and
precedent of the Conference, invite the Liberal leaders to consider
with us whether a national settlement could not be arrived at;
but we are not in office and under the circumstances the first step
must come from them. It would be rash for an Opposition, which

cannot carry out its own policy and which, if you be right, cannot even prevent the Government from carrying whatever they may propose, to propound a scheme without any knowledge how they would receive it and with the strong probability that the further we went towards them, the higher would the Irish demands be raised. This seems to me the danger of the campaign which you have undertaken in the *Observer*. As I said at the beginning, I am far from closing my mind to the possibility of radical changes in our system of government—still further from being unfriendly to the idea of a national settlement of the Irish question, but, just in proportion as you desire the success of this policy, I beg you to be cautious, moderate and restrained in what you may now write upon the subject.

Where there is so much agreement between us it is perhaps not necessary to dwell on points of difference, but I cannot pass by without a word your suggestion (as I understand it) that we ought to have come to terms with the Irish in order to defeat the Budget. In my opinion, nothing could have been more fatal to the successful attainment of your object, not to speak of the credit of the Unionist Party, than that we should have made this change in our policy towards Irish Government as part of a bargain to secure support in a Parliamentary fight on quite another subject. If the arrangement is to stand at all, it must stand on its own merits. Nothing could be worse than that it should have the appearance of a manœuvre to dish the Whigs.                    A. C.

*A. C. to F. E. Smith.*
*Secret.*                                                HIGHBURY,
                                                    BIRMINGHAM,
MY DEAR F. E.                                  21st *October* 1910.

Though not in Court I am as busy as you and cannot write as fully as I should like if my letter is to catch the post tonight. But let me make one or two points clear.

(1) That each one of us recognises the gravity of the decision we have to take. There is no need to dwell on that.

(2) We equally recognise the vast importance of the results which Lloyd George holds out to us. To place the Navy on a thoroughly satisfactory basis, to establish a system of national

service for defence, to grant at once Preference to the Colonies on the duties immediately available, and to enquire, not with a view to delay but with a view to action at the earliest possible moment, what further duties it is desirable to impose in the interests of the nation and the Empire—these are objects which silence all considerations of personal comfort and all individual preferences or antipathies.

And in saying this please understand that I am as assured as you are yourself that Lloyd George has made this proposal in perfect good faith and without any unavowed or unavowable *arrière pensée*.

Nor am I at all less inclined to give the most attentive and even friendly consideration to these proposals because as I now understand from you and Bonar Law they are dependent on another consideration, namely, on agreement for a settlement of the Irish question on the lines of what I understand Lloyd George calls Federal Home Rule for the United Kingdom and what I should call Provincial Councils. On the contrary I think this adds to the value of the proposal and increases its possible advantages. I have never been averse in principle to very considerable changes in Irish Government, and I see that it would be safe and wise to go further, as part of a national settlement which both Parties would maintain, than it could ever be if the plan were the work of one Party only and regarded by that Party as a minimum capable under pressure of parliamentary or political necessity of being indefinitely exceeded.

Although, therefore, this is a most important addition to the proposals laid before Balfour by Lloyd George, and although every addition adds to the difficulties as well as to the advantages of agreement, it does not materially alter the position at the moment, at least as I see it, namely, that if we can come to some agreement at the Conference on the points which we are there discussing, then there is open to us the possibility at least that a very much wider agreement and closer co-operation might be attainable.

But Lloyd George seems to have spoken to you as if he had already invited us to consider with him whether some such form of Devolution could not be agreed to by both Parties, and as if there was a present danger that the Conference would break up because we refuse even to consider such a proposition. This is a complete and I think dangerous misunderstanding. No such proposal has been made to us or even hinted at either inside or outside the Conference. What we have been considering there is not *what changes* in our system of Government should be made but *how* such changes should be effected. This is a wholly different though perhaps a not unrelated question, for what we desire is not a guarantee against all change but security against changes in the machinery of Government *which the people do not approve.* If they clearly do approve them, they must have them. Whether we think them good or bad, we make no pretence under such circumstances to any power to prevent their passage into law.

It seems to me that Lloyd George has failed to recognise this, and that if he recognised it his path and ours might be considerably smoothed. For consider the position: If the country clearly approves any proposal they make on *e.g.* the Irish question, they *could and would carry it within a reasonable time and without a dissolution* under the plan which we have proposed with the honest desire to meet them as far as possible, *even though we as a Party were wholly opposed to the change*; whilst, if the change were one agreed upon by both Parties, it would go through as easily and as swiftly as any great Bill has ever gone through Parliament.

Such security as we have asked therefore does not prevent change when Parties disagree and does not render change one whit more difficult when Parties are agreed.

What more can he reasonably ask? And what is it that he fears if this system be adopted?

My reply to your letter has grown far longer than I intended. Even now it has been written in such haste that my thoughts are badly and inadequately expressed, but at least it will serve to show you the temper in which I approach the consideration of these great issues and the momentous proposal made by Lloyd George to Balfour.

It will I hope also enable you to clear up the misunderstanding which seems to exist in Lloyd George's mind as to what he actually proposed to Balfour and what was our attitude to it.

Yours sincerely,

AUSTEN CHAMBERLAIN.

*A. C. to Lord Cawdor.*

21st October 1910.

Bonar Law dined with me on Wednesday night to discuss what in his letter asking for the appointment he called "the thunderbolt" of which he had just heard. As soon as we were alone after dinner, he said,

"Well, I suppose you were as much surprised *by it* as I was?"

So as a preliminary to any further talk I asked him what he meant by "it" and what he knew. It then appeared that Lloyd George had authorised F. E. Smith (who I understand was the original intermediary between George and Balfour) to inform Bonar Law of the whole proposal; and I found that Bonar Law knew everything that I knew. But he knew more, for he added two important items to the account which Balfour gave us of Lloyd George's state of mind.

1. It appeared that in addition to giving a preference to the Colonies on the existing rate of duty, Lloyd George was ready to consent to the appointment of a Commission which should be required to report within six months on what further duties it was desirable in the interests of the Empire to impose, and he was prepared to bind himself to accept and act upon the report of such a Commission.

This is important. But Bonar Law's next addition to my knowledge is of even greater consequence.

2. Lloyd George, it appears, according to F. E. Smith, puts in the forefront of his programme the settlement of the Irish question on the basis of Devolution, Federal Home Rule, or whatever you like to call it, and he had left Bonar Law under the impression that the Conference was in danger of breaking off because we on our side refused to consider any such proposition. This is of course quite untrue, for no such proposition has ever been made to us, nor has it ever been hinted, either in the Conference or in the communication which passed with Balfour, that we were invited to confer on the possibility of such a solution. I thought this *mal entendu* was important, and after some reflection I authorised Bonar Law to inform F. E. Smith (who would of course report it to Lloyd George) that no such proposition had ever been made to us. What we were discussing in the Conference was the conditions under which such

changes should be made, not what the changes themselves ought to be; and I said for myself that I by no means closed my mind against the friendly consideration of proposals on that subject if the Government chose to make any to us.

I need not dwell upon the circumstances which make me think that much would be safe as part of a national settlement strictly upheld by both the great Parties in the State which would be in the highest degree dangerous if it were extorted by the Nationalists from the Parliamentary necessities of one Party and were merely a stepping-stone to further concessions. Nor need I now dwell upon the great change of opinion in regard to Home Rule which has taken place both in Ireland and Great Britain since the battle was last fought out, nor on the profound alteration which time and legislation have worked in the conditions of the problem. Such considerations as these will easily present themselves to your mind, and I only write now to give you the earliest information that I can of the very important addition to Balfour's account of Lloyd George's state of mind which I received from Bonar Law.

I wrote to Balfour on Wednesday night and saw Lansdowne on Thursday morning and have given both of them a full account of this conversation.

What a world we live in, and how the public would stare if they could look into our minds and our letter-bags.

*P.S.*—I should add that Lloyd George told F. E. Smith that the Liberal Party was pledged to Devolution in some form or another and could not abandon the pledge, but if a scheme agreed on between the two great Parties were rejected by the Irish, the Liberals would then wash their hands of the whole affair and leave the Irish to stew in their own juice.

A. C.

*Balfour to A. C.*
*Private.*
WHITTINGEHAME,
PRESTONKIRK,
22nd October 1910.

MY DEAR AUSTEN,
I enclose a letter from Alfred Lyttelton, and my reply. Evidently your conjecture is right, and Lloyd George has talked in a

manner which suggests that the Conference is divided upon a subject which has never been before it, and, so far as I can see, never *can* come before it as a separate question. For, surely, whatever our views may be upon "Home Rule all round" or Provincialism, or whatever it is to be called, this is emphatically a Constitutional change of the greatest import, and, like other Constitutional changes, deserves to be carefully safeguarded.

Garvin has written me a long letter, very nice in tone, putting forward the same general views as were expressed in his article. I have had it typed and send it to you, with a copy of my reply.

I think Lloyd George in his statement to F. E. must have mixed up, or caused F. E. to mix up, his conversation with me and the proceedings of the Conference. It is quite true that he mentioned (in his airy way) that he thought something would have to be done for Ireland, probably as part of a general scheme of Devolution, and I remember asking him how, in those circumstances, he proposed to deal with England. Was there to be an English House of Commons as well as an Imperial House of Commons sitting at the same time at Westminster? He said he supposed England would have to be divided; and I did not pursue the subject.

It is also true, as I think I told you, that he mentioned Colonial Preference. I forgot to tell you that he also talked about a Commission of Enquiry into Fiscal relations, *but he said nothing about reporting in six months, etc.*; and as I have always resisted the appeal of our own Free Traders to hang up the subject until a Commission had reported, I did not receive this part of the suggestion with any enthusiasm. But in truth we touched on so many questions, and the initial difficulty of forming a Coalition seemed so fundamental, that I did not think it worth while coming to close quarters as to the exact nature and limitations of the programme which a Coalition could carry out. Defence, Education, Licensing were the things on which he laid stress, and on none of these, of course, any more than on the others, had he precise suggestions to make.

I did not take up a *non possumus* attitude upon any of them. I think it quite possible, though perhaps improbable, that a *modus vivendi* might be arrived at on the substance of a common policy if the enormous initial difficulties of a coalition could be overcome.

288

But I saw no object in a detailed discussion about the pattern of the wall-papers which are to adorn this new political structure when the foundations have not been laid! Yrs. ever,

ARTHUR JAMES BALFOUR.

*Balfour to A. C.*
*Private.*
WHITTINGEHAME,
PRESTONKIRK,
MY DEAR AUSTEN, 27th October 1910.

Lloyd George has written to ask me to see him before the Conference—on Monday if possible. I have wired to say that Monday is very difficult for me, but that, if the Conference was put off till Tuesday *afternoon*, I could see him Tuesday morning. If he accepts this arrangement, we four should be able to have a preliminary talk at your house at Monday's dinner and you will receive my report of Lloyd George's conversation in time for the afternoon meeting.

I enclose you a little (!) budget of letters:

1. F. E. Smith's letter to you, herewith returned. I am in entire agreement with your answer to him.

2. A pair of Irish Unionist Letters—the first drops in the storm which will assuredly break over us if any new departure be admitted.

3. A long reply by Garvin. He puts his case well as you would naturally expect; but I do not know that his original sketch becomes more attractive in proportion as its outlines are filled in!

Yrs. ever,

ARTHUR JAMES BALFOUR.

*P.S.*—I should be glad if you would return to me Garvin's letter when you have read it.

I supplement these letters by one which passed at a later date.

*Lansdowne to A. C.*
*Confidential.*
DERREEN,
KENMORE,
MY DEAR AUSTEN, 22nd August 1912.

I wonder whether you noticed the letter headed "Unionists and Ulster" which appeared in yesterday's *Times*?

Upon the whole I am disposed to take no notice of it, but I am perhaps inordinately prejudiced against newspaper controversies. This with all respect to Winston!

I am, however, reminded of a conversation with you on the subject of the Constitutional Conference of 1910. We were both shocked at the absence of all record of its proceedings, and I think we both believed that from the notes which we had made (yours were much fuller than mine) it might be possible and desirable to draw up a kind of *procès verbal* of great value for historical purposes. When we next meet we might discuss this project.

We should of course be precluded from making our document public, but we ought not to be precluded from stating categorically whenever it may seem necessary that the Unionist members of the Conference never contemplated, or discussed with an open mind any "settlement of the Irish problem on the lines of Home Rule." This is what Mr. Hawkin in effect suggests, and on this assumption he bases his contention:

(1) that we were aware that the General Election of December 1910 was to be a Home Rule Election, and

(2) that for this reason we feel ourselves precluded from standing by Bonar Law.

I feel just as strongly as Bonar Law does about Ulster, although I should personally have used language rather less suggestive of readiness to carry a rifle in her defence. We shall probably all of us have to speak a good deal in the autumn and there will be plenty of opportunities for showing the public that the alleged differences between us do not exist. At any rate I am not much inclined to publish anything at this moment either as to the Conference, or as to my attitude towards Ulster. I should be glad to know what you think.

Your horticultural speech delighted me. Horticulture has its dangers. Lady L. put her foot in one of my drains a few days ago, and sprained her ankle so severely that she is still on her sofa and likely to remain there.

Yours ever,

LANSDOWNE.

*A. C. to Lansdowne.*

HIGHBURY,

MY DEAR LANSDOWNE,                        *26th August* 1912.

A correspondent sent me Hawkin's letter to *The Times* and I replied shortly that there was no foundation for the statement that I differed from Law about Ulster. Like you, I should have expressed myself differently, but I hope that Ulster will offer a stubborn passive resistance. I think she will be right to resist, and I believe her resistance will be successful if Ulstermen will keep cool, resolute, and, as far as may be, silent as to their exact intentions. My only fear is lest the train should be fired too soon, a few of the demonstrators get blown up prematurely, and the whole movement be crushed in ridicule. This is not a great danger, but the Ulster leaders should bear it in mind. The cooler, nay the colder, the resolution of Ulster is, the more impressive it will be and the more terrifying to the Government. If Ulster is hard, but cold as steel, Government cannot go on, but if Ulster gets "jumpy" the Government will have an easy victory.

Them's my sentiments.

As regards the Conference of 1910 I have very full [1] and (I am certain) very accurate notes. They were written out immediately after the meetings from jottings taken at the meetings themselves. I have not looked at them since, but they are very much at your service whenever you want them.

These notes cover everything that went on in the Conference. We tested their accuracy once when you and I compared notes as to a particular formula suggested for finance and found we had each independently recorded it in the same words. But they do not even allude to Lloyd George's secret proposals made first through F. E. Smith and subsequently directly to Balfour. Of these, as you will remember, you, Cawdor and I heard nothing for about a week (or more?). Then Balfour said he must inform us, and Lloyd George informed Asquith and later Birrell and Crewe. Up to that time the secret was confined to George and Winston. [2]

[1] They are less full than I supposed, but adequate.
[2] This was the impression left on Balfour's mind at the time. Asquith later told me that he had known all about the proposals from the first.

My recollection is clear that when we first heard of them they appeared so favourable that we could not understand how George could face his Party after agreeing to them. At this stage as reported by Balfour, they included :

(1) Placing the Navy on a satisfactory footing.

(2) Compulsory Military service.

(3) Dealing with the Poor Law.

(4) Some vague reference to Insurance, which, if done by common agreement, could be done better and cheaper than if done by one Party.

(5) Immediate Preference to the British Dominions on existing duties and an enquiry to see if anything further could be devised.

In return we were to settle by agreement the Constitutional crisis; and the Irish question was, I suppose, also to be settled by agreement, but I cannot recall exactly what was said at first about Ireland. I know that George several months later said to me that his idea was "something on your father's lines"—a sort of National Councils "scheme," and that he stated to Balfour that if the Nationalists would not take what was offered he would break with them. The Liberal Party would have kept its word and done all it was bound to do and would thenceforth be free.

But as first put before us, it was more evident what we should get than what we should give, and I believe that Ireland was hardly mentioned to us *at first*. I remember that Welsh Disestablishment was also brought in, and that Balfour was referred to something the Archbishop of Canterbury had said as showing that he was not irreconcilable on the subject if the majority of the people clearly desired it.

After some of you left town I had an interview with Bonar Law, whom F. E. Smith had, with Lloyd George's permission, told of these overtures. From Law I learned some additional conditions and these I at once recorded in a letter to all or some of you, a copy of which I have in London. I believe that this letter will show :

(1) That Law explained that the Tariff enquiry was to be finished and to report *in six months*.

(2) That it was through Law that I first got an idea that Home Rule in some form was a condition of the agreement.

I know that when Balfour first told us of the overtures we were astonished at George's concessions and someone asked, "But how can he justify such a *volte face*! What will his people say of him?"

To which it was replied that after all that was his business and not ours. But that later, when he had fully developed his ideas, we said that it would be as impossible for us to justify our acceptance of them to our people as it would be for him to justify his acceptance of them to his people. And we summarised the whole position by saying that each side was to do what it most disliked to please the other, whereas the only possible basis of a compromise would be to put aside the most contentious measures and be content (at least as a beginning) to take up the less contentious ones.

I believe (but do not *know*) that it was on this ground that Balfour finally broke off the negotiations *outside* the Conference, adding also that his whole history forbade his being a party to any form of Home Rule, though younger men less involved in the controversies of '86 and '93 might be free to contemplate what he could not accept.

To conclude the recollections, you will remember that George had considered even such details as the distribution of posts in a coalition Government and suggested that Asquith should be First Lord with a peerage, Balfour President of the Committee of Defence with the lead in the Commons, you Foreign Secretary, and I First Lord of the Admiralty; but if it was thought that his remaining Chancellor of the Exchequer would be a difficulty he would retire in my favour and take some other office.

It was for these reasons that the Cabinet (some of whom would of course have had to retire) were not at first informed of what was toward, but before the end we were told that they had been informed and had agreed.

No word as to these secret and extraneous negotiations was ever spoken in the Conference by any of the eight who sat there. All conversations in regard to them were held between Balfour and George alone, and in the Conference we all acted by common accord as if nothing of the kind were in progress.

I am not sure of the date, but my letter referred to above must have been written, I think, at the end of the week in which Balfour first told us of George's overture.[1]

I go to London today and abroad on Wednesday—but what weather for a motor tour!

I am sorry to hear of Lady Lansdowne's accident, and I hope that it will not keep her a prisoner for long.

Yours ever,

AUSTEN CHAMBERLAIN.

*Lansdowne to A. C.*

DERREEN,

KENMORE, CO. KERRY,

MY DEAR AUSTEN,             *27th August* 1912.

I am sorry to have imposed upon you the task of writing to me at such length—but your letter is of great value and I shall place it carefully among my archives.

Of the proceedings which took place in Conference, I have a fairly distinct recollection, but it is much less distinct with regard to the even more important and much more extraordinary proceedings which took place *pari passu* between Balfour and Lloyd George and of which we subsequently became aware. I am sure you are right in saying that, during our formal and official sittings, no reference was ever made by any of us to the informal conversations which had been in progress outside.

The main point, however, is that we none of us treated Home Rule as an open question, and, unless I am mistaken, the official breakdown took place because we were entirely dissatisfied with the Government proposal for treating Home Rule under the Constitutional machinery which they were prepared to set up.

But we must have a talk about all this when we meet, as we shall before we are much older.

I have made my secretary write to Mr. Hawkin a short note to the effect that there is, so far as I am concerned, no foundation whatever for the statement to which he called my attention.

With thanks,

Yours ever,

LANSDOWNE.

[1] This was not so. It was written some weeks later.

*Copy of Sir R. Finlay's Notes of the Meeting of the Unionist Leaders to hear Balfour's Report of the Proceedings at the Constitutional Conference.*

*Notes as to Conference:*

(These notes are made by me, 18th December 1910, from rough memoranda made by me of A. J. B.'s statement at the meeting at Lansdowne House six weeks or so earlier. *Present*: A. J. B., Halsbury, Cawdor, Lansdowne, Austen C., Selborne, Walter Long, Finlay, Carson, Alfred Lyttelton, Akers-Douglas and others.)

Legislation was to be divided into ordinary, financial and constitutional legislation.

(1) As to ordinary legislation:

If a difference arose on two occasions in two sessions in two years between the two Houses of Parliament it was to be settled by a joint sitting of the two Houses. The joint sitting was to consist of the whole of the H. of C. and 100 peers, 20 of them members of the Government and 80 to be selected on a system of proportional representation.

(*N.B.*—This would give the Unionists, when the Radicals are in office, a majority of 45 only or thereabouts in the 100 peers.)

Not more than a certain number of peers to be created in any one year.

(2) As to financial legislation:

The Budget not to be rejected by the Lords unless in case of tacking.

Legal tacking presents little difficulty.

But as to "equitable tacking" the Government proposed such a Bill or part of a Bill should be treated like ordinary legislation.

*But* (*a*) How define?

Proposed definition: "Finance is the sole business of the H. of C. provided that if it appears that any provisions of a Bill though dealing with taxation would effect important social or political changes through expropriation or differentiation against any class of owners of property these provisions shall not be treated for the purposes of this Act as provisions dealing with taxation."

(The result would be that Government would have to bring it in as a separate Bill; it might be rejected twice by the H. of L. and then it would come before a joint sitting and it might be amended.)

(*b*) Who to decide?

Not a legal tribunal but a joint committee of the two Houses—14 members, half from each House, to be elected at the beginning of the Parliament for the duration of the Parliament—the Speaker of the H. of C. to be in the Chair with a casting vote only.

(3) As to constitutional legislation:

Asquith said no differentiation was possible between that and ordinary legislation. But the Government were willing that Bills affecting the Crown or the Protestant succession or the Act which is to embody this agreement should be subject to special safe-guards—if the two Houses differed the Bill would drop—if they agreed there should be a plebiscite.

On the 16th October the Conference broke off on the difficulty of Home Rule. A. J. B. proposed that if a Home Rule Bill was twice rejected it should go to a plebiscite. Lloyd George, while admitting the reasonableness of this, said it was impossible for the Government to assent to this.

The Conference met again last Tuesday. Government proposed compromises.

One was that a General Election should intervene on the next occasion on which a H. R. Bill, having passed the H. of C., was rejected in the H. of L., but only on this occasion, and that H. Rule Bills if introduced afterwards should be treated like ordinary Bills.

The meeting at Lansdowne House was of about twenty pro-minent members of the Party.

A. J. B. made the statement which I have outlined in the above notes and asked whether we should go on or break off.

A. J. B. expressed no opinion but from an expression he let fall I inferred that he was averse to going on on such terms.

Lansdowne, Cawdor and A. C. were for breaking off.

This was the decision arrived at. Alfred Lyttelton gave no opinion and Walter Long had doubts though he concurred with the majority.

I expressed myself strongly against the proposed settlement and in favour of breaking off the negotiations. My chief grounds were :

(*a*) The joint sitting with the whole of the H. of C. and a selection from the H. of L. giving Unionists only 45 or so of a majority was purely illusory.

(*b*) There was no principle in the proposal about Home Rule, that only one attempt should be safeguarded by a General Election and it would leave it open to any Government to get H.R. passed on subsequent occasions without consulting the people, for such subsequent Bills would be treated as ordinary legislation, and there was no safeguard whatever as to constitutional changes other than H.R. unless they touched the Crown, the Protestant Succession or the Act embodying the agreement arrived at by the Conference. I said that I did not believe that the Unionist Party in the H. of C. would give their support to carry into law any such arrangement.

After we broke up, Gerald Balfour who was present told me he doubted whether we had come to the right conclusion.

R. B. F.

*Note by A. C. after copying the above, 25th December* 1913.

My principal objections were to confining the security for Home Rule to a single occasion and to the absence of any general provisions securing that constitutional changes should be specially safeguarded.

I thought better of the joint sitting proposals than most of my colleagues and felt sure that we could get Asquith and Co. to raise the numbers of the House of Lords delegation. I did not, however, like leaving the H. of L. wholly unreformed.

*Sd.* AUSTEN C.

## 1910: NOVEMBER, DECEMBER

### *Autumn : Second Election*

9 EGERTON PLACE, S.W.,
*13th November* 1910.

Our meeting of colleagues [1] was unanimous that the Government's terms would not do and so at last the end has come. Everyone except Curzon is as gloomy as the weather, and you know what this despondency in the crew means in strain and collar work for the Captain and officers.

Yesterday, for instance, A. J. B. sent for me in the afternoon. The editor of the *Express*, Buckle, Norton Griffiths, M.P. for Wednesbury, some others and Garvin—Garvin of all men!—had all been in quick succession to tell Balfour that we could not win with the Food Duties, that he must—not indeed abandon them altogether, but announce that if returned to power now, he would not impose any new food duty without yet another appeal to the country!

B. said he didn't like it. He had come slowly to the Food Duties, but having come to them, he didn't like to go back on them. The Party had shed some members by adopting Tariff Reform, he wouldn't split it by abandoning it. He wouldn't say that I was the only person he wished to consult—that would be invidious— but I was of course the person he wished most to consult. He didn't cite Free Fooders; he thought nothing of them, but what was he to say in face of all these Tariff Reformers?

We spent an hour and a half together. He said he liked it and found it "most interesting and refreshing. I am so tired," he added, "of talking to people who can't answer my arguments!"

I told him:

(1) That if he now took Preference off his flag, he could never put it back again.

---

[1] To consider the terms offered by the Government for the Constitutional question.

(2) That if he was thinking only of the Corn Duty, he would find meat and other duties even more difficult of platform treatment.

(3) That whatever was the case with corn, these were necessary to any effectual Colonial Preference.

(4) That not only would no Party ever again face the difficulties of the corn tax, if we now even temporarily abandoned it, but that all the Colonies would say (with truth) that the game was up.

(5) That the policy urged on him would be a mere repetition of the mistake of 1906. We should still have all the odium of the Corn Duty attaching to us. The only difference would be that we should not defend ourselves!

(6) What should we gain? We were all told before the last election that the towns might be all right but we couldn't persuade the agricultural labourer. The artizan understood risking a penny to win a shilling but the labourer only thought of the penny spent and didn't believe in the shilling to be won. Yet we had won the labourer in the purely agricultural counties. I need put it no higher than this: Tariff Reform and Food Taxes have not prevented us from getting his vote. Now if you give up all agricultural protection and keep industrial duties, you may lose the labourer. You will certainly lose the farmer, who will cry out that agriculture is betrayed.

(7) And now for the north. You won't placate your Manchester merchants. They talk Food Duties, but their real objection is to the interference of the other duties with their cosmopolitan interests. And if we could gain them, who are they? and how many? Tens or scores! And we want the hundreds or thousands —the working men. Now Tariff Reform is not keeping them from us. It is the only thing we offer that brings them to us—the only thing that makes us converts among them.

(8) The trouble is not that they are thinking too much of T.R. or of Food Duties. The trouble is the opposite. They are not thinking enough of them. If they did, they would vote with us.

(9) Food is a bogey—a cry—a term of abuse. Treat it properly and you need not fear it—and then I made him a speech to show how it should be done! And he listened with appreciative interest.

Well, I was dog-tired after it; but I guess he was well pleased to find someone who said, "Stick to your guns," and who could give him intelligent reasons for the faith that is in him.

*16th November* 1910.

Every spare moment of my time is spent at my writing-table and I cannot get it clear of unanswered letters. Just now we are all flooded with letters from "ardent" but wobbly Tariff Reformers begging us to play hankypanky somehow with the Food Taxes, to run away from them today that we may live to fight for them again, etc. etc., till I am sick of them. The answer is very simple, no doubt. "We wouldn't, if we could. We couldn't, if we would!" and much more all to the same effect. But dear me! it is an arduous work to teach men to face facts. Here is G. promising Balfour the support of the whole Unionist Press except the *Morning Post* and the *B.D.P.* if only he will promise that no new taxes on food shall be imposed if we win this election until we have had yet another election, and explaining that we would thus keep the counties, because they would believe that they would get agricultural protection after all, and win the towns because *they* would believe that they wouldn't! Is this confused ? So is G.! Here is Buckle urging the same "as a Preferentialist." Here is Northcliffe do. do. and of course lots of others. But Balfour stands firm and will nail the flag to the mast tomorrow, so all is well. The fools! to think that they could get rid of the Food Tax tar by putting a coat of whitewash over it "for this occasion only." Balfour called Bonar Law and me in yesterday afternoon to persuade Northcliffe and we spent an hour and a half talking to him. I don't suppose he was persuaded, but *he* could not explain how the thing could be done and happily he will back Balfour whatever he says.

Well, that is all hard collar work, pulling your fiercest to keep the cart from running backwards downhill; but in other ways we have made very pretty progress. When the Houses met, our Party were looking up and the Government men were looking down. And by the time Lansdowne's notice of motion was known in the lobbies our men were jubilant and the Radicals very much the reverse. And the papers made very satisfactory reading this morning.

I did a deal of thinking about the situation on Sunday and the result was to convince me that we must move quickly and dramatically if we could, but above all quickly and decisively. So on Monday morning I wrote out the enclosed draft resolution[1] and spent my day, or at least a good part of it, in interviewing separately Lansdowne, Balfour and Cawdor. Curzon alas! I couldn't get hold of, but I wrote to him and by Tuesday morning I got the assent of all the others to the amended form in which the resolution was published. Even Salisbury concurred, Long was enthusiastic, Beach thinks it "admirable," and it has in fact met a long-felt want.

Salisbury was the original prompter of Lansdowne's move. I supported his suggestion strongly and together I flatter myself we have made a pretty splash. For we have taken the offensive and thrown the enemy's plans into confusion. So far so good. The rest is in the lap of the gods.

I cannot learn anything of what is passing with the King, but it is evident that there is an unexpected hitch in that quarter. So much the better. By Jove, if we *could* drive them into resignation! Their people are in a mortal funk of it.

### Draft Resolution

That this Conference, believing that the maintenance of an efficient Second Chamber is essential to the protection of our liberties, expresses its satisfaction at the evidence which the House of Lords have already given of their desire for reform.

That we shall heartily welcome any reasonable proposals for increasing the efficiency and representative character of that House by the addition of Peers for life or of representative Peers elected for a term of years.

That we believe that there need be no serious difficulty in reasonably adjusting such differences as may from time to time arise between the House of Commons and a reformed Second Chamber.

But that if such differences arise in connection with proposed changes in the Constitution, affecting not merely a particular law

[1] Printed below.

but the law-making power itself, it is the people and the people alone who have a right to decide, and their opinion should be sought by a special Referendum or a General Election on the point at issue.

HIGHBURY,
*30th November* 1910.

Balfour sent a special messenger to Edinburgh on Monday night to ask my opinion.[1]  I telegraphed back strong disapproval and wrote more fully by the messenger giving reasons and suggesting an alternative.  He ought to have got my letter before he spoke. Now we must make the best of it.  It won't do to quarrel among ourselves.  But I wired him stiffly this morning :

"See *Daily Mail*.  Tariff Reform not an issue.  Doing much mischief in doubtful seats here where electors care for nothing else.  Has probably lost us one seat already.  Please stop this misrepresentation of your speech."

He replied :

"Will do what I can with *Daily Mail*.  So far as I am concerned shall make it quite clear that Tariff Reform is one of the greatest issues."

Edinburgh was an extraordinary success.  6000 people seated, 1000 admitted to stand, overflow of 1500 next door full the moment the door opened, overflow in the street besides—three speeches—and so many turned away that people coming to the meeting thought it had been abandoned.  The *Scotsman* said the crowds and the enthusiasm recalled the old Midlothian times when the desire to hear Gladstone was at its height !  *Veggy* flattering !

I am speaking every night this week—Dudley to-night ; West Bromwich tomorrow ;  Darlington Friday ;  Newcastle-on-Tyne on Saturday.  Very well so far and amazingly fresh considering all things.

---

[1] The opening paragraph of this letter refers to Balfour's Albert Hall Pledge to submit a Tariff Reform Budget to a Referendum.  The letter itself is printed on the next page.

*Balfour to A. C.*
*Private.*                                          4 CARLTON GARDENS,
                                                        PALL MALL,
MY DEAR AUSTEN,                              28*th November* 1910.

I have received the enclosed letter from Bonar Law.

The suggestions by the Government speakers to the effect that
Tariff Reform should be submitted to a Referendum of course
misses the obvious point, that the Referendum is intended as a
method of settling deadlocks between the two Houses when they
differ, not as a means of upsetting the decision of the two Houses
when they agree. But, putting aside this argument, what do you
say to Bonar Law's suggestion?

The following reflections on it occur to me:

(1) There are strong objections to dealing with taxation by
Referendum, which were often mentioned at the Conference.
These still seem to me conclusive against making it a part of our
ordinary practice to refer the annual Budget to this kind of tribunal.
They are not so conclusive against referring to it new principles
embodied in the Budget on the *first* occasion when those principles
are adopted. If it be asked who is to define this occasion, the
answer would be, I suppose, the standing Joint Committee of
Fourteen, though this is not a point which we need at the moment
consider. I presume the body which should have a right to refer
the matter for decision to the Joint Committee would be the
minority of the House of Commons which had unsuccessfully
opposed the Budget. By hypothesis the majority would be in
favour of the change.

(2) If the new Budget principles were brought forward by a
Radical Government, then presumably the House of Commons
Unionist minority would have the alternative of either treating
them by Joint Session of the two Houses, or of submitting them to
a Referendum, whichever they thought best. If, on the other
hand, the new principles were brought forward by a Unionist
Government, the Radical minority would have the same formal
chance open to them, but almost certainly they would choose the
Referendum if the majority in the House of Lords remained
Unionist, and was in favour of the change.

(3) Evidently there is a great deal to be said on both sides with

regard to such a scheme as this, and we have but little time to think it out. Still I believe something practicable could be devised if there was any chance of our obtaining an important electoral advantage by not making the proposal. Bonar Law and Garvin evidently think there is such an advantage. Fabian Ware has written to me very much alarmed about it, but as he wants us to submit the question of Home Rule to the Colonial Conference (a most futile idea) his opinion leaves me untouched!

I am sending this by special messenger to catch you in Scotland. If Bonar Law's idea is to be carried out at all, it should find expression in my speech at the Albert Hall tomorrow night. You will not have time, therefore, to send me an argued reply, but a telegraphic message based on this letter will probably be made intelligible.

I have kept a copy, and I have numbered the paragraphs.

Since dictating the above I have seen Lansdowne. He is clearly, and strongly, for Bonar Law's proposal. I now understand that the *Daily Mail* has taken it up. So many of our candidates get their speeches out of that paper; and so many others (poor dears!) are utterly floored by the question, "Are you going only 'To trust the people' when Radical legislation is in dispute?"—that I am convinced at least a large minority of our Party will find themselves pledged to the new project before we know where we are. We shall then be exactly in the position we were in about letting in Colonial corn free. In other words, the unpledged portion of the Party can never hope to be strong enough to resist the pledged portion *plus* the Radicals.

On the whole I am disposed to think that I cannot be silent about the matter tomorrow—that I cannot wisely plead for delay and further consideration—that I had better therefore boldly accept the challenge thrown down to us, and say that we do *not* shrink from an appeal to a Referendum in the case of Tariff Reform.

Yours in haste,

ARTHUR JAS. BALFOUR.

I kept no copy of my reply to this letter, which was written at midnight from my hotel in Glasgow, and the original cannot now be found. It was, however, as strong a remonstrance against the proposal as I could make. If the Government had accepted our proposals, it might have been necessary to make this concession to them, but since compromise and agreement had proved impossible, I saw nothing to gain and much to lose by what I regarded as a fatal change of front just as we entered on the election campaign.

To this remonstrance Balfour replied next day:

*Balfour to A. C.*
*Private.*
4 CARLTON GARDENS,<br>PALL MALL, S.W.,<br>30th November 1910.

MY DEAR AUSTEN,

I am really distressed at having had to take a line last night of the expediency of which I know you are very doubtful. I hate doing anything important without carrying my most trusted colleagues with me, but, in truth, a decision had to be taken one way or the other. Silence was impossible, and, indeed, would itself have amounted to that which I firmly believe is the best for Tariff Reform, as well as for the other articles of our political faith.

I kept Lansdowne here till 7 o'clock, when your letter arrived, and we anxiously discussed it in the short time then available. I am fully impressed with the important arguments you use, and unquestionably the difficulties of a Referendum are great. At the same time, had I refused the Referendum, we should have had to meet a broad line of argument of peculiar plausibility at a time like this—I mean the contention that while we provided a machinery for preventing a House of Commons, elected, as all Houses of Commons are, on a mixed issue, from deciding some great new departure against the people's wishes when the majority in the House of Commons was Radical, we refused to provide any such machinery when the majority in the House of Commons happened to be Unionist. To this I believe there is really no effective electoral answer, and my own personal conviction—right or wrong— is that we could venture upon a Tariff Reform Budget with a narrow majority in much greater security if there were a Referendum behind it than we could under any other conditions.

You are so busy, and I am so busy, that I do not argue the matter

U

305

further now. But I hope you will understand the precise conditions under which the decision was arrived at.

I do not know whether it will or will not influence you to know that all the colleagues I have been able to see were strongly in favour of the course I took, and that Lansdowne in particular is more emphatic in his expression of opinion than I have ever known him upon any subject whatever.

Yours ever,

ARTHUR JAMES BALFOUR.

*P.S.*—I am told—and, if true, it is interesting—that in Switzerland, where the ordinary Budget is of course not submitted to a Referendum, their Penal tariff *was* submitted on its first introduction, and carried triumphantly.

*Private.*　　　　　　　　　　　　　　　4 CARLTON GARDENS,
　　　　　　　　　　　　　　　　　　　PALL MALL, S.W.,
MY DEAR AUSTEN,　　　　　　　　　　13*th December* 1910.

It certainly is very much to be regretted that we could not consult further before my Albert Hall statement, though possibly consultation might not have altered the views of either of us.

As you know, the decision had to be taken one way or the other within a very few hours. We were 400 miles apart, and I could do no more than I did to collect the views of the Party leaders. I suspect that if a Shadow Cabinet could have been called, the whole trend of its opinion would have been nearly unanimous in favour of the course which, on my own responsibility, I did actually adopt.

Nor, in truth, have I been at all shaken by the course of subsequent events. I do not believe that our candidates could have faced the question which was being put to them at every meeting— "Are you going to have a Referendum only where the Liberal measures are concerned; are you going to give Unionist revolutions a free run?" You remember that this point was constantly put during the course of the Conference by Lloyd George, and I always expressed my willingness to see the Referendum extended even to cases where the two Houses were agreed. It is true that none of the eight were of opinion that Budgets were suitable subjects for a Referendum; nor, speaking generally, do I think they are. But it is extremely difficult to argue that when a new way of looking at national finance is for the first time adopted, the Referendum (by hypothesis to be used for other purposes) should not be employed. If you ask me whether it will hurt Tariff Reform, my own opinion is that it will not. If you ask me whether it will delay it, again I think it will not, except for the time required to take the Referendum. I am convinced that in all the countries which have adopted a tariff it would have been endorsed by a popular vote. I do not see why this country should be an exception, and I doubt whether you would ever get a majority for Tariff Reform in the House unless there was every prospect of the policy being endorsed afterwards at the poll.

As regards the electoral effect at the present juncture, it must, of course, be a matter of conjecture. I have done my best impartially to weigh all the testimony available, and I am myself convinced that if I had taken a different line the Government anticipations would have been fulfilled, and we should have lost heavily. I admit, however, that this is necessarily a matter incapable of demonstration, and I only give it as my own very strong opinion.

I cannot tell you how grieved I am at finding there is even this shade of difference between us. You know how I hate feeling that in any particular there is anything but absolute agreement between us. I am just off to Scotland, where I make my last speech tomorrow —hoarse and rather tired.

Yours ever,

ARTHUR JAS. BALFOUR.

I examined the effect of the pledge on the elections as soon as the results were known in the following memorandum, of which I sent a copy to Balfour and Lansdowne. I did not, I am sorry to say, convince either of them. A final appeal to Lansdowne closes the year.

*Memorandum by A. C. on the result of the Albert Hall Pledge*

*Monday, 5th December 1910.*

Now that we have the results of the first day's elections, it is I think worth while to consider what evidence they offer of the strength of the Free Trade Unionists and of the advantage which the Party has gained by endeavouring to conciliate them by the offer of a Referendum on Tariff Reform.

Lord Cromer has taken to himself the credit of this suggestion. He boasted loudly of the number of voters who followed his lead and of the strength that he could bring to the Party. What has the support of himself and his friends been worth? If the Free-Food Unionists are numerous anywhere, we ought to see clear evidence of it in the polls. Where do we find it?

Manchester is their stronghold. What have they done there? The Unionist vote has increased in only two of the Divisions—the North-east and the South-west. I dismiss the latter, where we lost a seat, for in January last there was a three-cornered fight. This time there was no Labour candidate. Both the Liberal and the Unionist polled more votes than before, but the Liberal increase was greatest.

But the case of North-east Manchester merits attention. The Labour vote has gone down. The Unionist vote has gone up 429; but is that—the only real advance in Manchester—due to the Referendum? The Unionist candidate definitely repudiates it!

We have won seats at Ashton-under-Lyne, Warrington, Wigan, South Salford, Darlington, Grimsby and King's Lynn. At Ashton-under-Lyne, Mr. Aitken, a Canadian by birth, stuck to Colonial Preference "almost to the exclusion of every other topic." Does he owe the seat to Unionist Free Fooders?

At Darlington I addressed some ten thousand people in two meetings on the eve of the poll. At the second I asked what I should talk about. The meeting called for Tariff Reform and nothing else. I spoke on the Food Duties at both gatherings. "If we win," said both the Chairman of our Association and the candidate, "we shall owe it very largely to you." The candidate himself fought almost entirely on Tariff Reform.

At South Salford the candidate, now the Member, said after the poll:

"The real issue was not the House of Lords. It was the question of the Tariff."

He added that he found meetings listened impatiently to speeches on the House of Lords; they always listened attentively to Tariff Reform.

I have no special knowledge of Warrington, but it was expected that we should win it before the Referendum promise was given. At Wigan I spoke to two great meetings in November. They both came to listen to Tariff Reform. They both heard all about the Food Taxes. The seat was won without the Referendum and I do not hesitate to say that it was won by Tariff Reform.

I say nothing of King's Lynn and Grimsby. If anyone believes that they were won by the Referendum, I should like to see the evidence on which his belief is founded. But turn to Lincoln. Here last time there was an Independent Unionist Free Trade candidate. He has maintained a Free Trade Unionist organisation with the help of a large expenditure. He is one of Lord Cromer's followers and, like Lord Cromer having done all the mischief he could for several years, rallied at the last moment because the Referendum satisfied him. What was the value of his support? The Liberal polled more votes than ever and has a majority of over 600.

Lord Cromer has a family connection with Glasgow. There, if anywhere outside Manchester, the Unionist Free Fooders are strong. They boast that it is their defection which cost us many seats. Lord Cromer himself claims that they have great influence there. Wait and see! I shall be surprised if the results establish his claim.

*6th December* 1910.

The second day's polls are now available. We have lost seats at Cheltenham and Wakefield. Mr. Brotherton was a Free Fooder till a short time ago. He has never been a genuine Tariff Reformer. He probably thought the Referendum was his salvation. It has proved his undoing. And Cheltenham? Here in the home of retired officers, civil and military, living on small fixed incomes, Tariff Reform was said to be a bugbear; yet Tariff Reform won last January. Here, if anywhere, you would expect to find the "moderate man" who is afraid of Tariff Reform. How many of them rallied to the cry of the Referendum? What are they worth? We have lost the seat.

*9th December* 1910.

I have kept this paper back till the Glasgow results were available. We now have them. The position is unchanged. We have not succeeded in winning a single seat.

It would be wearisome to go through all the results in the same way, but the result at Durham is, perhaps, worth notice. It is a University and Cathedral city. The "moderate" voter ought to be in evidence there if anywhere. In January last there was no contest. We have therefore to take 1906 as our comparison. Now it happens that in 1906 the sitting member was Mr. Arthur Elliot, a Unionist Free Fooder. He was opposed by Mr. J. W. Hills as a Tariff Reformer. Mr. Hills won the seat with 1313 votes to Mr. Elliot's 880. Mr. Hills now polls exactly the same number. The Liberal candidate polls 877 or three less than Mr. Elliot. In a straight fight between two Unionists on the single issue of Tariff Reform against Free Trade our majority was 433. With the help of the Unionist Free Traders and the moderate men, placated by the offer of the Referendum, we have raised it to 436. Was it worth while?

After weeks and even months of careful consideration the Unionist members of the Conference decided to restrict their proposal for the use of the Referendum to constitutional changes defined as being changes in the law-making power. We agreed that there were great difficulties in extending it to any other matters, and, in particular, we were unanimously of opinion that it was unsuitable for a Budget, whether Tariff Reform or not, for if it were applied to Budgets we foresaw that the temptation to turn these Budgets into a bribe to the many at the expense of the few would be irresistible.

Following the lines on which we had worked, Lord Lansdowne moved and carried his resolutions in the House of Lords. It is true that they left open an extended use of the Referendum, but finance was still specifically and deliberately excluded from its operation. On these lines we went into the fight. Nottingham gave us our battle-cry and all the omens were favourable.

Then came the suggestion of the *Observer*. Garvin and others, in the hope of conciliating so-called "moderate" opinion, raised the cry for the extension of the Referendum to Tariff Reform. If that were done, all would be well. Free Traders and Free Fooders would flock to our standard; the moderates would rally to us in their thousands and victory was certain.

Again, I ask, was it worth while? What evidence is there that we have gained any real strength in the constituencies by this new policy?

I earnestly hope that it is not too late to ask that the whole question should be carefully considered before the Party is further committed to a proposal the disadvantages of which are obvious and the advantages still to seek.

*Sd.* AUSTEN CHAMBERLAIN.

CLIVEDEN,

MY DEAR LANSDOWNE, 18*th December* 1910.

Many thanks for your letter. I, of course, knew that you had been consulted by Balfour before his Albert Hall speech and that you had agreed with him. I confess that his declaration there was a great blow to me—the worst disappointment that I have suffered for a long time in politics. Had we won seats, it would have thrown all the credit for our victories into the hands of the little band of Free Fooders who have done nothing to help and much to hinder us ever since 1903. It would besides have saddled us with a proposal which, as applied to Budgets, I believe to be almost, if not quite, impracticable. But the paper I sent to you and him was not meant as a complaint over spilt milk but as a very earnest appeal that our position should be most carefully reconsidered before anything is said to pledge us as to the future now that it is obvious that we have not won this time and that we are therefore free to reconsider the pledge.

I wish very much that I could accept your invitation to come to see you, for I should like to talk the position over with you, but I am tied up with engagements in London up to Thursday and must then go down to Highbury for Christmas.

It is of course impossible to *prove* one way or the other what the effect of the pledge has been. You and Balfour both believe it to have been justified by the results, and you will find a great many people to support your opinion. I am profoundly convinced of the contrary, but all timid folk—and there are so many of them —will agree with you, but timid folk don't win elections. We gain half a dozen well-known names and we lose our chance of winning hundreds—and it is hundreds and not half-dozens that we need to win. You may not rate his judgment very high, but Hewins wrote to me that it ruined his chances and Colefax that it did him harm in Manchester. It encouraged people everywhere to put Tariff Reform in the background and the House of Lords in the forefront and that played straight into the hands of the Government.

Well, it's over for the moment, but do, I beg, think very seriously before you tie yourself permanently to a proposal which we deliberately rejected on its merits and which Balfour only accepted provisionally in answer to a "challenge" which in fact proved to be only a trap.

Yrs. ever,<br>Austen Chamberlain.

1911

1911

THE year 1910 had been one of continuous domestic crisis and hot political contention which two General Elections within the twelve-month had done nothing to allay. Its successor was a year of both domestic and foreign crisis and brought us to the verge of war with Germany. I wrote of it in *Down the Years* [1]:

> "On July 2nd the world had been startled by the announce-ment of the sudden despatch of the *Panther* to Agadir, and some three weeks later by the grave warning addressed to Germany by Mr. Lloyd George (then Chancellor of the Exchequer) at the Mansion House. Peace, he had said, was the greatest of British interests, but if Britain was to be treated where her interests were vitally affected as if she were of no account in the Cabinet of Nations, peace at any price would be an intolerable humiliation. Such words coming from the mouth of a Minister who was supposed to belong to the most pacific section of the Cabinet produced a profound impression, which was not lessened when it became known that the King had postponed his visit to Good-wood and that the Atlantic Fleet, which had been on the point of starting for a cruise in Norwegian waters, had been ordered to Portsmouth. A brief statement was made in Parliament on July 27th by the Prime Minister, who appealed to the House to postpone all further discussion. Balfour at once declared that the Opposition would observe the rule that no party differences should prevent national agreement where British interests abroad were at stake, though he added (for it was at the height of the Constitutional crisis and party feeling was running very high) that adherence to it had never been more difficult; and he reinforced the Chancellor's warning by saying that if anyone was counting on their acting differently, he had utterly mistaken the temper of the British people and the patriotism of the Opposition.
>
> "It would have been well for Germany if her rulers had re-membered this declaration in August 1914 when it is supposed that they reckoned on the violence of the passions aroused by the

[1] Pp. 63-4.

Home Rule question to paralyse British action and to prevent us from entering the war to defend our own interests or to come to the assistance of France or Belgium.

"It was not till towards the end of November that an agreement was reached between the French and German negotiators. Meanwhile the air was full of rumours, some true, some false, of military and naval preparations, and all Europe was kept in a state of strained and dangerous tension. When on the last days of that month the House of Commons was able to proceed to the discussion which it had been promised and the Government made a full statement on the events of the last few months, it was clear for all who had eyes to see and ears to hear how grave the situation had been and how perilously near the nations had stood to the brink of war."

There is little trace of these anxieties in my letters, for at the height of the crisis my father was in London and I saw him frequently.

Before the danger was past, Italy startled the world by a sudden declaration of war against Turkey on 24th September and by the annexation of Tripoli. My wife and I were staying on the Italian Lakes at the time and saw the first signs of mobilisation as we journeyed from Como to Baveno. It was the holiday season, and the Press and Diplomacy seemed equally taken by surprise. There was no Covenant or Pact of Paris in these days, and my sympathies, as will be seen, were wholly with the Italians.

Parliament met this year on 6th February. As my letters show, I was exhausted by the long fight over the Budget and by two General Elections (then a more lengthy affair than now as the polls themselves were not yet all held on one day) in which I had spoken nightly.

But worse than the physical fatigue and in part its cause was the intense depression which settled down on me as a result of the Albert Hall Pledge. To have fought so long and so hard to keep Tariff Reform in the forefront of our programme and to prevent its being whittled away or postponed, to have come so near, as it seemed to me, to success and then to see this new obstacle suddenly interposed in haste and at the last moment, though we had deliberately rejected it earlier after full consideration, left me miserable and exhausted. Only once before in my political life had I felt so beaten and *humiliated*, and that was when Balfour's Cabinet decided in its last year not to meet the challenge of a Private Member's motion on Food Taxes, but to abstain from speech and vote, and I had come to the conclusion that nevertheless it was my duty not to resign and that I could best serve the cause of Tariff Reform by remaining in the Government. On that occasion I sought my father's advice. He listened patiently and with loving sympathy to all I had to say, but at the end he replied :

"I am sorry, my boy, but this time I can't advise you. You have your own position and responsibilities ; they are different from mine, and you must make your own decision."

I left his house where I had dined and went back to 11 Downing Street to go to bed but not to sleep. In the morning I wrote to him that I had decided that I must "eat dirt." That decision cost me one of the two sleepless nights which political worries have caused me in my whole career. The other was when I resigned the Secretaryship of State for India during the war, in face of great pressure from the Prime Minister, from Balfour himself, and from Bonar Law.

But all this is a digression, though there is an allusion to the earlier case in one of these letters.

The opening of Parliament found the Unionist leaders ill-prepared and their councils in much confusion. We had declared for the reform of the House of Lords, but there was no agreement as to the extent and character of the change to be made. We had adopted the Referendum, but even among those who welcomed it there was no agreement as to the circumstances in which it was to be applied. The Budget dispute was ended and the Budget which had roused such fears had become law, but we were now to face the battle over the Constitutional issue which the rejection of the Finance Bill by the House of Lords had brought to a head.

The proposals of the Government were embodied in the Parliament Bill introduced by the Prime Minister on 21st February. They have long been the law of the land and I shall not recapitulate them here, but they gave rise to a more serious crisis than the Budget itself and one which this time sharply divided the Unionist Party within its own ranks along unaccustomed lines, for I and other strong Tariff Reformers found ourselves now in hearty agreement and close co-operation with Lord Salisbury and his brothers and separated from some at least of those with whom we had worked during the struggle over Tariff Reform.

The Parliament Bill was introduced on 21st February and with the aid of a rigorous use of the closure was read a third time on 15th May. All attempt to reform or reconstitute the Second Chamber was abandoned and the Bill was confined to a rigorous curtailment of its power to reject Bills passed by the Commons.

The struggle was interrupted for a few days by the celebration of the King's Coronation, which took place on 26th July, but it was already generally known that the Peers intended to introduce amendments in the House of Lords altering the Bill on two or three important points, and in particular insisting on special safeguards against organic change in the Constitution without previous consultation of the people. On 20th July, however, Asquith wrote to Balfour that he thought it courteous and right before any public decisions were announced to let him know how the Government viewed the political situation. They would, he said, ask the House of Commons to disagree with the Lords' amendments. "In the circumstances," he added, " should the necessity arise, the Government will advise the King to exercise his prerogative to secure the passing into law of the Bill in substantially the same form in which it had left the House of Commons, and His Majesty has been pleased to signify that he will consider it his duty to accept and act on that advice."

In view of this pledge, which, as it subsequently appeared, had been obtained from the King as far back as the previous November when it had been made a condition of the advice tendered to His Majesty to dissolve Parliament, Lansdowne held that the Peers were no longer free agents and that they could only submit to *force majeure*. A section of the Party, dubbed Die-hards, comprising many of the most active and keenest of our younger men, took the opposite view and the Party was divided, according to the political slang of the time, into "Hedgers" and "Ditchers." Lord Halsbury became the central figure of the minority who desired to fight out the struggle to the end and to force, if necessary, the creation of peers. He was supported amongst others by the Dukes of Bedford, Westminster and Marlborough, by Lord Selborne, Lord Salisbury, Lord Milner and Lord Willoughby de Broke, and among the Commoners by Carson, Wyndham, Lord Robert and Lord Hugh Cecil, F. E. Smith and myself. Party passions ran very high; when the Lords' amendments were discussed in the Commons, the Prime

Minister was refused a hearing, Lord Hugh Cecil of all men taking a marked part in the disturbance. A little later, Balfour described the action of the Government as a "felon's blow" struck at our liberty, and the advice given to the King as "traitor's advice." It became clear that the King had accepted the advice with great reluctance, and so moderate a man as Archbishop Davidson, as appears in his *Life*, felt strongly that an improper advantage had been taken of his inexperience.

A Banquet, organised in honour of Lord Halsbury, gave an opportunity to the Die-hards or "Ditchers" to express their views, and an active campaign was undertaken among the Peers to secure recruits. Lansdowne himself advised the Unionist Peers to abstain from voting, though he would not discourage those who wished to vote in favour of the Bill. A middle body, led by the late Duke of Norfolk, were ready to abstain if that course was followed by all the Unionist Peers, but announced that they would vote against the Bill if any Conservative Peers voted in its favour. Up to the last moment the issue remained in doubt. Finally, on August 10th, the House resolved not to insist on its amendments by a majority of 131 to 114, and the Bill became law. Thirty-seven Unionist Peers voted with the Government, and the Duke of Norfolk and some of his friends cast their votes against it.

A few days before the final decision was taken, Balfour addressed a letter to Lord Newton stating that he agreed with the advice Lord Lansdowne had given to his friends. "With Lord Lansdowne I stand; with Lord Lansdowne I am ready, if need be, to fall." After arguing the merits of the issue he added: "Let us, then, if we can, agree. Let the Unionists in the Upper House follow their trusted leader. But if this be impossible, if differ we must, if there be Peers who (on this occasion) are resolved to abandon Lord Lansdowne, if there be politicians outside who feel constrained to applaud them, let us all at least remember that the campaign for Constitutional freedom is but just begun. . . . It would, in my opinion, be a misfortune if the present crisis left the House of Lords weaker than the Parliament Bill by itself will make it; but it would be an irreparable tragedy if it left us a divided Party."

This letter was naturally regarded by *The Times* and other papers as a rebuke to the Die-hards, and was interpreted as charging them with disloyalty. The letter and the comments which it aroused drew a strong remonstrance from me, which I print, together with Balfour's reply, on pages 348-351.

Reviewing the whole controversy after the lapse of years I suppose that it must be admitted that it was a mistake for the House of Lords to throw out the Budget in the first instance; but once this action had been taken, I remain of the opinion which I held strongly at the time and for which I had my father's full support, that having entered into the struggle we were bound to see it through. A Constitutional revolution was worked without the mass of the people apprehending then or since what its effect would be. The fundamental Constitutional laws of this country are left at the mercy of a House of Commons majority in a single Parliament without any of the safeguards which have been thought necessary in every other great democracy. The House of Lords was left unreformed and shorn of its powers. If the creation of peers had been forced it would have brought this Constitutional issue to a head, and a serious effort must have been made to reform the Second Chamber as a necessary step to giving it the powers which it ought to possess.

This struggle was scarcely over when a strike broke out on the railways which for a time gave great anxiety. It was finally settled by Mr. Lloyd George, as it was believed, by an appeal to the patriotism of the railway directors based upon the critical international situation. The negotiations had been long and difficult. It was nearly midnight when agreement was at last reached, and the story went that Lloyd George had burst into the Cabinet room, where other Ministers were waiting to hear the result, triumphant, but exhausted, exclaiming:

"I've done it! Don't ask me how, but open a bottle of champagne." [1]

Owing to the determination to get the Parliament Bill through the House of Commons before entering on consideration of the Finance Bill, the Budget was not introduced till 5th May. Its principal features were the initiation of the National Health Insurance scheme and the introduction of Payment of Members. At the time I opposed the latter proposal, which the changed composition of the House has since rendered necessary.

The only other parliamentary business which I need mention was the fight over the Government's Naval Prize Bill, giving effect to the Declaration of London. It was strongly opposed in the House of Commons and by Chambers of Commerce and Shipping

---

[1] See letter of March 1st, 1912.

throughout the country, but was carried by large majorities. Fortunately for the country it was rejected by the House of Lords and the Declaration remained unratified. Though three years later, on the outbreak of war, the Government declared their intention of observing it, they quickly found this course impossible and, thanks to the action of the House of Lords, we were bound by no international engagement.

In the early months of the year a Reciprocity Treaty was negotiated between the Governments of the United States and Canada, and caused much anxiety among Tariff Reformers in this country, who felt that we were missing our opportunity and that the door might soon be closed against us which the Asquith Government had, in Mr. Churchill's famous phrase, "banged, barred and bolted" in the face of the Colonies at the Conference held three years earlier. In a letter subsequently published, President Taft claimed that it "would have made Canada an adjunct of the United States." That was what we feared, but the agreement was strongly opposed by the Opposition in the Dominion and caused considerable defections in the Government ranks. As a result Sir Wilfred Laurier's Government was decisively defeated at the General Election of this year and its place taken by a Conservative Government under the premiership of Mr. Borden.

I had taken a motor-trip to Cannes with my wife in April, and when Parliament at last rose in the third week of August she and I went to Switzerland and the Italian Lakes for a more prolonged holiday. My return was hastened by the telegram from my brother printed on page 356. During the year dissatisfaction with the condition of the Party and with Balfour's leadership had been growing and the cry, "Balfour must go," had been raised by Leo Maxse with all his accustomed vigour in the pages of the *National Review*. I had been urged by many of my friends among the younger men to take a more independent attitude and to announce an "unauthorised programme" of my own as my father had done before me. My attitude towards Balfour was defined in my letter of August to F. E. Smith and from that attitude I never swerved. It had been painful to me to differ openly from him on the question of the House of Lords, and scarcely less so to find myself, as I had done so often since 1903, out of harmony with the course which he had marked out for himself, but I had a deep and affectionate regard for the man and had received much kindness and unfailing consideration from him, and as long as he was prepared to retain the position, I could have no other leader and could lend myself to no movement directed against him.

I was not therefore very happy about the new movement started in my absence to form a "Halsbury Club." It was intended to unite in closer and more effective action the fighting spirits of the Party, to adopt generally a less negative and purely critical position than that which had commended itself to Balfour and was natural to his temperament, and, whilst adopting a more aggressive attitude towards the Government in Parliament, to advocate a more constructive programme in the country. In pursuing these aims, however, it ran the risk of keeping alive something of the divisions which had crept into our ranks, but I was in sympathy with the objects which its founders proclaimed and, on the definite understanding that it was not to be directed against Balfour and indeed in the belief that I could preserve the observance of this condition better from inside than from outside its ranks, I agreed to join.

But events were precipitated by Balfour himself. Parliament reassembled on 24th October and on 8th November Balfour publicly announced his resignation of the leadership at a meeting of the City of London Conservative Association. The story of this decision and of what followed is told as far as was known to me in my letters to Mrs. Chamberlain and one or two from other sources which I am permitted by the writers or their representatives to publish.

Balfour had been the leader of the Unionist Party as well as leader in the House of Commons. It was now for the members of the Party in the House of Commons to choose a new leader in that House only. Whether he or the leader of the Party in the House of Lords would eventually become leader of the Party would, in accordance with precedent, be left unsettled until the time came for the Party to take office, when it would probably be decided by the action of the King in inviting the one or the other to form a Government.

The choice of the Party appeared to lie between Walter Long and myself, but two other names were quickly mentioned. In view of the imminence of the struggle over the coming Home Rule Bill, for which the Government was actively preparing, the candidature of Sir Edward Carson was proposed by the Irish Unionists and might be the choice of the Party, particularly if it was very evenly divided between Long and myself. Sir Edward Carson, however, refused to allow his name to go forward, but another

322

candidate appeared rather unexpectedly in the field in the person of Bonar Law. I think it is true to say that my colleagues in the late Government, including the Whips, the keener Tariff Reformers and many of the younger men, thought that I was the better fitted to fill the vacancy, but I still called myself a Liberal Unionist, I had only joined the Carlton Club a little time before, and the part which I had taken in recent events had certainly aroused some passing antagonism. Long, on the other hand, was a lifetime Conservative, a typical country gentleman and senior to me both in length of service in the House and in Cabinet rank and he aroused none of the jealousies or doubts which were inseparable from my position. I have told the story of my part in these events in the account sent to my father and written in all the stress and the emotion of those critical days. I have added a few letters to and from others to complete the picture.

As a result, Bonar Law was chosen by acclamation and quickly justified his selection by the new vigour of his leadership.

The stage was now set for the culmination of the struggle over Home Rule which continued to be the dominant factor in domestic politics until the outbreak of the Great War.

1911 : February, March

9 Egerton Place, S.W.,
28th February 1911.

Here comes out the familiar blue pad of writing paper and here
begins a new series of letters. What will they have to record and how
far will things have marched to their appointed end before you come
back? I wonder! I wonder too what that end will be. I feel certain
that the Government are uncertain; that is all that I do feel sure of.
Well, time will show, and meanwhile we will keep up a merry fight.

I hope that you have had a good journey and are safely and
comfortably housed at the Villa Victoria[1] by this time. At any
rate you are well out of London. It is a pouring wet day; London
is a sea of mud and all that you can imagine disagreeable.

Neville dined with us at the House last night and heard Arthur
Lee make one of the best speeches he has ever made. Today we
two went to the Levée where I saw many friends whilst waiting
for Neville to pass, and received many congratulations on my
speech of yesterday. It passed off very well—the speech I mean—
though I felt bad about it beforehand. I enclose a note which Ivy
passed down to me from the Gallery. You will laugh at her naïf
surprise at Lady Londonderry's habit of passing remarks.

At the Levée the Bishop of Uganda begged to be remembered
to Father, and the new Greek Minister sent his and his country's
respects and best wishes. Sir D. Morris was there too and gave
an amazing account of the revival of the West Indies. He is to
send through me an address of his for Father's perusal.

1st March 1911.

The debate on my amendment[2] drags itself rather wearily
along. There is no lack of speakers and a good deal of rather

[1] At Cannes.
[2] Regretting that the persistent refusal of the Government to modify the
Fiscal System was imperilling the preference granted by the Dominions, de-
ferred closer commercial union of the Empire and deprived the country of the
most effective method of inducing foreign countries to grant fair treatment to
British manufacturers.

324

good speaking—young Astor [1] for instance making an excellent maiden speech yesterday—but the interest of the House centres not in the debate but in the rumours and button-holing of the lobbies. No doubt tomorrow, when the end comes, there will be more excitement.

We dined last night with the Aveburys—not very lively as you may think, but I had some very pleasant talk with the Archbishop of Canterbury. By the way, his brother of York overwhelmed me at the Levée with congratulations on my speech. His speech for the Budget made him appear more of a partisan than he wishes to be thought and he is anxious to restore the balance.

You know Haldane's penguin-like gestures when he is speaking —elbows pressed in and fat hands splayed out with upturned palms. Somebody said of his speech on Monday:

"His gestures always remind me of a conjurer doing his tricks."

"Yes, and he keeps up the same meaningless patter all the time," added someone else. Not a bad description of him as a House of Commons speaker!

*2nd March* 1911.

There is no news here. Two lovely spring days have succeeded the storm of the early part of the week and make the idea of the House of Commons more abhorrent than ever. Clyde finished a good speech yesterday and Anson spoke thoughtfully as always and unusually well, but the debate is flat, though thirty men rise every time to catch the Speaker's eye. I brought Collings home to dinner and left him here with Ivy when I returned for the afterdinner speeches. He was very pleasant as always and seemed in good spirits, having just had a successful fight at the Central Chamber of Agriculture over Land Purchase.

Ivy and I thought we would like a jaunt in the morning so we went to the National Portrait Gallery and then lunched at the Carlton to give ourselves a holiday feeling. We enjoyed it!

Sifton's speech seems to have produced a great effect in Canada.

[1] Now Lord Astor.

Oh! if only we could move a little faster and if the Canadian Government would move a little slower! All the news seems to show that feeling in the Dominion is hardening against the Reciprocity Agreement, but I fear that it will not have time to make itself fully felt. Still it is very satisfactory that the feeling is there.

*4th March* 1911.

In the evening I dined at the Palace, sitting between Lord Herschell and Sir A. Nicolson. The former was very pleasant and we spoke appreciatively of our fathers' regard for each other. Nicolson [1] was gloomy, foreigners didn't understand what we were about or why we were rushing to change a constitution which had been the envy of all the world. They couldn't make the present England out; the fact was, as Cambon had said to him, the English character was changing and we were no longer the sober, steady, conservative people that we had been. And withal our people were very hard to rouse to a sense of their danger (in foreign affairs). France was entering on a new period of uncertainty and ministerial instability. Cruppi knew nothing of foreign affairs; Delcassé would guide the foreign policy of France as far as any man could who was not foreign minister. He should not be surprised if in the end it resulted in Clemenceau's return to power, but meanwhile——!

"People ask me," he said, "whether I think that Germany means to make war on us. Not in the least, I reply, but she means to have the dominant word in all international questions!"

Altogether, as I say, he was gloomy and disquieting.

Admiral Beaumont was there, very angry at the publication of "A. K. W.'s" [2] notes on invasion, and General Smith-Dorrien equally angry at the publication of Ian Hamilton's book on Compulsory Service.

I talked with Bigge [3] after dinner; he too took to me a gloomy view. What could the Crown do if Asquith pressed for the creation of peers? I sketched a programme for the House of

[1] Later Lord Carnock.
[2] Admiral Sir Arthur Knyvet Wilson.
[3] Private Secretary to the King, afterwards Lord Stamfordham.

Lords: read the Parliament Bill a second time, limit its duration to two years and provide that no Home Rule Bill should be submitted during that time for the Royal Assent without previous reference to and approval by the people. If they took up that position, I did not believe that Asquith could ask the Crown to exercise its prerogative in a revolutionary way; if he did, I could not believe that the Crown ought to do it; and if the Crown refused, I was certain it would find ministers to risk everything in support of it and believed, though no man could *guarantee* success, that in such circumstances another General Election would produce very different results.

Here we were interrupted and I gossiped with Halsbury. He had a story that John Burns, being told that Lloyd George had produced a most favourable impression during his stay at Court and been most conciliatory and attentive, had replied:

"Yes, and he's had housemaid's knee ever since!"—which at least has the merit of being just what Burns would be likely to say of one of his colleagues.

The King, who looked very well and seemed in good spirits, didn't leave us till nearly midnight. He sent most friendly messages to Father and told me Asquith had spoken in warm praise of my speech.

Dr. Jowett of Carr's Lane was there as a representative of Nonconformity and I had a pleasant chat with him. He is going to leave Carr's Lane in a few weeks, having accepted the charge of a large church in New York. They have not yet chosen his successor in Birmingham.

*5th March* 1911.

The longing for a holiday and above all for Italy is strong upon me. Being unable to gratify it, I do the next best thing. I have been very idle since Friday. Yesterday morning we went to the National Gallery and spent an hour among the pictures of the Umbrian School, amongst which we noticed particularly a beautiful little St. Catharine by Fiorenzo di Lorenzo from the Salting collection. I vaguely remembered the artist's musical name but nothing more about him. However, in turning over my photographs in the evening, I found I had already made acquaintance with his art at Perugia where there are several episodes from the life of San Bernardino and an Adoration of the Shepherds by him.

We came back here to lunch, took Joe out in the afternoon, and dined alone together. Another lunch and dinner alone today have given us a pleasant homely feeling. We have been so little alone for a long time past. But we have a busy time in front of us. I have a speech to make each of the next three weeks and we have three dinner-parties arranged and fear that we must have two more. We are so much in debt! Besides I want to entertain a few Members, some informally, bringing them home from the House, and some more formally with their wives. I think we have worked off 80 people with the three already arranged!

*12th March* 1911.

Here is a shocking state of things! My last letter to you was dated the 6th and here we are at the 12th with never another word written. But indeed the silence has not been due to idleness; there was not a moment at which I could have written till yesterday and even yesterday I felt too tired. But I must go back to Tuesday and tell you how the week passed.

That morning I spent at a Committee meeting of the L.U. Council where we did a good deal of business. Our Scottish representatives were more hopeful than they have been for some time. The approach of the Home Rule danger, they said, was beginning to make itself felt in that country and they thought it would produce considerable effect before long. J. C. Williams told somewhat the same tale of Cornwall, but he thought that nothing short of the introduction of an actual Home Rule Bill would make much change there.

I got back home just in time for lunch and then went to the House and sat through the Budget discussion, though I did not take part in it. I dined with the Royal Navy Club as their guest and had to respond to the toast of my health. I enjoyed the evening with them, meeting many old friends and being very cordially received, and then I returned to the House to vote.

On Wednesday I went to my Bank and then took the 5 o'clock train to Durham where Storey met me at 10.30, and I passed the night at his house. Next morning I motored into Newcastle,

shook hands with his 500 guests, lunched and made them a speech
and then took the 5 o'clock train back to London. But alas!
I got no rest, for friends came into my carriage and talked with me
nearly the whole way—a bad preparation for the all-night sitting
which followed. I drove straight from the train to the House
and there we battled fiercely from midnight till 10 o'clock next
morning. Winston was leading for the Government and either
of his own motion or at Elibank's instigation broke the Government's repeated pledges that we should have "full opportunity of
discussion" and should only sit "a little late." As a result of their
obstinacy they got in the end one more clause than they might
have had without a fight at 12.30—a very important clause, it
is true, but a very brief one. Some of their men went home,
openly saying that they would not stop for such dirty work.
I have never known such an episode before, for it was a clear
breach of one of those parliamentary understandings which all
leaders have hitherto so carefully guarded.[1]

I came home, had a bath and was down at the House again
at noon, but I only stayed till lunch time and after lunch I went to
bed and slept heavily till dinner. Alas! we had a dinner-party,
but I was dog-tired and my digestion was upset so that I could not
enjoy it and our guests must have thought me very stupid. I kept
very quiet yesterday, having another dinner-party here in the
evening, and felt more equal to taking part in that, but both our
parties were rather upset by people falling off at the last moment
owing to "flu" of which there seems to be a great deal about.

*12th March* 1911.

Well, we have spent a quiet Sunday together and we feel all
the better for it, but to tell the truth we are both tired and we need
a holiday, so that I have pretty well made up my mind that at
Easter I will take one. Rumour says the Government will give
us a week and I think that I shall take a second week; and if I can
swell it to nearly three weeks in all, so much the better. It is long
since I have felt in such continuous need of rest. I can of course
do my work and do extra work at a pinch; but I am fairly tired

---

[1] I believe that Mr. Churchill was not in the House when the pledge was
given and was misled about its terms.

out. I have had bad indigestion for three weeks or more—unprecedented with me, but I suppose that, art having stopped my sciatica, nature has to find a new outlet for my fatigue. And "Cope" can only say that to give me medicine (which he does) is like flogging a dead horse and that a holiday is all I need.

My original idea was ten days at Paris alone with Ivy, but we agree that motoring is really a better holiday and that if we take more than ten days it is too much for Paris, so we incline to go with Leverton who presses us to take another motor-trip with him. We think of Provence, and if the idea materialises, we shall perhaps call on you, but it will be little more than a call. Still it would be nice to see you if only for a couple of days.

It rained as soon as we started for Kew today, but we pursued our way all the same and enjoyed our visit to the greenhouses. Ivy has very wide interests—"you will have noticed it yourself"—and is a capital companion for a holiday, whether it be spent in looking at flowers or pictures or china or old furniture or what not.

I have been reading *Pie Powder*, the book of which I spoke to you.

"I remember an election petition," says the author, "in which one allegation was that a number of rosettes had been kept in a table-drawer in the central committee-room. To meet this charge, it was thought desirable to call witnesses to swear that the only table in the room consisted of planks laid upon trestles. 'So that the table had no proper legs?' said counsel. 'Never mind whether it had proper legs,' said the judge. 'The important question is, had it proper drawers?'"

*16th March* 1911.

Ivy went to a hen lunch yesterday with the wife of the American Naval Attaché and found it very agreeable. Mrs. Harcourt told her that Loulou was in great need of a holiday and that Winston's nerves had quite given way after the all-night sitting. The prolonged strain of these last years seems to be telling on everyone. Eye-witnesses say that at the Board of Trade party first one male "suffragette" created a row and was removed by two detectives and then another who also occupied two detectives, and then—all the detectives being occupied—two women got close to Winston and called him every possible name.

*19th March* 1911.

I am proving a very bad correspondent this year and fear that Father must often be saying: is there still no letter from Austen? But indeed there is nothing to say and half the time I don't feel equal to saying it. I believe I posted a letter or at least a makeshift for a letter last Thursday. On Friday I went to Manchester by the noon train and motored out to Middleton where I was to speak for Hewins. Thereafter the programme was—dinner of twelve people at 6; meeting at 8; overflow meeting at 9; visit to a club and a "few words"; another visit to another club and a few more words; back to my host's and twelve more men to sandwiches and tobacco. At last, soon after midnight, to bed. Came down in the morning to find my host had accepted an invitation for me to lunch at the Club—but at this point I struck and said I must go back to London by the mid-day train, which I did, travelling back with a defeated candidate and a triumphant indigestion as my *compagnons de voyage*. I got to Euston just after four, where Ivy and Joe met me in the brougham.

We had a dinner here in the evening which went off very well after the most palpitating accidents. Three people fell off from illness on the actual day, the last of them at 6 p.m. leaving us thirteen! But we laid violent hands on B. and made her throw over Mrs. Chapin; and, as I say, though it wasn't the party we had planned and didn't *look* very lively on paper, it turned out very well and passed off very pleasantly.

*22nd March* 1911.

Ivy and I lunched yesterday with the Malmesburys and I sat next a dreadful woman, a writer who also does some speaking for us (or for the Central Office). She assured me that the electors were appallingly ignorant, that the Scotch would much prefer being governed by Germany to being dominated by England, that the greater part of politics was settled and arranged beforehand by Mr. Balfour and Mr. Asquith when they met at Lady Elcho's (of course the public did not suspect this, but she knew it), that Asquith's visit to his daughter had nothing to do with her health—"Did I really think it had? Of course not! It was just a political move"—that Lloyd George had for a certainty consumption of the throat and later on, cancer, that Queen Alexandra to her certain knowledge was suffering from an abscess on the brain and was quite mad, that she would probably die in a month and the Coronation would be put off, etc. etc. Nothing would stop her and I subsided into dumb indifference.

*23rd March* 1911.

We have "chucked" our engagements for Thursday and Friday next and our own dinner for Saturday and are going to leave by the night boat on Wednesday next. Every day I seem to get some new little warning that it is time I was off—a most irritating rash all over my body being the last symptom, which "Cope" says is only a form of nettle-rash (urticaria) caused by my being run down. But my real illness is known only to Ivy and myself. It's Referendum sickness! Balfour's Albert Hall speech knocked the heart out of me and I have been fighting without pleasure ever since. Up to that time I was clear we were right and I could go on with good courage if not with particular hopefulness—but since then the bottom has fallen out of the world. Now I think we are wrong and the stimulus to work and fight has gone. I shall see things more sanely when I have had three weeks' change of thought and scene.

We did very well in the House yesterday in a small way, upsetting the Government's programme of business again, forcing them to promise us another extra day for estimates after the 31st and involving them in the necessity for a second Consolidated Fund Bill before Whitsuntide which will still further impede their progress and add to the restiveness of their men below the gangway, who show more and more impatience, who don't back them very well when they try to fight and are furious when they give way to us. Our people calculate that we have now put them a fortnight out of their reckoning and that they *cannot* provoke a crisis before the Coronation.

10 p.m. My day's work has been: to the Bank; to lunch with the Duckworths; to the House of Commons; Shadow Cabinet from 4.45 till 7.40 and to meet again at 11 a.m. on Saturday, which means that I must come up from Birmingham by the 8.45. Oh

damn! And it is all as unsatisfactory as it can be! The world is out of joint and I *can't* set it right. Well, I'm off for a holiday and if only I get away, they may do what they please, bless them! But it aggravates me to attend discussions where I don't agree and can't carry my view. I foresee defeat and can't stop the herd from rushing down the nearest steep place.

Don't be alarmed if you see a paragraph in the papers that I have gone abroad "under medical advice." It only means that I must have a holiday and that I must explain my desertion of my post at the present moment.

We have stopped Joe Lawrence's idea of pressing for a Commission on Preference.

My speech? Well, "*j'ai un commencement d'idée. C'est déjà quelque chose*," as Monsieur Jean[1] said of his new liqueur. But I'm very tired. Well, I will go to bed and sleep on it.

*26th March* 1911.

We came up by the breakfast train yesterday morning[2] and I went straight to Carlton Gardens where we had a Shadow Cabinet —my last, thank goodness! for four weeks at any rate. At last I found myself in a majority again and, strongly supporting Curzon's objections, succeeded in defeating the project of introducing a Referendum Bill of our own as well as a Lords Reform Bill. As to the latter, a Committee of four or five on which I sat produced one Bill; then that was referred to another Committee under Balfour's presidency, and on the ground that our House was too Conservative and didn't look fair as between the parties, they have produced another and more Radical one, and that is now adopted, I dissenting on the ground that we are giving away a great deal too much, in which Douglas as usual agreed with me, and Brodrick dissenting because we were not giving away enough! What a topsy-turvy world, is it not? Even in my present mood, I can't help seeing the humour of it. Well, now, thank goodness! I can leave them to their own devices and they must find their own way out of the wood.

[1] Of the Restaurant Henri IV in Paris.
[2] From Birmingham where I had been for the annual meeting of our Unionist Association held in the Town Hall.

It would have rejoiced you to see and hear the warm welcome given to Neville and Annie at the Town Hall and to feel, as we all felt, how strong were the ties between the meeting and the family.

*28th March* 1911.

I must tell you my week-end record—rather a good one, I think. You already know how we came up from B'ham by the 8.40 and how I had a long Cabinet. Now listen to the record of the last 36 hours. I went to bed at 11 on Saturday and slept till 9.30 on Sunday morning. Then coffee, bath, a game with Joe— and back to bed and *to sleep* till 1.30. After lunch wrote till 5, played with Joe till 6—and *slept* till dinner. Went to bed at 10.30 sharp and slept without waking till 9.30 on Monday morning— say 25 hours' sleep out of the 36. It isn't everyone who can do *that!*

## 1911 : MAY

9 EGERTON PLACE, S.W.,
*1st May* 1911.

The rain did not come and yesterday was a beautiful warm spring day. After a morning spent in clearing off arrears, I went down to the House and found it very dull. The Committee Stage of the Parliament Bill is nearly over and all life has gone out of the discussion if there ever was any life in it. Debate there has been none. On each amendment Asquith or another minister makes one speech and thereafter the ministerial benches are dumb. Our men continue the discussion alone and after a time the closure is moved and the same thing begins again on the next amendment selected by the Chairman for discussion, for all the time the House is working under "kangaroo" closure and vast numbers of amendments are passed over by the Chair.

I found my colleagues, or some of them, still tinkering at a Lords Reform Bill which Lansdowne is to introduce on Monday. But I feel a happy detachment about it. It is not my Bill and I take no responsibility for it or its consequences. If it does not shock Conservative opinion (whether with a big C or a small c) it will show what an amazing distance public opinion has travelled in the last twelve months. But indeed I am inclined to believe that Conservatism now finds a refuge only in the hearts of old Radicals like myself. *A propos:* Balfour related an amazing conversation which had passed between Morley and George Curzon. Morley observed that it would be a great assistance to him in framing his reply for Monday if he could have some kind of indication beforehand as to the scheme Lansdowne would propose. Curzon laughingly replied that it would of course be a great convenience to all of us to know beforehand the nature of the speeches that we had got to answer.

"Of course," he said, "I can't tell you anything about our Bill, but I should have thought you could have gathered sufficient indications of its character from the speeches of Unionist leaders. If it differs from them at all, it will be in the direction which I suppose you approve—*i.e.* more democratic."

"Well, my dear George," said Morley, "there's no reason why I shouldn't tell you that we haven't a draft or a shadow of a draft of a Bill or any idea on the subject. And if your Bill is really of the kind you describe, I don't see why we shouldn't accept it— of course if you accepted our proposals in return."

Curzon did not take up this observation or point out the impossibility of our accepting the Parliament Bill on any conditions, but he said:

"Perhaps I ought to warn you that we retain a measure of the hereditary principle."

"I should hope so," exclaimed Morley, and then he went on to say that in all these matters he was a Conservative and so forth.

"The trouble about our dear John," commented Balfour, "is that you can't trust him. He talks to you like this in private and then lets you down in public."

Gwynne of the *Standard* and Max Aitken have both been in Canada for some time. Chaplin and Bonar Law tell me that both are convinced that Laurier will be beaten on Reciprocity. The Opposition have unlimited powers of obstruction and are determined to use them—even to the extent of refusing supply— so as to force a dissolution before November, and they believe that at a General Election Laurier would be defeated. Heaven send it be so!

There appears to be plenty of work waiting for me—three Committees of the T.R. League and one against Payment of Members tomorrow and a speech to make on Invalidity and Unemployment Insurance on Thursday.

It is grey and cooler (but not cold) today.

*5th May* 1911.

My impression: the Sickness-Invalidity scheme is bold, sound and comprehensive and in many respects original. This is Lloyd George's part. The Unemployment scheme is, I think, hazardous, tentative, incomplete and probably bad, but it is Llewellyn Smith's and not Ll. George's and I believe L. G. not only knows little about it but thinks ill of it.

*7th May* 1911.

I think more and more of what I owe to Father, and I do not know whether I owe most to the counsel he has given me when I needed it or to the extraordinary self-restraint and courage with which he has refused to advise me sometimes when the temptation must have been very strong but when it was necessary—though I did not think so, perhaps, at the moment—that I should take my own decision and steer my own course. The result has been that, for better or worse, I have my own career, my own life and influence, and have not been wholly overshadowed by his great personality, though always trying my own actions and decisions by the thought (not exactly of how he would act— that is a different thing) but by what principle and ideals he would be guided. He has *made* me in every sense of the word and, if I accomplish anything in my career, it will be due to his teaching and his example. I have a good deal of the Kenricks in me by nature. Left to myself, I don't think I should have done much ill to anyone; but if I work and persist and fight with political beasts at Ephesus or elsewhere, it is because I am his son and because "*Noblesse oblige!*" And though in these last years there has been an added pleasure in what I have done, as well as additional ease in doing it, through Ivy's sympathy and help, it is my deepest joy to feel that whatever successes I have won my Father has witnessed and enjoyed, and that *if* any further advancement comes to me in the course of years he will have foretold it and, as it were, enjoyed it too. Never did son owe more to his father and never did father more generously or more wisely help his son's career. He has been more ambitious for me than ever I have been for myself—infinitely more ambitious for me than he was for *himself* —and that is the only point on which I have ever had to resist his counsels. Well, I don't know myself how I am led into saying all this, but give him, please, dear Mary, my deepest love, full alike of gratitude and reverence. God grant that I may be to Joe something of what he has been to me for nearly fifty years! And when I think of what my birth cost him, I am the more amazed and humble. I hope and believe he knows what a profoundly grateful and loving heart his kindness has made.

Confound Ll. George. He has strengthened the Government again. His Sickness scheme *is* a good one and he is on right lines this time. I must say I envy him the opportunity and I must admit that he has made good use of it.

*9th May* 1911.

Further extracts from the provincial Press confirm my first idea that Lansdowne's Bill has been well received by our papers, but the House of Lords itself was very cold. I am told that L. was rather too apologetic and would have had a better reception if he had been bolder. Curzon had a meeting of Unionist Peers at his house and is said to have handled them very well and carried them with him. But I am out of politics!

Talking of agreement, what is one to say of Morley's speech rejecting *any* hereditary element in the reformed H. of Lords after his conversation with Curzon already reported to you? Well, as Balfour said then, the trouble with "our dear John" is that he agrees with you in private and then throws you over publicly.

*11th May* 1911.

I have told Wilson to send you a copy of a letter of Hartington's written when Salisbury was sent for after Gladstone's defeat in 1886. He asked Hartington to form a Government but barred consultation with Father. It would be "too sharp a curve for C. and him to sit in the same Cabinet" then. Very true, and of course, as H. says, Father would have refused; but this, says H., was conclusive against the idea in any case, as, if a Government were formed without consultation with Father, nothing would make it anything but a Conservative administration in popular estimation. I was interested to get at this bit of inner history.

*11th May* 1911.

The ceremony at the Cordwainers [1] was very simple and pleasant, the Master and the Lord Mayor both referring in the

---

[1] The opening of their new Hall, built on the old site.

kindest way to Father's and your absence, and I was asked to convey all good wishes to you both (Master too nervous to be very coherent—Lord Mayor speaking very nicely) and a pair of silver candlesticks to you as a memento of the occasion. They are about six inches high—writing-table size—a replica of an old pair in the Company's possession.

A similar pair was given to Ivy.

*12th May* 1911.

I hurried off a scrap of writing to you last night to tell you the nature of the "memento" destined for you by the Cordwainers. They really treat the family as if we were permanent honorary patrons of the Company and I think they feel that they have got additional credit and a new standing in the City since Father renewed the old association with them and made a speech for them at the unveiling of John Came's window.

Their present dining-hall occupies with the kitchens the top floor of their enlarged new building. It is a fine room panelled with oak and Father's portrait [1] hangs at one end in a good light. We sat just opposite it and once again I thought *how* good it was. Its incompleteness does not trouble me, for what is unfinished is so obviously incomplete that the eye does not dwell on it. As a pendant they have hung a full-length portrait of an old Master, and between the two on a bracket rested the large cup we gave them as a memorial of my Grandfather and Great Uncle. They had invited Lilian and Alfred Cole and Leo and Emmeline, and all four came. I made them a little speech and told them the story of William C. and his broom.

*16th May* 1911.

The Parliament Bill finished its weary course last night and we divided rather badly—majority 120. I came down to vote but did not attend the debate. I seemed unable to pick up any interest in it on my return, and, to tell the truth, did not try very hard. Other men were already engaged on the work; I had not heard the earlier discussions and did not know what had taken place and it seemed best to leave the completion of their work to them.

[1] By Charles Furse.

I hear that the country has taken and still takes very little interest in it.

This morning Ivy and I attended one of the prettiest ceremonials I have ever seen, the unveiling of the Queen's Memorial. We had places on the platform of the Memorial itself and could move about freely so that we saw everything to the best advantage.

In the Mall were massed companies of the Guards, Lifeguards and I think all the regiments having a direct connection with Queen Victoria. Over the flower-beds chairs had been set and the space was gay with uniforms and ladies' dresses.

On the platform facing east the *Corps diplomatique*, Ministers and ex-Ministers and their wives and, grouped below, the choirs of the Royal Chapels.

The Royalties walked from the Palace in procession headed by Beefeaters, etc., and returned in the same way when the ceremony was over. But the two prettiest episodes of all were the general salute as the statue was unveiled, when the massed colours of all the regiments present were lowered as the bands played "God Save the King," and the parade of the troops round the monument before the King and Emperor. The sun shone brightly, the men did their difficult wheel round the circle admirably and colours waved and pennons fluttered on the lances and all looked as splendid as splendid could be.

From the Palace to the new central gate in the Palace railings and again on the steps of the Memorial and its platform *blue* baize was laid instead of the usual red and this greatly added to the beauty and harmony of the scene, but the roadway round the Memorial itself was uncovered and must have ruined the dress of every lady in the procession.

I hear that the day after the last row in the House, when Winston was leading, John Burns had an audience of the King. As he was leaving, the King said:

"I fear that the Home Secretary has not been quite successful in conciliating the House."

"Well, Your Majesty," said Burns, "Winston Churchill does not exactly walk about the House with an oil-can in his hand!"

9 EGERTON PLACE, S.W.,
*16th June* 1911.

11 p.m.  All has gone off very well.  We have every reason to be thankful and none to be anxious, but it has been an awful day and Ivy's courage at once astounds and humbles me.  If I felt for the boy, what must she have felt!  Yet though I saw traces of tears when she had been with him after the operation, she did not let me see a tear all day.  If she had broken down, I ask myself: Could I have held out?  It is so pitiful to see a little fellow like Joe feeling he has been ill-used and afraid of being ill-used again, and his little quivering lip and piteous face when I went into the bedroom after he had been put to bed again haunts me.

They found more adenoids than they expected and the tonsils were swollen as well.  So while he was under the anaesthetic they cut the tonsils a little, also, which of course means a little more pain for poor Joe.  But about 4 o'clock he drank a cup of milk and ate three slices of bread and butter (not very thin) and a biscuit, so his throat cannot be giving him much pain.  He has not been sick at all.  He drowsed away the rest of the morning and played quietly with Ivy and me this afternoon, but of course he is suspicious and afraid of everything—crying even when Miss O'B. took his temperature this evening.  And my heart aches for him and neither Ivy nor I—do what we will—can think of anything else for more than a minute at a time.  B. came in to lunch.  It was very pleasant to see her and her presence was a help.  She must have thought me fretful!  I contradicted and misunderstood all she said but she will have understood.  And now I seek relief, as so often before, by telling you all my troubles, and I don't think I add to yours for your thoughts will have been much with us all day.

*17th June* 1911.

Well, the bad day is over.  Joe is much better this afternoon and will be much better again tomorrow.  I have not passed such

341

a bad day since he was born. Poor little mite! But after all a child's memory for trouble of this sort is short. I am confident that it was right to have it done and he and Ivy and I will all grow stronger from tomorrow.

*31st July* 1911.

I am glad you are safe in Birmingham. It is still very hot here.

Please thank Father for his message. Both Ivy and I are very touched by his consideration and love. We know how in this as in all else you are at one with him and we are more grateful to you both for this fresh token of your love than I can express.

I have been and am fearfully busy and cannot finish my day's work in the 24 hours. But I am very glad to hear of Father's strong approval of our action.

Lansdowne has so far refused to express *dis*approval of anyone voting *for* the Bill or even to *dis*suade anyone from taking that course. But I believe that Balfour and Balcarres have shaken him this afternoon. Meanwhile I am now the lamb which troubles the waters. I hear that Balfour is hurt by my letter to W. de Broke though he has not spoken to me about it. Well, I didn't suppose that he or L. would be exactly grateful for it.

*8th August* 1911.

10 a.m. Many thanks for all your letters. I am so busy that I have not time to write fully even now.

The latest idea is that Asquith is going to accept some amendments—of course not really important ones. It is suggested and pressed by Balcarres and Steel-Maitland that this gives L. a new opportunity which he ought to seize, viz.: to confine his own amendment to the Crown and Protestant Succession—this will probably be accepted by Asquith—and Home Rule, omitting from it the section dealing with grave questions.

This is what I have always wished to see done (I never liked the general use of the Referendum and only accepted it to keep in line with Balfour) and I hope Halsbury and his friends will agree.

If so, Lansdowne and Halsbury and the bulk of their friends will vote together on Wednesday; the Lords will insist on so much of L.'s amendment as refers to Home Rule and it will then be for the Government to create its Peers *before* the Bill goes back a last time.

I don't know whether this will come off. L. is ill and much bullied by Curzon; but I understand from Balcarres that Balfour pressed L. to do it at a meeting held in his room yesterday. What a curious ending if it does come off. If it doesn't, Halsbury would beat the Government but for Unionist rats and *may* beat them anyway. The Government count on getting 25 or more Conservative Peers. But if the House of Lords is capable of organisation, the Duke of Norfolk should in that case put at least as many and probably more "abstentionists" into Halsbury's lobby!

I will wire if I can on Wednesday, but if this doesn't come off, and perhaps if it does, the division is likely to be quite late; and if it comes early I may be engaged on the Budget and Payment of Members. You see how full my hands are.

Joe looked very well and enjoys himself. Ivy too is well—she told me of Father's kindness—but I shall be glad when Miss O'B. is back to take Joe off her hands.

What would be good places to stay at in Switzerland, 25th August to beginning of October—say three with a fortnight or so at each—not relaxing—for a quiet time?

HOUSE OF COMMONS LIBRARY,
*8th August* 1911.

It's a toss up in the Lords. Read Salisbury's examination of the extent of the pledges.

Division bell. No time for more.

Ninety-six degrees in the shade!

PHILPOTS,
*12th August* 1911.

Thank you for your letter. Ivy says all the family are very good in writing to her except B. who is in disgrace—not a word having come from her since Ivy left town a month ago.

I came down here yesterday in time for lunch, very glad to

get a little of the quiet of the country after the excitement of the last week in town.

Well, we are beaten but certainly not disgraced. The satisfactory features of the result are that every Peer on our list voted with us except Sutherland who went to America, and that with the exception of Minto and Harrowby there is not I think a man among the rats who is worth a cuss! Norfolk himself played the man and came over as he said that he would, but only four other Peers did the like. When the result was known, I think the two unhappiest men, in our House at any rate, were Balcarres (whose father voted with us, as by the way did Rayleigh) and Steel-Maitland. Balfour and Lansdowne between them have produced the one result which Balfour least desired and Balcarres and Steel-Maitland most deplored—the victory of the Government by Unionist votes. Lansdowne himself, I fear, was quite willing that this should happen and, as he wrote to me, did not *dis*suade Unionist Peers from supporting the Bill.

I have a note from F. E. Smith this morning describing the result as a calamity. I do not take this view. I think it is a misfortune, but it seems to me that Halsbury's fight has averted the calamity which a total surrender would have been. No doubt there will be much heartburning and many angry threats of men who feel that those for whom they fought failed them when their own time for fighting came; but I hope that our struggle will soften their soreness and will keep them true to the cause.

Meantime it has been a very unpleasant time for all of us, and our enemies and critics within the Party (and some of our so-called friends too) have been saying all they could against us behind our backs. My letter in particular gave much offence and was seized on by these folk to work mischief. But I should have left it to speak for itself and not broken Father's good rule of "Never explain!" if I had not seen clearly that both Balfour and Lansdowne —particularly the former—felt themselves directly attacked in their honour. This was too much for me, and bad as I think Balfour's leadership has been and unwarrantable as his own letter was, I could not leave things on that footing and so took the occasion of Long's speech to repudiate all charges on their honour whilst leaving their "statesmanship," which he said I had also attacked, to speak for itself. But how is a Party to win with a leader who not once but twice calls for abstention on a critical division? Can he never learn? Curiously enough Long himself has been particularly civil to me throughout. He made a remonstrance very briefly but very quietly and in the most friendly way about the letter to me privately before he spoke, but he could not have been pleasanter about it if he had been my best friend. Yet Balcarres tells me: "He is furiously jealous of you and hates you like poison." I expect he is jealous but he is a queer mixture. He is hot-headed, often wrong in opinion, a bad counsellor and not, I think, a particularly loyal colleague to Balfour, for he grumbles freely in the lobbies and often is the nucleus round which grumblers gather. But our personal relations have always been very friendly and he has never shown a sign of jealousy to me when I have got on.

> 9 EGERTON PLACE, S.W.,
> 18th August 1911.

Meanwhile our plans are in abeyance. I hope if all goes well to bring Joe down to Birmingham on Tuesday, to return here myself the same day and to leave with Ivy for Basle on Wednesday. She wants to break the journey for a few days, then we shall move on to Axenfels or some other place yet to be decided on. Chamounix, I hear, is very crowded, but so I expect is all Switzerland.

Of course we can make no definite plans till we see what happens with the railways. What a state of things it is!

> 19th August 1911.

You will have seen that the House is to meet again on Tuesday next. The latest talk is that the Labour Party may move a Vote of Censure on the Government. I think the Government would have done better to get rid of the House altogether, for I do not see that our discussions help them or anyone to keep order or restore it where it has been disturbed, and I warned Elibank that he could not expect to get our people back to support him. But I feel that someone must be there to represent the Opposition whether the Government is attacked for showing energy or whether it has to be criticised for weakness, or whatever be the situation, which may of course alter many times between now and then.

So Casabianca has decided to remain on the burning deck. It would look very bad for our Party if none of us were there, and having stayed so long I feel I must stay on.

The Railways have more men out than they expected, but if they keep the rest I expect the strike will soon fizzle out. The men seem to me to have put themselves decisively in the wrong first by the suddenness of the strike, secondly by the refusal to use the Conciliation Boards and lastly by refusing to accept the Government offer of enquiry.

The Labour Party have been trying to bring the strike to an end, but they report that the strike "leaders" say that they are only "following" their men and that the men would not go back if ordered. Ramsay MacDonald, from whom I have this, tells me Asquith infuriated them. He marched into the room where they were met at the Board of Trade and, without as much as saying "good morning" to them, sat down and read in his most aggressive tones the published statement. Then he added a few words which they interpreted as a threat to shoot them and, without giving any time for a question to be asked and without a further word, marched out of the room.

There are rumours of dissension in the Cabinet—Asquith and Winston for strong measures, Lloyd George against them—but these I disbelieve, for that is not my reading of Lloyd George's character.

Meanwhile, apart from these domestic troubles Foreign Affairs are very ticklish and I much fear that the strike will encourage Germany. I gave private notice of a question on Morocco which brought me a letter from Grey and a talk with George. The latter at least has learned something since he got into office and does not, like that ass ——, affect indifference to Foreign Affairs. He was puzzled and anxious about Germany's intentions and held— rightly, I think—that nothing but the clear intimation that we should take a hand in any fighting had restrained Germany from attacking France. I heard, by the way, from Arthur Lee that the French mobilised on the frontier with extraordinary smoothness and rapidity, their arrangements working distinctly faster than the German. *Tant mieux!* Their artillery very good. Their *morale* poor, but if they won the first victory, they would be all right. This from a military friend of his who saw the trains going off one after another at three-minute intervals packed with soldiers.

Grey wrote: "The negotiations between France and Germany go very slow. They are a little nearer each other than they were—we are kept fully informed by the French—the Germans make a great point of secrecy. I don't want to hinder the negotiations by any stiff language about Germany so long as there is a prospect of a settlement between her and France on reasonable terms; at the same time I don't want to say soothing words that might be interpreted in Germany as a weakening of our attitude."

So he preferred not to have a question asked and of course I did not ask one.

I see that *The Times* Lobby man is talking today of the preparations made to have Westminster Hall for a session of the Peers if 400 "puppet" peers had been created. Bigge told Steel-Maitland and others that the King would not create one more than was necessary.

"But who will decide what *is* necessary?" asked Steel-Maitland.

Bigge replied: "Asquith will say how many he needs but the King will *make him prove it*!"

And F. E. Smith last Monday said to Lloyd George:

"We have been friends. Do you mind telling me now that it is all over what you would have done if we had beaten you?"

"Don't you know?" asked Lloyd George. F. E. said he had thought he knew till Morley made his declaration but had since been doubtful.

"You weren't taken in by that bit of bluff, were you?" asked Lloyd George. "Asquith would have sent to Lansdowne to ask how many of his men would still abstain. I suppose they would all have done so and we should have created 50 or 75 to overcome the Halsburyites!"

Was ever a Party so badly led as ours was on this occasion? Thank goodness, they are now beginning to find out what a mess they have made of things, *e.g.* the Chairman of one of the big Conservative Associations writes to Steel-Maitland:[1]

"I am a loyal man and will do what I am told, but don't, I beg,

[1] Chairman of the Conservative Party organisation.

347

ask me to call my Association together to approve the leader's action or I shall have a contrary motion carried against me!"

And again: the L.U. Association cannot hold its annual meeting at Bedford as arranged because neither Bedford nor St. John of Bletsoe (Lord Lieutenant of the County) will take the chair for or even go on the platform with Lansdowne!

"So," says Savile Crossley,[1] "let us go to Derby. Victor can't refuse to receive or support his father-in-law."

Did Ida tell you of Lady ——'s costume at Osterley? She came across the lawn in a skirt of the very latest fashion, very narrow and very thin with no room for any petticoat under it and *with the sun behind her*.

"Look," said Sir J. D. Rees to me. "Look at that lady. *Exposition universelle*, I should call it!"

*A. C. to Balfour.*
*Private.*

MY DEAR BALFOUR,[2]                                    *26th July* 1911.

As soon as I was able to leave the debate yesterday afternoon I went to your room to see you. You were absent and no one could tell me where I could find you.

It now appears that you had retired to the Travellers where you were at that moment composing the letter to Lord Newton in which you accuse us of "abandoning our leader," whilst encouraged by your language *The Times* this morning roundly brands some of your most earnest and, I will add, most loyal colleagues, as "rebels."

I have read your letter with pain and more than pain. I think we have deserved better treatment at your hands. You cannot say that those whom you thus pillory have ever been wanting in loyalty to yourself. Might they not have asked in return at least for such ordinary consideration and frankness as a leader customarily extends to his followers? I have discussed this matter with you in

---

[1] Chairman of the Liberal Unionist Association, afterwards Lord Somerleyton.
[2] See Introductory Note to this year, p. 319, *supra*.

council of your colleagues and in conversation. Nothing that you have said on any of these occasions has prepared me for the line you have now taken up or given me a hint of your intention to treat this as a question of confidence in the leadership of either yourself or of Lansdowne.

On the contrary, you have repeatedly stated that this was a question which must be decided by each individual for himself. The crisis at which we have now arrived has been visible for a year past. We have frequently discussed it. Yet till this morning you had given no lead and had never suggested to those whose views you knew to differ from those which you now express that you desired that they should alter or abandon a course of action to which they were publicly committed.

It would be worse than useless to recapitulate at this stage the arguments which have convinced us that acquiescence by the whole House of Lords in the passage without amendment of the Parliament Bill would be disastrous to that House, to our Party, and to the country. You have confronted us not with a reply to our arguments but with a denunciation of our conduct, and to make the pill more bitter you have addressed that denunciation not to us but to the public Press.

Under these circumstances I only desire to recall to your recollection that you have repeatedly stated that you had no objection to enforcing the creation of some peers if that did not of necessity carry with it the creation of such a number as would make a majority for the Government on all questions in the Lords; that you even stated more than once that you believed that that would be the best solution; and that as late as Friday last after our council you corrected a list which included your name among those in favour of unconditional acquiescence, saying that it was not correct to interpret what you have said in that sense. We now know from the King's declaration to Salisbury that his promise only extends to the creation of such a number as will carry the Parliament Bill and that he will not consent to make more, and therefore the only danger which you feared from our action does not now exist.

Is it fair under such circumstances to talk of "standing or falling" by a policy which is not your own and which, till this moment, you have never asked us to adopt, or to accuse of "abandoning their leader" men who are carrying out a policy with which you have repeatedly expressed sympathy and even agreement?

It was the determination of us all that there should be no criticism of yourself or of Lansdowne at the Halsbury dinner. It is still our determination and not even your letter will shake it. But our relations would be less frank and confidential than they have always been if I did not tell you privately that you have given deep and I think undeserved pain to men who have served you with affectionate loyalty both by the manner and the matter of your communication.

Ever yours,
AUSTEN CHAMBERLAIN.

*Balfour to A. C.*   4 CARLTON GARDENS,
*Private.*   PALL MALL, S.W.,
(*Undated,*
MY DEAR AUSTEN,   *probably 27th July.*)

Your letter—which I have read with feelings of pain which you will readily understand—seems written under a misapprehension.

There is nothing in my letter which was intended to suggest— or which on a fair interpretation ought to suggest—that I accused any friends of mine of disloyalty to myself. I certainly advised the Unionist Peers to follow their leader, Lord Lansdowne; I certainly hinted—nay more than hinted—that if Lord Lansdowne felt that, through his lead not being followed, he must resign his leadership, I should follow his example. But I never for an instant thought, I never for an instant allowed anyone to say in my presence, that old and tried friends like yourself, like Selborne, like Salisbury, like George Wyndham, either were, or could conceivably become, guilty of disloyalty.

I think you underrate the difficulties of a situation which I at least did nothing to create. The Shadow Cabinet showed irreconcilable differences of opinion. Had it been a real Cabinet one of two things would have followed. Either the dissentient minority would have resigned or they would have silently acquiesced in the decision of the majority. There could of course be no question, in the case of a Shadow Cabinet, of resignation. There certainly has been no silent acquiescence. Members belonging to the two sides at once set actively to work. They used all the means which printed correspondence or the public Press placed at their disposal, and in the face of all men the Party fabric was, for the moment, violently rent from top to bottom.

In these circumstances I could not remain a mere spectator. I had to speak, and if I spoke I could only say in public what I had already said at the Shadow Cabinet. You state that I "have confronted you, not with a reply to your arguments but with a denunciation of your conduct." How differently the same document strikes different readers! I certainly endeavoured to indicate why I think the so-called fighting in the last ditch is not fighting at all;—and as for "denunciation" I had thought that my letter—especially the final paragraph—made it perfectly clear:

(1) that the importance of the issue had to my thinking been exaggerated;

(2) that the division of opinion it has occasioned, even if inevitable, could and should be temporary.

Denunciation was never intended and was never used. It may be difficult to express differences of opinion when feeling runs high without giving quite unintentional pain. Your father, for example, observes that "the country owes a debt of gratitude to Lord Halsbury because in this crisis of his country's fate he has refused to surrender his principles." Many people will read this as meaning that in Mr. Chamberlain's opinion those who follow a different course from Lord Halsbury *had* surrendered theirs. I do not so read it. *That* would be "denunciation" indeed. But without going into these or other collateral questions I beg you to believe that while I did most assuredly advise the Peers to follow Lansdowne, I never for a moment intended to express, or did express, anything at which my friends in or out of the House of Commons have reason to take umbrage.

Yrs. v. sincerely,

ARTHUR JAS. BALFOUR.

The following letter to F. E. Smith is printed in the *Life of the Earl of Birkenhead,* vol. i. p. 220, but it is necessary to my story to reprint it here.

9 EGERTON PLACE, S.W.,
*20th August* 1911.

I confess that Balfour's leadership at times makes me despair of the fortunes of a Party so led. He has no comprehension of the habits of thought of his countrymen and no idea of how things strike them. But I have been very closely and intimately associated with him for the past eight or nine years. I know his strength as well as his weakness. I have received much kindness at his hands as well as some hard knocks, and I am too much attached to him ever to join any combination against him or his leadership. I took this decision long ago. I have held fast to it in spite of many difficulties and some provocation, and I am going to hold fast by it still.

All I can do to put more fight into our policy and to strengthen the fighting and constructive section within the Party, I will do, but what I do must be within the limits set out above and must not be directed against Balfour personally or against his leadership.

I don't think you will have expected me to act otherwise, but it is better for us both to make the position quite clear.

Let me add that I think the Party in the country will look increasingly to the fighting section and that, bad as the present situation is, the action of those who supported Lord Halsbury has saved us from a catastrophe.

1911 : September, October

Baveno, Italy,

*23rd September* 1911.

I gather from *The Times*—the only paper which I read—that politics have been very dull since we left home in spite of the efforts of the German Foreign Office to keep everyone in a state of anxiety and bewilderment. I must say it is pleasant to see France keeping cool and resolute and to know that all the panic has been on the side of Germany. The more panic and loss there is in that country as a result of their restless machinations the better it will be for other countries. What bad neighbours they are! And one cannot see how this restlessness is to be stayed without a deal of blood-letting. If we come in they will be dangerous, but it is an unmixed benefit that the Government Liberals, at least, should have learned what manner of men they are and what dangers we have to confront. I don't think that Lloyd George will forget his lesson, and on the other hand the Germans have learned something, for they now know that even a Liberal Government won't give them a free hand to make hay of treaties and re-arrange the world according to exclusively German ideas. I expect you noticed Bebel's speech. It was evidently a noteworthy performance and specially interesting after hearing Angst's account of his conversation.[1]

*24th September* 1911.

What is this I saw in someone else's paper (Italian) of a Tripoli question, of naval and military preparations and the rest? Is this complication to be added to the difficulties of Europe and what on earth can the pretext be for re-opening the question of Tripoli at this moment? It is tantalising only to see these things on the back of a paper someone else is reading in the train. I must see if there are any Italian papers in the hotel. I loath the beastly German things which are everywhere!

[1] See *Down the Years* by Sir Austen Chamberlain, p. 61.

z

353

*26th September* 1911.

Saturday's *Times*—the last we have received—had a note tucked away in a corner that the Porte intended to ask Italy for explanations of her intentions as regards Tripoli, and that is all that I have seen of this question in the English journals. Here the papers are full of nothing else but the naval and military preparations of the Italian Government—calling up of 80,000 men to the Colours, mobilisation of the Fleet, appointment of an Admiralissimo, etc., with articles on the historic connection of Tripoli with Sicily and on the recent offences of the Turks. I asked a young Signor Vare, who is here with his English wife, whether he read the Italian papers and what it all meant.

"I don't need to read them," he said, "for I have just come from the Foreign Office. I suppose they (*i.e.* the Italian Government) have just made up their mind to take it somehow."

I think that jealousy of French expansion in Morocco is the exciting cause. Of course, Italy has long looked to Tripoli as its eventual share of African plunder. But it is curious to find the papers so much occupied with it here and not a word in *The Times* to prepare one for what was coming.

BELLAGIO, ITALY,
*30th September* 1911.

I see the papers, both English and foreign, have waked to the fact that there is a Tripoli question, and a very serious one too. The Italian papers are very bellicose and I should think that the Government here would have difficulty in accepting any solution which does not give Italy practical control of Tripoli. Every country is represented by them as favourable to their demands, though these demands are not yet formulated.

*1st October* 1911.

So war is declared between Turkey and Italy and the first shots fired on some Turkish torpedo boats. Well, I really should have felt a little disappointed if nothing had come of my discovery that there was a Tripolitan question. I missed the *Corriere* one day and so did not see the first news of the Italian ultimatum, but at Como yesterday I heard a newsvendor crying: "War declared," etc., and at once bought a penny's worth of sensation. There is a strict censorship here and no further news is published this evening. This must be anxious news for Austria and provoking for Germany. I really cannot be sorry for the Young Turks, who have certainly done nothing to keep our friendship, but I trust their eyes may be opened a little to the value of German assurances.

> LUGANO,
> 4th October 1911.

10.30 p.m. Your letter of Sept. 30–Oct. 1 somehow missed us at Bellagio but reached my hands this afternoon. I had already received the *Observer* this morning and wondered why it "*me tombait des nues.*" I heartily agree with its comments and your observations on the Italian–Turkish war. The attitude of most of the English Press seems to me gross folly. As we are not in any case going to intervene on behalf of the Turks, we shall not win their good-will and we are in danger of losing that of Italy. The Italians certainly counted on our approbation or at least our most favourable consideration; and we preach and scold in angry impotence and affected moral superiority in a way that must be most aggravating. They claim—I do not know with how much reason—that they alone of European Powers were sympathetic to us during the Boer War and, though their action was sudden and high-handed, they have not at all a bad case on their side now. France and ourselves have each recognised that Tripoli was their eventual sphere. They have larger interests there and many more subjects than any other Power. These very facts have made the Young Turks peculiarly jealous of them and have caused the Turkish Government to throw every obstacle in the way of Italian enter-prise and industry in Tripoli. Then they see France absorbing Morocco as it has already absorbed Tunis and as we have absorbed Egypt. They have an immense emigration annually and no Italian colony to which it can be directed. Austria has taken with equal violence and still less provocation its share of the Balkans. Turkey, badly governed though it is, was taking a fresh lease of life, was beginning to train a Navy and to develop a national feeling. Germany, the friend of the Turks, was alleged to be showing, and might any day develop, a real interest in the economic development of Tripoli; and when German papers talk of the Mediterranean as "a German sea," Latin Powers may well begin to consider how far the Triple Alliance will serve their interests. Add the usual incidents of the Jenkins's ear kind to inflame the public—a vessel seized and its captain mishandled, a girl carried off, converted and placed in a Harem—and should we act very differently? I doubt it, and I am sure that no other Power would. And then we, whose statesmen have talked of turning the Turks "bag and baggage" out of Europe and who have hailed with delight almost every release of any people or place from Turkish sway as a gain to humanity and civilisation, hold up our hands in pious horror and express ourselves as unutterably shocked. I think it would be not at all a bad thing for some English statesmen to express open sympathy with Italy. As it is, we are likely once again to fall between two stools.[1]

What I do not understand is why all Europe was so taken by surprise. There was certainly enough evidence here to show that a storm was brewing; and I imagine that their own want of foresight makes the Press and politicians of other countries all the more angry with Italy. And this little blow to their conviction that we were just entering on the millennium has no doubt been peculiarly bitter to our own Liberal Press. Heaven send that we take the lesson to heart!

I am much intrigued and a little disturbed by a telegram from Neville received this morning:

"Expect telegram this afternoon urge you to return as soon as possible join movement feeling in country real and widespread."

Now what does that mean? No further telegram has come to explain it and *The Times* has given one no idea of anything being afoot. Only yesterday I was saying to Ivy that it was striking how quiet everything was and that it was clear that this year, at any rate, every politician meant to have a clear holiday. Now comes N.'s message and as I suppose he knew that I was returning on Tuesday next, it looks as if he thought it very urgent.

---

[1] My father did so express himself.

In ordinary circumstances we should put ourselves in the train at once and go straight through to London, but I want to spare Ivy the night journey if possible, and cannot conceive how a few days can make any difference when the papers give no indication of any domestic happenings to call for such haste. So I don't know what to do. I have wired Neville to ask him to telegraph to Basle (whither we go tomorrow morning) whether it is necessary that I should be in London on Saturday and have added that, if not, I shall arrive on Tuesday. But what is it all about?

*Balfour's Resignation and the Question of the Leadership of the Party
in the House of Commons*

9 EGERTON PLACE, S.W.,
11*th October* 1911.

On my return home on Saturday I found letters from Selborne
and others begging me to attend a meeting of the Die-hards
summoned by them for Thursday.

On Monday Wyndham came up to town to see me by Selborne's
wish.  S. and he had been in communication with Milner, Carson,
F. E. Smith, Amery, Willoughby de Broke and others.  Briefly
their conclusions were that the Die-hards must keep together and
act together so as to have their proper influence in the Party and
prevent the leaders being stampeded as they were last August by
Curzon.  They wished therefore to form a Die-hard Club (name
yet to be settled) not hostile to the Party organisation or to Balfour
and Lansdowne but to work out and proclaim a forward policy.
They regarded Lansdowne's scheme of Lords' Reform as dead
and the Albert Hall Pledge for a Referendum on Tariff Reform
as void and expired after the events of this summer.  They had
come to the conclusion that a purely elected Second Chamber was
the only one to which we could now persuade the country to
give effective and sufficient powers.  Such men as W. de Broke
and Northumberland shared this view now and preferred to trust
their fate to the electors rather than to some "hanky-panky"
nomination scheme which Curzon would manipulate.

They wished to speak more plainly about national dangers
and National Defence ; to give more definite form to the Unionist
programme of Social Reform ; and in all things to take a more
vigorous fighting line ; to act in common within the Party and to
speak in unison both in the House and out of it.  They had decided
to back Carson for all they were worth in his resistance to Home
Rule.

They had had two or three meetings, had issued a summons to forty or fifty people for Thursday, were of opinion that I must join and were agreed that they could not go further without me.

W. gave me a special account of Milner's views, embodied in a memo. sent me today.

I said I was sorry that it should be necessary to form any fresh Club or Committee in the Party, but there was force in the reasons urged for it. I should of course join with them.

I agreed about the House of Lords, Tariff Reform and Ireland, as also on their general principles. I should be glad to see National Defence more frankly discussed and more closely studied. I knew very little about military subjects and thought it extremely difficult to form a just judgment on them without special information. I could not at present pledge myself to National Service as I had not seen how to work it with the requirements of the Regular Army, those of the Navy and Finance. But I should not quarrel with free speech on the part of those who saw their way.

I asked W. if he had heard or seen anything of Balfour. He said very little. I had heard (from Sandars before I left London on 23rd August and from Steel-Maitland since my return) that he was very tired, not well and thinking of retiring. I told W. that I was most anxious that he should not retire now and that great care should be taken not to allow our movement to appear to be directed against him. I thought he had got the Party into a great mess and he should help to extricate us before he left us. It would be extremely difficult for the Party to unite under any-one else just now. Suppose for instance Lansdowne were to retire. Could Selborne accept Curzon as leader in their House or Curzon accept Selborne just now?

W. agreed that neither would now willingly accept the other and turned back to the situation in the Commons. He said that Balfour had spoken to him at Clouds in the spring about his own possible retirement, had indicated me as perhaps the best successor, and asked W.'s opinion. W. had then preferred Bonar Law whom he thought, as he is, the best speaker on our side, but he now wished to say that he thought I was the right person. B. L. did not develop. Long's judgment was often bad and his temper hot. Therefore it must be me.

I said that for either of us it would be extremely awkward to succeed now. There were special obstacles in my way—notably that I was a Liberal Unionist and not a Conservative. But apart from this we should each find it difficult to accept the other. I could not yield opinions to Long as I had yielded them more than once to Balfour; nor would he yield to me. It would be very difficult for either of us at any time and particularly so in the present state of Party feeling and after the recent dissensions. I was most anxious therefore to avoid any change in the leadership now.

W. said he understood and agreed. In the course of our talk he said that neither Bob nor Hugh Cecil would give any more trouble about Tariff Reform. Hugh had said that he would never be a Tariff Reformer but that he wished now that we should carry T.R. and that quickly. Bob, he regarded as even more advanced.

*12th October* 1911.

Selborne and Wyndham dined with me last night. Long and interesting talk. S. confirmed and amplified what W. had told me. He had been with Halsbury that afternoon and had told him how his views were shaping *re* composition of Second House. H. offered no objection.

S. agreed very much with the views I had expressed about National Service. He had never committed himself to it, but what happened in August had convinced him that the present system wouldn't do and he wanted enquiry. S. and W. are both railway directors. They got the following through their railways, confirmed by Gwynne of the *Morning Post*, by information given to W. at the War Office, and by facts known to them as officers of the Territorial Army.

During the strike negotiations, Asquith, Haldane, Winston and Ll. George met the railway representatives and showed them a telegram from the French Government to the effect that the demands of Germany were intolerable and the German Government most threatening. The French were prepared to resist on one condition. If that were not accepted they would have to give way. It was that England should at once (within ten or fourteen days) send its whole expeditionary force (160,000 men?) to pro-long the French left. Our Government agreed. Are we now, they asked the railways, to be confronted by a strike? This was why Claughton and Granet gave way. It explains Granet's remark to me at Axenfels:

"What can you do when you are appealed to as patriots?"

This had changed Selborne's views. Hitherto he had always supposed that there would be time (not perhaps Haldane's six months, but sufficient time) after the Regulars left to train and equip the Territorials. He now saw that the difficulty would come upon us quite otherwise. The Territorials would have been quite disorganised—all horses and many officers gone, and 20,000 invaders might, once landed, have marched from end to end of the country.

We discussed land policy with much agreement. They were anxious for a more fighting policy on the Insurance Bill. I told them my idea of moving at once to report progress on the 24th. They warmly approved.

We left Referendum for another time, agreeing that we differed but must find a way to agree. Some concession on each side.

We agreed that we were free from the Albert Hall Pledge.

They both said that Balfour is not what he was—must be protected against Curzon, etc. I again stated my strong view that, apart from feelings of affectionate regard for Balfour which they shared, the time was not opportune for a vacancy in the leadership of either House. They concurred.

*22nd October* 1911.

Balcarres lunched here. We discussed Insurance Bill policy and prospects, the strikes, Parliamentary procedure, etc.

I told him my view of the Halsbury Club. Question of leader-ship in either House was not raised by us and was not, in our opinion, open and we did not mean it to be opened. Neither in the Party's interests nor Balfour's was the moment well chosen for his resignation.

Balcarres said the question *was* open. Balfour was very restless under the criticisms made upon him and might go in a few months.

I re-enforced my views and added that, if the question was open, it had never been raised in any speech of ours and was not kept open by us. It was Long's blundering and most *offensive defences* of Balfour which made people think that there was a movement among leading men against Balfour.

Balcarres said,

"Oh, Long! Well, if I have anything to do with it, I don't mean the Party to have Long for leader."

Balcarres said,

"Balfour bears no grudge against you but he is furious with Selborne. Why? Well, I asked him, and he wouldn't give any reason; but he is. He laughs at your Halsbury Club. 'They don't agree on anything. What will they do?'" And Balcarres added, "You aren't agreed about Reform of the House of Lords or Tariffs or anything. You can't get your people to agree to an elected Upper House such as I and Steel-Maitland want."

I replied: "Don't be too sure. We are not going back to our differences of last August. They belong to history and we who are actors can't write that history. But the Parliament Bill is a fact. It alters the whole situation and you will find that men who thought L.'s Bill went too far, now recognise that after the events of the summer you cannot get the powers we think necessary entrusted to or wielded by anything but an elected Second Chamber."

"Oh," said Bal., "if you can convince Halsbury of that!"

"I don't say that H. is convinced, but you would be surprised to learn the names of some of the men who are."

Bal. went off to see Balfour, with my consent to his telling as much as he liked of our conversation.

*23rd October* 1911.

I send you some hasty jottings of conversations. Father has heard already from me the substance of that with Hewins on the 17th. He will not altogether approve what I said to Balcarres about the leadership, but I am convinced it is right and in my case I must work in my own way among these very difficult problems. I am quite clear in my own mind that I *don't* want a vacancy in the leadership.

I have read the part of Bernard Holland's Life of the Duke of Devonshire dealing with the fiscal controversy. It is, I think, very fairly done and calls at any rate for no answer from us. I was anxious to make sure of this at once. I understand that you want to keep the book for Christmas but I thought you would be glad to know this much at any rate.

*23rd October* 1911.

Called on Balfour by appointment at 12.15 to discuss our policy tomorrow and on Wednesday. We were quickly joined by Forster, Steel-Maitland and Balcarres.

Balfour said that he had just heard from Lord Rothschild that France and Germany had settled all outstanding points.

He told me before the others arrived that at Balmoral he had seen Grey, George and, I think, Asquith. They had talked freely about Foreign Affairs. Grey serious but moderate. L. George very bellicose—Germany meant war; wouldn't it perhaps be better to have it at once? and so on. Balfour was "rather shocked" by his violence.

I asked him if he had confirmation of the story I had heard from Selborne about the French demand for assistance. He said, yes, though not in the exact form told by Selborne of the telegram shown to the Railway Companies' representatives. Forster had heard it from a Pressman.

Balcarres said that he had been staying at North Berwick. The *Neptune* was moored just opposite. Looking out one day with his glasses he saw that it was cleared for action. That night the whole fleet went to sea. He thought it was 9th September but couldn't remember the exact day. About a fortnight ago his wife was told by the Captain of the *Colossus*,

"Oh, yes, we were all out that night; lights out and cleared for action, strung right across the North Sea looking for the German torpedo-destroyer squadron which had disappeared. The Admiralty didn't know where it was!"

*23rd October* 1911.

11 p.m. Here are the jottings of another conversation—very hastily penned—to add to those already sent. I will try when I

have anything interesting to record to send more as I know they interest Father and you.

Some of them I may need for reference at one time or another, so will you please file this series together in a big envelope, so that without trouble you could send them to me if I needed them.

I enclose today the notes of my earlier conversations with Selborne and Wyndham.[1] I read them to you and Father, but they are so much referred to in my later notes that you may want to look at them again.

### 23rd October 1911.

Gwynne, now of the *Morning Post*, called this evening and we had a long talk, covering much the same ground as my conversation with Selborne and Wyndham—the Halsbury Club, the leadership, Tariff Reform and National Defence. He had been afraid that the Halsbury Club might stifle Tariff Reform; said we must fight on everything but could only win on that; thought much could be done in Scotland by an active T.R. campaign. I agreed, but he need not fear that the H.C. would burke T.R. I had told Selborne last June or July that I stood pledged that the first Unionist Budget should be a T.R. Budget and that I could not move from that position. Selborne had then and there accepted that position, dropping at once an alternative involving delay which he had then suggested to me. I was asked to join the H.C. with the assurance that T.R. was one of the things for which it would fight—"the full policy, preference for all."

As to the Second Chamber he was in favour of election but could not take that line in the *M.P.* because of Bathurst. Lady B. had almost come to take the same view, but B. talked "as if he had promised his father on his death-bed to stand by the hereditary principle." I said I had heard a rather different account of B.'s views, and told him in effect what Selborne and Wyndham had told me, adding that these men had had their faith in the hereditary principle rudely shaken by the surrender of last August. The staff had broken in the moment of stress. You might perhaps splice it, but it would never be as strong as before. The hereditary peers having yielded once would yield again under similar or lesser

---

[1] See above under date October 11th.

strain. I thought Bathurst and others saw this and that (1) the country wouldn't restore the old powers to the old House, and (2) that, even if they could, the old House wasn't strong enough to wield them. Gwynne agreed and hoped he would get Lady B. to the same point of view. I might help with B.

Turning to National Defence, G. said he had always lived much with soldiers and trembled at our present position. Haldane's scheme had broken down, as would soon be manifest. He heard Ll. George was terrified about Germany "and the Foreign Office tell me Winston is still more alarmed." We ought to be able to put 120,000 men into the field at once but when the crisis came we had officers for only 85,000. Clemenceau had said to Gwynne in September :

"My dear Gwynne, the difference between the 120,000 men you ought to have been able to put into the field and the number you could put in is the measure of the concessions we have had to yield to Germany."

I sketched my views—again as sketched to Selborne.

G. said, "But we are not so very far off National Service, but it can only be carried by an agreement of both Parties."

I rejoined that we had always done our best to keep Defence clear of Party, but Ll. George's platform style and the aggressive policy of the Government made co-operation in any close sense almost impossible.

Gwynne said, "You know Haldane's plan. If recruiting for the Territorial Army breaks down, he proposes to fix a quota for each county and to say, e.g., to Rutland :

"Your quota is 1000 ; you have only recruited 500. 500 more must be taken by ballot."

"But that is compulsory service," I said.

I told Gwynne that I thought a good deal of the criticism against Balfour was wrong. For instance, some of our people wanted a regular "Newcastle Programme" for the Unionist Party. I agreed with Balfour that we had work enough in hand ; Tariff Reform (itself the basis of all social reform), Constitutional Reform and Land Reform (purchase first but purchase accompanied with other measures necessary to its success). This was pretty well enough and the first thing and main thing was to make our policy on these clear and sufficiently definite.

G. agreed "especially if you emphasise the fact that T.R. is at the root of all Social Reform."

*24th October* 1911.

11 p.m. The first meeting of the House was as usual rather flat. There was a momentary "breeze" between Asquith and me—he saying that I administered pettifogging enquiries and I retorting that we had accepted his pledge once this session only to find it broken by a colleague. I don't think I had been provocative (not seeing an opportunity to be so) but I wasn't sorry that he took it so!

This is a horrid situation that we are in. The T.R. League have recently issued a fresh appeal for money (they are *very* short) in my name. Of those who reply, one-half refuse alleging that we are anti-Balfourian, and the other half out of disgust at Balfour's surrender last August. Result £700 of outstanding subscriptions paid up, but only £17 of fresh money. Cheerful!

The response to the invitation to the Annual Conference is poor and instead of the 600 Vice-Presidents who attended the last dinner only 250 have applied for tickets for this one. And the League has taken a room that holds 1000! Bonar Law, Duncannon and I decided we couldn't abandon it or let it fail. We must pack it and packed it shall be. Oh! "Bother, or words to that effect."

What do you say to the Cabinet changes? No strength to the Government in their announcement, for they appear to the public meaningless. But I infer that:

1. the Cabinet had lost confidence in McKenna,[1] as well they might do;

2. that the chief men are really anxious about what they have seen of the spirit of Germany;

3. that Winston feels the Home Office is getting too hot for him, and

4. that he has definitely decided that he cannot rival Ll. George

---

[1] Mr. McKenna was succeeded as First Lord of the Admiralty by Mr. Churchill.

as demagogue and will cultivate the rôle of statesman and strong man instead.

It's curious, by the way, that when I met him at Dunrobin in 1902 he asked me what I wanted to become. I had then just been made P.M.G. and I said that since I had known it, I had always thought the Admiralty one of the pleasantest offices and the post of First Lord one of the proudest positions that any Englishman could occupy. Winston pooh-poohed it as a "poor ambition."

I am grieved at Onslow's death. What troubles poor Lady O. has had of late.

*26th October* 1911.

At the Bank of Africa yesterday we had a curious story, relating of course to events now several weeks old, of feverish German military preparations in West Africa—soldiers landed and pushed up country in bodies of two and three hundred and exorbitant premiums paid to contractors to hasten progress with the railway.

*A propos* of this St. Aldwyn told the same story about the British fleet in the North Sea which I had heard from Bal. St. A. had it from "a naval officer."

I spoke yesterday on the Gag resolution. Bonar Law said "the best speech I ever heard you make" and Walter Long said the same thing. I don't honestly think it deserved that praise; still, as Father used to say, it was pleasant to get it.

I started work about 9.30 and got to bed a little after 1 o'clock— at work the whole time. No fear that I shall rust for want of use.

Fred Oliver called this morning ostensibly to bring Horace Plunkett, but P. arrived late and did not seem to have anything novel to say when he did come. But before he arrived Fred told me that he had heard the following account of the reasons for the interchange of offices between Winston and McKenna.

When the situation with Germany became acute the Defence Committee was agreeably surprised by the preparedness of the War Office. Numbers were deficient but the W.O. had all its plans ready and could say at once what it proposed to do and what additional stores it required, which were at once granted.

The Admiralty, on the other hand, had all ships, men and stores complete but had no plans for a campaign, had in fact no General Staff worth the name and, though it had all the means, did not know in the least how it would use them. Up to a point McK. had done very well, but this defect he had never discovered or never remedied. So without passing any censure on McK. the Committee of Defence thought there had better be a change.

I am sorry to hear this of the Admiralty, but Heaven send the report of War Office preparedness is true. How different from what we have seen in past times!

Oliver also told me that he had repeated to Milner what I had said about M.'s position. O. had previously told me that M. and Balfour were antipathetic, that M. did not complain of being left out of the councils of the Party but that he felt he was not wanted, his advice not sought and his counsel not desired. I had said how much I regretted this and that I had begged both Balfour and Lansdowne to summon him to Shadow Cabinets but had met with no success. I added that I must in fairness say that M. had held ostentatiously aloof and given them some excuse and that personally I found him a very difficult man to get hold of— he was so constantly engaged.

But now, I said, here is his chance. He has been consulted about and joined the Halsbury Club. We, and I in particular, are most anxious to have the benefit of his knowledge of finance, experience in administration and above all—ideas. He would be invaluable if he will really attend Committee meetings and give time to it. But hard as I have tried to get him into our councils and much as I long for his assistance, it is no use if he won't attend. If he will attend and put his back into it, he will have all the influence he has a right to claim and we shall gladly yield to him.

Fred repeated this, telling M. "it was in fact a very special personal appeal from me," as indeed it was, for I had begged Fred to use all his influence to get M. to throw himself into this work and take his rightful place.

Now Fred reports that Milner in effect says: How can I work with them? My views on Home Rule are not theirs; how can we work together?

Please look at the abstract of Milner's views sent you with the first of these papers. It was drawn up by Amery after a conversation between himself, Milner and Wyndham, and it was approved by Milner. You will see that he then said that if we were really in earnest on other matters, he could be more or less silent on this one question and work with us.

*Now the only man who has any real influence with him is Father.* I understand Milner is with you now. Can Father do anything (1) to persuade him to give us the help we need from him especially in considering social reforms and National Defence, (2) to dissuade him from making any false move on the Irish question?

*Brief Summary of Lord Milner's views given on night of 18th September 1911.*
This represents my views in brief.

## M.

1. That it is desirable that the Die-hards should remain a working body, acting together "separate but not hostile." (This need not necessarily include every one of those who co-operated last session nor exclude others joining.)
2. That it is further desirable that they should strike a common note and have an agreed general line of policy.
The main features of that policy should be:

(a) Tariff Reform.
(b) Imperial Unity.
(c) Defence.
(d) Social Uplifting.
(e) A sound Constitution.
(f) A real United Kingdom.

(a), (b), (c) and (d) are all closely interconnected, and are the big Imperial issues and primary issues of principle; (e) and (f) are concerned with machinery and in a certain sense derivative. Fighting upon them is forced upon us by the attempt of log-rolling factions to pervert the Constitution and the Union in order to help to put themselves in power here and in Ireland and to burke the real Colonial and Imperial Policy.

On (c) Lord M. would welcome a bold and whole-hearted

POLITICS FROM INSIDE

adoption of National Service, but would be content with less as long as individual members of the group are left free to urge it.

Under (d) he is very keen on including agricultural improvement.

Under (e) he is for a completely elective Second Chamber on such lines as to eliminate the ordinary party motives as far as possible.

Under (f) he is ultimately for a Federal United Kingdom on Canadian or South African lines, and meanwhile for a line of vigorous criticism and attack which will effectively demolish the Radical advocacy (which is certain to rely mainly on loose talk about Devolution and Colonial precedent for a measure utterly unjustified by such precedents) and which, *without producing any scheme*, will not absolutely preclude our bringing it forward later. If others demur to this, he is prepared not to make a prominent feature of this but dwell chiefly on the other matters that interest him most, provided, that is, that a really vigorous line is taken on the other main points.

9 EGERTON PLACE, S.W.,
*27th October* 1911.

I had Garvin to lunch yesterday. Said the last two or three weeks had been on the whole the most depressing he had ever known. He despaired of Balfour, hated the attacks on him and the manner of them and in fact found comfort nowhere. I "emptied my sack for him as I have done for others and he went away comforted or at least saying that he was so."

"You made me a Balfourian," he said more than once, "and I followed him on Referendum even against your father and yourself. It was your doing, but——!"

Well! I have learned some lessons from Father, and I remember the motto he chose. *"Je tiens ferme!"* It's a great thing to have a line. It's a greater to stick to it. And since he urged me to stop in the Cabinet when he resigned in 1903, I have had mine. Balfour is my leader as long as he will lead. And nobody can fairly say that I haven't given him in public and in private as loyal support as any man can ask.

I was no sooner back from the House than Alfred Lyttelton

370

came to see me and I had to forfeit my Friday afternoon's play with Joe.

Alfred said that the Party was in a mess—there was no use disguising it—that the Halsbury Club tended to keep alive differences, that he thought he pretty well knew my position in regard to it, that I had "joined the train after it was in motion" and he supposed that it was too late for me to withdraw or for the Club to be abandoned, and that I "couldn't make a declaration." But "the old chief" felt things more than he used to do, that his health wasn't good and ("though, mind you, I speak only for myself and know nothing, yet I know the chief pretty well") he was thinking of early retirement. There was "the killing winter" before him and then too he is very chivalrous, he thinks the fortunes of the Party are on the mend and that it is therefore a favourable moment for a successor to take up the leadership. But the events of August had made divisions, the Halsbury Club tended to keep them alive, and we should all like him to go, if he does go, "in as great a blaze of glory as a man could who had been leading the defeated Party for seven years" and with full sympathy and cordiality for the Party (so that they might still profit by his counsel and help) and for his successor. Nor would I and Carson and—well, it didn't matter about the peers—join in a kind of round-robin of them all to assure him of our loyal and whole-hearted allegiance.

I replied that I had never said, done or thought anything which would make it in the least difficult for me to do what he asked, but was it the best thing to do? One didn't take that kind of formal step towards a leader unless one thought that he was really menaced and it seemed to me that to assure him that he was our leader, etc., was to show that there was a doubt about it. My position had been from the first that there could be no question about Balfour's leadership as long as he was willing to lead. The leading spirits of the Halsbury Club knew my views and shared them. Alfred had said that I "couldn't make a declaration" but we were going to have a public meeting of the H. C. and at that meeting I had intended to say publicly what I had already said privately to individuals, viz. :

The leadership of the Party is not in question. There is no vacancy *and we desire none.* If and when one comes, neither this

371

nor any Club will choose the successor. That is not the object of the Club. Neither is it our object to continue a controversy which now belongs to history. But whatever view is taken of the wisdom of our action, all will agree that it evoked a spirit in the Party which they would not willingly see die. It is to preserve that spirit and to direct it to purposes now common to the whole Party that we found this Club . . . and so forth.

I added that in the idea of its founders the Club had two other immediate purposes not so easily expressed in public—to retain the "Die-hards" (hateful name but brief) in the Party and prevent them throwing up their positions in the local associations, etc., in disgust as they were doing (Steel-Maitland and Balcarres would confirm this) and to prevent the wilder ones running amuck as Leo Maxse did.

Alfred said that was very satisfactory. If I meant to say that, he would like to think over it a little but probably that would be sufficient and nothing more would be required.

Then I told him fully my views about the Halsbury Club and about the leadership and why I thought it was neither in the Party's interest nor in Balfour's that he should retire now. Alfred agreed and talked of my position, saying that I must be B.'s successor when the time came, that Walter Long couldn't do it, it would kill him. We all knew Walter's good qualities and "if he could always have three drives off the tee, he might do very well, for his third shot was generally a good one, but the first two went here and there and all over the place." He changed his mind so often and was always so hot. And then he simply couldn't do the work that was required, witness his speech at the close of the debate on the Parliament Bill.

I said I wasn't going to make any pretence of the *nolo episcopari* kind. I supposed I did want to succeed if it fairly came my way, though, like anyone else who thought of what it meant, I was appalled by the difficulties of the position and well aware how many of the necessary qualities I lacked. That, therefore, if my name were before the Party when the time came I should not withdraw it in favour of anyone else. But if the Party preferred another man, there were other men under and with whom I had no doubt I could work harmoniously, but that if Long were to be the choice I must frankly say that though our personal relations had always been most pleasant, I did not think it would be easy for me to serve under him and I certainly couldn't surrender my opinion to him as I had several times done to Balfour.

Altogether Alfred spent an hour with me and said he was delighted to hear what I had told him.

The day before, Bonar Law had asked me to see him as soon as I had seen Carson. On Friday he had asked if I had yet seen Carson but I had not. He then said that he was "so much in two camps" that he hardly liked to invite our confidences lest he should be thought to be playing a double game but when I had seen Carson he would really like to see me.

After the above conversation with Alfred and the suspicion which was evidently at the back of Alfred's mind when he came that it was possible that I might not be willing to give any public support to Balfour's leadership, I determined to see Law at once, and wrote to him that he had better know my whole mind without waiting for Carson.

So on Saturday morning I called on him. He began at once by saying that he feared from my letter I had misunderstood him, that it wasn't about my position but about that of the Party he wanted to speak.

I said that so I had supposed, but I was quite ready to talk frankly about both. He then went over pretty much the same ground as Alfred had done in opening, but with this important addition and variation: that it had been felt that the Halsbury Club was an attack on Balfour and that something must be done to counteract its effect, that accordingly there had been a meeting of "anti-Die-hards" summoned by Curzon to which Law went; that it had there been proposed that there should be a meeting of the Party to reaffirm its confidence in Balfour; that he had pointed out that unless the "Die-hards" would join, this would only make matters worse and they had eventually decided that he and Alfred should see Carson ("I proposed that it should be Carson and not you," he said, "because Long was there and I thought he would more readily agree to Carson") and ascertain what we would do. He had seen Carson, who had said he could say nothing definite without consulting me. That was what he had wished to tell me.

373

I hesitated for a moment whether I would tell him about Alfred's coming to me, when he said something which showed me that I should be revealing nothing—at least as long as I did not speak of the personal part of his talk. So I told him of Alfred's proposal for a round-robin. He at once said, "Oh, no. I don't like that. That wouldn't do," but he thought a Party meeting would be a good thing. I then went over just the same ground as I had done with Alfred. We hadn't raised and didn't wish to raise the leadership question. On the contrary we desired that there should be no question about it. I told him what I proposed to say at the Halsbury Club, told him that there was nothing in my mind which would prevent me from cordially joining in any recognition of Balfour, but was it desirable to make a demonstration about what wasn't in dispute? Didn't it rather suggest that there was a doubt, where my whole object was to maintain and show that there ought to be and was none?

Law expressed himself well satisfied with all I told him, but thought that Balfour should be told that if he would like to have a Party meeting all would concur and support him and he could choose whether to have it or not.

I said I had no objection to that, but that as I had intended to make a declaration at the Club I wished that nothing should be said about a Party meeting till after that. If they attached value to what I said, as they evidently did since they consulted me, they would see that it would have much more force and grace if it were clearly my spontaneous act and did not appear to be wrung from me at a Party meeting. This he said was very fair and he agreed to it.

We then talked more about Balfour and I gave my reasons why he ought not to retire now. Law here gave the conversation a personal turn by saying that I personally and in particular ought to wish that Balfour should not retire now as the Halsbury Club militated against me; it had thrown some men into Long's arms and Long would just now collect too many discontented men to admit of my being chosen if a vacancy occurred. He had said to F. E. Smith ("who was very flamboyant at the time") as far back as last August: "Yes, it's all very fine for you. You stand to gain in any case, but Austen's position is different. A man who

374

may be leader of the Party mustn't get identified with a section or take the lead in sectional fighting."

As he had thus raised the question I thought it well to have it out with him, so I repeated to him exactly what I had told Alfred the evening before as to my personal feelings and position, and after a little more talk we parted.

Garvin told me that he had been estranged from Law but they had made it up again, that he had been surprised to find how much Law had strengthened and developed since he had gone through his great sorrow, that he was now concentrating on politics, was becoming ambitious and thought I had neglected him. G. begged me to see him more often and talk to him more. I told G. that I had long ago told him, when he and I were together fighting one of our difficult moments in Tariff Reform and when I thought B. L. was either a little jealous of me or suspected me of being jealous of him, that between him and me no personal question could arise; and B. L. ought not to have any feeling of the kind now described by Garvin, but of course we hadn't talked quite so much lately because we took different views of the crisis of the summer.

I think that B. L. does feel that if Balfour retired and I were too unpopular with a section of the Party to be chosen to succeed, the leadership must fall to himself, and I have no doubt that he would like it in exactly the same sense as I should. And indeed he practically said as much to me last August; but he is thoroughly straight and will do nothing underhand.

This is finished at Hackwood, Curzon's place. Lansdowne, Cromer, Roberts, Dunmore, Lord and Lady Manners, Lady Edward Cecil and Harry Chaplin our party.

I have had a little explanatory talk with Lansdowne which I think was useful.

*30th October* 1911.
*(Late.)*

I have little more to chronicle. I have seen Carson. It was Law and Long (not Alfred Lyttelton as I wrote) who were deputed to call on him.

375

Carson, I found, as I expected, entirely agreed with me. If things could be left to take their course, they would soon fall into their proper perspective. A Party meeting was not only unnecessary but in his opinion *very* undesirable, and so we have told Law and Alfred.

I can't tell you how hateful this whole business has been to me with its underlying references to my own position and prospects, and the background of intrigue and back-biting which one feels in them all the time. Well, these things have to be lived through and lived down; but it is hateful to feel that one's record counts for nothing against the stupid or malicious whisperings of men who never formulate a charge or come into the open.

The North Herts vacancy has brought up again the question of Bob Cecil's position. It is a natural seat for him, many of the people would like him, but there are difficulties with the local Tariff Reformers. He certainly does not mean to give any trouble, would be a valuable accession to our debating powers in the Commons, and many good T. R.'s are very anxious to see him get in. F. E. Smith appealed specially for my help on Friday and Balcarres today.

I have told them both that personally I should be very glad to see him in, that I will raise no kind of objection and make no trouble, but that as long as he did not publicly accept T. R. I could not publicly urge his candidature. As I say, I think it would be a real advantage to us to have him in. He could be very mis-chievous if convinced that he was permanently ostracised, whilst he and all the Cecil clan will be bound over (and very willingly too) to good behaviour by his admission. But I feel that I stand as Father's son in a very special way for Tariff Reform; that men look to me to hold that citadel and yet (not unnaturally, considering that I stayed in the Government when Father went out and con-sidering all the concessions I have had to make to Balfour and Party unity) that those who are Tariff Reformers before everything do not wholly trust me as they could trust Father, and that if I yield a point they will exclaim that Tariff Reform is definitely sacrificed to other questions and will throw up the sponge. If I had Father's record, I could speak the word and carry weight.

As it is, I should not much help Bob and I should destroy the confidence of Tariff Reformers in me and in the sincerity of the Party in regard to Tariff Reform.

I tell you all this so that Father may know my exact mind. If I were he, I would speak the word if I saw the opportunity and if I were appealed to. But I do not know whether he will be able to bring himself to do so, and I cannot press him against his will.[1]

In any case Steel-Maitland and Balcarres regard Bob's (as I do) as a special case and will not allow it to be a precedent. They refused to consider the admission of young Bowles on similar terms.

You will remember that Bob has never, like Hugh, opposed the Party on other questions or said an unfair or, as far as I know, unkind word about Tariff Reformers. He wants to join us but as he said to Smith, "I am a proud man" or as Alec Hood once said to me, "It's that damned Cecil pride and obstinacy which makes all the difficulty."

I shall assert once more the full Tariff Reform position and its primacy of place in our programme at the T. R. meetings on 8th November.[2]

*Secret.*

*4th November* 1911.

The blow has fallen and I am as sick as a man can be. Balfour has definitely decided to resign the leadership and he will announce the fact at a meeting of the Council of the City Conservative Association which he will summon on Wednesday to meet on Friday. By Friday afternoon therefore his resignation will be public property and on Monday morning the Party in the House of Commons will be summoned to meet and select a leader of the Opposition in that House. He is now communicating his decision

[1] My father replied that he would write in this sense if appealed to and urged me to make the same declaration publicly.

[2] I spoke both at the morning conference and the evening banquet, an immense gathering which by its numbers and enthusiasm entirely belied my earlier misgivings. At the banquet I declared that Tariff Reform had been fully discussed in the country and that a Unionist Government would "without any further mandate, sanction or approbation" embody it in statutory form.

to his colleagues individually—a task which I think he finds very painful—and he asked me today to tell Father of his decision and to give the reasons for it. At the same time he particularly begs that not a word may be said about it till he makes the public announcement. This is obviously desirable, but it will be a miracle if the secret is kept.

There is the great news, sad news to me whatever happens for I love the man, and though as you know he has once or twice nearly broken my heart politically, I now can think of nothing but the pleasure of intimate association with him, the constant personal kindness he has shown to me and the great qualities of mind and character he has brought to the discharge of the tremendous duties of his post. Well, it is another milestone in my life. The last of the elder generation resigns his post and to no other man can I feel again what I have felt towards him.

It appears from what Sandars [1] has told me that he went away to Gastein with his mind pretty well made up, but S. thought that rest and change might alter his purpose. But he came back more determined than ever, wanted at first to announce his resolution at his Scotch meetings last month, was persuaded to wait till he could see his colleagues, then thought of announcing it at the Leeds meeting of the National Union on Thursday week and has now come to the conclusion that his successor in the leadership of the Opposition in the Commons ought to make his début on that occasion and that to announce his resignation there would be to throw a chill on what ought to be a great rally of all the forces of the Union.

He told Lansdowne of his decision before he went to Wynyards this week. He told Londonderry at Wynyards and he has told Curzon and others besides myself today.

In the course of my conversation with Lansdowne on Thursday, the subject came up and L. said that he thought B.'s resignation might be very near. I said:

"You know my views about it. I think it would be a great misfortune—almost a disaster at the present time."

"Have you ever written to tell him?" asked L.

"No," I said, "but I will if you think it would be well. I think

---

[1] Mr. Balfour's private secretary.

he knows my views about it, but I have not liked to obtrude a letter without any particular cause."

L. thought it might be well that I should write and I wrote accordingly urging him at least to remain till the end of next session. He got my letter on his return from the north yesterday evening and Sandars came round to see me on my return from the Guildhall at 11 p.m. and Balfour sent for me on my return.

Sandars went through B.'s reasons and B. repeated them this morning. But S. said it was a definite decision, that nothing would make him alter it, and that the discussion of it with his colleagues was very painful to him and he accordingly begged me to take it as final and not to add to his worry and to the painful strain of the separation.

Balfour's own reason for going is his health. He says that he cannot do the work of a leader as now understood; he strained his powers to the uttermost at the last election. Even more will be required of the leader in future.

"It is perhaps the greatest danger of democracy, wherever you look, that without knowing it they are overstraining the men who give themselves to the public service." He does not believe in being an occasional leader, making an occasional speech and giving occasional help. Very likely if he offered to continue on such conditions, the offer would be accepted. But it ought not to be accepted. It would be bad for the Party. He must therefore go very shortly. He could never form a Government again. And if he must go, what better time can there be than now? If he stays to fight Home Rule, the Government *may* be beaten on it. He could not then go at the moment of a dissolution, and if he fought the elections and won, he could not then retire and leave another man to form a Government. So he came back to the point that if he meant to go—and he must go—now was the best time. Separation was always painful. It wouldn't be less so because we postponed it.

I made a few, very few observations, but after what Sandars had said to me, I couldn't say much more than :—You know what I feel. I have already said my say. Sandars tells me I must not press it, and to try to say more would only be painful both to you and me.

379

Incidentally he said that the Halsbury Club movement had nothing to do with his decision, and Sandars says the same, but I think the restlessness in the Party, particularly outside the House, has affected him, as requiring more labour than he can give to deal with it satisfactorily and as indicating demands on the leader's strength and time to which he no longer feels equal. Sandars says specifically that Long has "something to reproach himself with," and that he wrote a letter which was "simply insolent." B. therefore feels that the dissatisfaction, such as there is, is not confined to one section of the Party, but that on all sides demands are being made which he has not the strength to satisfy. L. says that his heart is weak and that for some years now he has never made a big speech without taking a strong heart tonic to fortify him for it.

I have felt so badly about the whole business and slept so ill last night on the shock of this news that I could not muster up courage to write the whole story to you this afternoon. Now you will not get my letter till Monday. I may add some more to it tomorrow.

*5th November* 1911.

I do not think that there is anything to add to what I wrote yesterday as far as Balfour is concerned.

Now as to myself and what Father said the other day.

There has been so much talk of late about the possibility of B.'s resigning that I think I know fairly well how the ground lies. As far as I can tell, all the Front Bench with the exception of Long and possibly of Law think, with more or less misgiving, that I am the best man to succeed to the leadership of the Party in the Commons. Lansdowne, it is hoped and believed, will go on in the Lords. Who will be leader of the Party time will show. It may be either or neither of us according to our deserts, but till we are called upon to form a Government that question does not arise.

Against me, however, there is Long's strong objection to my selection, his special group of friends, swelled for the moment by some others who are angry about the Halsbury Club, and the fact that I am both a Liberal Unionist and a Nonconformist. I cannot find that there is anyone in our councils who thinks that

Long himself would do, but he will throw all his weight into the scale against me and might get Bonar Law chosen. Sandars says that he and Balcarres had never supposed that Law would allow his name to be put forward. I think they are mistaken and that Law would allow it and like it if he thought there was a chance of his being chosen.

As to my own feelings I think you pretty well know them. I wish there were another Balfour, clearly superior to us and obviously marked out for the post. How gladly would I play second fiddle to him! But there is no such man at present, and having given my life to this work and got to the position I now hold, I cannot shirk fresh responsibilities or heavier labours if they fall to my lot.

*10th November* 1911.

My telegram will have told you what by the time you receive this will, I expect, be public news; that I and Long have withdrawn our names and that we shall propose Bonar Law as leader.

I did not take this decision without a pang, but I am clear that it was the right thing to do, and this morning I told Balcarres to make the proposal in my name to Long.

I discussed it with Ivy and she agreed.

I fear it will be a great disappointment to my Father. But for that thought, the decision would be an unmixed relief to me now that it is once taken.

Give him my dearest love, tell him that I am sorry to have grieved him, but that I am sure that he would have done the same in my position and that I have at least brought no discredit to the name.

I will write full particulars when I can for him. At this moment Bonar Law is coming to see me.

## Note on the following letter

I beg readers to remember that the following letter was written in the stress of an emotion perhaps excusable in this crisis of my political fortunes. I have omitted a phrase or two which I could not now repeat. Even so the letter does less than justice to Walter

Long or to our friendship and co-operation, which became increasingly close as the years passed. My feeling towards him is better expressed in two entries in a few pages of diary which I kept at a later day to occupy my thoughts at a moment of great domestic anxiety:

*31st January* 1917:

A fine letter from Walter Long to whom I had written on the death of his eldest son killed in action. Nothing finer in this war than the spirit in which people bear their losses. I marvel at their fortitude. Poor Walter, he was devoted to him and rightly proud of him. How should I bear such a loss? I wonder if I could bear it as gallantly and fling myself like Walter into my work with increased vigour.

*3rd February* 1917:

Walter and I have had our tiffs—one at least at the time of Balfour's resignation of the leadership. But I like him. He is hot-tempered and easily angered and at times there has been a queer streak of jealousy—at least of me—in his character. Bonar Law often complains of it. But I like him for all that, and his letter on his son's death by its simple piety and manliness would break down all prejudices if I had any. After all, I think, the jealousy of me was not so much a growth natural to the soil as seed diligently cultivated by others.

I have added to my own letters passages from two letters written to me by Mrs. Chamberlain, two letters from Walter Long and one from Bonar Law written to me at this time, together with my reply to Law. I have no copy of my answer to Long's friendly notes.

*11th November* 1911.
(or 11 / 11 / 11 as I shall never
have an opportunity of so dating
a letter again in my life.)

Your letter received this morning has been a great relief to me. I admit that I don't give up the leadership without a pang, but my chief regret has been the thought that it would be a severe disappointment to Father, who has always been more ambitious for me than he ever was for himself and who, I feared, might take my decision hardly. I am glad that he can look at it as your letter tells me he does. I now have some regrets but no remorse. I am thankful the thing is settled and not ashamed of my part in it. Personal questions are out of the way again and I can work unhampered for the success of our cause.

Father and you will want to know all that has happened, so I now give you the story of events since my return.

*Wednesday, 8th Nov.* I got back from Birmingham at 2 o'clock. Found Bal.[1] had already been to see me, had seen Ivy and Ivy had promised that I would go on to the House to see him immediately after my speech at the Tariff Reform Conference at 3.0.

Bal. told Ivy that Balfour had been forced to precipitate his declaration and was going to make it that afternoon at 4 o'clock in the City. This decision was taken on Tuesday and at once made known to colleagues in town. Bal. had prepared telegrams to summon a Party meeting for Monday at noon when Long had come into his room dragging Chaplin and Lyttelton with him to protest. He was in a very angry and excitable state. All three urged delay—at least till Monday week. Said that otherwise there would be a split. Bal. pointed out the dangers, difficulties, even impossibility of delay. They were obdurate. They then challenged his right to summon a meeting at all! Finally Long, in that or a subsequent interview (I think a subsequent one), threatened that if the meeting were called for Monday he would at once move the adjournment and, if the motion were rejected, would leave the room and advise all his friends to do the same. Bal. had no one else to consult and didn't know what to do.

Long was furious about me, said the Whips were trying to foist me on the Party, and was going about everywhere saying that he would not stand it.

Bal. thought there were four men whose names would be put forward :—Long, Law, Carson and myself.

In these happy circumstances I hurried off to make my 3 o'clock speech with the pleasant knowledge that I had to make another in the evening !

[1] Lord Balcarres, Chief Whip, now the Earl of Crawford and Balcarres.

Made my speech (and for once I thought a very good one though I say it as shouldn't) and retired at once from the meeting. Chaplin was waiting to see me in the Committee Room and asked me to drive with him to the House. Told me that he, Long and Alfred thought delay necessary to avoid serious division; I told him I thought it essential that the decision should be taken at the earliest possible moment. *Any* decision taken early was better than leaving the question indefinitely open. The position would be intolerable for those whose names would be canvassed and most injurious for the Party where every difference would be sharpened and exacerbated. Besides if the M.P.s didn't decide on Monday, the Leeds Conference would take it out of their hands; there would be resolutions, speeches, every kind of lobbying and intrigue. The Party must be summoned to decide at once.

"Then," said Chaplin, "I very much fear there will be a split."

At this moment we reached the Ladies' Gallery entrance and at the same moment Long walked up.

"Ah! Here is Walter," said Chaplin who had just got out.

"Chaplin picked me up at the Tariff Conference," I began, "he was just telling me——"

"Oh!" interrupted Long, "you don't think it necessary to explain why you are in a taxi with a man, do you? You haven't come to that, have you?"

You may imagine my feelings, but I got a grip on myself, turned round and went in with Chaplin.

At the top of the stairs I turned to Long and said:—"You interrupted me in the middle of a sentence. I was going to tell you that Chaplin was telling me of his conversation with you. Will you join us? We had better go into Balfour's room."

C. and I went straight in. Long hung up his hat and coat elsewhere and followed in a moment, having recovered both his temper and his manners.

Characteristically enough he began by saying what a hash Balfour had made of matters and how badly Sandars had managed. After a few sentences I led the conversation back to business and thenceforward kept the lead of it. We went over the ground already travelled with Chaplin with the same results. I then said that I took the situation to be as follows:—We all deplored Balfour's decision; we all thought the moment ill-chosen for it; we had all done our best to prevent it, but in vain. It was quite definite. Balfour wouldn't go back on it and we had now to deal with the new situation created by it.

There were, I understood, four men whose names were before the Party. It was unfortunate that there was no one whose qualifications were so pre-eminent as to make him the obvious and necessary choice, but, that being so, the Party must make their election between them. It might be that between then and Monday Balcarres, in whom all streams of feeling in the Party would naturally centre, would be in a position to tell us that there was a clear majority of the Party for A, B, C or D, or even for Z whom none of us had yet thought of. In that case I thought that all of us who were not the one indicated ought to go to the Party meeting to support the one so selected. If Bal., on the other hand, could not gather a sufficient consensus of opinion before Monday, then our names must go before the meeting and we ourselves must remain away. I did not consider that either of us (*i.e.* Long or myself) was bound, or indeed in the circumstances ought, to withdraw his name. Even if Long were willing to withdraw, his friends would not allow it, and similarly, if I were, my friends would refuse their assent. "But I repeat: I don't think that either you or I can or ought to withdraw at this stage. We shall both desire that if a vote has to be taken between us or between us and others, the name of the successful man should then be put again to the meeting and the nomination made unanimous and whoever is not chosen will then do his best to support the man who is."

In discussing the question of date I had already said:—"You know I think it is very likely that the result of an early meeting will be that neither you nor I will be chosen. I do not believe that if either *you or I were out of the way,* Law would be chosen. But since we are both in the field, I think that Bonar Law with his admittedly great qualities may be their choice. If we divide the Party too equally, I think that very possibly it will be felt that your friends and mine will more easily unite in support of some third person than accept either of us by a narrow majority of votes. In such circumstances the *tertium quid* will probably be the right solution and the *tertium quid* can only be Bonar Law."

To all of this Long assented. Chaplin murmured his approval and we sent for Bal. to come and join us.

He at once began by saying that the news was out already in the lobbies and that the Party was overwhelmingly in favour of the earliest possible decision. Walter Long said that settled it and he and Chaplin withdrew their objections. I said that had been my view from the first.

"Had we not better now tell Bal. what we have been saying?" I asked. And Long said, "Yes, you tell him." So I did.

(More to follow when I have time. A. C.)

(Diary of the last few days continued.)

I accordingly told Bal. that we had discussed the situation together and were agreed that of the four men whose names were being canvassed, none was so clearly marked out for the post that we either could or ought to withdraw our own names at that stage; that we both hoped a vote might be avoided, but that if one were necessary, we both desired that the choice of the majority might then be made unanimous and whoever was not chosen would give all the help he could to the one who was; that meanwhile the lobbies were no fit place for either of us and that we could not ascertain the drift of Party feeling, but all members of the Party would naturally confide in him, that by Saturday or Sunday he might be in a position to tell us that the general opinion of the Party clearly favoured some one person and that in that case the one who was not chosen, or both of us if a third person was chosen, would go to the Party meeting to support the favourite of the majority.

Long expressed entire concurrence and said he had nothing to add or alter in my statement.

Bal. expressed himself as much gratified and much relieved. Chaplin asked if Law and Carson would follow our example. Bal. replied that they could not do less. In any case they must be made to.

As we were on the point of leaving the room I said I was going home. I should not come to the House again till the matter was settled and should not go to any of the Clubs. But if anyone came to see me, I should repeat in substance what I had just told Bal.

In the evening I went to the Tariff dinner—a huge success after all—and deliberately burnt my boats on the Referendum for Tariff Reform, determined that before I or another was chosen I would make it clear that I would no longer be bound by Balfour's Albert Hall Pledge either as leader or as follower.

*Thursday, 9th Nov.*

Bal. called early to say first that the Irish said they must propose Carson as a demonstration; they did not expect to carry him. Secondly that many members of the Party wanted a ballot taken at the Party meeting. Did I object? I replied that I regarded the method of taking the decision of the meeting as the affair of the meeting. I authorised him to give my consent to any course which he himself approved.

He made no secret of his desire that I should be chosen. Long would be "impossible." "Where," he asked, "should I be with him changing his mind every hour?" But he went on to say that of course Long had been bitter against me, the "squires wanted him because he was a squire, and of course you know all the things they say about you. But you may like to know, Austen, for it's a compliment to you, that all the men who have served with you think you are the best man. All my colleagues in the Whips' room do and so do all who know your work and Long's. Mind, I don't say they will all vote for you. Their feelings are played on and they're told they must stick to the man who was loyal to Balfour and stuck to him."

I snorted at this idea of Long's loyalty who, as Bal. knew, had been the centre of every coterie of grumblers for the last five years. Bal. said it was so, and any way Long would break down and be obliged to resign in less than a year.

As to Law he regarded him as "lamentably weak." "I want what's best for the Party. I think you are the best man and therefore I want you."

In the course of the day Gwynne and Garvin called to see me. I told each of them what Long and I had said to Bal. Garvin had been with Law trying his hardest to persuade him not to allow his name to be put forward. He reported that he had found Law inflexible, quite determined to get the position if he could and quite satisfied that he was fully qualified for it.

*Friday, 10th Nov.*

Bal. came again at 11 o'clock in the morning. He said that Carson would not allow his name to go forward. Bonar Law was determined that his should be submitted. "I am furious with him," Bal. said; "of course it injures your chance. Mind, I think that if the vote could be taken on Saturday you would be elected. Long would be furious, but, after the way you have behaved to him, he would have to support you. But the lobbying is all on his side." By Monday, therefore, he could not say what the position would be. We should each poll something over 100 votes and then the votes cast for Law would have to be distributed between us. What the result would be he couldn't say. Either of us might be chosen with a majority of between 10 and 20.

I replied that that was very much what I had expected to hear; I was therefore prepared for it and had made up my mind what I ought to do:

Of course I had had my ambitions, but the acceptance of the position in my private circumstances would have involved heavy personal sacrifices to which I did not now feel called upon to submit. If a clear majority of the Party had desired me to take the position, or if I could have expected loyal support from the minority, I should have felt bound to make these private sacrifices and should have undertaken the task as a duty. But neither condition was fulfilled. There was no clear call from the Party and it was evident that if chosen I should not be heartily accepted by Long or his friends.

On the other hand, I had no confidence in Long's judgment and shared the opinion which he and so many of the men in the councils of the Party had expressed to me that Long's leadership would be a brief but disastrous fiasco.

Bal. suggested that for this very reason I should retire in Long's favour now, let him have it and expose his incapacity. Before six months were over, he would be done for and the leadership would fall to me.

I replied that the same thought had occurred to me the day before, no doubt at Satan's suggestion. But I definitely and at once rejected it. The Party was on the eve of a really critical year. Our fortunes for years to come depended on the fight we made next session. To choose a leader whom we all thought would be so mauled and mishandled that he couldn't retain the post for six months would be disastrous to the Party and to our cause and I could have nothing to do with it.

"I therefore ask you," I concluded, "to go now to Long and to say to him from me that I understand from you that we divide the Party very evenly and that the result of a vote on Monday is uncertain but that whichever of us won would win by a very small majority. Tell him that I think that such a result would be bad for the Party, that it would accentuate differences and make it difficult for the friends of the one who was not chosen to give the full and cordial support which is necessary to the one who is chosen. That I therefore propose that he and I should both withdraw our names and that he as the senior Privy Councillor should propose and I should second the election of Law."

"Do you mean that?" asked Bal.

"Yes, I do."

"You have really made up your mind?"

"Yes, and that you may not doubt it or think that this is only a hasty conclusion on the spur of the moment, I may tell you that, expecting your report to be what it is, I discussed this decision with my wife this morning and she agrees with me and approves what I'm doing."

"Well, Austen, you're a great gentleman. I only wish I had half a dozen more like you in the Party."

And so we parted—I not wholly unmoved by the feeling with which he spoke his last words—and he went direct to Long.

A little later he telephoned that Long "very cordially accepted my proposal" and would like the decision known at once. I said that so should I.[1]

---

[1] Compare *Walter Long and His Times*, by Sir Charles Petrie, pp. 171-2. Sir Charles states on the authority, as he tells me, of a diary kept by the late Sir Harry Samuel that Long wrote to Chaplin asking him "To see Lord Balcarres and say that if Mr. Chamberlain would withdraw, Mr. Long would do likewise. The message served its purpose." I can only say that no such message ever reached me. If Lord Balcarres had received it when he called on me on this Friday morning it is inconceivable that he would not have communicated it to me at once.

(Story finished.)

On Friday afternoon, when I supposed that the news of our decision was already public, Bal. telephoned to me from the H. of C. that Law was there, that he was undecided about accepting and wished to see me. I replied that he *must* accept; he had allowed his name to be put forward and it was too late for him to withdraw. I regarded the matter as settled, but would of course see Law if he wished.

Law accordingly drove here at once. "Well, Austen," he began, "this is a very serious thing for me. I am not sure that I can accept."

"My dear Law," I said, "you must. You have no choice now. You allowed your name to go forward. Don't think that I blame or criticise you for it—I long ago said that there should be no personal rivalry between you and me about offices—but you altered the situation by doing so; you cannot now shrink from the consequences."

"You know, Austen, I think you and Bal. are rather hard on me in saying that because I allowed friends to put forward my name, therefore I have no choice now. I assure you that that wasn't in my mind in the least. I always thought that you would be chosen as a matter of course. My only idea was that if I refused to have my name put forward now, I should be regarded as definitely deciding never to be a candidate for promotion and as being out of the running for all time."

These are not quite his words but they give the sense. The underlying idea was :—You would get the leadership now, but you might fail and I wanted to make good my position as your successor.

As he went away, he said he had written me a letter to explain his position before this sudden change in the situation. It was not posted but he should send it to me to show me exactly what he had been thinking. I send it to you. You will see that in fact it hardly supports his verbal account of his reasons. I dare say that both ideas--the present and the future—were floating in his mind.

But to go back to our conversation. We argued a little more, then suddenly he got up from his chair and said :—"Now look here, Austen! Can't you let Walter Long have it? He couldn't keep it for six months. He'd be an obvious failure and in six months or less the leadership would be vacant again and the whole question would be open."

*Et de deux.* What a world! The same proposal that Bal. had made. Let Long show himself for what he is and in six months the prize will be yours. And the Party and our Cause meanwhile and long after? And my position—watching Long's mistakes, powerless to stop him and accused, as of course I should be, of trying to trip him up? What a prospect of confusion, intrigue and discredit for everything and everyone! And we all the while in the middle of the critical fight against Home Rule, etc. in the campaign which will decide our fortunes for years to come.

No thank you. I may not love Long and have no cause to spare him, but——!

So I told Law that that wouldn't do and I wouldn't play on those terms. He must now be leader. He would have all the help we could give him and a united Party behind him. He might fail as any of us might have done. I believed he would not, but it was possible, and just as (if I had been chosen) I could not have bound him as a condition of my acceptance to have abandoned once and for all the right to have his name again considered in that event, so he could not ask for such an undertaking from me. "But don't think," I said, "that I don't know what I am doing. We are nominally only choosing a leader in the Commons, but I believe that we are in fact choosing the future leader of the Party and appointing the man who will sooner or later be Prime Minister. Either of us would have had to face great difficulties and take some risks, but I believe that, once in the saddle, the one who is placed there will get a firmer and firmer seat and the probability is that once there he will remain there."

"Yes, I think that is so," he said.

We talked on about his qualifications and disqualifications a little longer and then he left, his last words being, "Well, I suppose that I shall have to accept, but it will make no difference to our personal friendship, will it?"

"No," I said, "none." And that promise I must keep. I confess I feel a little grieved. I don't think that if our positions had been reversed I could have acted as he did, but I must just get that feeling out of my mind and keep it out.

And there is the end of one chapter—not without some disappointment and some regrets, but I am well satisfied that I could do no differently.

I believe that if I had held on, I should have won at the second ballot by a small majority. That is Sandars's belief—we had a long and pleasant talk last night—and he tells me that it was Bal.'s also. I would have faced all the risks for the sake of the authority and influence the position would have given me, if I could have been assured of one thing—really loyal co-operation and support from all my colleagues and the exercise of their influence with their friends to give me a fair chance. You know that Long wouldn't have given me a dog's chance. While I stood up to fight the enemy, he would have stabbed me in the back and knowing what I do . . . of the feelings in his *entourage* I do not think that anyone can say that I shirked a duty when I decided to withdraw my name.

And now as to the future. I sent Bonar Law a very friendly acknowledgment of his letter yesterday and then I plunged into policy. I called his attention to my statement on Wednesday evening about the Referendum, told him it was made deliberately *at that moment* in order that if the Party chose me they should choose me knowing what that choice involved and that, if I were not chosen, my position should at any rate be clear before any other choice had been made. The Party ought not to be bound and would not be bound by the compromises on that question or on the House of Lords which were put forward before or at the last election. A stricken field had changed the situation and we couldn't go back to our old position. He knew that the Albert Hall Pledge had been given against my earnest advice and entreaty. I had swallowed it for that election out of loyalty to Balfour and regard for Party unity. But I thought then and thought still that it was a great mistake, and I couldn't be a party to a repetition of the mistake and I could never join a Government which intended to handle Tariff Reform in that way. I believed he agreed, but at any rate he had a right to know my mind and, to prevent any misconception, I wrote to him fully and at once.

And thus we turn at once from the past to the future, from all these personal questions to the great issues. Heaven send that

Bonar Law act wisely! I don't think he has a conception of the questions that press for an early decision. Sandars is very unhappy and very anxious about him. I must do my best to keep (or get) an influence over his mind.

Love to you all. I do hope Father's gout will go quickly. It is beastly weather here—constant squalls of wind and rain. Your letters and Father's opinions have been a great help and comfort to me and Ivy is a tower of strength. I cannot tell you how splendid she has been—full of courage for any difficulties, wise and steady in counsel, infinitely loving and sympathetic through all the ups and downs of these tumultuous days whilst we sat at home and let the storms rage round us. We have just lunched together and smiled over human nature and its humours as illustrated by ourselves and others.

I suspect that if you could peep into all our houses today you would find Walter Long not a little relieved that he is not to be put to the test, me happier than you would have seen me at any time in the last ten days, and Bonar Law for the moment as unhappy a being as exists in all London. I've just had another telephone message from him; must see me before tomorrow's meeting to tell me only terms on which he can accept are that the Party should be absolutely unanimous and so forth. I have replied they will be. But he has got to accept *now* whatever happens.

Lord what a funny world it is when you come to think about it!

Well, we Highbury folk at any rate are a very happy, very united and very loving family. So if they wish to know the inner history of these days please let the girls and Neville see these letters. They can keep secrets who have known so many.

Once again love to you all,

Ever yrs. affectly,

*Signed:* AUSTEN CHAMBERLAIN.

*Mrs. Joseph Chamberlain to A. C.*

HIGHBURY, MOOR GREEN,
BIRMINGHAM,

MY DEAR AUSTEN,                    11*th November* 1911.

Just a hurried note to catch the post, to send you and Ivy our love.

I took your letter in to your father this morning, and he received your news as he always does, in his strong firm way. "I do not see that under the circumstances he could do otherwise." That is his verdict, and I hope you will feel it is the one you wish from him. It would not be in human nature not to wish that a position which is so full of the possibilities of distinction, and of which he considers you worthy both in character and ability, could have fallen to your lot—the more that if filled well it may lead to a higher position still—but, as I wrote to you last night, he feels the present situation is full of difficulties and they might have so hampered you that it would have been impossible to do what you felt ought to be done, while had you been chosen by the Party you could not have refused to do your best. It is always unfortunate when such a question is prejudiced by rival claims (though I hate the word) and things being as they are I feel the position might have been made intolerable. Bonar Law is the best solution for the cause, I believe, since you could not have a free hand, and after all that ought to be and is the first consideration.

*Mrs. Joseph Chamberlain to A. C.*

MY DEAR AUSTEN,                    12th November 1911.

We have read your budget with breathless interest and sympathy with you through every moment of this trying week, and every phase of its development. We should be more than human did we not feel regret and disappointment that the position we had hoped for you is to go to another, the more that we know you are the better man. But the circumstances were so strong against you that we recognise there was no other way for you—and we are proud of all the fine qualities of loyalty, dignity and unselfishness which you have shown throughout and which can only command the respect and admiration of your friends—for you have been true to yourself.

.        .        .        .        .

Perhaps today as your father thinks of it more and more the sense of disappointment is uppermost in his mind, and he can even conceive that possibly the *dénouement* might have been different, but he says to tell you that in a matter such as this your decision must be your own, and he approves whatever it is. "In his place I do not think I could have done differently." But he recognises the extent of the sacrifice and he wishes you had not been called upon to make it.

Tell Ivy we are thinking of her a great deal and are so thankful she is at your side. "I think it (the decision) will make for Austen's happiness" and that your father feels it such a precious possession that it reconciles him to much for you.

. . . . . .

Of the letters you sent, those from Walter Long interested him most. "I consider his announcement that he would be willing to serve under Austen very important."—It will I hope and believe tend to make your relations easier.

9 Egerton Place, S.W.,
13th November 1911.

Thanks to you all for your letters and messages received this morning. We played out the last act of this little drama this morning. There was some restlessness up to almost the last moment, some talk of forcing a vote at all costs even in the hall of the Carlton itself; but, as I was sure would be the case, it all came to nothing after our speeches, and Bonar Law was nominated unanimously and with acclamation. Long's speech was unexceptionable—not distinguished but straightforward and sincere and I could say ditto to every word of it. I knew, for I had heard it from several quarters, that there was some feeling that we had taken the decision out of the hands of the Party, some resentment at the idea that it was settled—they didn't know exactly how—behind their backs. So I thought the best thing was to tell them just what had happened. So I told them that Long and I had met on Wednesday, that we had discussed the situation and, finding ourselves agreed, had sent for Balcarres. I then told them what we had said to Balcarres, of my sending for Balcarres on Friday, of his report to me of the state of feeling in the Party, of my decision and message to Long and Long's reception of it.

I think this plain tale impressed them all, and that the Party felt the whole episode to be not discreditable to them and to call for a like spirit in the rank and file. Bonar Law has a good hearty send-off and the Party will go to the country in good spirits and rather proud of itself than otherwise.

Bonar Law came to see me again before the meeting this morning to say that he could only accept if the Party were unanimous, etc. What is more important, he said that he agreed with me about the Referendum and recalled the fact that he had expressed himself in the same sense at a Shadow Cabinet. He also told me that after seeing me on Friday he had gone to see Long and he added,

"You know Walter is a funny fellow. He talked of you— well, as I might have done."

So you see there will be no breach there. But Father in thinking over the course of events must not attach too much importance to Long's letter to me. That letter no doubt was written, as Long said, overnight and before he had my message, but it was not sent to me till after Bal. had taken my proposal to him. And the fact is that after our talk on Wednesday he could not allow it to be said that he would not serve under me if I were chosen, and when he wrote it, and now, I do not doubt that he believed and believes he would have accepted loyally such a result. He is a curiously passionate and emotional man, a creature of impulse and at his best his impulses are generous and straightforward. But for months beforehand he had said he would never consent to my leadership, that he wouldn't have a Liberal Unionist, that it would be a disgrace to the Tory Party and much else of the same kind. And if I had been chosen by a ballot, as I believed and still believe I should have been, I am convinced that he would never have rested under my leadership. Whatever proposal I might have made he would have been un-consciously biassed against it. Whenever there was a difference in council, he would have held the view opposed to mine; and his friends (I don't mean by any means all who would have voted for him but a passionate and not uninfluential nucleus of them) would have been unrestrained and bitter critics of every step I took. I cannot have as much or as direct an influence on policy as a follower as I might have had under happier circumstances as leader, but I believe that I can now exert more influence on the policy of the Party and do more for the causes I have at heart than if I had been promoted to the first place by a narrow majority after an angry fight leaving bitter memories and unappeased enmities behind it.

So I hope that Father won't grieve. Some regrets we must have but the sooner we forget them the better for us all. I at least have not had one moment's doubt that my decision was right in the circumstances since that decision was taken.

*Copy of letter from Walter Long.*

65 EATON SQUARE, S.W.,
*9th November* 1911.

*Written last night but omitted to post it.*

MY DEAR AUSTEN,

This is damnable! I have heard two statements today. First that you and I have had a long and unending feud. Second that I would not "serve under you." I hope I need not say that there is no more foundation for the last than you know as well as I do there is for the first.

Yours ever,
WALTER H. LONG.

*Copy of letter from Walter Long.*

65 EATON SQUARE, S.W.,
MY DEAR AUSTEN, *11th November* 1911.

One line to say I think you have behaved splendidly; your sacrifice is immeasurably greater than mine.

I suppose our friends will all curse us!

Yours ever,
W.

*Copy of letter from Bonar Law.*

PEMBROKE LODGE,
EDWARDES SQUARE,
KENSINGTON, W.,
MY DEAR CHAMBERLAIN, *10th November* 1911.

I enclose the letter I had previously written you of which I spoke to you, but it expresses very fully what I now feel after our conversation this afternoon.

Yours sincerely,
A. BONAR LAW.

397

*Bonar Law to A. C.*
*Private.*
PEMBROKE LODGE,
EDWARDES SQUARE,
KENSINGTON, W.,
MY DEAR CHAMBERLAIN, 10*th November* 1911.

The enclosed letter from Hope [1] came to me through Goulding and suggests the possibility of a misunderstanding which I should always regret.

My position is a very simple one. A number of my friends in the House expressed their intention of voting for me, and while I did not solicit their support I felt after the most anxious consideration that I had no alternative but to say that if I were offered the leadership I should accept it, and I was justified in this decision by meeting our friend Gwynne of the *Morning Post*, who told me that he knew from a conversation with you that you not only had not felt hurt by my candidature but that you considered I had no alternative under existing circumstances. I should like to add that from what my friends tell me my candidature is likely to prejudice another competitor more than you; but however that may be I am sure that the loyal co-operation and personal friendship which has always existed between us will not be affected by the present contest.

Yours sincerely,

A. BONAR LAW.

*A. C. to Bonar Law.*
*Private.*

9 EGERTON PLACE, S.W.,
MY DEAR BONAR LAW, 11*th November* 1911.

Many thanks for your letters. Do not think that I did or do criticise your decision to allow your name to be put forward.

We have long been friends. You are now my leader as well. This change is not the breach of an old tie between us; it is only the addition of a new one. I shall give you all the help I can. You have got a "good press" this morning. I hope and believe you will find a united Party on Monday.

My great regret at the moment is that I cannot go with you to

[1] James FitzAlan Hope, now Lord Rankeillour. The letter said that he had heard with dismay of Law's candidature, that he did not think Law had any chance and that his standing must gravely prejudice my chances.

Leeds. I have long been engaged to speak that night in Leigh. It was a stupid oversight to fix the day of the National Union meeting, but I am afraid that I should do more harm than good if I now tried to put it off. But you will know that whether at Leigh or Leeds I shall back you.

There is one question of great importance to which you must give your serious consideration at once—I mean the question of the Referendum in connection with Tariff Reform.

You heard what I said on Wednesday. Balfour's decision on that point was taken in spite of my earnest entreaty and with the knowledge that I was profoundly opposed to it. To keep the Party together and to support him, I swallowed my objections and accepted his platform for that election.

But the constitutional fight has now been fought out. His offer was not accepted. There was no compromise, and we as a Party ought not and cannot now be bound by that offer or by the scheme of House of Lords Reform which was then suggested.

A stricken field changes the situation. We start afresh. The Party will not and ought not to go back to its old position.

It was therefore not by an accident or from thoughtlessness that I made that declaration when I did. I wished my colleagues in the House, if they chose me as their leader then, to know clearly where I stood. I thought it not less important that my position should be clear before anyone else was chosen.

I did not read Mr. Balfour's Albert Hall Pledge at the time as binding him in any contingency except that of immediate success at the Polls. Even so, I thought it then and I think it now a fatal mistake which gained us nothing and lost us much. I could not be a party to a repetition of the mistake or join a Government which proposed to handle Tariff Reform in that way.

I believe that though you took a slightly different view from me at the time, we are in agreement now as to the future. But you have the right to know my mind and lest there should be any possibility of misapprehension I write it to you fully and at once.

Good luck, good courage and good friends!! That is my wish for you in the arduous days now to come.

Yours ever,

AUSTEN CHAMBERLAIN.

*Lord Balcarres to A. C.*

7 AUDLEY SQUARE, W.,

AUSTEN,                                   13*th November* 1911.

I would wish you to have heard many things which have been said of your speech this morning. It struck a tone of dignity and calm which leaves you within an environment of strength held in reserve.

People (and Press too) are urging me to publish the full text of our proceedings—well I haven't got it yet, for I never anticipated such a demand. And I do not think consent would be wise. The meeting was so harmonious that with the most subtle malice it will prove difficult to misrepresent the proceedings—so no necessity can dictate publicity.

Moreover, the freedom and spontaneity of the two speeches (wasn't Walter's good ?) were based on the privacy of our gathering. Once we begin to edit here and to excise there, we should lose the authenticity as well as the charm.

Furthermore, I would like to retain the vagueness which in the future will magnify rather than depreciate the *personality* of our proceedings.

Finally we should set a precedent which might haunt us in future. I will send you a transcript as soon as possible.

BAL.

# 1912

## INTRODUCTORY TO 1912 LETTERS

"ALIKE in foreign and in domestic politics the year opened in gloom. Anglo-German relations showed no visible improvement, the Turco-Italian War had been happily localised but . . . a prolongation of hostilities might easily set up a conflagration in the Near East and even in Europe. At home there was a general labour unrest unparalleled since 1848. . . . The Government seemed to be weakened by the recent by-elections; the agitation against the enforcement of the Insurance Act in the coming July was increasing; . . . Moreover, Ministers were pledged to three vast measures: the Manhood Suffrage Bill, which involved some embarrassments connected with Women's Suffrage; Welsh Disestablishment; and Home Rule."

So runs the opening passage of the summary of the events of the year in the volume of the *Annual Register* for 1912. It is a gloomy picture, but not more gloomy than the year itself. As I closed my introductory note to the letters of 1911, it seemed to me in memory that the field was cleared and the lists set for the final struggle over Home Rule and for that series of events which led the country to the very brink of civil war before the greater peril of external aggression for a time stilled all domestic strife and made us again a united people with a common purpose and an undivided will.

But as I turn over the early letters of this year, I find they are occupied with quite other matters. There are indeed signs of growing tension with Germany, of the constant preoccupation of both Government and Opposition with the failure of all attempts, including Haldane's mission to Berlin, to find a basis of agreement which might end the race in naval armaments and place our future relations on a friendly and secure footing, such as we had reached with France by the Entente of 1903. There is still the backwash of the domestic controversies of the preceding year and our troubles about the application of the Referendum to Tariff Reform and the undercurrent of unrest in the Unionist Party on the subject of the Food Taxes, which was to boil up again with disastrous results at

403

a later stage; there were the questions raised by the decision announced at the Coronation Durbar in the previous autumn to transfer the capital of India from Calcutta to Delhi and by the unconstitutional manner, as the Opposition thought it, in which the Government had used the King-Emperor's authority to secure this change, and there was the kindred question of the reversal of Curzon's partition of Bengal.

But all these matters were for the time being overshadowed by the growing industrial unrest which culminated in the great coal strike. The railway strike of the previous year had been followed by an extensive strike in the Lancashire cotton mills which was not settled until it had caused, as was estimated, a loss to the operatives of £1,000,000 in wages and to Lancashire trade a loss five times as great. Scarcely had this dispute ended, when it was announced that a ballot of miners had decided in favour of a strike for a minimum wage by a majority of nearly four to one. Early in February the negotiations between the two sides broke down, and all attempts by the Government to promote a voluntary settlement failed. "By 4th March about a million workers in and about mines had left work, while another million in various industries were threatened with enforced idleness through lack of coal."[1] The Government, which only a week or two before had declared against a Private Member's Bill for a minimum wage, now announced their intention to introduce legislation to provide for the fixing of district statutory minima whilst refusing to include figures in the Bill itself.

The Suffragists, or Suffragettes as the extreme and violent wing of the Women's movement came to be called, chose this moment to break the windows of a number of shops, and the danger of violence thus disclosed and the rumour of further outrages caused the closing of the Winter Exhibition at the Royal Academy and the British Museum.

No sooner was the coal strike in course of settlement than a strike broke out among the transport workers which paralysed shipping in the London docks. It was not settled till early in August. Suffragette disturbances continued throughout the summer, the agitation becoming steadily more violent.

It is a strange story which unfolds itself in these daily letters, and one which, let us hope, may never be repeated in this land of ours. Even the General Strike of 1926 provoked less bitterness

[1] *Annual Register.*

and roused less fear. Work in the mines was not fully resumed till after Easter.

In the course of this year, after twenty-five years' close co-operation between the Conservative and Liberal Unionist Parties, their separate organisations were at last united in the National Union. The new arrangement took some time to complete but worked smoothly from the first. The astonishing thing is that it should have been necessary to maintain the distinction so long after a united government had been formed, in view of the strength of the prejudice for and against the old Party names.

The Easter recess was spent by me in a visit to St. Petersburg, undertaken in connection with a recently formed Anglo-Russian Bank, in the course of which I met both the Foreign and the Finance Ministers.

It must have been as the result of the contacts thus made that I received during the war an invitation which I had entirely forgotten until reminded of it by finding the following reference in a letter dated 7th June 1916:

> I can think of nothing but Kitchener's death, so sudden, so wholly unforeseen. I was actually invited by the Russian Government to go with him to discuss allied finance, but declined, as I felt I should be in a false position, expected to decide and agree to proposals which in fact could only be decided by the Chancellor of the Exchequer himself. I never dreamed of danger.

In *Down the Years* (Chapter III, 3) I have told how on my return from Russia the dangers to European peace caused me to suggest to Grey that the time had come to turn the Entente with France into an Alliance. I urged the same proposal on Balfour, who was deeply concerned about the increasingly menacing character of German policy, and I find in going through my papers that in July of this year he actually submitted to Grey a memorandum on Anglo-French relations in which he reviewed the situation and put forward the same proposal and made practical suggestions for carrying it into effect. The matter is dealt with is Mrs. Dugdale's *Life of Balfour*.

The Home Rule Bill was introduced by the Prime Minister on 11th April and the debate on its Second Reading began on the 30th of the same month. Meanwhile a Bill for the Dis-establishment of the Church in Wales had been introduced by

Mr. McKenna on 23rd April, and the Franchise and Registration Bill followed. It was known that these measures would be rejected by the House of Lords and must be passed again under the procedure of the Parliament Act. This detracted much from the reality and interest of the debates in Parliament. The real issue would, it was felt, now be determined by events outside Parliament. Ulster held the key to the situation. If Ulster were resolute, it could not be coerced. No settlement which did not include Ulster would satisfy the Irish Nationalists; any settlement which subjected the Six Counties to a Dublin Parliament would be resisted to the death. The Government never faced up to this dilemma and the situation became steadily more menacing and the danger of civil war drew nearer.

In Easter week, Carson and Bonar Law were present at a great demonstration held near Belfast when 100,000 men, admirably disciplined, marched past in military order, and at the meeting subsequently held repeated after Carson the pledge that they would never in any circumstances submit to Home Rule. In September the Ulster Covenant was signed. In October the first Balkan War broke out.

I spent the summer recess in another leisurely motor-tour with my wife and Leverton Harris, in France and Italy. Parliament reassembled early in October. The Home Rule Bill was made subject to a "guillotine" resolution, but was still unfinished at Christmas and after only a few days' holiday the House reassembled on 30th December.

On 18th November Lansdowne at a meeting in the Albert Hall announced that the Unionist Party definitely dropped the offer of a Referendum on Tariff Reform and clearly defined the Unionist attitude to Food Taxes, and Bonar Law, who followed him, endorsed his declaration. A fortnight later, he repeated and amplified his statement at another great meeting at the Alexandra Palace and next day I spoke in the same sense at another Unionist meeting. These speeches roused some fears among the Unionists of Lancashire and Yorkshire and there was a recrudescence of the movement against Food Taxes. The Northcliffe Press, headed by *The Times*, went over to the Free Food side, and at Ashton-under-Lyne on 16th December Bonar Law announced that the Party had adhered to Food Duties for the purpose of Imperial Preference which was itself a step to Imperial unity, and that "this was not the time to haul down the flag"; but he promised that a Unionist Government would call a Colonial Conference and would impose such duties only after the Conference and if the Colonies regarded them as essential for Preference. The speech failed to satisfy dissentients at home and was ill-received in the Colonies as involving them in our domestic disputes.

The last letter of the year deals with this matter, but comment will be better reserved for 1913, which opens with Bonar Law's reply.

9 EGERTON PLACE, S.W.,
*17th January* 1912.

I lunched with Bonar Law yesterday and had a pleasant talk.
He is beset by letters asking him to abandon Food Taxes altogether
but admits that he doesn't see how it can be done and volunteered
the promise :

"Well, Austen, if ever I do think that any change ought to be
made in our policy on this question, I promise you that I won't
propose it till I have your assent. You and I stand too much
together on this question for us to have any difference about it."

*11th February* 1912.

Yes, I quite agree, Mary. You *ought* to have had more of a
letter from me before now, or at any rate more of politics, to
show Father that I have not altogether ceased to be a politician.
But I care more about the union of this household than about the
Union of the Kingdom and am more deeply thankful that Ivy
and her babe go on so well than that the Government are tossed
on a stormy sea and have begun their last voyage. I *am* doing
my work. Besides my two speeches and much talk at Birmingham
with my constituents I have seen and discoursed with Lansdowne,
Hubbard, Gwynne and Robbins. But this is all a little unreal
and shadowy (except at the moment of the speech or conversation) ;
my thoughts are elsewhere and—well, it's perhaps a good thing
for me that Parliament meets on Wednesday (though I hate it!)
and that my days are full of appointments and business.

From all of which I hope you will draw the right inference,
which is that I have been taking Dr. Luff's beastly depressing
medicine ! [1]

*13th February* 1912.

I hurried off my note yesterday to catch the post as soon as
I got back from an organisation meeting at Law's, and forgot

[1] For sciatica.

even to acknowledge the receipt of your delightful letter. But you know what pleasure *your* letters give me. No others can take their place.

I hoped to be all right again today but am still headachey in spite of all proper remedies. The weather—wet, raw and foggy—perhaps in part accounts for it. Perhaps too it is due in part to reaction after a strain of anxiety greater in fact than I felt it to be at the moment. All has gone and continues to go well. Dr. P. says Ivy is a model, is doing everything for herself and needs no doctor and that Diane is "splendid," so well formed and growing so well. But though everything has gone well from the first, of course I have been anxious.

I have dictated a long screed on politics which shall go with this, as also some newspaper cuttings—Robbins is sometimes interesting in the *Birmingham Post*, and I will send you anything of his worth sending.

*13th February* 1912.

I saw Lansdowne on Wednesday morning, and yesterday Selborne, Curzon, Bonar Law, Long and I met at his house to discuss the situation and the line to be taken at the opening of Parliament. Our Front Bench amendment in the Commons will this year take the form of a motion calling upon the Government to complete their reform of the House of Lords and denying their right to proceed with such legislation as they contemplate whilst the Constitution is in abeyance. There will also be a full-dress debate in the Lords upon the Indian changes. Curzon made us a statement on the subject from his point of view which I must say was extraordinarily well done. He of course takes a very strong view on the subject—first, because, whether right or wrong in itself, it was improper that an act of such great political importance, and open under any circumstances to so much criticism, should be made the personal act of the Sovereign and that it should be thus rendered impossible to modify or alter the decision without in some respect lessening his prestige with his Indian subjects. The constitutional impropriety is, it seems to me, singularly heightened by the fact that, as now appears, the changes cannot be carried out without an Act of Parliament. Lansdowne had been summoned to see the King on Wednesday afternoon and I had begged him to put this aspect of the case strongly before the King, urging him to tell the King that whilst he and his friends were particularly anxious on all occasions to keep the Crown out of our discussions it was impossible to protect the Crown as we should wish when His Majesty's Ministers used him to shelter them in acts which without his authority they could not have carried through.

"Do tell him," I urged, "in plain language that no Tory Minister, not even Dizzy, at the height of his power, would have dared to make such a use of the Crown. Just imagine what would have happened if Dizzy had caused Queen Victoria to proclaim herself Empress of India at Delhi without a word of prior communication to Parliament, and had come three months later to the House of Commons for the necessary legislative sanction. Mr. Gladstone would have hurried back from his retirement at Hawarden and would himself have moved a vote of censure on the Ministers, which would have been supported by a solid vote of the Opposition of those days."

Lansdowne told us that the King took a special interest in this policy. . . .

Curzon is altogether opposed to the changes, believing, as he does, that a very considerable centralisation of power is necessary to the security of British rule in India.

Curzon's second objection is the expense. This is placed by the Government at four millions—I presume for Delhi alone. Curzon himself says that including the expenditure necessary in other places it will cost not less than ten millions, more probably twelve and possibly fourteen, and this at a time when the Government of India, owing to the prospective loss of the opium revenue, are struggling with financial difficulties and striving to cut down expenditure alike on the Army and the Civil Services. He told us that the site chosen for the capital is one on which he had wished to erect a monument and form a public park as a permanent Memorial of the last Durbar, but that after three years' interest in the work he was obliged to abandon it because the ground was saturated with alkalis, was liable to annual floods, and had no water supply, and the whole proposal was declared by his advisers to be dangerous to health. Owing to the secrecy with which the plan was matured, and to the fact that no one outside the Council of the Viceroy and the Secretary of State were so much as informed of the intention until it was publicly announced, none of these difficulties have been discussed and probably they have not been foreseen.

Curzon's third objection is that in Delhi, as at Simla, the Government will be wholly cut off from all the active streams of Indian life. They will live in a purely official environment, and the fault which has been found with their previous seven or eight months' residence in Simla will now be continued throughout the whole year. He adds—and this is confirmed by everyone to whom I have spoken who knows anything of India—that the Mohammedans are entirely untouched, or at any rate fail to be pleased by the thought that British rule is now to be conducted from the old Mogul capital and associated in that way with the traditions of the last great Mohammedan Empire in India.

Lastly, there is the reversal of the partition of Bengal. Apart from the waste of money involved in this change and from administrative inconveniences which he believes will make it impossible to carry it out, or at least to maintain it in the form proposed, his information and the letters he receives from highly-placed Mohammedans there, such as the Nawab of Dacca, confirm the view put to me by Theodore Morison that they regard it as a deplorable breach of faith. The Nawab writes, for instance, that Government officials from the highest downwards have pledged themselves to him that the partition was irrevocable and that he has so pledged himself to his people, but now his face is blackened. How can he or his people trust the British Government again?

Lansdowne appears to share all Curzon's objections, although, as is natural to him, he expresses them with less vehemence. It is believed that Minto takes exactly the same view. The measure was driven through the Councils both of the Viceroy and of the Secretary of State by the force of authority. Neither of them were, properly speaking, consulted. The Secretary of State's Council, for instance, were summoned in. The dispatch was read to them and they were informed that His Majesty and the

Cabinet had approved it. I am told that even so the most significant protest came from the Bengali representative, himself a Hindoo, against the proposal.

I wonder what you have thought of Haldane's mission to Berlin? I hear a rumour that he was invited by the Emperor, but I must say that the visit seems to me singularly ill-timed and the representative ill-chosen. I hope, however, that no harm has been done. Churchill's speech must, I think, have damped down the extravagant ideas which were beginning to find expression in the Berlin Press. In my opinion the time has not come for any overtures to Germany, and I wish our Government would take to heart the advice given by Sir Frank Lascelles that patience is the quality now needed by our diplomacy and an avoidance of unnecessary provocations. Everything that I hear goes to show that at present the German idea of what is necessary for a better understanding between us is too widely separated from our own to permit of any good results from present negotiations. It is all very well to talk of not envying Germany her place in the sun, but it is another thing when translated into German it is taken to mean that they are to have as much as they like of the African Portuguese possessions—that we are to surrender Walfisch Bay— and that having done this, we shall not indeed have arrived at a settlement but shall have given sufficient proof of good intentions to make it worth while for Germany to make proposals to us. The attitude of a portion of the Liberal Press and Party, and indeed of people who ought to know better, like the Bishop of Winchester, seems to me incredibly foolish and ignorant.

"Why," the Bishop asks, "cannot we settle outstanding questions with Germany as we have done with France?" The real answer, of course, is that by a series of agreements, completed before the French negotiations were begun, we removed every practical cause of friction and disagreement between us and Germany. Heligoland, Zanzibar, Samoa, our respective boundaries in West Africa—all these were dealt with and settled in the same way as we settled our differences with France. The distinction between the two cases is that in return for the concession we made to France we have her sympathy and friendship; whereas our agreements with

Germany, so far from promoting closer union between our peoples and Governments, have not succeeded in preventing a serious and growing estrangement.

And yet that section of the Liberal opinion of which I have spoken, represented particularly by the *Daily News*, values no friendships except those which are for the moment unattainable. When our relations with France were bad, and even critical, they were the earnest friends of France and passionate advocates of an Anglo-French Entente. When Russia was supposed to be our enemy, and our relations with her were difficult and anxious, they preached the duty and advantage of an agreement with Russia. Now that we are friends with both Russia and France, these friendships have ceased to interest them or to have any value for them, and they are ready to risk both in a wild-goose chase after a German understanding. They behave exactly like a rake whose whole ardour is in pursuit of his mistress and who ceases to care for her the moment she has yielded to his importunities.

My mind, on the other hand, works in exactly the opposite direction. I believe that our true policy would be to develop our Ententes into a triple defensive alliance. I expounded this view to Lansdowne for his consideration when he lunched with me. Lansdowne was of course non-committal and I did not attempt to do more than put the idea into his mind. Gwynne, to whom I also spoke of it, was enthusiastic and begged me to make a speech on Foreign Affairs! I must come back to this subject in another letter, for this one has already grown to inordinate length. It will, I hope, excuse me in your eyes for the absence of political news in my earlier letters.

*14th February* 1912.

10.30 a.m. We had a pleasant dinner at Bonar Law's last night. Everybody was in good spirits at the improvement in our own fortunes and the obvious uneasiness and distress of the Government. It is reported that they have had some most stormy meetings of the Cabinet on the suffrage question. It appears that Asquith's statement about adult suffrage was made without any previous consultation with the Cabinet, and in this Government it appears that the Prime Minister at any rate is not allowed to declare a

413

policy until it has received the assent of his colleagues. Meanwhile the Suffragists in the Cabinet are very angry with those of their colleagues who are to take part in the Albert Hall meeting, but I hear that Asquith turned fiercely on Lloyd George and told him that it was all his fault for trying to commit the Government and the Party at his Bath meeting. It seems quite likely that the Franchise Bill will never get presented and that the Government will confine itself to producing a Plural Voting Bill and giving time for the reconsideration of the Conciliation Bill. Robbins, however, suggested to me that the Government already begin to feel that they may get into such difficulties that they will be beaten on something, and if so they may produce an Adult Suffrage Bill and ride for a fall on the Women's Franchise in the belief that, as we are as much divided as themselves upon that subject, it would be the least favourable issue from which we could proceed to a dissolution.

The agitation in Ireland for full financial autonomy seems to be increasing, and such a defence of Home Rule as was provided by Dr. Horton's letter in *The Times* the other day to quiet Nonconformist consciences is not likely to smooth the path of Ministers. F. E. Smith tells me that Willie Redmond's language about Lloyd George is unprintable. Redmond and his friends thought that, having helped the Government to get the Veto out of the way, they would proceed on a straight course without any disturbing element to Home Rule. Now he says Lloyd George has queered the pitch, completely altered the whole situation, and jeopardised the success of Home Rule by the unpopularity of his Insurance measure.

F. E. Smith, who probably does not speak without knowledge, also told me that he did not believe there was any foundation for the rumours of Asquith's resignation. If it were to come about, he thought that both Lloyd George and Winston Churchill would agree to serve under Grey whom they thought they could displace at any moment convenient to themselves. He did not believe that at the present moment Winston would be willing to see Lloyd George made Prime Minister, for Winston Churchill thought his own star in the ascendant and regarded Lloyd George as a waning force.

Bonar Law did very well with his speech, but he made a hash of an answer to a challenge of Asquith's about the Insurance Bill, which fluttered the lobbies a great deal and out of which he will have to get somehow.

"Would you repeal the Bill?" asked Asquith.

"Yes," said Law without thinking what that meant. If we came in *now*, we should be obliged to suspend its operation and amend it. But in a very short time, repeal will be an impossibility, for the Friendly Societies are already rearranging themselves to work it and before long all sorts of vested interests will have grown up under it.

It's rather provoking that he made this slip which may give him a little trouble; he has plenty of pungency and pugnacity which was lacking in Balfour's speeches, but he is rather rash and has not yet realised the difference between his old position and his new one. He is too much inclined to use *any* weapon against the Government, as he would have done in former days when he was little reported and less studied, without considering that now he must be ready to support and prove any charge he makes. He was awfully wrong about finance at the Albert Hall and not on very good ground in his charges of corruption. The Government have done some bad jobs but he drew his charges much too wide. Similarly, today he asked: Had the Government spent public money on their Party agitation? Now that isn't a question you should ask unless you can follow it up with proof. And he had no proof—at most a suggestion or a clue which it would have been worth while to follow up privately to see if it led to anything further, but which he could not produce as it came to him confidentially and indirectly from an anonymous Treasury official.

*Monday morning,*
*19th February 1912.*

I send you a copy of a letter about the Referendum which I have just sent to Bonar Law. I fear that he, as I told you, is rather weak. Had he spoken out at Leeds I believe the country would have applauded him and he would have had no trouble with the Party. But he let that opportunity slip, and before another

415

came along Walter Long had been to him to protest that the Party was committed to the Referendum on Tariff Reform and that it must not be abandoned. Bonar Law is anxious not to quarrel with Walter Long and now finds it very difficult to reject his advice. He told me that he had spoken to Lansdowne on the subject and that he thought Lansdowne would have preferred to continue the pledge, but he had told Lansdowne that he (Bonar Law) was personally in a position which made that impossible. He would be considered to have renounced his faith and sold his conviction, and that therefore on personal grounds he could not repeat his pledge. He had ascertained from Balfour that Balfour would not consider the abandonment of the Referendum offensive to himself. This was all satisfactory enough, but two days ago he suddenly asked me whether I should mind his saying in the course of the Tariff Reform debate this week that we should submit a Tariff Reform Budget to the Referendum if even now Asquith consented to take the same course with Home Rule. He said that he did not think it was possible for Asquith to accept this suggestion and that it could therefore do us no harm. At the same time it would make his position easier with Long.

I at once entered a caveat but he asked me to think it over and not give my answer immediately. I told him however that I thought his right course would be to put his personal position to Walter Long as he had done to Lansdowne, and to say to Walter Long that under the circumstances he must appeal to Walter's good feeling and loyalty to support him in the only course which he could take with honour. This is what I hope he will do and I believe that, thus appealed to, Long would waive his objections.

*A. C. to Bonar Law.*
*Private.*

My dear Bonar Law,                                    *17th February* 1912.
    I have been thinking over what you said to me about the Referendum. I earnestly hope that you will make no such announcement. It is surely sufficient to say that the offer which Mr. Balfour made was not accepted—the compromise embodied in it was rejected—the situation has been changed by subsequent

416

events, and the Party can be no more bound to the exact solution then proposed than to the next form, let us say, of the Lansdowne Bill.

I am sure that any revival of the Referendum in connection with Tariff Reform will lead to great trouble. I do not mind saying that a Tariff Reform Budget should be treated like other Budgets, that if every Budget was to be subject to a Referendum, of course a Tariff Reform Budget could not be an exception to the general rule; but I am most profoundly opposed to singling out a Tariff Reform Budget from all others and imposing upon it this additional difficulty.

I am most anxious to keep exactly in step with you and I do not think that it should be difficult for me to do so, but on this subject I burned my boats before you were leader and I cannot unsay what I have publicly stated.

Yours very sincerely,

A. C.

This ought to have been posted on Sat. but the servants overlooked it.

*19th February* 1912.

I will now give you the promised account of our fusion negotiations. They began with a meeting at Bonar Law's house at which 5 Liberal Unionists deputed by our General Purposes Committee met 5 Conservatives. The members of this Conference were on the Conservative side, Bonar Law, Lord Chilston (Akers-Douglas), Lord Kenyon, Balcarres and Steel-Maitland; and on our side Savile Crossley, Pike Pease, J. C. Williams, Jardine and myself.

After settling some preliminary points we asked Crossley and Steel-Maitland to draw up, with the help of Boraston and Jenkins, alternative schemes for the complete fusion of the Unionist organisations, and for the fusion of the central offices only.

When this had been done the Committee met again at Bonar Law's house and after considering the two schemes came to the conclusion that the larger one alone was worth consideration. The smaller one would probably involve nearly as much inconvenience and criticism without the corresponding advantages.

2 D

417

We then discussed the larger scheme in some detail and provisionally agreed to it subject to some modifications.

The scheme, so modified, was laid by us before a full meeting of the Liberal Unionist Committee on Friday last. We went through it and made some further alterations which are indicated on the draft which I enclose. We agreed that we could not bind the Scottish organisations in any way, that the case of Scotland must be separately treated, and that the Scotsmen must settle it for themselves. Subject to this exception the Council decided that if the scheme proved equally acceptable to the Conservatives, we would recommend it to our people. As a first step, and by way of both sounding and educating Liberal Unionist opinion, it was decided that both Crossley and Boraston should devote a week to interviews with leading Liberal Unionists from all over the country. Our largest subscribers had already been consulted and signified their assent.

You will see from the draft that the new organisation is to be called the National Unionist Association. Until the first Conference is held next November a provisional Committee will be formed of the two existing Committees. After the Conference is held in November it is proposed that the names of the committee-men should be proposed *en bloc* to a smaller body, the Council, elected by the Conference, from the chair or by distinguished members of the Party who would emphasise the fact that it was an agreed list, fairly representative of both the former wings, and would use all their influence to get it carried in that form. It is believed that there would be no difficulty in getting this done and the Conservatives are very anxious to adopt our plan of electing the Committee *en bloc* so as to avoid the canvassing and intrigue which has played so disastrous a part in their organisations in the past. You will notice that the Presidents (that is the leaders of the two Houses) are to have power to appoint four additional members, and, in selecting these, they are to have regard to the fair representation of both the former wings. On the Council we are to have during the first year about 80 Liberal Unionist representatives to about 220 Conservatives. This is more than our proportion according to any existing standard. It is almost impossible to say what is our exact strength in the House of

Commons at the present time as several Members appear in both lists, but by no calculation can we make it one in three. Again, if you take the test of finance, where we have of late incurred joint liability for expenditure, Crossley had established the rule with Hood that we should pay one-fifth only. For the first year, therefore, we are generously provided for. After the first year we feel that we must trust to our merits to secure us proper representation. Where, as is generally the case, joint associations already exist in the locality little or no jealousy has been shown of Liberal Unionists. These men who were held at arm's length by the Conservatives as long as they belonged to separate organisations have been welcomed to the positions that their merits deserved as soon as the Associations were fused, and we hope and believe that the same will happen under this larger scheme. In any case as the ultimate object of the amalgamation is to bring us all under one common name, and to obliterate the divisions and jealousies of the past, we should defeat our own purpose if we attempted to lay down in perpetuity a fixed proportion between Liberal Unionists and Conservatives. I am sure that the leaders of the Conservative Party will use their best endeavours to secure the fair and amicable working of the proposals if they are adopted, and I do not think that we could ask for any further guarantees.

As regards the fusion of funds, it may be found convenient that each of us should reserve sufficient to meet our existing or prospective liabilities, but it is intended that in future there should be a common purse. Crossley would prefer to fuse the funds completely at once and to make the outstanding liabilities of both sections a first charge upon them.

*20th February* 1912.

I dined last night at Grillions—a small but pleasant party. Balfour of Burleigh, who was there, told me that he had had an interview with Harcourt about some business and that Harcourt had mentioned to him with evident pleasure that he had received a long and interesting letter from Father. B. of B. thought that Father would like to know what obvious pleasure his letter had given as illustrated by Harcourt mentioning its receipt to him.

I had Lord Sanderson on one side of me and tried to pump him on foreign affairs, but I could not get much out of him. He seemed very doubtful whether the republic would endure in China owing to their habit of ancestor worship which seemed to require as its keystone an hereditary monarch. But he agreed that whatever happened the Manchus would not return.

He told me (and he is the first person who has given me this account of last year's history) that no offer of assistance was ever made to France. According to him what the British Government feared was that the demand of Germany for a share of Morocco must bring in England with a counter-claim and in that way they might be dragged into the field. He admitted that in view of such a contingency the French and British General Staffs had worked out a joint plan of campaign, but he thought that things had gone no further. I asked why in that case had the War Office not merely warned regiments to be ready but actually assigned to them billets in France. His reply was that that was just like the War Office who were always over-hasty. I give you this for what it is worth. Personally I do not believe it is a correct account of what took place, and Sanderson when pressed did not seem sure of his ground.

The explanations of Haldane's visit given at Westminster and in Berlin rather change my view of that episode. It would, I suppose, have been impossible to refuse the German invitation that a British Minister should visit Berlin, but I remain very anxious as to the nature and scope of the *pourparlers* which are going on. In any case it was singularly foolish to begin by pretending that Haldane's visit was purely private and caused only by his interest in University affairs. If this had been true, it was the wrong time for the visit, for no one would have believed it, and as it was not true and was immediately demonstrated to be false, it appears to have been a wholly unnecessary and useless departure from the truth.

I found a good deal to agree with in the notes of last Sunday's *Observer*. There is no sign that the naval or military increases of Germany will be stayed, whatever the result of the negotiations, and if that be so the outstanding rivalry remains whatever territorial adjustments may be contemplated. As to these, I still believe that the German public is opening its mouth far too wide at the present time and that until they come to a more reasonable view of the situation all conversations on the subject are extremely dangerous. Meanwhile there is one advantage that has accrued to us from German rivalry and German ambitions. It is to them that we owe the loyalty of the Boers, and of Botha in particular, to the British connection. If Germany had not been a South African Power I would not have given much for the chances of that connection after the establishment of self-government. It is the fear of Germany which has driven Botha into our arms.

Here is a link with the past. B. of B. went over the field of Waterloo with his father in 1863, his father having carried the Colours of (I think) the 3rd Battalion of Grenadier Guards at the great battle. Balfour's son went through the whole three years of the South African War without being on the sick-list for a day.

9 EGERTON PLACE, S.W.,
*21st February* 1912.

Our debate yesterday went off very well. I was satisfied with my own speech and Bonar Law wound up for us in the most successful speech he has yet made—full of vigour and spirit and loudly applauded by our men at all points. The Party backs him heartily. The cheering left nothing to be desired and he responded to the encouragement given to him and was in admirable fighting form. The Party went into the lobby in high spirits and we had a very good division.

*Wednesday, 21st February* 1912.

I forget whether I told you that Lansdowne had asked me to see him yesterday, when we had a free exchange of views both on the subject of Food Taxes in general and the Referendum in particular. He would have liked to get out of the Food Taxes if possible, but I think accepted my view that that was out of the question. On the Referendum I found him less difficult than I had expected. He is not, I think, an enthusiastic supporter of it for any purpose and he was quite prepared to take the line that the events of last year had entirely altered the situation and cleaned

421

the slate for us. The difficulty with him is, I think, entirely caused by Curzon who appears altogether to dominate him at the present time.

Since writing to you about foreign affairs I have received a most interesting report of Grey's account to Cambon of the nature and scope of Haldane's conversation in Berlin. It comes to me on first-hand authority. The only question is did Grey disclose everything to Cambon and did Cambon disclose everything that Grey said to my informant? Subject to these qualifications the story is as follows:

Cambon began by saying that Grey had on this, as on all occasions, behaved with the utmost loyalty to France. Haldane had been to see Cambon before he went to Berlin, and Grey had informed him afterwards of all that took place.

The Berlin conversations had begun by a disclaimer on each side of any intention to attack the other, Haldane adding that he presumed that the German disclaimer applied equally to any unprovoked attack upon our friends since such an attack *pourrait nous engager*. Haldane had then sought to secure some arrangement about armaments but had rapidly discovered *qu'il n'y avait rien à faire de ce côté*: they then turned to the question of English co-operation in the Baghdad Railway, and the Germans had indicated that they would be willing to recognise and to allow to us a predominating influence in the Persian Gulf section. To this, Haldane is reported to have replied that we already had that predominating position in those parts and did not require German permission to exercise our rightful influence! It was added that, the Turks having got wind of or suspecting the fact that the conversations had in part turned upon the Baghdad Railway, the Turkish Ambassador had called upon Grey immediately after Haldane's return with instructions to say that the Turks had given no concession to Germany for that part of the line, that they did not recognise the right of England and Germany to discuss it or to settle it between them and that any conversations or proposals on the subject must be addressed directly to the Porte. "*Et c'est tout—absolument tout. Il n'y avait plus rien.*"

This is certainly very interesting. I wish I felt certain that it *was* the whole truth.

*23rd February* 1912.

Our sub-committee on organisation had a long interview yesterday with the principal officers of the National Union. Please tell Father not to trouble with the scheme I sent him and not to reply to Bonar Law's letter until I write again. The representatives of the National Union were quite willing to meet us generously as to our share of representation, but though they have reorganised their own constitution it remains very cumbrous and there is some difficulty in getting them to make the adjustments which we think necessary. It is a very curious situation, for the truth is that Steel-Maitland and Balcarres want what we want and are inviting us to stand out against their own National Union. We had, as is usual, a most interesting and instructive conversation among ourselves after the Conservative delegates had left us, and it was arranged that Crossley and I should see Steel-Maitland and Balcarres at the earliest moment and try to hammer out a common policy. The National Union offered us half the representation on all the working Committees, which will really exercise control, but they propose to retain their own method of selecting the other half, which in fact gives them rather inferior men, and Balcarres is humorously alarmed at the thought that the type of men we should put on would wholly overshadow what he calls the "aldermen" who come to the front under the Tory system. When I can report anything definite, I will write again.

Tryon made an admirable speech yesterday in moving the Tariff Reform amendment and we had a good debate though in a thin House. Mildmay, who, as you know, has been a rather reluctant convert, seconded the amendment in a speech pleasantly and easily delivered in which he tried practically to convince the House by the arguments which had convinced him. It marked, I think, some advance in his position and a real desire to keep in line with the Party. Lyttelton wound up in a non-contentious and closely reasoned speech in which he put extremely clearly the arguments arising from the combined effects of the fiscal autonomy of the Colonies and the existence of the most favoured nation clause.

Macnamara and Robertson, for the Government, made characteristically bombastic and empty speeches. In fact, as someone said to me, the most striking feature of the debate was that our speakers were all up to date in their facts and arguments whilst our opponents seemed to know nothing of what had been passing in the world.

F. E. Smith attended a meeting in the Lord Chancellor's room to discuss the speeches they would make at the anti-suffrage demonstration in the Albert Hall. He said he found the Lord Chancellor boiling with rage. "I shall say," said the Lord Chancellor, "that to pass such a measure without the clear sanction of the country would be a great outrage on the Constitution." He added that he saw an attempt made in some quarters to twist the Prime Minister's words into meaning that if a Women's Suffrage amendment were inserted in the Government Franchise Bill it would thereafter have the whole force of the Government behind it. "That," said the Lord Chancellor, "is not the case. I can name seven of my colleagues who will oppose it, and I myself will join a committee in the House of Lords to put down obstructive amendments."

I think the Government are in a great mess over this question and will be in a worse position still before they have done.

The Suffragists want the Bill kept in the House of Commons for the Committee stage. So naturally do we. The Government have promised to give, if necessary, a week or ten days for its consideration. This will play havoc with their business arrangements, whilst at the end of the time I should hope that we should have succeeded in preventing a conclusion being reached. The Government will then either have to give more time, and so further disarrange their programme, or they will be exposed to the bitterest hostility of the supporters of the Bill. The present inclination of myself and others who think like me is to support all extensive amendments in Committee. In that case, I think, they will be carried and I should hope that those who are prepared to go as far as the Conciliation Bill, but no further, will on the Third Reading, if it be ever reached, vote with us against a measure which would involve Adult Suffrage. In any case it is a very pretty Parliamentary prospect, for, although the question divides the Opposition, division among them is far less injurious than division in the ranks of a Government who are at the same time trying to carry such large controversial measures.

*24th February* 1912.

I have not given you any account of our conversation with Pernolet when he dined with Beatrice and me last Sunday. We talked a good deal about the situation in the summer. I observed that on this occasion we had done, or had been ready to do, everything that French statesmen have desired. We were on the verge of giving them not merely the diplomatic support which we had promised but actually military aid, and all arrangements had been made by our military authorities for placing our Expeditionary Force in France within ten days of the outbreak of war. I dwelt upon the fact that this was going far beyond our obligations under the Anglo-French Treaty, which were confined to merely moral support. I did not pretend that it was done wholly from disinterested affection for France; on the contrary I thought that the justification of the English policy from the English point of view was that in the present state of Europe we could not afford to see France beaten to her knees. If my diagnosis was right it followed that, even though the Moroccan question were now settled, we should be obliged to act again in the same way if France were again similarly threatened. The result in the last instance had been to excite German feeling singularly against ourselves. No doubt if similar circumstances recurred, the animosity against England would be even greater, and the question arose whether our Entente were not a one-sided arrangement which in practice committed us to the defence of France but involved no corresponding obligation on the part of the French Government and people. If, as a result of our action, war broke out between Germany and ourselves would France afford us like assistance and make common cause with us as we had done with them?

This is a problem which is much exercising my mind at the present time. I keep asking myself whether it would not be an act of wise statesmanship to endeavour to replace the Entente with France and Russia by a triple alliance for mutual defence.

To my question about the attitude of France, Pernolet replied by saying that for many years after the Franco-German war England was still very unpopular in France, even more so than Germany. With the short exception of the time of the Crimean War, there had never been any friendship between the two peoples. Bonapartists remembered us by Trafalgar and Waterloo. The Legitimists bore us ill-will on the ground of the too great sympathy of our Court with the Orleanists, and no party in France had any real attachment to us. Then at last came the Entente, and feeling really changed—first slowly, then more rapidly and completely. But, said Pernolet, even then the *bourgeoisie* desired peace before all things and were inclined to suffer almost anything rather than risk war. Clemenceau had, however, administered a tonic at the time of the Casablanca incident *quand il avait envoyé promener les Allemands.* This had produced an extraordinary effect. Had the French people been appealed to beforehand, they, or at any rate the whole of the *bourgeoisie*, would have replied at once, "For Heaven's sake do nothing that may provoke a rupture." But when they saw Clemenceau's action and its effect they took quite the opposite view. They felt tired of the constant *tracasseries* of German diplomacy and began to feel that it was time to make an end of so intolerable a situation. Every Frenchman recognised the absolute loyalty of England in these events. In addition they found much more common ground with the individual English-man to-day. He was less insular, less aloof, more approachable, in short, less different from Frenchmen than his fathers had been; and, most of all, Frenchmen who came to England were struck by the cordiality with which Frenchmen were now received and by the obvious dislike and animosity which they found everywhere existing towards Germany. These different circumstances had produced a great change in French public opinion. No doubt international finance was a dangerous element in their politics, as he thought it was in all countries nowadays. Caillaux had been its instrument. What exactly he had done remained a little mysterious. It had not been thought desirable to probe the matter too far, and his fall had been therefore arranged by means of the scene which we know, but as answer to my question he would observe that it was French public opinion which had made that fall necessary and driven him from office, because it was considered that he was trying to give French policy a new direction and was not true to the friendships of France.

Pernolet is very intelligent and sees many politicians and public men of all classes. This makes his views interesting even if one finds a good deal to criticise in them.

*26th February* 1912.

Many thanks for Father's letter to Law about organisation. I shall hold it back till we have reached a definite agreement and will let Father know how we proceed. The real difficulty is between the Conservative Central Office and the National Union, not between either of them and us.

Yes, it is really irritating to hear Balfour's "friends" speak of him as they do, but indeed they have always done it. Selborne told me for instance that two or three weeks before the "Die-hard crisis" he met Walter Long at Winchester's where Long spoke of Balfour "in terms that no Die-hard ever thought of using." It appears that on the same occasion Long said that there would be no trouble when Balfour retired, that he would not serve under me but was prepared to serve under Law. I hear that he is now very anxious for fusion and says that if it had taken place a year or two ago there would have been no trouble about my leadership! He is the one leading man who seems to have had a real jealousy of Liberal Unionists as such.

*26th February* 1912.

Since I wrote to you about foreign affairs last week I have received some more information as to the events of the summer from the same unimpeachable source. According to this statement Lansdowne approached Cambon with a suggestion for a closer union between France and England just before we left office, but by the time Cambon was ready to proceed the change of Government had taken place and Grey said he could not take up the project. At that time Grey said there were only four members of the Cabinet who favoured the Entente—the Prime Minister, Crewe, himself and one other. There has since been a complete change of view in the Cabinet but Grey says that they could not make an alliance without communicating it to Parliament and for that he is not prepared.

As regards last summer, the story confirms what Sanderson told me at Grillions. It is denied that the French Government sent

427

any such dispatch as that which was alleged to have been shown to the railway directors, but Grey told Cambon that if Germany provoked France by aggressive demands England would stand by France. We regarded the sending of the *Panther* to Agadir as a provocation, but if it were a question "of a few square miles" of territory in West Africa we should regard that as a matter for conciliation and compromise, and if they quarrelled about that we must reserve our liberty. I am not sure whether it was in this connection, or at the time when they took office, that Grey made the statement above recorded about the alliance. In any case the account of the division of opinion in the Cabinet refers to the earlier time. So far, therefore, as last summer was concerned, no very definite engagements were made, but it was agreed between the two Governments that in order to be prepared for immediate action if the occasion should arise the General Staffs of the two countries should elaborate their plans together. The relations between the two General Staffs were exceedingly cordial; all these arrangements were worked out easily and successfully, and according to this story, as according to Sanderson's, it was from this circumstance that the rumour about the dispatch of the Expeditionary Force to France arose. Cambon emphasised the absolute straightforwardness and loyalty of Grey throughout. Of Russian diplomacy he did not speak with the same respect or confidence.

1912: FEBRUARY–APRIL

*The Coal Strike*

9 EGERTON PLACE, S.W.,
*27th February* 1912.

I do not think that I told you Asquith had invited me in flattering terms to take the Chairmanship of a Royal Commission. Last year some 400 members of the House of Commons, drawn from all parties, presented a memorial to the Prime Minister asking for an enquiry into the method of recruiting for all branches of the Civil Service. The Government have decided to grant the enquiry by means of a Royal Commission, and Asquith was anxious to have me for its chairman in view of my old position at the Treasury and I suppose of other qualifications which he thought he saw in me. I considered the matter carefully but have definitely declined it—not without some reluctance, for it would be a useful piece of public work, but it would involve the sacrifice of two mornings a week at least for a long time to come and I cannot afford that amount of time.

I dined at Grillions again last night and he came up to express his great personal regret though he said he quite understood and accepted my decision. I was very much among the Government, for I sat opposite to Harcourt, to whom I gave Father's message, and Grey; and Haldane also sought me out to talk about the administration of the University Grants. He is trying to get them put under the Board of Education which he says has now been reorganised and has an admirable University branch, through which he urges they would obtain much larger grants than they do from the Treasury. Against him he said Lloyd George quoted me as being strongly opposed to the transfer of these grants from the Treasury to the Board of Education. This is quite true, for I have always feared that the Board of Education would seek to impose their views of what ought to be taught upon the Universities and would stereotype the University courses : whereas the Treasury, not being in this matter a department of specialists, was content merely to ascertain that the work carried on was of a University standard and that certain other necessary financial conditions were observed.

Everyone here is much exercised over the prospects of a coal strike, but as I know no more than the Press tells us, I have said nothing to you about it. The situation looks extremely threatening but I somehow remain of the belief that a general strike will be avoided. On the whole, however, public opinion seems to grow more gloomy as the days pass by.

*29th February* 1912.

Here is the coal strike apparently upon us, but I cannot help believing even now that it will be of short duration and that some kind of compromise will in the course of a week be arranged or imposed on the disputants. Whether that would really be a good thing is another matter. There is so much unrest in the labour world that I feel that we shall never have settled peace until one struggle at least has been fought out to a finish. But I confess that the coal trade is not the field of battle I would select if I had my choice.

We had a capital anti-suffrage meeting at the Albert Hall last night, the most remarkable features of which were the composition of the platform and Miss Markham's speech—one of the very best—indeed the best—that I have ever heard on the subject. There are so many things which a woman can say, and which she said well, which a man cannot utter without offence. Loulou on his colleagues was also very interesting and Loreburn on "a constitutional outrage." I had a few words with Mrs. Harcourt afterwards. It is evident that they are furious with Lloyd George.

I have had put into my hands within the last few days the most curious and interesting account of a conversation between an Englishman, whom I know slightly, and two Germans—both officials and one a naval officer. The Englishman, who has taken a special interest in naval affairs, saw these gentlemen several times last spring at the time of the discussion on our naval estimates. The German naval officer had then pointed out that English Ministers and Opposition leaders had both fallen into error in describing the German programme and had urged the Englishman to put the real facts clearly before the public. Encouraged by these overtures the Englishman reopened communications last month and suggested a fresh exchange of views. His proposal was accepted and I have his report on the conversations which ensued. He reminded his two friends of the statement made to him last year that Germany had no intention of altering or accelerating her naval programme and asked if that declaration still held good. Each of them in reply stated that the situation had entirely changed, and that in view of England's recent attitude towards Germany public opinion in that country had become intensely Anglophobe and thousands of thoughtful Germans who had previously disagreed with the Naval party were now convinced that England was not only prepared to support France by force of arms but that she strongly resented any attempt on the part of Germany to extend her colonial possessions. In consequence of this great change in public opinion the Navy party had received a considerable accession to its ranks, even the Socialists, or at least the greater part of them, falling into line.

They made no secret of the fact that German aspirations lay in the direction of colonial expansion and the acquisition of coaling stations. They denied that Germany had any design on Holland or Belgium or, through Austria, on the Adriatic. They insisted that colonial, not European, expansion was what Germany desired. "Yet," said they, "wherever we look we find England blocking the way and insisting that her interests are adversely affected."

The Englishman suggested that in the event of Portugal selling her African possessions a mutually satisfactory arrangement might be possible. "Yes," said the German naval officer, "but what would England require? Doubtless Delagoa Bay and Beira; leaving us the worthless territory to the north." When asked what he would propose as a fair arrangement, the reply was "Why not let Germany have Delagoa Bay and Beira?" The Englishman then referred to the preamble of the German Navy Law. They replied that he had misunderstood it. Germany, they stated, had no hope of being able to defeat England at sea. What they aimed at was a fleet strong enough so to cripple the English navy that, though victorious, England would be impotent to resist the encroachment of other Powers after the war and not strong enough to prevent Germany recovering her position in the course of time. In other words they desired a fleet so powerful that the cost of its defeat would be too great a price to pay for the advantage gained. They entertained no designs of invading or robbing England of any of her possessions, but they intended to place themselves in such a position that they could carve out their own destiny and acquire fresh outlets for expansion in various parts of the world without finding England barring their path.

When asked what, on this basis, they would consider a fair proportion between the strength of England and that of Germany, they replied a proportion of 3 to 1. This is the standard advocated by the German Navy party.

There is an interview *qui donne à penser*. It is not indeed a new idea to me, as you know from the letters I have already written, but it is a singular and striking confirmation of my fears. At my suggestion this account of the interview has been communicated to Asquith and Grey and I can only hope that the Government will act with the vigour and decision that the situation demands.

*1st March* 1912.

Asquith announced at five o'clock that the negotiations to close the strike had failed—all English owners accepted, the Scottish and S. Wales owners refused the Government terms. So did *all* the miners. He would make another statement on Monday. Is it legislation, and, if so, of what kind?

*1st March* 1912.

As I hastily noted last night our Shadow Cabinet was extremely successful. It was, I think, the best meeting of the kind that I have ever attended. There was an obvious desire for agreement and for the avoidance of anything that would make difficulties, and the final decision was what I had hoped to secure. Lansdowne began by stating that the meeting had been summoned to consider the question of the Food Taxes, and, assuming that they were retained, of our attitude towards Balfour's pledges on the Referendum. He said that personally he could not but feel that the Food Taxes were a great difficulty to us, but he had come to the conclusion that it was quite impossible for us to abandon them at the present time. He thought, however, that it would be well if it could be stated definitely that we would not propose a higher duty than 2s. on foreign wheat and 5 per cent. on other food stuffs. In short his opinion was that we must keep the Food Taxes but be as specific as possible in our declarations about them.

Then as to the Referendum. He must say that Balfour's pledges were very unreserved. We must consider, however, the circumstances which led to them and in which they were given. The conditions were now completely changed. The action of the Government, and especially the declarations of the Lord Advocate and Solicitor-General in the debate last week as to the intentions of the Government in regard to House of Lords reform, had in his opinion cleared the slate for us. We must therefore reconsider our position and he thought that we should declare that we would not now undertake that any special subject and in particular Tariff Reform should be referred to a Referendum. Bonar Law, Chaplin and I expressed our entire concurrence with what Lansdowne had said in a single sentence. Londonderry did not wish to separate himself from his colleagues, but said that he would view with dismay any appeal to the country while we were still saddled with the Food Taxes. Derby agreed with Londonderry with a difference. He would do anything to be able to drop the Food Taxes but admitted that it was impossible. Long expressed his agreement with Law, but added that the prevalent feeling both of candidates and of officers of associations in his part of the country was that Food Taxes were a tremendous and growing handicap. The coal strike rendered the situation much worse as it might force up prices. Was it therefore necessary or desirable to make any statement at the moment? Could we not at least delay until the strike was over? Law then gave his view of the situation which he summarised in the sentence that "in short these taxes are a handicap, but we must carry our handicap and carry it boldly." Selborne and Wyndham briefly expressed their entire agreement. Balcarres, being appealed to, admitted that the Food Taxes were a difficulty and that many of the Party would be glad to be free from them but considered that it was a point of honour that we should not abandon them.

Lyttelton then said that he wanted to make two suggestions. In the first place would it not be possible, now that we had a friendly Government in Canada, to approach them through Milner or some such person and explain our difficulties to them and ask whether under the circumstances they could suggest any alternative. Chaplin was strongly opposed to this suggestion which he thought would produce the same kind of division in the Party as the abolition of the 1s. duty had done, and Law destroyed the suggestion at once by stating that he had recently met two Canadians—one, Borden's whip, and the other a gentleman from Calgary to whom a seat in the Cabinet had been offered and whose partner actually sat in Borden's Cabinet. Law had asked both of them what would be the effect in Canada of our giving up the corn duty, and that both had replied "Canadians would consider it a great slap in the face after the results of their election."

Lyttelton's second suggestion was that the whole proceeds of the Food Taxes should be given away in relief in one form or another to working-men. One or two made some short observations on this suggestion during which it was really amusing to observe Walter Long clamouring for an expression of opinion from me. I said that I had no objection to a pledge being given that whatever we got from wheat should be taken off tea, but for reasons which I gave it would not be safe to go further.

Reverting to the general question, Finlay observed that he thought that we had got over the worst of our difficulties and that to abandon the Food Taxes now would split the Party and be a great slap in the face to Canada. As to the Referendum, he had always thought that the proposal to submit the whole scheme of Tariff Reform to it was impracticable. It would no doubt be practicable to submit the corn taxes only if they were separated from the rest, but this would be suicidal. He thought that the proper statement to make was that this was part of a general question which must be considered and in regard to which we should not pledge ourselves to details at the present time.

I then asked leave to say a few words as to the occasion on which the declaration should be made. I ought to have mentioned that Bonar Law said that his intention was not to make any definite statement on the subject at the present time as he was most anxious not to do anything which appeared like throwing over Balfour, though Balfour had stated that he himself would not view it in that light. Law therefore proposed merely to speak on Tariff Reform as a policy with which we should proceed at once on entering office but without any specific declaration as regards the Referendum. In other words he would continue to follow the line taken in his Albert Hall speech which he had intended to indicate that he considered himself freed from the Referendum pledge though he had not expressly stated the fact.

I now said that there were some general questions on which it was useless to try and gather the general opinion of the Party or to be finally guided by it: that I thought this was one of them and that the leaders must decide for the Party and convey their decision clearly to the Party. I did not object to Law's proposal if members and candidates clearly understood what he meant, but, whilst people like ourselves might be skilful enough and have authority enough to compel a meeting to be satisfied with such a statement as he had suggested, the ordinary candidate was confronted with the necessity of answering "yes" or "no" to a plain question—"Would he promise to submit Tariff Reform to a Referendum or would he not?" No ordinary candidate could or would avoid giving a plain affirmative or negative answer, and under these circumstances I was afraid that unless Law made our intentions perfectly clear many men would commit themselves to a course which Law did not intend to follow without knowing that they were placing themselves in opposition to him. These men would desire to take the plain Party line whatever it was. They would be placed in a position of much difficulty and one of which they would rightly complain if the leader's views were not made known to them, and I therefore urged that an early unequivocal declaration of Law's intentions was necessary. To my surprise I found Walter Long heartily agreeing with the whole of my statement with which he at once expressed his concurrence. Steel-Maitland also observed that an early declaration was necessary as he was being constantly asked for directions by candidates. He had told all of them that they must support the Food Taxes whatever the difficulties, and he wished to be able to give them an equally clear lead upon the Referendum. There was a murmur of agreement round the table only broken by the repetition on the part of Londonderry and Derby of their previously expressed opinion, and Law wound up the meeting by saying that the general sense of it was obvious and that he would find some formula that would make the position perfectly clear and would express it at Liverpool if his meeting there did not have to be postponed on account of the strike.

*1st March* 1912.

After the Shadow Cabinet Lansdowne took Devonshire and myself into his room to discuss a letter which he had received about Party organisation. We settled this point rapidly and I then took the opportunity of telling him all I had learned of Cambon's conversation. Lansdowne had no recollection of his ever having suggested to Cambon that we might develop the Entente into an alliance. He was certain that he would not have done so without consulting the Cabinet, and my recollection agreed with his that he had never brought such a proposal before us. It is possible, however, that in the course of conversation some phrase may have been dropped to which Cambon gave more importance than it was intended to have, and that on thinking it over he may have considered it worth while to consult his own Government and then been prepared to formulate some suggestions.

I pointed out to Lansdowne that C.'s account of the military events of the summer coincided with that given me by Sanderson, and I asked him whether he thought Sanderson knew anything of what now went on in the Foreign Office. He replied "A good deal." He told me that C. lunched with him recently and had told him something of what I had heard about the Berlin interview, but C. had also informed him that there had been some talk (upon what basis I don't know) about Zanzibar. Surely our Government cannot be thinking about giving up the protectorate. In conclusion I observed that I could not reconcile what I had learned from C. and Sanderson with the statement emanating from railway directors that they had been shown or informed of a dispatch from the French Government asking for military assistance. Lansdowne then turned to Victor and said, "I think you should now tell Austen what you heard at Leeds." It appears that Victor was at Leeds a short time ago as Chancellor of the University when Haldane after his return from Berlin attended a University function. He said that Haldane talked very freely both in public and in private about his Berlin visit without telling them really anything about it. "But," he added, "we afterwards were entertained at the Judge's lodgings by the Lord Mayor. There were several people present and we were asking him about the prospects of the coal strike." Haldane said that of course he could tell them nothing about that, "but," he said, "I will tell you something about last August" (*i.e.* the railway strike). He said, "I was left alone in London one day in charge not only of the War Office but of the Foreign Office also, the Prime Minister having gone to Wiltshire and particularly requested that he might not be summoned back unless his presence was imperatively necessary. There I sat in the War Office," said Haldane, "with a General in each room with his ear glued to the telephone receiving reports as to military arrangements. At last I felt that the situation was too grave for me to take the whole responsibility on my own shoulders and I telegraphed for the Prime Minister. Suddenly Lloyd George burst into our room exclaiming, 'A bottle of champagne! I've done it! Don't ask me how, but I've done it! The strike is settled!' And," concluded Haldane, "from that day to this I have never known and none of his colleagues have ever known how it was done."

You will have learned from the papers all that I can tell you about the coal strike. I view with profound misgiving the action of the Government. What the outcome of it all will be no man can yet say. Nothing will bring the miners back to work for some days, but I still do not believe in a prolonged strike.

*Evening, 2nd March* 1912.

What do you think I am going to do at Easter? I am going to Petersburg for a week with Balfour of Burleigh on the business of our Corporation and the Bank of Russia and England which we control. We are to attend a dinner at the Embassy to meet the Prime Minister who is also the Finance Minister, as the Foreign Office here is backing our Bank against a German syndicate for some pending business. In any case the visit should be interesting politically as well as from the business standpoint.

I enclose a letter from Leo Maxse which "eventuated" (as the Harvard Professor would say) in a long talk on foreign affairs after tea today. Leo trusts that I am not so set on being Chancellor that I would not take the Foreign Office. He and I found ourselves in great agreement on all matters of substance. I did not get any news from him, but he confirmed a very serious report I have already heard that the new Navy Estimates are quite inadequate. I *cannot* understand Winston taking any risks on that score, for, as it seems to me, his personal interests coincide with the nation's and both point to the maintenance of unquestioned naval strength. You can destroy Maxse's letter. I don't need it again.

*Sunday, 3rd March* 1912.

Here is a bore! No sooner do I write to you that I am going to Petersburg than it appears that their Easter so nearly coincides with ours this year that it is useless to go before the 15th April. This, of course, is an impossible time for me and I shall have to give it up. Well! I will go to Crowborough or elsewhere with Ivy. There are consolations.

*3rd March* 1912.

The above was dictated yesterday morning before I went out. Last night I added a P.S. to my No. XIX letter telling you of the breaking off of the negotiations. There is no fresh news on that subject this morning. But now we learn that educated women of position and means chose this moment to go window-smashing up and down streets. Was ever such criminal folly? With the greatest strike we have ever known in progress, great distress and unemployment, not in the coal trade only, in sight, and serious danger of rioting in some districts at least, the women set the example of disorder and wanton destruction. There is but one redeeming feature. Surely among even such feeble folk as our politicians of today this will provoke resistance and defeat their cause.

*5th March* 1912.

You will have seen from the papers that there was more window-smashing again yesterday. It is significant that public opinion is now turning actively against the Suffragettes. Hitherto the crowds seemed to view their conduct with indifference or even treated it as a joke, but both inside and outside the House of Commons a much more serious and hostile opinion is now beginning to prevail. I hear that several men in the House who were going to support the Conciliation Bill now declare that they will have nothing to do with it. I can only hope that they will remain in this frame of mind. If they do, it may alter our tactics when the measure comes on for discussion. Even the *Daily News* this morning declares the Conciliation Bill is jeopardised and any larger measure is dead— or *vice versa*. I do not follow their reasoning and am not sure which they think in most peril.

Asquith's statement on the coal strike was the best thing he has done for a long time. It was spoken instead of being read which has become far too much his habit. The impression it produced upon myself, and I think upon most careful observers, was that he desired to bring the pressure of public opinion to bear against the miners. I confess I still view the interference of the Government with great anxiety. But what else they could do it is extremely difficult to say. I doubt whether public opinion would have allowed them to stand absolutely aloof, but I certainly do not share the feelings of people like Garvin and *The Times* who blame the Government for not interfering earlier.

I dined last night with about 30 or 40 Unionist members at one of their weekly dinners at the House of Commons, and having to say something in response to my health, I discoursed to them briefly on foreign affairs. They agreed at any rate that I had given them something to think about—which was what I intended to do. I think my suggestion rather took them aback, but it is well that men's minds should be directed to the problem of foreign policy.

*5th March* 1912.

I also send an article from the *Pall Mall* (which illustrates the very large and vague ideas about an Anglo-German understanding now prevalent in Berlin and finding an echo here) and Robbins's account to the *B.D.P.* of the "Gloom at Westminster." There is no doubt a very uneasy feeling abroad and much to justify it. But I am an optimist by heredity and profession.

439

After all, I believe I shall go to Petersburg for a flying visit at Easter. It is not a very convenient time, but they are so anxious that I should go that I believe they will make my time theirs.

*6th March* 1912.

So here comes a defeat at Manchester close on the heels of the serious drop in the Liberal majority at Glasgow. What a blow for the Government! The Tariff Reform League was very active in the Manchester Division, but I think the result must be attributed mainly to dissatisfaction with the Insurance Bill and in part to a general and growing discontent with the Government. People do not reason very closely, but they think, and think rightly, that the Government has some responsibility for the widespread unrest with which they seem unable to cope. In the Glasgow contest Clyde tells me that Home Rule also exercised considerable influence. The Government are now clearly on the downgrade. I do not think they will again recover. As I told the Unionist dinner-party the other night, our business now is to hold tight to our own principles with the assurance that before long the country will give us our chance if we have not previously tied our own hands by foolish pledges.

Mr. Wilson tells me that you take in the *Round Table*. There are two remarkable articles in the March number—one on the Balkans, and the other on Lombard Street and War. They are both singularly well informed and well written. You will find the former of them at any rate interesting reading. The latter, perhaps, deals with too technical a subject, although it deals with it in a very clear and popular way. The Balkan article was written by Philip Kerr. I don't know who wrote about Lombard St.[1]

I rather share your regret that I could not see my way to take the chairmanship of the Royal Commission on the Civil Service, but consideration of time made it impossible. I should have had to give up to it at least two mornings a week and the enquiry will last for a year or more. It will be useful and indeed necessary work, but not very interesting. Still, I should have undertaken it if I could. There was, however, a further complication which I should have had to consider seriously, had I not been prevented from

[1] The Hon. Robert Brand.

accepting by lack of time. This is that incidentally the Commission will certainly have to try, or at least indirectly to decide upon, the charge that the Government have abused their patronage. It might have been very embarrassing for me to have to declare either for or against Bonar Law in this matter. Personally I am inclined to think that he has been on very weak ground, and this is now I fancy his own opinion. The Government have done some bad jobs, but it is not easy to bring home proof of them; whilst in regard to the great majority of appointments in connection with Valuation, Labour Exchanges and Insurance, I do not believe that any charge of extensive political partisanship can be sustained.

*7th March* 1912.

I agree with all Father says about the strike. Law said to me today there were only two courses—one to hold aloof but to say and *to prove* that absolute protection by police, special constables, military or whatever was needed, would be given to those who were willing to work; the other compulsory arbitration with effective penalties by imprisonment and by attachment of funds against all who aided, abetted or procured resistance to the award. He thought the first course the right one and I agree; the second he thought possible and justifiable and I agree again. But we both thought that it was not our business to hurry the Government and that the mass of the public must feel the effects of the strike before it would give the necessary support to the Government for such drastic action. It is said that other Unions are beginning to perceive how hard their funds will be hit by the colliers' strike throwing other industries out of work and that they are beginning to put pressure on the miners' Unions. You will be interested to see Neville's answer to my query.

Your account of Balfour's health is not very encouraging. There isn't in reality a shadow of reason for bringing him back now. Today Asquith finally postponed the Home Rule Bill till after Easter. All the Government parties are very sick and there is a good deal of recrimination in their papers. Robbins's London letter shows the trend of opinion.

Have I told you already? After all I believe I am going to Russia. They are so anxious that I should go, and attach so much importance to it on this side and there, that I believe they will insist on making my time their time if it can be done with any chance of meeting the right men. So everything now points to Balfour of Burleigh and another director and myself leaving London on Saturday April 6, reaching Petersburg on Monday 8th, leaving again on Saturday 13th and being back here on Monday 15th. Asquith, I am delighted to say, indicated today the Government's intention to have only a few days' recess at Easter and to take extra time at Whitsuntide. I think this is a good distribution of our parliamentary holidays.

*8th March* 1912.

I have been this evening to make my bow to my Sovereigns. I saw Miss Balfour, who gave a good account of Arthur B., and the Halsburys, who are just off to Cannes so you will see them. Naturally I arrived simultaneously with the Lloyd Georges. Said he: "You gave us a nasty knock in Manchester. There has been nothing like it since Gerald Loder's defeat at Brighton. And it wasn't one thing only—everything contributed, the strike and even the women." All which I think is very true, and of course I encouraged him in the view that the Insurance Act was only a minor factor. Each man on our side attributes it to his own particular pet project or antipathy, but the wise man like myself knows that it is the *general* distrust of the Government.

The Fusion Committee, *i.e.* the 5 Conservatives and 5 Liberal Unionists, met on Friday and adopted as their own recommendation the L.U. scheme set out in the memo. which I sent you, and it is to go to the National Union as our joint recommendation. The L.U.'s had met and adopted it in the morning. I told them it had Father's approval, with which they were much pleased, and I also confided to them his share in the establishment of the huge Committees against which we were fighting, and with this they were hugely amused.

*9th March* 1912.

It was fine and dry this morning though cold, and Ivy and I drove out in the open carriage. The almond blossom and forsythia are lovely and the crocuses are still very gay though a

442

good deal spoiled by the rain. We went to Agnew's water-colour exhibition and saw some good Coxes of which Uncle Arthur has secured the two finest, real beauties, which will be a great addition to his collection.[1]

Copley Fielding was also very well represented and there were some excellent examples of Collier, a beautiful "Palace on the Giudecca" by Holland, and several other things of interest, including one de Wint which reminded me more of the drawing in Father's library than any other I have seen both as regards colour and handling.

I have seen by *The Times* of this morning that the report that the Government are again reducing their Naval Programme is confirmed. It is inconceivable to me how they can take such risks at such a time. And, as Hilda said, what is the good of all their brave words if this is the outcome? I am disappointed with Winston. I had thought that when his interests coincided with those of his country, the latter would not suffer! I do not understand his attitude.

If you did not read it at the time, look up the article on the foreign page of yesterday's (Friday's) *Times* called the Shensi Relief Expedition. It is an interesting account of successful daring. Brave men these nine! What risks they must have run!

*12th March* 1912.

As you know I have been very optimistic about the coal strike, but I am bound to say that the situation now looks very gloomy. Asquith did indeed tell Law yesterday that he thought that the situation was more hopeful; but I think this means little more than that the miners' leaders saw that they had put themselves in the wrong with public opinion and are manœuvring for a better position without altering their demands in the substance. Law told me that Sir George Askwith,[2] whom he saw on Sunday or yesterday morning, was very gloomy. Law asked him if it would not be a good thing that the Government should at once announce in the firmest terms that they would afford every protection for any man who wished to work. In reply Sir George said, "But

[1] Bequeathed by him to the Birmingham Art Gallery.
[2] Then of the Board of Trade, now Lord Askwith.

how can they do it? There are only 80,000 troops available for the purpose, and the Territorials cannot be trusted." I asked Law what he meant by the figure of 80,000, and how it was arrived at, as there is nominally an Expeditionary Force of 160,000; but Law could not tell me. Sir George had gone on to say that he had the gloomiest reports about the transport and dock labourers. If they were severely pinched by the cessation of work they would take to looting. He regarded Cardiff and Hull as the most dangerous centres.

In this connection I may tell you a story I had from Jardine on Friday. He said, "I think the situation so serious that I went this morning to a wholesale armourers' to buy five revolvers. I intended to take them with me to the country this evening. When I gave my order the shopman said, 'We had a hundred yesterday; we had fifty when we opened this morning; we have not one left now.'"

It is strange to have such experiences in England. We are living in a new world, and the past gives us little guidance for the present. More works are being closed down every day. More trains are being taken off the railways. The whole machinery of national life is slowly stopping, and it must be remembered that, even if the strike were stopped this week, it would be a fortnight or three weeks before any substantial recovery could be made, though indeed the moral effect would at once become apparent. It is indeed a grave situation, yet the worst thing that could happen would be the triumph of the miners. They would then be neither to bind nor to loose for the future, and the example of successful blackmailing of the nation which they had set would breed a plentiful crop of imitators.

I think it was Sir George Askwith who told Law on this same occasion that someone (I think the Prime Minister) had suggested to the Cabinet that Asquith and Bonar Law should be joined as arbitrators, but that Lloyd George had at once rejected this proposal on the ground that the responsibility was the Government's and that they could not devolve or share it without grave discredit.

This topic now overshadows all others. The Suffragette disturbances become almost an episode of it. Men dwell not so much on the general folly of their action as on its wickedness at this particular moment. All political questions are thrust into the shade and little interest is taken in the House of Commons debates. It seems to me that very strong action will be needed to restore order in industry and that we of the Opposition had best be silent and patient until public opinion is sufficiently roused to support the vigorous measures which will be necessary; but much depends on the tact and skill of the owners, for it is all-important that they should keep public opinion on their side. The Government would be ready enough to put them in the cart if it saw the chance of doing so.

I lunched with Haldane today to discuss another question but we naturally did not escape the strike. I said: "It seems to me that the Government having announced that it had come to a certain decision which it embodied in the Four Points, having invited the employers and men to accept them and having threatened to impose them on the employers by legislation if they refused to accept them voluntarily, cannot now press the great bulk of the owners who have accepted the Government's own terms to go beyond those terms and make further concessions." He assented and said the men understood that, Asquith had plainly told them that he would not accept their schedule without examination and arbitration and the men by coming into today's Conference tacitly acknowledged and accepted that condition. I do not feel confident of this, but give it for what it is worth. In answer to something I said about guarding the mines, etc., Haldane said, "Yes: I have been most anxious to keep the soldiers out of it as long as possible because we had information at the beginning from some of the railways that their men would strike if they were asked to move troop trains. But that danger is less now and getting less every day, for they are feeling the pinch. Trains can't be run and railway-men are being turned off. Other Unions are being hard hit by having such heavy demands on their funds for out-of-work pay. They are beginning to put pressure on the miners and that is what is changing the miners' attitude."

11 p.m. I am summoned to a meeting at Lansdowne House tomorrow at 11.30. About what? I can think of no explanation except that Asquith has applied to Law or Lansdowne for co-operation in regard to the strike.

*13th March* 1912.

I went to Lansdowne House at 11.30 and found L. himself, Bonar Law, Curzon, Finlay and Selborne. There had been no communication from the Government as I had last night surmised, but Law wanted our opinion (1) as to whether he should not ask a question today—were the Government taking all possible steps to alleviate distress and were they arranging to give protection to any man who wished to work ?—and (2) as to the lines of his speech tomorrow if a debate on the strike should then take place.

We approved the question, but it was not put because Asquith was at a conference and could not be present. Meanwhile the situation has changed somewhat as you will see by the papers. I think it is only manœuvring and that there is no real change of substance at present. But the miners had found out that their position was untenable. They are seeking to win back public opinion and the Government are trying to get them just enough over to enable the Liberal Party to range itself on their side—in other words, the Government want to *hurler avec les loups* if they can and not to quarrel with organised labour.

*14th March* 1912.

The coal situation remains very obscure. I share Father's rooted distrust of the Government and am afraid that they are manœuvring to get the miners on to tolerable ground in order that they may take their side and turn upon the masters. Public opinion is beginning to grow more restless and a good many people are demanding that something shall be done without, I think, a very good appreciation of the dangers of interference, or at least of such interference as the Government is most likely to contemplate. I send you Robbins's London Letter of today. He came to see me yesterday in the Lobby to know why we did nothing. His son is at Cardiff for *The Times* and dare not leave as he thinks disorder may break out any moment.

We had a joint meeting of Liberals and Unionists opposed to Women's Suffrage the day before yesterday. It is estimated that in our Party there are 110 absolutely trustworthy Anti-Suffragists, and 70 confirmed Suffragists. This leaves 95 doubtfuls, of whom I dare say as many as 30 will vote for us and a good many more will not vote at all. The return of the Liberal Party is far less satisfactory. They have a great majority of supporters of the cause, but Harcourt is very busy lobbying among them with good results. He is made for that kind of work which I cannot endure. He is pretty confident that he can get a large number of the Irish to vote against the Bill and he is hard at work intriguing with them. No doubt what he says to them is that if the Bill gets past a Second Reading, and the Government in accordance with their pledge have to find time for it, it will seriously jeopardise the prospects of Home Rule. No one knows exactly what the result will be, but there is a growing feeling that it may be possible to defeat the Bill on the Second Reading. If a few more windows were smashed the Bill would be smashed at the same time, but I expect we shall hear nothing more of the militants till after the vote has been taken.

*15th March* 1912.

Something—I forget what—led to our gossiping about maiden speeches yesterday. Law said: "My maiden speech was the only one I have ever made in the House about which I was not in the least nervous. That was because no one knew me." Long said: "Did I ever tell you about mine? I remember it well. It was in the dinner-hour and there were only eight people present. It was on the Irish Land Bill of 1881. When I went out, Ashbourne (then Gibson) came to me in the Lobby and, putting his arm through mine, said: 'That was a capital speech of yours, my dear fellow, and devilish clever too! Oh! you'll go far, and so forth.' Quite charming. But the next night I found him with his arm through that of another member saying to him too: 'That was a capital speech of yours, my dear fellow, and devilish clever too. Oh! you'll go far.' In short the very same words. And then, as the member moved off, he added confidentially to me, 'You know one's obliged to say these things to these new members, my dear fellow, to encourage them, but I never heard such rot in my life— never!'"

You must try to read into this little tale Ashbourne's fine brogue. It greatly enhances its effect.

I send you a cutting from the *B.D.P.* I am very uneasy about these German negotiations. I don't know where Robbins gets his information but he is generally not far wrong, and our Government seem to me to be on very dangerous ground.

*15th March* 1912 *(contd.).*

The coal strike drags its weary length along and the situation remains for the moment very obscure, though there are some signs of growing division in the miners' camp. Meanwhile there is one curious side effect. After the panic of January when everyone filled their cellars, the demand for coal for household purposes in London has fallen off in a marked degree. I am informed that the merchants have tremendous stocks and had expected to charge still larger prices. They find, however, that the rich no less than the poor are cutting down their consumption to a minimum and there is even some question whether the present prices can be maintained. It is curious how one hears on all sides of people not lighting their fires in the morning or keeping a fire in only one room and everyone making economies of which in ordinary circumstances they would never think.

*16th March* 1912.

So the Government have declared their negotiations at an end and have announced their intention to legislate! Not altogether unexpected but not, I think, altogether wise. The fixing of minimum wages by legislation is a perilous path on which to enter, and try as the Government may to distinguish between coal-getters and all other workmen, it will not be easy to maintain that distinction when once the principle of legislative interference is admitted. The due working of the railways and other forms of transport, of gas and lighting and power companies, of bakers—these at any rate are quite essential to our modern life and the law may be just as well invoked for each and all of them in turn in the event of a national stoppage. I believe therefore that the right course would have been to declare the negotiations at an end, to state plainly where the blame lies and to promise in the most definite terms full protection for all men willing to work. I believe that then the English and Scottish pits would quickly have got to work again. There might have been rough work in places, but the law would have been vindicated, the crisis quickly over and no dangerous and embarrassing precedent created for the future.

However, *Dis aliter visum!* Asquith and his colleagues have decided otherwise. Now the chief interest lies in guessing what the Government Bill will be. What are the "adequate safeguards" to ensure a fair day's work? What, above all, the means taken to secure "the stability" of the settlement? in other words what punishment is to fall on workmen and Unions which refuse to accept the legal settlement? I know of none but the power to sue the Unions for damages for breach of contract and a veto on the payment of strike allowances to any workman out against the award. Strong meat this—much too strong, I think, for digestion by a Liberal Government and certain to provoke the fierce opposition of the Labour Party and perhaps of *all* the Unions.

It does seem to me that State interference is bad and that it can only be rendered tolerable if, in trades where the State does interfere, strikes are forbidden and rendered illegal and all disputes are compulsorily referred to arbitration. If the Government adopted that line, their action would be the less harmful because other Unions would think twice before invoking or compelling interference of Parliament. This is the Australian system—open to many objections, no doubt, but at least not open to as many as the plan which I suspect the Government of contemplating.

*16th March* 1912.

Macquisten, who fought the Glasgow vacancy for us the other day, was talking to me last night about a former Glasgow member, who boggled at Tariff Reform. "Sir William Laird," said he, "once said to me: 'B—— has a weakness and he calls it a conscience.'" I like this epigrammatical observation. One knows so many people to whom it applies.

*18th March* 1912.

We now know enough to be sure that the Government Bill is what I have forecast above. It is more like the Canadian plan than any other but has two fundamental differences: (1) In Canada it is forbidden to strike *till* the enquiry has been held and the award given, but (2) after that the parties *may* fight the quarrel out if they like and the terms of the award are not binding on those who wish to work. Here (1) the strike takes place first and (2) after the award its terms are binding on anyone who gives or takes work, though no one is forced to do either.

The policy I am pressing is that we should vote against the Second Reading. I believe this to be right in itself and I believe also that in the long run it is the safest for us as a Party as well as for the State. I think Balfour agrees. So does Balcarres. Law hesitates and is to my mind unduly timid. In my opinion there are only three reasonable courses :

First, the one we have hitherto pursued in this country— abstention from interference and protection for those who wish to work *coûte que coûte*. This is the best.

Second, the Canadian plan, limited as in Canada to the ascertainment of the rights and wrongs of the dispute by an impartial tribunal, leaving the pressure of a public opinion thus instructed to force the parties to agree. There is much to be said for this plan, but if it was to be adopted, it ought to have been enforced before the strike began.

Third and last, the Australian plan. This is logical but only to be adopted in the last extreme.

The Government's *via media* seems to me to have no merit except that it will in this particular case and for the moment stop the strike, and that only because the miners' leaders know that they could not keep the men out beyond another fortnight, if so long, for the funds are running out. So they will be only too glad to claim, as they may well claim on these terms, a victory, and call the strike off for the present. Then it will reappear again among the railway men and transport workers. The Government plan not only gives no chance of finality or stability but by paying blackmail encourages fresh claims.

I should like therefore to vote against the Second Reading and then leave the Committee stage pretty much alone. It is not a case where we should be supported in obstruction or delay, but I think we shall be expected to oppose and that we *ought* to oppose.

On the other hand I think the Lords ought to let the Bill through, not necessarily without amendments but without any wrecking amendment.

19*th March* 1912.

You and I did Winston Churchill an injustice. His statement yesterday was very good and as far as I can judge all the changes he proposes will make for the strength and readiness of the Fleet. Indeed, granting the basis on which he starts, nothing could have been better; but I still think the Government have made the initial mistake of relying too much upon the pre-Dreadnought ships.

*Mrs. Chamberlain to A. C.*

VILLA VICTORIA, CANNES,

MY DEAR AUSTEN,                    19*th March* 1912.

I believe I wrote to you on Saturday and therefore have not acknowledged your letters marked XXX and XXXI. You are a trump, and your reward must be the knowledge that on your letters turn the interest and profit of our days. Of course we are following this unhappy state of affairs with the deepest interest. Your father is much perturbed over the Government action and feels with you that their course will probably be the worst one. He was pleased at the inclination of the leaders to oppose it if such should be the case. "Tell Austen, if he has to speak, to speak against it. I think he ought not to bear any of the brunt of the trouble which the Government have brought upon themselves." His view of the situation is contained in his words of two days ago, when deprecating the idea of interference. "I think and have always thought that the present movement must be fought—and that being fought there can be no doubt who will win. It may take longer than we thought but whatever time it takes it should be fought."

Last evening Mrs. Wemyss came in at tea-time and he discussed it with her with the greatest animation. Then he turned and glanced at me, his expression keen and clear-cut, a regular House of Commons look "I *wish* I were there!" and a ring in his voice that made my heart thrill and ache at the same moment. But he knows he has a substitute—and a colleague and a representative to fight all good causes in the way he would have him, and so he can rest content on his laurels—and so can I.

HOUSE OF COMMONS,
*22nd March* 1912.

How well I understand Father's longing to be back here and to take part in such a fight as yesterday's. And how many men, both in and out of the House, have said to me in these last weeks:

"We need your father."

"If only Mr. Chamberlain were here," and endless variations on the same theme.

Well, we had a good debate and much the best of the argument. It was evident that both ministers and especially Asquith hated the Bill and disliked their task, and when you don't like your own case it is not easy to make a good speech in support of it. We thought their speeches very weak. There was not even any attempt to answer us. They could only exclaim pathetically: We must do *something*! The most striking thing about them was the divergence of attitude between the two—Asquith insisting that this was a purely temporary expedient with no ulterior consequences and Grey throwing this pretence to the winds and admitting that it "opened the door" to further demands and a new state of things. How they have drifted!

Following my usual practice I shall not hesitate to tell *you* that I made a good speech, very warmly received by my own side who gave me an ovation when I sat down and the subject of many congratulations from opponents as well as friends since. Indeed when the *Daily News* calls it "a cogent powerful speech; one of the best he has ever delivered" and the *Daily Chronicle* says: "The point was driven home with a genuine eloquence which aroused an enthusiastic demonstration. It was far the best statement yet made of the Anti-Labour case," you will feel that it won recognition in unexpected quarters, and I think I may say seriously that it interested the whole House. Of course it was delivered too late for Press comment, which is confined to Balfour and Asquith.

Today the Government have plucked up courage enough to resist the inclusion of the 5s. and 2s. minima as well as the hewers' schedules, though their attitude was doubtful up to the last moment and Grey carefully left the question open last night. The fact is that the strike is rapidly breaking down. Vast bodies of miners cannot be kept from going back to work any longer, and if this

Bill had never been introduced the strike would have ended as rapidly as it now will, without leaving us this disastrous precedent of unscrupulous pressure and feeble surrender.

I send you under separate cover the rules of our new National Unionist Association, as finally agreed upon, contrasted with the old rules of the National Conservative Union. I have authorised Crossley to publish a notice whenever desirable that "Mr. Chamberlain, who approved of the negotiations and has throughout been kept informed of their progress, concurs in the result and is prepared to recommend its acceptance to the L.U. Council."

The chief alterations are in the name and in the new Rule XX which takes the place of the old Rules XXIII-XXIX whilst the special arrangements for guaranteeing proper L.U. representation in the early stages are to be found in the new Rules XXVII-XXVIII. We have in short got our way in the main.

*Mrs. Chamberlain to A. C.*

VILLA VICTORIA, CANNES,
MY DEAR AUSTEN,                   20th March 1912.

Your XXXIII has just come—intensely interesting! but I have not yet read it to your Father, as your Aunt Lina and Nellie were there when it arrived and I like to look your letters through first for only portions do to read to anyone out of our *own* family. But I must send you a brief line to say I am sure your Father will approve of your line—in fact it is what he said yesterday in other words, which I wrote you, only I remembered afterwards he prefaced them by saying : "the best thing is to let the thing alone— vote against it, and do nothing to help them—if he must speak, etc. etc." This morning we telegraphed—not in any way to influence your decision for he feels you are on the spot and can judge as circumstances arise—but to let you know his mind.

At dinner last night he said : "They are in a hole—don't do anything to help them out !"

"Shall I telegraph that ?"

"Well—um—yes, you might—he will know I trust him to do what he thinks right, and do not mean to interfere," and therefore I wrote it then and there signing "Tibbs" for the sake of auld lang syne and also as a less identifiable message. The first thing he asked me this morning was, "Have you telegraphed to Austen?" So you see how interested he is.

Now I am interested to find how clearly he has gauged the situation and that he came to that view before having the advantage of the fuller and later letters for I wrote yesterday before he had seen your XXXII. He is very anxious that you should not be involved in any of the Government's suggestions either to support or defend or meet—and by you I mean the Opposition. He hates the weakness of the Government and their interference and with you sees that it is a bad precedent to establish and wants the Opposition to be as free as it can make itself. As usual he is full of fight and courage and would give anything to be able to take his part. "I believe I could smash them!"

I do hope Bonar Law will stiffen up—his being timid in a crisis is just what your Father always fears about him. But by the time this reaches you the whole thing will be settled. I wonder what the effect of it all will be on the Government? Possibly good at first, but I don't see how that can last.

9 EGERTON PLACE, S.W.,<br/>23rd March 1912.

What a correspondent you are! Here today comes your letter of the 20th. I could not resist telling one or two friends of Father's message. It was so characteristic and showed so shrewd a grasp of the situation! I should not have been surprised if my letters had been at times inconsistent, for filling as I have done several sheets daily with running comment on the passing phases of the coal dispute, the thought of the moment must necessarily be recorded before it has been weighed and judged, and first thoughts are not always best in such difficult circumstances. But as you say, I think there has been a pretty steady line of policy running through them all and happily it has prevailed. It is curious, however, how difficult I still find it to read Balfour's mind. I thought at first that he favoured a motion for the rejection of the Bill whilst Law certainly hesitated about it and was afraid of its having a bad effect on public opinion. But in the end Law saw clearly that nothing less would do, whilst Balfour, though willingly assenting to the course we chose, would, if left to himself, have spoken against the Bill but not voted. As it is, all has gone well. We have made no mistake so far and kept our hands free for the future, whilst the Government may easily find their policy break down as explained in the following dictated sheets, and cannot now derive much *kudos* even from a settlement of the strike if such is yet brought about.

There is, I think, nothing to add to my dictated account of the situation at the moment except this—that as it became apparent on Thursday that the Irish were trying to put pressure on the Government to yield the 5s. and 2s. minima so as to please Labour and keep it sweet for Home Rule, some Liberals at last mildly revolted and waited on Asquith to protest against any further surrender. I do not think that Asquith can now put any figures in the Bill but one never can tell. I do not trust Grey, whose speech on Thursday was amazingly extreme.

"If that speech had been made by Lloyd George," said Law to me, "I should think that he had decided to go to the country at the next election with a cry for a general minimum wage."

Arthur Lee himself regrets that Roosevelt has allowed himself to be nominated this year, for he thinks that he will be beaten. He tries to defend the "recall" but I don't think he really likes it.

*Dictated.*

Since I wrote to you yesterday afternoon the situation has become more obscure than ever. I had scarcely written the words "the Government have at last decided to stand firm about something" when on going into the House I found the whole question of the minima again under discussion and a lively interchange going on between Asquith and Grey on the one side and the Labour men on the other. You will see exactly what took place from the papers. Apparently Ramsay MacDonald spoke without consultation with the miners and they are reported to have been very angry with him. However, Asquith maintained his position that he would not put figures into the Bill and the amendment was negotiated without a division. But immediately afterwards

455

Asquith called out Law and enquired whether, if the owners and the men came to an agreement as to what the minimum should be, we should be prepared to support its insertion. Law replied, as I gather, sympathetically, but happily said that it was a point on which he must consult his colleagues. He called us to his room and we had a hasty consultation when we unanimously decided, with Law's full concurrence, that we would do nothing of the kind. I observed that the only object of the proposal was to save the face of the miners and that that was not our business. If the Government gave way to them, I urged that we should denounce Asquith in the strongest terms for his surrender and I should base myself on the very arguments which he himself had used in resisting the amendment an hour or two before. Law said that it would not do for us to offer opposition to a mutual agreement between masters and men. In this we all agreed but added that we had nothing to do with their negotiations or agreements, which might be anything they chose—we were only concerned with the general interests of the country and with the provisions of the Bill before the House, and we would have nothing to do with putting figures into that Bill whether they were agreed or not. Law communicated this to Asquith, who accepted the position and said that he should now devote himself to trying to secure a fresh conference between masters and men in the hope that they would agree upon a minimum which they might jointly recommend to the Conciliation Boards. It was announced later in the evening that a conference between masters and men would take place on Monday, but at present there is little probability of their coming to any agreement, and late last night the Government appeared to be seriously considering whether failing an agreement it was worth while to proceed with the Bill. They are indeed between the devil and the deep sea! If the Bill is carried but does not settle the strike, their policy stands condemned. On the other hand, if they now withdraw the Bill on the ground that, as the miners rejected it, it has no chance of success, their policy has equally failed. For the moment all I can say is that the discussion seems only to have exacerbated feeling and that the prospects of an early and widespread return to work are less good than they were.

Congratulations on my speech continued to shower upon me

all day from all quarters of the House. I admit that I thought it a good speech when I made it, but it was one of those happy occasions when one finds one has done better than one knew. I cannot resist adding to the newspaper quotations that I sent you one from the *Standard* which particularly pleased me for a reason that you will easily guess:

"For cogency and lucid reasoning I have never heard Mr. Chamberlain speak more effectively than he did tonight. More than ever did he remind one of the crystal clearness which was so characteristic of his father."

Members tell me it changed the votes. At any rate it sent some of our men happily to our Lobby who would otherwise have abstained.

I dined last night with George Wyndham and had no intention of going back to the House, but seeing the light still burning as I crossed Hyde Park Corner I was attracted to it like a moth to the candle. The result was curious.

Just at the close of the debate last night Banbury was putting to me some point of order about the Bill. I was not sure whether it was a good one or not, but I said:

"If you want a point of order, consider this. The title of the Bill confines it to coal mines, but the definition clause extends it to underground ironstone mines; is it in order in the clause of a Bill to go beyond the title?" Banbury took my point and raised it. The Speaker, to whom we were only able to give about five minutes' notice, was bothered by it and evidently thought the objection a good one, but before deciding asked Asquith to explain why the words were introduced. Asquith, relying upon the Attorney-General, who in his turn as I heard took it from Masterman, announced that coal mines were defined by other Acts to include not only coal but ironstone mines and shale and fireclay mines.

"Accordingly," said Asquith, "the words are a restriction and not an extension of the scope of the title," and on this the Speaker ruled against Banbury. Yesterday morning Finlay pointed out to me that this statement was wholly unfounded. The other Bills referred to expressly included these other mines as well as coal mines both in their titles and in their clauses. "Coal Mine" in point of law conveys what it means in ordinary language and no more. As you may believe I was pretty angry about this, the more so because it is characteristic of the conduct of Members of the present Government. If they are in a hole they give the first convenient answer without stopping to enquire whether it is accurate or not. This was not an isolated instance. We have had several such, and it is a new and bad practice introduced by the present Ministers. Accordingly I went to see the Speaker on the subject and he at once, without waiting for me to say anything, said that he thought that his ruling was wrong and that Asquith had completely misinformed him. I replied that of course the ruling could not now be changed and I did not now desire to change it, but I did desire to bring the Government to book and asked him how and when I could do it. He suggested that my best chance would be on the words of the clause itself. Getting back from my dinner, I arrived just in time to move an amendment omitting the words. We had a short but stormy discussion in which, to say the least of it, the Attorney-General was disingenuous. There the matter might have ended, but as I was leaving the House with Law to go to his room, the Attorney-General came out with some other Member of the Government and accosted me on the incident with rather boisterous merriment. I did not want to continue the discussion but I could not allow him to suppose that from my point of view the whole episode was merely a joke. The result was that in a moment tempers boiled up on both sides and a fierce altercation took place. However, with the aid of Bonar Law the tempest subsided after a time and we parted on terms which make it possible for us to meet again without an explanation. It certainly was a scandal that the Government, being solemnly appealed to by the Chair for information on a matter of fact to guide the Chair in its judgment, and being therefore in a position of peculiar responsibility and trust, should carelessly and without verification make a wholly unfounded statement. On the other hand, the Attorney-General and his colleagues know what I think of it and will not in future suppose that I regard such methods as a natural incident of Parliamentary warfare.

*24th March* 1912.

Sir A. Nicolson dined with me last night to meet B. of B. and talk about Russia. We had a very pleasant chatty dinner but nothing notable to record. B. of B. is very genial and from something he said I should imagine much less Anti-Tariff Reform than he was. Nicolson says Grey is very gloomy, can talk and think of nothing but our present industrial troubles and "speaks as if we were on the eve of a social revolution." All the Liberal papers speak of "his masterly intervention" in the debate yesterday. I don't see it, but I may be wrong. You never can tell what may happen, but I don't believe that masters and men will come to an agreement on Monday, and in that case it's only so many fresh hopes raised only to be disappointed and the net result of these new negotiations will be to increase irritation and to delay the return to work.

In my opinion a settlement now is not really to be desired. The fire will smoulder and break out in other places. I hear that Sir George Askwith says the next thing will be a strike of seamen. Better fight it out now whatever the cost and have peace thereafter at least for a reasonable time.

Do you know these stories? Winston Churchill when Under-Secretary at the Colonial Office is said to have written a long memo. for Elgin ending, "These are my views." "But not mine" was Elgin's minute on the paper.

The other is older. Mowatt when a young man at the Treasury was called in by Lowe, then Chancellor of the Exchequer.

"Mr. Mowatt," said Lowe, "I have read this long correspondence of yours with the —— Office. It won't do; it won't do at all. There are only four letters which the Treasury can write in such a case. First, 'You can't have the money.' Second, 'I have nothing to add to my previous letter.' Third, 'This correspondence must now cease.' And fourth, and last, ' Go to Hell!'"

Sir A. Nicolson was gloomy about the Turco-Italian war. Italy was losing 1000 men a week and the hot weather was yet to come. The prolongation of the struggle cost the Turks nothing. Italy was making little or no progress, she could not advance into the interior and the country was not worth having. At present the Italians were still extraordinarily united and enthusiastic but he feared a great and dangerous reaction if the struggle was long continued. Meanwhile our position also was very difficult for, whilst we did not want to do anything to lose Italian friendship, Hardinge wrote from India that Mohammedan feeling there was running very high—it being held that England ought to compel Italy to desist from the attack. Sir Arthur did not believe in Young Turks or Young Chinese, which does not surprise me.

*25th March* 1912.

The Coal Bill is again postponed! The conference met this morning and I understand that nothing came of it, but the Prime Minister asked for a further meeting this afternoon—of which also I expect nothing will come. In my opinion this prolongation of negotiations, like the introduction of the Bill, only delays the ultimate resumption of work by helping the firebrands to persuade the men that they are still masters of the situation and that the Government dare not finally break with them. To have the strike beaten and broken is now as much the interest of the older leaders as of the employers. If the men can claim any victory, all the credit will go to the Smillies, Hartshorns, and such-like, who have thrust on one side the advice of Burt, Fenwick, "Mabon" and others of their stamp. I expect men to begin to break away from the Federation soon and then will come the real pinch—everything depending on the efficiency of the protection which the Government will and can give. It is said that they will draw a military cordon round a number of the mines. But at best the resumption of work will only be partial at first and it will be long before the coal supplies are normal. Happily there are large supplies of coal and coke at Highbury—the Corporation only stopped supplying coke last week—and I have sent down orders that they are to be carefully husbanded, wood to be burned in the servants' hall as much as possible, the heating of the green-houses being restricted to what is necessary to prevent damage—forcing of grapes, peaches, etc., to be delayed till we see how long it is before we can buy fresh stocks at reasonable prices. I think you will approve. Wilson is informed that the coal which we bought at 21/- is now being charged 37/6 wholesale to the merchants and almost unprocurable at that.

The Attorney-General has behaved like a gentleman, which I

really believe he is. He called me out today to explain that he had been to the Speaker to say that he thought he ought to offer an apology to him and an explanation to the House for having misled the Prime Minister and through him the Speaker about the inclusion of ironstone in the Coal Bill and that he would do so by the Speaker's advice on a motion to amend the preamble. He added a few friendly words about our tiff, so now the incident is closed. He never ought to have answered such a question from the Chair unless he knew the facts, but he is doing the right thing now and doing it handsomely. Indeed he says he had meant to do it on Friday but he thinks that I got "nettled" by the interruptions— which is true—and so used language which "nettled" him, which is also true, for I said that his statement to the Speaker was "false" which would certainly seem to impute intention to deceive and not merely ignorance and carelessness. Altogether we parted good friends again, of which I am glad for I hate a personal row.

*26th March* 1912.

I send you a part of Robbins's letter to the *Daily Post*. I cannot confirm his account of the division of opinion in the Cabinet from my own knowledge but it is not improbable in itself. How they wobble! On Friday evening Asquith said to Law:

"If the men don't agree, it doesn't seem much use going on with the Bill."

Law replied: "Well, that is what we have always thought," and Asquith turned his back on him and marched off. On Monday morning it was announced that the Government meant to go on with the Bill in any case "to strengthen their hands," but by the afternoon all was in doubt again. All this shilly-shally only tends to prolong the struggle. It would be well if the Government could make up its mind *and stick to it*! Today it is said that the miners want the Bill in any case, even though they will not declare the strike at an end. Naturally! for they can lose nothing and do gain something by it. I can imagine no worse policy than to pass it under these circumstances. It seems to me criminal weakness on the part of the Government.

*Evening:* The House met in perfect uncertainty as to the position. The conferences were still going on, Asquith wasn't present and McKenna, who was in charge, could only say that though the Government thought it right not to go on with the Bill in similar circumstances yesterday, they thought it urgent to finish the Bill now. This was intolerable. No one knew what was happening or what the Government meant to do. Laurence Hardy hurried across to say that at 2.45—just as the House met— the Government had asked the owners to meet the men in district sections and discuss minimum rates, district by district, in a series of Committees. We felt the House could not go on like that and privately intimated that Asquith must come down and make a statement. We were told he was coming, but he didn't come; so just as the 5/- and 2/- amendment was about to be moved, Long moved the adjournment and Asquith arrived while he was speaking. You will read his statement in the papers. The House sat absolutely silent. He himself laboured under great emotion, his voice breaking and tears in his eyes if not actually running down his cheeks. I confess I was not edified. On his own lines, as Law said, he has done his utmost to settle the strike; but he has acted weakly and this emotion seemed, to me at least, a further display of weakness, not the regret of a strong man, disappointed certainly but still resolute, but the lamentations of a weakling who feels the world is out of joint and that he is not the man to set it right. However he stood fast to his decision not to include any figures in the Bill. Law said a few words in reply and said what Asquith had more than once seemed on the very point of saying—that it must be made clear that all the resources of the State would be used to protect men ready to work. Then the debate dragged on till nearly 8.30. I stayed to vote but not to hear the result. The Government Whips were saying that one-third of their Party or more would vote against the Government but this I think a great exaggeration.

It has transpired that at the conference Smillie, the Scottish Miners' Agent, tried to raise the minima to 5/9 and 2/6 and on this the owners refused to go on. No wonder! This is the result of the Government's policy. I think they have done everything possible to confirm the men in the belief that they were absolute masters of the situation.

There is no doubt Lloyd George wanted to give way. So too,

I believe, did Grey. Balfour met him yesterday. He says Grey was gloomy in the extreme, did not conceal his detestation of the Bill or its dangers, but we were on the brink of revolution, we must sacrifice principle and let the future take care of itself. We must do anything to end the strike. London would be without water or light, etc. etc. It is deplorable to hear of a man like Grey talking in this strain. Do you wonder that a Government, in which he ranks as a strong man, is not equal to such a crisis?

There was one sentence in Asquith's speech indicative of the dissensions in the Cabinet. "The Government," he said, "cannot consent . . ." and then correcting himself, "I at least could not consent" to insert figures in the Bill.

*27th March* 1912.

I have been busy in the City from 12 o'clock till now and have not been to the House so I know no news. I expect a gradually increasing break-away of the miners, accompanied probably with serious rioting in some places, but public opinion is ready to see any such violence put down without mercy and if only the Government will act with vigour and at once—not waiting for the Local Authorities to be defeated before they intervene—I believe that matters would soon mend. The all-important thing is that the miners who have gone to work or may now go back should not be driven out of the mines again by force or intimidation. If the Government do not act vigorously now, the last shred of excuse for their long hesitation and constant surrenders will be gone. Even at best I remain of opinion that their policy has delayed the resumption of work besides leaving us a legacy of future trouble. Asquith's speech yesterday may have been pathetic but what we need is not pathos but government.

I am very pleased that you liked my speech. I could not tell how *The Times* report would strike a reader. It was, as always in that paper, well done, though a hash was made of one or two sentences, but in spite of the first person style it was not verbatim and the author at least thought that he did it better than the reporter !

Yes, I think our policy has been right. Nothing but our

negative on the Second Reading justified us in leaving the committee stage alone; yet to have moved large amendments in committee under the peculiar circumstances would have involved us in endless difficulties. The country would have become impatient at the length of time taken up by the discussions and we might have had visited on us their displeasure at the continuance of the strike on the one hand, whilst on the other questions of great importance now and of still greater importance for the future might and would have been hastily debated and voted down under circumstances most adverse to their proper consideration thus preventing them from getting the full support which they will receive if, as a Government, we ever have to propose them. Lastly we should have united all sections of the Government Party among themselves and with Labour in a vote against us whilst, as it is, they are sore, divided and disheartened.

Lyttelton said to me yesterday:

"Looking back on it, I think we have made no mistake and I think, my dear Austen, that that is very largely your doing."

And so I believe it is—not only with the leaders but also with the Party.

What you say of Balfour is very true. I am always reminded of the Frenchman's saying about Cavour:

"*Cavour comprenait qu'on ne gouverne pas sur un point d'épingle.*" That is a truth that Balfour has never understood. Not only does his mind work differently from other men's but he never has the least conception how other men's minds are working or will work in any given circumstances.

But this was not intended to be a political letter at all.

I go to St. Petersburg on Saturday the 6th and leave again on the 13th, getting back here on the 15th. My address there will be at the British Embassy. B. of B. and I stay with the Ambassador, Sir George Buchanan, who was at the Embassy in Rome (as First Secretary, I think) when I was there with Father and you in Currie's time.

The programme arranged for us is:

Monday, dinner with the Ambassador.

Tuesday, dinner with the Directors and Council of the Anglo-Russian Bank.

Wednesday, to the Imperial Ballet with the Ambassador.

Thursday, Banquet given by the Bank.
Friday, Banquet given by the Ambassador.

The only fly in the ointment is that so many of the principal people will be away for their Easter holidays, which are long and much observed.

*28th March* 1912.

Your reference to Hewins reminds me that I have said nothing of his maiden speech. It was unexpectedly good and I hope he is going to do well. He spoke again last night but I did not hear him and have not yet read the report.

Well, I thought we had done with the Minimum Wages Bill for the present at any rate, but this morning comes a note from Balcarres summoning me to a conference at Lansdowne House in regard to the difficulty which has arisen in respect to one of the Government amendments. All I know is set out in *The Times* this morning. It appears to be a precious muddle and I do not at all feel inclined to press the House of Lords to swallow at the dictation of the miners words which the Government had agreed to alter. However, *nous verrons*.

I wish I knew the inner history of the Cabinet during these last weeks. I believe that there have been strong and even acute differences of opinion among them, and I fancy that by this time all of them are discontented and disappointed and each section feels that things would have been better if they had had their own particular way. Rumour says, and I think truly, that Winston and the Lord Chancellor, with perhaps Morley, were strongly opposed to any legislation. Harcourt's name is also coupled with this group. They were beaten at an early stage by the rest of the Cabinet. Then came the fresh division of opinion as to putting the minimum figures into the Bill. On this question I hear that Lloyd George and Buxton at first stood alone, but that between Friday and Monday under the pressure of events they had won over several of their colleagues, but not enough to make a majority. Both these sections are said to be highly discontented and to taunt each other and the rest of the Cabinet with an "I told you so." On the other hand, Asquith and the middle section would seem, from what Asquith said to Law, to have very little more reason for satisfaction. I imagine that on Friday or Saturday it was just touch and go with the Bill, and that but for the humiliation of dropping it after having proceeded so far, the Government would not have been sorry to abandon it. The general impression now seems to be that the men will vote to go back to work but that there may be trouble in some of the districts. I share this view, but I have been wrong before and may prove so again.

Today we have the Conciliation Bill. Nobody knows what will happen on it, but it is expected that the division will be rather a close one, as the Nationalists have decided to vote against it to prevent its blocking the way for Home Rule. I was asked if in view of this fact and of the obvious advantage to us as a Party of getting the Bill into Committee where it would take up a week or ten days of Government time, I would consent to warn some of our friends to stay away from the division; but whilst recognising the Party advantage which would accrue from this course I said it was quite impossible. In the first place it would not be loyal to Harcourt and other Liberals who have fought the battle strenuously and straightforwardly in their own Party in the midst of great difficulties. This was to me a conclusive answer, quite apart from the fact that we should destroy our moral credit as opponents of the Bill and really put ourselves out of court for any future struggle. What a curious situation it is! I am very anxious to avoid speaking, but if Bonar Law speaks for the Bill I may be forced into a few observations against it.

*29th March* 1912.

*The Times* of this morning explains the details of the Government's last muddle over the Coal Mines Bill. It illustrates the haste and carelessness with which the Bill was drawn up and passed, and the real ignorance of the Government as to essential facts of the trade with which they are dealing. And what is if possible worse, it shows them once again the slaves of the extremer section among the miners' leaders. They put words into the Bill on Report in our House which either mean nothing or mean what they themselves do not intend and admit to be unfair. On this being pointed out by the owners they agree, after consultation with the President

and Secretary of the Miners' Federation, to insert other words in
the Lords, and Crewe makes a great point of this concession in
moving the Second Reading. Then the other miners' leaders find
out what is being done and object to the alteration, and the Government after much secret and fruitless negotiation with them simply
announces to the owners and the House of Lords that it can't keep
its word because the men object!

I was quite prepared to support the Lords in insisting that what
they had promised they must perform, but Law, Lansdowne and
F. E. Smith thought differently and I did not attempt to press it
on them against their will. So the Bill has gone through unaltered
and will receive the Royal Assent today.

In our House the Women's Suffrage Bill was defeated by 14
votes. We made a compact that none of us would speak from our
Front Bench and so kept both Balfour and Law out of the fray.
I think Balfour really wanted to speak but refrained out of loyalty
to Law and from the wish not to embarrass him. There was much
excitement during the division. Both sides thought the Pros had
won, and it was said towards the end of the debate that their
majority would be as much as 50. We were just out of our lobby
and when we saw our numbers were 222 we knew it would be a
close division. "We've won." "We've lost." "We are beaten
by one." "No, we're beaten by nine." "Nine is it? No, eight."
Such were the exclamations all round me and the House crowded
and excited, but still the tellers from the Aye lobby did not appear,
and the excitement grew. It appears that Mond who was telling
for the Bill called 231 as the last man passed through the Aye lobby.
"No," said the other teller, "it's 221." "Yes," added McKenna
who was standing by, "I heard you slip ten—thus: you counted
200, 1, 2, 3, 4, 5, 6, 7, 8, 9, 220." Mond was doubtful, couldn't
be sure what he had done, was thoroughly bemused in fact. "It's
free trade arithmetic," said I to Loulou afterwards. "Oh!" said
Loulou, "he's only accustomed to count in millions!" Finally
the tellers went to the Clerks' lists and counted (twice over, for
they couldn't believe the result) the names ticked off at the desks
and found only 208!

Now, it is easy to slip or to add ten and make 221 into 231 but
how can you make either out of 208? Several men were in a

desperate hurry to catch the night mails to the country—indeed the Closure division was deliberately engineered by some of the Antis in the belief that 8 or 9 Pros would be obliged to go before the second division was called. But the figures in the second division don't show any falling off. On the contrary they are higher than in the first, but it is just possible that some men voted but did not get marked. Father will know how in a late and crowded division some men always get past the table before the Clerks are in their places and call their names out to the Clerks when they come. It is just possible some of these were not marked though of course they would be counted by the tellers. No doubt today when the division lists are open to examination, it will be found out if this is the explanation. But I don't think that it can account for as many as 14 votes.

*2nd April* 1912.

Of all the dreary days in the year I think Budget Day is the dreariest, and of all odious tasks that of following the Chancellor of the Exchequer immediately he has made his statement the most odious! It is a dull Budget and bad finance. Lloyd George will be, if possible, a little more unpopular in the City than he has hitherto been, and there the political consequences of this Budget begin and end.

*3rd April* 1912.

So much I wrote last night and then feeling "tired and disgusted" I resolved not to write any more but to read the *National Review* and went to bed early. This morning, having read through *The Times* report of my speech, I don't see that I said anything foolish and so am comforted and think better of the world at large. Besides last night's rain has altogether stopped, the barometer stands high and the sun is now making a gallant effort to dispel the fog. Lastly I have a nice letter from Ivy and a bunch of wild flowers from Joe, but dear me! the house is very empty with no perambulators obstructing the hall, no children and no Wife! Man was not made to live alone—not this *man* anyway! I must be off very soon to the Shareholders' meeting of our Bank and after that I have nothing to do but answer the accumulation of dull letters until I start on Saturday. Then there will be a busy, bustling time.

The Coal ballot is full of surprises. South Wales, where by general admission the grievances were greatest, the spirit on both sides most unyielding and the extreme socialist and syndicalist views most rife, declares overwhelmingly in favour of resumption. Lancashire, where there were no grievances, where the "abnormal places" case was already fully met and the 5/- and 2/- minima in actual operation, is equally strong against resumption of work. I asked Balcarres for an explanation. You know he sits for Lancashire and owns mines there. He could only suggest that it was a struggle for mastery among the miners' leaders in which Walsh, Ashton and the older school were being worsted. At Grillions on Monday, where chance placed me between Grey and Asquith, Asquith replied to the same question in the same sense but added that another and decisive factor was that the Lancashire men still had large funds. He then thought, however, that the Scottish miners would vote like the Welsh for resumption. Now it appears that they have gone the other way, and there is every probability that on balance the majority of the whole of the voters—not by any means the same as the whole of the miners—will be for continuance of the strike. Grey observed that the results showed that it was not, as sometimes alleged, a leaders' strike but a spontaneous revolt of the men. Asquith thought this true only of certain districts. I have no doubt the men will go back to work, but it is clear that their leaders had led them to expect a much easier and a more complete victory and those who in the first instance came out "in sympathy" are not content to go back without tangible benefits for themselves. Of course any idea that, with the immediate difficulty removed, the Government would settle down to prepare legislation to protect the community in future has disappeared. "Enquiry" is still in the air, but of practical results we have nothing but the mischievous precedent of this Minimum Wages Act.

We had a small but most pleasant party at Grillions—Finlay, Haldane, Balfour, Lansdowne and Welby in addition to those already named. Much House of Commons gossip. Asquith propounded the question why has —— no hold on the House though we all recognise his great ability and the skill with which he not only administers his office but does all the many other tasks entrusted to him. "Now what do you say, Austen?"

"Oh! if you ask me, I say at once: because he can't look you in the face. No one can like or trust a man with such shifty eyes. He may be perfectly straight, but you can't believe it of him."

Grey interjected: "I think there's another reason. I am reminded of what Lloyd George once said to me of one of your Back Bench men when I asked a similar question: 'Why, when he is so good, will he never be in the Front rank?' 'Because he is too relevant,' said Lloyd George."

Come to think of it, that's an extraordinarily shrewd remark, and no one uses the weapon of irrelevancy more successfully than Lloyd George himself. It is his constant defence—an offensive defensive, as the strategists say.

"But you haven't given us your real reasons, Austen. Now what are they?" repeated Asquith.

"Oh, but I have," I said. "Add Grey's reason and you have an excellent explanation of the coldness of the House to him."

"Well, let us ask Balfour." And he called down the table to Balfour, "What do *you* think of —— ?"

"A first-class official but he will never be more," said Balfour.

"But why?"

"Because he is always moving his eyes without moving his head!"

"Now that's what Austen said. That's very curious," exclaimed Asquith.

I walked back to the House with Balfour and Finlay.

"I'm afraid, Austen," said Balfour, "that both you and I are too relevant." I think it is one of my weaknesses from a House of Commons point of view.

I send you Robbins's comments on the situation. But I do not agree with him or *The Times* that George is holding up this six and a half millions simply for the Navy. George did not say so nor did Masterman, and I don't believe they mean it. If they do, then I must reconsider my attitude, but I suspect that very little of it will go to the Navy. It is much more likely that George will use it for less admirable but, politically, more advantageous purposes. We must return to the subject and try to get it cleared up.

PETERSBURG,
*8th April* 1912.

M. Sazonoff, Minister of Foreign Affairs, dined at the Embassy. After dinner I entered into conversation with him. He asked me almost immediately :

"When will your present Government go out ? They are not going to last long, are they ?" And then : "Who will your Foreign Minister be ?"

"Lansdowne if he is willing."

"But they tell me he is getting old. If it is not he, who then ?"

In that case, I said the succession would be open, but the most probable choice seemed to be Curzon. At this, as Buchanan had led me to expect, he wrinkled his eyebrows into the middle of his forehead, shrugged his shoulders and mutely but very expressively indicated his dislike of the choice. He fears that Curzon is anti-Russian and would break off the Anglo-Russian friendship.

I combated this view, told him we thought that Russia had had the best of the agreement and, being in Opposition, we had naturally criticised its provisions; but now that it was made, England would be absolutely loyal to it whatever Party was in power. He could not have a better example of English policy in this respect than the Anglo-French agreement. Our Government made it and many Liberals had thought it committed us too deeply to France, but no one could say that the Liberal Government had not carried out all its obligations in the spirit as well as the letter.

S. admitted this but said that the Russian friendship was evidently very unpopular with the Liberal Party and its maintenance depended on the willingness of our Party to support it whole-heartedly. They were criticised in Russia on the ground that it was too favourable to England, but he envied Isvolski the honour of having signed his name to that agreement. Peace depended upon the maintenance of the balance of power in Europe and that in turn depended on the Triple Entente.

I agreed. That was the only possible basis for our policy. I had much regretted Haldane's visit to Berlin because it was capable of being interpreted as an indication of instability on our part.

S. said he had regretted it too. Benckendorff had been very frightened by it, but Grey had been very frank and loyal. He admitted that the English Government could not have refused such an invitation from Berlin and "after all nothing has come of it. The negotiations do not advance."

I painted Berlin as the mischief-maker always ready to begin negotiations, not with a genuine desire to bring them to a successful conclusion but as a means of making mischief between friends and always carrying mischievous gossip from one to another.

He assented and then abruptly asked me if it was true that England had been prepared to send troops to France last summer. I replied, "Yes, to my knowledge all the arrangements for co-operation were worked out between the two General Staffs and billets on the Northern Frontier actually assigned to English regiments." I added that this was done in prevision of possible eventualities and because it seemed not unlikely that need would arise for action but that the exact moment of such action was not defined. In fact I told him frankly the conclusions I had formed from all the information that came to me, without telling him what that information was or whence it came.

We then talked a little about the Baghdad Railway, Persia, the Balkans and the Turco-Italian conflict.

He did not think that the last (Persian Gulf) section of the railway would ever be made. England's demand was that France, Germany, Austria, Russia and herself should each have one-fifth of the capital. To this the Turks would not consent because they objected to Russian participation and offered one-fourth each to the others. We refused this because we then had not a majority. He thought the other railway now talked of, though perhaps not very useful commercially, would be very important strategically to us.

He was hopeful of peace being preserved in the Balkans; he had spoken very bluntly to the King of Montenegro, who did not like it, but was now using his influence to preserve peace in Albania. The dangerous moment of the melting of the snows was passing.

He deplored the unskilful diplomacy of France just recently *vis-à-vis* of Italy. They had done everything to thrust Italy back into the arms of Germany. He said Poincaré's name should be *Contrecarré*. He had entirely thwarted or undone all the good work accomplished by Barrère in Rome who was an able man and had in recent years greatly improved the relations between France and Italy. He was again at work trying to promote peace and was hopeful that a basis might be discovered in the proposal to give Italy the coast and some considerable hinterland but to leave the further hinterland with its Arabs and a small opening to the sea to Turkey.

Our conversation lasted from the moment of our leaving the table till the guests departed. He was very pleasant, but I am told that he is not a strong man. He does not produce the impression of much strength or force of character.

Russia "at present" is doing nothing to counter the German army increase on their frontier.

9 EGERTON PLACE, S.W.,
*16th April* 1912.

Here I am at home again and a bigger change than this sudden plunge back into English life and politics no one could wish for. Our stay in St. Petersburg continued most interesting to the end, but I think it was well that it did not last any longer for it involved an amount of eating and drinking which, if much further prolonged, must have sufficed to undermine any constitution. As it is, however, I am feeling very fit and have not had a single twinge of pain since I left home. Two journeys of 48 hours' duration with only an interval of five days between them sound rather formidable, but they were very easy and comfortable.

We were very much struck by the extraordinarily rapid financial and commercial recovery of Russia after all its troubles internal and external, and by its vast natural resources which are only beginning to be developed.

Neither Sazonoff nor Kokovtsoff[1] appeared to me strong men

[1] Minister of Finance.

473

nor have they that reputation. Indeed everyone seemed to agree that Russia had had only two really strong men of late—Stolypin, a really big man whose death was a great misfortune, and Witte. Witte would like to get back into office, but it is said that the Emperor has not forgiven him for the constitution into which the Emperor thinks he was unnecessarily driven or, alternatively, that the Emperor has not forgotten or forgiven the brusqueness with which Witte on more than one occasion lectured him. Very likely both stories are true.

I could not really make out how far there was a genuine joint Cabinet responsibility now. On the one hand, Kokovtsoff incidentally mentioned that the full Council of Ministers met regularly every Thursday and generally sat from two till seven, and on my expressing surprise at the long duration of these Cabinet meetings said, "*Ah! avec un cabinet unifié comme le nôtre—qui n'est pas unifié du tout—ça prend du temps.*" On the other hand Buchanan told me that Sazonoff had refused to allow an important conversation which B. had had with the President of the Council when S. was away on sick leave to appear in an English blue-book, on the ground that Foreign Affairs were not the P.M.'s business and that B. ought not to have gone to see him about them. Both K. and S. are said to be very amiable but to be weak and to change their minds bewilderingly often.

What dreadful news this is of the *Titanic*!

*17th April* 1912.

I have not yet had time to look at the text of the Home Rule Bill circulated this morning but I may say I share the general feeling on our side that the last form of the proposal is even madder than Mr. Gladstone's original plans. I cannot conceive anything more embarrassing to a British Chancellor of the Exchequer or more certain to create friction, and worse, than the financial arrangements. I do not think that there is any enthusiasm for the Bill on the Liberal side, though no doubt, as far as the House of Commons goes, the Party will accept it with a more or less reluctant acquiescence. I hear on all hands that Asquith's speech was depressing and that Balfour's was very good. Bonar Law last night made one of the severest attacks on the Prime Minister that I have ever heard in the House of Commons, but it was very well done, his bitterest sayings being not mere taunts flung out in the heat of debate but a summons as it were or a grave arraignment gravely delivered. I cheered myself hoarse. I should think you must almost have heard my voice at Cannes!

I happened to be sitting next Balfour, who turned to me in the middle and said, "This man is extraordinary. He is not an orator and yet I always find him interesting." I gave my explanation. "It is," I said, "because his arguments always close with a snap." Birrell's reply was contemptible.

Asquith told Harry Chaplin that he should not take the Second Reading till nearly Whitsuntide. He said that he himself was absolutely done up and must go away for a change. Meanwhile Grey has gone and is fishing in Scotland.

We have a meeting of Liberal Unionist Peers and Members of Parliament at Lansdowne House tomorrow to consider the fusion scheme. I think it is generally well received among them.

*18th April* 1912.

I never knew a Government with so little power of resisting small Parliamentary pressure. Yesterday the Chancellor of the Exchequer moved a resolution to establish a Committee on Estimates. Just before doing so he leaned across the table to me and said:

"I suppose you are going to oppose this. I have a minute of yours here arguing strongly against it and I cannot say I differ from you."

I asked him to let me look at the papers and found he referred to a minute I had written for the Cabinet in 1905 and left on record at the Treasury in which I advised the Cabinet to reject a similar proposal. Asquith also apparently shared my view, but now the same motion is put down by the Prime Minister and moved by the Chancellor of the Exchequer!

I took Collings to dine with me at the Club on Tuesday night. He is full of "go." The Rural World Publishing Company have just brought out a second edition of his Home Rule pamphlet of 100,000 copies for which they are already paid. He told me he was contemplating another book on the land question, and I spent some time in sympathetically but firmly trying to instil into his mind that he did not know as much about the City as he knows about land, and that his ideas of the facility with which you can borrow money have no foundation in fact. He took it all very nicely, but it produced of course no more permanent effect than water on a duck's back.

It may interest you to hear that I had some talk with our Ambassador in St. Petersburg about the Persian situation. He is very gloomy about it, for trouble succeeds trouble, and the present Persian Government is quite unequal to its task. He told me that he thought the Russian Government was acting quite loyally, but their agents on the spot disregarded their instructions and forced their hand, and they themselves adopted methods which did not square with English ideas. For example the other day he had had to go to M. Sazonoff to say that Grey was greatly disturbed about the bombardment of the Mosque at Meshed by Russian troops which produced a bad impression in England and a still worse one among our great Indian Mohammedan population. Sazonoff replied, "But we did not bombard the mosque—we were very careful not to." Apparently what they did was to spare the mosque itself and to throw shell into the crowded sanctuary lying all round it. On Buchanan pointing this out, Sazonoff said, "But we have a letter from the priests thanking us for what we did and for the care we took of the shrine."

"But, Excellence," said Buchanan, "it really is no use your telling me that because I know that that letter was written in your Consulate and that the priests were forced to sign it by your Consul."

"Still, what does that matter?" exclaimed Sazonoff, "it is just as useful and answers all complaints."

Buchanan complains that the Minister is very changeable and often accepts or refuses one day what he refused or accepted a few days before.

We had a meeting of the L.U. Peers and M.P.s at Lansdowne House this afternoon and they unanimously approved the proposed fusion arrangements. The Council of the National Union simultaneously held their meeting and did the same. Conservative and L.U. conferences will now be held on 8th May to sanction it finally.

*22nd April* 1912.

I don't write to you about the *Titanic* for we all think alike and our thoughts are sad thoughts, tempered with a solemn pride that human nature is so great in the imminent moment of death. By nature I *know* myself a coward. But every time I read such a story, I feel that if ever my time came in the midst of a catastrophe, it would be—I will not say easier for me to do my duty—but less possible for me not to do it, by each glorious memory of what our race has done and endured. I bow my head solemnly to the memory of brave men and women lost, and I feel that human nature is the better and nobler for the sacrifice they made.

*24th April* 1912.

Alfred Lyttelton made a good speech on Welsh Disestablishment in reply (to McKenna) with one really fine rhetorical passage, but he never closes his arguments "with a snap." He never talks nonsense and there is always thought in his work, but his speeches never come off. He lacks freedom himself, so his hearers are never at their ease and cannot let themselves go.

Today I went again—a dull debate on insurance in a House of 30 Members. The only breeze stirring the stagnant atmosphere was at question time when Carson (in whose madness there is always method) came into conflict with the Chair. For the moment, as I say, the House is as dull as ditchwater. No doubt it will get more lively next week with the Second Reading of the Home Rule Bill. Our people are all in good spirits and the other side are not. But how get them out—there's the rub!

*27th April* 1912.

Weariness has descended on Ministers and the whole House is a prey to lassitude. We have had a surfeit of excitement and are, as it were, trying to sleep off the effects of it. Asquith's introductory speech on the Home Rule Bill was by common consent altogether unequal to such an occasion. Of McKenna's on the Welsh Bill I have already written. Balfour and Law's speeches on the former occasion alone stood out—each very good in their different ways and Balfour showing all his old mastery of the House. I did not hear Lloyd George on the second day of the Welsh Bill, for I had gone to Birmingham, but to a reader it seemed poor trash. You will have seen how the Government majorities fell away on each occasion. They will pick up again no doubt, but it is the beginning of the end. It is thus that Governments die—of sheer exhaustion. Asquith has been away since the Home Rule division, utterly worn out. They are getting to the end of their tether, but the end will not come this year—next year perhaps!

I addressed the evening meeting after the Annual Conference of the Midlands L.U. Association yesterday at West Bromwich. I found the speech very difficult in anticipation, being caught I suppose by the general flatness; but we had a capital meeting and the speech itself went off very well, and Neville said it was really a very good one. There is no report worth mentioning in the London papers so I send you a *Birmingham Post* which please return as it is my only copy. I heard from several people that the Conference was a great success and the strong old L.U. feeling was very marked over this revival of H.R., though the Associations outside Birmingham have already fused and quite approve our reorganisation plans.

*29th April* 1912.

Now it comes to the point of winding up, I share all Father's regrets at bringing the L.U. Council to an end. It has been an excellent body and done excellent work, but we really had no choice for we cannot recruit enough young men. The sons of L.U.s have not their fathers' memories of the pre-'86 times and naturally join the largest section of Unionists. Often indeed no other choice is open to them and in any case it gives them the best chances and the widest field. And as to the moment, though I would sooner have done it after the close of this final fight over Home Rule, we had now an opportunity, owing to the re-organisation in progress in the Conservative Central Office and staff, which would never have recurred. Indeed when you come to think about it, it is an amazing thing that their two chief officers will now be Boraston and Jenkins! What jealousies this would have awakened a little time ago.

Budget this afternoon and I shall probably have to speak, so I must get to work. I am going to lunch with Gwynne, who wants to talk foreign affairs with me.

*30th April* 1912.

You will see by the papers that we took up the question of the use of the surplus again, and though Lloyd George wriggled a great deal we managed to pin him down to the point. As I expected he entirely refuses to bind himself to use the money only for the Navy or to make good an extraordinary deficiency in the revenue owing to the strike, and insists upon reserving full discretion to himself to propose any allocation of it that he may find convenient. He uses the Navy as a stalking-horse but he obviously has other things in view. You will remember that the day after the introduction of the Budget *The Times* loftily rebuked me for having misunderstood his good intentions. Naturally today it is silent on the subject. We are indeed badly served by our Press.

Gwynne missed his train yesterday and was unable to give me lunch so I do not know what it was he wished to say about the Foreign situation. I notice that Sazonoff's hope of discovering a *modus vivendi* between Turkey and Italy has not as yet been realised, and the general situation of Europe must, I think, be causing a good deal of anxiety in the Chancelleries.

10.45 p.m. I have had a busy day with an L.U. Committee at 11.30, then a business interview with Boulton, lunch with him at my Club and Board meeting of the I. and F. at 2.0, on to the House where I stayed till past 7.0; then an hour with Steel-Maitland about Boraston's engagement, relations with the T.R. League and other plans and suggestions. So home to dinner with Ivy at 8.15 and busily writing ever since.

Winston moved the Second Reading of the Home Rule Bill. He was delayed for three-quarters of an hour by supplementary questions, points of order, etc., but when he at last rose at 4.30 he produced a pile of notes an inch and a half high (literally!) and proceeded to read for rather over an hour the dullest and most irrelevant political essay that I have ever heard—not one word of exposition of the Bill, not a single attempt to clear up any obscure point, not an argument in support of this Bill and scarcely any argument at all. I *never* heard a worse performance. There was a fairly full House and they sat him out, but there was scarcely a cheer from his friends throughout the whole speech—at most a murmur of approval now and then from the Irish Nationalists— and the whole performance was as dull and ineffective as—ditch-water!

Long, who had at his own request been entrusted with the duty of moving the rejection of the Bill, did a little better but not much. The Liberals deliberately trooped out when he rose (I think by a preconcerted plan); he had one or two good points but he did not make them well, and, like Winston's, his speech was lamentably beneath the occasion though, unlike Winston, he did at least speak and not read it. Our men sat tight and tried to cheer him, but he gave us little opportunity.

Altogether it was a bad beginning to what ought to be a great historic debate and one felt humiliated by the contrast with other times and other men.

*1st May* 1912.

The Home Rule debate goes on very languidly in a thin House. Cave[1] made an admirable speech yesterday evening and Finlay[1] a very good one this afternoon, but there were scarcely 30 Members on the Government side of the House while he spoke. Tonight some of our young bloods are going to try to catch the Government napping and to beat them on a resolution on the Insurance Act, but they won't succeed. I have told Balcarres how it was done in 1893 and commended the example to him. They might be caught one day on Supply but only if, as in '93, Members undertake to be present unless properly paired for a whole month of Supply days. I shall go back for tonight's division, but I expect no good from it.

*2nd May* 1912.

Of course last night's attempt to beat the Government came to nothing. Lloyd George adopted the simple expedient of accepting

---

[1] Each became Lord Chancellor.

the resolution so there was no division, but we should not have beaten them if there had been.

The Taft-Roosevelt campaign is becoming exciting. I confess that my sympathies remain with Taft though his Reciprocity policy is now shown to have been directed in intention, as we always said it was in effect, to making Canada an "adjunct" of the U.S.A. I should think that the publication of the "adjunct" letter will finally damn Reciprocity in Canada if it needed anything more to give it its quietus, and that the Canadian Liberal Party will now desire to forget it as soon as possible. It was an extraordinary indiscretion to publish such a letter. It ought to make Asquith rather sick over his own hasty approval of the policy.

*3rd May* 1912.

An off-day for me, pleasantly spent in digging in plants into my little patch of dried-up garden, but the plants themselves are wretched stuff and match the garden! I need hardly add that I ought to have been excogitating a speech on the Home Rule Bill for Tuesday, but never do today what you can put off till to-morrow is a golden rule in the matter of speechmaking at any rate, for the pains of composition grip one quite soon enough in any case. Balfour made a good speech yesterday, perhaps not so fine as his first but full of thought and grit. Grey's reply was poor and thin and had no particular relevance to this Bill. Indeed that is the striking feature of all the Ministers' speeches on it. They are on it but not about it, and Grey's, like Winston's, left on my mind the impression that though he was vaguely of opinion that some form of devolution was necessary to set free the House of Commons for Imperial Affairs he did not really like this Bill, did not really feel any confidence that it would work and felt at heart, as many others have felt, that though Devolution or Home Rule sound very well in theory you cannot put them into a Bill! A suspicion crosses my mind that he thinks that if Labour and Social questions could be relegated to provincial or national parliaments, the Imperial House of Commons would get rid of some elements which do not make for strength or wisdom in foreign and colonial affairs—which is quite possible though by no means certain.

The *Birmingham Post* observes that his speech was coldly received by his own side, he being at present out of favour with his Party on both foreign and domestic subjects. No doubt there are many of them who do not like his policy, but he was quite as well received as his colleagues have been and the House was fuller than it has been on any day yet since the debate began.

Gwynne, who lunched here today, tells me that Lloyd George is very much at a discount with his Party just now. To tell the truth I think the whole Government is below par and falling still.

*3rd May* 1912.

As I told you Gwynne lunched here today and as I expected wanted to hear news of my Russian visit, so I gave him some accounts of my conversations with Sazonoff and Kokovtsoff. When I had finished he said he would tell me the other side of the story. My visit had produced a great effect and I had made a most favourable impression in Russia. This he had learned both from the *Morning Post* correspondent and from Tyrrell of the Foreign Office, who is Grey's secretary. Sazonoff had sent for his correspondent and told him that he dreaded the effect of Curzon's becoming Foreign Minister. This was not on account of his speech on Persia but because of his general attitude and because they thought him difficult to deal with and overbearing. G. says he hears that our diplomats don't like him and very likely they convey their dislike of him to foreigners. S. had gone on to say, "Now, can't you tell your Editor and can't he convey a hint that the man we should like to see at the F.O. would be Chamberlain? With him the Russian Entente would be safe," and so on. All very flattering, no doubt, but I told Gwynne that I thought the suggestion would surprise my colleagues and that I regarded myself as bound to undertake the duties of Chancellor of the Exchequer to see Tariff Reform through. Gwynne then developed the view, which I confess I share, that Curzon would be a very bad Foreign Minister, partly because he does in fact cherish all his old suspicions of Russia and the old policy of the 'eighties and 'nineties, and partly because his judgment is bad and he himself rash. This lack of foresight, or rather deliberate refusal to contemplate possible eventualities because they are disagreeable to him, was illustrated in Tibetan affairs and, still more strikingly, during the Constitutional Crisis last year. It is a bad fault in Home politics and a danger in Foreign Affairs, and Gwynne thought he would get us into war before two years of his régime were run. G.'s own solution was that Lansdowne should return for a year whilst I carried a Tariff Reform Budget and that he should then retire and I be transferred to the F.O.! "You know," said he, "that you are the man whom Grey would like to see as his successor. Anyway we must not have Curzon."

I suggested that Selborne was an alternative. "Yes," said G. "or Balfour. Is he thinking of it? I saw Sandars the other day and was talking over these things with him and he asked, 'What's the matter with Balfour?' Does that mean that he wants it?" G. finally said that Tyrrell (no doubt with Grey's knowledge) wanted to see me. "I think," he added, "that he wants you to make a speech on Foreign Affairs. May I bring him round and leave him to talk with you?" Of course I said yes.

Now there is a matter for speculation for you if you care to speculate. Anyway it will interest you.

My own policy is the maintenance and development of the Triple Entente as being in the present condition of Europe the only possible policy for Russia, France or Great Britain. I don't trust the Russians far, because I think their Ministers weak and because, after all, the last word still rests with the Czar, and a weak autocrat much subject to personal influences and yet difficult to reach (for he lives in great seclusion) is about the worst and least trustworthy of all forms of Government. But I believe that, though very timid and much too subject to German influences, the Russian Government means well, and though many of its minor representatives and officials in Persia and elsewhere are quite unreliable and even false, we must make the best we can of it and them, and that a policy of suspicion and aloofness would be most injurious to our interests in the East and West alike. Russian opinion has undoubtedly become much more friendly to England of late.

Meanwhile the big railway issue which was proposed to us in St. Petersburg by the President of the railway has been given at a worse price to the Berlin house of Mendelsohn against the President's wish by order of the Minister himself, probably acting on superior orders! We can do very well without it as we had cut the price very fine, but it illustrates the difficulties of both business and public dealings where the Russian Government has a say in the settlement. But then as a Russian friend said to me, "We are governed by German barons."

I must go to dress for the dinner at Buckingham Palace.

*4th May* 1912.

At the King's dinner last night I sat between Sir George Reid and General Sir Douglas Haig, the latter just home from India and now commanding at Aldershot, I think. Sir George was dull but I found Haig interesting. We talked a good deal about Persian affairs and the projected trans-Persian railway to India. He is very suspicious of Russian intentions and thinks both Hardinge in India and the F.O. at home far too ready to accede to Russian wishes. He would find Curzon in cordial agreement with him. My own idea—I can hardly call it an opinion for I am not sufficiently informed to have one—is that the mischief was done by the original agreement when we gave away a great deal too much; but we can't get that back now and it is not good to adopt a policy of grumbling over spilt milk.

After dinner I had a long and very interesting talk with Sir Arthur Nicolson on Foreign Affairs. He began by asking about my Russian visit, thought Kokovtsoff an able man "but he talks too much." Sazonoff, he thought weak and not very able. Witte would never be recalled to office. The Emperor would never forgive him. I asked why? Because of the constitution? No, because he had told lies to the Emperor, and the Emperor, like his father, would never forgive a man who had deceived him. Witte had lied to him; he had undoubtedly been playing with the extreme revolutionaries.

Then we turned to Sazonoff again and I told him of our conversation and S.'s anxiety about Curzon and my answer. "And he didn't believe you?" said Nicolson.

"Did I altogether believe myself?" I asked. "But I was talking as an Englishman to a foreigner, and it was the right thing to say."

"Oh, certainly, but if Curzon becomes Foreign Minister there will be a flare up!"

I said that whoever was Minister—Curzon or another—we must maintain the Triple Entente. Then he carried me off to a sofa in the long gallery and we continued our conversation till sent for to talk to the King. He insisted that the Triple Entente was our only possible policy. I told him the account I had given Sazonoff of the events of last summer. He confirmed it. "Perfectly right," he said. I said I had told S. that this threefold friendship was the only possible basis of English policy now and I added that I thought it ought to be developed into an alliance for the reasons I have already given you. He most cordially and warmly agreed.

"Of course; of course, but this Government will never do it." He went on to speak of the position in the Mediterranean. "We have abandoned it! And Italy and Austria are going on building Dreadnoughts and we haven't an alliance. I think it very dangerous. Once before we abandoned the Mediterranean in 1796 to fight the Dutch and when we had fought them Nelson went back—to find what? Napoleon's successful Italian campaign completed, Malta occupied and a French Army in Egypt! It isn't safe! It would only be safe if we had a firm alliance. We have abandoned the Pacific, we have abandoned the Far East, we have abandoned the Mediterranean. I don't call it safe.

"'What then would you do?' Lord Morley asked me only a few days ago, but when I said, 'Make an alliance with France,' he threw up his hands and walked out of the room."

I put to him my view that we supported France last summer not because our Treaty obligations compelled us to do so but because we could not afford to see France go under; that if this was so, we must equally support France on other occasions if she were attacked, and that we had proved in the summer that we could and would do the one thing all my French friends had previously thought we couldn't do—namely bind ourselves to put our whole expeditionary force into France within fourteen days. We were therefore a really valuable ally to France, and France must see that our own interests would force us to support her in a defensive war. Would France do the like for us if we were the party attacked?

"Not unless we have an alliance," he said.

"Then why don't the Government take the question up? I think I could promise the support of our Party and certainly, even if I had to separate myself from my Party, nothing would induce me to join in an attack on the Government for such action."

Nicolson again said they couldn't hold together if they tried it.

"Well, who would be against it? Asquith, Grey, McKenna (he would follow Asquith), Lloyd George and Winston would support it."

"Lloyd George and Winston, yes, but I know one who wouldn't."

I suppose Morley or perhaps the Lord Chancellor. And then he went on to say that the fact was they were worn out and felt it and couldn't do anything.

Incidentally, he referred to Haldane's "most unhappy visit" to Berlin. I was very interested and pleased to find him developing exactly the ideas which, as you know, I have been trying to spread, and confirming so closely both my history of last year's events and the deductions I drew from them.

11.30 p.m.—As I told you, we were called away in the midst of our conversation to go to the King. To me he said, "I hope there is not going to be any violence in the House of Commons this session."

"Well, Sir," I said, "I don't think Your Majesty can suggest that the Opposition has forgotten its duty to the country or the Throne in the midst of our sharp Party fights."

"Certainly not," he interjected.

"But you must remember, Sir," I continued, "that we not only very strongly object to what the Government are doing but that we think that they have pursued their objects by trickery and fraud."

I retired and he passed on. A few minutes later, as I was talking to St. John, Law joined us.

"I think I have given the King the worst five minutes he has had for a long time," he observed; and this is his account of their conversation as noted by me as soon as I got home.

The King began, "I have just been saying to Sir E. Carson that I hope there will be no violent scenes this session."

"May I talk quite freely to Your Majesty?" asked Law.

"Please do. I wish you to."

"Then, I think, Sir, that the situation is a grave one not only for the House but also for the Throne. Our desire has been to keep the Crown out of our struggles, but the Government have brought it in. Your only chance is that they should resign within two years. If they don't, you must either accept the Home Rule Bill or dismiss your Ministers and choose others who will support you in vetoing it—and in either case half your subjects will think you have acted against them."

The King turned red and Law asked, "Have you never considered that, Sir?"

"No," said the King, "it is the first time it has been suggested to me."

Law added, "They may say that your assent is a purely formal act and the prerogative of veto is dead. That was true as long as there was a buffer between you and the House of Commons, but they have destroyed the buffer and it is true no longer."

Ivy went to the theatre last night also with Mrs. Walter Jones. A very fat gentleman, coming in late to the seat behind her, managed to get his waistcoat button caught in her back hair as he stood laughing at the actors on the stage. Ivy struggled in vain to free herself or to hit him in the waistcoat to attract his attention, and in a moment he sat down dragging out a wisp of her hair. Ivy now consoles herself with the hope that he got into trouble when he went home and was asked by his wife to explain how he came to have a lock of golden hair round his button! Poor man! he would probably be unable to give any explanation that would have the least semblance of truth.

*5th May* 1912.

Our dinner passed off pleasantly but I got less talk with Hesketh Bell and Dunlop Smith than I had hoped, for General Winslow has become very deaf and could not join in a general conversation, so that he monopolised my attention after dinner. He fought under Grant in the Gettysburg campaign and subsequently was in command of Sherman's cavalry. He had a very high opinion of Grant's services and was rather interesting in his comments on the two Generals. Hesketh Bell, as Neville will probably have told you, is going to the Leeward Islands, very naturally disappointed at his transfer. Though he does not criticise Lugard's appointment to United Nigeria, he thinks the Colonial Office might have shown him more consideration. Certainly he is hardly used.

*6th May* 1912.

My morning and evening have been devoted to arranging my ideas for a speech on the Home Rule Bill tomorrow and my afternoon to listening to Campbell and the Attorney-General. I am overwhelmed with material and cannot free myself from the overplus. Perhaps a night's rest will make things clearer.

*7th May* 1912.

I got off my speech. I scarcely know whether it was successful or not. Maurice Healy was in possession of the House and, having spoken for half an hour last night, dribbled on for more than an hour today. He absolutely emptied the benches and bored the few of us who were left to tears, but Members came in to hear me and remained to the end of my speech, so that I had a good though not a crowded audience. Half way through I thought it was a failure—I seemed pulling a very labouring oar—but it went better afterwards, and though the effect was marred by my own feeling that I had too much to say (so that I left out things I ought to have said) it was, I think, on the whole successful and I received gratifying congratulations afterwards.

Both the George Murrays and the Morants were at the Burgh-clercs' dinner. If we hate the Government, what words will express the feelings of these Civil Servants?

"They lie," said Morant, "they *lie* and then they put the blame on us. I have been three hours with Lloyd George today trying to get him to tell the truth (about the Insurance Act) and all he would do was to smile and say, 'I shan't say that!'"

What men! What manners! They are disorganising the whole Civil Service.

*8th May* 1912.

I send you two extracts from the *Birmingham Post* about my speech from which I think I may conclude that it was successful in spite of my last evening's doubts. I also send the report of the City Council meeting as it gives the debate on Neville's Town-

Planning scheme. The *Morning Post* has been making good use of Taft's "adjunct" letter to point a moral and adorn a tale. I regret the attacks on Bryce for, though I have no love for him, he was bound to act on the instructions of his own Government and to support the Canadian Ministers as long as the Home Government approved their action. And to attack him as Ambassador not only looks ungenerous but gives the *beau rôle* to Grey. It is the Home Government who should be attacked, and Heaven knows! Taft and they have laid them open to it.

9 EGERTON PLACE, S.W.,
*9th June* 1912.

Bonar Law is contemplating a Vote of Censure on the Government for McKenna's refusal to protect "free" labourers. I have encouraged him, but we must wait to see how things develop tomorrow before absolutely deciding. McKenna's speech on Thursday evening was certainly very bad.

HEREFORDSHIRE,
*9th August* 1912.

I was up till four on Monday night and till three on Tuesday. We wrung some concessions from Lloyd George, who yielded sooner than have us sit up and on to the bitter end. One of them is really important to men like my host here who has a great lot of timber on his estate. He reckons that it will lower his death duties two per cent.

The Sugar Convention debate was very tame, as the Government speakers did not attack the Convention but justified their leaving it on the ground that it had done its work so thoroughly that bounties would never be revived! As I said, I should be quite content to rest the defence of our policy on Acland's speech.

9 EGERTON PLACE, S.W.,
*13th October* 1912.

I have been very busy since my return; first the City, then Tariff Reform, then the debate and my speech, and then the Halsbury Club gathering at Hatfield to discuss the lines of House of Lords reform and the use of the Referendum. I was much better pleased with the discussion than I expected to be and do not feel it to have been the waste of time and vexation of spirit which I had anticipated.

What is to be the end of the trouble in the Balkans? They must fight it out, I suppose, and, indeed, I hope. But I distrust Austria profoundly. It is an anxious time for all the Chancelleries.

### Note to letter of 12th November 1912

The following letter needs some explanation.

On the previous day the Government were beaten in an early division on an amendment moved by Sir F. Banbury on the Report stage of the financial resolution for the Home Rule Bill—228 votes being cast for the amendment and the Government mustering only 206 against it. Mr. Asquith at once moved the adjournment of the House. The next day he announced that he would move the following day to rescind the decision taken on the 11th.

Accordingly on the 13th he made a motion to this effect, the Speaker declaring that the motion, though without precedent, was not out of order. The debate which followed gave rise to one of the most disorderly scenes ever known in the House of Commons. Member after Member was refused a hearing, and the Speaker, after fruitlessly adjourning the debate for an hour, was finally obliged to terminate the sitting. As Members filed out an Ulster Member, Mr. Ronald McNeill, threw a book across the table which hit Mr. Churchill in the face. Such a scene had not been witnessed since the fight which took place in the House in 1893 in the course of the discussion on Mr. Gladstone's Second Home Rule Bill. It was a sign of the rising temper on both sides of the House and of the exasperation which the methods of the Government had aroused among the Opposition.

Next day this incident was settled by a handsome apology from McNeill, and the Speaker suggested that he should himself confer with the Prime Minister and Bonar Law in the search for a solution which should accord with past precedents and not create a new one, and the House then again adjourned till the following Monday, the 18th.

12th November 1912.

I am a weary man after a long and tiring day—much correspondence, a Board meeting in the City, a visit to the House of Commons to hear Asquith's decision and a speech to, I suppose, 6000 people in Lambeth Baths tonight. But I must send a line to thank you for your letter and to reciprocate your feelings on the occasion which called it forth.

Humpty Dumpty is cracked and even the best seccotine won't make him whole again. Our Whips had observed that for some time past the attendance on the Government side at the beginning of the Monday sittings was very slack, so last Thursday we settled the fateful amendment and the procedure. Samuel was as hoity-toity and superior as we expected, the thing "didn't deserve argument" etc. etc., *et voilà*! the Government was in a minority of 22! It will scarcely add to their moral authority though they have found a shorter way out of the difficulty than I supposed existed.

*15th November* 1912.

All passed off very quietly in the House today. We said nothing and so there was no debate. There was something which it was desirable to say, but that something would necessarily have been in substance controversial and as Asquith was studiously uncontroversial in matter and even more so in form, we did not move. To tell truth, if I had been sure that Law could state our position firmly but not in a combative way, I should have urged him to speak; but I feared that he would act as an irritant on the majority and they on him and that the whole might put us in the wrong with the Speaker and the country.

As it now stands, we enjoy our victory and the Government programme is—printer's pie!

*16th November* 1912.

What excursions and alarums! What a week of emotions and what luck that at least our own crisis coincided with a lull in the war news and so got fair attention from the public and the Press! The Government may get their old horse up again and mend the broken shafts but they can't mend their horses' knees. Their authority is sadly shaken and the last shred of moral authority gone from their legislation. Next week, no doubt, after the loss of ten days, the Bill will be as it was before the Banbury amendment was voted, but the Government time-table is hopelessly upset. They dare not, I think, drop any of their chief Bills; yet if they persist in trying to carry them all, they will one day be caught in a minority again. The Welsh Bill grows more and more unpopular, and McKenna who is in charge of it has failed signally in the conduct of his two departmental measures and is as much disliked on his own side as on ours—which is saying a great deal. A cheerful prospect truly! The Labour men are very sore at the Government's acceptance of the Speaker's suggestion. They were not consulted or even informed beforehand, for the Government (or Lloyd George at least) has a great contempt for them, and whilst Redmond and Dillon are admitted to the Government's Councils, they are left out in the cold. The more extreme Radicals are equally angry and I dare say there will be angry words on Monday. They will of course always vote with the Government in critical divisions, but the sore is kept open and they trust each other ever less and less.

We are told that the Chairman of Committees on being consulted stoutly informed the Government that what they proposed was out of order and would certainly provoke a row, but that then Rufus Isaacs devised the form of words which the Speaker (wrongly as we all think from Balfour downwards) would not rule actually out of order though he showed his evident dislike of them.

There is little or no "secret history" to tell you in connection with the week's events. There was no ambuscade on Monday, though there were special efforts to get the men up. Asquith said in the Parliament Bill debates that the real protection of the minority against the forcing through of several highly contentious measures in a single session was that the attempt to do so would break down the limits of physical endurance, and that is just what happened. He had overworked his men and sooner or later was bound to reap the penalty which he had himself foretold. But his own degradation is distressing to anyone who knows him as I do and has never received anything but kindness at his hands, and equally distressing to all who care for the honour of the House and its leader. He no longer leads, but is dragged this way and that by Lloyd George and his crew and with the manners of Mr. Turveydrop unites the methods of the Artful Dodger. The "debt of honour" remains unpaid. No attempt is made to redeem it. He tells us that the Parliament Act presupposes the "unswerving support" of a majority in the House and of a "stable public opinion" outside it. He loses by-elections one after another and then announces that by-elections will not make him swerve from his path whilst he is undefeated in the House. He is beaten in the House on a vital point after clear warning by the Minister in charge that it is vital and then, to save his face and to enable him to carry that mass of measures of which he had told us there was "no fear," he proposes forcibly to abrogate the whole common law of Parliament. Our men feel and rightly feel that he keeps no faith with us. Do you wonder at the result?

They would have howled him down on Wednesday but that Law very properly insisted that he should be heard. They were determined to stop the proceedings somehow, and I think they were right. The Government had brought us to a stage where violence could only be checked by violence, the disease could only be stayed by its own virus. Yet after the division on the adjournment, it looked as if our game was up and the whole affair would end in smoke. I offered myself as a last resort to make a violent personal attack on the Prime Minister, directly charging him with breach of faith to the King and breach of faith to the House and the country. The charges are true, but it would have been a hateful task, from which I was saved by the Attorney-General and Helmsley on Wednesday night and by the Speaker's intervention on Thursday.

I believe the Government meant at first to try to go on on Thursday and use the closure if there were any further row, but the Speaker would not stand it and threatened resignation, and this, possibly combined with the King's intervention, brought them to reason.

The first inkling of what was going to happen on Thursday came from Ivy in Mrs. Lowther's gallery. She sent me down a note: "The Speaker is going to resign. He has written to P.M. and King." This came of course from Mrs. Lowther who was beside herself with excitement, furious alike with the Opposition and the Government. Mildred Lowther whispered to Ivy, "You must take what my mother says with a grain of salt. She is so upset."

I gathered Law and two or three others into the room behind the Speaker's chair and told them, and then Balcarres came in (it was almost the end of questions) with a message from the Speaker that he was going to make a suggestion. And so the curtain was rung down! Now I think we must hold the fort in the House with a reduced garrison for a time and spread our forces in the country. We shall not catch the Government napping again this side of Christmas.

Lansdowne spoke admirably at the Albert Hall and disposed of the Referendum most neatly. So that is off my mind, but if you knew how often Law has doubted and hesitated since our decision was taken just after he was made leader, you would know what a weight is off my mind. These declarations were to have been made nearly a year ago and were very nearly *not* made this week. But all's well that ends well! And while other people were uncertain, it was some comfort to feel no uncertainty oneself.

### Note to letter of 24th December 1912

The following letter was written in reply to a note from Bonar Law enclosing a letter from a man who had been among the strong Tariff Reformers. He wrote that he was afraid that the divisions in the Party would not mend but that the trouble might grow as the Unionist Opponents of Tariff Reform and Food Taxes were active and meant to continue so. He suggested, therefore, that if it would be of any help to Bonar Law, he could get a large number of Tariff Reform M.P.s to sign a private letter to him approving of a Referendum limited to Food Taxes. He added that a simple dropping of Tariff Reform and Food Taxes could not be done without grave trouble in the Party throughout the country and that it would take the heart out of the active workers. In sending me this letter for my information, Bonar Law wrote: "It seems to me the last straw."

*A. C. to Bonar Law.*

HIGHBURY,
*24th December* 1912.

MY DEAR BONAR LAW,

I do not wonder that G——'s letter draws a cry of distress from you. He is a good fellow and the best of friends, as you know, but he was always a pessimist and he is not always a good counsellor. On this occasion I cannot conceive worse advice than he offers. Its adoption would cover Tariff Reformers with ridicule and destroy every shred of character with which we are yet blessed. I do not understand how after your recent speeches anyone can think it compatible with your honour to withdraw from the position you have taken up, and I am certain that it would be fatal both to yourself and to the Party if you were to do so.

Just consider what our history has been. Balfour handicapped us at the beginning with the promise of a double election. That did not prevent the Free Fooders from voting against us, whilst it puzzled and discouraged keen Tariff Reformers. That pledge was happily for the 1906 election only, and with our failure to win that election we were automatically free from it. Then in December, 1910, in spite of previous decisions to the contrary, Balfour imposed on us the new pledge of the Referendum at the very last moment. The results were very similar. It did not enable us to win any seats and it puzzled and disheartened earnest men. Now we are at least free from that embarrassing condition also. For Heaven's sake do not let us resume the burden from which we are just free or place ourselves under any fresh disabilities. We have got a bad quarter of an hour to go through. The disaffection of *The Times* is serious and I do not underrate it; but weakness on our part would be fatal to all of us. I cannot too strongly press upon you my conviction that you can save the Party by firmness and courage at this crisis and that any change of plans would be fatal to our success. If you stand firm the Party will rally to you. The country will recognise a man of courage who knows his own mind and is prepared to risk all for his convictions. It is just because the Party has felt that it was not being led boldly and with confidence that we have had so much trouble, and it is because the country did not believe in our sincerity and conviction that we have remained out so long. I prefer your Albert Hall speech to your Ashton speech, and in so far as the second detracted anything from the first, I cannot but think it was a mistake. But I do not want to criticise or add to your worries. I am ready to defend both speeches on the lines laid down by you in your conversation with me last Friday, and to maintain their perfect consistency. On these lines I will do everything to help you and will stand by you whatever happens. It is a moment of rather fiery trial but courage and firm faith will bring you triumphantly through, stronger in yourself and stronger in the esteem of your countrymen than ever before.

I hate to write you a political letter on Christmas Eve, but I hope that the New Year will bring you better fortune and more happiness than the past has done.

Yours ever,

AUSTEN CHAMBERLAIN.

1913

1913

MY letters for 1913 are fewer than usual, for in May Mrs. Chamberlain had to undergo a sudden operation at Cannes and I hurried out to join my father and sisters at this time of great anxiety. The operation was successfully performed before I could reach Cannes, but I remained with the family for some little time. Again, in the autumn my father was in London longer than usual and there are consequently fewer letters, but the doings of that time are described in other letters.

The illness of Mrs. Chamberlain also prevented my wife from performing the ceremony of launching the cruiser *Birmingham* which Mr. Churchill had invited her to do. To compensate for this disappointment, Mr. Churchill very kindly invited her to launch the *Warspite* at Devonport in November. In the Battle of Jutland the ship flew the silk ensign which my wife had presented in memory of this occasion.

The first Balkan War was finally closed by the signature of the Treaty of London, but the Second Balkan War broke out at the end of June. It ended in the complete defeat of Bulgaria by her former allies now joined by Roumania. The London Conference of Ambassadors, presided over by Sir Edward Grey, reconciled with difficulty the rivalries and jealousies of the Great Powers and succeeded for the time in preserving peace among them.

The House of Commons resumed its sittings on 1st January after the briefest adjournment over Christmas. The debates on the Home Rule and Welsh Bills dragged their weary length along under a sharp guillotine, only to be rejected as soon as they reached the House of Lords.

Parliament was at last prorogued on 3rd March, but for three days only. The new session opened on 6th March and set about the weary task of once more passing the two Bills in accordance with the terms of the Parliament Act. The Franchise and Registration Bill was dropped by the Government on the Speaker's ruling that the adoption of an amendment on Women's Suffrage would so alter the character of the measure as to require the introduction of a new Bill. Suffragette outrages continued.

A minor issue of some constitutional importance was raised by the decision of the High Court in the case of Bowles versus the Bank of England. It had been customary to collect taxes on the strength of the resolutions passed in Committee of Ways and Means when the Budget was opened, the collection being subsequently regularised by a clause in the Finance Bill. In consequence of the great delays which had attended the passage of the Finance Bill in the last two years, Mr. Gibson Bowles, a former Member of Parliament and a man of very considerable ability and ingenuity, now challenged the practice in his action against the Bank of England and it was declared illegal. The Government was obliged to meet the situation thus created by a new legislation, on the merits of which I had the misfortune to differ from my Party.

My wife and I paid a ten days' visit to Paris at Easter and, after the summer adjournment of Parliament on 5th August, again took a long motor-tour with Leverton Harris in France and Italy.

All these things are touched upon in these letters, but their main interest lies in the account they give of the new crisis which arose within the Unionist Party over Food Duties at the turn of the year, and the attempt towards the close of the year to reach some agreement between Parties for the settlement of the Home Rule question. A few words must be said about each of these matters.

It has already been noted that the speeches of Lansdowne and Bonar Law at the Albert Hall with their definite abandonment of the Referendum had caused some unrest and dissatisfaction in the Unionist ranks. When a fortnight later definite proposals were made by Lansdowne at a meeting at the Alexandra Palace for free Colonial wheat and a 2s. duty on foreign corn and repeated and further developed by me the next day, the smouldering ashes of controversy burst again into flame. Bonar Law's speech at Ashton, in which he stated that the Unionist Party had stood by Food Taxes as necessary to secure the largest measure of Preference for British producers in Empire markets and would not now haul down the flag, only added fresh fuel to the fire. *The Times*, then owned by Lord Northcliffe, and the *Daily Mail*, which had formerly supported Food Taxes, declared for their abandonment; the Party in Lancashire and Yorkshire, including great Unionist newspapers like the *Manchester Courier* and *Yorkshire Post*, took the same line and so did opinion in Ulster. It was urged that Food Taxes were unpopular, that the Party could not win if saddled with their unpopularity, and that by clinging to them we should seal the fate of the Irish

Unionists and the Welsh Church and destroy all prospect of successful resistance to the Government's policy. In a few weeks, almost in a few days, the revolt had become general; the panic had spread to all but a few stalwarts. When we examined the lists we found that we could only count on the constancy of some thirty to forty men, including the veteran Henry Chaplin but mainly drawn from among the younger and more active spirits of the Party, not a few of whom had been drawn into politics by the call to public service on behalf of a United Empire which was the theme of my father's great Tariff Campaign in 1903.

Confronted by this revolt, or rather by what in the slang of the Lobby we should have called this "rot" in the Party, I urged Bonar Law himself at once to undertake a six weeks' campaign in the country to deal boldly with the question of food taxation and to lay once and for all this bogey, as bogey I believed it to be. I offered to do the same and suggested that he should call on all the ex-Cabinet Ministers to take their share in a great organised campaign throughout the United Kingdom. I did not deny the general unpopularity of Food Taxes, but I urged that where this difficulty had been faced boldly from the first, there the Party had been most successful; that our embarrassment arose from the fact that from the leaders downwards we had shirked the question in our platform speeches, and that our supporters had been left too long without a clear lead and without facts and arguments with which to meet the arguments or misrepresentations of opponents. The organisers of meetings had often tried to warn me off the subject as too unpopular, but my experience had been that the meetings themselves longed to have the case boldly argued and never failed to respond. I was convinced then, as I remain convinced now, that if this had been done we could have killed the "dear food" cry and that the Party would have emerged stronger and more respected from the ordeal.

But Bonar Law had no stomach for such a fight. He was by nature a pessimist and he did not now believe that victory was possible as long as we were handicapped by the name of Food-Taxers and by the "dear food" cry. The pressure upon him to abandon the taxes was immense and came from all quarters. Under it he gave way. He said that he still believed the full policy was right but that he could not drag reluctant followers after him in a course which they believed fatal to their chances of success. He should, therefore, summon a Party meeting and resign the leadership. As soon as this decision became known, a memorial was circulated in the lobbies and in a few days signed by nearly every member of the Party praying him to modify the programme and to retain the leadership. I would not sign the memorial for I entirely disapproved the change of policy, but, as will be seen from my letters, I told him that he had no right to resign. Bonar Law's final decision was conveyed in a letter to our Chief Whip, Lord Balcarres, in the course of which he wrote:

*13th January* 1913.

"I have discussed with Lord Lansdowne the memorial presented to me by Unionist Members of the House of Commons. That memorial, in effect, asks that we should retain the leadership of the Party while altering in one very important particular not indeed the policy of Imperial Preference, but the method by which the policy can be most effectively carried out. The modification requested by those who have signed the memorial is that if, when a Unionist Government has been returned to power, it proves desirable after consultation with the Dominions to impose new duties on articles of food in order to secure the most effective system of Preference, such duties should not be imposed until they have been submitted to the people of this country at a General Election. This modification does not seem to us to involve any principle the adoption of which would have prevented us from loyally supporting the course of action desired by the majority of the Party. It would, nevertheless, have been more agreeable to ourselves, and in our view more for the interest of the Party, that the change of method should be accompanied by a change of leaders."

The memorialists had, however, declared that such a change would be fatal. Bonar Law and Lansdowne therefore felt it their duty to comply with the request that they should retain the leadership and were prepared to do so.

This letter was published on 14th January. The night before I had stated my position in a speech to my own constituents at Acocks Green in East Worcestershire, within a few weeks of the 21st anniversary of my first election to Parliament. I venture to quote a few passages from this speech:

"A political Party, if it is worthy of the name, is an association of men brought together for public action by a common faith in great principles of policy, for the defence and advancement of which the Party exists, and without which it would lose all the dignity and usefulness that distinguish a party from a faction. But with such a Party there must always be room for honest differences of opinion, sometimes on questions of considerable importance, more often upon questions of detail. . . ."

After tracing the course of the agitation I admitted that the proposed new duties were unpopular but, I added, "for great ends and in a great cause . . . I was willing to face that unpopularity, to fight it and to meet it till we had conquered it."

It was urged that the Food Duties were not needed by the United Kingdom or necessary for Preference, but I continued :

"I did not share those views. I do not share them now. I believe that those duties are needed if we are to do justice to our own agriculture . . . and that though you may have Preference without any new taxation, you cannot have any complete or permanent community of commercial interest between the different parts of the Empire unless you are prepared to vote these new taxes. I altogether deny that those views are not capable of clear explanation and of full justification at any gathering of our countrymen, or that they have been proved by anything which has taken place to be incapable of acceptance by them. It is not true to say that we have been beaten because we fought upon this issue. It would be much truer to say that we have been beaten because we did not fight upon this issue and because we left the field in too many cases open to the misrepresentation of our opponents. . . ."

But I had to recognise facts.

"I have to recognise that the decision, for the time at any rate, is against me. I have to acknowledge that the great majority of the Party took and take a different view. But for the first time in my long connection with it, for the first time in the eleven years that I have been permitted to sit in the councils of that Party, I am unable to take any share of responsibility for the decision to which they have come. I cannot turn my back upon myself. I cannot unsay what I have said. I cannot pretend to like the change of attitude. I cannot pretend to view without misgivings its possible effect.

"I am afraid that this change may be a calamity for the Party with which all my public life has been associated. I am afraid it may prove a misfortune for the Empire which it has been my earnest desire to serve. But I have been too long engaged in politics to suppose that I can always have my own way, too long to sulk because I cannot now persuade the Party to take a course in this one matter which I believe to be alike the right course and the wise course; and though I have to admit my disappointment and acknowledge my fears, I will do my best in the future as I have done my best in the past to support my leaders and to co-operate with my political friends. I care too much for the other great causes whose success is bound up with that of the Unionist Party to sit idly by and not render what help I can in their defence or their promotion." [1]

I apologise for quoting my own words at such length, but I am prouder of that speech made at the moment of the greatest disappointment of my public life than of any other that I have made. It had been my consolation when Long and I withdrew our names and proposed Bonar Law as leader that he had made his reputation by his Tariff Reform speeches and that the cause was safe in his hands. Now that consolation was taken from me.

. . . . . .

There were no letters to my family this autumn, or at least none that can now be traced, but I was engaged with others in an attempt to find a compromise on the Irish question which both Parties could accept. Mr. Churchill was the prime mover in this overture and again suggested a coalition to make a national settlement of some of the great problems of the day. My wife and I stayed with him on the Admiralty yacht after the launch of the *Warspite* and later, after a speech of mine at Bromsgrove, he arranged a dinner at the Admiralty to enable F. E. Smith and me to meet Morley.

Asquith had made a conciliatory speech which expressed a willingness to consider concessions. My Bromsgrove speech was a friendly response, and with these conversations and in the letters here published we sought to follow up these advances.

Asquith and Bonar Law met privately three or four times and their occasional meetings were continued into January 1914. Unfortunately, they came to nothing; but I venture to think that the whole episode is creditable to those concerned in it—not least

[1] *Peace in Our Time*, p. 266 et seq. By Sir Austen Chamberlain. (Philip Allan and Co. Ltd., 1928.)

to Mr. Churchill and Lord Carson, whose moderation and earnest desire for a settlement would have surprised the public on both sides if they had known of it.

The situation in Ireland was daily becoming more tense. The sands were running out. We were moving quickly to the catastrophe which I foresaw. The story of the "Mutiny" at the Curragh is told in the next chapter.

## 1913 : JANUARY–MARCH

9 EGERTON PLACE, S.W.,
*7th January* 1913.

I have prepared you and Father for what this letter has to tell, yet I find it a very difficult one to write. I have done my best, but the game is up. We are beaten and the cause for which Father sacrificed more than life itself is abandoned! It is a bitter confession to make and it is difficult for me to speak calmly about it.

I found a note from Lansdowne on my return to town yesterday asking me to see him. We could not meet till nearly seven o'clock and then he had been closeted with Law, Carson and Balcarres for two hours.

Law's decision is to call a Party meeting on Thursday and to resign on the ground that his policy is impossible. I presume that he will be re-elected, though he says he means to make this impossible.

I will try to write more fully another time, but I have not the heart now. The Whips' report was that though fifty or sixty Members would gladly support Law if he determined to stick to his guns, not more than twenty-five wished him to do so. Law says that so good a Tariff Reformer as Page Croft confirms this estimate. Three weeks of hesitation have destroyed the chance of a successful fight!

*8th January* 1913.

Every hour the situation changes. I believe now that practically the whole of the Back Benches will sign a letter to B. L. pledging him their support on a certain statement of the position. The movers were Carson and F. E. Smith. They feel that there is no alternative to B. L.

They read me a draft of the letter and I said I would not sign it. I could accept defeat but I could not invite it. They explained that they did not mean to ask me or any Front Bench man to sign, but if I objected to their proceeding they would not go on. I replied that the matter was out of my hands; I had no objection to their proceeding. I would do nothing to dissuade men from signing. More than that I would not promise. They had better take the letter first to men like Hewins, Amery, Page Croft and George Lloyd and see if they would sign, or sign after alteration.

They refused to sign the letter as it stood and altered it materially. Now I think it is being almost universally signed. Hewins is far more sanguine than I am as to the future and the amount we save from the wreck, and I have told friends that I could not *urge* them to sign if they felt that they ought not to do so and that I was in no way responsible for the terms, but that on the whole I should be glad if they could sign. Hugh Cecil came to me and said:

"I'm very sorry to hear you are not happy about this. I think you ought to be. I've signed a great deal with which I'm sure I don't agree!"

Time will show what the outcome of it all will be. We have, I think, a very bad time to go through, but when history comes to be written I think its verdict will be that whatever was the fate of particular items of Father's programme, he breathed a new spirit into the Empire, changed the course of our Imperial development and made possible a future of union which but for him would never have been realised.

*Bonar Law to A. C.*

PEMBROKE LODGE,
EDWARDES SQUARE,
KENSINGTON, W.,
8th *January* 1913.

MY DEAR AUSTEN,

Carson has told me something of his conversation with you yesterday, and I wish to say to you how well I understand what all this means to you. You cannot fail to look upon it as if it were going back upon your father's life-work, and though I believe that the tendency towards closer union on the part of the Colonies is the direct result of what he did, yet that cannot at the moment soften the blow much.

It is to me a great misfortune that I should be in such a position that it is I who seem to deal the blow at his policy. I have told you, and I am sure you believe me, that if you or your father wished it I should gladly resign my position but I have not the courage to go on and be responsible for a policy which, with the feeling in the Party such as it is, I am sure is bound to fail. If I had been your father, I might have carried it through successfully, but I cannot.

In this crisis as in the earlier one, you have acted as what I know you are, a great gentleman.

Yours sincerely,

A. BONAR LAW.

I enclose the memo. I gave to Lansdowne of which I spoke to you.

*Enclosures*

*7th January* 1913.

My Ashton speech has been criticised from two points of view; the first criticism is that it throws the burden of deciding whether or not there should be Food Duties on the Colonies.

This is a criticism which seems to me so absurd that I cannot believe that any one who uses it really believes it. Every time a nation makes a commercial treaty with another country the nature of the negotiations is decided by the advantage which the one country is to obtain in trade relations with the other. If, therefore, we were making such a treaty with a foreign country, and made any modification in our tariff for the sake of the trade with that country, then it could be asserted with as much truth as in this instance, that our tariff was dictated to us by that foreign country.

If we entered into such a conference with the Colonies probably the first thing which we would ask from Canada, for instance, would be that the free list which Canada now has should be continued as free to us, while a tariff should be imposed against all other nations; and if Canada agreed to that proposal, then the Canadians would be just as entitled to say, as our people can say now, that we were dictating the tariff policy of Canada.

The second criticism is that at Ashton I went back on the declarations which we had made at the Albert Hall. This criticism is made on the ground that I left it uncertain whether or not Food Duties would be imposed. I had then, as I have now, no doubt that if a preferential arrangement is to be carried out by means of tariffs Food Duties are necessary, and after reading over the report of my speech, it seems to me perfectly plain that was the view which was conveyed by that speech.

I was dealing with a statement which has been constantly made by our opponents, and which in the last few months was repeated by our friends, that the Colonies do not want Food Duties. Dealing with this view, I said that if that were true we should find out, and if the Colonies do not think Food Duties necessary for Preference then they would not be imposed. Not only is that declaration not inconsistent with what we said at Albert Hall, but it is the view which I have constantly advocated throughout the whole fiscal controversy.

I have looked back some of my old speeches on this subject, and I find that I have always said that the Food Duties were not proposed by us for the sake of Protection, but solely for the sake of Preference; and obviously if they are not necessary for Preference then they would not be imposed. This is not only the view which I have always advocated, but so far as I can remember it was the view invariably taken by Mr. Chamberlain himself.

While, however, I am anxious that it should not be supposed that at Ashton I had gone back on my previous views the real question is what course is possible now for Lord Lansdowne and myself? It seems to me that we have only two alternatives: one is to go forward without hesitation with the policy which we have announced, and the other is for us to resign.

I am told, and from the conversations which I have had with very many Members of the House I think it possible that if I were to call a meeting of our Members in the House of Commons their objection to a change of leadership just now is so strong that I might succeed in carrying a majority of that Party in favour of steady adherence to our present policy. I might succeed at the meeting; but in my belief the success would only be temporary. I have had interviews with some of the strongest and most consistent Tariff Reformers, as for example, Mr. Page Croft and Mr. George Lloyd, both of whom came to me in order to express their readiness to support our policy, and Mr. Lloyd told me that he thought that at least fifty Members would be willing formally to state their adherence to that policy. I put to both of them, however, this question : Did they take that line because they believed it can succeed, or because they wished to support their leaders, and neither of them was prepared to say that he thought the Members of the Party to whom he referred believed that we could succeed on that line.

To carry a Party meeting in itself would be of no advantage. What we have got to do is to win the election, and I have not myself any doubt that as our Members are afraid of the Food Duties, they would go into such a fight expecting to be beaten, and what is perhaps of more importance, at the first sign of disaster, the first time a by-election seemed to be unfavourable to us, there would be a recurrence in a more acute form, if possible, than at present of the desire to get rid of Food Duties.

The first alternative, therefore, seems to me impossible, and I think we must adopt the second, and for us the sooner that course is taken the better.

My conviction, therefore, is that I should call a meeting of the Party at the earliest possible moment. At that meeting I would say, that in my belief if the Party had been united we could have won, and won easily, on our policy; but that since the Party does not itself believe in the possibility of success if we adhere to the present policy, then it is the duty of the Party to change that policy. With the change of policy there must be a change of leaders, for after the declarations made by Lord Lansdowne and myself it would be simply impossible for us to announce a change of policy and to continue to lead the Party.

I should say, also, that though I cannot be responsible as leader for a policy of which I do not approve I should be perfectly ready to accept the decision of the Party, and to support as well as I can the policy on which the Party has decided. If Austen Chamberlain could take the same view—though, of course, it would be more difficult for him to do so than for me, because he could not fail to be influenced by the feeling that the change of policy meant the abandonment of views which his father had considered vital, and for which, indeed, he had given his life—but if he were prepared to take the same line and agree to support the Party in their changed policy, then we should have a completely united Party, and in that way there would be certainly the best chance which circumstances admit of, of securing victory at the election.

It would, of course, be a great disadvantage to have another change of leader so soon, but after all that is a comparatively small price to pay for a united Party, and at all events, in my opinion, the only possible course which is now open to us.

Some of my friends think that it is possible to go on saying nothing, with the understanding that the policy will be changed later. This is impossible. I shall have to make speeches, the first on the 24th of this month, and it is simply out of the question that I should ignore the controversy, or pretend that the position is unaltered when I know in my own mind that it will have to be changed.

*A. C. to Bonar Law.*
*Private.*

9 EGERTON PLACE, S.W.,
MY DEAR BONAR LAW,                    *8th January* 1913.

Many thanks for your letter. I reciprocate the spirit in which it is written, for in the midst of my own deep disappointment I can appreciate and sympathise with your feelings and difficulties.

As you know I wish that you could have felt differently and I still believe that the advice which I tendered you was the best for your reputation and for the Party, and that if it had commended itself to you and been acted on at once the position of the Party would have been stronger in three months' time than it will be now and your own reputation immeasurably enhanced.

But I recognise that if you couldn't believe what I believed you could not advocate it with success, and I saw that I could not make you share the confidence that I felt.

If you and I now consulted our own wishes, we should leave politics to others; but neither of us *can* do that and you least of all.

You must make your sacrifice as well as others. I think you had the right to invite the Party to fight on your lines or get another leader. But, forgive me if I pain you, I don't think you

2 K                    513

have a right to say to the Party, "I see that my line is impossible and I cannot pursue it further, but I will not lead you on any other."

The whole Party desires you to continue your leadership and I do not think you have the right, as things now stand, to withdraw.

I have said more than I meant to. Indeed I only wished to tell you that if I have not sought you out yesterday or today it is only because I could not help you by anything I could say and I felt that things had now passed altogether beyond my control and that it was now for others to find a solution since the cause which I supported was definitely rejected.

I am deeply sensible of the difficulties of your position. I will try not to make them greater, and if you do not altogether like what I have to say when I come to speak, you must make allowance for a man whose dearest political hopes and personal affections have received from fate a cruel blow.

Yours ever,

AUSTEN CHAMBERLAIN.

*Lord Lansdowne to A. C.*
*Private.*

LANSDOWNE HOUSE,
BERKELEY SQUARE, W.,
MY DEAR AUSTEN,                                   15th January 1913.

You must allow me to tell you how much I admire your speech. It was a difficult one to make, but you seem to me to have said with all possible frankness and dignity all that was necessary in order to vindicate your own consistency without a trace of disloyalty to the Party.

The whole episode has been indescribably painful to me, and I should have been glad if it had the effect of releasing me from the somewhat ill-defined responsibilities of the joint leadership, but that was not to be.

I am afraid the "sequels" will be troublesome, in spite of assurances to the contrary from Derby and others.

Yours ever,

L.

*A. C. to Lord Lansdowne.*
*Personal.*

9 EGERTON PLACE, S.W.,
MY DEAR LANSDOWNE, 16th *January* 1913.

It is a great pleasure to me to receive your letter. It was not an easy speech to make but the praise you give it is just that which I should have wished to earn.

I am very unhappy about the prospects of the Party, for I fear that our new position is and will be proved to be an impossible one—a half-way house combining all the disadvantages and none of the comforts of either terminus. However, we shall know better in a few weeks' time. Do you see that the *Irish Times*, which clamoured for the abolition of the Food Duties, now claims the whole produce—and more—of the other duties as compensation to Irish agriculturists for their abandonment! Of such men is our Party made!

Well, I did not mean to write all this but only to thank you for your unvarying kindness and to assure you that my own troubles have not made me insensible to yours. I do indeed understand that you are making a real sacrifice in retaining the leadership. It adds to the great debt which the Party already owes you. Your retirement now would be an absolute disaster. But what would not we all give to be allowed to cultivate our cabbages in peace?

Yours ever,

AUSTEN CHAMBERLAIN.

*A. C. to Mr. Chaplin.*
*Private.*

9 EGERTON PLACE, S.W.,
MY DEAR CHAPLIN, 15th *January* 1913.

Thank you very much for your kind letter and telegrams. We have been passing through a most difficult and anxious time and I am afraid that as a Party we come badly out of it. The weakness and vacillation shown by so many of our men must be damaging to our political credit, and will, I think, influence events far beyond the immediate subject on which it was displayed.

I had it in my mind to write to you earlier but I really did not

515

know whether you were in a condition to care to receive what must have been a rather worrying letter. I am glad to hear that you are mending, but I am afraid from what you say that it is not only a slow but a painful process. I hope, at least, that political anxieties will not make it slower.

If I may venture to advise, I would suggest that you should not be in a hurry to make any public declaration. I believe that if Bonar Law could have found it in his heart to do it, he could have stopped this trouble at the very beginning by a bold appeal to the Party and by offering himself to lead a campaign in explanation and defence of our position, but I am bound to admit that he received very little encouragement to do so from the Whips or from any considerable section of the Party in the House, and he himself did not believe, and could not be persuaded, that such an effort could be successful. This was really to me the conclusive factor of the situation; for if it was bad to feel that the army thought itself beaten before it had fired a shot, it was still worse to have the conviction forced upon one that the General was equally depressed. As long as I thought there was a chance of getting Bonar Law to fight on our old lines I pressed that course upon him to the utmost of my power; I only ceased to do so when I found that he would not fight under any circumstances and that the only result of my persistence would be to make him resign. No other leader was possible at the present time and I had no choice but to submit. We must now wait for his Edinburgh speech and see what he makes of it. I don't think there is anything more to be said until we have that before us and I hope that then I may have the opportunity of seeing you and talking over the whole situation; meanwhile I have to confess that I am bitterly disappointed and very depressed, but if one gives way to feelings of this kind one should not be a politician. We must make the best of a bad job and see what comfort we can draw even from defeat.

*Mr. Chaplin to A. C.*

BRIXWORTH,<br>
16th January 1913.

Many thanks, my dear Austen, for yours.

I have spoken on so many platforms on the inestimable boon

of Preference to the Working Classes that I am not willing, and can't allow it to be supposed that I am indifferent to the hauling down of the Flag of Preference, for it is that and nothing else in my opinion and I do not say this without good reason. I *wish* I could see you—this is only one and a half hours from London and there are heaps of trains every day to Northampton from where you are.

Ever yours,

H. CHAPLIN.

We must take some decided line or the T. R. League will tumble to pieces.

9 EGERTON PLACE, S.W.,<br>22nd January 1913.

Selborne dined with us last night to talk over the situation. He was very pleasant, as always, and I have asked him and Hewins, George Lloyd and Amery to come on Saturday, when we shall have B. L.'s speech before us. Selborne feels very much as I do and will, I expect, say so when he next speaks; but he dwells, as others do, on the progress which Imperial Union has made since Father began his campaign and on the much greater readiness now shown by the Dominions to co-operate in other ways than trade. All this is true and comforting as far as it goes, but it does not yet go far enough. S. shares my fear of the impetus which will be given to foreign countries to try to negotiate trade treaties with the Dominions in consequence of our defection and, also, on the importance of showing to the thousands of foreign emigrants into Canada that there is a tangible benefit in Empire if we are to make them not only good Canadians but good Imperialists also. B. L. does not like the speech he has to make and I am not surprised; but I am rather avoiding him at the moment, as he must find his own way of dealing with the situation and I do not want to incur responsibility for a declaration which, whatever it is, cannot represent my views.

Well, we did not win Flint. I am not surprised and not altogether sorry. Cowardice and funk should not have their way made too smooth for them all at once. I see that in spite of the candidate's going "dead against" Food Duties from the first, his opponents made all the play they could with them and he attributes his defeat to them. Well, what did he or anyone expect? If you won't fight on them, you will be beaten by them, as I have always said.

We are going down to Windsor for the night—the date of our visit having been altered by the King, at Harcourt's suggestion, to allow of my voting on the Women's Suffrage amendments next Monday and Tuesday.

*23rd January* 1913.

It snowed hard yesterday evening as we went down to Windsor, and though the snow had all gone this morning the weather is raw and damp.

We were a small party, it being the anniversary of Queen Victoria's death—the Rufus Isaacs, the Iveaghs and ourselves being the only guests besides the members of the Household. Lady Minto was in waiting. I sat next the Queen at dinner and the King talked to me for a long time afterwards but without saying anything of consequence.

This morning we went over the library with Fortescue and saw as much as we could of the drawings, pictures and other treasures in the hour or so between breakfast and our departure. Did you ever see the King's collection of jewels, cameos and so forth in one of his small private apartments? We had only time for a hurried glimpse at them, but they are marvellous. By the way, I saw in (I think) the White Drawing-room the original bronze equestrian statuette of Louis XIV, of which Mrs. Endicott gave Neville a copy. The original statue was in the Place Vendôme but was destroyed in the Revolution.

*25th January* 1913.

Well, Bonar Law has made his speech. I wonder what you think of it. "As good as the circumstances permitted" is my verdict, but I cannot help feeling that the position of the Party is a very false one. Food taxes will not be imposed or defended, but they are not abandoned. They may never be revived, but the Party still carries the load and I am very much afraid that we shall have all the disadvantages without the advantages of either clear course. In short it is the half-way house policy which never saved anyone or anything. Well, it is not my choice nor is it a good choice, but I am rather glad, since they would not fight boldly on my line, that they have yet not wholly abandoned the policy and keep the flag still flying somehow. But it would amuse me to make the speeches which Government candidates can now deliver!

I spoke on the Women's Suffrage amendment yesterday. Ivy, who came down to the House to hear me, says it was a good speech, but of course the sensation of the debate was Loulou's outspoken attack on Grey and George.

The Speaker has now definitely told the Government that the adoption of any of the Women's Suffrage amendments or of their own amendment to abolish the occupation franchise would make the Bill a new Bill, and so necessitate its withdrawal and re-introduction in the altered form. This is regarded on all hands as giving the death-blow to the Bill for this session. It puts the Government in a horrid mess and is very humiliating for them. The advocates of Women's Suffrage will be very angry and we are threatened with a recrudescence of violence in even worse forms than hitherto.

*26th January* 1913.

We had a regular *tabagie* last night—Selborne, Wyndham, Ridley, Hewins, Amery and George Lloyd—and sat talking in the dining-room till the air was thick with smoke and then adjourned to the drawing-room, where we continued the discussion under Ivy's presidency. Hewins was sanguine but not, as we thought, very practical; Wyndham was loquacious but not very helpful; Selborne was silent but sensible, though not at all hopeful, and George Lloyd was pessimistic, whilst Amery took a cheerier view of possibilities. In the end we arranged that Hewins should draft instructions for our League speakers, that Lloyd, Amery and Wyndham, who all had ideas, should write a four-page leaflet apiece, whilst I drafted a resolution, which with some modifications was adopted as suitable for a declaration of opinion and policy by the Committee of the T.R. League. And having accomplished so much we separated about 11.30, feeling, I think, that after all we had had a pleasant evening and that Ivy had given us a very good dinner and been very good to allow us to turn the drawing-room into a smoking-room, as mine was too small for the party.

This morning I went to Stafford House to see Chaplin, who came to town yesterday. At present nothing short of a manifesto of protest will satisfy him, and he is determined to go to work among the farmers. I told him that some remonstrances from them to their members and candidates would be very useful, for the County members had been among the worst funkers.

What do you think of the latest Turkish revolution?[1] I incline to the belief that a renewal of the war will be prevented, or, at least, that it will not spread to other combatants. I think the German Government is genuinely anxious to preserve peace and she can keep Austria quiet if she wishes. But the mobilisation must be costing Austria a pretty penny and the temptation to her to try to get something to show for her expenditure must be very great.

*27th January* 1913.

I am glad to feel that my letters give you pleasure even though they be, like the recent ones, rather laboriously put together as who should say making bricks without straw. Your own letters are always welcome, dear Mary, both for your own sake, because as you know I set great store by your judgment, and because I value all the messages I get through you from Father. I was just dictating a note to Selborne when your letter came, so I took the liberty of transcribing for him Father's expression of pleasure at learning how his views coincided with our own and Father's hope that he would give expression to them—to encourage him in well-doing.

What you say of the reception of my Acocks Green speech is, I think, very generally true. The stalwarts are pleased because I spoke out and they do not feel wholly abandoned and betrayed, and the funkers and pure Party men are pleased because I promised not to sulk and put my own position without offence to them. So as far as I personally am concerned the speech was successful

[1] A coup d'état by Enver.

and I think under difficult circumstances it was the best thing I could have done, not only for myself but for the cause.

Asquith buried the Franchise Bill this afternoon—lock, stock and barrel. The Suffragist members of the Cabinet would not go on with it without Women's Suffrage, and after the Speaker's ruling they could not proceed with Women's Suffrage. I left the House at dinner-time and have not been back. Then all was quiet in the streets, though there were many sightseers about Westminster expecting a row. All the police of London seemed mobilised even at 3.30 when I walked down—a *posse* of constables by the Duke of York's steps, others in Great George Street, Downing Street and so forth and police thick on the ground in Parliament Square, which by dinner-time they had cleared and were holding with cordons drawn across the different roads.

We lunched with old Lady Lawrence [1]—ninety-three, but very well and her mind as keen as ever. She was vehemently anti-Suffragist and I was interested to find that she was equally strong in denunciation of the removal of the capital of India to Delhi.

WESTBOURNE, BIRMINGHAM,
*1st February* 1913.

Speeches, speeches everywhere and nothing new to say! I have still two speeches immediately in front of me, one this afternoon for the Women's Association and one this evening for the Jewellers who, bless them! dine at 6.30 and will not let us get away before eleven—a really monstrous imposition.

We had a very good meeting at Redditch and a satisfactory gathering of the Grand Committee of our Association yesterday afternoon.

Uncle William and Aunt Mary dined here last night. Both seemed very well, and Aunt Mary was much interested in reading the second volume of Disraeli's Life and in revising all her earlier ideas of that great man. She was impressed by his greatness, his breadth of view and foresight and felt how much there was in common between his ideas and Father's.

[1] Widow of the first Lord Lawrence.

*3rd February* 1913.

I am dreadfully distressed at the loss we suffer in Balcarres, who goes to the House of Lords. He has done wonderfully well and I have found him particularly pleasant to work with and a good friend in all my troubles. I suppose that Pike Pease or Edmund Talbot will be appointed to succeed him—both thorough good fellows. I shall miss Balcarres very much, for politically we had become very intimate.

*3rd February* 1913.

Gwynne also says that some communications have been passing between him and Lloyd George and Winston with a view to the two latter having a conference with Bonar Law and me about Compulsory Service; that their military advisers and they themselves recognise that the Territorial Force is breaking down, but that the Government are hoping it will last out their time and that the difficulty will stand over for us to cope with. They are, however, nibbling at his suggestion, but object that this is a proposal for common action on one point only and that one rather pleasing to our side but most obnoxious to their own. G. thinks that they both would like a coalition; but to this I gave no encouragement, saying that I did not think anything of the kind was possible whilst they stood committed to the Home Rule Bill. If they were ready to come down to three or four Provincial Councils for doing some of the work of the Dublin Castle Boards it would be a different thing. But I said, as Law had already done, that if they wished to have a private talk about our defences I would certainly meet them.

HOUSE OF COMMONS,
*4th February* 1913.

I went to the Levée this morning and had a few words with Spring-Rice. He said Father was in splendid form when he saw him, and that he had gone straight to Grey with Father's proposal for settling the Panama difficulty and that Grey had been delighted with it and had been working on those lines ever since.

This is the last day of the Report stage of the Welsh Church Bill and I have come down in response to a special private whip for 4.45. The mystic hour is drawing near, but it looks to me as if the Government had plenty of men about.

5 o'clock: We have just had our division. The Government majority fell to twenty-eight!

*8th February* 1913.

It cleared up a little by lunch-time and both the children were able to get out for a little. Joe walked with us to the Victoria and Albert Museum and after looking at a few things joined the perambulator on the other side, whilst Ivy and I went upstairs to look at the oriental china of the Salting bequest. Then we looked at his miniatures—quite lovely. What a charming art it was and what a pity that there is no great professor of it today. Most notable of all perhaps was a portrait of Anne of Cleves by Holbein —so attractive and so unlike the heavy German face I associated with her in my mind.

All the museums and galleries are in terror of the Suffragettes, and no wonder! You will have seen the account of their destruction of glass and plants at Kew. I think it has made me more angry than anything they have yet done. In sheer childishness and naughtiness it outclasses all their other misdeeds.

*10th February* 1913.

On our way home this afternoon our eyes were caught by the placards announcing the disaster to Captain Scott and all his southern advance party and we can think of nothing else.

We went to Christie's this morning to look at some Worcester china and found besides a delightful collection of pictures and drawings—Cox, Prout, de Wint, Copley Fielding and Lewis among Englishmen, and Meissonier, Israels and Harpignies among foreigners. There were beautiful things among them. Then we went on to the Diploma Gallery, where I have only been once before. Do you know the lovely drawing of a Holy Family by Leonardo? It is more beautiful than any picture of his that I have ever seen. There is, too, a capital Millais—A Memory of Velasquez, the portrait of a little girl—a beautiful Raeburn boy, a Sargent and some other fine pictures, besides a half-finished Holy Family in bas-relief by Michelangelo, a fine work none the worse for not being finished.

*10th February* 1913.

We have finished a pleasant day pleasantly at C. Lawrence's.[1] I sat between Lady Bessborough and Mrs. Langenbach, a sister of Mrs. Bischoffsheim and as like her as two peas. They were both chatty and pleasant—Lady B. particularly so—and the dinner was very good, and I thoroughly enjoyed his pictures. Amongst others he has two small Etty's.

"Now don't you think," I asked, "that Etty was a great man and is bound to come into fashion again?" And I was delighted by his answer: "Millais said to me he was our greatest English colourist." Some day Etty will again be brought down from the ceiling and hung on the line in all our public galleries. There is my prophecy. Do you know Lawrence's pictures? He has a lovely Romney boy, a capital Gainsborough landscape, his last acquisition, and an Allan Ramsay of Queen Charlotte, which gives you quite a new and pleasant idea of her. There is a Hogarth portrait, too, a Millais and others, all good and chosen for their merits and not for their names. Ivy sat between C. Lawrence and Lord Moulton.

It was very foggy this morning, but is now brightened up a little.

(*Continued on Wednesday morning.*)
And thereupon, as it really was brightening up and I felt the need for air and exercise, I walked out and across the Park to the Arthur Lees, where we met the Spring-Rices, Jack Hills and Mrs. Lee's sister at luncheon—a bright and pleasant party. Springy says that in America now when the question is asked: Is marriage a failure? the answer comes pat, No, only a temporary inconvenience!

I hurried off to the House to see Asquith about my question in relation to Captain Scott. What a noble message that is and

---

[1] Hon. Charles Lawrence, afterwards Lord Lawrence of Kingsgate.

what a fine story—the men who were hale standing by their sick comrades to the last, knowing that they were giving up their own lives, and Captain Oates walking out to his death so that they might yet have a chance, with just the words: "I may be gone some time." Was there ever anything finer or simpler? Both Mrs. Scott and Mrs. Wilson are left utterly unprovided for. I do not like the idea of a Mansion House appeal. This is a debt owing by the nation, and Parliament ought to discharge it.

*12th February* 1913.

We go over to Paris on the 20th and our address there will be Hôtel de Crillon, Place de la Concorde. We shall stay there at least a fortnight and, if the weather is good, probably pass a day at Amiens on our return journey. Here it has been foggy all day. We were in one of the worst fogs that I have seen for a long time and I had a funny experience driving home at 1 a.m. I thought I had seldom been in so pungent a fog—it was like bonfire smoke—when suddenly I discovered that the mat was on fire, some careless person having thrown down a lighted cigarette end. All's well that ends well. We put out the mat before any serious damage was done.

PARIS,
*22nd February* 1913.

We went to the Cluny Museum this morning and spent an hour most agreeably in the lower rooms. My travels with Leverton have very much increased my interest in many of the things one finds there, and we were fascinated in turn by shoes, lace, velvets, tapestries, early wood and stone carvings, especially the French, so much more graceful and tasteful than the Flemish and German, and, finally, by a case of miniatures in painted wax of Marie de Medicis, Henri III, Charles IX, Henri IV, la reine Margot and so forth. Quite delightful! I should like to have carried them away.

PARIS,
*23rd February* 1913.

We dined last night with Monsieur Pernolet—a little family party—two nieces and their husbands, all very pleasant and an excellent dinner. He is trying to arrange two other dinners—a "*Dîner d'intelligence pour Austen*" and a "*Dîner de robes pour Madame.*" We chaffed him gaily on the distinction.

PARIS,
*24th February* 1913.

We lunched at Henry's and walked back here. Finding an invitation from Madame Dietz to dine on Wednesday to meet Millerand, I sallied out again to leave cards and our acceptance and then went with M. Pernolet to the Sunday reception for men only of the new Director of the École des Sciences Politiques where I had some pleasant conversation, meeting amongst others M. Tardieu, the publicist, and finding them all much interested in, and mostly strongly in favour of, the proposal to revert to the three years' service with the Colours, so as to strengthen the immediate readiness of their army for war.

France seems to me thoroughly warlike and very tired of German interference and threats. In fact just as a few years ago she was too much devoted to peace at any price and too much inclined to submit to anything, she has now, I think, swung over too far the other way, and is inclined to be a little too impatient.

One or two people expressed to me their inability to understand what was going on in England. What puzzled them was the growing lawlessness—first in the strikes and now among the Suffragettes. This seemed to them a new feature of English life and singularly in contrast with our past history. I must say that to me, also, it is the most disquieting feature of our internal situation.

PARIS,
*25th February* 1913.

This morning I spent a long time at the Louvre. My special object was the Chauchard collection—such Millets, Corots, Troyons, Rousseaus, Isabeys and Meissoniers. But Millets above all; not so much the " Angelus " for that has been spoiled for one by too frequent reproduction, but a *fileuse*, a peasant girl sitting on a bank spinning, and another, a girl walking in front of her sheep. Such charm, such poetry!

The representation of the English School is improved but still leaves much to be desired. I wandered through room after room, only looking at a few old favourites or new faces. One of the Rothschilds has left a splendid Hobbema to the gallery, but there is no Hobbema so beautiful as ours in London. On the other hand, the Louvre family group by Hals puts ours effectively into the shade. Indeed, it is to our murky one as sunshine is to fog. The nude recumbent woman by Manet, formerly in the Luxembourg, is now in the Louvre, but I need someone to explain to me wherein his merit consists.

Your account of Steel-Maitland paints him very much as I have found him; very keen, very hard-working, very anxious that others should work as hard, still rather "young" and anxious to get things more cut and dried than I think they can be. Of course, the Shadow Cabinet, which is inordinately big, is also extraordinarily useless, and B. L. rightly avoids summoning it as much as possible. But then I think he ought to take rather more upon himself and define, as far as he wishes to define at all, what his policy on some big questions is going to be—the Second Chamber, for example, the land and perhaps housing. But he is convinced that if we are united we can win on the faults of our opponents and I doubt whether he cares much or knows much about any of these questions. I will of course give him any help I can whenever he seeks it, but I am tired of urging people to do things which they will not do, or only do half-heartedly, and I feel that in the main I am wise just now to let him work out his own salvation.

PARIS,
*27th February* 1913.

. . . We dined last night with the Dietz—a party of fifteen and made as much noise as if we were fifty, for after the manner of French people everyone talked at once and at the top of their voices. M. Dietz was just back from Vienna, which he found much more peacefully inclined than three months ago. Dr. Dillon, of the *Daily Telegraph*, who has been there since the crisis began, was writing very pessimistically a couple of days ago, but the majority of our papers take the more hopeful and, I believe, the truer view.

Millerand was at the dinner and I had some friendly conversation with him on Anglo-French relations. He was till just lately Minister of War, but resigned owing to the mistake he made in re-admitting Du Paty de Clam to the Army. Pernolet thinks that he was the strongest man in the Cabinet—a man of character and good reputation. He was formerly a Socialist and I knew him twenty-eight years ago as a writer on Clemenceau's then paper, *La Justice*.

I met also M. Pallain, one of the French members of the International Group who are "studying" Persian railway projects —a difficult subject of which I do not know very much, but by his desire I gave him my views for what they were worth, and he said that they coincided with the project which they had determined to put forward after hearing the views of their English colleagues, whom they had found rather inclined to draw back. A director of the Bank and the Editor of the *Débats*, a Major, now I think retired and writing for the same paper, were also members of the party, and with all I had a little talk as well as with an American-Parisian, who happily massacred the French language worse than I did.

PARIS,
*1st March* 1913.

We had a very pleasant party last night and an excellent dinner. M. le Bon, formerly Minister of the Colonies, and M. Noetzlin, Director of the Banque de Paris et des Pays Bas, were the two most distinguished guests. Everyone discusses the proposal to revert to three years' service, for which they say the "*jeunes gens*" are quite ready. They tell me public opinion will impose it on the Chamber as it imposed Poincaré on an unwilling Assembly. I find them tired of the constant pin-pricks of Germany, of its constant threats and bullyings.

"*Eh bien, Monsieur, et à quand la guerre?*" was M. le Bon's opening when we left the ladies.

"*Pas cette fois, Monsieur, à ce que je crois du moins.*"

"*Eh bien, le plutôt serait le mieux selon moi,*" he replied.

I asked why, and he said first because of the growing disproportion of population between France and Germany and the falling birthrate of the former. Secondly, because public opinion changed. It was in the right mood now, but it might not always be so. Lastly, if war had arisen out of the present situation, Russia, being the most directly interested of all the powers of the Entente, it was certain would act promptly and with vigour. Meanwhile, Austria was neutralised by the agitation among her own Slavs and by fear of what might happen in her Balkan possessions, and Italy had shown great military weakness in Tripoli. I suggested that France might do more to cultivate a good understanding with Italy—not that Italy would leave the Triplice to join the Entente, but her connection with the Triplice might be weakened. He admitted that during the war in Tripoli public opinion in France had been unduly excited and the hand of the French Government had been forced.

M. Noetzlin asked about the prospects of the Channel Tunnel under present conditions. I told him that it was much better that the question should not be raised again. I am not very convinced of its military dangers, but I think its construction would largely increase our liability to scares if relations with France ever took a less favourable turn.

I don't think Ivy told you that we went to see *L'Habit Vert*, a skit on the Académie, which we found very amusing with good acting, pretty dresses and pretty faces—the best play that we have seen yet. We dined that night at Maire's, an excellent restaurant far up the Boulevards by the Porte St. Martin, not known to English visitors to Paris.

I nearly forgot to tell you that the night before last we dined with General and Mrs. Winslow. We met the American Ambassador, Mr. Herrick of Cleveland, Ohio, and his wife, both very pleasant. He is an interesting and intelligent man. He spoke with much respect and feeling about Father. There were also there young Mr. and Mrs. Bliss, he a contemporary and college friend of Phillips, she very pretty and attractive; the Marquis and Marquise de Chabron (?). She is American and said she had known William well in his later years at Washington. Her father was Minister at Brussels and afterwards in Spain. I asked but have forgotten his name. She came out after you left Washington.

Both she and the Ambassador told me that the old parties were "rallying" now more than they had ever done. The Ambassador says that several of the Faubourg have been to write their names at the Elysée since the new President assumed Office. The Ambassador took this, as I did, as a sign that they felt the old game was up and that now that they had a President of more culture and position who was, besides, supposed to be a strong man of more conservative leanings than his predecessors, they were prepared to be reconciled. The Marquise, however, took quite the other view. Her husband is a *rallié* of old date, but she said it was the fact that Poincaré had been imposed by public opinion on the Assembly that had given new hopes to the Right. They thought that if he could succeed so, others might, and that he was, as it were, a preparatory stage. I wonder how much it all amounts to. Not much, I expect!

PARIS,
*2nd March* 1913.

Oh, the "wild loose life" we are leading! It has been a charming day, sunny and brisk without being too cold. It was lovely when I closed my letter this morning and we drove in an open taxi out to the Bois to lunch at the Pré Catalan. I had not been there before—Armenonville was my special house of call—but we found the Pré Catalan excellent, a large bright room with a pretty view of trees and lawns. After an excellent lunch, we went on to the races at Auteuil and found the crowd, as always, entertaining.

We went to tea at the Ritz with Madame Bouvens, whom I was very glad to see again, for she was very hospitable to me when I was here. She has had much trouble since. M. Koechlin and the eldest son, Richard, who were both my friends, were there, too. We got back to our hotel just in time to receive M. Pernolet, who called at six o'clock. He has been kindness itself. I asked him about the Faubourg rallying. He did not think that there was anything in what I had heard on this subject and I expect that he is right. We are to meet one or two of the Faubourg at his dinner on Tuesday, though he has not been able to collect all whom he wished at such short notice.

PARIS,
*3rd March* 1913.

Our dinner-party at the Ribots was unexpectedly interesting, containing among others, M. Jonnart, lately Governor-General of Algeria and now Minister for Foreign Affairs, Monsieur Denis Cochin, who is, I think, Chairman of the Committee of Foreign Affairs, M. Gabriel Charmes and M. Lepine, the very successful Prefect of Police, who is just retiring. Only two ladies besides Madame Ribot and Ivy. I tried to draw M. Lepine on the Suffragettes. How would he treat them? But he evaded the challenge.

M. Jonnart is much exercised over the problem of the educated native, which threatens to be as troublesome for them in a few years as it already is for us in India. Incidentally, he observed that the relations of French and natives in Algeria would be much better if it was not always thought necessary to staff the country with Southerners, whose vulgar coarse ways were highly displeasing to the stately Arab, who did not like being poked in the ribs or slapped on the back when you were pleased with him, and met with *des injures* when you were the reverse. He says that the position in Morocco is disquieting. They have only just troops enough there for the work and will have to vote considerable credits.

M. Ribot is much aged since I last saw him. He particularly begged to be remembered to Father.

PARIS,
*5th March* 1913.

Have I ever told you that we leave tomorrow morning, spend the night at Amiens, and are in London on Friday evening? Well, all good things must have an end. We have certainly enjoyed ourselves thoroughly. If we have seen less of the theatres and museums than we intended, we have seen more society than we expected and it has been very interesting. Last night we dined with M. Pernolet, again a Faubourg dinner, *"des gens un peu empaillés, hein?"* he said to me, but we found them very pleasant. Le Comte Louis de Ségur and his Comtesse, old people with beautiful manners, Orleanists, great friends of the Comte de Paris and the Duc d'Aumâle; she was a Casimir Périer; the Comte et Comtesse de

Clermont Tonnerre, she born a de Kerguelen, of Legitimist origin, and now bitten by *Le Socialisme Chrétien* ("*je trouve ça un peu dangereux, moi,*" says M. Pernolet) ; Monsieur Herbette, formerly Ambassador at Berlin, whom I met there, and his wife ; M. et Mme de Boislisle ; le Comte E. de Billy, and others, to the number of sixteen. An excellent dinner again and much pleasant conversation. Ivy's green dress much admired and especially her way of wearing her rope of seed-pearls (invented for the occasion) over the left shoulder and knotted under the right arm at the waist.

9 EGERTON PLACE, S.W.,
*8th March* 1913.

I was no sooner home than Duncannon rang me up on the telephone to seek an interview and came round directly after dinner. He wanted instructions how to deal with the Westmorland election, where the local people have rejected the Central Office nominee and adopted a very popular local Free Trader, who rejects the Edinburgh programme altogether. Boraston has withdrawn all his help and I told Duncannon to do the same. The worst of it is that it is said that by his personal popularity the candidate will increase the majority.

D. is rather anxious about Friday's conference and I have therefore promised to attend it. He says that *our* people are furious at the change of policy, that they have lost all respect for Law and are only restrained from an open breach with the Party by respect and regard for me. Cheerful, is it not ? and *I* do not know how to defend the new platform, effectively, before agriculturists. Hewins, who was very confident that he could do it, was (according to D.) laughed down at Canterbury when he tried.

Law rang me up to ask me to come early to his dinner tonight, so that we might have some talk before the other guests arrive. "We have got a lot of troubles in front of us. I'll tell you about them this evening." So that, too, was cheerful !

*9th March* 1913.

Our dinner last night at Bonar Law's was a dull affair, for of course we had but recently parted and there was no curiosity about a King's Speech which each of us felt we could foretell without difficulty. The inclusion of "a large measure" on Education was, however, a surprise, but I expect it is only put there for window-dressing purposes.

Law had sent for me mainly to talk about the Kendal Division.

Robbins came to see me this morning. He had the same impression that everyone was tired and everything would be flat and dull that I had formed. He did not see what could upset the Government, but they were weary and exhausted and some accident might occur. He found widespread uneasiness about our land defences, but admitted that the Government would always have a majority on any question of that kind. Lloyd George's land campaign might cause a split: It had been postponed from last autumn against George's will because Asquith was not then prepared for it; but George was straining on the leash because he was determined to be the Radical candidate for the succession, and Asquith had *baissé beaucoup*, was very tired and almost ready to go. No one could stand against George. Grey might have done at one time, but not now. He was cold and had no following and never got the credit of his Radicalism with his own party. He was, by the way very Radical on the land. George feared Winston. But at present he couldn't rival George. He was absorbed in the Navy, but would not get any sensational increase as he had contemplated and begun to work up a Press campaign for. Harcourt hated the idea of the land campaign—but George could of course beat him into a cocked hat if he pleased.

As to us, he agreed that we made little progress. There was no marked revulsion of feeling to our side.

"Such enthusiasm as there has been has been among *your* people (*i.e.* the Tariff Reformers) and they have done all the work that has been done; and all this damping down of Tariff Reform and postponement and so forth does not tend to encourage them."

La! la! I hate the echo of my own dull thoughts.

Steel-Maitland came home with me from Law's dinner to impress on me what he had said to you of the absence of forethought and the necessity for prevision in our Councils. I told him that, having a longer experience, I was perhaps less sanguine than he was, but that otherwise I agreed entirely. But, I added, there is only one man who can do or get done what you want, and that is the leader. I had tried for years to get other men to adopt my policy (or their own for that matter), but at least to have *a* policy and to make it *the* Party policy; but I had failed and was tired of trying. I would help Law all I could, but *he* must take the initiative. S.M. observed that A. J. B. may have been maddening in his refusal to act but at least he always took a wide and comprehensive survey of the situation. Bonar Law was so worried with daily details and so tired of them, and besides, his mind was so differently constituted, that with all his virtues he didn't attempt anything of the sort and I must help him.

The fact is, I think our present position illogical and indefensible, our recent history cowardly and disgraceful, our prospects of winning poor, and our prospects, if we do win, alarming; and I say to myself that it would be better that we should be beaten again and learn in that fiery trial to find faith and courage and leadership such as may deserve victory first and be able to use it afterwards. I am really sickened by this double surrender—first the House of Lords and now all that I care most for in the fiscal question. Well, when I have been in harness again for a time, I suppose these sores will chafe less and that I shall re-find some of the old spirit. But the cup has been dashed too often from my lips, and just now *le jeu ne vaut pas la chandelle*.

*11th March* 1913.

The session opened yesterday as quietly as I expected. The benches were not full in any quarter of the House and Members chatted with each other rather than listened to the speeches. Of course, the first day of a session is always apt to disappoint those who want excitement, but this was a degree duller than usual. On our bench Balfour, F. E. Smith, Carson and Alfred were all absent. Carson came to a consultation later, but does not feel equal to speaking. F. E. has got a bit of his broken rib in his lung and will be *hors de combat* for some time. Balfour is at Cannes and Alfred in East Africa. What is left of us is not a very formidable force. Walter Long has had a return of his trouble and is far from well. Law seems to me very low-spirited—not without reason, as I think—and I—well, I give my help when it is wanted but without enjoyment or confidence. Harry Chaplin alone seems very much better and is full of plans for somehow rehabilitating the cause. He has just been with me to discuss suggestions, some of which he has abandoned almost as soon as formed, but others he is to discuss with the Tariff Commission and see what they think of them.

It was arranged that we were to have two amendments to the Address—the first, on which Long and I were to speak, on Home Rule, etc., and the second on Tariff Reform.

Meanwhile the Government have asked me to take the Chairmanship of the Royal Commission on Indian financial management. I would certainly accept a seat on the Commission,[1] but I am doubtful about undertaking the very onerous duties of Chairman. I am to see Crewe on the subject this afternoon. Before I decide I must learn what are the terms of reference. It should be a very interesting enquiry.

Please thank Father for his message. My constant prayer is that I may be for my children something of what he has been for his and that Joe, as he grows up, may feel for me a part at least of what I feel for my father. Can I say more? If I could, I would; but this tells you what and how deeply I feel.

I will give your message to Captain Tryon when we meet.

A telephone message from Talbot tells me that the Speaker means to give Thursday to the Labour Party, so we shall only get in one amendment on the Address and I shall not have to speak.

The man who hesitates is lost—no less than the woman. As you will have foreseen, I have agreed to take the Chairmanship of the Commission on Indian Finance as a result of my interview with Crewe today. It is to enquire into all manner of things which I have never studied and of which I know nothing; so at least I shall learn something—and knowledge is *always* interesting and *sometimes* useful. But ah me! it means a deal of work, I fear.

*12th March* 1913.

What a violent ill-tempered outburst is this of the *Cologne Gazette's!* It is curious how completely France and Germany

[1] The Royal Commission on Indian Finance and Currency.

seem to have changed characters—the former self-reliant and calm, the latter blustering and yet panicky. I was enormously struck by the changed spirit in Paris which, as far as I could learn, extended equally to the provinces. Everyone spoke to me of the readiness of the people to make the heavy sacrifice [1] asked of them and told me that the Chamber was being driven forward by public opinion. I see this morning that the Vienna Press says Asquith was too sanguine and that the difficulties are far from being arranged. But I cannot believe that they would or can provoke a great war now, for the mutual disarmament of Russia and Austria is at last to take place and Austria's financial situation must be almost desperate. I hear that she got some money from Speyers here in London, but only after depositing security here, as S. feared that they would be forced to proclaim a moratorium in Vienna. Meanwhile, here are Greeks and Bulgarians fighting among themselves. How these allies love one another! Could one have a greater proof of the ineptitude of the Young Turk Government which allowed them to come together? If poor old Abdul Hamid knows what is going on, how he must smile over the folly of his successors.

*15th March* 1913.

I have had a busy conclusion to my week. On Thursday I joined the Empire Parliamentary Committee's luncheon at the House of Commons in honour of Colonel Allen, New Zealand Minister of Defence, and Mr. Mackenzie, their new High Commissioner.

Thence I hurried to the meeting of the Executive of the National Unionist Association; from there I walked on to the Club and wrote my birthday note to you (we shall drink your health tonight). Then I returned to the House, to learn that the fiscal amendment was blocked, went to dine with Duncannon and was carried by him to the Smoking Concert arranged for the delegates to the T.R.L. Conference, where I made a speech, which I thought was unreported, at ten o'clock at night, but was gratified to find that it had all been taken down.

Yesterday I attended a morning sitting of the Conference, an

---

[1] The extension of service with the Colours to three years.

afternoon "collogue" in B. L.'s room, the T.R. dinner in the evening and Lady Newton's reception afterwards—four speeches, two
conferences, a concert, a dinner and a reception in forty-eight
hours. It is just as well that I have trained myself to think and find
my words when on my legs, for naturally this had to be done
without notes and without preparation. I hope that what I said
will be useful and I am sure that it was necessary to say it.

At the House of Commons luncheon Seely was in the Chair
and made a graceful reference to Father's work for Imperial Union
"to whom it owed more than to any other man." It was quite
spontaneous and very nicely done.

At the Executive of the N.U. Association I was glad to find
our old L.U. friends properly installed—Agnew, J. C. Williams,
Lord Lawrence and Jardine, all taking an effective part in the
discussion, and the Committee very sympathetic to me and very
ready to act on any hint of mine, whilst the Conservative part
of it begins, I think, to feel that we are adding to its importance
and efficiency and showing it how its influence can be usefully
exerted.

16th March 1913.

Now I must return to the account of our Tariff Reform gatherings. The meetings were all large and enthusiastic, but there was
a deep and sometimes loud undercurrent of anger and discontent
in them. They gave me a great reception at each function, perhaps
most remarkable of all at the Concert, which was almost exclusively attended by working-men. If I had not spoken as I did,
I verily believe that there would have been a revolt the next day
at the Conference, and even as it was, the feeling of the Conference
that the mere repetition of the Birmingham Resolution moved by
Chaplin was not enough was so evident and so general that I
advised Duncannon not to resist additions, but to let them do as
they pleased, and contented myself with securing privately the
withdrawal of a Scottish amendment which I thought ill-worded
and likely to make difficulties. As you may believe I was not sorry
that they should make a demonstration. Father's letter read very
well. Wyndham made an admirable little speech—just saying the
right things in the best way—and we had a good letter from

Selborne. In the end, after hearing me, they carried Chaplin's resolution unanimously and then did the same by Maxse's, which censured no one but declared the adherence of the rank and file to the full programme.

I thought that I could not do better at the complimentary dinner in the evening than emphasise the meaning of the day's work and tell the Free Traders bluntly that we would budge no further. Chaplin, who was in the Chair, did not make my path easier, for he took a most gloomy view of the situation and argued at length that the position was untenable and success impossible—a view which finds only too much response in my own breast, though I do not proclaim it from the housetops. But what a lovable old boy he is and what a gallant fighter! If I had gone through all he has done during the last few months, I should feel myself excused from taking part in political demonstrations—above all when things are so unsatisfactory as they are now.

Well, I think that the net result is good. Our men are encouraged, the Free Fooders are warned and the great middle mass see that I have done all that I can for union and know that if they cannot keep the Party up to the Edinburgh line, there will be a prodigious split. It was time to let them know that I neither would nor *could* avert a split any longer unless they would second my efforts.

*18th March* 1913.

We dined with the Duchess of Somerset last night and found a pleasanter party than we had expected. Lady Halsbury and the Duchess were my neighbours—the former very lively, whilst Lord Halsbury merrily complained that he was getting old and deaf and blind. He certainly is rather deaf, but he is a fine old fellow and full of spirit.

Lady Ermyntrude Malet was there.[1] I had not seen her for many years and was very glad to meet her again. She spoke of the tremendous change in Berlin since we were there—its luxury and vice in place of the old simplicity. She says there has been a great deterioration.

[1] Widow of Sir Edward Malet, British Ambassador in Berlin when I was there as a student in 1887-8.

*19th March* 1913.

What bad news this morning! The King of Greece assassinated by a madman and, as if there were not trouble enough in Europe, the French Government overthrown by Clemenceau on a question of domestic politics in the midst of the dissensions on their army proposals and regardless of the state of the world! Poor Queen Alexandra, she is sorely tried. For the King himself I feel that he, at least, died in the hour of triumph and with the happy knowledge that the throne was more secure than perhaps ever in his long reign and the Crown Prince now the hero of the army and the nation, instead of its scapegoat. But what a tragedy it is that such a useful and honourable life should be cut short by a madman's folly. It is a perilous *métier* is that of King in these days.

Camilla Lacey,
*22nd March* 1913.

Just so far had I got when Ivy came in.

"Don't you think you had better come out now while it is fine and do your writing this afternoon?" So out I went and stayed out till lunch-time, and after lunch I went out again and stayed till tea-time; then I spent an hour with the children and then—well, then I dozed till dressing-time and after dinner listened to John Evelyn's account of his passage of the "horrid" Simplon and then went early to bed. So my letter was unwritten and now it is Easter Sunday, 23rd March.

We motored down on Thursday afternoon just in time for tea. On Friday morning Joe's heart was set on going to "the wood"; so through Lev's woods and the woods of Norbury Park we went, hunting for rabbit holes, looking for squirrels and generally enjoying ourselves.

I wish you had a more stable government in France just now. The European situation needs a strong France not too much preoccupied with internal differences. I do not think I much desire to see our Government defeated. I should like to kill the Home Rule Bill, but we should be in the most awful mess if we came in and I know that they would make it impossible for me to refuse the Exchequer, just as they have made it impossible for anyone to be successful there !

We are going to lunch at the Northcliffes'.

9 EGERTON PLACE, S.W.,
*25th March* 1913.

This morning's news is sad—two old friends passed away. Lady Dorothy Nevill and Lady Cowper, so unlike but both in their different ways so lovable. And now comes the evening's paper with Lord Wolseley's death. . . . I always regret the old Panshanger parties.

Pike Pease has organised a snap division for tomorrow at 3.45 and is, I hear, very hopeful of success. I must go and vote.

Here is a horrid bore. We had just got out invitations for a dinner on the 18th when the Speaker changes his Opposition dinner from the 4th, for which date I had already made excuses on account of the Birmingham meeting, to the 18th, and I cannot beg off again, so we have to alter our feast to the 25th.

Winston has asked Ivy to allow her name to be submitted to the King to launch H.M.S. *Birmingham* at Newcastle on 7th May. I need not say that she accepts. Very proper I think.

*30th March* 1913.

It is twenty-one years today since I was first returned Member for East Worcestershire and I think just about twenty-five since I first became a Parliamentary candidate for the Border Burghs. Twenty-five years are a long spell when they are the second twenty-five in one's life, but looking back I cannot say that I regret the choice I made among the alternatives offered to me by Father, in spite of present discouragements and occasional disappointments in the past. They have been years full of interest and activity for me and not wholly useless, I hope, to others, and taken as a whole, as I look back upon them, they have been happy years and since my marriage very happy ones. And, incidentally, my choice of a political career combined with my late marriage has given me an intimacy and friendship with my Father, which I think are rare in such a relationship, and certainly make it very beautiful and precious in our case. Give him my love and duty and my thanks for opening this life to me and for his constant help and encouragement. And for yourself too, dear Mary, accept my grateful and loving thanks for all the encouragement and support you have given to me. Dear me, what a happy and united family ours has been.

I am reading Cobbett's *Life and Letters* and find a good deal of interest and amusement in them. He was a vain, inconsequential fellow, but he was a *man*. This morning I came upon his account of the success of a speech he delivered at Winchester.

"In one part of my speech," he writes, "an attorney of the Rose party, who stood just under the window, made an attempt to excite a clamour; but I fixed my eye upon him, and pointing my hand down right and making a sort of chastising motion, said, 'Peace, babbling slave,' which produced such terror amongst others that I met with no more interruption." It sounds simple enough, does it not? but I do not think it could be recommended to beginners as a safe way to put down opponents.

9 EGERTON PLACE, S.W.,
*1st April* 1913.

The amount of speaking required of one is one of the most serious problems of modern political life. As Balfour once said to me, Democracy threatens to kill its servants by the work it requires of them—not that it means any harm, but what is play to it is death to us! By the way, the more I look at the work before my Royal Commission—and I have only just begun to look at it—the more I see how big a task I have undertaken. To think of me of all people presiding over an enquiry into currency! I do not know the elements of the subject and have already received a small library from the India Office as a foretaste of what is to come. I suppose that I shall be able to feel my way as I go along. At any rate, I shall begin by simply eliciting what the witnesses themselves wish to say and leaving cross-examination to others, though there are one or two questions to which I want an answer already. I asked Crewe, before I consented to take the Chairmanship, whether it would be necessary for us to take evidence in India and he said not. But I begin to wonder whether we can get through without going there. What would you say to that if it seemed desirable? I am very anxious to avoid it, as I do not see how I could reconcile my absence for the time required for such a visit with my other obligations.

I think I drew your attention to the very remarkable debate on Preference in the Viceroy's Legislative Conference. Fleetwood Wilson told Hewins when he was here last year that with the new representative element they were "up against" Indian feeling against the present fiscal system and he could not defend the existing state of things. He made a cautious speech on this occasion, but it is miles in advance of anything since Sir E. Law's minute. It is curious that just when Preference seems rather to have lost its interest for Colonials, it should spring into prominence in India. No doubt you saw Hewins's comments in the *Morning Post* of Tuesday, 25th

March. I really believe that that good old fellow, Sir Roper Lethbridge, has had no little influence in this matter. He is indefatigable in correspondence in the Lancashire papers, in the *Westminster*, in the *Asiatic Quarterly*, *The Times* and the Indian papers themselves.

*2nd April* 1913.

I went to the Chapel Royal Service today for the King of Denmark. Poor Queen Alexandra was there in the gallery with the King and Queen, but I hardly dared to look at her, she looked so sad.

I have had Boraston to lunch and we have enjoyed a roaming talk over the political field. Things are going better in his office,[1] but like the rest of us he cannot help sometimes regretting the old Great George Street gatherings.[2] *That* was a model Committee. As George Murray said of my Committee on a National Guarantee, "It is very remarkable. I don't remember ever to have seen one like it before. Every man knows his business!" and what is more, in Great George Street every man met to do business and for nothing else.

*4th April* 1913.

I went to the House for the Tariff Debate on Wednesday night and was very pleased with it. Tryon made an admirable speech, Hewins quite a good one and Law came successfully through a very difficult situation. The mover and the seconder on the Government side were both very poor and ineffective. Simon made a clever forensic speech—perhaps the best thing he has yet done—but the honours of the debate were on our side and the division was a good one from our point of view, the Government majority being only 83. Our men came up well for it.

*5th April* 1913.

The hoped-for but unexpected has happened. I talked my headache away![3] It hung about me all yesterday till I actually

[1] The Unionist Central Office.
[2] The offices of the Liberal Unionist organisation had been in Great George Street till the amalgamation of the two parties.
[3] At our annual meeting in the Birmingham Town Hall.

rose to speak, and whenever I tried to concentrate my thoughts on what I was to say half my head throbbed as if I had a small motor engine inside it. Any proper preparation was impossible and I had to content myself with the general idea of a contrast between 1913 and 1903 and an account of the progress made. I have looked hastily at the report and I do not think that I talked any nonsense, but it was hard work, for I naturally felt tired and I was anxious about my voice as my throat was still rough and had felt quite sore after conversation at dinner the night before. But this morning the speech is over and done with, the headache gone after a week of constant discomfort and the throat none the worse for the exertion. Altogether, my reply to Edmund Talbot when he told me on Wednesday night that I ought to chuck the meeting and go to bed has been justified. I said: "I think I want a tonic and I'll try the effect of a meeting as a pick-me-up." This morning the sun shines and though there is a disagreeably high wind, I am, as you will perceive, in a thoroughly post-oratorical mood.

The meeting called loudly for Neville and gave him a great reception and he made a very neat little speech. I will send you a *Birmingham Post*. You will realise how the meeting rejoiced in his reference to how much brothers do for each other in these days.

*6th April* 1913.

Are you not laughing over the vexation of the Germans at the descent of their new Zeppelin in France? It must be provoking to them, especially just after they had been emphasising the necessity for greater secrecy as to all that concerned their air fleet. But they are not dignified in their disappointment. Indeed, German national dignity seems to have been altogether lost for the present. Their nerves are evidently in a very jumpy state, and one must admit that the European situation is not a pleasant study. We are apparently far from having reached a solution of the Balkan embroglio. I must say that my sympathies are all with the Montenegrins. It is hard that they should see an agreement patched up by the great Powers at their expense and that they should be robbed of the prize for which they have fought so hard. I suppose it was necessary to allow that satisfaction to Austrian *amour-propre*, but I don't like it, and still less do I like seeing a British ship in the coercive squadron.

*Que diable allons-nous faire dans cette galère?* All the Albanians in the world are not worth the bones of a British Grenadier, and why we should pull the chestnuts out of the fire for Austria is not clear. It is the price of peace, I suppose, and, if so, it must be paid. But what if it does not lead to peace? Ah! What then? The strain on Russian sentiment must be very great and this coercion of Montenegro cannot be very palatable to Italian feelings, one would think.

*7th April* 1913.

Many thanks to Ida for her long letter received this morning. Your weather seems like an echo of ours. We too have a raging north-east gale and it is very cold and grey today, though not at present raining. I am glad to hear that the fame of the book continues to spread.

Your thoughts like your weather seem also closely to resemble ours. Ida writes of the blockade of Montenegro very much as I have felt. But I was wrong yesterday about Germany and her Zeppelin. The German Government at any rate appears to have acted with perfect dignity and courtesy. The general feeling here was that Seely's statement about our air fleet was very unsatisfactory and that he was juggling with figures. He spoke, too, with his usual air of ineffable complacency, which is annoying when he speaks of himself and really alarming when applied to matters of defence. The attitude, "*I* am at the War Office, so all is well," does not reassure the doubtful. I *know* that the Admiralty were much concerned about the German dirigibles a year ago, for indeed it was Prince Louis himself who told me so and of their extraordinary progress in the previous few months.

I must go down to the House today for the discussion on Lloyd George's Revenue Bill, which is the result of Bowles's success in his Income Tax action against the Bank of England. All my sympathy from past Treasury training and from present Tariff Reform proclivities is on the Chancellor's side, but I don't like helping him and the Party won't like my doing it. Perhaps I will watch the game and take refuge in silence from the embarrassments of speaking either way.

We are just off to lunch with the Leo Maxses.

*Evening*. Well, I went to the House and, of course, I did speak and my Party did not like what I said, as was to be expected. And the debate went on and finally I made a suggestion which Lloyd George was fool enough to refuse and, thereupon, I cleared out and came home to dinner, lest seeing that he had missed an opportunity he should repent and come back to me with my own proposal. At present my position is really a very good one. I have shown my desire to find a solution of the difficulties by friendly arrangement and my desire to do all that is required to enable "the King's Government to be carried on" as the Duke of Wellington used to say, and Lloyd George has refused my offer. So I wash my hands of the affair.

The most interesting feature of the debate was Lloyd George himself. He was *pianissimo*, and not merely that, he was almost incoherent. As Law said to me: "B—— couldn't have done worse!" and Father will appreciate what that means. For the moment at least he is a cowed man. Usually he is the most ready of all men for a reasonable deal and I offered him a good one. What struck me was that he seemed unable to deal with it or to grasp its meaning. He kept consulting the Attorney-General—who looked even more ill than he did—and once again the A.G. advised him badly.

*8th April* 1913.

You will have read in the newspapers Sir Edward Grey's important statement on the Montenegrin blockade before this letter reaches you. It was very badly received on his own side where this action is obviously unpopular. But from the moment that Grey became a party to the agreement between Austria and Russia which left Scutari to Albania on condition that Djakava was given up, I do not see what else he could have done. But the situation is critical. Russian opinion is growing more and more restive, whilst it is said that the forcible conversion of Roman Catholics to Orthodoxy by the Servians in the conquered territory has profoundly affected the Emperor Francis Joseph, who hitherto had stoutly insisted that he would not have war in his time. I was talking yesterday to John Baird, formerly in the diplomatic service and always in close touch with the Foreign Office. He was very gloomy. He did not see how any effective pressure could be put on Montenegro by the blockade and did not believe that the Allies would accept the proposed boundary in Thrace. He has quite lately been out there. He says the Greeks hate the Bulgarians who, they allege, massacre systematically and in cold blood, whilst the Turk only did it occasionally when his blood was up. The Bulgarians had lost all faith in Russia and were now animated by very hostile feelings towards her. There had been an extraordinary change in this respect. He spoke most highly of the Servians. They had always got all they wanted for themselves, but their spirit was extraordinary and they were quite ready to go on. He had passed train-loads of them going off towards Scutari, singing and laughing in the best of spirits. They were quite as fine soldiers as the Bulgarians. I expressed surprise at this and he said everyone was surprised at it, but he had it on good military authority. Finally, he said that he should not be surprised to see the Allies break up and Austria with Bulgaria fight Russia, Roumania and the other three Allies! And then we could not keep out of it. Germany and France would, of course be drawn in, and, if we held aloof, all our influence would be gone, the old cry of Perfidious Albion would be raised more loudly than ever, and in the end peace would be made by the union of all the Powers at our expense.

The summary of the German Chancellor's speech in this morning's *Times* is very interesting. It appears to have been a temperate and as far as possible non-provocative statement of the German case. I wish that Grey could see his way to lay down in the House of Commons the principles of British policy in a similar way. It would be a ticklish task, but I cannot help thinking that if well done it would be very useful. Our people would then know what they had to prepare for and other nations would better understand what they had to expect.

I do not wonder that the Germans are uneasy at the rise of these new Slav states. It may seriously affect the power of their ally, Austria, with her enormous and discontented Slav population. But no one, I suppose, can confidently predict what the attitude of the Czechs would be in a crisis, for though Slavs they are Roman Catholics, and it is impossible to be sure which tie would be the stronger with them. In Albania, for instance, religion is comparatively nothing and race everything, whilst in Macedonia race barely counts and religion is everything. What a "pie" the southeast of Europe is! Printer's pie, I mean!

8th April 1913.

I spent the morning (amid interruptions) searching for ideas for Hull and Lincoln. Except at election time, I *will* not again take two meetings on successive nights. No sooner do I get a sketch of an idea for one than I feel that it will "queer the pitch" for the other, and the two so jostle one another in my thoughts that I cannot buckle to either. I suppose that somehow something will emerge, for the ways of evolution are mysterious. Neville said the other day: "I envy Austen. He sits in an easy chair, reads a chapter or two of a novel, scribbles a note or two and goes to sleep—and his speech is made!" There is a superficial air of *vraisemblance* about this description, but who looks deeper would see the fierce internal pains! And in this case there are overflow meetings as large (or nearly so) as the original ones at both Hull and Lincoln. Oh—well, let us say: "Dash my wig and burn my breeches!" That is really quite as helpful as any other expletive. I should like to say with old Mr. Phipson when he played whist with my grandfather: "There's corn in Egypt, Mr. Kenrick. There's corn in Egypt." But I seem to have hit on the famine years!

HULL,<br>11th April 1913.

It is just noon and I am expecting a deputation of Tariff Reformers in a few minutes. We left London at 1.30 yesterday, got here at 6 o'clock, dined at 6.45 with the Mark Sykes and some of the local leaders. At 8 o'clock we were at a splendid meeting in their fine City Hall, containing 4000 people or more, with hundreds turned away from the doors. There I spoke for fifty minutes and then I was hurried away with Ivy to an equally large meeting in the Drill Hall in West Hull, where I again spoke for half an hour, received a deputation, and was otherwise detained till nearly 11 o'clock; then we came here and had supper, and went to bed and slept the sleep of the just on the hard beds which are the portion of the just!

And this morning I have made notes for another speech at Lincoln and since this letter began I have spoken, conversationally, for half an hour to the deputation—and, wonder of wonders, I haven't got a headache!

Now for lunch and then for a three hours' journey to Lincoln—and then to begin again.

*12th April* 1913.

I am greatly encouraged by your approval of my Birmingham speech. I felt so unfit for anything of the kind that I was more than usually discouraged about it. Now that I have got rid of the other two—the other four, I should say!—the relief is enormous. I send you reports of both. The Lincoln paper is the Radical journal, but it gives the best report of the speech, though its opening statement about the smallness of the meeting is sheer nonsense. The Corn Exchange, holding about 3500 people, was packed almost entirely with men, and the volume of their smoke—for smoke they did as well to while away the hours of waiting as during the meeting itself—absolutely obscured from my view the further end of the hall. I gave them a solid, a *very* solid hour on Tariff Reform and they listened with a pleased and eager interest that was most encouraging and entirely confirmed our view that *that* is the subject which most appeals to them—and you will see that I put it on no mean or selfish grounds and never once "played down" to them as the saying is.

At Hull I took Home Rule for the first meeting and Tariff Reform for the second. At Lincoln I reversed the order. Ivy says that, as a speech, the first Hull one was the best; and this is probable, considering how ill I still was when I spoke at Birmingham and how much fatigue I had undergone before I spoke at Lincoln.

*13th April* 1913.

I agree with all you say in your last letter about the Indian Preference Debate. You will see that I dwelt upon it at some length at Lincoln, for I think it very important. It is certainly embarrassing for this Government that the first subject to which their newly elected Members of Council turn should be the fiscal and economic question rather than, as expected, the political and administrative questions. It is, I think, clear that Sir Guy Fleet-wood Wilson, who has always been, I believe, an economist of the old school, feels that it will not be possible to maintain for long the present fiscal system in face of the intense dislike of it felt by native opinion, which now has both a voice and vote in the administration. Sir Roper Lethbridge is in high spirits. He is just bringing out a new booklet on the subject, for which I have promised to write a "Foreword." I shall have to write to him tomorrow and I will rejoice his heart by telling him what you say.

*14th April* 1913.

The European news seems rather better and at any rate Europe is more hopeful. If you read today's *Times* you will see signs of the friction among the Allies of which I wrote a few days ago—especially between Bulgaria and Servia. Meanwhile, English newspapers are recalling Gladstone's denunciation of Austria and I should say that everyone here hates the coercion of Montenegro; but most people feel that it is better that Montenegro should be coerced than that Europe should be involved in war. It is noteworthy and characteristic that when Grey made his statement the other day—in a condition of (for him) quite unusual nervousness, and when Asquith and Law had united in deprecating immediate discussion as highly inexpedient and probably dangerous—the sixteen Members who rose to support the adjournment of the House all belonged to that Little-Navy party, which always joyfully affronts the possibility of war in quarrels which are *not* our own, but always opposes any strengthening of our forces to meet the dangers they so light-heartedly provoke.

There is no doubt that Grey's prestige now stands very high in Europe. It has been greatly increased even by this Montenegrin business, for they have felt that here was a man of courage and action, who knew his own mind and was perfectly straight and resolute, all through.

I send you part of the *Birmingham Post*, London Letter. There is no doubt that Berlin wishes that Grey would "travel more," if by more is meant to Berlin. I heard that some time ago he received a semi-official invitation through a lady from the Emperor. If he had gone, it would have been represented that he had seen the error of his ways and was now seeking them. But the Foreign Office had an overdose of this sort of thing with Haldane's visit and will not allow themselves to be caught a second time. Grey very properly simply ignored the invitation. If they want to make it, it must be made with all the forms.

*15th April* 1913.

When Alfred Moseley went I hurried down to the Treasury to consult about the Secretaryship of my Commission and then went on to the House, where I enjoyed myself, as Stuart-Wortley said, in the character of *Athanasius contra mundum*, denouncing a concession which Lloyd George had made to pressure from both sides of the House.[1] It was quite wrong and he knows it. It abandons the whole principle of his Bill, which is to give legal sanction to the old unlegalised usage by sacrificing just that part of the usage which has been valuable because the occasions on which it was used were always occasions of public emergency. I made a really convincing speech and actually convinced and changed the votes of a few people, but of course in the end we were beaten by an overwhelming majority, 224 to 75, most of our men not voting and the Government Party going almost solid the other way. And with that I wash my hands of the Bill and shall vote against the Third Reading, for there is no answer to my argument that if you can afford to wait for the collection of your new taxes till the Budget is passed you can equally afford to wait for the old ones—especially as, setting aside the case of the introduction of Tariff Reform to which this procedure would not be applied, new taxes will only be imposed when there is pressing need for money to fill a deficit, or, most likely of all, to carry on a war. And yet this, which is the case of greatest difficulty and urgency, is by George's "concession" expressly excluded from the benefits of the Bill. Well, the world is wrong and Athanasius-Austen cannot set it right, so it must jog along as best it can.

[1] On the Collection of Taxes Bill.

*16th April* 1913.

I had a more interesting dinner last night than I expected—only my host, Oliver Locker-Lampson, and two other men. But one of these was a Mr. Harrison, formerly a maker of agricultural machinery, and, as such, a member of the Tariff Commission, and now business manager to Buchanan of whisky fame. He was disgusted at our change of policy, like so many of us, and felt it to be both so unnecessary and so foolish, but he interested me by illustrations which he drew from his own experience of a favourite thesis of mine, that the great advantage to be derived by manufacturers from Protection is not increased prices but greater facilities for getting capital, and, above all, production on an increased scale enabling the goods to be produced and even sold more cheaply. *The Times* has a startling announcement this morning that French shipbuilders have actually carried off a tender for three English ships—surely an unprecedented thing and a prodigious triumph for them.

*17th April* 1913.

Who would be a politician—at any rate who would be a politician who cared about getting anything done? It is heartbreaking to see how we are treated by our friends. There is another row on in Hertfordshire about a successor for Hildred Carlile, and it will be a wonder if it is settled without a split. And it is all such stupidity and folly! Why on earth select a man who is suspect from his past opinions and who is known now to be reluctant to take the Edinburgh policy as a whole, when you can get any number of good candidates who present no such difficulty? Why go out of your way to seek trouble?

And then *The Times*! Geoffrey Robinson is, I understand, still away on a holiday, but meanwhile all the mischief possible is done! Could anything be worse than their article this morning on the Indian debate? They drive the Indians back on a policy of pure Protection and lay it down *now*—fifteen years after Lord Salisbury's denunciation of the Belgian and German treaties—that all dependencies must be excluded from the scheme of Imperial Preference, lest foreigners should be displeased by our recognition of Imperial Unity! It's enough to make the angels weep! Everyone else may do what he likes with his own, but we must do nothing for fear of giving offence to somebody whom we have no chance of conciliating, however supple our backs may be. Oh! it makes me sick. How can one fight against such "backing" by one's friends? The moment that the climate seems to be becoming a bit more endurable, back veers the wind and we get these nipping frosts again. I wonder how long it will be possible for me to remain a Party man. I am weary to death of these constant troubles and should be far happier if I were quit of a Party who seem to me determined to ruin their own fortunes and most of what I hold dear with them!

I had a pleasant dinner with the "Round Table" last night— a mixed company, including two Canadians, Milner, Lovat, Albert Grey, Abe Bailey, and others. I went there determined to let them know as politely as I could that while they had done a lot of good work, they had also, in my opinion, done a lot of mischief and to beg them in future not to "crab" *any* movement which led in the direction of Imperial Union. I expect some of them did not like it and it was not exactly a proper guest speech, but I am sick of being told that this or that Round Table man, or the Round Table as a whole, does not want Preference. It is really all traceable to Curtis, of whom they have a tremendously high opinion, who is certainly very much in earnest and wholly unselfish, but seems to me to think that he discovered in 1909 what Father preached from 1895 onwards, and because he had a share in framing the South African Constitution thinks that he can settle a policy for us on every conceivable subject. If the cobbler would stick to his last, I should have no complaint, but he at once annoys and amuses me when he tells me that what Birmingham needs is a parliament for the midland counties, and he does not amuse me at all, but simply irritates me—nay rather, angers me—when, because he thinks he can get organic union without our policy, I have him flung at my head at every turn as saying that Preference is unnecessary, undesirable, bad. His business is, on his own showing, to encourage *every* movement towards Union and to discourage none.

*19th April* 1913.

I dined at the Speaker's last night and had some pleasant talk with Balfour about my Committee and other things. From the

Committee to the Indian Council debate (which Balfour had of course not seen), from that to Curzon and from Curzon to the Die-hard movement seemed natural transition.

"I do not want to revive old differences," I said, "for though the fates put you and me in opposite camps on that question, I have always thought that we were in much closer agreement than appeared to the public. But have you ever thought what would have happened since if the Die-hards had had their way then?"

"No," said he, "tell me."

"Well, in the first place I don't think the King would have given them one peer more than they could show to be needed. That, after all, is what he said to Salisbury and authorised Salisbury to tell us——"

"Oh! but Salisbury was quite wrong," he interrupted. "He misunderstood the King. The King had put himself entirely in the hands of the Government, who had treated him *abominably*, and he could not help himself then."

"Very well," said I, "then suppose he had created five hundred new peers or whatever number was required to give them a majority of one over all the Unionists in the House of Lords. Still, neither the Home Rule Bill nor the Welsh Bill would have passed through such a House. They would, of course, have carried the Parliament Bill, but then the reaction would have begun. Some of the new peers would certainly have voted against either of the other Bills, and then among so many there would have been some deaths and, though you may take pledges from the fathers, you cannot bind the sons. Home Rule and the Welsh Bill would have been defeated in their own House of Lords. What then? They could not have asked for a new creation; they would have had to dissolve!"

He observed that that was very interesting—he had not thought of it. Yes, it was probable; certainly, it was very interesting.

Oh lord! our lost opportunities! And here is Curzon now, informing us that it is urgent to "change the *venue*," to alter the issue; that the country is wearied and stale and will not be impressed by the Lords simply rejecting the Bills a second time, so we must do something dramatic. And his idea of "the dramatic" that will rouse the country to frenzy is that he should introduce into the

Lords a Bill to refer Home Rule to the people before it is sent up a third time from the Commons. What childishness!

Thank goodness Sydney Peel has withdrawn his name at Mid-Herts so I hope that we shall escape a row there. You will have seen Hugh Cecil's speech reported in today's *Times*. It is not worded as I should have wished, but, like utterances recently reported of Bob Cecil's and Derby's, is obviously a real attempt to play up and I am sure, from private conversation, was intended to be a response to my request for some sign from their side that they would meet us in the spirit in which we had met them. Hugh, I think, gave me his real mind when he said: "I not only want a Tariff Reform Government in in order that this Government may be out, but I want it to settle Tariff Reform, so that that question may be out of the way."

*19th April* 1913.

We went this morning to Agnew's gallery where they have got together a wonderful collection of Turner drawings, having bought the best part of three collections—the Taylor, Swinburne and Farnley Castle collections. They represent all his periods and are, therefore, a very interesting study, and many of the individual pictures are lovely. Then we lunched with Mrs. Clive, who was enthusiastic about everything in the girls' book, except the azure binding, and said that everyone praised it. The great Elwes was lost in admiration of the colours, which, he said, far excelled the plates in his monumental work on lilies. Mrs. Clive trusted that the girls really knew how good it was and how it delighted everyone.

From Mrs. Clive's we went on to South Kensington, where Ivy wished to see a loan collection of old English glass, but alas! the loan court where it was and much of the rest of the museum was closed to visitors for fear of the Suffragettes. So I bought some lupins and wallflowers and planted them in my garden, where I hope they will flourish.

*20th April* 1913.

It has been a lovely day. We got our motor early and were at Camilla before twelve, after a delicious drive with a spring feel in the air and every green thing bursting into leaf. Joe and I picked cowslips in the field till it was time for him to rest, and after lunching in their warm dining-room, with the windows wide open, we sallied out to a little wood close by where we picked great bunches of bluebells, a few belated primroses, cuckoo flower and anemones, till we had our basket full and a big bunch besides. The sun shone all the time, the birds were loud in song and altogether it was charming. We had a lovely time. Ivy says that both the boys enjoyed it, but she thinks the bigger boy enjoyed it most! We had an early tea with the Harrises and got back here soon after six. Diane was watching for us from the window and *shouted* to us as we came upstairs. She had felt lonely without Joe. I have just planted some more lupins and oriental poppies given me by Leverton.

*20th April* 1913.

I have written you some rather despondent letters lately, as if all the world were grey and everyone in it a "bad hat." Don't you believe a word of it, my dear Mary! The world is a very pleasant place and, if some things go wrong in it, others go right. Dear me! I *have* enjoyed myself today, and what are politics to a man who is happily, most happily, married and has two delightful children and a very united, very lovable, family circle? I don't care a snap of my fingers for them! And yet that is not true. I care a great deal, but I am seeking for words to tell you how divinely happy I am this evening. I have had a day after my own heart, driving down to Camilla with a wife who enjoyed everything with me and a small boy who prattled away the whole way down; then looking at Leverton's flower garden and then again gathering wild flowers to my heart's content, and the small boy's talk and his smile and his dimple all the way back and a glance or a word exchanged with Ivy from time to time. It is too early to go to bed and I am too lazy to work and it is pleasanter to chat with you than to read whatever novel is lying on my table. I have read two chapters and I do not even know its title, but I am sure it is trash. I read Benson's *Weaker Vessel* and finished it last night. That was not trash. It was well written and the characters were well drawn, but just for that reason it gripped me too much and took too much out of me. There is a great deal of "sensibility" in my composition. So I took down John Evelyn's *Diary* as a relief and hit by chance on a visit to Paris, 1649 and 1650, where, within a couple of pages, his intelligent curiosity led him first to go to a hospital to see an operation and then to the Châtelet to see a malefactor put to the question to make him confess a robbery. Gurrrh! It made my blood run cold and woke me up at night; but honest John Evelyn only observes, after describing the horrors, "There was another male-factor to succeede, but the spectacle was so uncomfortable that I was not able to stay the sight of another." But the good John, who was a genuinely pious body and loved besides to draw a lesson or moral from all he saw, adds, "It represented yet to me the intolerable sufferings which our Blessed Saviour must needs undergo when his body was hanging with all its weight upon the nailes on the crosse."

Apparently, if the accused did not confess, they could not hang him, "but did use in such cases, where the evidence is very pre-sumptive, to send them to the gallies, which is as bad as death."

A pleasant age! but I think I would have confessed at once, guilty or not guilty, and been hanged and done with it. What stuff to make a letter of! But it isn't a letter. It's just a talk.

*21st April* 1913.

And why does Monday succeed to Sunday—a dull day to a sunny one, a wet day to a fine one, a work day to a holiday and politics to all the delights of life? I believe Monday merely comes round to vex me, or at least to allow the unspeakable *Times* to irritate me almost past endurance. Not a word in its article today to recognise that Tariff Reformers have made sacrifices. If I were not the slow, phlegmatic, lazy beast I am, I would have given them a piece of my mind and left them to find out where and what they are without us. No, I am really too indignant for polite letter-writing.

*22nd April* 1913.

Budget day, and of all days in the year I dislike the day on which the Budget is opened most of all. For the eighth time in succession I have to follow, with my faculties as alert as I can make them, the Chancellor's statement through all its details, learn from his lips what it is he proposes to do and, when he sits down, rise in an exhausted House, which hurries out to tea, myself exhausted and thirsting for a cup of that refreshing beverage, and comment on what he has said. And Lloyd George does not make the task easier, for he is a very bad exponent of details. He can make an impassioned plea on behalf of reform as well as anyone, but he cannot state details clearly and, to my mind at least, his arrangement of his material is habitually bad and does not follow the natural and logical course.

I am very curious to know what he will do this time. He is faced with a deficit of probably two or three millions, I should think, on present taxes—it might even be more. Will he simply put up Income-tax or Super-tax, or will he try anything new? We shall know in a few hours.

*Evening.* No new taxes! By carrying forward a million from last year and by putting his estimates of revenue very high, the Chancellor just makes both ends meet. But what about next year? Well, I think the inference is that he expects an election will have been held before next year's Budget.

*24th April* 1913.

As you see, I have no news for you today. They have been trying another "snap" at the House tonight, but I do not know with what result, as I am paired. I cannot say that I am anxious to turn the Government out, for though they do a lot of mischief we have made a pretty hash of our affairs, and I do not see clearly what we should or could do.

"We dig our graves every morning," Birrell is reported to have said, "but Bonar Law fills them up every evening." By the way, the mention of his name reminds me that Wyndham said to me the other day:

"You will like to know that you changed my vote the other day on the Collection of Taxes Bill and you convinced Birrell, too. He told me that he thought your speech so unanswerable that he went out without voting"—though the Government had named their own tellers. So speeches still affect votes sometimes.

A telephone message from the House just received explains that there was no "snap." I got a private telegram from Lockwood asking me to go down and inferred there was a plot against the life of the Government, but it was only a whip for a Private Bill!

*A. C. to Arthur Steel-Maitland, then Chairman of the Party.*

9 EGERTON PLACE, S.W.,

MY DEAR STEEL-MAITLAND, 25th April 1913.

I have carefully read your memorandum. The Edinburgh policy is of course an extremely difficult one to work and unless it be worked with absolute loyalty it is merely a trap for Tariff Reformers. I think you know that I have done my best to get those who are called extremists to support that policy, and the Tariff Reform League at my suggestion promised to give its support to all candidates who advocated it. I do not know what more can be asked of them, nor do I understand the constant complaint which is made of their action. I think that they, or perhaps I should say "we," have much more reason to complain of the treatment we have received than others have to complain of our action. After all, our policy was the policy of the Party and its leaders. It is not we who upset the coach or made difficulties about it, and it is a little hard that when there has been a revolt in the Party the stalwarts who caused no part of the trouble should be singled out in *The Times* and elsewhere for constant rebuke.

As regards the details of your memorandum I do not like the way you put the third point. It seems to me the proper wording would be "The summons of a Conference with the proviso that if Food Duties are found desirable they shall be submitted to the people for the purpose of obtaining a mandate for their imposition." This puts the policy positively. Your words put it negatively. There is a great difference between the effect of the two, and a definite assertion of this support of the policy is as necessary to the maintenance of the Edinburgh compromise as is the negative condition that the new Food Duties shall not be imposed without such an appeal.

Of course the great difficulty is that our future policy is now uncertain. It is difficult to ask candidates for a pledge to support that which cannot be definitely explained to them, but everything depends on their intention. If a man desires to support the whole policy he will find means to do so if a Government proposes it. If, on the other hand, he desires to oppose it he would accept your words and yet vote against the Government when it was proposed. For my part I do not understand under these circumstances why candidates should be chosen with a highly suspicious past and a doubtful present when there are plenty of good men who are not subject to any such disqualifications.

By all means let Hayes-Fisher see Duncannon. I will send Duncannon a copy of our correspondence.

*27th April* 1913.

11.0 p.m. Why is it not Sunday every day of the week? *Such* a good day we have had, and such wild flowers we have brought back with us. At this moment we have only just finished arranging them and setting out the vases. Primroses and anemones on my chimney-piece, purple orchis, cowslips and polypodium fern on my table; and in the drawing-room bluebells, king-cups, cut-glass dishes with primroses, wood-sorrel and wild violets floating in them, and vases with big sprays full of the tender green of young beech or bunches of wild broom just breaking into blossom. I should like to sit at home all day tomorrow and enjoy them, but no such luck awaits me. We started this morning in driving rain, but it soon ceased. We drove over Wandsworth Common, Tooting Common, Mitcham Common, and everywhere where there was a bit of wild land it was ablaze with golden gorse; then through Purley and Caterham into the lovely country beyond, and so over Ashdown Forest, acres of gorse in full bloom, or young beech or birch with their tenderest green, to Crowborough where the Colefaxes have a cottage this year. We got there just in time for lunch, after a two hours' drive, and found the Garvins staying with them. We lunched amidst agitated and agitating political talk and then I said to Mrs. Colefax: "You know what you are going to do with me? You are going to take me to pick wild flowers!" And so she did. And we all enjoyed ourselves like children—except perhaps Mrs. Garvin who, I think, cares little for flowers and less for walking. Then at five o'clock, after an early tea, we took to the car again and by seven o'clock we were back here in time to say good-night to Joe. A heavenly day! That Ashdown Forest district is a wonderful country—such rolling landscapes, such skies, such flowers! It is there that I want a cottage when my ship comes home, or politics become unbearable. Who taught me to love flowers? Auntie and Father, I think, and I owe them a deep debt of gratitude for it.

*30th April* 1913.

I have learned nothing new about foreign affairs. The Bourses are nervous and everyone in diplomatic circles seems grave, if not anxious. But my French co-director said yesterday that in Paris men were more hopeful than they were two or three months ago, and the lawyer of our Russian Bank said that public opinion in Russia was less inclined to go to war about the Balkans. But his reason was ominous: "Because they think there must be war with China!"

"But do you think there will be a China?" asked B. of B., "or will it be split up?"

"Well, if they hold together there will be war, because they will be strong enough to fight; and if they break up, we think they will be a good cake," he rather quaintly replied, meaning that that would be a favourable moment for Russia to cut her slice in Mongolia. I should have thought that Russia had territory enough in Asia and that wise statesmanship would tell her to develop her resources as rapidly as possible—they are immense and as yet only scratched—and to keep those resources for use in Europe.

*2nd May* 1913.

We had a very pleasant dinner [1]—Prince and Princess Louis, Lady Kitty Somerset, Lady Meux, Cave, Mrs. West and the Benckendorffs. Winston was very gloomy about the situation. He seemed to think it almost impossible to keep Austria and Russia from going to war, but hoped that Germany and France might be kept out of it. If they, however, joined in, England must be involved. If we stood on one side, we should be hated and despised throughout Europe and should "never be forgiven."

[1] With Mr. and Mrs. Churchill at the Admiralty.

To add to all Grey's other difficulties in working for peace came "the fear of being left on the wrong side" in case it came to war. Benckendorff was enthusiastic about Grey's skill in managing the conference of Ambassadors.

Winston was very confident about our naval strength at the present time and Prince Louis told me that we were well ahead of all the nations in hydro-aeroplanes. He did not greatly fear the airships as bomb-droppers. Their use would be as scouts. For example, fog is habitually so shallow that even when two fleets are quite hidden from one another by a thick sea-mist on the water, they are both plainly visible from an aeroplane flying above them.

*24th May* 1913.

Here we are at home once more and thoroughly enjoying it! You know—indeed you must know—all we felt as we journeyed out to Cannes and with what different thoughts we return. I shall not dwell now on all you are to us. You know it by this time, or we are all of us even more coldly reserved than I think. We say little but we feel much, and you, dear Mary, have made us all your loving admirers and devoted friends. We cannot picture our world without you and we are deeply grateful that you have been spared to make life beautiful for us and to help us all now and in the future as for so many years past.

God bless and guard you, dear Mary,

Ever yours affectionately,

AUSTEN CHAMBERLAIN.

*26th May* 1913.

I found three books waiting for me on my return; the first, Lord Milner's new volumes of his speeches, with a very interesting introduction. The second, Trevelyan's *Life of John Bright*, into which I dipped hastily for the history of Committee Room 15. Trevelyan has told it practically in the words of the letters and without any comment. The third book was an album sent by George Wyndham for Father, which I shall give to Mr. Wilson to keep against his return. In it are pasted selections of the letters received from subscribers to the Chamberlain Birthday Fund. I opened it at random at this letter:

"I send you a shilling because I am very sorry for what I made my husband do. When they told me our food would cost us more I would not let him vote Conservative, as he had always done. Now we find food so much dearer and we begin to understand the foreigner does all the Englishman's work, so we hope Tariff Reform will come soon. Now my son and lots of others are going back to the Conservative side. I would have sent it before, but it takes a long time now for a poor woman to save a shilling.

"ANN GREEN (Widow)."

It seemed to me very touching and I think it is characteristic of many of those contained in the volume.

*28th May* 1913.

I attended the first meeting of my Commission yesterday morning, when we sat from ten till nearly two o'clock. Thence I went direct to my Board meeting and it was past three before I was able to get anything to eat, with the result that I did not feel particularly well for the rest of the day.

As regards the Commission, I suppose I shall see my way more clearly as we go along, but our first witness, Mr. Abraham, of the India Office, though a very clever man, proved a very bad witness. It was impossible to get a direct answer from him and after listening to his answers for nearly three hours I felt that I knew rather less than I did at the beginning.

*3rd June* 1913.

I went straight to the Club to keep a business engagement, and then on to the House of Commons, over which I had undertaken to conduct about twenty-five boys from one of the elementary schools in my constituency. They were an admiring band and I think thoroughly enjoyed themselves.

After that we had a long day at the Budget, winding up with an amusing panic in the Ministerial ranks when they found that we were in great force and assumed that we were going to vote for Snowden's amendment. They were so afraid of being beaten that they put up men to ask for an adjournment of the discussion and gave an extra day for the debate. As a matter of fact, nothing would have induced me or any of the Front Bench men to vote with the Labour Party, and I doubt whether twenty of our men would have been found in that lobby. The whole episode, however, serves to show how nervous they are. Altringham is very unfortunate for them, coming, as it does, on the top of the Newmarket result.

*4th June* 1913.

I was invited to the Crewes' dinner for the King's birthday last night and found myself placed between Lord Morley and Sir Thomas Holderness. Morley, who said he had asked to have me next him, was most pleasant and chatted so freely that I scarcely got a word with Sir Thomas. He asked with much feeling about you and Father and all the family and finally said, "Now, Austen, we are just going to break up, but if you and your wife will ask me to dinner again I will come!" So we certainly will do so.

On the other side of our round table sat Sir James Willcocks, just home for four weeks after four years' absence in India. He spoke with deep and touching gratitude of Father. He is going to Scotland, but said, "I would come back from the end of the world just to get a sight of him again. I owe everything I am to him. I had been in eight campaigns (I think it was eight), but *he* gave me my chance." It would have warmed your heart to see the light in his eyes and hear the tone of his voice as he spoke of Father.

*8th June* 1913.

Just think. All last week I never went to the House except on Monday. This week we have the Home Rule Bill (and I must attend though I shall not speak) and the Budget which I must also attend though I shall not speak *again* on that.

Is not this Marconi business incredible? . . . And if we had stage-managed the whole affair we could not have devised any scheme for dribbling out the truth in a way more damaging to the reputation of the Government.

And here while *they* are cutting their own throats and destroying themselves, *we* have been fools enough to tie our hands with needless pledges, and when they put themselves out and us in, as they are now doing, we have deprived ourselves in advance of freedom to act! Oh——!!

*5th July* 1913.

What sad news this is about Alfred![1] I feel wretched about it.

*12th July* 1913.

The last weeks in London have been saddened by the losses of friends and I think an added gloom has hung over the House of Commons which has been dull enough all the session. No one thinks of anything except when the holidays will begin and indeed we all need a long rest both of mind and body after such hard years as we have had since 1909.

Have you heard that half a dozen of my friends—George Duckworth, Percy Clive and others connected with my Treasury days—are giving Ivy my portrait by Laszlo done in the same style as Admiral Beatty's? I only hope it may be half as good-looking. I shall have to get Laszlo to do a companion one of Ivy. Thus are extravagances forced upon one! But it is kind of them and Ivy is of course delighted.

*7th August* 1913.

My Commission adjourned yesterday until 23rd October—all in good spirits and I am hopeful that when the time comes I shall get a unanimous report. Kilbracken, who was unable to attend, sent me his congratulations on the way I had handled them and Sir Shapargi insisted on proposing a vote of thanks to me which he did extraordinarily nicely. Moreton Frewen looms large as an autumn bugbear, but may be satisfied if he gets a good opportunity to blow off steam.

*10th August* 1913.

I was so tired that I slept in bed from 11 till 1 o'clock and in my chair from 3.30 till 5 o'clock! I ought to be thankful for

[1] The death of Alfred Lyttelton, a man loved by all who knew him. Asquith paid a noble tribute to his memory in the House of Commons.

a nature which can recuperate itself after this fashion.   Yet I still feel very tired and listless though not sleepy.   The fact is that politics have slipped back into the bad rut of 1903–5 and I cannot get over the disappointment of last Christmas.   I have no joy in trying to defeat the Government for though they do much mischief I have no confidence that we should do good.

*A. C. to Lord Lansdowne.*

*Copy.*

9 Egerton Place, S.W.,
*29th October* 1913.

The course of events since I last saw you had not rendered me less anxious. I saw Bonar Law three times—on the last occasion, on Monday, in company with Selborne and Bob Cecil. He then showed to us a draft of the crucial passage of his speech and very briefly sketched the lines on which he would lead up to it.

As planned by him the preliminary portions of the speech would have dwelt wholly upon our case for a General Election and upon the Ulster question, but we all represented to him that it was very important that he should make it clear that we object to the Home Rule Bill as an Imperial danger quite apart from the Ulster opposition. I must say that he received our criticisms angelically and in some minor matters agreed to meet our wishes. What the result will be I do not know, though as finally sketched we all concurred in the general line which he proposed to take.

I wonder how Asquith's and Grey's speeches have struck you. I confess that I have taken a quite different view from that which seems to be held by the Press. I thought Asquith's far the more conciliatory of the two in substance though not perhaps in form, and I was very sorry that Grey entered into any discussion of possible proposals, for I think that the more we discuss alternatives in public the more rigid will the lines of separation become. Grey's speech indeed almost fills me with despair, and I am sorry that *The Times* should seem in any way to countenance his suggestion. Surely if one thing is clear about Ulster it is that Ulster will not submit to Dublin, and any proposal for Home Rule within Home Rule is only another way of saying that in the last resort Dublin is to rule Belfast.

In my first conversation with Bonar Law last Friday morning he and I went over the ground which you had covered the evening before with the amplifications which you invited me to seek from him. In the course of that discussion I made him a suggestion which I want to put before you. It is one in which, as I have subsequently learned, Selborne entirely agrees, though I am sorry to say Bob Cecil does not.

Starting from the premises that Asquith had probably in mind the offer of the exclusion of Ulster, and that such an offer would both satisfy British public opinion and pacify Ulster itself, whilst yet leaving the dangers of Home Rule almost untouched, I suggested to Bonar Law that the only way in which we could successfully meet such a proposal would be to draw Asquith on to the lines of general Devolution. I do not for one moment pretend that I am in favour of Home Rule all round, but I think it would be infinitely less dangerous than the present Home Rule Bill even with Ulster excluded.

If such a settlement were contemplated it would surely be necessary in the first place utterly to recast the Bill and to omit some of its worst provisions such as those dealing with the Customs and the Post Office.

Secondly, it would be impossible for a Dublin legislature, even though called a Parliament, to establish any kind of rivalry with the Imperial Parliament of Westminster if it were not an isolated excrescence on our system but merely one of several provincial legislatures.

In short, though I think that Home Rule all round would be inconvenient and often worrying, I do not believe that it could be dangerous to our unity or would materially lessen our strength.

Apart from these arguments on principle, I suggest that this course has great tactical advantages for us and I think can fairly be represented to Asquith as the most advantageous for him. I assume that we cannot possibly assent to any settlement which does not exclude Ulster, but surely to alter his Bill merely by the exclusion of Ulster is the most difficult course for him, for it is the one against which the Irish most unanimously protested, and as attention has been specially concentrated upon that point, it would appear to the public and his friends to be giving us all that we had asked. It would therefore be regarded as a humiliation for the Government and a triumph for us. But as I have already said, and I know you share that view, it would indeed be but a hollow victory. It seems to me, therefore, that if there are to be conversations, and if those conversations are to have any chance of a successful result, the best plan for both Parties is to try to reach a new solution, or in other words so to change the issue that each will be able to claim that they have substantially got not indeed all they desire but the essentials of their claim, whilst in such a case a lethargic public would probably say that it did not care who had triumphed but was thankful the business was settled.

I wish you would think this over and let me know your views upon it. I entirely agree with Bonar Law that no suggestion of this or any kind should be made public by him, and indeed I urged him to say, after expressing his willingness to enter into conversations if Asquith so desired, that he thought the worst possible way to carry them on would be to shout questions from Fife to Newcastle and to hurl back answers from Newcastle to Fife. It is not therefore with a view to any public indication of our attitude that I make this suggestion, but because we ought to have a clear idea in our own minds whither we are tending, and if my suggestion were approved we ought carefully to avoid any expression of opinion that would make it more difficult of adoption.

I have seen in strict confidence a copy of a letter written by Carson to Grey on the 26th of last month. Please do not mention it to anyone, but it is highly important as Carson clearly indicates that he thinks that this is the right solution and expresses the hope that if there is a conference it may proceed on these broad lines.

Yours ever,<br>AUSTEN CHAMBERLAIN.

*Lord Lansdowne to A. C.*

*Confidential.*

MEIKLEOUR, PERTHSHIRE,<br>31st October 1913.

MY DEAR AUSTEN,

Thanks for your letter of the 29th.

To my mind, as to yours, the recent course of events has lately brought more and not less anxiety. So long as we were fighting for a General Election we were upon solid ground, but from the moment that the *venue* was changed and we began to talk about the exclusion of Ulster, we found ourselves in a quagmire. I am afraid that we may have to choose between either assuming responsibility for proposals which we know perfectly well will be unworkable and fraught with danger, or, if we will have none of them, laying ourselves open to the charge of being reckless and obstructive. It is for this reason that I have always dreaded the entanglements of a conference.

Like you, I do not take at all kindly to Grey's suggestion of "Home Rule within Home Rule" and I do not believe in a solution upon those lines. The only consideration which leads me to tolerate the idea of the exclusion of Ulster is that, if the exclusion is to be substantial and effectual, the result must—so it seems to me—be the destruction of the present Bill. It would have to go into the crucible, and would probably not come out of it alive. But I realise that the experiment would be full of danger.

As to an attempt at a solution on the lines of general Devolution or Federation, we are, I suppose, in the abstract, all of us supporters of Devolution, and should like to see Parliament relieved of a good deal of the burden of work which overwhelms it; but I hesitate to talk glibly about the adoption of the Federal principle until I really know what I mean by the words. Asquith would be sure to reply that he has an open mind on the subject, but that he is not going to let his Home Rule Bill be sidetracked while someone is hammering out a colossal scheme of Federal Government for the United Kingdom or perhaps for the Empire.

I think however that I can detect a gleam of daylight in the direction indicated by the third of Asquith's "governing considerations." This was, you will remember, that he recognised the importance of the extension of the principle of Devolution in appropriate forms to other parts of the United Kingdom, but that the claim of Ireland is prior in point of urgency and must be dealt with first. Might we not fasten upon this, and say that we are prepared to allow Ireland to be served first, but only upon condition that whatever system of self-government is granted to her must be one applicable to other parts of the United Kingdom?

This would, to use your words, make it necessary "utterly to recast the Bill and to omit some of its worst provisions."

But I am afraid that we shall make nothing of this plan so long as the Ulster red herring is being trailed backwards and forwards across the track. I should therefore not be sorry if the result of the discussion which is now proceeding should be to elicit the fact that Asquith will not offer anything which Carson can afford to look at. We might then begin again upon different lines.

There is of course a general desire in the minds of all of us, from the King downward, to avoid bloodshed in Ulster, but from all other points of view I am disposed to believe that Home Rule would be a less bad thing, both for Ireland and the rest of the United Kingdom, if Ulster were *not* left out, and if other local Administrations were to be set up for Scotland, Wales, etc., than if the Bill were to pass in anything like its present shape and Ulster to be excluded from its operation.

The situation is becoming so difficult that I have made up my mind to strike my tent here and come up to London next week. I shall hope to see you soon after my arrival, and it might be desirable that we should have a good talk before a larger conclave is summoned.

Yours ever,

L.

*A. C. to Lord Lansdowne.*

*Private.*

9 EGERTON PLACE, S.W.,

MY DEAR LANSDOWNE,                    *2nd November* 1913.

Many thanks for your most interesting account of your views. I am off to Wales for two speeches (a great nuisance just now) and only return just in time for my Committee on Thursday. I am afraid therefore that I cannot be available for consultation before 6 p.m. on Thursday or the same hour on Friday.

I assume that Carson could not touch anything short of the exclusion of the six counties and that nothing less than this would avert civil strife; and though I think that to carry the Bill with this change only (if such a thing be possible) would be little short of disastrous, I do not hesitate to say that I think it would be infinitely better than the Bill as it stands, not only for Ulster but also for southern Loyalists and for the United Kingdom.

Otherwise I think I entirely agree with you.

Asquith, as you say, would of course demand that Ireland should be dealt with first, but it must make a vast difference to his method of dealing with it if he knows that he must apply the same medicine to England, Scotland and Wales. And my *great point* is that one other parliament must be a rival to Westminster. Four or five "parliaments" may be a nuisance but can hardly be a serious danger to Westminster sovereignty. One parliament might claim equality; five could not.

I very much regret that B. L. after all said nothing of this side of the question and confined himself entirely to Ulster. I wonder whether it was accident or design.

Yours ever,

AUSTEN CHAMBERLAIN.

*Memo. of Conversation with Mr. Winston Churchill.*
*Secret.*

*27th November* 1913.

I went on board the *Enchantress* yesterday evening but I had no private conversation with W. till this morning, when we spent half an hour in his cabin. The conversation was resumed in the train as soon as we left Portsmouth and continued till we reached London. It was very frank but also very discursive. W. "orated" a good deal and there was much that was irrelevant to the present situation; but what follows is I think worth record.

In answer to W.'s opening remark I said that I had assumed that Asquith's Ladybank speech meant that he was prepared upon conditions to exclude Ulster. He replied, "We have never excluded that possibility—*never*." Of course Redmond hated it, but they were not absolutely bound to R. and he was not indispensable to them. They would not allow Ulster to veto Home Rule, but they had never excluded the possibility of separate treatment for Ulster. This was repeated more than once in the course of our talk. He added that he and Lloyd George had proposed to the Cabinet Committee on the Bill to exclude Ulster from the first. Loreburn had been particularly opposed to this.

"I asked, then," said W., "'But how far are you prepared to go? Are you ready to plant guns in the streets of Belfast and shoot people down?' Loreburn would only say pompously, 'I shall be prepared to do my duty.'"

W. said that there were three ways of dealing with Ulster:

(1) Home Rule within Home Rule, *e.g.* grant to her the nomination of all executive officers within the province.

(2) Exclusion for a fixed term—say so long that two general elections must have intervened—and then inclusion if Parliament had not otherwise decided in the interval.

(3) Exclusion till Ulster voted herself in—the Bill to provide that a vote should be taken in five or ten years.

I replied that I thought it quite useless to enter on conversations at all unless the Government was prepared at least to take the third course, *i.e.* exclusion till Ulster voted for inclusion.

He pressed a little for (2) saying that some concession on this point might make it much easier to meet Carson's wishes on the boundary question. There was a fringe of Covenanters in counties whose exclusion Carson could not ask for. They would be a great difficulty to Carson. Concession by us on (2) might enable them to solve this difficulty on terms more favourable to Carson. I did not ask what the counties were, merely saying that I thought Ulster would regard the suggestion as a trap. She would say: We are to disarm now that we may more easily be gobbled up afterwards.

W. repeated more than once that exclusion was possible as part of a compromise or settlement by common assent—even, as I understood, if the assent was merely passive. And he said more than once that though he was prepared to put down disorder ruthlessly, he did not consider that they "had the right" to coerce men in the position of Ulstermen into submission to Home Rule.

I spoke of my speech at Bromsgrove on Thursday last. ("Very important," said W. "Oh, *very* important—yours and Lansdowne's. We had them before us at the Cabinet.") I said I had better say at once that it was made—not indeed without some knowledge of my colleagues' views—but without any consultation with them. It was done wholly on my own responsibility and committed no one except myself. I had received strong remonstrances on the subject (here I rather exaggerated their number and importance) and delay was not making for peace. "If the House once meets, the opportunity for peace will be gone. You will break the H. of C. in the process. That is bad, but worse remains behind. You will break the Army, and then how is Government to be carried on by anyone at home or abroad? That is why I spoke."

He elaborated this argument, dwelling on the dangers of strikes and so forth, and on the effect in India, South Africa, etc.

I said that my idea was that the bare exclusion of Ulster was the worst and most humiliating solution for them and it did not satisfy us. The Bill without Ulster was only one degree less bad than the Bill with Ulster. So we must change the issue. They would say: We always wanted Home Rule all round. "That is true," he interrupted. "We only adopted this course because in face of your opposition it was the utmost we could hope to carry."

"Very well," I rejoined, "you would say that and I should say that this was the old Liberal Unionist policy."

W.. attached great importance to my statement that though the scheme must be "equally applicable and equally applied" Ireland might be dealt with first. I said: "I put that in to meet Asquith's condition."

He suggested that it would be well to find out exactly what delegation of powers we had in mind and whether my Federalism was or was not at all equivalent to what they had in mind. I replied that I had not thought it my business to make a plan, but why did not A. resume his conversations with Bonar Law? He would then find out whether B. L. was prepared to consider such a solution and how far he could carry agreement.

He said that A. could not make any advances at present. He did not think that the time had come. Leaders might be prepared but Parties were not. Public opinion had got to have a shock. Both sides had to make speeches full of party claptrap and no surrender and then insert a few sentences at the end for wise and discerning people on the other side to see and ponder. "A little red blood had got to flow" and then public opinion would wake up and then——! "And you must remember that we think that time is on our side. We shall give no provocation. The Ulstermen will have no excuse, and we think that public opinion will not support them if they wantonly attack."

I said that this was very dangerous. It was a gamble on bloodshed. They might win or we might win, but either way there was a national disaster. I did not suggest that A. should make public advances but why should he not at once resume his conversations with Bonar Law?

"Oh," said W., "he means to do that. He will do that. But they could not scrap their Bill before they knew that there was agreement as to a substitute."

"Well," I replied, "you asked me for a scheme. I have not got one. But suppose A. were to go to B. L. and offer as part of a Federal settlement by consent:

(1) To reserve all powers not specifically delegated.

(2) To reserve customs and excise.

(3) To reserve the Post Office.

(4) To reserve the judiciary or at least all appointments to the High Court.

(5) To give Ulster its own parliament.

I believe that B. L., who doubtless would be in consultation with his colleagues, could not refuse such an offer, and I do not think that A. would find it very difficult to draw up eight or ten propositions as to the powers remaining to be delegated."

We discussed (1) and (4) a little. W. did not raise any objection. To (2) and (3) A. had already agreed. (5) followed from our whole conversation.

W. again spoke of the feeling of Parties, that we must wait, etc., and then said (and this he repeated more than once) that we ought to be prepared to "turn the corner" by the exclusion of Ulster and afterwards we could see what more could be done, whilst I again pressed the danger of delay if anything was to be done at all. And so we travelled more than once over the same ground, but this concludes all that is important in regard to Ireland.

Incidentally he told me that A. was "supreme" in the Cabinet but very self-contained, reserved and slow to speak. "He holds the casting vote and he thinks it unfair to use it till all have spoken."

Also A. had told him that B. L. was "a much better man to do business with than Balfour."

I see that I have omitted to say that in the course of our conversation I said to him that, though I would try to find a more conciliatory way of expressing myself if our talk were more formal, he must understand that my root objection to Home Rule was to the idea of "Ireland a Nation." That was separatism and must issue in separation. He replied that that was to deny to Irish sentiment any satisfaction in the enjoyment of its parliament. "You are like the R.C. Church which admits the necessity of the marriage bed but holds that you must find no pleasure in the enjoyment of it. But," he went on, "there can be no 'nation' as long as they accept a subsidy and we can always bring them to book by withholding supplies."

The impression left on my mind by the whole conversation is that W. genuinely wants a settlement and that so do Lloyd George, Grey and Asquith, but that as to the means they have no clear ideas and that the hot and cold fits succeed one another pretty quickly; that A. means to "wait and see" and will not give his "casting vote" till the last moment.

In endeavouring to collect those parts of the conversation which dealt with the immediate situation I have omitted all else. But Winston very early alluded to the Lloyd George–Balfour negotiations at the time of the Constitutional Conference and indicated very clearly that he would like to see them renewed now. He recurred several times to the idea. I turned away from this discussion as much as possible, saying that events had not made it easier. Anyway that could wait. Settlement of the Irish question could not. I alluded to Oliver's pamphlet. If we agreed on a solution of the Irish question, we might perhaps ask some guarantees for its permanence and stability. This *might* lead to some agreement on the constitutional question. And *if* we agreed upon both of them, public opinion *might* be so pleased with the result as to demand and enforce further co-operation. But sufficient for the day was the Irish question. He said that left to themselves they could only make a very bad Second Chamber, far too radical and revolutionary, breaking with all the traditions, etc., "and then all the restrictions of the Parliament Act would have to apply and continue." The idea of fusion with an extreme wing left out on either side is obviously constantly in his mind and would be greatly liked by him.

Some allusion by him to the terms originally proposed by Ll. G. led me to say I thought Balfour's account of them had been rather imperfect. "Did you not see," he asked, "the long and detailed memorandum of fifteen pages or more which Ll. G. drew up?" I replied in the negative. No such memo. had been shown to us. "Well," said W., "there were two copies of it and Ll. G. does not know where either of them are now!"

Incidentally he said that Asquith had been fully informed of the conversations from the first but, until Crewe and Birrell were informed, had maintained an attitude of strict reserve and aloofness. The Cabinet as a whole were never informed. "How could we tell them? Some of them would have had to go!"

I said that Balfour had finally rejected the idea because the basis of the proposal was that each side should do what it most disliked to please the other. Balfour thought that the only possible basis of fusion would be that we should both set aside the contentious proposals which divided us and unite to carry non-party measures. Winston demurred to this conclusion and argued that the country would only approve fusion if by its means great controversies were settled and great national issues set at rest.

As already noted I did not attempt to follow up this issue, but sought to bring the conversation back to the present situation of the Irish question as often as Winston raised the larger problem.

A. C.

*Lord Lansdowne to A. C.*
*Secret.*

BOWOOD, CALNE, WILTS.,
MY DEAR AUSTEN, *30th November* 1913.

I have to thank you for two extraordinarily interesting letters, and for the memorandum enclosed in the first of these. This I return herewith, and also the copy of your note to Winston. Your comments upon Asquith's Leeds speech were perfectly justified, but I am inclined to think that Asquith probably believed himself to be doing exactly what Winston apparently thinks the leaders of both Parties ought to do, viz.: "to make speeches full of party claptrap and No Surrender, with a few sentences at the end for wise and discerning people to see and ponder." He was, no doubt, bound to drag in a repudiation of the idea that he would make any surrender on questions of principle, but principles are not always capable of exact definition. I am glad however that you pointed out that, in our view, the grant of *National* Home Rule does involve a question of principle to which we attach the first importance.

I have no time to comment upon your conversation with Winston Churchill. It leaves me under the impression that we have by no means done with overtures yet, and that we shall find Asquith ready to go pretty far. Meanwhile I hope we shall proceed upon the assumption that the position is unchanged, and that while we are justified in pressing for a general election, Ulster is also justified in continuing her preparations.

I should say that we were a long way from the realisation of Winston's fusionist aspirations. It does not seem to me inconceivable that the moderates of both Parties should some day or other combine, and I think Winston is right in holding that, if this were ever to happen, the country would expect a Government called into existence in such circumstances to deal with the greater controversies, *e.g.* the reconstruction of the Second Chamber and the adjustment of its relations with the House of Commons, and not merely with non-contentious measures, if there be such. If such a fusion ever took place, it would, I should think, probably be as the result of a General Election ending in "a stalemate."

We ought really to make an effort to resuscitate Lloyd George's 15-page memorandum, of which both copies have, it appears, been so disastrously mislaid. I should not wonder if Short could produce one of them.

Yours ever,

L.

*A. C. to Mr. Winston Churchill.*
*Secret.*

9 EGERTON PLACE, S.W.,
29*th November* 1913.

MY DEAR WINSTON,

"And what do you think of it all?" as Rosebery once said to a meeting. You told me that Asquith would say nothing at Leeds. I thought that dangerous, but he has done infinitely worse.

When he spoke at Ladybank we thought his offer was made in good faith and that he meant business. Selborne, Lansdowne and I, in the order named, all advanced to meet him. Thereupon he withdraws. He may say what he likes, but he *has* slammed the door in our faces. It is difficult now to think that the Ladybank invitation was made in good faith and impossible to believe that he means business. He has blown conciliation to the winds. Could I have foreseen the terms of his speech (which I have only just been able to read in full) I would have talked Navy shop with you as long as you would have cared to continue—or the fashions or feminism or anything *except* the Irish question!

Well! he has chosen, but I would not have his responsibility on my hands. He would scarcely have spoken differently if he had deliberately set himself to provoke strife. I presume he knew what he was doing.

Yrs. sincerely,

A. C.

*Mr. Churchill to A. C.*
*Secret.*

THE ADMIRALTY, WHITEHALL,
30*th November* 1913.

MY DEAR AUSTEN,

The Prime Minister has not withdrawn in the slightest degree from the Ladybank position. I am quite sure of this. Neither in fact nor in mood has there been any change.

I am sorry you take such an unfavourable view of his speech. I am confident we shall get to a settlement when the time comes. Anyhow you said nothing in your talk with me which weakened in any respect the integrity of your fighting position; and all shall be buried in secrecy.

It was a real pleasure to me to entertain you both and I greatly value the kindness which you have showed me.

Yours very sincerely,

WINSTON S. CHURCHILL.

*A. C. to Mr. Winston Churchill.*

HIGHBURY,

MY DEAR WINSTON, *2nd December* 1913.

Many thanks for your letter of the 30th. Our fathers were friends in spite of political differences and I hope that you and I can preserve our friendship through like difficulties.

Your letter of the 30th only reached me after my return from my meeting last night though I do not think I could have spoken differently even if I had had the chance of reading your words first. I can only say that if the Prime Minister's position and meaning are indeed unchanged his words were singularly unhappy. He has managed to convey to everyone the opposite impression, whilst Lloyd George's outburst is beyond characterisation.

You will see what I said—much interrupted by a defeated Socialist Councillor and a little knot of opponents organised by him—and you will understand that though always delighted to see you and Morley on any pretext I should prefer not to be asked to meet Lloyd George—at present.

Yours sincerely,

AUSTEN CHAMBERLAIN.

*Mr. Churchill to A. C.*

THE ADMIRALTY,

MY DEAR AUSTEN, *1st December* 1913.

Monday night would suit me and Morley best if you are free. Failing this, let us fix on Saturday.

The Prime Minister was much concerned to hear from me what I thought myself justified in telling him, namely how much you had been upset by his speech; and he most cordially agreed with my reply.

Yours very sincerely,

WINSTON S. CHURCHILL.

580

*Mr. Churchill to A. C.*
Secret.

MY DEAR AUSTEN,

THE ADMIRALTY,
1st *December* 1913.

I send you herewith a couple of papers I circulated to the Cabinet two years ago. They are purely speculative; but for what they are worth, you may care to turn them over in your mind. Will you send them back?

It is so easy to talk vaguely about Federalism, but few people try to face the obvious difficulties or provide answers to the first questions which arise.

Yours very sincerely,

WINSTON S. CHURCHILL.

*A. C. to Mr. Winston Churchill.*
Secret.

MY DEAR WINSTON,

HIGHBURY,
2nd *December* 1913.

Your two memoranda are very interesting. I do not altogether share your views as expressed in the earlier one on the impossibility of having an English Parliament and Executive side by side with an Imperial Parliament and Executive. I incline to think that in practice your forecast would not be realised.

But this is less important and to me at least far less interesting than the second paper. I do not fully comprehend the scheme in all its aspects and am brought up rather short by para. four which appears to propose something different *in kind* for Ireland, Scotland and Wales from what is intended for England. But as regards the powers to be devolved I see much agreement and no insuperable difference between us.

I attach great importance to the retention by the Imperial Parliament of all powers not specifically devolved (para. 7).

The real difficulty in the way of devolution is finance. How to surmount this I do not know.

All that I meant by saying that, if I had foreseen the terms of the Leeds speech, I would not have discussed the Irish question with you was that that speech was so uncompromising as to make such conversations between us a waste of time. I raise no objection to your having told or telling the Prime Minister anything that passed between us. Indeed I thought it quite likely that you would feel bound to do so.

Yours sincerely,<br>AUSTEN CHAMBERLAIN.

*Bonar Law to A. C.*

PEMBROKE LODGE, KENSINGTON,

MY DEAR AUSTEN, *2nd December* 1913.

Many thanks for your note with the enclosures, which are excessively interesting, and I read your speech last night with pleasure for I agree with every word of it and thought it was extremely well put. I have kept a copy of your conversation with Winston, of which I hope you approve.

As regards the Tariff deputation, I feel most strongly that it would be a great mistake just now when we are all saying (in my case, and I am sure in yours too, sincerely) that the Irish question is leading directly to civil war. Surely at a time like that it ought to be above everything else our business to concentrate attention on that one issue; and such a deputation, with an account of it in the papers afterwards, would simply be playing into the hands of our enemies. I do think also that it is very unreasonable for them to press me in this way. I have made it absolutely clear in two speeches that if we come into office we shall at once deal with the tariff question; and in addition to that I am doing everything in my power to make it easier to carry the Party for a tariff. For instance, yesterday I got Lord Faber to come and see me and spoke to him about the hostile leaders in the *Yorkshire Post* and he definitely promised that he would put an end to them. Whether he will keep the promise or not I do not know. As you are coming back tomorrow I should like to see you before I reply to Duncannon, so perhaps you might telephone me when you arrive.

Yours very sincerely,

A. BONAR LAW.

*Earl Grey to A. C.*
*Confidential.*

22 SOUTH STREET, PARK LANE, W.,

MY DEAR CHAMBERLAIN, *4th December* 1913.

I have telephoned to say I shall be delighted to lunch with you tomorrow Friday, 1.30.

582

Oliver will have told you I saw Haldane on Tuesday. I had just arrived from France and I called as an old friend to lament over Asquith's rude reception of your offer to consider the Federal solution.

He told me Asquith had not withdrawn at Leeds from the Ladybank position and that he, Asquith, would be very glad to discuss with one of the Unionist leaders, who could speak for the Party, preferably Bonar Law as being the official leader, the whole situation.

I had hoped to see you this morning—otherwise I would have written to tell you what I now write.

I received this morning enclosed private letter from Haldane which I think you ought to see. I have not written to B. L. as I do not know whether he is in town.

There is probably nothing in Haldane's letter which B. L. does not already know, but you will know whether he ought to see it. If you think so you can show it to him.

> Yours very sincerely,
> GREY.

*Enclosure.*
*Private.*

*3rd December* 1913.

I saw Asquith yesterday before going to Birmingham and told him of your talk. What I said at Birmingham is substantially what he thinks and it seems to me that conversation on these lines might be practicable. Bonar Law is the natural conversationalist.

*Earl Grey to A. C.*

22 SOUTH STREET, PARK LANE, W.,
*6th December* 1913.

MY DEAR CHAMBERLAIN,

I enclose copy of a letter I wrote to Haldane, and his reply. I also wrote to Stamfordham telling him I had seen you. In my letter to Haldane I thought it better not to mention your name. I had intended to tell him of my conversation had I seen him this morning.

583

I would rather like to tell Lansdowne of my correspondence with Haldane and I assume you have no objection.

Yours very sincerely,

GREY.

*Enclosure.*
*Very Private.*

5th *December* 1913.

MY DEAR HALDANE,

Can I see you tomorrow, Saturday, any time that may be convenient to you? Please telephone place and hour to Mayfair 5418.

Edward's Bradford speech is to me a very great disappointment. It does not help matters. The position as it is seen through Unionist eyes is as follows :

The Unionists have made a big concession. Although preferring the *status quo* they are prepared to swallow the Federal Plan in order to avert civil war. Instead of accepting this offer with both hands, Asquith and Grey pooh-pooh it. I cannot understand why.

You tell me that provided the Unionists are prepared to accept a Dublin Parliament with an Executive responsible to it, there is hardly any concession the Government is not prepared to make.

I am under the impression that the Unionist leaders will not make any difficulty over this. A couple of hours' talk between Asquith and Bonar Law would probably satisfy both that the essentials of a settlement exist. Every day that this conversation is postponed makes compromise more difficult. Edward Grey is altogether wrong when he says there is plenty of time. Unless an agreement is reached before Christmas the situation will become extremely anxious and difficult. It is in the power of the Government if they desire it, to arrive at an understanding on the basis of a Parliament in Dublin and Equality of Treatment for all parts of the U.K. *qua* delegated powers.

If the Government do not desire such a settlement, or do not act upon that desire in such a way as to arrive at a basis of an understanding before Xmas, you must expect to see the Unionist Forces take the field in serious earnest in January, after which the chances of any agreement, however reasonable, will be very slight.

To me as an outsider the Unionists appear to be acting patriotically. They have shown their desire to meet you, and to rescue you, the Country and the King from the position for which certainly they are not responsible.

To me it seems that Asquith has an opportunity of gaining for himself the reputation of being the biggest statesman of our time, the statesman under whose guidance a permanent and satisfactory settlement of our Constitutional Problems was reached by General Consent, or the alternative reputation of being worse than Lord North. The moment is favourable for making safe the first alternative and as no one can tell how long that moment will continue, I again urge upon you the importance of despatch.

I will keep myself free tomorrow and Sunday to see you or Asquith should either of you wish to see me.

Yours ever,<br>GREY.

*Lord Lansdowne to A. C.*

BOWOOD, CALNE, WILTS.,

MY DEAR AUSTEN,                      *7th December* 1913.

I feel that it would do me good to have a talk to you.

I wonder whether you and Mrs. Austen would spend a weekend with us here before Christmas.

The next one, or that which follows, would suit us, and if you made it Friday instead of Saturday so much the better; you would find no party.

Consider this as favourably as you can.

Asquith's last speech is I should say a *bona fide* advance, but how innumerable are the loopholes and pitfalls which lurk beneath his plausible generalities, *e.g.* "Exceptional treatment for Ireland? Oh! dear no, but we must have the spirit of equality with modifications suited to the peculiar conditions economic, social and historical of Ireland."

Yours ever,<br>L.

*A. C. to Lord Lansdowne.*
*Private.*

9 EGERTON PLACE, S.W.,
MY DEAR LANSDOWNE,                    *9th December* 1913.

I too should like a talk with you. May I come down on Saturday the 20th (the first day I have free) by the train reaching Calne at 6.15 and return by the 6 p.m. on Sunday?

My wife would have liked to come also, but we want to move the family down to Highbury on the 22nd, and as that always involves a good deal of fussy work, the double journey would be too much for her and I have dissuaded her from attempting it.

I dined with Winston last night to meet Morley. F. E. Smith also present. I declined to meet Lloyd George.

I gathered:

(1) That Morley and Winston were very averse from coercion of Ulster—Morley even more so than Winston.

(2) That Dillon had told Morley that Devlin would stick by Redmond whatever happened.

(3) That Dillon and Redmond were in a chastened mood. They might sulk a bit but would not oppose.

(4) That Morley hates Federalism. "Am I to have all these local devilments of parliaments in my country?" he cried.

(5) That there is a real danger of the Government trying to solve the difficulty by the mere excision of Ulster and attempting to cast on the House of Lords the onus of rejecting this by not accepting the Second Reading of the Bill. This idea smiles to Winston more than it does to Morley.

(6) That both Morley and Winston are seriously anxious about Asquith's delay in getting to business with Bonar Law, and that they have urged him without success to move more quickly. They begged me to write Morley a letter repeating what I said in conversation—that if we had not seen our way to a basis of settlement before the House met, all chance of agreement would be gone. Morley most heartily concurred.

Yours ever,

AUSTEN CHAMBERLAIN.

*Note.*—I dined at Winston's on 8th December to meet Morley

and F. E. Smith. This letter was written at the request of Morley and Winston to be shown to the Prime Minister.

*A. C. to Lord Morley.*
*Private.*

9 EGERTON PLACE, S.W.,

MY DEAR LORD MORLEY, *9th December* 1913.

The conversation at Winston's last night offered much food for reflection both in the present and the future, but there is only one point in it to which after a night's reflection I want now to recur.

You and Winston want Home Rule but you want it to come peaceably and with reasonable prospects of its working successfully and proving a healing measure.

I dislike Home Rule but I dislike still more the prospect of civil war with its necessary consequences, the destruction of the House of Commons and the demoralisation of the Army.

So it comes to this: that we all see serious peril ahead and we are all willing to make some concessions to avert the calamities which threaten the nation.

I believe that our views so expressed are shared by the responsible men in both Parties. But if this be so, what will be said of us if we let the opportunity of a national settlement slip by?

And this brings me to my point. There is no time to lose if anything is to be done. I quite understand the Prime Minister saying that he won't be hustled by anyone, but it is not persons but events which will hustle us all. Every day which is allowed to go by without progress renders agreement more difficult. Speeches have to be made and they tend to emphasise differences and to commit disputants still further to their own particular line. Opinion hardens and time is given to the forces hostile to a settlement by consent, to organise and agitate.

Again look at Anson's letter in this morning's *Times*. It represents a feeling universal in our Party. We cannot afford to wait till the last hour to take or to leave what may then be thrown to us.

If Bonar Law cannot tell us by Christmas that the conversations offer a fair prospect of success, our whole Party must turn out on the stump as if a General Election were in progress.

Imagine the temper in which we shall then meet the House of Commons. Nothing but the persistent and strenuous personal exertions of Law (I speak what I know) kept our men quiet last session. If the House meets again with things as they are now, nothing can prevent the destruction of the House as you and I have known it.

And finally who among us can guarantee the continuation of peace in Ireland? When feeling is wrought up to the pitch which it now is, no man can say how, when, or by whom revolution will be begun. A street brawl, a clumsy policeman, a too zealous official, a nothing may fire the train, and no man can foretell the consequences, except that all the chances of a settlement by consent are then gone at once and for ever.

What I urge therefore is that, if there is no hurrying, at least there should be no time wasted. Asquith has met Law three times, I believe. This isn't business. If our leaders proceed in that leisurely way events will take the reins out of their hands. I believe that in less than half a dozen conversations they could settle the basis of an agreement or find out that agreement is not possible. I believe that agreement is possible but I am convinced that time is working not for but against a settlement. *Liberavi animum meum.* I can do no more. If Asquith does not press on his private negotiations now, it will be in my opinion quite useless to try later—and you know I speak as one who desires that these conversations should succeed.

Yours very sincerely,

AUSTEN CHAMBERLAIN.

*Lord Lansdowne to A. C.*

BOWOOD, CALNE, WILTS.,

MY DEAR AUSTEN, *10th December* 1913.

By all means come to us on the 20th, but I will send a car to meet you at Chippenham at 5.52, so as to avoid a tiresome change on to the Calne line. I wish you would stay longer.

Where we shall be by that time Heaven knows. B. L. has not yet sent me his report of his conversation with Asquith. At this moment I can see nothing ahead but rocks—reefs upon reefs of them!

The account of your symposium interests me immensely.

I dare say you have heard of a correspondence between Grey (Albert) and Haldane, in the course of which the latter insists and not without reason that none of the Unionist leaders have yet produced anything intelligible in the shape of a Federal plan.

We are very sorry that Mrs. Austen cannot pay us a visit.

Yours ever,

L.

*Lord Morley to A. C.*
*Secret.*

FAIRMEAD, WIMBLEDON PARK,

MY DEAR AUSTEN,                              *10th December* 1913.

I am very glad to have your letter, and I showed it to the P.M. He read it with close interest, and felt both the force and good faith of it.

What you mention as having happened three times, has today happened a fourth time. *This of course is for yourself alone;* I pledged myself to that, unless you learn it from other sources. It will satisfy you that they are not letting the grass grow under their feet. The advance is not effective, and it looks as if it might never be. They recognise that terms of adjustment of a secondary kind (Post Office, Customs, etc.) might be settled, were it not for the fact which becomes more, and not less, prominent as time goes on, that what the Covenanters, Carsonians, etc. hate and loathe is the naked idea of a Dublin Parliament whatever adjustments you make about optional exclusion and the like. This is now more and more apparent to both my leader and yours.

That is the Irish difficulty. The English difficulty for Bonar Law is, as you well know, the anger that would be felt among his own friends apart from demerits of H.R. if he were to abandon a commanding battery in the electoral struggle, and at the same time accept a modification of Unionist policy in which he could not profess any faith on the merits.

For the moment, then, the bed-rock difficulties are apparent. The P.M. may naturally think that he knows better than Bonar Law what the effect of any particular move is likely to be in England and Scotland, but he is painfully aware that neither of them is equally well informed about the true state of the various forces in Ireland. Carson really holds the keys of knowledge, and I consider that until and unless we (and you too, for that matter) find out how far he believes that he can go to prevent the political mischiefs of H.R. (as he thinks them), in order to prevent the mischief and ruin of a sanguinary collision, we are really in the dark. I wondered the other night whether F. E. (if done with Bonar Law's knowledge) might be a direct channel with Carson. This is only my own notion, and may not be worth noticing.

I feel the force of your saying that "a nothing" may lead to an explosion that would fire the whole ruinous train. I am amazed that people don't see this, or else are recklessly indifferent.

The P.M. is entirely alive to the cogency of all your points. And so, no doubt, is B. L. But for the moment the signals are adverse.

If you think any day you would care for a further "free and frank interchange of views" be sure to command me. It is far the most tremendous crisis of my long life, and will prove itself the same, I fear, in yours. I often ask myself whether your father's strong and bold will could have carried the country through. We need intrepidity, though intrepidity without taking soundings and bearings might easily wreck our British ship.

Yours always sincerely,

M.

*A. C. to Lord Morley.*
*Secret.*

9 EGERTON PLACE, S.W.,

MY DEAR LORD MORLEY, 10*th December* 1913.

Your letter is most interesting but it is not reassuring.

I had heard from B. L. that there was to be another meeting this week. I counted it (perhaps wrongly) as the third.

I agree with you that Carson very largely holds the key of the position, and the only reason I write again is to say that in the conversations I have had with him, as well in letters to others shown to me in confidence, he has proved himself most moderate and deeply sensible of his heavy responsibility.

I believe him to be one of the factors and perhaps the most

important factor making for peace, and if the P.M. gets a different idea of him at second-hand I think that they ought to meet. I venture to suggest that the P.M. should ask B. L. to bring Carson to the next or an early meeting. I believe that the P.M. will find the solution of Carson's difficulties if he can accept the formula that Ulstermen shall not be treated differently from other citizens of the United Kingdom.

One other point; the P.M. has chosen a conversation *à deux*. This puts a fearful strain on Law. It is quite true that many, indeed most, of our Party will be furious if he surrenders what they consider a winning position. To put on him the undivided responsibility for the negotiations is perhaps unwise. Just consider this. But above all make no mistake about Carson's object. He wants peace—on terms of course, but on terms which I believe the Government could accept.

Yours very sincerely,

AUSTEN CHAMBERLAIN.

*P.S.*—If it is thought well to follow up either of these ideas, please have them started spontaneously and not as coming from me. I should have no objection to making them directly to B. L. but I should not like the P.M. to present them as my suggestion. For the moment the Carson point is the important one.

*Lord Morley to A. C.*
*Secret.*

PRIVY COUNCIL OFFICE,<br>WHITEHALL,

MY DEAR AUSTEN,       *11th December* 1913.

I am glad to have your letter, which I showed to the P.M. He sees all your points, and the force of them.

After my conversation with him yesterday afternoon he wrote to Carson (with whom he is well acquainted), suggesting a direct interview. The reply had not been received when I left him before luncheon.

I am not sure that I grasp what you call the Carson principle, that "Ulstermen shall not be treated differently from other citizens of the United Kingdom." Like all the other principles, it becomes vague when you try to resolve it to chapter and verse.

I will let you know, if I am acquainted with the Carson reply.

Yours very sincerely,

M.

Your remark on the ineffectiveness of conversation *à deux* is extremely just.

*A. C. to Lord Lansdowne.*
*Secret.*

9 EGERTON PLACE, S.W.,

MY DEAR LANSDOWNE,                    *11th December* 1913.

I have not heard anything as yet from B. L. but from the other side I learn that "the advance is not effective, and it looks as if it might never be. They (*i.e.* B. L. and A.) recognise that forms of adjustment of a secondary kind (Post Office, Customs, etc.) might be settled, were it not for the fact which becomes more, and not less, prominent as time goes on, that what the Covenanters, Carsonians, etc. hate and loathe is the naked idea of a Dublin Parliament whatever adjustment you make about optional exclusion and the like."

This letter is in reply to one I wrote to the eldest of my companions [1] at Monday's dinner urging that this was no time for "wait and see" and that if a basis was not arranged before Parliament met it could never be arranged at all. I did not volunteer but was *begged* by them to send it in order that it might be shown to A.! Apparently they thought that such a letter from me would strengthen their hands.

My correspondent continues: "The P.M. is entirely alive to the cogency of all your points. And so, no doubt, is B. L. But for the moment the signals are adverse," and he throws out as his own idea the suggestion that F. E. "of course with B. L.'s knowledge" might be a direct channel with Carson.

I have replied that Carson feels his responsibility and is most sober and reasonable; that he wants peace—on terms of course, but on terms which I believe that the Government could accept;

[1] Lord Morley.

and I have suggested that if A. has got any other opinion at second-hand he should ask B. L. to bring Carson to an early meeting. I have added that I should not mind making this suggestion direct to B. L. but if A. makes it, he must produce it as his own and not as coming from me.

Lastly I have said that I believed A. would find the key to the solution of Carson's difficulties if he could accept the principle that Ulster was to be treated like the other parts of the U.K.

The real difficulty here is that my correspondent hates what he calls "all these devilments of local parliaments in my country" and says he thinks he would have to resign if Federalism or Home Rule all round were to be proposed!

What a jumbled world it is!

I will bring these letters down to you. My correspondent begs me to command him if I think another conversation would be useful, but at present I have nothing more to say publicly or privately—to them, I mean. I have more for your own ear. I wish we could meet earlier, but I have to go to Manchester on Monday and my Commission sits on Wednesday, Thursday and Friday next week.

I will look out for your car at Chippenham.

Yours ever,

AUSTEN CHAMBERLAIN.

*Lord Lansdowne to A. C.*
*Private.*

BOWOOD, CALNE, WILTS.,
12th December 1913.

MY DEAR AUSTEN,

Your letter of yesterday is most important.

I hope that you have by this time seen Bonar Law's note of what passed between him and Asquith when they last met. He is, I suppose, sure to come to London after his Carnarvon meeting, and I hope you will give him the information which you have been good enough to impart to me. Meanwhile your language ought to disabuse your correspondent's mind of the idea that the difficulties in the way of a settlement are due entirely to the objections of "Covenanters, Carsonians, etc."

I do not at all like the proposal that F. E. should be brought

2 P

in as an intermediary. Our relations with Carson are of a kind which make the employment of an intermediary quite unnecessary.

I do not know the extent to which Carson will allow himself to be influenced by the attitude of the Unionists outside Ulster. They are beginning to get their heads up, and I should not wonder if we had serious trouble with them if a transaction of which they did not approve were to be forced upon them. Even if Carson were to be invited to an early meeting, I doubt whether he would be in a position to accept terms on behalf of the outside Unionists. I dwell upon this point because I notice that you expressed your belief that the key to the solution of Carson's difficulties might be found in the acceptance of the principle that Ulster is to be treated like the other parts of the United Kingdom.

I do not think Bonar Law likes "these devilments of local parliaments" much better than your correspondent. I have always myself felt that no one has yet worked out a scheme for the establishment of such local legislatures, and unless we have definite ideas as to how they are to be constituted the proposed reservation as to the equal treatment of other parts of the United Kingdom would leave everything quite in the air. It must be remembered that Asquith has told us twice over that he refuses to standardise Home Rule. If Ireland is to be served first (and this, I take it, would have to be conceded), and if she is to be given a special brand of Home Rule suited to her social, economic and historical peculiarities, the reservation that Ulster is to be treated like other parts of the United Kingdom will not afford us any real protection.

Hoping to see you next week.

I am,

Yours ever,

L.

*Lord Morley to A. C.*
*Private.*

FLOWERMEAD, PRINCES ROAD,
WIMBLEDON PARK,
MY DEAR AUSTEN,                                    20*th December* 1913.

This mystification about your letter is the most desperate I ever knew. So far as I am concerned, I showed your letter to the P.M., to Winston, and to nobody else. I made a copy of

594

my reply to you with my own hand, not even trusting my secretary with it. That the leakage as to the letter—of which I saw signs in the *Irish Times* three or four days ago—came from you, I never dreamed, any more than I could have assigned it to Downing Street. It is extremely perturbing, because though several people knew about the meetings, very few indeed can possibly have known about the letter. One ordinarily asks in such a case *cui prodest*; but I don't know who gets any good out of this particular divulgation except the newsmongers. I shall be truly sorry if it causes you an atom of embarrassment.

The substance of the leakages comes to nothing discreditable or dangerous to anybody. But they are troublesome and may be mischievous in a situation so delicate for the half-dozen men who are charged with the handling of things. I found Winston violently disturbed at the dinner having got out, but this particular detail of your letter to me is much more provoking and mysterious.

The prospect is about as ugly as it can be.

Yours always sincerely,

M.[1]

[1] I cannot recall the incident to which this letter refers, but there had evidently been some allusion in the Press to one of my letters to Morley—probably to that of the 10th December.

my reply to you with my own hand, not even trusting my secretary with it. That the leakage is to the letter—of which I now fight in the Irish Times three or four days ago—came from you, I never dreamed, any more than I could have assigned it to Downing Street. It is extremely perturbing, because though several people knew about the meetings, very few indeed can possibly have known about the letter. One ordinarily asks in such a case no question; but I don't know who gets any good out of this particular divulgation except the newspapers. I shall be truly sorry if it causes you an hour of embarrassment.

The substance of the leakage seems to nothing discreditable or dangerous to anybody. But they are troublesome and may be this historic in a situation so delicate for the half-dozen men who are charged with the handling of things. I found Winston violently disturbed at the dinner having got out that this particular detail of your letter to me is such there are provoking and mysterious.

The prospect is about as ugly as it can be.

Yours always sincerely,

M.[1]

[1] I cannot recall the incident to which this letter refers, but there had evidently been some disturbance in the Press or some of my letters to Morley—probably to that of the 10th December.

# 1914

"AH 1914! 'Oh! that a man might know the end of this year's business ere it come!' I see not a patch of blue sky—not for the country as you rightly put it." [1]

Gloomy indeed was the prospect at the beginning of 1914. The conversations between Asquith and Bonar Law were continued but ended in failure to reach agreement. Carson could accept nothing less than the total exclusion of the Six Counties; Asquith was unable or unwilling to concede as much. Relentless Fate, as in a Greek tragedy, seemed driving us all to a catastrophe. A blunder, as I had foretold in one of my letters to Morley, put the spark to the powder, and the country was shocked and alarmed by the so-called "Mutiny" at the Curragh. The story of that event is told here breathlessly, as I learned it, almost from hour to hour. It needs to be checked by the accounts given by others. Something of the passion of those months and of the quickly-alternating moods of hope and despair of any peaceful settlement seems to me still to live in these daily chronicles, hastily written in the tumult and confusion of the time. The actors were in the grip of forces stronger than themselves, whirled round and downwards like frail craft caught in the maelstrom of inexorable fate.

In January my father announced that he would not again stand for Parliament, and by his urgent wish I secured the permission of my East Worcestershire supporters to leave them in order to succeed him in West Birmingham. A connection of twenty-three years was thus brought to a close. They had taken me a young and untried man and throughout had shown me the most generous confidence and kindness. I have since been as fortunate in West Birmingham where the tradition of my father is still a living force, but I felt the separation from my old friends deeply at the time.

The letters cease on the return of the family from Cannes early in May. My father died on 2nd July. A month later we were at war with Germany. When that struggle ended four years later, we were in a new world.

---

[1] Extract from letter from Lord Morley dated 2nd January 1914.

*Bonar Law to A. C.*

PEMBROKE LODGE,
EDWARDES SQUARE, KENSINGTON,

MY DEAR AUSTEN,                          *8th January* 1914.

I am very sorry that I will not have a chance of seeing you before your meeting, because I had hoped that you would be back in town and that we would have a talk soon, and for that reason I had not written you.

The easiest way of letting you know how matters stand is to send you the enclosed letter[1] which I forwarded to Balfour yesterday, and the enclosures[1] referred to in it. The enclosures are the only copies I have, so you might please send them back to me after you have read them.

It is really very difficult to know what I ought to say at Bristol, but if, as I feel sure will be the case, there is no further interview with Carson, and nothing new has happened, my present inclination is to say that there have been conversations, but that no proposal has been made, and that I am sorry to say I see no prospect of a settlement. I suppose, however, I should not be free to say that without telling Asquith that I meant to do so. I shall write you therefore on Tuesday if I can, but in any case not later than Wednesday, telling you exactly what I propose to do. I should be much obliged if you would tell me whether you think what I have suggested is the best that I can do at Bristol.

I was of course not surprised to see the news of your father's retirement. I hope he does not feel it, though I am sure he must to some extent.

Yours very sincerely,

A. BONAR LAW.

*P.S.*—I enclose a communication which I have received from Lord Roberts, which taken in conjunction with your account of the interview at the dinner with Morley seems to me amazing. What do you make of it?

[1] I have no copy of these.

600

FOLKESTONE,
*23rd January* 1914.

Our correspondence has begun very badly on my side this year. I have not dared to put a number to the hurried scraps I have written to you. And now another day has passed and still no letter to you written. I have been busy all day and done nothing.

Ivy says she sent you the *Daily Telegraph* report of the Southampton speech. It was not a good speech—woolly and badly put together—but it was saved from failure by the interrupters, who gave me some good openings and livened the thing up. Its chief result so far is that Hagenbeck's manager tenders his thanks "For your allusion to the Wonder Zoo in your telling speech of yesterday" and places a box at my disposal whenever I like to visit it!

The meeting itself was a tremendous affair—a vast skating rink, with a lofty narrow gallery on one side, from the middle of which I spoke to an audience of seven or eight thousand people, a big meeting as it were to right of me, and a big meeting to left of me, and a fearful sputtering gas lamp just in front of me that seemed to be repeating my words in morse signals all the time. They said that they had not seen such a meeting in Southampton since Balfour spoke just after the Dogger Bank incident, when everyone went expecting a declaration on Tariff Reform and got only high diplomacy. Young Sidney Herbert spoke well and he and Lady Herbert were greatly pleased with the message from you and Father.

9 EGERTON PLACE, S.W.,
*27th January* 1914.

I got here at lunch-time and have been busy ever since. First letters. Then at 3.15 Horace Plunkett with a plan for settling the Irish difficulty—Ulster to consent to try Home Rule for ten years and to vote herself out at the end of that time if she did not like it! This being accepted as a basis of compromise, a conference of Irishmen might then discuss "details." The futility of well-meaning goodness!

Tomorrow I have to face my East Worcestershire friends and I don't like the job and shall be glad when it is over. Thursday

I stew over Skipton and on Friday I go there, returning by a night train, without any sleeping accommodation, so as to get down to Folkestone in good time on Saturday.

All reports agree in saying that the Irish question is beginning to stir the voters, but I feel talked out on it and find it extraordinarily hard to get a line for another speech. By the way, the Southampton local paper was enthusiastic about my performance; but though pleased that they should be so, I know better. It was *not* good! I may sometimes think that good is better, but I know *bad* when I hear myself doing it.

Arthur Lee pleased me with a story of his experience. He had spoken at Ipswich—rather well as he thought—and two working-men of the Committee congratulated and thanked him.

"I do a bit of speaking myself, Sir," one of them said, "and I shall make free to use some of those witticisms. Indeed, the 'ole speech was 'ighly ludercrus if I may say so!"

HARBORNE,
*29th January* 1914.

I got through my East Worcester farewell yesterday—very painful to them as to me, though they were in some sort prepared for it. I dwelt upon the importance of keeping Birmingham straight and on its need for help now that our two great men[1] were withdrawing, and I spoke of our family's obligations to the City and its claims on me. They listened sympathetically and showed that they felt there was much to be urged on their side also. Then I told them frankly that it was Father's earnest wish that I should succeed him and that he would be deeply grieved if I were to refuse, and this they felt to be unanswerable. Several of them spoke very nicely and they passed the resolution which you will see in *The Times*. I spoke a few words of thanks in reply and told them that Beatrice[2] would continue to work with them. I wish B. could have seen how their faces brightened. It was the only happy moment of a painful interview. To me the strain was so great that I came out after a short hour with them with a racking headache.

---

[1] My father and Jesse Collings.
[2] My eldest sister.

I suppose I have done right. At any rate, with Father's strong feeling before me I could not do otherwise. But had he not felt as he does, I could not have brought myself to this decision. I feel as if at fifty I had got to begin life again, and the pain of Father's parting from West Birmingham is enhanced by the pain of my own parting from East Worcestershire. They have been so good to me, and in its way my association with them has been as remarkable as Father's with Birmingham. Well, I am glad it is done since it had to be. I must, as soon as I can, publish an address to the East Worcestershire electors.

I am all right again this morning. I got my speech for Skipton roughed out in the train yesterday morning and have the rest of the day to work it up. I think the line is all right this time, but it is as heavy as the cakes that B. used to make in her toy stove! I want another "Wonder Zoo" but cannot hit upon one.

General Botha's short way with Labour leaders [1] has fluttered the Liberal and Labour dovecotes here considerably. Poor anaemic Liberalism did not expect such Russian despotism from its protégés and whines and yaps where it cannot bite. I doubt if Botha has been altogether wise about the deportations, but I smile over Liberalism's discomfiture.

9 EGERTON PLACE, S.W.,
*31st January* 1914.

What a life! I left Birmingham at 12.20 yesterday. Luncheon basket in the train. Arrived at Leeds at 3.12, left at 3.30, reached Skipton at 4.30, cup of tea at the Castle and changed clothes, dinner by Walter Morrison to two or three hundred of the workers at 5.30 (!), meeting at 7.30, spoke for an hour (good meeting, good speech) meeting over before 9.30; to the Castle, changed again, supper; left at 11 o'clock by train; no sleeping accommodation, but got a carriage reserved, too short however to lie down; was waked three times to show my ticket and, finally, being waked again at 4.30 at Bedford, could get no more sleep;

---

[1] The South African Government deported ten of the leaders of the railway strike including the President of the Trades Federation and the Secretary of the Railwaymen's Society.

train late—got here at 7 o'clock; coffee, letters, papers, bath. And now I am off by the 11 o'clock to Folkestone.

Well, it was a capital meeting—3000 in the hall and 2000 applications for tickets refused for want of space. Most cordial message sent to Father by the meeting through me. And as I say, I think that this time I made a good speech.

FOLKESTONE,
*1st February* 1914.

At Walter Morrison's dinner Lord Wharncliffe, who was to be Chairman of the meeting and is a good fellow, leant across Morrison to say to me :

"Are you going to say much about Tariff Reform tonight ?"

"No," I said, "as a matter of fact I am going to talk almost entirely about Ulster."

"That's all right," he said, "because I was going to say that they are very full of work here just now and don't care much about Tariff Reform."

"You tempt me," I rejoined, "to try whether I can't make them care about it, and if it were not for the great importance of Ireland at this moment I would do so."

Well, I began my speech with the deeds of the Government, then spoke of the work which lay before the Opposition—the restoration of the Constitution, land reform and Tariff Reform—and at that a great cheer went up. It was all nonsense about their not caring! Their paper, the *Yorkshire Post*, was against it; their great local man, Walter Morrison, was against it; and I dare say their "influential people" as well; but they were obviously interested and could easily be made very keen about it.

I am sorry there is no good report about the speech. *The Times* has, I think, the best. As I told you, I thought it was a good one, with a well-knit argument, well delivered, and a capital audience to speak to. A Mr. Whittaker Thompson, candidate for West Bradford, proposed and Major Roundell, candidate for Skipton, seconded a vote of thanks to me. Both spoke well and nicely. One of them made himself the spokesman of the meeting in sending a special message of affectionate regard to Father through me. As I returned thanks and acknowledged their kindness to me, a voice called from the middle of the hall, "Don't forget about your Father," and they all cheered again. It was so genuine and so heartfelt. It was delightful to witness.

FOLKESTONE,<br>
5th February 1914.

I need not give Father any account of our talk at Law's, as we were all agreed upon the course which was subsequently approved by the Shadow Cabinet at Lansdowne House this morning. Law opened the proceedings by giving an account of his conversations with Asquith.

They first met on 15th October (before Ladybank). The conversation was general. The interview ended with Asquith summarising Law's position as being that, if Ulster were excluded and if proper precautions were taken to protect the Loyalists of the South and West, Law would be willing to consider a settlement.

They met again on 7th December after Ladybank. They went over much the same ground and at the end of the conversation Law asked what would be the next step. Asquith replied: "The next step will be in a few days I shall make this proposal to the Cabinet. I do not know if my authority will be sufficient to carry it there, but I think it will. There remain the Nationalists, but without us they are helpless. You may expect to hear from me again in a few days."

Law, however, heard no more from Asquith. Then came the Leeds speech, which we all interpreted as a banging of the door. Then at Manchester Asquith reopened it. There followed one more interview, but in this Asquith had gone back altogether from the exclusion idea and only talked of Home Rule within Home Rule. Meanwhile, he had opened communications with Carson, of which C. would tell. Law had only to add that, on reading Birrell's speech with its allusions to the offer which had been made and refused, he had written to Asquith, calling upon him to prevent his colleagues from alluding inaccurately (or accurately) to secret conversations.

Carson had seen Asquith twice, I think, and had had three letters from him and a very important memo. At the first meeting they had discussed some details of exclusion and the steps which might be taken to make the Bill more palatable to the Loyalists of the South and West.

This was followed up by a letter from Asquith enclosing the memo.  A. explained here or subsequently that he had so far consulted no one except Simon and Crewe.  He had had no communication with any of the Nationalists.  He particularly said that he made no offer and that he was not in a position to make one.  But he submitted suggestions for meeting the case of Ulster which he more than once described as "veiled exclusion."  Their main features were: the Post Office and Customs to be retained by the Imperial Parliament, Ireland to have some financial compensation; factory legislation and administration and education to be managed by Ulster, I think, under the supervision of the Imperial Parliament.  The police are reserved for six years; if then handed over, Ulster could have its own police.  All legislation and taxation affecting Ulster to be subject to the proviso that if a majority of the Ulster members objected to it, it was to have no effect in Ulster until it had been submitted to and approved by the Imperial Parliament.  An Imperial High Court to be established in Ireland, to which anyone conceiving himself aggrieved might appeal against any legislation or executive action.

Carson replied that neither he nor Law thought there was any use in submitting these suggestions to their respective friends, as Ulster would not accept and they could not advise any solution short of exclusion.

Asquith sought another meeting with Carson.  In this he said that he did not know whether he could carry these suggestions, but he thought that he had gone a long way in them and that if he were in a position to put them forward they would do a great deal to influence public opinion and to meet the objections felt by moderate people in the country—in fact, he intimated that they would put public opinion on his side.

Carson repeated his objections.  A. then said that he thought he was entitled to ask for C.'s suggestions.  C. replied that he was there to listen, not to make suggestions.  It was useless for him to make any suggestions, unless the principle of exclusion was accepted.  Then he would give any help in his power in dealing with details and ways and means.  Asquith finally closed the correspondence by taking note of what Carson had said, adding that he hoped later to communicate with him again. Carson had heard no more from him.

On this we decided that, immediately the Address had been moved and seconded, Long should move an amendment to the effect that it would be disastrous to proceed further with the Home Rule Bill without a General Election. Asquith will doubtless follow and then publicly make an offer more or less on the lines already indicated. Law in turn would follow him, perhaps moving the adjournment of the debate, but not till he had given a clear lead to our men and the Press that we thought the terms in-admissible. We should in any case carry on the amendment till Thursday, when we might divide. Thus we shall plunge *in medias res* and, abandoning the ordinary first-night fencing, mark the exceptional nature of the crisis by exceptional action. There is, however, an exact precedent in '84, when Bourke moved an amendment in the same way on Egypt by Stafford Northcote's desire.

The Lords will follow exactly the same course. Law would have liked me to move the amendment, but felt that he could not pass over Long. As it is, I shall speak later—possibly even follow Asquith instead of Law.

We further appointed a Committee to consider in all its aspects the proposal to force a dissolution by an amendment of the Mutiny Act.

The candidate at Skipton writes that a mill-hand said to him: "If you get that there Austen here for three more Fridays, we've done t' trick!"

FOLKESTONE,
*6th February* 1914.

I was so full of my budget of news last night that I scarcely answered your letter. Yes, I do not really doubt that the decision to go to West Birmingham is right. Everyone seemed to expect it and everyone seems glad of it, except the East Worcester people, and even they, who do not recognise the special claim of Birmingham, do recognise the binding force of Father's wishes. I ought to be of more use in Birmingham than I could be in the county, and Birmingham, which for sixty years or more has been represented by Bright and Father, feels the need for one man at least of the front rank among its members. Neville pressed this upon me strongly and I think that there is much force in his argument that since they have been without Father's speeches they have felt "out of it"—they who were accustomed to feel that they were the hub and centre of all that was most important in the Unionist Party.

9 EGERTON PLACE, S.W.,<br>
8th February 1914.

The Jewellers' Dinner went off very well last night. I spoke briefly and to the last was uncertain what line I should take. However, I got off some thoughts on the Parliament Act and on Foreign Affairs, which I have long had a desire to express. I think that they went well and that they possessed good sense and some originality. Incidentally, being urged thereto by Gwynne, I emphasised our loyalty to the Triple Entente. For the rest I pleaded that the Secretary of State should deal more frankly with the House and with the country. I have always thought that the secrecy preserved in the Morocco crisis was dangerous, for had war broken out when it threatened most seriously, it would have found public opinion here (though not, I hope and believe, our Government or our Army and Navy) wholly unprepared for such a possibility. It is indeed a strange thing that the oldest and most democratic of European Parliaments is the only one to which the Foreign Minister of his country does not annually and as a matter of course give an account of the policy and position of the nation and of its relations with other countries.

9th February 1914.

I am just back from Law's dinner. Balfour was there, greatly to my satisfaction.

We had an unusually interesting conversation about our plans and proceedings across the table after dinner and, I am inclined to add, as useful as it was interesting. We were all agreed in essentials, and in the end all agreed on details also; but I thought at one point that a suggestion of Balfour's involved too much finessing and was, therefore, bad and might besides compromise our position with the public and, at another, that Bonar Law, discussing a remote contingency, was too ready to think that, if the unexpected happened, the game was up. I have not the time, and it would not be worth while if I had, to go into all the details, but you will get an idea of my line if I tell you that I said to Balfour: "Let it be a *challenge*, not an invitation (to Government). Then I don't mind." I protested against the idea that the House of Lords must pass the Bill if Ulster were excluded. I urged that they should even then reject the Bill, refusing to take any responsibility for its other evil consequences. If the Government once proposed to leave out Ulster, they *could* not coerce her into submission to Dublin. The Lords might reject the Bill and, if it were passed over their heads by means of the Parliament Act, they might intimate their willingness to pass an Amending Act excluding Ulster before the Bill came into force. But they ought not to allow themselves to be made assenting parties to anything like the present Bill, even if Ulster were excluded.

*10th February* 1914.

There is nothing to add before I go down to the House, unless it be to note a statement in the *Morning Post* that the Royal Irish Constabulary are discontented and that there is a movement among them to refuse service against Ulster on the ground that they were not enlisted and are not paid to take the risks of fighting a drilled and organised army. I was asking Carson about them last night. Supposing the Army Act were so amended that the Government could not use troops in Ulster, could they concentrate the R.I.C. there and use them? C.'s reply was threefold: first, that there were not enough of them; secondly, that they wouldn't do it; and thirdly, that the Ulstermen would love to fight them for they were all Catholics! In answer to another observation of mine that the Government were at times, at any rate, calculating on an explosion in Ulster taking the form of riot instead of revolution, Carson said that he could guarantee that they should be disappointed in that expectation. The discipline was admirable and the need for it completely understood.

11*th February* 1914.

Yesterday was certainly more interesting than the opening day of a new session usually is, but, as generally happens, public expectations were disappointed. We were all convinced that Asquith would at once announce the proposals for dealing with the Ulster difficulty on which the Government had decided. He did nothing of the kind. The first half of his speech was a weak, rambling and undignified defence of the Government's past and almost technical criticism of the amendment. It was only in the latter portion that he came to business, when, changing his tone and speaking very quietly and solemnly, he admitted the gravity of the situation, and for the first time admitted also that the obligation of taking the initiative rested with the Government. He said that he would use "no last words" and would exclude no possible solution; but, having said that, he gave no further indication as to what was in the mind of the Government beyond dwelling on the fact that any concession offered must be the basis of peace, not merely in Ulster but apparently over the whole field of Irish government. The passage was very obscure and no one knew exactly what interpretation to place upon his speech as a whole.

Bonar Law had come down in the full expectation that he would make to the House of Commons the proposals for Home Rule within Home Rule which he had foreshadowed in conversations with Carson, and had spent a morning preparing a careful reply to these propositions. He was entirely taken aback by Asquith's line and decided not to follow him. Carson pleaded that he was unwell and not fit to speak at all that day, and the result was that I, who had supposed that I should not speak at all till today or tomorrow, and therefore, had prepared nothing, was thrust into the breach and rose to speak a little after ten o'clock. I did not like the position, for I felt that I was falling between two stools. The arrangement gave me either too little or too much time for preparation. I felt that I could have followed Asquith at once with more effect, and I should have done so, had I been the leader; whilst if I was to prepare a reply in the quiet hour which I had to think it over before dinner, it was not sufficient for the purpose.

I think Bonar Law made a great mistake in not himself following

Asquith. It is the second into which he seems to have fallen in this affair. The first was the failure to follow up at subsequent interviews Asquith's parting statement at their second conversation that he should at once lay before the Cabinet a proposal for the exclusion of Ulster and that Bonar Law might expect to hear from him in a few days. They did not meet again for six weeks, and then Bonar Law allowed Asquith to ignore altogether what had previously passed and to put the discussion on entirely different lines. It seems to me that it was a grave error of judgment not to bring Asquith to book at once and not to break off there and then if he announced that on reflection he had been unwilling to propose, or the Government to accept, the solution which he had foreshadowed.

As regards yesterday's debate, the result of Bonar Law leaving Asquith's speech unanswered was exactly what I had feared. Everyone passed out into the lobby without guidance and every tongue was set wagging and every head speculating as to what was the meaning of the speech they had just heard. It was rumoured, and I believe it is true, that the Irish Nationalists were much disconcerted and very sulky at his references to exclusion. That has increased the belief among our people in the readiness of the Government to adopt exclusion and they, not unnaturally perhaps, suspect that Asquith had already made acceptable proposals to Bonar Law in secret. I take Robbins as an example of a shrewd man and practised observer wholly deceived as to the realities of the situation. As I passed through the lobby I said to him, "Well, Mr. Asquith has disappointed our expectations. I thought that this time, at any rate, he was going to lay his cards upon the table." Robbins was evidently surprised by my attitude.

"We thought," he said, "from the tone in which he spoke and from the silence in which his words were received on your benches, that he was playing cards which had already been disclosed to you and that you were ready to play them too."

Nothing, in my opinion, could be worse than the spread of this idea. The suggestions which Asquith made in conversation were, as you know, wholly unacceptable and, though it is very probable that his speech was intended to give the opposite impression and to lull both our men and the country into a sense of security whilst he was gaining time and waiting for something to turn up, surely it was the business of our leader to destroy that impression from the outset and to show that nothing in the secret communications gave him any confidence in the intentions of the Prime Minister.

On the whole, I think our Press is better than might have been expected under the circumstances, but my speech was delivered too late to influence their leading articles, and I am afraid that an atmosphere of uncertainty has been created, which it should have been our business to avoid.

As to the speech itself I was not very pleased with it, and when I sat down was not quite certain how far I had succeeded in conveying my meaning, but my colleagues expressed warm approval and Arthur Balfour in particular was even enthusiastic. I found him and Harry Chaplin putting on their coats in the room at the back of the Speaker's chair. "I was just saying to Chaplin," he said, "that it is nonsense to talk about debating having degenerated in this House. It is as good—it is better than ever. You never made a finer speech in your life. It was a splendid piece of debating." All of which is very comforting, and as it will gratify my family as much as me, I report it for your satisfaction. It at any rate makes me hope that I did something to give our Party the lead that it required, but I have seldom had so much of the *esprit de l'escalier*. I could think of nothing as I drove home but the opportunities I had missed.

6 p.m. Simon's speech was a failure. Carson followed in excellent form. Both manner and matter were admirable—clear, strong and deeply earnest. Redmond followed. As he spoke I sat between Chaplin and F. E. Smith. "He is going to refuse exclusion," said F. E. in one ear. "He is going to accept," whispered Chaplin in the other. He ended without having done either. He also would use no "last words" but he argued against exclusion and said that the attitude of his Party towards it was well known. He recognised that there was a new situation, but he said nothing to clear it up. Speculation is very busy, but the general impression is that the Government will be forced to adopt exclusion, that

the coercion of Ulster has now been made impossible and that the Bill cannot pass in its present form. We are going to close the debate and take our division tonight.

I said "How-de" to the Speaker. He congratulated me on my speech and then expressed the view that the Government could not go on with this Bill, or must pass concurrently with it an amending Bill. What a farcical conclusion to the Parliament Act! He was confident that the coercion of Ulster was now out of the question. *A propos*, Long tells me that he hears on good authority that Harrel (son of Sir David Harrel, formerly the Under-Secretary in Dublin) came over to see Asquith a few days ago and told him to make no mistake about Ulster, that there was no bluff in her attitude, that she would fight, that the police could not deal with the situation, and that, though he was no soldier, he believed it would require 60,000 troops to overcome her resistance. What forces the folly or the weakness of this Government has let loose! What lasting injury they have already done to our institutions and to society!

I think I may say now that my speech was a success. It might well have been much better, but good judges like Balfour, the Speaker and Finlay have all praised it; and it pleased our Party and very much displeased our opponents.

*12th February* 1914.

Our great debate is over and has, I think, justified itself, and the exceptional action which we took. It is true that we are all left wondering what exactly the Government intend to do; but the impression is universal that they cannot now attempt the coercion of Ulster and that they must propose its exclusion. They professed to find in the debate, and especially in Carson's speech, a new situation which offered a prospect of a friendly solution. It was indeed a noble speech both in matter and delivery, but as Carson expressly stated that nothing short of exclusion of Ulster would induce her to lay aside her purpose, it is impossible to attach any meaning to Birrell's declaration that this was an eirenicon unless the Government have made up their mind to impose on the Nationalists a surrender to the Ulster demand. I must say that under the circumstances Redmond maintained a remarkable control both over himself and his followers. They have learned something from their past history and are no longer to be tempted by any attack into such outbursts as were common of old.

Assuming, as I think we may, that the Government will now propose the exclusion of Ulster and not Home Rule within Home Rule, there remain two important and difficult questions. In the first place, what is the Ulster to be excluded? There is an idea that they will offer four counties out of the nine, but I do not think that the Ulstermen could accept anything less than six, for there are large Protestant populations just within the boundaries of two others, and the Covenanters of the four counties could scarcely abandon the Covenanters of these two. If this difficulty be overcome it remains to be seen what consequent modifications the Prime Minister means to make in other provisions of the Bill, and what are the additional securities which he thinks he can offer to the Loyalists of the South and West. And if all these questions are satisfactorily settled, there is still the difficulty of arriving at the method by which they are to be carried into law. It is thought that the Government will put their proposals forward as suggestions for incorporation in the Bill by the House of Lords; but this pre-supposes the readiness of the House of Lords to give a Second and Third Reading to the Bill, and thus to accept some sort of responsibility for it. My own present inclination is to urge that the Lords should reject the Bill on Second Reading, but they should at the same time embody the suggestions in an amending Bill which they should send down to the Commons. Thus they would take no responsibility for the passage of Home Rule, but would provide the means by which, if the Home Rule Bill were passed over their heads under the Parliament Act, an amending Bill embodying the concessions would take effect at the same time. This would certainly emphasise the absurdity of the Parliament Act procedure, but I cannot make up my mind whether it is not too refined and complicated to meet with public approval.

After all, we may all be wrong, and the Government may still be hankering after Home Rule within Home Rule. The only mention of exclusion by Ministers was to deprecate it whilst saying that they did not absolutely rule it out, and it is rather the general tone of their speeches and the atmosphere prevalent in the debate which gradually confirmed the impression that they had made up their minds to give way on this point.

### 13th February 1914.

10.30 p.m. Bonar Law has heard rumours of Radical revolt against the exclusion of Ulster. It is said that they complain that that would be a humiliating surrender to us of all that we have claimed. Surely I was right in saying that *by itself* it was a most humiliating surrender for the Government and, at the same time, a most unsatisfactory result for us. That the Government mean to give way is, I think, now clear. They have made up their minds that they cannot coerce Ulster; but how far they mean to go and what the end will be I cannot guess. If they do not act quickly and resolutely, they may yet fall between two stools. St. John hears that the violent party are getting the upper hand in Ireland and even that Redmond's life is in danger, and Tim Healy swears that he will be ruined and destroyed if he consents to exclusion. But in Tim's case I expect the wish is father to the thought and I don't put much faith in St. John's gossip.

FOLKESTONE,
*18th February* 1914.

I think Asquith must have made up his mind that he cannot face the possible coercion of Ulster, but I doubt if he yet knows what he *is* going to do. To me it seems that delay is making his path not more but less easy. There are storm mutterings both in his own Party and in Ireland among the Nationalists there, whilst every week that passes hardens opinion in Ulster and makes any concession on their part more difficult. For myself the more I consider Federalism, understanding thereby something on the lines of Father's old scheme of provincial councils (for that is what it comes to) the more merits I see in it. But finance offers tremendous practical difficulties. Meanwhile Lansdowne, Selborne and I have given in public speeches some favour to the idea, for it would be absolutely destructive of the separatist features of the present Bill, would fulfil Carson's conditions and, indeed, has been privately favoured by him and might result in a more Imperially-minded

Parliament at Westminster. Certainly, if Home Rule in any form is once conceded anywhere, there is no possible solution of the question of Irish representation except in a scheme of general Devolution, which gives to each local parliament or council the management of the same local affairs, gives to each part of the Kingdom equal representation at Westminster and retains for settlement by the common Parliament the same subjects throughout the whole Kingdom. So, and so only, can Parliament be prevented from becoming a mart where Irish votes are put up to auction on questions that do not affect Ireland, and knocked down to the English party which is least scrupulous in bidding for them. But this means destroying the present Bill and building afresh on a new foundation.

9 EGERTON PLACE, S.W.,
*25th February* 1914.

Last night's debate was very interesting, but to my mind very unsatisfactory. There was a distinct hardening of Asquith's tone as compared with the first night of the session, and everyone draws the inference that Redmond has proved recalcitrant and that Asquith is not prepared to face his displeasure and the dissatisfaction in the Liberal ranks and has, therefore, decided against exclusion.

From secret information we gather that the present intention of the Government is to propose a very wide scheme of safeguards, giving to Ulster Home Rule within Home Rule and taking some special precautions for the protection of the Loyalists in the South and West; but they have decided that Federalism is too difficult and would take too long to be adopted now, and that they cannot risk exclusion. It is said that Redmond has informed them that he could not put up with it and that his life would be in danger if he were a consenting party. This information comes from a source in Dublin Castle.

*27th February* 1914.

So Leith has hammered one more nail into the Government's coffin! I begin really to believe that the Government will be forced to the country after all. Asquith is an enigma to me. When he told Bonar Law that he was going to propose exclusion to the Cabinet, why did he not insist on having his way? They all admit that he is master when he chooses to exert his authority. His Party are crying out at the folly of the Government in provoking unnecessary elections and the "stalwarts" exclaim that these defeats are the natural result and fitting punishment of truckling to the enemy. Proceed boldly with the Bill, drop all talk of concession and amendment and all will be well with us again, they say. It is not Home Rule that most of them are thinking of, but the success or failure of the Parliament Act. It is the keystone of the arch on which their house is built.

Your accounts of St. Aldwyn's and A. J. B.'s views are very characteristic. I agree with all they say as to the exclusion of Ulster being no settlement, though it is better than the Bill as it stands. No doubt, I, too, should prefer to leave things as they are, but Provincial Councils, even if dignified with the name of Parliaments and the style of Federalism, would be infinitely preferable to this Bill with or without Ulster exclusion. However, this is not a time for any counter proposals. All I desire to emphasise is that, as Balfour says, there is a United Kingdom question as well as an Ulster question, and that the former is the more important of the two.

*28th February* 1914.

I dined last night at the Speaker's and was fortunate in getting such pleasant companions as Arthur Lee and Anson for my neighbours at dinner. In the smoking-room afterwards I had some interesting talk with Law, Carson and F. E. Smith. Stamfordham sought an interview with Law a couple of days ago and urged that the violence of our speeches was rendering a peaceful settlement impossible. Law replied that we might be right or wrong, but that S. should understand that these speeches were not made in thoughtlessness or passion; they were part of a policy carefully considered and deliberately pursued. We were convinced that Asquith had gone back on the idea of excluding Ulster and now meant to force her in. This policy must result in civil war and the only way to stop it was to convince Asquith that we were serious and that we would go all lengths in support of the Ulstermen. "If we fail in that, he will go forward, the Bill will pass and Asquith will present it for the King's signature, assuring him that, as it will not immediately come into force, there will be a General Election before anything can happen. In this way, Mr. Asquith will get the responsibility off his own shoulders and will discharge his obligations to the Nationalists, but it will transfer the whole odium of what follows to the King. We are taking the only course which can by any possibility protect the Crown."

F. E. is to arrange for a great Lancashire demonstration today four weeks, to which we are all of us to go, and B. L. is favourably considering my proposal that we should all turn out for a week's campaign. Things are moving. Our amendment for the Army Annual Bill is drafted. Finlay told me that he was not very well satisfied with the wording, which proposed to forbid the use of troops in aid of the civil power in Ulster. I have suggested that it should forbid the retention of any troops in Ulster and their re-entry except to act against a foreign enemy, and this suggestion has been adopted. If the Nationalists persist in their determination to hold a demonstration at Derry, that will be a critical day. It is a most provocative proceeding and must be intended as a challenge.

*4th March* 1914.

I send you a letter from Charles Boyd with his first impressions of Father's speeches. You will be interested to see it and if you have any comments to make he will be interested to hear them. Please keep the letter for me. I have replied that I agree that Father's speeches were generally directed to persuading his audience to an immediate course of action and that I was afraid that, especially among the earlier ones, he would find few statements of general principles. As to the Free Trade speeches of 1884-5 I have observed that his view of them is curious, as Father has often told me that his doubts of the wisdom of our policy originated at that very time and in those speeches, when he felt that neither he nor Farrar[1] could produce an adequate answer to some of the con-

[1] Then Permanent Under-Secretary at the Board of Trade, afterwards 1st Lord Farrar.

tentions which they had to meet. Long before the Tariff Reform campaign of 1903, Father had told me that the inability of so able and convinced a Free Trader as Farrar to answer some of his questions satisfactorily had shaken his original unquestioning faith in the old Free Trade gospel.

You will have seen, before this reaches you, that Asquith has promised to make his Home Rule statement on Monday next, and that we therefore withdrew our motion yesterday evening. There is no doubt that he has secured the hearty approval of Redmond and Co. for whatever course he is going to take, and the Liberal papers seem to indicate pretty clearly what it will be. He will offer the widest Home Rule within Home Rule—what he himself called in his private conversations "veiled exclusion," but actual exclusion he will refuse. It will be a highly specious proposal and they count on its appearing to be so sweetly reasonable, so amply safeguarded, that it will place all moderate opinion on their side. Then when the House of Lords amends the Army Bill, they will resign and raise the cry of Peers against the People again. As far as the actual scheme of Home Rule is concerned, these new proposals can only make it more complicated, more absurd and more unworkable than ever; and the question is, can we make a jaded and often uninterested public think and realise all that is involved and how flimsy and useless all these safeguards will be in practice? In the last analysis they all bring you back to this dilemma. If Parliament or Government at Westminster tries to use them and to veto some Bill or Act of the Irish Government or Executive, how are we to enforce our will? The Irish Ministry resigns, no other can command a majority in the Irish Parliament, and we must either give way or suppress the Irish Parliament and re-conquer Ireland. Can anyone doubt for a moment what the result would be?

*5th March* 1914.

Rumour is very busy about Asquith's statement. Law tells me today that he is now convinced that Asquith means to allow any county to vote itself out. In only four counties would the Unionists have a majority, whilst in two others great numbers of

Covenanters exist, but would be outvoted by the Nationalists. Law says he cannot yet ascertain whether the exclusion, such as it is, is to continue or whether it is to be automatically ended at a fixed date. I imagine that the Customs and the Post Office provisions will be abandoned in any case.

*10th March* 1914.

I take off my hat respectfully to President Wilson! Just when I was criticising his foreign policy in regard to Mexico he does the right thing and a big thing, in a big way, in respect of the Panama tolls.[1] He seems likely to carry his point and I hope that he will, not so much for the sake of our trade and shipping as because his action reflects honour on him and his office, and its approval by the Senate will, I should think, greatly increase the respect in which the United States are held and inspire a new confidence in their good faith. The articles on his action in our papers were very pleasant reading. The reception of his message was most cordial and the response complete to the spirit in which it was penned.

*15th March* 1914.

I cannot but feel that the extraordinary Austro-German outburst of feeling against Russia at this moment is not wholly divorced from the spectacle of our domestic difficulties and that, if for any reason our participation were impossible, Germany might provoke a quarrel with Russia or France. And if we are to believe Lucy[2] in the *Observer* and other indications in Liberal papers, the Government could and would go on without an Army Act till they had passed their Bills and got the Royal Assent to them, so that we should not succeed even in getting an immediate dissolution. We had supposed that they must dissolve at once or resign. I am beginning to think whether it would be possible and wise to pass the Act for two months only. I am not at all certain that it may

[1] He urged the repeal of the exemption given to American shipping which Great Britain maintained was a breach of the Hay-Pauncefote treaty. "The large thing to do is the only thing we can do—voluntary withdrawal from a position everywhere questioned and misunderstood." (Message to Congress, March 5, 1914.)

[2] The late Sir Henry Lucy, the Toby M.P. of *Punch*.

not now be our best policy to take a leaf from Asquith's book and "wait and see." Something will depend on what he says tomorrow, when he has undertaken to answer several questions postponed from last week. There might be great advantage in leading him on and forcing, if we can, a disclosure of the details of his proposals. The Nationalists are evidently restless and many of his own men are uneasy at what he has already said. Yet by itself that is not a policy. If he has to put it in black and white it will surely mean that he will have to disclose further changes— Customs and Post Office for instance, Finance and perhaps Judiciary. And the strain on the allegiance of the Nationalists might prove too severe.

*16th March* 1914.

Winston's speech [1] is a curious commentary on the doubts and hesitations I expressed in yesterday's letter. If he indeed speaks the real mind of the Government and this is their last word, they will singularly simplify our course, for they will leave us no choice. If they are unyielding, the difficulties of deciding what is right for us to do will vanish.

*17th March* 1914.

"And Pharaoh hardened his heart." The old text tells the whole story of yesterday's proceedings in the House.

When Asquith rose to reply to the long string of questions addressed to him, his tone was curt and imperious, and the matter of his answer was not less so than the manner. "First accept the proposition I have already made; then and not till then, I will answer your questions" was in effect all that he would say. Conciliation vanishes and the forces are once more drawn up in battle array.

*19th March* 1914.

The day fixed for the Irish debate has come and once more we are all agog to know what Asquith will say. The rumours that

---

[1] If, he said, the issue was to be brought to the challenge of force, "Let us go forward together and put these grave matters to the proof." (Speech at Bradford.)

Government are contemplating active measures in Ulster become more definite and persistent, but I doubt their accuracy. I think that they are not unwilling to provoke Ulster, but they desire to avoid striking the first blow.

*20th March* 1914.

We had a very interesting sitting in the House yesterday. It was very tense and grave during Law's and Asquith's speeches, and very excited by Carson's, who spoke under the stress of considerable emotion, having just telegraphed *en clair* from the House of Commons to Ulster: "Resist by all means in your power any attempts to make arrests"; whilst Devlin's rude and bitter attack produced a scene which was only terminated by the Speaker's very skilful handling of it and, it must be added, by his allowing Carson to substitute one grossly unparliamentary (but richly deserved) phrase for another in giving the lie direct to Devlin.

Law made an excellent speech—quite the best he has ever done in that line of grave remonstrance and argument. George Cave also was excellent, but he is too briefly reported for you to judge of what he said. I rose at ten and spoke for forty minutes, too late for any comment by the Press, which already had its descriptive columns full, but *The Times* gives a very good report, wanting only a phrase or a sentence here and there which helped the connection or added to the dramatic effect. My artful little pause in the middle of the quotation from Dillon was very successful. Liberals and Nationalists tumbled right into the trap and looked very foolish when, on their applause subsiding, I finished the sentence. It was a successful speech and, I think I may say, a good piece of debating. Law told me that two men in the lobby had said to him that it was "the best I had ever made" and added: "It wasn't that, but it was very good. As will happen in a speech so little prepared, you did not always keep the interest of the House, but if you lost it for a moment you regained it the next minute." And he went on to say "I have been saying to Balfour that the nice thing about you is that you never feel slighted if I am obliged to leave you out of a debate and you never refuse if I ask you to step into the breach." This is true, and I am glad that he recognises it. This was the second important debate this session in which I have been told that room could not be made for me and have then been asked to take the job on in the middle of the debate itself. There is this, at any rate, to be said for the result, that if the speeches might have been better for more thought, I am saved a great deal of preliminary anxiety and labour.

On the whole, we as a Party were well satisfied with the day's work. We hammered Asquith's new position badly and there were more signs than ever before of restlessness and misgiving on his own side. His suggestions did not bear the scrutiny to which they were subjected.

I see I have not mentioned what was perhaps the most dramatic moment of the debate—that at which Carson left the House in the middle of Devlin's speech, to catch his train, all our men rising and cheering him as he went.

Illingworth told Talbot that there was no foundation for the rumour that Carson and others were to be arrested, but I think that there must have been serious discussion about taking action in Dublin, for Carson's warnings were based on intercepted telephone messages. It is just possible that the whole was a deliberate plan on the part of someone who wished to precipitate an outbreak in Ireland and thought that this was the way to do it. No one who knows as much of their intimate talk as I do can doubt that *some* members of the Government count on a riot in Belfast to help them out of their troubles.[1]

---

[1] Asquith's proposal was that any county in Ulster might vote itself out for six years. It would then come in automatically unless Parliament should have decided otherwise meanwhile. Carson had described this as "sentence of death with a stay of execution for six years."

Carson had telegraphed *en clair* to Ulster to resist arrests by all means in their power.

9 EGERTON PLACE, S.W.,
*20th March* 1914.

*Nearly Midnight.* These are indeed strange times. One does not know what to think or to believe. Let us put down events as they occur or rumours as they reach us and "wait and see."

I have been dining at the Salisburys. On arrival Lady Helen Cassel tells me :

"You know that the Fleet is ordered to Belfast and that Sir A. Paget is to be reinforced with 60,000 troops."

"No, I cannot think that that is so."

"But it is!" she said. "Miss Paget overheard her brother saying so. She at once told Almeric and he told Felix. Sir Arthur Paget was in London yesterday and left for Dublin today."

Just as dinner was over the butler said to me, "General Gough asks if he can see you. He is waiting in the hall." I went and found him and Mrs. Gough there. He was greatly excited. He read to me two telegrams from his brother,[1] who commands the Cavalry Brigade in Ireland. In substance, they were as follows : The first telegram said that he had been called upon to say whether he was ready to march against Ulster. If not, he was to send in his papers. He was given *two hours* to decide. The second telegram said the situation was unchanged. He and a large number of officers in the Brigade had sent in their papers.

General John Gough had come straight up from Aldershot prepared to send in his own resignation at once if the news were confirmed.

"They think," he said, "that we are poor devils with wives and children dependent on us and that our honour is in our pockets ; but it is not." He had seen General Wilson,[2] General French and Seely's Private Secretary. They all professed ignorance. He had been unable to find Seely.

[1] Hubert Gough.
[2] Afterwards Field-Marshal Sir Henry Wilson.

I begged him to do nothing until it was quite clear what had happened. He is to communicate with me tomorrow morning. I cannot believe that the Government wished to precipitate matters in this way. I suspect that Sir Arthur Paget has blundered, but that hardly lessens the seriousness of the situation. If once resignations have begun, how can the Government retreat, and where will the resignations end? The Government will be beaten, but what of the Army? We are very near the end of the Army and years will be needed to restore the *morale* and discipline of the troops.

*21st March* 1914.

10 a.m. The papers confirm the report of resignations at the Curragh, especially in the Cavalry Brigade. The movement of troops and ships appear to be on a small scale and directed solely to the protection of depots of arms, etc. Ministers are said to have received serious news of officers' resignations and to have been in conference late last night. More than that is not at present known. But to think that first the recklessness and then the hesitations and tergiversations of the Government should already have brought us to this point!

2 p.m. The news from the Curragh is confirmed. A meeting is being held at the War Office to consider what is to be done. I am off to meet Bonar Law and Lansdowne at Lansdowne House at once.

General Gough at the Curragh is sending his wife and children to England and asks are troops being moved? Evidently, the Curragh is in a ferment and wild reports are current.

I have sent *our* Gough (who is stationed at Aldershot) to see Lord Roberts.

*21st March* 1914.

*Saturday evening.* I cannot take my mind off the doings of the Army. The evening papers report 100 officers resigned at the Curragh. General Hubert Gough's first telegram to his brother at Aldershot began: "Have been offered dismissal service or undertake operations against Ulster. Two hours to decide." He added that he had resigned. A second telegram last night reported the resignations of the other officers and that all the resignations were being held up for the moment at Headquarters. A third telegram this morning said that he was sending his wife and children to England. John Gough interpreted this to mean that his brother expected trouble if any attempt was made to supersede, arrest or court-martial these officers. "Their men will stand by them," he said. He thought it possible that a whole regiment would march over to the Ulster side. "If the Government pursue violent measures, it is civil war and the Army is at an end."

I went to Lansdowne House directly after lunch. Bonar Law had just arrived. Balfour, Salisbury and Devonshire had been lunching there and joined us. I told my news. General Wilson, Director of Military Operations on the General Staff, had already been with Law and told him.

Law had telephoned to Stamfordham to say how grave he thought the position. Nothing now could stop the ruin of the Army, and civil war, but an immediate settlement. The Government ought to take a decision and make proposals at once.

Lord Roberts had gone to the War Office and, I believe, the King. He had already sent a letter to the Prime Minister on the dangers of the situation and forwarded a copy of it to Stamfordham (*i.e.* before the resignations).

Sir Edward Grey had told someone at lunch yesterday that the Government were considering the Referendum.

Balfour said, "I bet five to three now that the Government will take the Referendum."

We discussed the situation. It was agreed that Law should write with Lansdowne's express concurrence a letter to Asquith—not marked private though not necessarily to be published. In this letter, of which a copy would be sent to Stamfordham, Law would state the necessity for at once definitely omitting Ulster or consulting the electors by Referendum or otherwise. He would add that we might be asked at any moment whether, if we returned to office, we would reinstate the dismissed officers, and we could give only one answer—yes.

The difficulties associated with the Referendum are prodigious and we discussed them.

I should have liked to offer the Government the alternative of

Provincial Councils or Federal Home Rule on the South African model. I believe this now to be the only safe settlement and the only one which all parties could adopt with honour and reasonable satisfaction. But my colleagues, though thinking I was very likely right in saying that we must now come to this at the last, did not like to put it forward, although Carson had hinted at it again only last Thursday. Law had information that all the resigned or dismissed officers had been summoned to the War Office to meet the Secretary of State tomorrow.

Balfour mentioned that he heard that Steed and *The Times* Foreign Affairs room took a gloomy view of the foreign situation. The presence of our Expeditionary Force was a necessary part of all the military plans of the Triple Entente. Russia and France watched our difficulties with great anxiety. Germany was following them "with interest." No one could say what would happen if the crisis went further.

Lansdowne asked us all to meet again at dinner tomorrow night. We agreed and I left Law drafting his letter.

It is difficult to think that we are living in England. The tension is like that of the "black weeks" of the war—but this time the enemy is our own Government!

*22nd March* 1914.

*Sunday morning.* I continue my chronicle. I was wrong in saying that all the officers were summoned to the War Office. It was only Brigadier-General Hubert Gough and the three Cavalry Colonels from Ireland and Brigadier-General John Gough from Aldershot. They are now there. Here is Hubert Gough's account of what passed in Ireland—for the present private:

"All Brigadiers and Sir Charles Ferguson (General Officer commanding at the Curragh) were summoned to Headquarters on the morning of Friday, the 20th.

"Sir Arthur Paget said that active operations were to be commenced against Ulster; that he had been in close communication with the War Office and he had the following instructions from the War Office and the Chief of the Imperial General Staff to convey to the officers.

"Officers domiciled in Ulster will be allowed to disappear and

627

would be reinstated in their positions without detriment to their careers at the end of operations in Ireland. Other officers who were not prepared to undertake operations against Ulster from conscientious or other scruples were to send in their resignations at once and would be dismissed the Service.

"It was to be fully understood that any C.O.s or officers who avoided service on the incorrect plea of domicile in Ulster would be tried by Court-Martial.

"Resignations were to be sent in by the evening.

"All the Brigadiers were to go down at once to deliver this message to every unit of their Brigades and to collect and forward the results."

The above is copied from the account dictated by Hubert Gough.

Hubert Gough resigned and went back to the Curragh. He told his Brigade Officers what he had done and left them alone to consider their course. All resigned and so did several officers in the Artillery. On getting these resignations Paget came down from Dublin.

All this I heard from Mrs. John Gough this morning. I am expecting to hear the result of the War Office interview at any moment.

3 p.m. Mrs. Gough has just been in again. Nothing was decided at the War Office this morning.

The resigned officers in Ireland are:

1. all of the Cavalry Brigade whether at the Curragh or in Dublin;
2. all but five of the Horse Artillery;
3. about five in each Infantry Battalion.

General J. Gough has rewritten his resignation, which he no longer leaves in Sir Douglas Haig's hands but will post tonight. In it he says that he has heard what passed between Paget and his C.O.s and would in like circumstances have behaved as his brother did. General H. Wilson is writing a similar letter (he is Director of Military Operations) and all his younger officers follow him.

I may learn more tonight, but it will be too late for the post. I cannot write of other things.

*23rd March* 1914.

11 a.m. I posted full accounts of what was occurring here at 5.30 on Saturday, and again at midnight yesterday. I hope you will receive them safely.

Law, Balfour, Devonshire, Salisbury and I met again at dinner at Lansdowne's last night. Law had received a copy of the statement I sent you, with the added observation on Paget's part that all Ireland would be in a blaze next day. Law had written to Asquith that afternoon to say that the grave news from the Curragh had confirmed all our fears; that he might at any moment now be asked whether, when we came into office, we should reinstate the dismissed officers and that to this question we could only answer in the affirmative; that this announcement would totally break up the Army, and the only way out of the difficulties now was to take one of the two courses indicated in his speech on Thursday—that is to say, to make a clean cut of Ulster, or to resort to a plebiscite. He went on to say that he presumed that Asquith would make a statement today, and he trusted that he would facilitate an immediate debate upon it. To this, up to the present time, I believe he has made no reply.

In the morning the Archbishop of Canterbury had called upon Bonar Law. He had seen the Prime Minister and read to Law a report of his conversation with him. Asquith said that he had done everything that he could with the Nationalists about the time limit and that he could not persuade them to go a step further in that direction. He said that there were now only two ways of compromise, either to let the nine counties vote separately on their exclusion and to renew the plebiscite at intervals of say three years, or that six counties should be excluded. If the Opposition would make this offer he was prepared to say, without pledging the Government, that he would try whether he could get it accepted. Bonar Law had told the Archbishop that the first suggestion was ridiculous. Everything depended upon whether the Prime Minister was prepared to take risks and to stake his position definitely on the result. For himself he was prepared to do this. If Asquith

629

would bring him a definite offer to stand or fall by the exclusion of the six counties, he would take this suggestion to his colleagues. He could not pledge them before he had consulted them, but he was prepared to stake his own fortunes on the result and he believed his colleagues would accept. He added that some further concessions would be necessary, notably the exclusion of such anti-federal propositions as those relating to the Customs and the Post Office, and some protection for the loyalists such as the reservation of judicial appointments.

When he had finished, Lansdowne said, "I do not say you are wrong, but at the same time you know that this is what I always rather feared." We all agreed that there would be great dissatisfaction in the Party at any concession or compromise being made at the present time. At the same time, we were inclined to think that if Asquith did come to Bonar Law with such a definite proposal it would be impossible simply to turn it down.

The only further information we had before us was that Seely had asked General Wilson what would satisfy the Army and that General Wilson had replied, "the reinstatement of the dismissed officers and a declaration that the Army would not be asked to coerce Ulster to submit to Home Rule." We agreed that this was the right formula, and Wilson had been told that it was of great importance that the officers should not withdraw their resignations except on these terms.

Asquith told someone (the Archbishop I think) that there had been a misunderstanding and that everything would be set straight by eight o'clock this morning. Balfour observed, "Well, I tel¹ you what I think has happened. Paget has blundered in the execution of orders which he did not like, and by his blundering has saved us from a great disaster. I think that the Government meant, under cover of taking precautions to protect magazines, etc., to occupy all important positions in Ulster in such force that if they peacefully carried through the operation Ulster Unionists would be entirely split up and isolated. They hoped in so doing to provoke an attack on some detachment of the troops and that then blood would be up and they could put Ulster's resistance down ruthlessly." This seemed to all of us the most probable explanation of what had happened. Winston is reported to be using very fiery language and to be saying if the Army will not act, "his" marines will do what is necessary. Unless things are quickly settled resignations will probably begin in the Navy too.

This was all the information we had before us last night and we sat discussing it till 11.30. This morning I hear from Aldershot that all the regiments there are in a ferment and that there will be many resignations unless the matter is quickly settled, but on opening *The Times* I find that Asquith has authorised a statement which exactly bears out our anticipations. There has been an "honest misunderstanding," it is said. As to that, our test question will be in the form of Wilson's answer to Seely's question— "Will they reinstate the officers on the understanding that the Army will not be used to coerce Ulster to submit to Home Rule?" Unless Asquith can answer this satisfactorily we shall have to announce that we consider ourselves bound to see these officers righted and we shall have to push matters to a conclusion.

We have ascertained that the reports of orders for the movement of troops from England and preparations on the railways are unfounded.

I dictated these notes hastily, in order that you may follow the progress of events as closely as possible from hour to hour.

2.30 p.m.

24th March 1914.

"General Gough returned to Ulster last night with a written assurance that the troops under his command will not be used to coerce the people of Ulster into acceptance of the Home Rule Bill." So says *The Times* this morning and so the immediate crisis ends. But what immeasurable harm has already been done and what years of patience and of peace may not be needed to repair the evils already inflicted on both Army and nation.

I have tried to make you and Father sharers of our emotions by writing to you almost hour by hour each scrap of information as it came to me—true or false, confirmed or subsequently amended or discredited. And now the episode closes in Gough's return with his bit of paper initialed, I believe, by French and Seely after a long struggle lasting all yesterday afternoon. . . .

The net result of the whole is, as it seems to me, that the

Government have tried to use force and their weapon has broken in their hands; coercion of Ulster is now impossible and they will be forced to propose fresh terms of accommodation. So much to the good. But on the other hand, the discipline of the Army is seriously affected and a tremendous stimulus given to those syndicalists and socialists who want again to try conclusions with society in a general strike and who will echo Ramsay MacDonald's cry of "Class prejudice in the Army"; whilst the Army itself, if called upon again to act in a coal strike or railway strike, will have its *morale* badly shaken by the memory of what has passed, and whatever Government is in power will be confronted by "incidents" of the most difficult and delicate character. The fabric of society is loosened. It will take long to repair the rents.

*25th March* 1914.

Here at home one has watched the hours pass and news accumulate with deepening anxiety as to the future if with the growing certainty of relief in the present. What I have dreaded and, as you know, striven to avert in spite of some disapproval from friends, has now come to pass. The gravest of all questions—the limits to the duty of officers and men to obey orders—has been put to the test crudely and abruptly, and it has been practically admitted by the Government's action that in this case at least those limits were passed. But it is easier to admit this than to establish again what the true limits are and to set at rest all the dangerous questions which the criminal folly of the Government has raised.

*26th March* 1914.

These are strange times to live in and the problem of future government, by whatever Party it may be conducted, has been rendered far more difficult by the crimes and blunders of the last few days. I sent you a hurried note before I left for the House of Commons yesterday afternoon. Our suspicion that the White Paper did not contain all the documents that had passed was confirmed before the debate (on the Consolidated Fund Bill) began. The House was very full and met in a state of great tension and excitement. . . .

Seely's opening sentences convinced us, as they would convince anyone and as they must have been intended to convince the House, that he had paid for his share in the proceedings by his resignation, but . . . his resignation had already been refused by the Prime Minister and withdrawn by him.

Balfour followed and made a good speech.

Then came Asquith's statement—very weak in its explanations and laboured in its defence.

Bonar Law followed him and put some points extremely well.

Ramsay MacDonald followed in another speech on the same lines as that which he made in the debate, and I was told to be in readiness to answer any other Minister who might rise. About 7.30 I went to dinner, but was hurried back to the House in the middle of my meal by the cry that Grey was up. He spoke moderately and coolly, as he nearly always does. I should have been glad to have followed him at once, but it was a quarter-past eight when he sat down. There was a momentary interruption of the debate for private business and my colleagues urged that it was impossible for Members who had been in almost constant attendance during the afternoon to stay and hear my reply at that hour and they begged me to wind up the debate for them. I accordingly returned and finished my dinner and rose at ten o'clock, speaking to my surprise for an hour, though I had intended to be much more brief. . . .

When such grave issues hung on the debate I hardly liked to write of the purely personal aspect, but I know you want to be told about my own speeches, and so I add that this one was a great success. Bonar Law said to me, "This time it *is* the best speech that you have ever made," and he added, "you did what I did not think was possible after the earlier portion of the debate. You put us in as good a position at its conclusion as we occupied on Monday last." I overheard Balfour saying, "I never heard anything better done," and received many congratulations as I passed through the lobby to vote. I was particularly anxious beforehand, so that this was the more comforting; but when the excitement of the moment is over one's thoughts go back at once to the evil that has been wrought and to the dangers and difficulties which confront the country. . . .

*29th March* 1914.

*Sunday.* It is a pleasure to write thus after the hurry and excitement of the past week. I have seen no one and have no further news. The temper on both sides is hotter and feeling more bitter than it has been since 1886. I suppose the Radicals really do believe that there was an Army plot, whilst on our side, however reluctant some of us may be even to admit to ourselves that Ministers have lied, there is not one of us who can believe their disingenuous story that none of them contemplated anything more than putting a sufficient guard over valuable military stores.

If nothing was intended but to guard a few military stores would you move battle fleets and torpedo destroyers, cavalry and horse artillery? Would you give officers the choice of "disappearing" if they were domiciled in Ulster, and of sending in their papers and being dismissed the Service if they did not wish to take part in the movement? No jury would believe that statement on oath. Officers and men would have been ordered to go and been court-martialled if they had disobeyed orders. You only give officers a choice when you recognise that it is civil war and that ordinary rules and ordinary methods do not apply.

As for the Government, Law says it can't go on. Balfour rejoins: "You speak as if this were an ordinary Government," and in my belief Balfour is right.

*30th March* 1914.

French and Ewart insist on resigning. Seely has resigned again and this time his resignation is final and accepted; Asquith has taken the seals of S. of S. for War and his seat is therefore vacant. Morley admits that he not only saw the two paragraphs but altered their phraseology in small points; he is reported to have said that he thought they represented the decision or the mind of the Government and that he still thinks so; and being asked if he is to remain in office whilst Seely goes, he said he would make a statement as to his own position tomorrow.

What happened becomes more clear from Winston's speech today. Paget thought that the orders, when executed, would fire the heather. He discussed with Seely and a Cabinet Committee what in such case should be done. He then returned to Ireland

and began at once to put into operation instructions which were intended to be conditional on future happenings. And when the inevitable results followed, the Government tried every means to conceal the truth and to cover up their tracks.

These are my first impressions of the debate, confirmed by Balfour's. You will see, when the papers reach you, if they are borne out by a careful study of Winston's words.

The fact is that, as Balfour said on Monday week, the Government have raised questions which every wise man tries not to raise. Who shall satisfactorily define even at his leisure—much more in heated debate—the limits of obedience of soldier or civilian? These are most delicate questions of conscience. They are questions of degree, and every general statement is unwise and offers a pitfall to the unwary.

*31st March* 1914.

11 a.m. One thing stands out clearly from the debates in both Houses. The Government have been forced to admit that the Army and the officers have done no wrong. How, under these circumstances, they think they can raise the cry of the Army against the People with success I don't know, and how as honest men they can attempt it I cannot conceive. But I think it also appears from the debates that there are still two opinions in the Cabinet as to the future. On the one hand we have Morley and Haldane declaring that force will not be used to coerce Ulster— on the other hand we have Winston and Grey reiterating the statement that in the last resort all the forces of the Crown will be employed. As I listened to the speeches last night I observed to Long that I thought we ought to turn Saturday's demonstration into a meeting of support of the Lord Chancellor against the wilder spirits of the Government!

*1st April* 1914.

Diane arrived in Ivy's room this morning, the happy bearer of your postcard, and I received your interesting letter of the 29th last night. My information on the whole goes to confirm that contained in the letter read to you. I am told that the particular Battle Squadron selected to go to Lamlash was chosen because the

Admiral in command of it is the only one who would go gladly, or at least willingly, on such an errand. Some others would certainly have resigned whilst others, if they went at all, would have gone most reluctantly.

It is very difficult, even now, after all the disclosures and "full statements" and "plain tales," to disentangle the exact part played by the Government. That Paget thought his orders would provoke Ulster is clear; that he got instructions how to act in this case is also clear, and that the Government discussed this as a possibility, even if some of them did not count on it as a probability, is also established.

7 p.m. I met Robbins of the *B.D.P.* in Palace Yard. He thought that compromise of some kind was now inevitable.

As we were parting Robbins added, "May I say that in the Press Gallery, where they are pretty shrewd observers and discuss these things quite apart from Party bias, they think that your position in the House has been immensely strengthened by your last two speeches, and especially the last."

*2nd April* 1914.

I have no news for you, but letter-writing is like dram-drinking. The habit grows on you, and after the past fortnight it seems natural that some part of my morning should be given up to it. I am thinking much of our present situation. I am more and more convinced that an effort ought to be made to settle the Irish question and with it, or after it, some other questions. I do not think that things can be put back simply in their old position, or that even if we won a General Election we could blot out the memory of the last five or six years and go on as if they had never been. And if there is to be a settlement, then certainly I am sure that the only reasonable or promising course is to take up Father's interrupted policy of National or Provincial Councils and escape the dangers of a single, practically independent Parliament by a general system of equal devolution to all the units of the three kingdoms, treating of course Ulster as a separate unit. There is a growing feeling of sympathy with this idea in our Party and among the Liberals, say something like eighty men on each side of the House who openly avow their wish for it, besides many who would accept it or any other course advised by their leaders, and there is a large body of opinion outside Parliament which is increasingly favourable to it. But Balfour and Law, Lansdowne and Curzon all dislike it in varying degrees.

6th April 1914.

I will send you tomorrow two picture papers with views of Saturday's demonstration.[1] The speakers as usual look comical but the crowd is imposing. I feel that if I did that sort of thing three Saturdays running I should infallibly become a kind of third-rate Jim Larkin, incapable of argument or reason, husky-voiced and blatant. When one is strained to the utmost to make one's voice carry as far as possible and still cannot reach the limits of the audience, when one cannot tell indeed how much is audience, reason and argument go by the board. One abandons the idea of saying what one intended or trying to convert or convince anyone and one falls to demonstrating—a subtly degrading occupation. It is well to go into the country to recapture one's soul after such an orgy. I will pick primroses and forget politics for a week.

*Tuesday*, 2.30 p.m. I believe that last sentence sums up the difference between Father and me in our outlook on politics. Did he ever *want* to forget politics? I doubt it; but I constantly do. When I go for a holiday I want to get away from them, whereas he took them with him. For which reason, as well as for many other and bigger ones, I shall never be in politics what he was.

CROWBOROUGH,<br>8th April 1914.

Before those young men had left me, Albert Gray, K.C., was waiting to see me. He had asked for an interview to "give some important news from the Curragh" which turned out to be a statement from one of the Colonels as to what Paget said when he went down there. From the statement alluded to it clearly appears that when Paget went to the Curragh after receiving news of the resignations, he made a speech to the officers in which he

---

[1] In Hyde Park.

contradicted himself a good deal, but that he said two things, one of which was new to me and neither of which I have told you. First, that in trying to minimise what he was going to do, he said that there was one thing however the Government had ordered which he disapproved and thought would make trouble (Query: Arrests of leaders or seizure of their headquarters?), and secondly, that he was going to assemble an army or a force of twenty to twenty-five thousand men on the Boyne and that troops would be moved from England. Can any sane man believe that some members of the Government did not mean something very different from the four companies of infantry to guard small arms and guns? Paget does not invent all this without foundation.

You get all my news and most of my thoughts; and if the result is less good as history or philosophy than a considered judgment in the *Quarterly Review*, it helps you to share our daily emotions and to live our lives, and I know that that is what you want.

Did I tell you that Balfour found speaking in Hyde Park just as demoralising as I did, and in the same way? "I usually do a great deal of my thinking on my legs, as you know," he said, "but I *couldn't* think under those conditions."

CROWBOROUGH,
*Good Friday*, 1914.

I returned to Norton's[1] letters and came almost at once upon this to his eldest daughter, dated 10th April 1886:

"We have all been greatly interested in Mr. Gladstone's speech (introducing the Home Rule Bill). I have no idea that his scheme can be made to work; and generous as his design is, and powerful as his speech is, the project seems to me Utopian, and the speech an immense added difficulty in the way of a settlement of the Irish question. He has sown the wind, and it will blow a gale before it blows itself out."

It is the right moment to read such a prophecy! Curious that I should light upon it twenty-eight years later to the very day.

[1] Charles Eliot Norton, President of Harvard.

9 EGERTON PLACE, S.W.,
*29th April* 1914.

My time has been fully occupied in re-reading all the debates and cross-examination of Ministers in regard to events at the Curragh in preparation for yesterday's debate, the responsibility of which spoiled the pleasure of my Sunday in the country. I did not indeed do any work on Sunday and enjoyed the sight of the wild flowers which were perfectly lovely, but I could not get the speech out of my mind and I am greatly relieved now that it is over. It took, as you will see, a long time in delivery, being lengthened by the constant interruptions of the Ministers themselves in the first place and of the Government Party generally, who were extremely noisy throughout. I found it a very difficult task and was not well pleased with my performance of it. Bonar Law told me that Balfour had said to him that he thought it a very able statement, and he added himself that he thought it would read well, though it was not very effective in delivery. You will be able to judge of this from the reports. For myself, as I say, I am thankful that it is done and hope that I may not have to undertake a like duty again.

You will see that Winston gave the "go by" to the whole of my charges and practically admitted the truth of our case against the Government, but of course the interest of the debate from the moment he had spoken centred in his last phrase. What exactly he meant I do not know, and some attempt will be made today to elucidate his meaning, but I have information from a private source, which shows that Lloyd George at least had been consulted and had approved what he said.[1]

From the point of view of our motion the situation had already altered to our disadvantage by the gun-running of Friday night. Of course, if the Government had stated from the first that they had made, as was the fact, extensive preparations against the Ulster Covenanters and were justified in doing so, we might have had ground for criticism, but it would have been of a different kind; but from the moment of that episode the Government supporters changed their attitude and, practically abandoning the previous plea of the mere protection of stores against hot-headed persons dis-

[1] A very striking appeal for "peace with honour" to all concerned.

639

countenanced by the Ulster leaders, they admitted larger preparations and justified themselves by the events which have
subsequently occurred. To some extent, therefore, the motion
was out of date. No one any longer believed in the truth of the
Government's original story and no one on their own side cared
whether it was true or false.

I first heard of the moment fixed for the gun-running on Friday
afternoon. Had it been possible to postpone it, Carson would, I
think, have done so, not on account of our debate, but because the
situation in Ireland had changed so completely since the Curragh
episode; but the arrangements were too far advanced and the ship
and its crew could not be kept indefinitely waiting. We were in
some anxiety lest the attempt might result in bloodshed in spite
of all precautions, but, as you will have seen, the preparations were
made with a completeness and everything was carried through
with a smoothness and a success which reflect the highest credit
on the brains of the Ulster movement.

The Budget has been delayed till Monday, for what reason we
do not know. The result, as far as I am concerned, is that I cannot
escape my Wolverhampton meeting tomorrow and shall have to
speak both tomorrow and on Monday, so you will see that my
hands are still pretty full, and will forgive the meagreness of my
correspondence.

10 p.m. I am very tired and can say no more than this: Balfour
made a magnificent speech. His closing passages were intensely
moving. Carson was also very impressive; Asquith excellent in
tone and manner, very poor in matter and not only inconsistent
with but contradictory of Winston's central position; Bonar Law
very good in *very* difficult circumstances in his speech, but (I thought)
quite wrong in his attempted explanation of the phrase about the
duty of officers, when he interrupted Asquith. The whole situation
more obscure than ever.

*30th April* 1914.

Another kaleidoscopic change in the situation; and after the
blood and thunder of Bradford and the acute crisis of last month
all the talk is now of peace. No Vote of Censure ever had a

stranger history than that which I moved on Tuesday. Asquith had declared that the honour of Ministers was attacked and had demanded the formulation of the charges in the House; yet the Minister who was put up to reply made no pretence of defending their honour, and turned the whole interest of the debate from the proceedings of the past to the chances of the future. Once again, the more responsible people seem overwhelmed by the imminence and the greatness of the danger which confronts us, and once again, Winston has taken the first step towards reopening the paths of peace. How it will all end I cannot pretend to foresee.

Balfour's speech was magnificent. The case which he made against the Government in the polemical part of it was overwhelming, and stated by him with quite unusual lucidity and skill of arrangement, for it is not in such matters that his power is usually shown. But of course the real interest of his speech was in the closing passages, which formed one of the most moving episodes that I have ever listened to in the House of Commons.

Carson's speech was hardly less remarkable. Its frankness and its obvious sincerity made a great appeal to the House. He is convinced that he was only just in time to prevent the outbreak of civil war when he went over to Ireland on, I think, March 19th. When he got there he found that the bell-ringers had been in the churches all night, that signallers with rockets had been on every church tower, and that the slightest move on the side of the Government, or the least mistake on the side of the Covenanters, might have led to the last calamity. He feels, therefore, that we have been on the very brink of civil war, and that there is no time to be lost if the danger is to be averted. He is perhaps not less impressed with the impossibility, after all that has happened, of simply reverting to the old Unionist policy in the South and West, and, though opinions differ among well-informed people as to what would be the results in Nationalist Ireland of the rejection of the Bill at this stage, he himself takes a very gloomy view of the consequences.

Under the circumstances Bonar Law's position was extremely difficult. He was bound to repeat and to substantiate the charges which he had made; yet the kind of speech which he naturally would have projected would have been entirely out of place after what had gone before. I thought under the circumstances he did very well.

Asquith added nothing to the elucidation of Winston's suggestion and expressly stated that Winston acted on his own responsibility. But it is of course clear, and indeed I know it for a fact, that he had not spoken without Asquith's knowledge.

The Nationalists sat silent and disturbed throughout the whole proceedings. They are reported to have held a stormy meeting on Tuesday night and to have been with difficulty restrained by Devlin, who persuaded them that it was impossible for Carson to accept Winston's proposal. Many of the Liberals also were uneasy, and their demeanour throughout the debate was noisy and truculent, but the whole House was hushed into silence whenever anybody approached the question of peace proposals, and as you will see by this morning's papers, there is now in all quarters an impression that a settlement must somehow be made, though no one can see how it can be reached.

I am off to Wolverhampton to speak tonight.

*2nd May* 1914.

It is pleasant indeed to have your telegram with the news of your early return. How we shall welcome you back and how much there will be to talk over together—if ever we get an opportunity. But "out of the frying pan into the fire" is our life now. We jump from dangerous concession to still more dangerous strife and back again from talk of civil war to talk of patched-up peace, that would be only one whit less bad than war. The prospect varies from day to day. Ministers blow hot and cold without any apparent reason, and public opinion is confused and distracted by the kaleidoscopic changes in the situation. Meanwhile, the days pass, the time available for compromise shortens, and whilst men and papers exclaim that a way out must be found and there is much loose talk of Federalism, nobody attempts to concentrate opinion on the changes which must be made in the Home Rule Bill—apart from the exclusion of Ulster— to make it a tolerable or even a possible basis for that purpose.

I tried to do something to that end at Wolverhampton on Thursday, but I become increasingly afraid that, between the very

general dislike of any sort of compromise and the particular dis-
taste of several of our leaders for Devolution at large, we shall drift
and drift till we are again confronted with the imminent peril,
and perhaps the reality, of civil war, and then be forced by
public opinion to accept something which does indeed avert war
now, but leaves us with a scheme of Irish Government eventually
incompatible with national unity and almost fatal to national
strength.

*5th May* 1914.

I hear that Asquith has asked to see Bonar Law and Carson
again today. On our side I cannot see much light or leading.
As far as I could disentangle the attitude of different people it was
somewhat as follows :

Law thought that Asquith would demand as a condition of any
compromise that we should accept the settlement and give a pledge
that if returned to power we would give it a fair trial, or in other
words that we would not try to amend it, and he said that he
thought this would be a fair request on Asquith's part, and that
we, generally, had practically committed ourselves to this position.
He added that in his opinion it would be impossible to repeal the
Bill when once it has passed on to the Statute Book.

The rest of us demurred to his statement of our position,
Balfour in particular pointing out that the utmost he had said was
that they could avoid civil war by making a clean cut of Ulster
and could pass their Bill under the Parliament Act in spite of all
the resistance which we might make.

Carson said that this had also been his line and that he could
not be a party to any acceptance of the Bill even if Ulster were
excluded. But he agreed that it would be impossible to repeal
the Bill as far as National Ireland was concerned if once passed,
and he thought that the old Unionist policy, which would have
been successful if a little more time had been allowed it, was now
impossible.

Lansdowne agreed with Balfour as to his attitude on the
particular point raised by Law and was very anxious not to be
committed in any way to acceptance of the Bill as a condition of
the exclusion of Ulster. He did not take as serious a view of the

position in the South and the West as did Carson, but he admitted that he had held out in his speeches the idea that he would be ready to consider some scheme of Devolution as a possible line of settlement.

I said this was my attitude also. If the Government simply proposed to omit Ulster, and leave the Bill otherwise unaltered, I absolutely declined to undertake any responsibility for, or to accept in any sense, that proposal as a solution. But I put this question: "Suppose Asquith were to say, 'If I cannot come to terms with you I shall pass my Bill as it stands, but I am prepared to give you the exclusion of Ulster and to recast the Bill on federal lines if you will so far co-operate with me as to make that a settlement.' What would you say then?"

To this Carson and Bonar Law would only reply that Asquith could make no such proposal. Whilst Balfour said that if he did so it would put us in an extremely difficult position, and for his part his solution would be to cut Nationalist Ireland wholly adrift and give it full colonial self-government.

I added that both Lansdowne and I had from the first laid more stress than Carson and Law on the Imperial aspect of the Home Rule Bill, and that we had been anxious to prevent the impression growing that you had only to cut out Ulster in order to make the Bill safe. It was for this reason and to draw attention to its other dangers that I at least had spoken of the federal solution. I was constantly afraid that we should end by having Ulster cut out, but all the other evils of the Bill untouched.

Bonar Law thought that if Ulster was cut out the Customs and Post Office provisions must go also. He suggested that much might be done to reconcile the Loyalists of the South and West by repeating a proposal which he had already made to Asquith, that they should be invited to a conference to consider what securities could be devised for them. He apparently thought that they would sufficiently protect the United Kingdom, but I do not think that anyone else shared that view.

I tried to press my question on them again, but could get nothing from them beyond the statement that Asquith could never make or accept such a proposal—the Nationalists would not allow it.

"If that is so," I said, "then I go a step further, and I ask whether it would not be right for Law and Carson to play what I call the 'Great Game' and to make that suggestion themselves to Asquith. If he refused, we should be in a very good position. If he accepted, we should at least have averted the greater Imperial danger of the present Bill."

I suppose that Carson and Law will simply play a waiting game, and I doubt very much whether Asquith will press the conversation on very practical lines. It will be wonderful under the circumstances if we do not drift either into a civil war, which people are congratulating themselves on having escaped, or into some form of compromise which we shall be unable effectively to resist and which will be hardly less bad than the original Bill.

*6th May* 1914.

At yesterday's conversation with Law and Carson, Asquith said he wished to discuss only the machinery of settlement. He thought it would be useless to try to use the "suggestion" stage for compromise and proposed to pass the Bill unamended through the Commons, have it rejected by the Lords and become law under the Parliament Act and *then* pass an amending bill.

Law and Carson told him that this would not do. It was the worst possible plan. If it were once on the Statute Book the Nationalists would scarcely be brought to agree to any compromise, feeling on our own side would be worked up to its bitterest and hottest, and (Carson added) there would probably be an outbreak in Belfast. Incidentally, Law said to him that he had only three courses open to him : (i) to coerce Ulster, (ii) to omit Ulster, (iii) to have a General Election. He replied that (iii) would not help him, as, if he won, Ulster would still resist, and said as to (i) with emphasis, that he would never coerce Ulster.

I hear that Askwith (Board of Trade) on his return from a holiday says he finds the labour situation much more threatening than when he went away, that everything is working up for a storm in 1915. I told this to Law, who echoed my own feelings when he replied, "I am not surprised. I do not think that people generally yet realise how profoundly the social structure has been shaken by recent events."

*11th May* 1914.

I add a few lines to bring my record up to the date of your return.

I went to the State Banquet on Saturday and had a few moments' conversation with King George, Queen Mary, Queen Alexandra and the King of Denmark—all very pleasant but nothing of consequence. I also had some talk with Sir Charles Douglas, the new Chief of the General Staff. . . . I had avoided Ministers and their wives all evening, but when Queen A. sent for me I found myself close by Mrs. Asquith, who at once began a conversation. She said we were going to have a settlement. I replied that I saw no signs of it. We were worse off than in November and the P.M. was doing nothing to improve the situation—on the contrary he made it worse with his closure resolutions.

"Oh! but if *one* man is killed, Henry is done. We're done, Mr. Austen. We know that and we don't want a row. You didn't believe in the plot?"

"I beg your pardon. I did."

"None of my Tory friends do. You couldn't believe in it." And she added that I couldn't have believed in my motion or in what I said. "I thought it was very hard on you to have to move it, but of course you couldn't help yourself." This was just what I had feared and, of course, it forced me to say bluntly to her that I was not in the habit of saying things I did not mean, that I had chosen my words carefully and that I meant all I had said, though how much the P.M. knew of what had been going on I could not tell.

Grigg and Curtis came to see me again on Thursday to report progress. They have been very busy but I do not see that much progress has been made. We talked for some time. The net result was that I told them that Asquith could carry his Bill unamended *in spite of us* and proceed to civil war; or he could amend his Bill by the exclusion of Ulster and avoid civil war *without us*; but I for one would take no responsibility and enter into no agreement or negotiations for agreement, except on the basis of the reversal of all the anti-federal provisions of the Bill—Customs, Post Office, Judiciary to be reserved as well as everything else not specifically delegated.

646

"And what would the Unionist leaders say if he made that offer?" they asked.

"I don't know," I replied, "and no one will know till Asquith himself makes a firm offer to them on that basis. They will not tell me and they will not tell you or anyone else. Why should they answer a very difficult hypothetical question from irresponsible people? If Asquith wants to know, he must ask the question himself."

So far Asquith is just playing with the conversations and with Law and it is high time that Law brought him up with a round turn. He tells Law that he will propose the exclusion of Ulster to the Cabinet and believes that he can carry it. When he sees Law again, this, which he had described at parting from him as "the next step," is not mentioned and he begins on different lines.

He proposes to Law temporary exclusion of Ulster. Law says it will not do; he agrees, and three months later he proposes it in the House and solemnly assures us that he believed that we should accept it!

In his last conversation he tells Law and Carson that he thinks it useless to propose further concessions at this stage, that the Bill must go through unamended and be rejected by the Lords and *then* will be the favourable moment for a settlement. Law and Carson both tell him that this is the worst possible course, opinion will be hardening against any compromise and Carson adds that he may be unable to restrain Ulster.

Two days later Asquith gives notice of his guillotine resolution.

And all the time he feeds the Press and the King with talk of conversations and concessions! If I were Law I would have had this out with him before now, and I would certainly bring him to book before I discussed matters any further with him.

There are "a few last words" for you!

# INDEX

Abdul Hamid, Sultan of Turkey, 123, 176

Aberdeenshire, candidate for, 246

Abraham, Edgar, 563

Account, vote of, 231, 242–3

Acland, Sir William, 101, 490

Acland-Hood, Sir A. F., 172

Acocks Green, author's speech at, 504–6, 514, 520–1

Admiralty, dissensions at, 130; and new Dreadnoughts, 150–1, 166–7, 174; McKenna's conversion at, 234; Churchill takes over, 366–7; unpreparedness of, 368

Adult suffrage, 413–14, 424

Afghanistan, Amir of, 60, 106

Aga Khan, suggests permanent viceroy, 60

Agadir crisis, 315–16, 346–7, 353, 427–428; British support to France in, 346, 360–1, 363, 425, 472; Franco-British plan of campaign in, 420, 428, 472; danger from secrecy on, 608

Agnew's Gallery, water-colour exhibition at, 443; Turner drawings at, 555

Airships, German, 545; uses of, 562

Aitken, Max (Lord Beaverbrook), 308, 336

Akers-Douglas, A. (Lord Chilston), 22, 50, 110, 178, 295, 417; approves "Valentine letter," 37; and proposal of coalition, 193; and reform of Lords, 220, 255

Albania, 472, 545–6

Albert Hall, banquet to Colonial Premiers in, 56, 72, 77; Balfour speaks in, 72–3, 78–9, 302, 304, 306; Tariff Reform demonstration in, 56, 63; Lansdowne's speech in, 406, 495, 502; anti-suffrage meeting in, 414, 424, 430; Bonar Law's speech in, 496, 502

Albert Hall Pledge, 195, 302 n., 304, 306, 316, 332; effect of, on electorate, 307–12; considered void, 358, 361; author repudiates, 387, 392, 399; Bonar Law and, 392, 396, 399, 415–16; meeting to consider Unionist attitude to, 432–6

Alexandra, Queen, 543, 646; and death of Edward VII, 268–9, 275; at memorial service, 270; at funeral, 276; death of brother of, 539

Alexandra Palace, Lansdowne's speech at, 406, 502

Algeria, French relations with natives in, 531

Allen, Colonel, 536

Allison, Miss, 63

Amery, L. C. M. S., 358, 369; defeat of, 105 n.; and Food Taxes crisis, 509, 517, 519

Anderson, Mr., discussion on, 260

Anson, Sir W., 68–70, 325, 587, 617

Army, the, and the Curragh "mutiny," 625, 629, 634; shaken morale of, 632; limits of obedience in, 635

Army Act, 609, 620

Army Annual Bill, amendment to, 618–19

Army Estimates, Churchill and, 127

Army Reforms, Haldane's, 54–5, 361, 365

Arnold-Forster, H. O., 85, 141; as War Minister, 60–1; character of, 157

Ashbourne, Lord, story of, 447

Ashdown Forest, 560–1

Ashton-under-Lyne, election result at, 308; Bonar Law's speech at, 406, 496, 502, 510–11

Askwith, Sir George, 443–4, 459, 645

Asquith, H. H., 58, 109, 158, 171, 218, 234, 442, 469–70, 550; as Chancellor

Asquith, H. H.—*continued*
of the Exchequer, 66; Budget of,
67, 70-1, 74, 117; and Colonial
Conference, 78-80; inaccuracy of,
79-80; becomes Prime Minister, 93,
109 n.; at Home Rule debate, 101;
and reduction in Army and Navy
votes, 117-18; author's brushes
with, 131-2, 178, 244, 366; suffragists' hostility to, 135; and
Sinclair, 149; and Naval Estimates,
150, 153, 159-60, 164-5, 167, 171;
and financial muddle, 155; at
Speaker's Levée, 165; and Lloyd
George's Budget, 177, 203, 205;
abandons ex-Chancellor's speech,
177 n.; author praises speech of, 178;
good speeches of, 179, 202; and
Constitutional Conference, 190-1,
278; and creation of new peers, 199,
214-15, 241, 247, 254, 256, 318,
326-7, 347; and the Lords' Veto,
201, 203, 205, 212-13, 217, 243-4;
possibilities of defeat of, 210-11, 219,
256-9; surrenders to malcontents,
214-15, 217, 222, 252, 254; and
"reform" of Peers, 236; dull
speech of, 237; Irish dislike for, 242;
and Burns's speech, 253; in need
of holiday, 254; exposes Crown,
259; and King's death, 267; at
memorial service, 270; and Lloyd
George's proposals for coalition,
291 n., 293, 577; on constitutional
legislation, 296; and Agadir crisis,
315; praises author's speech, 327;
and Parliament Act amendments,
342; and railway strike negotiations, 346, 360; and suffrage question, 413-14; rumour of resignation
of, 414; challenges Law on Insurance, 415; and French Entente,
427; offers author Chairmanship of
Commission, 429; and coal strike,
432, 439, 443-5, 462; Home Rule
Bill of, 441, 474-5, 477, 607; and
Minimum Wages Bill, 452, 455-6,
461-3, 465; on definition of coal
mines, 457-8; on coal ballot, 469;

Asquith, H. H.—*continued*
tired out, 475, 478, 533; and closer
French alliance, 486; unprecedented
action of, 491; degraded state of,
493-4; and attempt to reach agreement on Home Rule, 506, 568-76,
583, 585; drops Franchise Bill, 521;
probable successor to, 533; pays
tribute to Lyttelton, 565 n.; speeches
of, on Home Rule, 567, 572, 578-9,
583, 585, 605, 610-12, 619, 621-3;
and exclusion of Ulster, 568, 572,
599, 616; and Devolution, 570, 572,
594; conversations of, with Bonar
Law, 574-6, 583, 586-93, 599-600,
605, 611, 643-5, 647; supreme in
Cabinet, 576; conversations of, with
Carson, 605-7, 643-5; proposals
of, 623 n., 629, 645; Bonar Law's
letter to, on Curragh incident, 626,
629; on Curragh "mutiny," 630-1,
633; becomes Secretary of State for
War, 634; on Vote of Censure,
640-2; alternatives before, 646-7
Asquith, Margot, and Navy debate,
164-5; at Prince of Wales's concert,
168; on author's Vote of Censure,
646
Astor, Lord, maiden speech of, 325
Athenæum, record blackballs at, 158
Australia, and menace of Japan, 29;
Deakin on army of, 82; strikes
illegal in, 449-50
Austria, 355, 491, 527; mobilisation
of, 520; agitation of Slavs in, 529,
547; financial situation of, 536;
and coercion of Montenegro, 544-7;
and war with Russia, 547, 561

Backhouse, Sir J., 109
Baghdad Railway, 123-4, 422, 472
Bailey, Sir Abe, 553
Baird, John, on Balkan States, 546-7
Balcarres, Lord, 39, 197, 363, 372,
376-7, 450, 465, 480, 494, 508; and
Parliament Act, 342-4; on Walter
Long's jealousy of author, 345, 387;
and Party leadership, 361-2, 381,
383, 385-90, 392; letter of, to

Balcarres, Lord—*continued*
author, 400; and fusion of Unionist Parties, 417, 423; and Food Taxes, 433; on result of coal ballot, 469; Bonar Law's letter to, on Food Taxes, 504; goes to Lords, 522

Baldwin, Stanley, on "Flight of Capital," 159, 161

Balfour, A. J., 55, 61, 87, 102, 110, 223, 252, 268, 275, 301, 363, 464, 534; and Joseph Chamberlain, 19, 23, 236; author's correspondence with, on Party policy, 22–34; on Colonial Conference, 29–30; outlines his policy, 31; and "Valentine letter," 37; and fiscal amendment to King's Speech, 48, 50–3, 141–3; speeches of, 57, 86, 97, 101, 145, 149, 157, 202, 204, 237, 239, 266, 474, 478, 481; and inter-Party conversation, 58; at Albert Hall banquet to Colonial Premiers, 72–3; Albert Hall speech of, on Preference, 78–9, 82; relies on Hewins, 80, 86, 143; in debate on Budget, 82, 86–7, 117; on amendment to Budget, 83; and Tariff Reform, 86, 97, 146, 157, 182, 253; on Sargent's water-colours, 115; on German menace, 117–18; speaks on "Religion and Science," 124; portraits of, 125; on Churchill, 126–7; borrows Cross's hat, 128; Birmingham speech of, 135; Education Act of, 135; Cecil on, 140; and Irish amendment to King's Speech, 140; in debate on Navy Estimates, 159–60, 164, 171; and Vote of Censure on Navy question, 162, 171; and New Zealand's offer of Dreadnought, 169, 171; speaks at Agricultural Hall, 172, 174; busy week of, 172; on Lloyd George's Budget, 177, 179; praises author's speech, 179, 248, 612, 633, 639; on Hicks-Beach, 183, 262–3; and Constitutional Conference, 190, 278, 295–6; and Lloyd George's proposal of coalition, 192–3, 284–6, 288, 291–4, 577; undertakes to submit Tariff

Balfour, A. J.—*continued*
Reform to Referendum, 194–5, 302–7, 310–11, 416; author's letter to, on lesson of election, 196–200; ill-health of, 196, 200, 207, 379–80, 441; advocates corn duty, 204; and reform of Lords, 205, 220, 237; and possibility of taking office, 206, 210–11, 213, 226–7, 231–2, 242–3, 247–8, 255–9, 264, 266; throws note to Asquith, 218; speech of, in City, 222; Mowatt and, 225; at Cannes, 225, 230, 236; and free Colonial wheat, 227–8; on reform of Poor Law, 228, 238; likeness of, to Duc de Broglie, 233; on Birrell's speech, 237–8; discusses financial difficulties, 242–3, 245; on beet-sugar, 245, 253; at meeting to discuss Land policy, 253; on creation of peers, 254–5, 319, 554; interviews brewers, 261, 265; speech of, at King's death, 267; at memorial service, 270; and Veto Resolutions, 277; Garvin's letter to, 279; letters from, on Lloyd George's proposal, 287–9; breaks off negotiations on coalition, 293; post for, in coalition, 293; consults author on Food Taxes, 298–300; correspondence of, with author, on Referendum, 302–7; agrees to sink Party differences in crisis, 315; and Parliament Act, 319, 342–4, 348–51; author's loyalty to, 321, 349, 352, 370, 374; dissatisfaction with leadership of, 321, 352, 361–2, 365, 370; resignation of, 322, 359, 371, 374, 377–80, 383; on Morley, 336; offended by letter of author's, 342, 344; correspondence of, with author, on Parliament Bill, 348–51; and Halsbury Club, 362, 371, 373, 380; proposed meeting to express confidence in, 374, 376; author's feeling towards, 378; suggests French Alliance, 405; at Belfast demonstration, 406; and Minimum Wages Bill, 450, 454–5; and Women's Suffrage, 467; "too relevant," 470;

Balfour, A. J.—*continued*
  and Foreign Office, 483; and Irish
  question, 608–9, 626, 643–4; on
  Curragh "mutiny," 630, 633, 635;
  on the Government, 634; and De-
  volution, 637; on speaking in Hyde
  Park, 638; speech of, on Vote of
  Censure, 640–1
Balfour, Gerald, 193, 297
Balfour, Lady Frances, 125
Balfour, Miss, 56, 442
Balfour of Burleigh, Lord, 419, 459;
  minority report of, 229; his link
  with Waterloo, 421; Russian visit
  of, 437, 442, 464
Balkan War, First, 406, 491, 501;
  Second, 501
Balkans, Sazonoff on, 472; unstable
  situation in, 536, 544–8, 550
Banbury, Sir Frederick, 51, 457, 491
Bank of England, Bowles versus, 502,
  545
Barber, Indian Finance Minister, 111–12
Barbers' Hall, 118–20
Barnes, G. N., 201–3
Barnstaple, author's speech at, 100–1
Barrère, M., 473
Bathurst, Lord, 364–5
Battenberg, Prince Louis of, 545, 561–2
Baxter, Sir George, 105
Beatty, Admiral, portrait of, 565
Beaumont, Admiral, 326
Beck, Cecil, 165
Beckett, Gervase, 73
Bedford, cancelled meeting at, 348
Bedford, Duke of, 318, 348
Beet-sugar, protection for, 111, 245–6
Beira, 431
Belfast, University for, 102–3; anti-
  Home-Rule demonstration at, 406
Bell, Hesketh, 487
Bell, Moberly, 232
Benckendorff, Count, 561–2
Bengal, reversal of partition of, 404,
  411–12
Benn, W. Wedgwood, 206–7
Benson, E. F., *The Weaker Vessel* of,
  556
Bentinck, Lord H., 98

Bentinck, Mrs. Cavendish, 63
Beresford, Lord Charles, 130
Berlin, deterioration in manners in, 538
Bessborough, Earl of, 181
Bessborough, Lady, 524
Bigge, Sir A., *see* Stamfordham, Lord
Billy, Comte E. de, 532
Bird, Alfred, 139
Birmingham, Joseph Chamberlain's
  Tariff Reform speech in, 26 *n.*;
  Balfour's speech at, 135; Joseph
  Chamberlain's influence in, 223;
  author speaks in, 240, 543–4, 549;
  meeting of Unionist Association in,
  333 *n.*, 334; author succeeds father
  in, 599, 602–3, 607–8
*Birmingham*, H.M.S., launching of,
  501, 540
*Birmingham Daily Post*, 239, 240;
  Robbins's letters in, 409, 439, 461
Birrell, Augustine, 158, 475, 558, 605;
  on unappreciated jokes, 63–4; part-
  ing words of, at Education Office,
  68; characteristic speech of, 101;
  Irish University Bill of, 102; Irish
  administration of, 158; on Constitutional Conference, 190; Balfour
  on speech of, 237–8; informed of
  coalition proposals, 291, 577; convinced by author's speech, 558
Bismarck, Prince, and London cabman,
  99–100
Blackpool, Tariff Reform campaign
  at, 131
Bliss, Mr. and Mrs., 529
Blumenthal, Count, 73
Boislisle, M. and Mme de, 532
Bon, M. le, 528
Boraston, Mr., 48, 99, 146, 172, 260,
  532; on election prospects, 151; and
  election policy, 239; and fusion of
  Unionist Parties, 417–18, 479, 543
Borden, Sir Robert, 59, 71, 321
Botha, Louis, gush over, 68, 76;
  meeting of, with Roberts, 70;
  speeches of, 72, 76; Duncan on,
  78; at Union Conference, 155;
  and Germany, 421; deals with
  strikers, 603

Bouvens, Madame, 530

Bowles, G. F. S., 98, 147, 377

Bowles, Gibson, praises author's speech, 245; versus Bank of England, 502, 545

Boyd, Charles, on Joseph Chamberlain's speeches, 618

Bracquemond, Pierre, paintings of, 147

Bradford, Churchill's speech at, 621, 640

Brand, Robert, 440 n.

Bridgeman, W. C., 26

Bristol, Bonar Law's speech at, 600

British Fleet, seeks German squadron, 363, 367

Brodeur, Louis Philippe, Canadian Minister, 71, 73

Brodrick, St. John, see Midleton, Lord

Bromsgrove, author's speech at, 506, 573–4

Brooks, Councillor, 182

Brooks's, record blackballs at, 158

Brotherton, E. A., 309

Browning, Oscar, 116

Brownlow, Lady, 64

Bryce, James, 68–9, 489

Buchanan, George, 464, 476

Buckle, G. E., 298, 300

Budget, Asquith's, 66–7, 70–1, 74, 117; author drafts amendment to, 83; author opens debate on, 109; Lloyd George's (1910), 135–6, 167, 174–5, 176–80, 201; rejected by Lords, 136, 181, 189; ex-Chancellor's speech on, 177 n., 557–8; receives royal assent, 189; London electors and, 197; Irish opposition to, 198, 201–3, 206, 208, 240; possible Government defeat on, 206–7, 240, 248, 251; a year overdue, 209–211; to follow Veto Resolutions, 212, 214–15, 217; passing of, 251–2; discussions of, 254; Licensing clauses of, 261; and the Lords, 295; Tariff Reform, and Referendum, 303–7, 310–11, 416–17; (1911) 320; (1912) 468; use of surplus in, 470, 479; (1913) 557–8, 563–4

Bulgaria, 536, 547, 550; army of, 170; defeat of, 501

Bülow, Prince von, 95

Burnley, Tariff Reform League at, 131

Burns, John, 57, 253; "the Hemperor," 41; Deakin on, 80; and Unemployment Bill, 98; on Lloyd George's Budget statement, 178; on Lloyd George, 327; on Churchill, 340

Butcher, S. H., 77

Butler, Dr. Murray, 191

Buxton, Sydney Charles, 179, 465; dinner with, 65–6

Cadogan, Lord, 149

Caillard, Sir Vincent, 43, 73, 79

Caillaux, M., 426

Caldwell, James, 183

Callow, William, 147

Cambon, M., 427, 436; on Balfour, 233; on English character, 326; on Haldane's mission to Germany, 422; on Agadir crisis, 427–8

Cambridge, Political Society of, 116

Campbell-Bannerman, Sir Henry, 52, 57; and Navy Estimates, 55; suggests inter-Party conversation, 58; Standing Orders of, 62, 66; guillotine motion of, 67; and Colonial Conference, 74, 77; death of, 93; illness of, 99; resignation of, 104; resolution of, on House of Lords, 199, 212, 236

Canada, commercial relations of, with U.S.A., 29, 40, 48, 321; Budget statement of (1906), 40; commercial relations of, with Germany, 40, 48; oriental immigration into, 103–4; rebellion in (1837), 104; development of industry in, 113–14; treaty-making powers of, 141; Nomination System in Senate of, 191; and Irish question, 280; and Reciprocity Treaty, 321, 326–7, 336, 481, 489; and Food Duties, 434; policy of, as to strikes, 449–50; foreign emigrants into, 517

Canham, Past Master of Cordwainers' Company, 94

Cannes, author at, 190, 247, 251, 253,
321, 501; Balfour at, 207, 225,
230, 534; Mrs. Chamberlain ill at,
501

*Canning Papers,* Captain Bagot's, 152

Cardiff, coal strike in, 444, 446

Carnock, Lord, *see* Nicolson, Sir A.

Carpenter, Boyd, 56

Carrington, Lord, 248; author's reply
to, 143, 146

Carson, Sir Edward, 295, 477, 534, 610;
speaks at Dublin, 39; on author's
speech, 179; a Die-hard, 318, 358;
and Party leadership, 322, 373, 375–6,
383, 386–8; resists Home Rule, 358,
406, 643; seeks to reach agreement
on Home Rule, 507, 569, 571,
573, 590–4, 599; and Food Taxes
crisis, 508–9; conversations of, with
Asquith, on Irish question, 605–7,
643–5; on use of R.I.C. in Ulster,
609; speech of, 612–13; and
Devolution, 615, 627; wires to
Ulster to resist arrest, 622–3; and
Ulster gun-running, 640; speech
of, on Vote of Censure, 640–1;
prevents civil war, 641

Casablanca, 122, 426

Cassel, Lady Helen, 624

Cave, George, 480, 561, 622

Cawdor, Lord, 167, 170, 291, 301; in
Constitutional Conference, 190, 295–
296; author's letter to, on Lloyd
George's proposal, 286–7

Cecil, Evelyn, 51, 83

Cecil, Lady Edward, 375

Cecil, Lord Hugh, 211, 237, 264, 377,
509; a Die-hard, 318–19; and
Tariff Reform, 361, 555

Cecil, Lord Robert, 77, 146, 147, 237,
264, 567; and Marylebone seat, 84,
138; negotiations with, 139, 142;
accepts terms, 181; a Die-hard,
318; and Tariff Reform, 361, 376–7,
555; and North Herts vacancy,
376–7; and Devolution, 568

Chabron, Marquis and Marquise of,
529–30

Chamberlain, Annie (Mrs. Neville), 334

Chamberlain, Arthur, 443

Chamberlain, Austen, early life of,
15–19; mother of, 15; relations of,
with his father, 17, 19–20, 337–8,
535, 540; engagement and marriage
of, 17, 37; religious instruction of,
19; Chancellor of Exchequer, 19;
correspondence of, with Balfour,
on Party policy, 22–7, 32–4;
Balfour's letters to, 27–31, 34;
drafts "Valentine letter," 37; Dublin
speech of, 39, 41, 43; new house
of, 40, 43, 54–5; on his wife,
42; and fiscal amendments to
Address, 48–53, 140–6, 201–2; on
speaking in the House, 53, 68, 163;
and new Standing Order, 58, 62, 66;
drafts amendment to Budget, 83;
birth of son to, 89; speaks at
Barnstaple, 100–1; speaks at Ipswich,
106–7; opens debate on Budget, 109;
youthful opinions of, 116; at Pepys
Club dinner, 118; brushes of, with
Asquith, 131–2, 178, 244, 366; re-
peals Land Tax changes, 136; many
speeches of, 136–7, 266, 302; speaks
at Wolverhampton, 138–9, 642–3:
and amendment on Unemployment,
142–3; election forecasts of, 144;
advises Sir J. Fisher, 150–1; speaks
at Stepney, 160; improves in
debate, 161, 179, 244–5, 247–8,
250, 265–6, 612: speaks at Leeds,
172; on making ex-Chancellor's
speech, 177, 468, 557–8; drafts
resolution, 182–3; at Constitutional
Conference, 190, 295–7; and proposal for coalition, 193, 283, 576–7;
views of, on Home Rule, 193, 281–2,
284, 286–7, 291, 568, 587, 644–6;
letter of, on lesson of Election, 196–
200; on reform of Lords, 220–1,
263–4, 297; dines with King,
221, 484–6; memorandum of, on
Unionist policy, 225–31; on Vote
of Censure, 234–5; helps draft
motion on Lords' reform, 237;
discusses financial difficulties, 242–3;
Southport speech of, 243, 249, 252;

Chamberlain, Austen—*continued*
and Veto Resolutions, 243–4, 250;
and beet-sugar protection, 246;
consulted by Balfour on finance,
261; letter of, to Queen Mother,
268; sees dead King, 269; advises
Lords to delay, 276–7; letter of, to
Garvin, on Irish question, 281–3;
letters of, on Lloyd George's proposal
of coalition, 283–7, 291–4; Balfour's
letter to, on Lloyd George's proposal,
287–9; correspondence of, with
Lansdowne, on Constitutional Conference, 290–4; post for, in coalition, 293; on Food Taxes, 298–300;
drafts resolution on Lords, 301–2;
correspondence of, with Balfour on
Referendum, 302–7; Edinburgh
speech of, 302; and Albert Hall
Pledge, 302 *et seq.*, 316, 332, 387, 392,
415–17; bitterest experiences of,
316–17, 506; his loyalty to Balfour,
321, 349, 352, 370, 374; joins
Halsbury Club, 322, 359, 374; and
Party leadership, 322–3, 359–62,
371–5, 380–3, 385 *et seq.*; on Parliament Bill, 327; busy days of, 328–
329, 331; in need of holiday, 329–30,
332–3; Balfour offended by, 344;
Long's jealousy of, 345, 382, 392;
correspondence of, with Balfour,
on Parliament Bill, 348–51; "poor
ambition" of, 367; withdraws his
name as candidate for leadership,
381–3, 389, 394–5; visits Russia,
405, 437–8, 440–2, 464, 471–4, 482;
invited to accompany Kitchener to
Russia, 405; writes to Bonar Law
on Referendum, 416, 495–7; refuses
Chairmanship of Civil Service
Enquiry Commission, 429, 440–1;
and Foreign Office, 438, 482–3;
speech of, on Minimum Wages Bill,
452, 463; quarrels with Attorney-
General, 458, 461; "too relevant,"
470; foreign policy of, 483; offers
to attack Asquith, 494; visits Paris,
502, 525–32; differs from Party,
502, 545–6; advises action in Food

Chamberlain, Austen—*continued*
Tax crisis, 502, 513, 516; speech of,
on abandonment of Food Taxes,
504–6, 514, 520; correspondence
of, with Lansdowne, 514–15; correspondence of, with Chaplin, 516–17;
spends night at Windsor, 518; takes
Chairmanship of Royal Commission
on Indian Finance, 535, 542, 563, 565;
speech of, at Tariff Reform League
Conference, 537–8; on his choice
of career, 540; speaks on Lloyd
George's Revenue Bill, 545–6, 551,
558; on preparing speeches, 548;
on gathering wild flowers, 556, 560–
561; portrait of, by Laszlo, 565;
correspondence of, on Home Rule
question, 567 *et seq.*; suggests
Devolution, 568, 572, 574–5, 581,
615–17, 636–7, 644; conversation
of, with Churchill, on Home Rule,
572–7; severs connection with East
Worcestershire, 599, 601–3; Southampton speech of, 601; Skipton
speech of, 602–3, 607; speech of, in
House, on Home Rule, 610, 612–13,
622–3; speech of, on Curragh
"mutiny," 633, 636, 639; moves
Vote of Censure, 640–1, 646; at
State Banquet, 646

Chamberlain, Beatrice, 115, 125, 145,
331, 341, 343, 425; takes charge of
household, 17; and her stepmother,
18; at the lying in state, 274–5;
works for East Worcestershire,
602

Chamberlain, Diane, 408–9, 556, 635
Chamberlain, Florence (Mama), 16
Chamberlain, Hilda, 80, 443; in
Dublin, 41, 43
Chamberlain, Ida, 171, 252, 545
Chamberlain, Ivy (Mrs. Austen), 42,
54, 58, 59, 86, 107–8, 110, 124–5,
145, 147, 172, 254, 267, 316, 321,
324, 325, 357, 519–20, 556; marriage
of, 37; author on, 42; and Albert
Hall Banquet to Colonial Premiers,
56, 67, 71–2; at Colonial tea-
party, 56; appreciation of, by cook,

Chamberlain, Ivy (Mrs. Austen)—*contd.*
78; birth of son to, 89; on Furse
portrait, 94; visits Tower, 98; at
Barnstaple, 100–1; on author's
speeches, 107, 173, 249, 519, 549;
At Home of, 110; hears author's
speech in House, 250–1; on procession to Westminster Hall, 271;
at lying in state, 275; wide interests
of, 330; Cordwainers' memento to,
339; and son's operation, 341–3;
Swiss visit of, 345; and author's
decision as to leadership, 381, 393,
395; birth of daughter to, 408–9;
loses lock of hair, 487; and Mrs.
Lowther, 494; asked to launch
*Birmingham,* 501, 540; launches
*Warspite,* 501; in Paris, 502, 525–32;
given author's portrait, 565

Chamberlain, Joe, junior, 328, 331, 345,
523; undergoes operation, 341–3;
at Camilla Lacey, 539, 555–6

Chamberlain, Joseph, first marriage of,
15; his love of flowers, 15; second
marriage of, 16; third marriage
of, 17; author's letters to, 18,
20; precepts of, 19; pioneer of
Tariff Reform, 19, 23, 89, 503;
retires from active work, 20, 38;
last hours of, 20; strives for Imperial Union, 23, 31, 223, 509, 537;
seeks agreement with Balfour, 23,
34, 37; visits author's new house,
54; suggests Committee on Business, 58, 65; quoted against author,
62; as Colonial Secretary, 74;
praise from, 77, 248; invited to
King's dinner to the Colonial
Premiers, 77; a *Radical Autoritaire,*
81; Furse portrait of, 94, 339; and
Gladstone, 96; on Canadian rebellion, 104; and Willcocks, 106,
564; letter of, to Goulding, 155;
and New Zealand's offer of Dreadnought, 171–2; letter of, 183;
letter of, to Freeth, 184; King asks
after, 221; Rosebery on, 223; on
Votes of Censure, 235; conversation of, with Balfour, 236; and

Chamberlain, Joseph—*continued*
death of Edward VII, 272; urged to
write to King George, 272–3; Irish
policy of, 282; refuses to advise, 317,
337; author expresses his debt
to, 337–8, 535; Hartington asked
not to consult, 338; Cordwainers'
memento to, 339; on Halsbury,
351; his influence on Milner, 369;
motto of, 370; and Lord R. Cecil,
377; and author's decision as to
leadership, 381–3, 393–5; and fusion
of Unionist Parties, 423, 427, 442,
453; on coal strike legislation, 451–
454; proposal of, for settling
Panama difficulty, 522; scheme of,
for provincial councils, 553, 615,
636; retires from Parliament, 599–
600, 603; Skipton's message to,
604–5; Free Trade speeches of,
618–19

Chamberlain, Mary (Mrs. Joseph), 17–
18; letters to, 38, 88–9; letters
from, 272, 393–5, 451, 453–4;
operation on, 501, 562

Chamberlain, Neville, 77, 324, 334,
478, 608; speeches of, 68, 165,
544; telegram from, 356–7; Town-
Planning scheme of, 488; on author's
preparation for speeches, 548

Chamberlain Birthday Fund album, 563

"Chamberlain's Ink," 94

Channel Tunnel, 529

Chaplin, Henry, 144, 151, 375, 434,
534–5, 612; and Irish amendment
to Address, 140–1; prowess of, 152;
speech of, 179; and summoning of
Party meeting, 383–4, 386; and
Referendum, 433; and crisis on
Food Taxes, 503, 520; correspondence of, with author, 515–17;
resolution of, at Tariff Reform
Conference, 537–8

Charmes, Gabriel, 531

Cheltenham, election result at, 309

Cherry, R. R., 39; "old Hugly," 41

Chilston, Lord, *see* Akers-Douglas, A.

China, republic in, 420; Russian aims
in, 561

Chippendale, account of, 173
Churchill, Lady Edward Spencer, 110
Churchill, Winston, 52, 57, 65, 105–6, 126, 146, 179–80, 248, 268, 486, 595; and fiscal discussion, 52–3; Lugard on, 79; promoted to Cabinet, 97; good speech of, 117; and Army Estimates, 126–7; Dryden couplet quoted at, 145–6; and Retaliation, 152–3; and new Dreadnoughts, 166, 174; and proposal for coalition, 192, 576–7; on imminence of defeat, 208; bon mot of, 225; and Veto Resolutions, 244; breaks Government's pledges, 329; in need of holiday, 330; Burns on, 340; and strike negotiations, 346, 360; and German menace, 365; moves to Admiralty, 366–8; and Lloyd George, 366, 414, 533; ambition of, 367; speech of, and Germany, 412; Navy Estimates of, 438, 443, 451; story of, 459; opposed to coal strike legislation, 465; bad speech of, on Home Rule Bill, 479–80; struck by book, 491; asks Lady Chamberlain to launch ship, 501, 540; seeks to effect settlement on Home Rule, 506–7, 572–6; seeks conference on Compulsory Service, 522; on possibility of war, 561–2; author's conversations with, on Irish question, 572–7, 578, 586; author's correspondence with, 579–81; fiery speeches of, 621, 631, 635; on Curragh blunder, 634–5, 639
Civil Service, Royal Commission on, 429, 440–1; and Liberal Government, 488
Clarke, Sir G., 100
Claughton, Sir Gilbert, 361
Clemenceau, Georges, 326, 426, 538; Delcassé on, 125; on strength of British army, 365
Clermont Tonnerre, Comte and Comtesse de, 531–2
Clifford, Lady, of Chudleigh, 110
Clinton, Lady, 101
Clive, Mrs., 250, 555

Clive, Percy, 565
Cluny Museum, 525
Clyde, Lord, 325, 440
Coal strike, 404, 430, 439, 443–6, 448; negotiations to close, 432, 448; possible courses as to, 441, 450; fears of violence in, 444, 463; legislation on, 448–58; resumption of negotiations, 456, 460; result of ballot on, 469
Cobbett, William, 541
Cochin, Denis, 531
Cochrane, Tom, 39, 51
Coke of Norfolk, 120, 126
Cole, Alfred, 339
Cole, Mrs. Alfred (Lilian), 339; anxious for Deakin to address meeting, 80–1; and Women's Liberal Unionist delegate, 110
Colefax, Arthur, 312
Colefax, Mrs., 560
Collection of Taxes Bill, 551, 558
Collings, Jesse, 56, 115, 143, 325, 602 n.; Land Bill of, 56; accident to, 161; and discussion on Land policy, 253; Home Rule pamphlet of, 475; contemplates book on land question, 476
Colonial Conference, author advises summoning of, 24; question of Referendum after, 25; Balfour on requirements of, 29–31; author on requirements of, 33; Canadian proposition for, 59; Colonial resolutions for, 65; general interest in, 67–8; question of President for, 74–5; and question of Preference, 75–80; publication of discussions at, 78; Asquith angers, 78–80; fit designation for, 82; and Food Taxes, 407, 559
Colonial Preference, see Preference
Colonial Premiers, Albert Hall Banquet to, 71; Stafford House dinner to, 75; King's dinner to, 77
Commons, House of, long sittings in, 63; distribution of Parties in (1910), 202; suggested joint sitting of, with Lords, 295–7, 303; finance the sole business of, 295; Payment of Members of, 320; disorderly scene in, 491

Compulsory Military Service, 365; coalition proposals on, 292; conference on, 522

Conciliation Bill, 414, 424, 439, 466

Conference of Ambassadors, London, 501, 562

Conservative Party, *see* Unionist Party

Consolidated Fund Bill, 234, 242, 632

Constitution, legislation affecting, 296, 369; changes in, and Parliament Bill, 318, 320, 409; reform of, as Unionist policy, 365

Constitution Conference, 190–2, 194, 277–8; no record of proceedings of, 191, 290; and Irish question, 284–8, 290, 294, 296–7; author's notes on, 291; Finlay's notes on Report of Proceedings at, 295–7; failure of, 296–7, 298

Cook, Captain, relics of, 173–4

Cordwainers' Company, 93–4; opening of new Hall of, 338–9

Corn tax, 58, 86, 146, 299; fixed limit for, 24; Balfour and, 204; and Colonial wheat, 227–8, 253; Lansdowne on, 433, 502

Cornwall, and Home Rule, 328

Cotes, Dr., 138

Cotton, duties on, and India, 111–12; strike, in Lancashire, 404

Cowper, Lady, 540

Cox, Harold, 253

Craig, Captain, 51

Crewe, Lord, 126, 158, 211, 248, 268, 467, 535, 542, 564; on Constitutional Conference, 190, 278; informed of coalition proposals, 291, 577; and French Entente, 427

Croft, Henry Page, 508–9, 511; maiden speech of, 204

Cromer, Lord, 109, 153, 170, 375; and Referendum on Tariff Reform, 308–9

Cross, Sandy, 128, 147–8

Crossley, Savile (Lord Somerleyton), 107, 151, 201, 348; and fusion of Unionist Parties, 417–19, 423

Crowborough, 560

Cruppi, M., 326

Curragh, "Mutiny" at the, 599, 624–8, 637–8; explanations of, 629–636, 639; reinstatement of officers after, 631

Curtis, Lionel, 553

Curzon, Lord, 298, 301, 333, 446; converted to Tariff Reform, 109, 113–14; and Indian attitude to Preference, 111–12; and reform of Lords, 220–1, 263–4, 338; fine speech of, 234; conversation of, with Morley, 335–6; and Parliament Bill, 343, 358, 554; and leadership of Lords, 359; summons meeting of "anti-Die-hards," 373; on Indian changes, 409; dominates Lansdowne, 422; as Foreign Minister, 471, 482, 484; lack of foresight in, 482–3; and Home Rule Bill, 555; and Devolution, 637

Czechs, 547

*Daily Chronicle*, on Navy Estimates, 153; on author's speech, 452

*Daily Express*, 115

*Daily Mail*, 105, 302; and Referendum for Tariff Reform, 304; turns against Food Taxes, 502

*Daily News*, 413, 439; on author's speech, 452

Darlington, 302; and Tariff Reform, 308

Davey, Lord, speeches of, 68

Davidson, Archbishop Randall, 325, 629; and Welsh Disestablishment, 292; on King's pledge to create Peers, 319

Deakin, Alfred, 67, 72–8, 80–2

Death Duties, increase in, 71

Defence Committee, 117–18

Delagoa Bay, 431

Delcassé, Théophile, 326; on Czar, 124; on Clemenceau, 125

Delhi, transfer of capital to, 404, 411, 521; unsuitable site of, 410

Denbigh, Lord, 245

Denbighshire, 175

Derby, Lady, story told of, 75

Derry, Nationalist demonstration at, 618

Desborough, Lady, 63–4, 170

Devlin, Joseph, 586, 622–3, 642

Devolution, 280–1, 370, 481; Lloyd George's scheme for, 282, 284, 286, 288; Liberal Party pledged to, 287; author's scheme for, 568, 572, 574–575, 581, 615–17, 636–7; Lansdowne on, 570–1, 594; leaders' dislike of, 637, 643

Devonshire, election results in, 196

Devonshire, 8th Duke of, 72, 101; death of, 99

Devonshire, 9th Duke of, 99, 436, 626, 629

Dickson, Scott, Hood's letter to, 142

Die-hards, oppose Parliament Bill, 318–19, 554; Balfour's "rebuke" to, 319; form Halsbury Club, 358, 372

Dietz, M. and Mme, 526–7

Dillon, Dr., on Austria, 527

Dillon, John, 206, 241, 493, 586

Diploma Gallery, 523–4

Djakava, 546

Dominions, examinations for Indian Civil Service in, 82; and abandonment of Food Taxes, 517

Douglas, Sir Charles, 646

Dreadnoughts, 55; "Phantom," 164–167; New Zealand offer of, 167–72

Du Maurier, Gerald, in Raffles, 58

Dublin, author's speech in, 39, 41, 43; Dillon's speech in, 241

Duckworth, George, 66, 67, 73, 100, 565

Duma, Russian, 129

Duncan, Patrick, on Botha and Smuts, 78

Duncannon, Lord, 366, 532, 536–7, 560, 582

Dundas, Colonel, 56, 58, 63

Dundas, Evelyn, 74

Dundas, Mrs., 58, 63, 165

Dundee, by-election at, 105–6

Dunmore, Lord, 375

Durham, election results in, 310

East Worcestershire, 540; author leaves, 599, 601–3

Edinburgh, Balfour's speech in, 34; Unionist chances in, 146–7, 175; deputation from, 156; author's speech in, 302; Bonar Law's speech in, 516–18, 559

Education Act, effects of, 25; alienates Nonconformists, 135

Education, Board of, and University Grants, 429

Edward VII, King, 54; death of, 190, 268–9; and creation of Peers, 199, 241–2, 247, 254–6, 264; author dines with, 221–2; memorial service to, 269–71; lying in state of, 273–5; verses on death of, 274; funeral of, 276

Edwards, Enoch, 267

Elgin, Lord, 59, 76, 78; and Winston Churchill, 79, 459; Deakin on, 80

Elibank, Master of, 59, 345

Elliot, Arthur, 310

Ellis, Tom, 58, 62

Endicott, William, 79, 529

England, in Devolution scheme, 288; growing lawlessness in, 526; see also Great Britain

Entente, Anglo-French, 403, 405, 413, 471, 483–5

Enver Pasha, coup d'état of, 520

Etty, paintings of, 524

Evelyn, John, Diary of, 539, 557

Ewart, Sir John, 634

Faber, Lord, 582

Farquhar, Lord, 172

Farrar, Lord, 618–19

Fawkes, Admiral Sir Wilmott, 130

Federalism, for Ireland, 193–4, 281, 574–575, 626–7, 642; for United Kingdom, 194, 370, 568, 570, 574, 581, 584, 589, 615–17; Lloyd George's scheme for, 284, 288

Ferguson, Sir Charles, 627

Fielding, W. S., 191; Budget Statement of, 40

Fildes, Luke, drawing of King Edward by, 274

Finlay, Sir Robert, 183, 191, 446, 469, 480, 613; motion of, 237; and legal position of minority Government, 255, 259; notes of, on Constitutional Conference, 295-7; on Food Taxes and Referendum, 434; on definition of coal mines, 457; and amendment to Army Annual Bill, 618

Fiorenzo of Lorenzo, paintings of, 327-8

Fisher, Admiral Sir John, 118, 165; quarrel of, with Beresford, 130; author's advice to, 150-1; and Naval Estimates, 150-1, 166-7; converts McKenna, 234

Fitzroy, Sir Almeric, 271

Flavin, M. J., 251

Flint, Unionist defeat at, 517

Food Taxes, 202; and election results, 197, 299; Balfour asked to abandon, 298, 300; author on, 298-300; Private Member's motion on, 317; Party disunion on, 403, 406, 502-4; Bonar Law asked to abandon, 408; Lansdowne and, 421, 432-3; Unionist discussion of, 432-6; use of proceeds from, 434; abandonment of, 503-6, 508-19; and the Colonies, 510-11, 559

Foreign Legion, Germans in, 121-2

Forster, Lord, 363

France, and Baghdad Railway, 123; effect of Retaliation threats on, 152-153; strikes in, 161; author's visit to, 190, 267; and Agadir crisis, 316, 346-7, 353, 360, 363; period of instability commencing in, 326; asks for British support, 360-1, 363, 425, 472; author seeks closer alliance with, 405, 413, 425, 485; British Entente with, 403, 405, 412-13, 425-426, 485; works out plan of campaign with Britain, 420, 428; Grey's loyalty to, 422, 428; relations of, with England, 425-6; relations of, with Italy, 473, 529; belligerent spirit in, 526, 528, 536; Government overthrown in, 539; English ships to be built in, 552

Franchise and Registration Bill, 406, 413-14, 447; Women's Suffrage amendment in, 424, 501, 519; dropped by Government, 501, 521

Francis Joseph, Emperor, 546

Free Fooders, 24, 28, 29, 135, 311, 496; and "Valentine letter," 37; *Morning Post* article on, 142; Balfour blames, 157; lose seats, 189; in Glasgow, 197

Free Trade, 30; Imperial, 29; principles of, 67; Unionists, and Albert Hall Pledge, 308-9; Joseph Chamberlain's speeches on, 618-19

Freeth, Sir E., Chamberlain's letter to, 184

French, General, 624, 634

Frewen, Moreton, 565

Gaelic League, 281

Garvin, J. L., 106, 182, 193, 232, 439; letters of, on Irish question, 279-80, 288-9; author's answer to, 281-3; against Food Duties, 298, 300; and extension of Referendum to Tariff Reform, 310-11; and Balfour, 370; and Bonar Law, 375, 387

Garvin, Mrs., 560

George V, King, 190, 225, 301, 315, 327, 340, 646; South African visit of, 201; receives address from Privy Councillors, 267; asks after Joseph Chamberlain, 268, 272; proclamation of, as Sovereign, 268; at memorial service, 270; at Proclamation Council, 271; at funeral, 276; Coronation of, 318; and creation of Peers, 318-19, 326-7, 347, 349, 554; announces transfer of Indian capital, 404, 409-11; author's conversation with, 486, 518; Bonar Law suggests prerogative of Veto to, 486-7; objets d'art of, 518; and Home Rule Bill, 618

George I, King of Greece, 539

George, David Lloyd, 66, 145, 183, 200, 202-3, 248, 254, 268, 360, 429-30, 455, 480, 486, 488, 490; in Tariff Reform discussion, 53; to address Colonial Conference, 79; and Free

INDEX

George, David Lloyd—*continued*

Trade principles, 87; Chancellor of the Exchequer, 87, 93, 155; and Asquith's Budget, 109, 111, 117; description of himself as Chancellor of Exchequer, 128; Budget of (1910), 135–6, 167, 174–5, 176–80; and new Dreadnoughts, 166, 174; Budget speech of, 177–8; Newcastle speech of, 184; member of Constitutional Conference, 190; proposes coalition, 191–3, 283–94, 576–577; characteristic speech of, 204; possibility of Government under, 211; and squaring of Irish, 212, 214–16, 241–2, 248, 251; inaccuracies of, 222; Land Taxes of, 229; on inevitable dissolution, 235; and Haldane, 245; proposes Federal Home Rule, 284, 286, 288, 292; misunderstands Unionist view of Irish question, 284–8; and Colonial Preference, 286, 288, 292; conversation of, with Balfour, 288; post for, in coalition, 293; on Referendum, 306; and Agadir crisis, 315, 346, 353; settles railway strike, 320, 437; his stay at Court, 327; Insurance measures of, 336–8, 414; on creation of Peers, 347; bellicose spirit of, 363; and National Defence, 365; and Churchill, 414, 533; on Manchester defeat, 442; and coal strike, 444, 462, 465; Budget of (1912), 468, 470, 479; on relevance as disability, 470; moves resolution to establish a Committee on Estimates, 475; on Welsh Disestablishment Bill, 478; unpopular with his Party, 482; Harcourt's attack on, 519; seeks conference on Compulsory Service, 522; land campaign of, 533; probable successor to Asquith, 533; Revenue Bill of, 545–6, 551; Budget of (1913), 558; suggests exclusion of Ulster, 572; seeks settlement on Home Rule, 576, 639; memorandum of, on coalition, 577–8; author refuses to meet, 580, 586

Germany, Canadian commercial relations with, 40, 48; animosity in, towards England, 95, 122–3, 425–6, 431; large navy of, 95, 123, 135, 153, 431–2; menace of, 117, 191; espionage system of, 175; visit of working-men to, 248–9, 265; and Agadir crisis, 315–16, 346–7, 353, 363, 428; author on, 353, 420–1, 472; and Turkey, 355–6, 520; and West Africa, 367, 412; growing tension with, 403, 405, 412–13; Haldane's mission to, 403, 412, 420, 422, 472; and South Africa, 421; colonial expansion of, 431–2; French irritation with, 526, 528; changed character of, 535–6, 544; airships of, 545; attitude of, to Balkan disturbances, 547; desires visit from Grey, 550–1; influenced by British domestic troubles, 620, 627

Girouard, Sir Percy, 79

Gladstone, Herbert, 59

Gladstone, W. E., 116; on Parnell as speaker, 68; oratorical power of, 96; story of, 224; Bills of, 224; Home Rule policy of, 282

Glasgow, Unionist chances in, 142, 144, 146, 154; Unionist defeat in, 197, 309–10; Government drop in, 440

Glasgow programme, 23, 25, 227

Godley, Sir A., 69, 224

Goldsmith, Mr., 107

Gordon, Evans, 73

Gorst, Eldon, 54

Gough, General Hubert, and "mutiny" at Curragh, 624–8; returns to Ireland, 631

Gough, General John, 624–8

Goulding, E. A., 48, 50, 142, 144, 149, 226, 235; and negotiations with Cecil, 138–9; Joseph Chamberlain's letter to, 155, 158; and land policy, 228

Graham, Lord and Lady, 107

Grahame, Lady Cynthia, 170

Granet, Sir Guy, 361

Gray, Albert, K.C., 637

Great Britain, German menace to, 95, 117, 123; obligations of, 169; asked to support France, 360-1, 363, 425, 472; works out plan of campaign with France, 420, 428; attitude of France towards, 425-6, 485; air fleet of, 545, 562; and possibility of European war, 547, 561; provincial legislatures for, 568

Greece, 536, 547; assassination of King of, 539

Grenfell, General, 60-1

Grey, Earl (Albert), 553; letters of, on Irish question, 582-5, 589

Grey, Sir Edward, 57, 73, 103, 106, 211, 363, 405, 414, 470, 475; on German menace, 122-3; and Naval Estimates, 151, 171, 174; and reform of constitution of Lords, 205, 236; surrender of, 213-15, 217, 236; on Agadir crisis, 346-7, 428; on Haldane's mission to Germany, 422, 472; and French Entente, 427, 486; and Minimum Wages Bill, 452, 455, 459, 463; on coal ballot, 469; on Home Rule Bill, 481-2; presides over Conference of Ambassadors, 501, 562; Harcourt's attack on, 519; and Panama difficulty, 522; and leadership of Party, 533; on Montenegrin blockade, 546-7, 550; European prestige of, 550; and visit to Berlin, 550-1; and Home Rule question, 567, 570, 584, 626, 635; on Curragh "mutiny," 633

Griffiths, Norton, 298

Grillions, 105, 116, 158, 254, 266, 419, 429, 469

Grimsby, 308-9

Guest, Freddy, 58

Guinness, Walter, 107-8

Gwynne, H. A., 138-40, 142, 226, 360, 387, 398, 479, 608; on Canada and Reciprocity Bill, 336; on Tariff Reform, Lords' Reform and National Defence, 364-5; on triple alliance, 413; on Unionist Foreign Minister,

Gwynne, H. A.—continued
482-3; on conference on Compulsory Service, 522

Gwynne, Rupert, 226

Habit Vert, L', 529

Haddock, G. B., 148

Haig, Sir Douglas, 484, 628

Haldane, Viscount, 105, 127, 158, 211, 236, 251, 360, 469; Army reforms of, 54-5, 361, 365; as a speaker, 69, 244-5, 325; on Lloyd George, 179; author's attack on, 244, 248; mission of, to Berlin, 403, 412, 420, 422, 472, 486; on University Grants, 429; on the settling of railway strike, 437; on coal strike, 445; Earl Grey's correspondence with, on Irish question, 583-4, 589; denies intention to coerce Ulster, 635

Halsbury, Lady, 538

Halsbury, Lord, 295, 327, 442, 538; leader of "Die-hards," 318-19; and Parliament Bill, 342-4, 351; and reform of Lords, 360, 362

Halsbury Club, aims of, 322, 358, 369, 372; formation of, 358; lack of agreement in, 362; and Tariff Reform, 364; "tends to keep alive differences," 371; and Party leadership, 371-4; gathering of, at Hatfield, 490

Hamilton, George, 68

Hamilton, Lady Ian, 170

Hamilton, Sir Ian, 102; in Bulgaria, 170; book of, on Compulsory Service, 326

Harcourt, Lord, 64, 268, 429-30, 465-6, 467, 533; and English Land Bill, 85; on Lloyd George's figures, 222; at lying in state, 274-5; in need of holiday, 330; Joseph Chamberlain's letter to, 419; lobby work of, against Women's Suffrage, 447; attacks Grey and Lloyd George, 519

Hardie, James Keir, 244, 259

Hardinge, Lord, 88, 460, 484

Hardy, Gathorne, Life of, 261-2

Hardy, Laurence, 51, 462

Harrel, W. V., 613

Harris, Leverton, 175, 179; visits to, 120, 539, 555-6; and author's Limehouse speech, 162-3; Fanny Burney's *Diary* of, 163-4; author's holidays with, 190, 267, 330, 406, 502, 525

Harris, Walter, Moroccan stories of, 120-1

Harrison, Mr., on advantages of Protection, 552

Harrowby, Lord, 344

Hartington, Lord, letter of, 338

Hartland, Dixon, 50

Hawkin, Mr., letter of, to *Times*, 289-91

Hayes-Fisher, William, 82, 86, 560

Hay-Pauncefote Treaty, 620 *n*.

Healy, Maurice, 488

Healy, Tim, 101-2, 203, 212; denounces Unionists, 214; brilliant speech of, 254, 260; sends message to Joseph Chamberlain, 260; on exclusion of Ulster, 615

Heligoland, 412

Henderson, Arthur, 98, 139

Herbert, Sidney, 601

Herbette, M., 532

Herrick, Myron T., 529-30

Herschell, Lord, 326

Hewins, W. A. S., 58, 80, 96-7, 106, 111, 113, 197, 209, 226, 312, 331, 542-3; and Canadian Budget Statement, 40; and fiscal amendments to King's Speech, 48, 141, 143; Balfour's reliance on, 80, 86, 143; on Balfour's speeches, 97; at Committee on Tariffs, 152; maiden speech of, 465; and Food Taxes crisis, 509, 517, 519; Canterbury speech of, 532

Hicks-Beach, Sir Michael, 138, 245, 301; Balfour on, 183, 262-3

Hills, J. W., 50-2, 310, 524

Hofmeyer, J. H., 65, 79, 155

Holderness, Sir Thomas, 564

Holland, author's visit to, 137, 176

Holland, Bernard, 76; life of the Duke of Devonshire of, 363

Holland, Sir William, 152

Home Rule, 567 *et seq.*; author's Dublin speech on, 39, 41; debate on, 100-1; Liberal pledge on, 135; Parties unable to agree on, 190, 293-4, 296-7, 522; changes in opinion regarding, 280, 287; and Ulster, 291, 406; Liberal proposal regarding, 296-7; commencement of struggle over, 323, 403; Parliament Bill amendment on, 342-3; Irish agitation for, 414; attempt to reach agreement on, 502, 506-7, 568 *et seq.*, 605; "within Home Rule," 567, 570, 573, 605, 614, 616, 619; exclusion of Ulster from, 568, 570-4, 586, 599, 605, 613-17

Home Rule Bill, 405-6, 474, 487, 564; postponement of, 441; second reading of, 477, 479, 481; author's speech on, 488; Government defeated on amendment of, 491-2; rejected by Lords, 501; Unionist opposition to, 567, 609, 618-19, 643; demand for general election on, 607; debate on, 610-13; prophecy on Gladstone's, 638; impossibility of repealing, 643; Imperial aspect of, 644

Hood, Alec, 85, 106, 110, 122, 144-5, 177, 181-2, 211-12, 214, 419; approves "Valentine letter," 37; and fiscal amendments to Address, 51-2, 142, 201-2; letter of, to Scott Dickson, 142; and election results, 197, 200; on Cecil pride, 377

Hope, James FitzAlan, 398

Hops, debate on, 207-8, 216, 221, 226

Hopwood, Francis, 54

Housing shortage, cause of, 136

Howick, Lady, 78

Hughes, Percival, 122, 142

Hull, author's speech in, 548-9

Hunt, Miss Brook, 56

Hunt, Rowland, 86

Hyde Park, speaking in, 637-8

"Impressionism," 147

Income Tax, differentiation in, 71, 74, 176; increase of, 175

India, Morley on problems of, 59; equality of races in, 60; Kitchener in, 68–9; Morley's repressive measures in, 87; frontier trouble in, 106; and Preference, 111–14, 542, 549–50, 552; transfer of capital of, 404, 410–11, 521; Curzon on changes in, 409–11; and Turco-Italian War, 460; Russian intentions towards, 484

Indian Civil Service, and Dominions, 82

Indian Finance and Currency, Royal Commission on, 535, 563, 565

Insurance Act, 320, 336, 338; unpopularity of, 403, 414, 440, 442; question of repeal of, 415; attempt to beat Government on, 480

Ipswich, author speaks at, 106–7; Lee's "ludercrus" speech at, 602

Ireland, and fiscal system, 42; amendment to Address on, 140–1; Birrell's administration of, 158; Federalism for, 193–4, 281; feeling against Budget in, 206; changed conditions in, 279–81; limited self-government for, 280–3; author's views on question of, 281–3, 284, 291, 576; question of, and Constitutional Conference, 284–8; Home Rule agitation in, 414; increasing tension in, 507; danger of civil war in, 584, 587–8, 615, 617, 626. See also Home Rule

Irish Nationalist Party, likelihood of split in, 102; opposed to increase in spirit duties, 136, 189, 198; Liberals dependent on, 189, 191; and Veto Resolutions, 189, 213–15, 241, 251; opposed to Budget, 201–3, 206, 208; "squaring" of, 212, 214–16, 236, 240–1, 246–7, 251–2; replenished funds of, 235; Lloyd George and, 287, 292; propose Carson as leader, 387; and Women's Suffrage, 447; and Minimum Wages Bill, 455; and

Irish Nationalist Party—continued exclusion of Ulster, 611, 621, 629; in debate on Vote of Censure, 642

Irish Times, 515, 595

Irish Town Tenants' Bill, 39

Irish University Bill, 102–3

Isaacs, Sir Rufus (Attorney-General), 493–4; misleads Speaker, 457–8, 461; author's altercation with, 458, 460–1; at Windsor, 518

Isvolski, Alexander, 128, 471

Italy, annexes Tripoli, 316, 353–6; author visits, 316, 321, 353–7; losses of, in Turco-Italian War, 459; relations of, with France, 473, 529; military weakness of, 529

Jamaica, incident in, 54

James, Mrs. Christopher (Aunt Lina), 433

Jameson, Dr. Starr, 72, 75; dinner with, 65–6; and Preference, 77; at Union Conference, 155

Japan, menace of, to Australia, 29; alliance with, 280

Japanese, in Canada, 103–4

Jardine, Sir Ernest, 417, 444, 537

Jewellers' dinner, 521, 608

Jonnart, M., 531

Jowett, Dr., of Carr's Lane, 327

Joynson-Hicks, Sir William, 97

Kato, Madame, on Queen Alexandra, 276

Kaye, Lady Lister, 170

Kendal Division, Free Trade candidate for, 532–3

Kenrick, Archibald, 16

Kenrick, Mr. and Mrs. William, 521

Kenyon, Lord, 417

Keppel, Derek, 168

Kerr, Philip, 440

Kew, suffragette outrage at, 523

Kilbracken, Lord, 70 n., 565

Kimber, Sir H., 40

Kimberley, Lord, 68

King, W. L. Mackenzie, 93, 103; and Japanese ex-Consul, 103–4

King's Lynn, 308–9

Kinnaird, Lord, 72

Kipling, Rudyard, poem of, on King's death, 274

Kitchener, Lord, in India, 68–9; at memorial service, 271; death of, 405

Koechlin, M., 530

Kokovtsoff, M., 473–4, 484

Kuropatkine, A. N., 102


Labour Party, 127; working with Liberals, 89, 198; and Unemployment, 98, 141; Liberals dependent on, 189; and Lloyd George's Budget, 189, 201; and Vote of Censure, 345; and railway strike, 346; and Minimum Wages Bill, 455; Government disregard of, 493; Budget amendment of, 564

Ladybank, Asquith's speech at, 572, 579, 583, 605

Laird, Sir William, epigram of, 449

Lambert, George, 234

Lambeth Baths, speech at, 491

Lambton, Fred, 86, 147, 181

Lamlash, squadron sent to, 635

Lancashire, and Tariff Reform, 109, 131, 144; and India, 111–12; election results in, 196–7, 200; and reform of Lords, 220; strike in cotton mills of, 404; attitude to Food Taxes in, 406, 502; result of coal ballot in, 469; demonstration in, 618

Land Bill, introduction of Collings's, 56; Harcourt's, 85

Land Taxes, and Lloyd George's Budget, 136, 174, 176, 228–9; and Ireland, 201; Unionist alternative to, 229; Lansdowne on, 230–1

Langenbach, Mrs., 524

Lansdowne House, Unionist meetings at, 37, 409, 445–6, 465; discussion on Lord's reform at, 219–20, 260–1, 263–4; Liberal Unionist meeting at, 475–6; meetings at, to discuss Curragh "mutiny," 625–6, 629

Lansdowne, Lady, 56, 185; sprained ankle of, 290

Lansdowne, Lord, 61, 143, 181–2, 185 n., 225, 245, 252, 300–1, 375, 446, 467, 469, 579, 626–7, 630; member of Constitutional Conference, 190, 192, 278, 287, 295–6; and reform of Lords, 199, 205, 220, 222, 230, 233–4, 255, 263–4, 265–6, 276–7; raises funds for Liberal Unionists, 201; and Unionist policy, 230, 406; on Scottish constituencies, 246; scheme of, for House of Lords reform, 249–50; correspondence of, with author, on Constitutional Conference, 289–90, 294; post for, in coalition, 293; and Referendum for Tariff Reform, 304–6, 310, 406, 416, 421, 433, 495; author's letter to, on Referendum, 311–12; and Parliament Bill, 318–319, 342–4, 349–51; moves Lords Reform Bill, 335, 338; unpopularity of action of, 348; and Balfour's resignation, 378–9; retains leadership in Lords, 380, 504, 515; and Indian changes, 409–11; and closer union with France, 413, 427, 436; and Food Taxes, 421, 432–3, 502, 504, 508, 511–12; as Foreign Minister, 471, 483; correspondence of, with author, on abandonment of Food Taxes, 514–15; correspondence of, with author, on Irish question, 567–72, 577–8, 585–6, 588, 592–4; on Devolution, 570–1, 594, 615, 637, 644; on possibility of coalition, 578; on Home Rule Bill, 643

Lascelles, Sir Frank, 412

Laszlo de Lombos, P. A., portraits by, 125; author's portrait by, 565

Laurier, Sir Wilfred, and Colonial Conference, 58–9, 72, 75–6, 78, 80–81; defeat of, 321, 336

Law, Arthur Bonar, 56, 85, 97, 110–11, 113, 142, 226, 231, 300, 409, 417, 466, 492, 494, 532–4, 543, 550, 558, 633; and fiscal amendment to

Law, Arthur Bonar—*continued*
King's Speech, 48–53, 204; admirable speech from, 66, 117, 421; on Empire Free Trade, 113; and proposal for coalition, 192–3, 284, 286, 292; and defeat or dissolution of Government, 226, 235; and rating reform, 229; and reform of Lords, 237, 239, 263; on author's speech, 245, 266, 367; and beet-sugar protection, 246, 253; and Ulster, 290; suggests Referendum on Tariff Reform, 303–4; candidate for Party leadership, 323, 359, 375, 380–1, 383, 387–8; chosen leader, 323, 389–96; author discusses Party's position with, 373–5; relations of, with author, 375; Balcarres on, 387; and Referendum, 392, 396, 399, 415–16, 433–6, 495; correspondence of, with author, on leadership, 397–9; and Food Taxes, 406–7, 408, 433–4, 502; slip of, 415; charges Government with corruption, 415, 441; author's letters to, on Referendum, 416, 495–7; on coal strike, 441, 443–4, 446; maiden speech of, 447; and Minimum Wages Bill, 450, 454, 456, 461–2, 467; attacks Asquith, 474–5; speeches of, 475, 478; conversation of, with King, 486–7; contemplates Vote of Censure, 490; author's advice to, 503, 516; abandons Food Taxes, 503–4; offers to resign, 503–4, 508, 512–14; and attempt to reach agreement on Home Rule, 506, 568–9, 589, 605, 629–30; correspondence with, on abandonment of Food Taxes, 509–13; Edinburgh speech of, 516–18; faults of, as leader, 527, 534; speeches of, against Home Rule, 567, 569, 600, 607, 610, 622; conversations of, with Asquith, 574–6, 583, 586–93, 599–600, 605, 611, 643–5, 647; letters of, on Irish question, 582, 600; dislikes idea of Devolution, 594, 637; on supporting Ulster, 617–18; on

Law, Arthur Bonar—*continued*
author's speech, 622, 633, 639; letter of, to Asquith, after Curragh incident, 626, 629; speech of, on Vote of Censure, 640–2; on Home Rule Bill, 643–4

Lawrence, Charles, pictures of, 524
Lawrence, Joseph, 109, 138, 332
Lawrence, Lady, 521
Lawrence, Lord, 537
Lee, Arthur, 50, 55, 82, 118, 120, 159, 167, 346, 455, 524, 617; portrait of, 125; and Navy dissensions, 130, 165; speech of, 174, 324, 602
Lee, Mrs. Arthur, 167, 174
Leeds, author's speech at, 172; Balfour's speech at, 378, 384, 399, 415; Asquith's speech at, 578–9, 581, 583, 605
Lee-Warner, Henry, 19
Leicester, Earl of, 126
Leith, Liberal defeat at, 616
Lepine, M., 531
Lethbridge, Sir Roper, 543, 550
Lewis, Leroy, 60
Liberal Government, difficulties of, 85; falling prestige of, 135; and Navy question (1909), 158, 160, 174; Votes of Censure against, 162, 171, 234–5, 345, 490, 640–1; dependent on Labour and Irish, 189; outcome of possible defeat of (1910), 206–13, 216, 219, 221, 226–7, 231–2, 240, 242, 247, 255–9; desires defeat, 206, 208, 212, 257; Veto Resolutions of, 212, 214–15, 239; supported by Opposition, 212–13, 344; surrenders to malcontents, 214–15, 251–2, 254; financial policy of, 231–2, 235; Naval programme of (1910), 233–4; and "squaring" of Irish, 236, 240–1, 251–2; rumoured dissensions in Cabinet of, 346, 461, 465; unconstitutional action of, 404, 409–10; and settlement of coal strike, 404, 446, 448–52; charged with corruption, 415, 441; on the down grade, 440, 478, 482, 492; weakness of,

Liberal Government—*continued* 452, 454–6, 461–3, 465–7; Civil Servants on, 488; beaten on Home Rule amendment, 491–4; Robbins on, 533; and Marconi scandal, 564; Balfour on, 634

Liberal Party, splits over Home Rule, 19; and Labour, 89, 198; and reform of Lords, 136; division in, 165, 167, 205; and Referendum, 194; well-filled war chest of, 201; and Chapel organisation, 250; and Irish question, 282, 615; pledged to Devolution, 287; Suffragists in, 447; and Russian friendship, 471

Liberal Unionist Party, hit by Education Act, 25; author's speech to, 115; funds of, 201; election policy of, 239; and Scotland, 328; and Lansdowne, 348; unites with Unionists, 405, 417–19, 423, 427, 442, 475–9, 543; strength of, in House, 418–19; and abandonment of Food Taxes, 532; model Committee of, 543

Licensing Bill, 67, 131; rejection of, 135

Limehouse, author's speech at, 162–3

Lincoln, election result at, 309; author's speech at, 548–9

Linlithgow, Lord, 50

Little-Englanders, 174

Liverpool, and Tariff Reform, 97; Bonar Law's speech at, 436

Lloyd, George (Lord Lloyd), maiden speech of, 204; and Food Taxes crisis, 509, 511–12, 517, 519

Locker-Lampson, Oliver, 552

Lockwood, A. R. M., 51

London, election forecasts in, 144; election results in, 196–7; coal economy in, 448; Treaty of, 501

London Chamber of Commerce, and Tariff Reform, 65

London County Council Elections, results of, 54; and Land Taxes, 228

Londonderry, Lady, 56, 324

Londonderry, Marquess of, 33, 63–4, 145, 378; and reform of Lords, 263; and Referendum, 433

Long, Walter, 58, 85, 110, 234, 238, 301, 344, 373, 409, 435; speaks at Dublin, 39; and Plural Voting Bill, 40; against fiscal amendment to King's Speech, 48, 50, 52; and reform of Lords, 220, 255; and Constitutional Conference, 295–6; candidate for Party leadership, 322–3, 359–60, 372–4, 380, 383, 385–91; his jealousy of author, 345, 382, 392, 396; character of, 345, 372, 382; and Balfour, 345, 362, 380, 384, 387, 427; praises author's speech, 367; withdraws his name as candidate for leadership, 381, 389; death of son of, 382; and calling of Party meeting, 383, 386; loses his temper, 384; unfitted for leadership, 387–8, 390–1; letters of, 395–7; speech of, at Party meeting, 395, 400; upholds Referendum, 416; and fusion of Unionist Parties, 427; and Food Taxes, 433–4; maiden speech of, 447; speaks against Home Rule Bill, 480; ill-health of, 534; amendment of, on Home Rule, 607

Lords, House of, to be strengthened or reformed, 70; rejects Budget, 136, 181–2, 189, 320; question of reform of, 136, 199, 201, 212, 364–5, 409, 490; agitation against, 189, 197; creation of new Peers for, 189, 199, 241, 254–5, 295, 318–19, 347, 349; proposal for elective element in, 201, 219–21, 230, 234, 249; committee of, to consider reform, 205; and Veto Resolutions, 209, 215, 241, 247, 254; attitude in, towards reform, 233–4; Finlay's motion on reform of, 237; proposal that P.M. nominate members to, 249–50; Referendum in reform of, 249–50, 263, 302; suggested joint committee of, with Commons, 295–7, 303; Unionist resolution on, 301–2; curtailment of power of, 318, 320;

Lords, House of—*continued*
and Parliament Bill, 318–19, 326–7,
343–4, 364; rejects Naval Prize
Bill, 321; purely elected, 358, 362,
370; and Home Rule Bill, 609,
614
Lords Reform Bill, 333, 335; Lords'
reception of, 338
Loreburn, Earl (Lord Chancellor),
278; on Women's Suffrage, 424,
430; and Home Rule question,
572–3
Louvre, the, 526–7
Lowe, R., on Treasury correspondence,
459
Lowther, J. W. (Speaker), 457–8,
461, 491, 493; threatens to resign,
494; and Home Rule debate, 613,
622
Lucy, Sir Henry, 174, 620
Lugard, Sir Frederick, 487–8; on
Colonial Office, 79
Lynch, Arthur, 165
Lyne, R. N., 79
Lyttelton, Alfred, 56–7, 67, 146, 155,
164–5, 167, 169, 177, 238, 287, 464;
and fiscal amendment, 53, 423;
approves amendment to Budget,
84; portrait of, 125; on Exchequer
Bonds, 235; and reform of Lords,
263; and Constitutional Conference,
295–6; proposes round-robin, 371,
374; and Party leadership, 371–2,
375, 383; suggestions of, on Food
Taxes, 434; speeches of, 477; in
E. Africa, 534; death of, 565
Lyttelton, Mrs. Alfred, 56
Lytton, Bulwer, 24

McCrae, Sir George, 175
MacDonald, Ramsay, 346, 632–3;
and Land Bill, 56; on Australia and
Preference, 76; and Minimum
Wages Bill, 455
Macedonia, 548
McKenna, Reginald, 86, 462, 467, 486,
490; on Lloyd George, 87; and
Naval Estimates, 150–1, 159, 166–7,

McKenna, Reginald—*continued*
234–5; leaves Admiralty, 366–8;
and Welsh Disestablishment Bill,
477, 493
Mackenzie, Thomas, 536
Mackinder, Sir Halford, maiden speech
of, 204
Mackrell, Mr., 87, 94
Macnamara, T. J., 423
McNeill, Ronald, 491
Macquisten, F. A., 449
McVittie, Mr., 260
Malan, F. S., 65
Malet, Lady Ermyntrude, 538
Manchester, and Tariff Reform, 198,
299; election results in (1910),
308; Government defeat at, 440,
442
*Manchester Courier*, 502
Manhood Suffrage Bill, 403
Manners, Lord and Lady, 375
Marconi scandal, 564
Marie, Empress of Russia, Delcassé on,
124; adviser and confidant of, 149;
at Edward VII's memorial service,
270; at funeral, 276
Marine Insurance, Committee on, 67 n.
Markham, Miss, 430
Marlborough, Duke of, 318
Marlborough House, dinners at, 56, 59;
concert at, 167–8
Marston, Mrs., 139
Mary, Queen, 270, 646
Marylebone, 110, 172, 184; and
Robert Cecil, 84, 140
Mason, A. E., 65
Mason, J. F., 51; speeches of, 161
Masterman, C. F. G., 146, 457
Matthews, Mr., 109
Maxse, Leo, 58, 80, 81, 110, 321, 372,
538; letter from, 438
Maxwell, Sir John Stirling, 24
May, Admiral, 150
Meat duties, 159
Mediterranean, Germany and, 356;
Britain abandons, 485
Menebbe, 121
Mensdorf, portrait of, 125
Merriman, J. X., 155

Meshed, Russian bombardment of, 476

Metric System (Compulsory) Bill, 63

Metternich, Count, 122–3

Meux, Lady, 561

Middlemore, J. T., 51

Middleton, author speaks at, 331

Midlands, Unionist chances in, 144; election results in, 196

Midleton, Lord (St. John Brodrick), 58, 262, 264, 615; and reform of Lords, 220–1, 333

Mildmay, F. B., 423

Millerand, M., 526, 528

Millet, paintings by, 526

Milner, Lord, 266, 553; speech of, 110; a Die-hard, 318; and Halsbury Club, 358–9, 368; views of, 368–70; volume of speeches of, 562

Miners' Eight Hours Bill, 99

Minimum Wages Bill, 404, 448–9, 452–8, 460–7, 469; Unionist opposition to, 450, 454, 464; author's speech on, 452, 456–7; insertion of figures into, 452, 455–6, 462, 465; point of order about definition clause in, 457–8

Minto, Lady, 518

Minto, Lord, 344, 411

Mond, Sir Alfred, 467

Monsell, Eyres, maiden speech of, 233

Montenegro, Russia and, 472; coercion of, 544–7, 550

Moor, Frederick, of Natal, 71–2, 77–9

Morant, Sir Robert, 68, 488

Morley, Viscount, 465, 485–6, 506, 564; on Indian problems, 59–60; dinner conversation of, 68–70; flashlights on weakness of, 70; repressive Indian measures of, 87; undependableness of, 335–6, 338; author discusses Irish question with, 580, 586–91, 594; dislikes Federalism, 586, 593; leakage concerning letter to, 594–5; and Curragh blunder, 634

Morning Post, 49, 152, 184; article of, on Free Fooders, 142; and Leeds speech, 172; prepared to believe the worst, 218–19; attitude of, to Lords' reform, 364–5; on Reciprocity Treaty, 489

Morocco, Foreign Legion in, 121–2; French in, 354, 531; Germany and, 420, 425; danger of secrecy in crisis in, 608

Morocco, Sultan of, 120–1

Morpeth, Lord, 68

Morris, Sir D., 324

Morrison, Walter, 603–4

Moseley, Alfred, 551

Moulton, Lord, 524

Mowatt, Sir Francis, 224–5, 459

Murray, Sir George, 73–4, 488; and placing of Treasury Bills, 218; on Model Committee, 543

Mutiny Act, amendment of, 607

Nasrullah, 60

National Defence, 533; Lloyd George's proposals for, 193, 283–4; and Halsbury Club, 358–9, 369; Gwynne on, 365

National Gallery, 327

National Government, Lloyd George proposes, 191–3, 283–94; distribution of posts in, 293

National Health Insurance, 320, 336, 338

National Review, 321

National Service, 359–61, 365; Milner on, 369–70

National Unionist Association, 405, 418; rules of, 453; meeting of Executive of, 536–7

Naval Prize Bill, 320–1

Navy, dissensions in, 130, 150–1; controversy as to sufficiency of, 135, 150–151, 153, 158–61, 164–7

Navy Estimates, discussion on (1907), 55–6; Cabinet deadlock on (1909), 149–51, 153; debates on (1909), 159–61, 164, 171; debates on (1910), 233; Churchill's (1912), 438, 443, 451

Nevill, Lady Dorothy, 541

New Hebrides Labour Ordinance, 52, 57

New Zealand, offers new Dreadnought, 167–72

Newcastle-on-Tyne, Lloyd George's speech at, 184; author's speech at, 302, 328–9

Newcastle-under-Lyne, 138

Newton, Lady, 537

Newton, Lord, 233; Balfour's letter to, 319, 348

Nicholas II, Emperor of Russia, Delcassé on, 124; and English treaty, 128–9; Pernolet on, 148–9; and Witte, 474, 484

Nicholson, A. W., on Lloyd George's Budget speech, 178

Nicolson, Sir Arthur (Lord Carnock), 458–9; on Russian conditions, 128–9, 484; on foreign views of England, 326; on Turco-Italian War, 459–60

Noel, Admiral Sir Gerard, 165–6

Noetzlin, M., 528–9

Norfolk, Duke of, 319, 343–4

Northcliffe, Lady, garden of, 124

Northcliffe, Lord, and Food Duties, 300, 502

Northumberland, Duke of, 358

Norton, C. E., letters of, 638

Nostell Priory, 172–4

Nys, Mlle de, 63

Oates, Captain, 525

O'Brien, William, 203, 236, 248, 251, 254

Observer, 106, 174, 182, 232, 310; and Federalism, 193, 283

O'Connor, T. P. (Tay Pay), 206; on Irish funds, 235; on Veto Resolutions and guarantees, 247

Occupying Ownership question, 230

Old Age Pensions Bill, 52, 71, 127; second reading of, 118; sliding scale of income for, 125; and Ireland, 278

Oliver, F. S., 84, 86, 170, 265, 367; and Federalism, 193; approaches Milner, 368–9; pamphlet of, 576

Onslow, Lord, 367

Orwell Park, 105–8

Paget, Dr., 108

Paget, Sir Arthur, and "mutiny" at the Curragh, 624–5, 627–30, 634–5, 637–8

Palgrave, Sir R., 178

Pall Mall Gazette, 439

Pallain, M., 528

Panama tolls, question of, 620

Paris, author's visit to, 502, 525–32

Parker, Charles, 246

Parker, Sir Gilbert, 48, 50–1, 84

Parliament Bill and Act, 189, 317–18, 339–40, 348–51, 493, 501; Lords' amendments to, 318; passing of, 319, 342–4, 554; Committee Stage of, 335; absurdity of procedure under, 613–14

Parnell, Charles, speeches of, 68

Parsons, Alfred, 147

Passive Resisters' Bill, 61

Paston Letters, 108

Patronage Financial Secretary, 243

Payment of Members, 320, 336

Pease, Jack, 49, 73, 206

Pease, Pike, 122, 417, 522, 540

Peckham by-election, 99

Peel, Captain, 107

Peel, Sydney, 555

Pepys Club, 118–20

Percy, Lord, 143, 176; speech of, 101

Pernolet, M., on Russia, 148–9; on Balfour, 232–3; on Anglo-French relations, 425–6; dinners with, 525–6, 530–2; on Millerand, 528; on Faubourg, 530

Persia, Germans active in, 124; Russia and, 476, 483; projected railway across, 484, 528

Petrie, Sir Charles, Walter Long and His Times of, 389 n.

Pie Powder, 330

Pilgrims, 72–5

Plunkett, Horace, 99, 601

Plural Voting Bill, 39, 40, 414

Plymouth, meeting at, 185

Poincaré, Raymond, 473, 528, 530

Political Society, Cambridge, 116

Ponsonby, Arthur, 149

Poor Law, reform of, 228, 230, 292; Committee Minority Report of, 238–9; discussion on, 253

Port Arthur, 102

Poynder, Dixon, 65

Preference, author advocates, 32, 58; discussed at Colonial Conference, 76, 79; Asquith refuses, 78; Balfour's speech on, 77, 79; and India, 111–14, 542, 549–50, 552; question of amendment to Address on, 141, 143; and corn tax, 146; Lloyd George's proposals on, 284, 286, 292; question of Commission on, 288, 333; amendment on, 324 n.; and Food Tax question, 406–7, 502, 504–5, 510–11; Round Table and, 553

Pretyman, E. G., 107–8, 159, 253, 261; speech of, 179, 180

Protection, dissociated from Colonial question, 31; advantages of, 552


Raffles, 58

Railway strike, 346; Lloyd George settles, 320, 437; and French telegram, 360–1, 436; South African, 603 n.

Rankeillour, Lord, 398 n.

Rating reform, 229

Rayleigh, Lord, 344

Reciprocity Treaty, 321, 326, 336, 481, 489

Redmond, John, 493, 586, 614; speech of, 101, 241, 612; and Lloyd George's Budget, 201–3, 206, 254; and Lords' Veto, 213, 217, 219, 241; Healy's attack on, 254; "Imperial" declarations of, 279, 282; and exclusion of Ulster, 572, 616; danger to life of, 615–16

Redmond, William, 414

Rees, Sir J. D., 165, 348

Referendum, 194, 361; enquiries into working of, 191; on Tariff Reform, 195, 302–7, 310–11, 358, 416–17; on House of Lords reform, 249–50, 263, 342; author declares against, 387, 392; Bonar Law and, 392, 396, 415–16; Unionists drop offer of, 406, 433, 495; Unionist meeting to consider, 432–6, 490; on Home Rule question, 626

Reid, Sir George, 191, 223, 484

Remnant, J. F., 51

Retaliation, Balfour and, 97; India and, 111–12; threats of, and France, 152–3

Revelstoke, Lord, 225, 232

Revenue Bill, 545–6

Ribot, M., 531

Richards, Judge and Mrs. Whitmore L. (Leo and Emmeline), 339

Richards, Hilda Mary, 63

Rider, Mrs., 165

Ridley, Matthew, 48–50, 110, 152, 225–6, 519; lunch with Curzon at house of, 109, 111; at Committee on Tariffs, 152; and Joseph Chamberlain's letter, 158

Ritchie, Richmond, 69

Robbins, Sir Alfred, 48–9, 141, 201, 446–7; London letters of, 409, 439, 461; on state of Liberal Government, 533; on Asquith's Home Rule speech, 611; on author's speeches, 636

Roberts, Field-Marshal Earl, 118, 375, 600, 625; meeting of, with Botha, 70; at memorial service, 271; and Curragh "mutiny," 626

Robertson, Civil Lord of the Admiralty, 55

Robertson, J. M., 423

Robinson, Geoffrey, 552

Roosevelt, President, 455, 481; portrait of, 125

Rosebery, Lord, 207, 236 n.; and reform of Lords, 70, 136, 219–22, 276–7; and Fanny Burney's Diary, 163–4; and rejection of Budget, 181–2; report of Committee of,

Rosebery, Lord—*continued*
199; proposes Committee to consider reform, 205; possibility of neutral government under, 210–211; on Joseph Chamberlain, 223; speech of, 233; letter of, to *Times,* 253

Ross, Judge, 42

Rothschild, Alfred, "French bonbons" of, 168

Rothschild, Lord, 363; on Mowatt, 225; promises loans, 258

Roumania, 501, 547

Round Table, author dines with, 553

*Round Table,* 440

Roundell, Major, 604

Royal Irish Constabulary, 609

Royal Navy Club, 328

Royds, E., 97

Rugby, author at, 19; School Speech Day at, 126

Runciman, Sir Walter, 184

Russell, George, and Gladstone, 224

Russia, 170; and Baghdad Railway, 122; Cabinet responsibility in, 128, 474; public opinion in, 129; M. Pernolet on, 148–9; author visits, 405, 437–8, 440–2, 464, 471–4; British Entente with, 471, 483; and Balkan affairs, 472, 545–7, 561; financial and commercial recovery of, 473; German influence over, 483–4; and India, 484; and France, 529; and war with Austria, 547, 561; and China, 561; Austro-German outburst against, 620

St. Aldwyn, Lord, 102, 367

St. Andrew in the Wardrobe, 163

St. George's in the East, Irish vote in, 206–7

St. John of Bletsoe, Baron, 348

St. Oswald, Lord, 172–4

St. Petersburg, author's visit to, 405, 437–8, 440–2, 464

Salford, South, and Tariff Reform, 308

Salisbury, 2nd Marquess of, letter of, on election results, 262; letter of, to Hartington, 338

Salisbury, 4th Marquess of, 157, 246, 301, 554, 626, 629; and reform of Lords, 220–1, 263; evening party of, 261; and Parliament Bill, 317–18, 343, 349–50

Samoa, 412

Samuel, Herbert, 492

Samuel, Sir Harry, 389 *n.*

Sandars, Jack, 142–3, 162, 182, 211, 259, 483; and "Valentine letter," 37; on Rosebery's speech, 233; and Balfour's resignation of leadership, 378–80, 384; and leadership of Party, 381, 392

Sanderson, Lord, 105, 116, 436; on British support for France, 420, 427

Sargent, John Singer, water-colours of, 115

Sauer, Dr. Hans, 155

Sazonoff, M., 473–4, 479; on Anglo-Russian friendship, 471; author's conversation with, 471–3; on bombardment of mosque, 476; on author as Foreign Minister, 482; Nicolson on, 484

"Scientific tariff," 24, 153

Scotland, forecast of election results in, 144, 146–7, 151, 154; organisation of Unionist Party in, 156; election results in, 196–8, 206; animosity against landlords in, 197–8, 206; and reform of Lords, 220, 222; deputation from, 246; type of candidate liked in, 246; Tariff Reform in, 246, 364; and Home Rule, 328; Liberal Unionists of, and fusion, 418; result of coal ballot in, 469

*Scotsman,* and election results, 206; on author's Edinburgh meeting, 302

Scott, Captain, 524–5

Scott, Percy, 130

Scottish Land Bill, 76–7, 85; Scottish tenant on, 61–2

Scutari, 546–7

Seaman, Owen, Coronation Ode of, 274

Seely, J. E. B., 206, 537; on British air fleet, 545; and "mutiny" at Curragh, 624, 630, 633; resignation of, 633–634

Ségur, Comte and Comtesse Louis de, 531

Selborne, Lady, 78

Selborne, Lord, 78, 155, 264, 295, 350, 409, 446, 483, 537, 567, 579; a Die-hard, 318, 358; and leadership of Lords, 359; on National Service, 360–1; and Tariff Reform, 364; and Food Taxes, 433, 517, 519; J. Chamberlain's message to, 520; and Devolution, 568, 615

Selby, Viscount, 105, 158

Servia, 547, 550

Shaw, Lord Advocate, 73

Sheffield programme, 28, 31

Shensi Relief Expedition, 443

Sifton, Sir Clifford, 325

Simon, Sir John (Solicitor-General), 432, 543, 612; Home Rule amendment of, 102

Sinclair, John (Earl of Pentland), Scottish Land Bill of, 61–2; peerage of, 149

Sinn Fein, 281

Skipton, author speaks at, 602–3, 607

Smartt, Sir Thomas, 71, 76, 78

Smillie, Robert, 462

Smith, Abel, 157, 181

Smith, Dunlop, 487

Smith, F. E., 57, 226, 344, 347, 374, 376, 467, 506, 508, 586, 590, 612; bon mot of, 148; and proposal for coalition, 192–3, 283–8, 291–2; speech of, 203–4, 237; on land policy, 228–9; author's letter to, on Lloyd George's proposals, 279, 283–285; a Die-hard, 318; author's letter to, on Balfour's leadership, 321, 352, 358; on rumour of Asquith's resignation, 414; broken rib of, 534; arranges Lancashire demonstration, 618

Smith, Llewellyn, 336

Smith, Parker, 40, 165–6

Smith-Dorrien, General, 326

Smuts, General, 65; and Predikants, 76, 78; at Union Conference, 155

Snowden, Philip, 564

Somerleyton, Lord, see Crossley, Savile

Somerset, Duchess of, 538

Somerset, Duke of, 178

Somerset, Lady Kitty, 561

South Africa, 76; Union Conference in, 155; opening of Union Parliament in, 201; fear of Germany in, 421; railway strike in, 603 n.

Southampton, Balfour's speech at, 23, 26; author's speech at, 601–2

South Kensington Museum, 555

Southport, author's speech at, 243, 249, 252

Soveral, Marquis de, 170

Spender, J. A., 73, 109

Spirit duties, increase in, 136, 189, 198

Spring-Rice, Cecil, 93, 522, 524; on German menace, 94–5

Stamfordham, Lord (Sir A. Bigge), 59, 583, 626; on creation of Peers, 326, 347; objects to violence of speeches, 617

Standard, 457

Stanley, Arthur, 83, 86

Steel-Maitland, Sir Arthur, 255, 347, 359, 362–3, 372, 377, 435; maiden speech of, 204; and Parliament Bill, 342, 344; and fusion of Unionist Parties, 417, 423, 479; character of, 527; criticises Party councils, 533–4; author's letter to, 559–60

Stepney, author's speech at, 160, 162–3

Steyn, President, 155

Stolypin, P. A., 129, 474

Storey, Sam, 57, 226, 328; and land policy, 228–9; seconds Tariff Reform debate, 245

Stradbroke, Lord and Lady, 107–8

Strathcona, Baron, 54

Stuart-Wortley, C. B., 58

Suffragettes, 62, 169–70; at Board of Trade party, 330; outrages of, 404, 438–9, 444, 501, 523; precautions against, 521, 555

Suffragists, hostility of, to Asquith, 135

Sugar Convention, 490

Sugar duty, repeal of half, 153–4

Super-tax, 176

Sutherland, Duke of, 344; Tariff Reform Party of, 139

Switzerland, use of Referendum in, 306; author visits, 321, 343, 345

Sykes, Mark, 548

Taft, President, on proposed Reciprocity Treaty, 321, 481, 489

*Tageblatt,* article in, 140

Talbot, Edmund, 522, 535, 544

Tardieu, M., 526

Tariff Reform, Joseph Chamberlain the pioneer of, 19, 23; need for Conservative unity on, 23–6; amendments to Address on, 48–53, 140–6, 199, 204; Albert Hall demonstration on, 56, 63; and Colonial Conference, 68; progress of, 95, 97, 105–6, 129, 131, 184–5, 204; and India, 111–14; and Lloyd George's Budget, 182–3; Balfour promises Referendum on, 194–5, 302–7, 310–311, 496; and General Election, 195, 196–8; debate on, 245; and beet-sugar protection, 246; and Scotland, 246, 364; and Food Duties, 298–300; and Halsbury Club, 364; basis of social reform, 365–6; author's position regarding, 376–7; amendment on, 423; popular appeal of, 549, 604; Cecil's attitude to, 555; question of deputation on, 582

Tariff Reform League, 43, 49, 50, 56, 57, 440; Conference and dinner of, 95; reports and figures of, 97, 131, 156; Balfour's speech to, 157; appeals for funds, 366; and abandonment of Food Taxes, 517, 519, 559; gatherings of, 536–8

Taxation, broadening basis of, 78; Budget amendment on, 83, 117

Tea, Preference on, and India, 110–11

Territorial Army, 55, 361; recruiting for, 365; lack of faith in, 444, 522

Thompson, Canon Denton, 230

Thompson, Whittaker, 604

Thornton, Percy, 147–8

Thring, Mr., Parliamentary draughtsman, 224

Thynne, Lord Alec, 58

*Times, The,* 143, 153, 232, 319, 439, 557; Arthur Lee's letter in, 130; letters of "Pacificus" in, 193; letter in, on Unionists and Ulster, 289–91; and Parliament Bill, 348; on Tripoli question, 354; opposed to Food Taxes, 406, 496, 502, 559; and Budget surplus, 470, 479; article of, on Indian debate, 552–3; and Home Rule, 567

Tirpitz, Admiral, 95

*Titanic,* loss of, 474, 477

Tobacco, preference for Irish, 111; increase in duty on, 136, 180, 183

Tosti, Signor, 96

Touche, G. A., 26

Tower of London, 98

Trades Unions, payment of members from funds of, 200; hit by coal strike, 445

Transport workers strike, 404, 444

*Trelawny of the Wells,* 261

Trevelyan's *Life of John Bright,* 562

Triple Entente, 471, 483–5, 608; and Irish question, 627

Tripoli, annexation of, 316, 353–6

Tryon, G. C., 110, 423, 543; maiden speech of, 204

Tryon, Lady, 110

Tullibardine, Marquess of, 61

Turco-Italian War, 353–6, 403, 459–460, 479, 529

Turkey, revolution in, 176, 520; Italy declares war on, 316, 354–6; development of national feeling in, 355; and Baghdad Railway, 422, 472

Tweeddale, Julia Lady, 73

Tweedmouth, Lord, 59, 65

Tyrrell, Sir William, 482–3

Ulster, 194; Unionist Party and, 289–290; author's views on, 291; and Home Rule, 406, 589; attitude to

Ulster—*continued*

Food Taxes in, 502; "Home Rule within Home Rule" for, 567, 570, 573, 605–6, 614, 616, 619; exclusion of, 568, 570–4, 586, 599, 605, 609, 611, 613–17, 629–30, 643–4, 647; boundary question of, 573, 614, 619; use of R.I.C. in, 609; amendment to prevent use of troops in, 609, 618; impossibility of coercion of, 613, 615, 632; prepared to fight, 613, 641; hardening of opinion in, 615; active measures of Government against, 622, 627, 630, 632, 634–6, 638–40; Asquith's proposal regarding, 623 *n*., 629; gun-running into, 639–40

Ulster Covenant, 406

Unearned increment tax, 176

Unemployment, amendment to King's Speech on, 140–1

Unemployment Bill (1908), 98

Unemployment Insurance, 336–7

Union Club, Birmingham, 240

Unionist Party, lacks constructive policy, 22–6, 28; need for unity in, 22, 26, 28, 30, 135; hit by Education Act, 25; Balfour's policy for, 30–1; defeat of (1906), 37; "a Colonial Preference" party, 53; feeling of elation in, 82–3; possibility of victory for, 135; gain of seats for (1910), 189; constructive programme of, 189; a united party, 189, 200; and Irish question, 190, 280–7, 290, 294, 567, 578, 584–5, 587–8, 617, 630; considers proposal for coalition, 191–3, 292–3; and Referendum, 194, 249–50, 317; land policy of, 200, 228–30, 253, 365; and possibility of taking office, 206–13, 216, 219, 221, 226–7, 231–2, 242, 247, 255–9, 266; discussion on policy of, 226–9; financial difficulties facing, 231–2, 242–3, 245, 257–8, 266; Kentish labourer's help for, 232; obtaining of loans by, 258; and Food Taxes, 298–300, 403, 406, 502–4, 508–19; disunion in, 317–19,

Unionist Party—*continued*

321–2, 371, 495; and Parliament Bill, 317–19, 351–2; choice of leader for, 322–3, 359, 377 *et seq.*; and reform of Lords, 333; Halsbury Club formed in, 358; programme of, 365–6; unites with Liberal Unionists, 405, 417–19, 423, 427, 442, 475–9; drops offer of Referendum, 406, 495; Anti-Suffragists in, 446

United Club, author's speech at, 58

United Irish League, 207

United States, commercial relations of, with Canada, 29, 40, 48; State Constitutions of, 191; and Irish question, 280–2; and Reciprocity Treaty with Canada, 321, 481

University Grants, 429–30

Ure, Alexander (Lord Advocate), 433

"Valentine letter," 19, 37

Vancouver riots, enquiry after, 103–4

Veto Bill, 206, 209, 214, 217

Veto Resolutions, 212, 239, 247; to precede Budget, 214–15; Irish and, 241; guillotine motion on, 243; debate on, 244; author's amendment on, 250

Victoria and Albert Museum, Salting bequest in, 523

Victoria Memorial, unveiling of, 340

Villiers, E. A., 165

Virchow, Rudolf, 94

Vivian, Henry, on Webbs, 239

Wakefield, election result at, 309

Waldegrave, Lady, 78

Wales, results of elections in, 196; result of coal ballot in South, 469

Walfisch Bay, 412

War Office, preparedness of, 367–8; "over-hastiness" of, 420; instructions from, on Ulster, 627

Ward, Sir J., Prime Minister of New Zealand, 71–2; and Preference, 75, 77; address to, 170–1

Ware, Fabian, 80, 304

Warrington, election result at, 308–9

*Warspite,* H.M.S., 501, 506

Wason, Cathcart, 170–1

Webb, Sidney and Beatrice, Poor Law report of, 238–9

Welsh Disestablishment Bill, 193, 292, 403, 405–6, 477, 493, 522–3 ; rejected by Lords, 501

Wemyss, Mrs., 451

Wenlock, Lord, 158

West, Algernon, on Curzon's speech, 234

West, Mrs., 561

West Africa, German military preparation in, 367 ; German ambitions in, 412, 431

West Bromwich, 302, 478 ; author speaks at, 302, 478

West Indies, revival of, 324

Westminster, Duke of, 318

*Westminster Gazette,* 173, 242, 257

Westminster Hall, memorial service in, 270–1 ; lying in state in, 273–5 ; preparations in, for new Peers, 347

Wharncliffe, Lord, 604

Wheat duty, *see* Corn tax

Wheatley, H. B., 118

Whiteley, George, 39, 85

Wigan and Tariff Reform, 308–9

Wilhelm II, Emperor, and war with England, 94, 122 ; at funeral of Edward VII, 276 ; invites Grey to Berlin, 551

Willcocks, General Sir James, 106, 564

Williams, J. C., 328, 417, 537

Williams, Vaughan, 225

Willoughby de Broke, Lord, 342 ; a Die-hard, 318 ; and reform of Lords, 358

Willoughby de Eresby, Lord, 261

Wilson, Admiral Sir Arthur Knyvet, 326 ; at memorial service, 271

Wilson, General H., and Curragh "mutiny," 624, 626, 628, 630

Wilson, Mr., 268

Wilson, President, and Panama tolls, 620

Wilson, Sir Guy Fleetwood, 542, 550

Winchester, Bishop of, 412

Windsor, King Edward's funeral at, 276 ; author spends night at, 518

Winn, Miss, 174

Winslow, General, 487, 529

Witte, Count Sergius, 102, 474, 484

Wolseley, Lord, 540

Wolverhampton, by-elections at, 105 *n.*, 106 ; author speaks at, 138–9, 640, 642–3

Women's Suffrage, 137, 403, 414 ; author's speech on, 169–70, 519 ; Albert Hall meeting against, 414, 424, 430 ; amendment on, in Franchise Bill, 424, 501, 519 ; estimate of number of opponents to, 446–7 ; defeat of Bill, 467–8

Workmen's Compensation, 39

Wrey, Sir Bourchier, 100

Wyndham, George, 85, 135, 226, 350, 369, 537 ; and Tariff Reform amendment to Address, 146 ; on position of Party, 184 ; and reform of Lords, 220, 237 ; rating policy of 229 ; and Veto Resolutions, 243–4 ; obscure speeches of, 255–6 ; on January election, 256 ; a Die-hard, 318 ; and Halsbury Club, 358–60 ; on leader for Party, 359 ; and Food Taxes, 433, 519 ; convinced by author's speech, 558 ; sends Chamberlain Birthday Fund album, 562–3

York, Archbishop of, 325

Yorkshire, and Tariff Reform, 97, 173 ; election results in, 197 ; and reform of Lords, 220 ; attitude to Food Taxes in, 406, 502

*Yorkshire Post,* 502, 582, 604

Young Turks, 355, 536

Zakka Khels, expedition against, 69

Zanzibar, 412, 436

Zeppelin, descends in France, 544–5

Printed in Great Britain by T. and A. Constable Ltd.
at the University Press, Edinburgh

*The*
*William McKean Brown*
*Memorial Publication*
*Fund*

POLITICS FROM INSIDE *by* Sir Austen Chamberlain is the tenth work published by the Yale University Press on the William McKean Brown Memorial Publication Fund. This Foundation was established by gifts from members of his family to Yale University in memory of William McKean Brown, of New Castle, Pennsylvania; who not only was a leader in the development of his community, but also served the Commonwealth as State Senator and later as Lieutenant-Governor of Pennsylvania.